D0871983

THE SOCIOLOGY OF RELIGION

The Sociology of Religion

A Study of Christendom

WERNER STARK

Professor of Sociology, Fordham University

VOLUME FIVE

Types of Religious Culture

FORDHAM UNIVERSITY PRESS

NEW YORK . 1972

First published in the United States of America
in 1972
by Fordham University Press
New York
© *Routledge & Kegan Paul Ltd. 1972*
Library of Congress Catalog Card Number : 66–27652
ISBN 0–8232–0935–0 (Fordham)
ISBN 0–7100–7240–6 (Routledge)
Printed in Great Britain

Contents

Preface

I started to work on my *Sociology of Religion* on or about 1 April 1963; I am writing this preface on 19 February 1971. Thus I have spent almost eight years on the five volumes, the last of which I am launching today.

My investigation has grown to considerable size: there are altogether close to 1,900 pages. The explanation, if not the justifiscation, of this bulkiness lies in the method which I have applied, and which might be called 'the method of significant detail'. It consists in giving for every proposition that is stated, for every assertion that is made, a number of illustrations which, between them, build up a comprehensive and realistic picture. I remember discussing this procedure once with the late Karl Mannheim; he gave his opinion that it is totally appropriate for studies in the area of cultural sociology. I certainly have found it rewarding. But its necessary consequence is an increase, sometimes steep, in the number of words.

What I have not attempted to do is to cover every nook and cranny of the field. Of course, most important aspects are discussed, but I have not made all-inclusiveness a major preoccupation. What is usually called 'the social function of religion' is first considered in the closing part, and then only partially. I have not, for instance, gone into the help which religion gives to the norm-system of a society and thereby to that society's functioning. The reason for this omission is not fortuitous. As I see sociology and its division and integration of labour, the relation between custom and law on the one hand and religion on the other belongs to the subject called 'social control', that is, to general sociology, and not to a speciality, the sociology of religion. I may announce, however, that my next research effort is to take in that very field. I intend to write a work to be entitled: *The Social Bond: An Investigation into the Bases of Lawabidingness.* In this wide framework, something will have to be said about the religious factor as it operates within the system of social control.

A special word of explanation must still be added about the treatment of the last hundred and fifty years. They are not allotted the same measure of space as the first eighteen centuries of our era. The reason is obvious or nearly so. This is a study of *Christendom,* but with the French Revolution there began a process of de-Christianization which makes the decades that followed it less interesting – not, of course, in themselves, but from our specific point of view. This applies particularly to the present volume. It deals with inclusive cultures, and the inclusive culture of the modern age, reckoning it from about 1800 onward, is increasingly and predominantly secular. Ernst Troeltsch felt exactly as I do: he brings his *Social Teaching of the Christian Churches* to a conclusion with the end of the eighteenth century because 'with the nineteenth century, church history entered upon a new phase of existence' (vol. II, p. 991). He has been criticized for this and so shall I be, for many are vitally interested in politics, taking the word in the widest sense, or in current affairs, to express it differently, and they prefer to read about the present more than about the past. With me, this incentive is very weak. What I set out to do was to achieve understanding of an historical phenomenon, and to present my findings to others so that they may understand also. The outline of my work was therefore determined by that historical phenomenon, and the main emphasis had to be placed on the periods in which it showed itself in its most evolved, most characteristic form. I have, however, given due, and, I hope, adequate attention to the years of comparative decline as well, as every reader will find who has the patience to hear me out.

Since the fourth volume was published, two of my kind helpers have assumed greater burdens. Dr. Madeline Engel is absorbed in onerous academic work of her own; she has also become Mrs. Thomas Moran; and Father Robert McNamara is now Dean of Loyola College, Chicago. Nevertheless, they have remained by my side, and thereby they have further increased my debt of gratitude to them. It is my hope that they will be rewarded by the possession of as good friends as I have. Father Quain has kindly read this manuscript as he has the earlier ones, and my wife has continued to slave for me as she has always done. In relation to all of them I am in the position of an undischarged bankrupt.

As this is the last volume of the series, I should like to thank the staffs of the two libraries on which I have mainly relied, Fordham University and Union Theological Seminary. Mrs. Mary Riley, Reference Librarian at Fordham, has been especially helpful.

The first concentrated thinking on the problems which are discussed between the covers of this book was done at the Rockefeller Foundation's House of Studies at Bellagio, the Villa Serbelloni, where I was allowed to spend the month of August 1968. It is difficult to think of a more ideal spot, and I wish those who gave me this opportunity to know that I appreciate the privilege which they bestowed on me. Not only is the landscape of surpassing beauty, but the culture which has come to dwell in it holds a deep fascination for the sociologist of religion, and I should be happy to think that something of its quality is reflected in the ensuing pages.

W. STARK

New York, February 1971.

Acknowledgments

As in the previous volumes, we list here, with thanks, the publishers who have been good enough to permit us to quote from books under their imprint. The authors' names are given in brackets.

A B P International (Wallace-Hadrill, M.); Archabbey Press (Panofsky, E.); A. & C. Black (Dix, G., Schweitzer, A.); The Bodley Head (Joyce, J.); Cambridge University Press (Coulton, G. G.); Jonathan Cape (Joyce, J., Origo, I.); Clarendon Press (Adkins, A. W. H., Mathew, D.); Concordia Publishing House (Hägglund, B.); J. M. Dent & Sons (Redlich, H. F.); William Eerdmans, Jr. (De Jong, P.); Farrar, Straus & Giroux (Redlich, H. F.); Fortress Press (Wingren, G.); The Hamlyn Publishing Group (Troutman, P.); Harcourt Brace Jovanovich (Jung, C. G., LaFarge, J.); Harper & Row (Niebuhr, R. H.); Harvard University Press (Greene, W. Ch.); Little, Brown and Company (Jung, C. G.); Longman (Butler, C., Treston, H. J.); Lutterworth Press (Dillistone, F. W.); Macmillan (Adam, K., Cox, H.); William Morrow & Company (Dupee, F. W.); Th. Nelson & Sons (Meikle, H. W.); New Directions Publishing Corporation (Trilling, L.); Oxford University Press (Geiringer, K., Pedersen, J.); Phaidon (Gombrich, E. H.); G. P. Putnam's Sons (Cardus, N.); The Press of Case Western Reserve University (Hanford, J. H.); Random House, Alfred A. Knopf (Cole, G. D. H., and Postgate, R., Joyce, J.); Russell & Russell (Nettl, P., Wilenski, R. H.); Charles Scribner's Sons (Maritain, J.); Sheed & Ward (Butler, B. C., Dawson, Chr., Hostie, R.); Editions d'Art Albert Skira (Battisti, E., Benesch, O.); University Books (Huysmans, J. K.); The Viking Press (Joyce, J., Quennell, P.); Franklin Watts (Hammacher, A. M.); The Westminster Press (Mehl, R., Niesel, W.); also Prof. Perry Miller.

Introduction

In the land which cradled Christianity, and in the lands to which it originally spread, life and thought were shaped and dominated by the principle which sociologists, since Ferdinand Tönnies, have come to call *community*. A community, in contradistinction to an association, as found in other, and especially more modern, societies, is a close-knit unity; indeed, it is a unit in the full and firm sense of the word. As Aristotle would have expressed it, in these formations the whole is before the parts, not only in the order of time, but also in the order of existence. By this last phrase I mean that the whole is considered to be more real than the part. Not only are the parents there before the children, but the very being of the children is derived, secondary, adventitious; and it is so, not only in relation to the immediate progenitors, father and mother, but in relation to all the antecedent generations back through the centuries. Real is in the first place the family tree; it is considered more real than its branches, twigs and leaves; real is the stream of life, the ongoing society, rather than the individual persons in which it finds incidental and ephemeral expression and incarnation.

This principle of community is first and foremost a fact and feature of social organization. Communities are different from associations in the specific way in which they order human relations: they are we-societies differing in their whole phenomenology from I-and-you societies. But their characteristics also have philosophico-religious implications of the greatest consequence for the sociology of knowledge and the sociology of religion. As we have seen already, the mind formed in the matrix of community is referred back to the origin of things: as it travels back up the ladder of descent, from father to grandfather, to forefather and to primal progenitor, it finds itself ultimately up against mystery, against the root-problems of all religion – where do we all come from? how have we been created? and why have we been created? what is the meaning of our existence, and what is the meaning of the suffering which our existence entails? – a complex of questions so insistent that it cannot be easily put to rest. The societies which we call communities will therefore spontaneously develop a metaphysical and mystical bent. Totemism was a fruit of community, and so was Christianity. So above all is Catholicism, together with those other variants of Christianity which are similar to it in decisive aspects, like Eastern Orthodoxy.

In a community-centred and community-inspirited atmosphere, the great twin-doctrine of Christianity – the doctrine of the fall and the doctrine of redemption – presents no difficulty to the questing mind. Nothing is more natural for the clansman (in the widest sense of the word) than to believe that *all* can be lost and *all* can be saved by the deed of *one*. The problem of transference which has plagued the Christian – the decreasingly Christian – world since, say 1200 or 1500 – how can the sin of Adam, and how can the merit of Jesus, affect me? – simply does not exist in community-type cultures. If there is only one life, if there is only one body of mankind, anything and everything that happens in it, happens to it – to it in its entirety. Wholesome food eaten strengthens all concorporate cells, as ingested poison will debilitate and threaten to kill them all. It is as simple as that. No wonder that the ages of community were the ages of Christianity as well.

No wonder also that the replacement of the principle of community by the principle of *association* created more difficult conditions for religion in general and Christianity in particular. An association, in contradistinction to other, and especially more ancient, societies, is merely a loosely knit unit; indeed, in truth it is no unity at all, if the word is taken in its full and proper meaning, but rather a multiplicity of individuals more or less co-ordinated for the pursuit of their common (and that means here: for their personal) benefit. In Aristotle's terminology, the part is, both genetically and ontologically, before the whole. It is genetically before the whole because, according to this mode of life and thought, a society is made by its members, and not the other way around. The attention is fixed on the marriage contract, not on the arrival and upbringing of the children. And it is ontologically before, or, as we might also say, above, the whole, because, under the changed dispensation, only the individual is truly real, while society as such appears logically as a non-entity, as merely a state or even a term of summation – the many, who remain the many, indeed, who remain unabsorbed, independent selves, brought under one definitional, purely verbal roof. Already this turn-about in social ordering and social outlook spells trouble for the religious world-view. If the individual is the *ens realissimum*, for instance, the human individual of blood, flesh, bristle and bone, then a tangible subject or object is the *ens realissimum*, somebody or something which you can see and grip and hold and weigh. Thus a relative materialism is apt to spring up which will contrast most sharply with the relative immaterialism or mystery-mindedness of the typical community whose anchor-ground in fact and thought is an *intangible* – the life in all, of all, and behind all.

It must not be thought, however, that the coming of association will, *per se*, lead to a secularization of society, and even less that it is bound to do so. For the great questions with which ancient and medieval society grappled are relevant, if in a modified manner, for modern man also. It is as natural to inquire: where do *I* come from and what is the meaning of *my* life, as it is to ask, where do *we all* come from and what is the meaning of human existence in general? True, an associational, i.e. individualistic, culture may not direct the eye back towards the origin of things, as a community-bred culture does, but it is all the more apt to draw it forward to the great fact of personal extinction: being may come to be conceived, as it is in so much modern philosophy and theology, as a being-unto-death. If a tragic element is thereby brought into life and thought – and the two great pioneers of modernized, archetypically individualistic religiosity, Luther and Calvin, are above all tragic thinkers, so far at least as man is concerned – this is not something which will, in and of itself, be detrimental to the continuation, and indeed to the continued vigour, of a life of faith.

Indeed, the onset of modern individualism brought, historically speaking, a temporary invigoration of religion, first by forming the Protestant denominations, and not much later by evoking, within the Catholic Church, such movements as the Oratorians and the Jesuits. The latter tried and succeeded in engineering an accommodation of the traditional communal theory and practice of Catholicism to the new associational atmosphere around it; the former expressed this atmosphere in a largely consistent, appropriate fashion. We have pointed out in our fourth volume,[1] that Luther returned, in his idea of the Christian Church, after a very short time to older, more organological conceptions, and that even Calvin moved in this retrograde direction, though not to the same extent. But there was one crucial issue on which he, and Calvin, did not retreat, and this precisely is the plank in the platform which makes Protestantism so different from Catholicism, whether medieval or modernized, as we find it to be. Whereas Catholicism, in a typically community-inspired attitude, taught and continued to teach, that there is a cistern of graces in heaven which the saints fill and the sinners empty so that men may and do help one another both in time and in eternity, Protestantism insisted that everyone had his own account in the book of life into which nothing could ever enter from outside. The sinning soul does not stand before the judgment seat surrounded by his friends, as Everyman does in the medieval play. Even the voice of Mary, whom Catholics are wont to call *advocata nostra*, is not supposed to be heard in this dread tribunal. The culprit has to meet his judge alone, and all he can hope for is a free pardon. In so far as this free pardon is thought to be based on Christ's self-sacrifice on Calvary, in so far as God does accept vicarious satisfaction through the Cross, even the new theology allows that the sinner partakes of the merit of One Other, and to that extent there is true unity and continuity with the older tradition. But the redemptive link has become bipolar only, the *solus-cum-solo* theory has arrived, and an essential element – the element

I Cf. especially pp. 20 et seq.

of collective guilt and collective merit – has dropped out. The saints count for nothing under the new dispensation. Even the prayers for the dead disappear, and logically so, for how can the living – other people! – hope to help them?

A consistently individualistic, more personal than communal form of religiosity will, of course, have to deal with the problem of the transference of Christ's redemptive merit, but it will not find it impossible to present a satisfactory solution to it. That solution will lie in line with its over-all intellectual direction. Whatever the starting point, e.g. in the Calvinistic doctrine of predestination, the inherent tendency of Protestantism has been, and has had to be, to preach that those are saved who (personally) take Christ for their (personal) Saviour – who, as we may also express it, associate themselves with Him. Whereas Catholicism has tended to be an inclusive culture, permeated in all its aspects and areas by a devotion to divine purposes, Protestantism has conceived itself, and has in fact been, more of an included Godward movement in an otherwise indifferent world. Thus we have two or more forms of Christianity instead of one; but we still have Christianity, even though its original parent reality, the close-knit community of the early days, is no longer with us.

As the reader has seen, the split of Christianity into two or more subvarieties did not have, as is popularly assumed, superficial causes, like the sale of indulgences and similar phenomena at the margin of religious life, but rather profound reasons, reasons connected with the very principle of socio-cultural ordering. It is one thing to believe that we are all in one boat; it is quite another thing to assume that each one of us paddles his own little canoe and is 'the captain of his soul' (to borrow from W. E. Henley). Yet both conceptions, concerned as they are with man's or men's relationship to God, are in equal measure authentically religious. If, therefore, nothing had happened in history but the replacement of a we-society by an I-and-you society, secularization need not, and probably would not, have taken place. But the coming of associationism and relative individualism was fundamentally connected with an even more momentous shift – a shift in the direction of what, in my terminology, might be called an I-and-it society. And this, indeed, has tended to cut the ground from underneath traditional religiosity.

Medieval man was above all attempting to build a pacified and warm, truly human, society. It makes no difference to our analysis that he did not succeed, that he did, in fact, fail deplorably. His intention, his order of values, at any rate was clear. To see how true this is, we need only think of the feudal 'state': it was no great abstract idea, no impersonal machine, no remote and fear-inspiring Leviathan. In its place stood close, neighbourly relationships, like those between peasant and squire, baron and earl, or duke and king. These arrangements did not work too well, but even in their hate-generating, and therefore de-generated, shape they were still decidedly and definitely human. With the Renaissance and Reformation, however, came a far-reaching de-humanization of life. What happened to the political system, the replacement of a chain of face-to-face confrontations by common subjection to a bureaucratic and later a law-regulated state (both bureaucracy and law are depersonalized, de-humanized forms of domination), is merely a symptom of a far more general transformation. The truth is that around the year 1500, society abandoned the ambition to create a love-informed and love-united community and settled for a rather different over-all aim – the aim to create a humanity that would learn to dominate and to exploit its physical habitat and thereby become powerful and rich. Associationism and individualism are themselves to some extent results of this most basic of all revaluations of values. For if technology and economy are to flourish, if the wheels of industry are to go round faster and faster and the shelves in the shops are to be piled higher and higher, the principle of competition must be called in to stimulate effort. But competition and individualism, competition and associationism, are Siamese twins. Where you find the one, there you will also find the other. And there you will assuredly not find a strong preoccupation with metaphysical and religious questions.

A manufacturing, matter- and man-manipulating society will not have much time for the first and last things. It will have no time for them in the direct and literal sense of the word, for it will feel that it has 'better things to do' than to rack its brains about remote and intractable problems; it will follow Martha rather than Mary; and it will have no time for them in the transferred and metaphorical sense either for it will, not unnaturally, regard religion and all it stands for as rather 'unproductive'. Thus a society which concentrates its attention and its efforts on the material sphere and its problems and possibilities – an I-and-it society as I have called it in an attempt to bring out its contrast to both we-societies and I-and-you societies – will produce a great deal of agnosticism, atheism and more or less atheistic pantheism, and it will even tend to hollow out the traditional forms of genuine religiosity whether collective or personal, whether Protestant or Catholic. As for a possible transfer of redemptive merit, such a society will be totally unable to grasp the very conception of it for, in a world with the slogan 'every man for himself', it simply does not make sense.

This has manifestly been the situation from about the time of the French Revolution, in which for the first time ancient attachments were openly destroyed in an uninhibited manner and on a large scale. Since then the process of erosion has proceeded swiftly. It is not only (as descriptive sociologists have emphasized) that church-going has declined everywhere; the secularization of life has gone far beyond such habits to the very kernel of the total world-view of industrial society. But mystery remains and will remain, however much man may come to learn and to achieve. It is like our own shadow which will inevitably follow us wherever we go, whether we like to look at it or not. Indeed, it will demand its meed of attention, and demand it insistently. It will give us no rest, and rest is what we all need. To live from day to day, to forget that we are but mortal, to be superficial, is not so easy as some seem to think. For this reason, religion may indeed recede, but it will never disappear; and the ground it has lost, or will yet have to yield, is apt to be taken up by kindred philosophies, such as existentialism, or by pseudo-religions of various kinds, which are still the legitimate concern of one who would like to combine the sociology of religion with the sociology of knowledge into an over-all 'understanding' approach. Our book will therefore range from the dawn to the dusk, from the birth of Christianity out of primary society to the state of evolution or involution which it has reached at the present time.

1 · THE AGE OF COMMUNITY AND ITS RELIGIOUS CULTURE

If a man loses his son, and especially an only son, this is to him in all normal cases a dreadful grief, and it might be thought that in a matter so natural, so universally human, there could be no difference from age to age or from society to society. And, indeed, the suffering of all bereaved parents will be similar, wherever and whenever such a tragedy happens; it will be similar – and yet it will not be quite the same. For in a modern, associational society, the death of a child is merely the loss of a near and dear one; it does not touch upon the personal survival of the stricken father. The primitive clansman, however, for instance the Jew of patriarchal days, feels differently. He will feel as if he has been directly, and not only indirectly, stricken; he will feel as if he has lost his own life. For the definition of the ego is not the same in all social systems. To modern man it means 'I'; to early man it meant 'we'; and it is only a slight exaggeration to say that the very instinct of self-preservation was attached to a different self. In any event, what mattered to the man bred in a community such as the clan and filled with its spirit was not the survival of one person, even his own, but the continuation of all, the survival of the house.

Many features of Israelite society, as they are reflected in the biblical record, are explicable in the light of this wider conception of the ego, for instance polygamy and levirate marriage. 'Polygamy is one of the ethical demands of old Israel,' Johannes Pedersen writes in his great work, *Israel: Its Life and Culture*,[1] 'because the maintenance of the family is the greatest of all.' Four wives are incomparably more likely to guarantee issue than one. Even more characteristic is the institution of levirate marriage. 'When brethren dwell together, and one of them dieth without children,' so the holy law ordains (Deuteronomy xxv, 5), 'the wife of the deceased shall not marry to another: but his brother shall take her, and raise up seed for his brother.' After what we have said, the intention is clear. By engendering a son for his dead brother, the living will, in a manner, countermand his brother's death. Though the man cannot give his brother back his individual life, he can yet continue – he can at any rate re-start – the stream of life which in and with his brother has come to a (possibly temporary) halt, and which was his deceased brother's real or higher life. A man is gone; but what is a man? The name, the house may still survive. Just how deep this idea was rooted in Israelite culture and society, can be seen from the pathetic story of

[1] Ed. London and Copenhagen 1954, p. 70.

7

Thamar, told in the Book of Genesis (chapter xxxviii). Thamar is the wife of Her, but Her dies before she can become pregnant. She hopes and prays that one of Her's two brothers, Onan and Sela, will step into his place, or rather into his marriage bed. But they do not; the family apparently cares little for their kinsman's name and house. And so Thamar does a desperate thing. She pretends to be a prostitute and attracts her deceased husband's father, Juda. To her joy, she conceives from him. According to modern mentality, her behaviour is, to say the least, bizarre. More than that: most would judge it crude and immoral. Yet to the Jew of Juda's and Her's time, it was deeply dutiful. Thamar was to her people a good woman, indeed, hard though this is to believe in the twentieth century, a faithful wife; and they kept her in loving memory.

It is immediately clear that much of the religious content of both Testaments is missed, if this collectivistic mentality is not kept in mind. God asks the patriarch Abraham to offer up to him, as a sacrifice, Isaac, his 'only begotten son', and Abraham is ready to obey (Genesis xxii). Great as such a sacrifice must be in any society, it is incomparably greater in a society such as Abraham's was than it would be in our own. For what the Lord demanded was not *one* life; much rather was it *all* life, life *itself*. But the slaughter of Isaac, happily avoided, is, to Christian theology, merely a figure, a prophetic foretelling, of the execution of Jesus, unhappily consummated on Calvary. When the Jewish converts of the first century heard the words of St. John (iii, 16): 'God so loved the world as to give His only begotten Son, that whosoever believeth in Him may not perish, but may have life everlasting,' they were more deeply moved than any modern man is ever likely to be (which does not mean, of course, that the same words may not strike a deep chord in modern souls as well). We see already here, on the very threshold of our investigation, that a full understanding of Christianity, and especially of Catholicism, presupposes a re-entry, at least in imagination, into the cultural context of another age.

The two institutions which we have mentioned by way of illustration, polygamy and levirate marriage, are, properly considered, effects rather than causes of Jewish, and hence of Christian, thinking. The last root of the Judaeo–Christian style of thought must lie, for the sociologist of knowledge, in the very constitution of the parent society, in the clan-organization of Hebrew life. This represents the substructure on which a whole mental superstructure, bearing in itself the seeds of both Judaism and original Christianity, must be shown to rest. We shall therefore first discuss the basic social facts involved, and then turn our attention to the spreading mental forms in which these facts found their fulfilment and their due completion.[1]

---

[1] In the present book I cannot discuss the problem of the relationship between a social substructure and a mental superstructure. All I can do is refer the reader to

THE SOCIAL CONSTITUTION OF COMMUNITY

The main point to establish, and at the same time the moot point most difficult to convey – to convey in a manner sure to carry conviction with modern readers – is, of course, the true unity of the primal group. Even historians are at times somewhat incredulous when they are told that man was in other societies rather different from what he is in our own: there appears to be a spontaneous and deep-rooted tendency to believe that 'human nature does not change'. True, human nature properly so called – man's flesh and bone – does not change over a relatively brief period of time such as recorded history; but human nature improperly so called, what sociologists are wont to describe as modal man, and what more simply might be designated typical man, or even prevailing character, *does* change with culture, for it is a product, a precipitate, of culture. Luckily there are more or less conclusive proofs that social coherence was much firmer two or two-and-a-half thousand years ago than it is now. One of them is the fact that ancient societies invariably thought of themselves as integrated bodies, either as quasi-organisms or as plants, such as the palm tree or the vine. This consistent organicism would never have arisen and would certainly not have maintained itself, if it had not been in substantial agreement with the facts.[1]

But there are yet more dramatic demonstrations of the hard and fast integration, of the near-fusion of individual lives in the archaic clan – features which belong to the realm of action rather than of thought and therefore carry a very high, nay complete, conviction. If man does not show what he is in what he says, he certainly does show it in what he does. Significant in the evidence is the blood feud. If a MacDonald touches a Campbell, and more especially if he kills him, the affair is at first – physically as it were – a quarrel between two persons. But if we look at the social implications, both clans are immediately involved. For what one does, all do: and what one suffers, is suffered by all.

Among the classical students of Hebrew society, the name of William Robertson Smith stands out, and however much we may have learned since his day, his voice still has the ring of authority. Studying not only the Jews themselves but also the other Semitic peoples around them, in order to arrive at a wider and truer picture, he has this to say about the social constitution of the desert tribes: 'At the time of the prophet . . . the tribal bond all over Arabia, so far as our evidence goes, was conceived as a bond of kinship. All the members of a group regarded themselves as of one blood. This appears most clearly in the law of blood-feud . . . If the slayer and slain are of different kindred groups, a

[1] Cf. Stark, W., *The Fundamental Forms of Social Thought*, London 1962, especially chapter VII.

---

my earlier study, *The Sociology of Knowledge* (London 1958 et seq), and to assure him that I reject determinism in any shape or form.

blood-feud at once arises, and the slain man may be avenged by any member of his own group on any member of the group of the slayer. This is the general rule of blood-revenge all over the world, and with certain minor modifications it holds good in Arabia at the present day, in spite of Islam, as it held good in the oldest times of which we have record . . . Under such a system the ultimate kindred group is that which always acts together in every case of blood-revenge. And in Arabia this group was not the family or household, not the relatives of the slayer and the slain within certain degrees of kinship, as we reckon kinship, but a definite unity marked off from all other groups by the possession of a common group-name. Such a group the Arabs commonly call a *hayy*, and the fellow-members of a man's *hayy* are called his *ahl* or his *caum*. To determine whether a man is or is not involved in a blood-feud it is not necessary to ask more than whether he bears the same group-name as the slayer or the slain. The common formula applied to manslaughter is that the blood of such a *hayy* has been shed and must be avenged. The tribesmen do not say that the blood of M or N has been spilt, naming the man; they say "our blood has been spilt!"'

These are strong and decisive words, and their impact is little diminished by the fact that the blood-feud does not always proceed but may be bought off, as it were, by the payment of compensation, be it in cattle or in cash. For it is again the whole offending clan which has to pay, and it is again the whole offended clan which is entitled to receive the blood-money. As 'every tribesman risked his life equally in the blood-feud,' so Robertson Smith writes, 'every tribesman might be called upon to contribute to the [blood-wit, composition or] atonement by paying which blood-feud could be healed. This is still the rule of the desert,' he adds, 'and so we often read of the "collection" of the blood-wit and find that it is offered, not by the manslayer himself, but by his people . . . Conversely it is Mohammedan law and doubtless ancient practice that the blood-wit is distributed to the kin of the slain . . . the *hayy* as a whole.'[1]

Rich as life is in luxuriant variations, there are, of course, other forms as well. The basic group may, for instance, be bilateral rather than patrilineal or matrilineal, and count the cognates as well as the agnates, as, for instance, Anglo-Saxon society did in its day. But this does not touch upon the salient point either: the integrated, operative collectivity is differently defined, but it is still a unity whose members stand 'in scot and in lot' with each other and must bear each other's burden like one man.

What, in the first place, does the term 'blood vengeance' mean? Modern man will be inclined to understand it as describing 'vengeance for

[1] Smith, W. R., *Kinship and Marriage in Early Arabia*, Cambridge 1885, pp. 22, 23 53, 54.

blood shed', and this cannot be totally wrong. But philologists have suggested that it meant originally 'vengeance of the blood', that is to say, vengeance exacted by the blood kin, and this derivation is much more likely to come close to the core. That the whole 'blood' or descent group is concerned is clear from the fact that the pursuers of the feud are inclined to wipe out the culprit's whole clan. The principle called Talion strikes us as cruel today: an eye for an eye; a tooth for a tooth; a life for a life. But if this last link in the formula is taken to imply that *one* life is to be taken in vengeance for the *one* life lost, then we have already a retreat from original collectivism before us. The Book of Genesis certainly does not think in such restricted terms. 'And Lamech said to his wives, Ada and Sella: hear my voice . . . I have slain a man to the wounding of myself and a stripling to my own bruising. Sevenfold vengeance shall be taken for Cain, but for Lamech seventy-times seven-fold' (IV, 23 and 24). Needless to say, 'seventy-times sevenfold' means an indefinite or infinite number, means in fact *all* the foes. For they are to Lamech merely one lot.[1]

The words of Lamech might easily be explained away as merely boastful, or as a song of defiance, but other parts of the Old Testament evince a similar spirit. Zambri deposes Ela, the son of Baasa, whom he kills. Now he must expect a blood feud against his whole family. He decides to anticipate it and to do to Ela's folk what they are sure to attempt to do to him and his folk. 'And . . . he slew all the house of Baasa: and he left not one thereof to piss against a wall [i.e. spared none of the male sex], and all his kinsfolks and friends' (III Kings XVI, 11). Even the end of the royal house of Saul is not much different. There is blood between the Saulites and the Gabaonites[2] and King David tries to resolve the menacing situation. The Gabaonites refuse to take a monetary composition: 'we have no contest,' they say, 'about silver and gold.' They stick to the traditional demand: extinction of the guilty house, the house of Saul: 'there [should] be not so much as one left of his stock in all the coasts of Israel' (II Kings XXI, 4 and 5). David does not fully comply, but he accepts the substantial justice of the Gabaonite claim. He hands them seven grandsons of Saul, preserving only the issue of his friend Jonathan. And the seven are promptly put to death.[3]

The record of this incident can, when it is closely considered, teach us even more about Jewish life and thought, and about the constitution of biblical society, than we can gather from the bare facts. Pedersen draws attention to the curious wording of the demand of the Gabaon-ites to David. He translates the Greek version of II Kings XXI, 5, as

[1] Cf. Merz, E., *Die Blutrache bei den Israeliten*, Leipzig 1916, pp. 9, 10, 69, cf. also 42, 43. Merz uses the terms *Gesamtrache* (collective and total vengeance) and *Geschlech-terrache* (kin and descent-group vengeance).
[2] As in our earlier volumes, we are using throughout this the transcriptions and translations of the English Bible known as the Douai version.
[3] Cf. Pedersen, loc. cit., 189, 383, 384, 390.

follows: 'The man (i.e. Saul) brought ruin upon us, let us destroy him from remaining within the whole of the territory of Israel.' *Him*, singular – not *them*, the members of the Saulite clan (plural). 'Though Saul long ago has fallen by his own sword on the mount of Gilboa,' Pedersen explains, 'the Gibeonites still demand *his* destruction by killing his successors, for it is his life that lives in them . . . Whether this rendering, from a philological point of view, is the very earliest text,' he cautiously comments, 'is a question apart, but at any rate it must have some sort of old tradition behind it, for it is entirely in the spirit of old Israel.'[1] The Saulites simply *are* Saul. He is alive while they are.

Why, we should perhaps ask, did David comply with wishes as cruel as those of the Gabaonites, especially in view of the fact that they were not Jews, but Amorrhites? The answer is simple: because he thought exactly as they did. The Lord, he says to Michol, Saul's daughter and his adversary, who taunts him for his humility, 'chose me rather than thy father and than all his house' (II Kings VI, 21). In other words, when he, David, became king, a family was preferred before a family, not an individual before an individual. This was also the way in which the Prophet Samuel saw such matters. He called Saul to the kingship, but it is a clan that he really called and not a person. 'For whom shall be all the best things of Israel?', he asks in a rhetorical question. 'Shall they not be for thee and for all thy father's house?' (I Kings IX, 20). The reference back to Saul's, the Anointed One's, father, Jemini, is particularly revealing here: Saul's personal great qualities or Saul's personal good fortune bring him to the throne, but the insignificant Jemini, as well as his insignificant kinsfolk, are elevated with him. And like David and Samuel, Saul himself thinks in collectivistic terms. When he looks for a champion of Israel who will slay the ferocious Goliath, he promises, as one of the rewards, that he will 'make his father's house free from tribute' (I Kings XVII, 25).

In all the cases which we have considered, and in the many others which we might still have put before the reader (such as Gedeon and his kin's feud against Zebee and Salmana, Judges VIII, 4 et seq., or David and Solomon's against Joab, II Kings III, 27 et seq., or Jehu's against Achab and Joram, IV Kings IX, 7 et seq.), it has been clan against clan, or, as the Bible likes to express it, house against house. But there is evidence that the concept of collective responsibility was also applied to the whole of Israel, the inclusive nation, and not only to kin groups included in it. Thus the Book of Deuteronomy (which otherwise shows already traces of a decay of these archaic conceptions) warns Israel 'that innocent blood may not be shed in the midst of the land which the Lord thy God will give thee to possess: lest thou be guilty of blood' (XIX, 10). This 'thou' is decidedly a plural; 'thou' are all the tribes. That a collectivistic interpretation is in order even here, can be seen from the

[1] Ibid., pp. 384 and 385.

Book's next chapter and 'When there shall be found in the land . . . the corpse of a man slain, and it is not known who is guilty of the murder,' the text runs, the elders shall pray for the whole people: 'Be merciful . . . O Lord, and lay not innocent blood to their charge' (xxi, 1 and 8).

One point which is particularly crucial in our present context is the religious foundation of the blood feud, and hence the collectivistic conceptions which are interlaced with it. David cannot immediately avenge Abner. 'I as yet am tender,' he complains (II Kings iii, 39), 'and these men, the sons of Sarvia, are too hard for me.' But he immediately calls on YHWH to bring to completion, on his and his kin's behalf, what he and they cannot complete. 'The Lord reward him that doth evil according to his wickedness' – so run the very next words. And he prays that the blood of Abner, the son of Ner, 'may come upon the head of Joab and upon all his father's house' (29). In other words, he utters a curse. In the end, indeed, it is a human agent, Solomon, who wreaks vengeance (III Kings ii, 29 et seq.); Solomon inherits the task from David.[1] He acknowledges without hesitation that the cause is his own for 'the innocent blood', he says, 'hath been shed by Joab from me(!) and from the house of my father.' Yet the deed he does, though in this fashion his own, is also owed to others. It is owed to the murdered Abner; it is owed to David who died before he could settle the score; and in a manner it is owed even to YHWH. It was a firm Jewish conviction that the carrying out of the blood feud is a religiously sanctioned, nay a fully religious duty – so much so that the hand of God will strike, in substitution, as it were, where the hands of the kinsfolk cannot.[2] Thus YHWH avenges Abel (Genesis iv, 9 et seq.); thus He punishes Abimelech (Judges ix, 23 and 56); and when David is in difficulties, a distant kinsman of Saul, Semei, sees this as a divine retribution for David's handing over of the seven to the Gabaonites: 'Behold thy evils press upon thee, because thou art a man of blood,' he cries. 'The Lord hath repaid thee for all the blood of the house of Saul' (II Kings xvi, 8).

The fact-based conceptions which we have just surveyed provided the firm foundations on which the belief that all men fell in and with Adam and rose again with and in Christ could securely rest. If the question is asked as to how a religion with this doctrine for a centre-piece could spread to Greece, it is not sufficient to reply that Jewish colonies were established all over the Grecian world. Men like St. Paul could indeed scatter the seed of the Word, but it would not have taken root if the soil had not been ready to receive it. It was ready, mainly because the Hellenic and Hellenistic cities were under the influence of life-forms and thought-forms similar to those found in the Judaic homeland.

[1] Merz, loc. cit., pp. 76 and 77, emphasizes, and that rightly, that both David and Solomon act, not as public functionaries, but essentially as private parties.
[2] Cf. Merz, loc. cit., pp. 63–6.

What William Robertson Smith was to Semitic studies, Gustave Glotz has been to Hellenic. Few have ever matched his learning, his penetration, his analytical power. We may therefore quote him with complete confidence. This is what he says about the blood feud in Greece: 'Homicide concerns the *genos* as a whole. The relatives of the dead man proceed against the murderer, be it as a group, be it singly. The question who is the next in succession is not raised. The father does not inherit; custom is against it. Nevertheless, he hastens to avenge his son, unless old age hamstrings his hatred. During the Homeric period, the collateral kinsmen have every right to receive the inheritance, if there is no son; but there is no evidence that they ever ask whether there is a surviving son, before they enter into the feud. They feel that they have been attacked; that is sufficient; they go for the foe. Blood vengeance is not a burdensome moral duty connected with the inheritance of material goods. It is an act of familial solidarity carried out according to rules which are older than the very principle of individual succession.' Glotz's chapter entitled 'General Characteristics of Blood Vengeance' begins with the following words: 'The *genos* forms, *vis-à-vis* other *gene*, a single body. If one of its members suffers, it suffers in its entirety. All those who are of the same blood have but one soul (*esprit*) and one flesh. They all resent an injury inflicted on any one of them. If one of them is killed, it is a pain and a loss for all of them. That is the reason why they help each other, and why they avenge their dead.'[1] Blood vengeance, Glotz says in summing up, 'is the most striking manifestation of primitive solidarity . . . It allows us to see the inner constitution of these societies where all fight together, linked to each other, whether they are living or dead.'[2]

Entering deeper into the detail, Glotz later points out[3] that the logic of life demanded and enforced complete solidarity even in the matter of blood-money or composition. Accepting *poiné* in cattle or cash instead of exacting the price in blood meant forgiving the murderer, signing away a right. But one man cannot sign away the right of a collectivity. The negotiator had therefore to speak and act in the name of all the kin. The perpetrator of the murder, on the other hand, and his family, had to be sure that they really would be secure once they had made the required payment, heavy as it usually was. They, too, therefore would see to it that the contract of release would be fully collective.

Needless to say, the Greek *genos* was, like its Jewish counterpart, an undying corporation. The duty of blood vengeance did not, therefore, spread only laterally, to more distant contemporary relatives; it also

---

[1] Glotz, G., *La Solidarité de la Famille dans le Droit Criminel en Grèce*, Paris 1904, pp 79 and 47. Cf. also p. 76. Our translation. Cf. also pp. 209, 210, 211, 213, 214.
[2] Ibid., p. 93.
[3] Ibid., p. 122.

continued in the line of direct descent to succeeding generations. 'However young the son may have been at the moment when his father was struck down, even if he was not yet born, the burden . . . rests on him. The passing years do not free him either . . . The [recorded] massacres of innocents have their main cause, not in a blood-thirsty bestiality, but in the fear of punishment to come. The daughters are spared, but they are condemned to perpetual virginity, for the duty of retribution passes on to the grandson. It is a heritable item, in the discharge of which men may take each other's place.'[1]

A terrible example of the hereditary, ever-new-bloodthirst-producing character of Greek vengeance and counter-vengeance can be found in Apollodorus. Porthaon had several children, among them four sons, Oeneus, Agrius, Alcathous and Melas. Oeneus came to rule over Calydon. His first wife was Althaea, daughter of Thestius, who gave him a son called Thyreus, and his second was Periboea, daughter of Hipponous, who gave him a son called Tydeus. 'When Tydeus had grown to be a gallant man, he was banished for killing, as some say, Alcathous, brother of Oeneus [his uncle]; but according to the author of the *Alcmaeonid* his victims were the sons of Melas [his cousins] . . . their names being Pheneus, Euryalus, Hyperlaus, Antiochus, Eumedes Sternops, Xanthippus, Sthenelaus.' However that may have been, the fat was now in the fire. 'Being arraigned by Agrius [another uncle], he fled to Argos and came to Adrastus, whose daughter Deipyle he married and begat Diomedes. Tydeus marched against Thebes with Adrastus, and died of a wound.' But this did not end the strife, for soon 'the sons of Agrius, to wit, Thersites, Onchestus, Prothous, Celeutor, Lycopeus, Melanippus, wrested the kingdom from Oeneus and gave it to their father . . . Nevertheless Diomedes [years] afterwards came secretly . . . from Argos and put to death all the sons of Agrius, except Onchestus and Thersites, who had fled betimes to Peloponnese; and as Oeneus was [by then] old, Diomedes gave the kingdom to Andraemon who had married the daughter of Oeneus, but Oeneus himself he took with him to Peloponnese. Howbeit, the sons of Thestius, who had made their escape, lay in wait for the old man at the hearth of Telephus in Arcadia, and killed him.'[2] There is enough tragedy in this circumstantial report to satisfy an Aeschylus, a Shakespeare and a Racine; there is certainly enough evidence in it to satisfy an historian.

Even at the hub and centre of civilized Greece, things were no different. 'In Athens, nothing is more frequent than hereditary enmities. The century-long and dreadfully bloody struggle carried on by the family of Alcmaeon against that of Cylon and that of Pisistrates is well known . . . Well known is also the long-drawn-out duel unto

[1] Ibid., p. 78.
[2] Apollodorus, *The Library*, I, VIII, 5 and 6, transl. Frazer, Sir J. G., ed. London 1921, pp. 71 and 73.

death in which the Lycomid[1] Myron of Phlya had the Alcmaeonids proscribed and they in turn took their revenge on the Lycomid Themistocles. These instances offered by the history of the great *gene* are by no means famous exceptions . . . The collection of invocations engraved on slabs of lead, published as an appendix to the *Corpus Inscriptionum Atticarum*, contains a whole series in which a curse is extended to the relations of the object, be they named individually or collectively, and even to the neighbours . . . After the sacrifice which, in Athens, preceded each assembly of the people and each meeting of the council, the herald condemned to perdition anyone who would hurt his homeland, "and with him his family (*genos*) and his house." [2]

We have so far spoken only of the blood feud between clans or *gene*, but the very same condition could and did exist between entire cities also. In a chapter entitled 'Extension of Responsibility to the Social Group',[3] Glotz simply restates, in slightly different words, the principles which he has shown us to have characterized inter-clan warfare. 'Any offence coming from a foreigner justifies a recourse to force, not only against the guilty person, but also against all those who are members of the same [wide] group. The rule is absolute. It is legitimate to pick, indiscriminately and simultaneously, on the people and the property of the opposed group; for the killer and the robber may, at the choice of the offended party, be killed, abducted as captives or stripped of their possessions, and the sanction which may be brought to bear on the offender may be extended to the whole group.' A series of historical illustrations is then given, and Glotz concludes: 'These examples are taken from different centuries, but a permanent principle of international *themis* is, in an identical fashion, applied in all of them. They show that the citizens who commit an anonymous murder on the person of a foreigner connect for ever their entire city with their personal cause.'[4]

In all this, the positive side must not for a single moment be forgotten against the negative side which is much more likely to loom large in the untutored modern mind. It is relatively unimportant that there was persistent strife between different descent groups – such strife was after all only intermittent, even if it was frequent – or that the geographical communities were so weak. But it is decisive that the bonds of brotherhood were so strong and remained so strong for ages and generations. Needless to say, this applies both to Hebrews and to Hellenes and must be appreciated as part of the precious common

---

[1] A Lycomid was a member of the priestly family which derived its descent from an eponymous Lycos.
[2] Glotz, loc. cit., pp. 421, 422, 572.
[3] The term 'social group' is used here in contradistinction to *genos* or family or clan. It therefore indicates what contemporary usage often describes as 'the entire community'.
[4] Glotz, loc. cit., pp. 209–11.

heritage which they left to the world in general and to Christianity in particular.

There can be no question that, by and large, Glotz's description of Hellenic conditions is correct: his great work, running to 621 closely-printed pages, is too well documented to allow any doubt. Yet there is a difficulty which is lightly alluded to on p. 191: 'In the *Iliad* and in the *Odyssey*,' Glotz says, 'strictly personal quarrels do not infallibly tie the offender's folk to his own fate.' And thereby hangs a general problem which a book like the present, which tries to derive Christianity from, or at least to explain Christianity's success by, the principle of ancient group-solidarity, must necessarily discuss.

We should, says Hubert Treston, who was Glotz's chief critic on this point, distinguish in Homeric society two distinct strata, the Pelasgians and the Achaeans. The Pelasgians were the aboriginal population of the land; the Achaeans were their recently arrived conquerors. All that Glotz says does apply with full force to the Pelasgian population. But the Achaeans were not equally committed to the principle of collective responsibility. Treston contrasts the 'unrestricted' and the 'personal restricted' vendetta and links the latter firmly and decisively with the Achaean class.[1]

So far, so good. However, we are told, the Achaeans stood on quite a separate plane. Following the lead of Walter Leaf,[2] Treston assumes that this military caste lived in an atmosphere foreign to the clan. Blood for blood was indeed the normal retribution, but individual blood only. The Achaean 'mode of vengeance . . . refuses to visit the sins of the father upon his children or upon his neighbours. The right to revenge remains with the relatives of the slain . . . but they dare not strike the innocent for the guilty . . . The vengeance is quite personal and individual, that is, the murderer alone is liable to the blood feud, which is therefore neither collective nor hereditary. Vengeance is a duty which devolves upon the dead man's sons or brothers, but we may include the possibility of support from a kindred of limited extent: a kindred which may be an embryonic clan . . .' This, Treston asserts, is the state of things in Homeric society: Homer was the poet of the Achaeans.[3]

Are we to conclude from this evidence that the Greeks were less collectivistic, by more than perhaps a shade, than the Jews, and there-fore less ready to accept a collectivistic creed such as Christianity? In weighing this question, there are several considerations. The first is that, after all, the basic, autochthonous population, the Pelasgian bottom layer, was every bit as collectivistic as the Israelites. The second

---

[1] Treston, H. J., *Poine: A Study in Ancient Greek Blood-Vengeance*, London etc. 1923, pp. 1 and 2.

[2] Cf. especially this author's *Homer and History*, London 1915.

[3] Treston, loc. cit., pp. 65, 69, 2, 27, 100; cf. also pp. 59, 107, 108.

is that, on Treston's own witness, later conquerors of Greece were not, like the Achaeans, relatively individualistic, but rather, like the Pelasgians, largely anti-individualistic. 'Leaf suggests that the Dorians may have followed methods of conquest similar to those of the Achaeans, yet he has no doubt that they were identical in social organization with the Pelasgians.' In this manner, the Achaean dispensation is in our opinion no more than an interlude, and Treston fully confirms the fact. 'In spite of conflicts and migrations, the dominant Hellenic or post-Homeric Greek society was based on clan and tribal organizations similar to those of the early Pelasgians. The militarist Achaeans of the *Iliad* and the *Odyssey* must then be regarded as a solitary accidental ephemeral phantom which crossed the stage of Grecian history never to return.'[1] In post-Homeric times, 'unrestricted' rather than 'restricted' vendetta became the norm.[2] In other words, the Greeks were now very largely like other nations.

These admissions would, in principle, be quite enough for our argument. But we should add that even the apparent individualism of the Achaeans was no real individualism, and that their restricted vendetta was no less a sign of firm group (if not perhaps clan) integration than the unrestricted feud. Why, we must surely ask, did the Achaeans restrict vengeance? Surely because, as a caste that conquered by force, and that was in all probability a numerical minority, they had to keep themselves numerous and united. The occasional loss of one could not be avoided since men will commit crimes; but they simply could not afford a wider internecine struggle. Theirs was the inner unity of a tribe on the move, of a military echelon, not the inner unity of a society settled on the soil, of an agricultural people. But it was a total unity all the same.

Among the points of detail which link Greek and Hebrew history in this particular is the decidedly religious interpretation of the blood feud, its guarantee, so to speak, by the higher powers. As YHWH watches over it so that it should not fail, so does Zeus whose will in this respect is often expressed by Apollo. Indeed, the Greeks had special divinities, or at least half-divinities, who would avenge a dead man in cases where there was no one else to avenge him: the dread Erinnyes, originally no more than the angry souls of the slain, but later much more than that, a pack of hunters, hounds from hell, who would give no rest to their wretched victims.[3] 'They are more particularly the avengers of murder committed within the family itself . . . When the son has slain his father or mother, who shall then carry out the blood-feud incumbent upon the nearest relation of the dead? This nearest relation is the

---

[1] Ibid., pp. 129 and 130.
[2] Ibid., pp. 61, 77, 115, 116, 122, 127.
[3] Cf. Greene, W. Ch., *Moira: Fate, Good, and Evil in Greek Thought*, Cambridge, Mass., 1948, p. 17.

murderer himself.' Here, then, the Erinnyes must intervene. But 'their absolute power extends in widening circle to all murder, even when it is committed outside the limits of the family',[1] and they go into action whenever and wherever the family concerned does not. Thus they implement, by way of substitution, the duties arising from the blood-bond, from the unity of the kin. A curse can call them upon the scene, as David's prayer was meant to bring down supernal aid when his circumstances did not allow him to pursue the killers of Abner. In Greece as in Israel, the coherence of the clan is the basic fact of the social constitution, and if there is a superintendent Providence which cares for the concerns of men, it must defend the key-reality on which all order, all society, is built.

While the distance between Palestine and Scandinavia is geographically much wider than that between Palestine and Greece, it was, at the time of which we are speaking here, sociologically to all intents and purposes as close, or nearly so. The reason is again the same as before. Kindred institutions and concepts centring on the essential unity of the basic social group made it easy for a doctrine asserting the solidarity of mankind in guilt and merit to pass from the shores of the Mediterranean to the shores of the Baltic and the North Sea. To demonstrate this similarity in attitudes, we can avail ourselves once more of the services of a top-ranking scholar. This time it is Frederic Seebohm.

From the welter of facts which he provides, we can only adduce a very few. We have chosen the regulations of the *Lex Scania Antiqua*, put on paper by an archbishop of Lund in Sweden in the first two decades of the thirteenth century.[2] Firstly, the regulations shed light on both Danish and Swedish custom, since the island of Skåne lies between them and belonged first to the one and then to the other country. Secondly, they preserve on the whole faithfully the ancient state of things, Romano–Christian influences being of but recent date.[3] 'From the tribal point of view,' Seebohm says in summing up, 'the solidarity of the family group was the chief interest regarded.'[4] By family we must understand in this context a group of descendants from a grandfather or great-grandfather. The kin so connected hold the land in common and are jointly responsible for any *wergild* that may have to be paid. With regard to the latter, article XLV, entitled *De Compositione*, records that until recently 'it always lay upon the slayer or his heir to provide the first portion [i.e. one-third] only from his own property. He might then exact the second portion from his agnates, and finally the third and last from his cognates.' And as the collection of the sum was ordered

---

[1] Rohde, E., *Psyche: The Cult of Souls and Belief in Immortality among the Greeks*, London 1925, p. 179.
[2] There is also an Old Danish version and hence the possibility of concluding back to an original common source of higher antiquity.
[3] Seebohm, F., *Tribal Custom in Anglo-Saxon Law*, London 1911, pp. 276, 277, 292.
[4] Ibid., p. 295.

THE AGE OF COMMUNITY AND ITS RELIGIOUS CULTURE

on the principle of sharing or collective responsibility, so was its distribution. 'In chapter XLVII it is stated that according to ancient law the distribution should be so made that each third should be divided again into subthirds, one of which should be paid to the [body] heirs of the slain, the second to the agnates, and the third to the cognates.' Trying to get rid of these forms and to replace them with more modern, i.e. more individualistic ones, King Waldemar II (who died in 1241) ordained that the murderer should find the whole *wergild* himself. But even this innovating ruler could not throw off the old collectivism. If the culprit fled, he stipulated, 'his relatives, agnates and cognates, were individually to offer their proper share of two-thirds . . . or be liable to the vengeance of the relatives of the slain.'[1]

So far as the basic facts are concerned, the rest of the Germanic world was not too different from its Scandinavian border area. Taking one step to the south, we come to the Frisians strung out along Europe's northern shores from the Zuider Zee to the island of Sylt. A source of the thirteenth century, the *Apes* of Thomas Cantiprantanus (a piece of edifying literature), relates that these tribes did not at once bury a man who had been slain; they kept him, or rather his corpse, in the house and preserved it by desiccation until such time as it was possible for them to avenge him. Only then did they commit him, proudly and with pomp and circumstance, to the earth. This gruesome custom was followed all over the area which is now called Germany and then included Switzerland as well. It was already a reform when, instead of the whole body, only the severed right hand was preserved.[2] We can let these things rest here; the wide distribution of the habit to delay burial until vengeance was secured shows with sufficient clarity that we are confronted with a widespread cultural trait.

With the softening of manners, compensation tended to take the place of feuding, but the collective character of the transaction remained, as can easily and impressively be seen from the detail of the pacification procedure which developed. 'After agreement had been reached, a day was set for ritual reconciliation. Usually a Sunday morning was chosen, or the day of the "burial with honours" which had to be paid for by the murderer. At the end of the religious service the parties concerned repaired to the open grave of the dead man where his nearest relative on the sword side and his other kinsfolk took up their place on the one edge, and opposite them, on the other, the murderer and his sib. Here the murderer asked his opponents three times for forgiveness and prayed, together with his relatives, a *Pater*

---

[1] Cf. ibid., pp. 285, 286, 289, 290; cf. also pp. 287, 288, 276, 267 and 243 (concerning the ancient North Frostathing law), pp. 246 et seq. (concerning the oldest of the North laws, the *Galathingslög*).
[2] Cf. Frauenstädt, P., *Blutrache und Todtschlagsühne im deutschen Mittelalter*, Leipzig 1881, pp. 10 and 11 (with notes).

Noster and an *Ave Maria* for the poor soul of the slain. Thereupon the leader of the other group handed him, in sign of reconciliation, the "dead hand" across the open ditch. The murderer let it drop into the earth and then paid over the first instalment of the composition money.'[1] The German phrase 'to give burial to the dead man's hand' is, as can be seen, a virtual equivalent of the English phrase 'to bury the hatchet'. Although there is no longer bloody warfare, the spirit of the blood feud at least is still present.

Foremost among the foes of the blood feud, needless to say, was the Church. Peaceful arbitration was her prescription, not cruel vengeance. Yet it is precisely a great churchman who shows us that the Germanic tradition also carried the conviction which we have observed in both Israel and Greece that God Himself will intervene where human justice fails to do what custom ordains. 'Look through his writings for the view of Gregory of Tours on divine vengeance,' writes Michael Wallace-Hadrill, 'and it will be found that he visualizes it as nothing less than God's own feud in support of His servants, who can have no other kin. God will avenge crimes specially heinous in the Church's eyes – parricide for example, crimes within the family generally and crimes involving all who lack natural protectors. The agent of vengeance may be God Himself directly intervening to strike down the culprit (for instance with sickness) or it may be a human agent, as the king. At all events, God's vengeance is of the same nature as that of any head of a family . . . The Frankish churchmen cannot in any other way see *ultio divina* in a society dominated by the bloodfeud.'[2]

The mention of Gregory of Tours, who died in the year 594, brings us to the last point we wish to make in this section, namely the long continuance of the blood feud, and of its associated collectivistic conceptions, not only in a marginal area such as Scandinavia, but even in the heart-lands of the European continent. St. Boniface was to die in the year 755, and, naturally, he was greatly concerned as to who would succeed him, who would carry on his work. He thought he had the right man, yet he hesitated. 'Why did St. Boniface become doubtful about the propriety of regarding Gregory of Utrecht as a likely successor? Because, it seemed, Gregory might have become involved in feud, his brother apparently having killed the uncle of the *Dux Francorum*; and nobody knew how the *discordia* would end. The *Dux* might decide to avenge his uncle's death fairly widely on Gregory's family. We may assume that this did not, in fact, happen; but the career of Gregory of Utrecht might have been very different had it not been for the threat overhanging his kin at a critical moment.' Rome had become influential by this time, both the Rome of the lawyers and the Rome of the popes.

[1] Ibid., pp. 127 and 128.
[2] Wallace-Hadrill, J. M., *The Long-haired Kings, and Other Studies in Frankish History*, London 1962, p. 127; cf. also p. 126.

Yet ancient collectivism still stood its ground. 'Not even Charlemagne saw feuding as a positive evil in the empire of his Augustinian *pax*,' Wallace-Hadrill writes, and he ends by saying that 'feuding in the Carolingian world [still] had a long future before it.'[1]

As with the Franks south of the Channel, so with the Anglo-Saxons to the north of it. A competent researcher has recently studied the kin structure there from about the seventh to the beginning of the eleventh century and has come to rather carefully weighed conclusions. 'The picture that emerges is complex: the system appears to have been less rigid than has frequently been thought; the circle of effective kin smaller; the lack of descent groups probable, despite patrilateral bias; the stability of marriage uncertain; and the corporateness of kindreds as landholding and residential units to have been unproven.'[2] Yet when it comes to the core phenomenon, the principle of social organization is seen to be largely the same as in other Germanic societies. 'What duty did a kin group owe to Ego? First and foremost, they owed him the duty of avenging his death, either by prosecuting a feud, or by exacting wergild payments. On the other hand, if Ego had killed or injured a man, he could expect some support from his kinsmen in helping him bear a feud or pay a wergild.' Echoes of Israel! Echoes of Greece! Indeed, even the most decisive detail is identical: 'In feuding the legal solidarity of the kin group is demonstrated by the fact that one member of the slayer's kin group is as good a victim for vengeance as the slayer himself.' So the final verdict is, and has to be, that 'right up until the accession of Edward the Confessor [i.e. A.D. 1042], the kinship system remained a potent force of social control' in the tribal area of the Anglo-Saxon stock.[3]

Where a strong state developed, both blood feuding and the wergild system had to yield to the kind of criminal prosecution which we are practising at present. But where feudalism survived, the old collectivism survived, too, and the private tort did not become a public crime. Rightly does Frauenstädt explain that the new condition could only take hold after the old 'sib consciousness' had died off, and that did not happen until the end of the Middle Ages.[4] Indeed, even after the fifteenth century, the legal authorities still showed a tendency here and there to leave the 'composition' of a case of manslaughter in their territory to the parties, or rather to the collective power of the parties. To the middle of the sixteenth century, we are told, court and town records exhibit instances 'a-plenty' (*in Menge*) in which the parties were officially encouraged to compose their difficulties themselves. In more

---

[1] Wallace-Hadrill, loc. cit., pp. 144, 188, 146.
[2] Lancaster, L., 'Kinship in Anglo-Saxon Society', *The British Journal of Sociology*, vol. IX (1958), pp. 375 and 376; cf. also p. 231.
[3] Ibid., pp. 368, 371, 376; cf. also p. 370.
[4] Frauenstädt, loc. cit., p. 7. Cf. also pp. 11, 14, 18, 86.

conservative countries, like Schleswig and Switzerland, it was only the middle of the seventeenth century that brought the disappearance of this last vestige of the once flourishing clan constitution of social life.[1]

We have now amassed and adduced sufficient evidence to prove that community was, according to all three dimensions, geographical width of distribution, historical length of prevalence, and socio-cultural depth of organizational penetration, a system strong enough to provide a sound substructure for a religious superstructure such as Christianity. It is true, as we shall see, that the alternative principle of association made powerful bids for domination even in the ancient world, even in Israel and Greece, indeed, that it gained a number of temporary victories long before it finally succeeded in establishing itself as the master of social life in modern times. Yet *every* society, as Tönnies has emphasized, has an element of community in it, first of all as a matter of fact (for no social system can well survive without some sympathetic fusion in the interrelation of its parts), and then above all as a matter of aspiration (for no society will easily give up the hope and the longing for a truly integrated common life without human antagonisms); every society contains therefore at least a potential basis for a strongly social religiosity such as original Christianity. The difference between the ages is therefore merely one of degree. Yet degree is important: it may decide the form and even the fate of religiosity. To demonstrate to what *high* degree the fully-fledged communities of the past prefigured and preformed, in their organization and in their outlook, the Christian faith, is the next task with which we have to deal.

THE MENTAL CULTURE OF COMMUNITY

If we may and must assume that the principle of community is in some societies not only a basic outer fact, but also a basic inner experience, we cannot be surprised to find that these societies produce an inclusive mentality to match it. Their whole style of thinking will be integrational. There will be a pervasive tendency to see and find coherence everywhere, in nature no less than in human life; indeed, this tendency may overshoot the mark and assert unity where the facts no longer warrant it and speak of diversity, perhaps even of irreducible diversity. In such cases we get ideology, a sad deviation from the truth. But before that borderline is reached, many insights will have been gained under the inspiration of the principle of unity and community which will represent secure achievements and possessions. Much in early man's outlook may be explained in the light of his addiction to the life- and thought-form of totality, due or undue, sound or ill-advisedly exaggerated, as the case may be.

One area in which the hunger and thirst for coherent patterns can

[1] Ibid., pp. 168, 172, 173.

clearly be seen at work is that of the great creation myths. According to the Nordic tradition, all that exists was made from the body of the giant Ymir. From his flesh the earth was formed, from his blood the sea, from his bones the mountains, from his hair the forests, and from his skull the heavenly dome, roof of the universe. The Vedic hymn known as the *Purushasukta* has a similar character.[1] The philosophical implication is plain: our senses show us a far-flung diversity, but in the depths of being the manifold is truly one. Multiplicity is but phenomenal, appearance; unity alone is noumenal, real.

What is true of mythology, is true of magic also. It can never make sense to a scientific age, but it can at least be sympathetically understood. What induced the people of another day to believe that they could bewitch a man if only they had a piece of him, a hair-lock, for instance, or even a droplet of spittle? Surely it was the idea that what happens to a part of him, will happen to the rest of him as well; differently expressed, it was the inability to see the part other than as an ingredient in the whole, the enslavement of thought to the inclusive pattern at the expense of the included element. 'The part, in mythical terms, is the same thing as the whole,' writes Cassirer, 'because everything which it incurs or does is incurred or done by the whole at the same time.' And again, in another context: 'Outward form and physical character can so easily be regarded as a mere mask [by primitive man], because from the outset the feeling of the community of all visible things effaces all visible distinctions and all distinctions which can be postulated in analytical-causal thinking ... Even where there is a strong tendency towards separation [for instance] of the spiritual from the physical, towards a dualism between body and soul, the original mythical feeling of unity continuously breaks through.'[2]

These assertions, as every sociologist knows, come very close to Emile Durkheim's theses as developed above all in the classical closing pages of *Les Formes élémentaires de la vie religieuse*. Nevertheless, Cassirer polemizes against him.[3] Why? We need not enter deeply into their disagreements because they touch only lightly on the sociology of religion, but we should like to specify our own point of view which is, in a manner, a reconciliation of the two.

Ernst Cassirer came from an idealistic tradition, the tradition of Immanuel Kant and his Marburg disciples. He freely acknowledged that intramental and extramental forms of thought and fact stand in a mutual relationship, that fact generates thought and thought, fact. But he was inclined, as are all of his general outlook, to attribute the primacy of being to thought. For him it was more true to say that

---

[1] Cf. Cassirer, E., *The Philosophy of Symbolic Forms*, vol. II, 'Mythical Thought', transl. Manheim, R., New Haven 1955, p. 54.
[2] Ibid., pp. 50, 187, 191.
[3] Ibid., pp. 192–4.

social relations set into a determinate pattern because men think in a certain way than vice versa, that people think in a certain way because the social relations which enclose them have set in a determinate pattern. Characteristically, he calls myth, in the very title of his part III, a 'form of life' rather than a form of thought. Myth then is the parent reality from which there emanates a social organization which, if it is a determining element, is yet in the first place itself determined. Cassirer asks 'whether it is not the pure forms of thought and intuition which make possible and constitute . . . the content of reality,' and answers this question in the affirmative. 'The structure of society is a mediated and ideally conditioned reality,' he asserts. 'It is not the ultimate, ontologically real cause of the spiritual and particularly the religious categories, but rather is decisively determined by them.'[1] That is where Durkheim disagreed, at least up to the very last period of his life. He read the equation between social and mental forms from the other side. Social facts are first, and from them flow mental forms which appear to be essentially secondary – epiphenomena only. The reason for this attitude lay in Durkheim's adherence to the materialistic philosophy of his day, and more especially in his debt and discipleship to Herbert Spencer. His approach appeared to Cassirer necessarily as a bad case of sociologism, i.e. as an exaggeration of the social element in the causal nexus. Indeed, it appeared as something worse, as a bad case of materialistic determinism, in so far namely as the social system itself, which ontologically anteceded and only subsequently dismissed a mental universe, was to Durkheim for many years simply a product of brazen laws of nature, no freer in its formation than any organism, any frame of flesh.

The sociology of knowledge needs to overcome the onesidedness of both Durkheim and Cassirer, especially if it is to become fruitful in our chosen field, the analysis of religion. Intramental and extramental forms can, after all, be divided and contrasted only in the mind of the scholarly observer; in reality itself they form an indissoluble whole. Men think in a certain way because they live in a certain way; men live in a certain way because they think in a certain way; both propositions are equally true, and it is only because we cannot pronounce or write down two different sentences at the same time that we must make the one statement before the other. It certainly does not matter which we place first.[2]

While the present book, therefore, proffers and propagates a sociological explanation of the origin of Christian culture-forms and ideas, it is yet in principle opposed to all sociologism. Sociology can contribute much to the understanding of the genesis of Christianity and of the various modes in which it incarnated and expressed itself, and a book entitled *The Sociology of Religion* must see how far it can possibly carry the sociological principle of analysis, if it is to fulfil its purpose and

[1] Ibid., p. 193.
[2] Cf. on all this my *Sociology of Knowledge*, as already quoted.

promise. But it must not overstep its logical and fact-given confines. Where other factors enter in, they must be freely and fully acknowledged.

It is not our duty to pursue these other factors, but it must be permissible, by way of illustration, to cast a brief side-glance at one of them, in order to prove that undue narrowness is not a charge which can be laid at the present author's door. If primitive man thought in terms of totality, one of the reasons for it is that he wished to be back in the great warmth- and security-giving womb of nature from which he had but recently emerged. A birth-trauma besets not only the individual whose first cry protests his ejection from the cosiness of the maternal flesh, it beset the race also when it awoke to the fact that it had to fend for itself in a hard and unfriendly habitat. Many of the early rituals try to mediate an experience, however momentary, however fleeting, of enclosedness in nature, of a total merging of the individual self in the universal life – an experience which is valuable both in itself and in its consequences. Cassirer mentions the Babylonian cult of Tammuz, the Phrygian cult of Attis, and the Thracian cult of Dionysus, but we would refer above all to the Totemic dances which are mimetic imitations of animal movements, hence identifications with a creature still securely held within the framework of nature, and hence again experiential re-insertions, within that framework, of man himself. 'In none of these cults does man stop at the mere contemplation of the natural process,' Cassirer comments. 'He is impelled to burst through the barrier that separates him from the universe of living things, to intensify the life feeling in himself to the point of liberating himself from his generic or individual *particularity* . . . Here we have no mere mythical-religious interpretation of the natural process but an immediate union with it, an authentic drama which the religious subject experiences in himself.'[1]

If the last paragraph was, as must be admitted, something of an aside in a sociology of religion, it was a necessary and not a frivolous one. Any man's assertions are more convincing if it is clear to his hearers or readers that he is aware of his proper limitations and anxious to remain within them. We can therefore return, with doubled confidence, to our main task, namely to show up the mental mirrorings of community which, between them, set the scene in whose ambit Christianity came to birth.

We have already distinguished three culture-areas which mark the progress of the Christian religion from an early provincialism to a final world-wide spread. We shall now survey them in succession, in order to find out how the unity of the basic social group had in each of them given outline and content to thought and feeling, and how the thought and feeling thus created and institutionalized could receive, accept and further unfold the Gospel message when it came through Jesus Christ.

[1] Cassirer, loc. cit., pp. 188 and 189.

The case of Israel

The spirit of a society, and especially the system of values which provides its inner structure, its stiffening, its backbone, as it were, is best expressed in its language, though even in this its expressed form it often remains somewhat elusive. Words have different undertones and overtones; some strike a richer chord than others; those that have the fullest undertones and overtones and that strike the most resonant chords, indicate where the heart and the treasure of a community lie. Philologists assure us that the three terms which, to the Jew of classical times, had the highest and the deepest significance were *mishpaha*, *bayya* and *eleph*, all describing, in one way or another, the extended family, the kin or clan. 'None of the social definitions is so living as that of the *mishpaha*,' Pedersen assures us, and he was a Hebraist of no common stature; the word is always used, he asserts, in an 'extremely living manner'.[1] The last phrase is particularly apt, and that in more senses than one, for *mishpaha* means in the first place a common source of life, a community of being. In this word, a physical and a psychic element are totally united, merged to such an extent that it almost seems wrong to separate them and set them down next to each other. The *mishpaha* is a unity in the flesh (one body) and a unity of the mind (one soul). It is, in other words, a total unity.

But can a society, can even a family, be a total unity, one body and one soul, as the individual person is? The Jewish sources assert it, however little modern man may be inclined to believe it. In the Bible Joseph (or Jacob, or Dan, or any other name) may sometimes designate an individual, and sometimes a tribe – so small is the difference in meaning to the Hebraic mind. When we hear that Joseph's father Jacob made him a present of a fine new coat, nobody is, and nobody can be, meant but an individual; but when the same Jacob declares that 'Joseph is a growing son, a growing son and comely to behold,' and when he adds, in the *same* breath, 'the daughters run to and fro upon the wall' (Genesis XLIX, 22), he clearly refers to a whole *mishpaha* stretching down into a distant future penetrable only to the inspired vision of an aged patriarch close to God. The one is the many, the many is the one; there is no need to make fine distinctions.[2] Again, when Jacob addresses Joseph with the words: 'Behold I die, and God will be with you, and will bring you back into the land of your fathers. I give thee a portion[3] above thy brethren which I took out of the hands of the Amorrhite with my sword and bow' (Genesis XLVIII, 21 and 22), he means now himself as a person,

---

[1] Pedersen, loc. cit., pp. 49, 50; cf. also pp. 48, 259, 263, 206, 217, 340, 475.
[2] Cf. ibid., pp. 13, 14; cf. also pp. 47, 48.
[3] Literally: the shoulder of a mountain.

now himself as a collectivity. 'The first part [of this passage] shows us a scene in Egypt: Jacob lies on his death-bed in his chamber and takes leave of his son Joseph who has brought his two boys Ephraim and Manasseh. But the next word transfers us to quite a different sphere. The old man suddenly grows into a tribe which has conquered an important part of the land of Canaan and leaves it to another tribe, Joseph, including two more tribes, Ephraim and Manasseh, who in the historical periods actually lived in those parts.'[1]

We cannot, and we need not, pile example upon example here, or else we should get a mountain as high as Ossa added to Pelion. But one further passage should be brought up because it is particularly instructive – Genesis xxxiv, 30: 'Jacob said to Simeon and Levi: You have troubled me and made me hateful to the Chanaanites and Pherezites, the inhabitants of this land. We are few: they will gather themselves together and kill me.' In this translation, the lines make perfect sense, and we can hardly blame the authors of the Douai version for rendering them in this fashion. Yet Pedersen, with the high sense of precision built into every true philologist, translates differently: 'I being few in number, they shall gather themselves together against me and slay me . . .'[2] To us 'I' is always 'few in number', for one is but one; but to the Hebrew 'I' and we' are convertible, identical terms.[3] 'I' can mean many, because the many always means one. They are so above all in the clan group, the *mishpaha*.

Spreading out from this vital centre, the *mishpaha* or clan, Jewish collectivism underlaid other words describing pluralities of people with the same configurational, integrational, unitary meaning, changing them, so to speak, from plurals into singulars. The so-called tribes had been clans once, but subdivision had, by David's time, loosened them to a considerable degree. Yet they are still seen in the same light as the proper *mishpaha*, the narrower circle deriving, not from a distant, but from a nearer forefather, the grandfather's grandfather perhaps.[4] When David addressed the ancients of Juda through the mouth of Sadoc and Abiathar, he assured them: 'You are my brethren; you are my bone and my flesh' (II Kings xix, 12). It was not, on this occasion, the narrower circle of the clan he was speaking to; it was the wider circle of the tribe. More indistinct than the term for tribe is the word *am* which is usually translated as 'people'. When Jacob feels that his day has come, he expresses this by saying: 'I am now going to be gathered to my people' (Genesis xlix, 29). The Holy Book uses the same phrase when recording the decease of Abraham: 'He died in a good old age . . . and was gath-

---

[1] Pedersen, loc. cit., p. 15.
[2] Pedersen, loc. cit., p. 289.
[3] Ibid., p. 275.
[4] Cf. Merz, loc. cit., p. 20. The biblical passages adduced there think in terms of a family-founder and four generations after him. Cf. esp. IV Kings x, 30.

ered to his people' (Genesis xxv, 8). The English version makes no difference between the two passages, and rightly so, for the essential meaning is the same. Yet the Hebrew text speaks in the later text, concerning Jacob, of people (singular), in the earlier, concerning Abraham, of peoples (plural) – a characteristic distinction and indistinction. 'One of the peculiarities of this word,' says our guide through philology, 'is that it can be used both in the singular and in the plural, very nearly with the same sense . . . This fluctuating *usus loquendi* expresses the Israelitic conception of the relation between the whole and the unit. The whole is entirely in the individual and *vice versa*.'[1]

The widest circle to which the collectivistic, the clan-like, the familial, conception of unity is applied in the Old Testament is the 'House of Israel'. Many are the passages in which the conviction that all Jews are brothers is asserted, and there is no need to parade them. We can clearly see at this point that Christianity both continued Israelitic thought and feeling, and went beyond them. It continued the Israelitic tradition by seeing societies as wholes; it went further in that it defined *all* men as a community in guilt and merit – all men without difference and distinction. Sinners are sometimes jocularly described as 'sons of Adam' and 'daughters of Eve'. The significance of the formula is, in the Christian's mouth, entirely serious. *All* men are Adam's clan, his *mishpaha*, not only those who derive further from and through Noe and Abraham; it was the race that fell when the first man, father of all, set his will wantonly against the will of his Maker. 'In Adam's fall,' as the hymn has it, 'we sinnèd all.'

But if the Jewish conception left something to be desired on the score of extent, not reaching the unity of human kind, it left little to be added on the score of depth. Leviticus xix, 18, enjoining that we should love our neighbours as ourselves, is common to Christians and Jews – indeed, the supreme commandment of both Judaism and Christianity. 'Love is not a more or less superficial sentiment,' writes Pedersen, in trying to plumb the depth of this biblical passage as it lived in the minds of pious Jews. 'The life which the individual holds is not private property, but something common, which he shares with others . . . In love the soul acts in accordance with its nature, because it is created to live in connection with other souls . . . The commandment to love is thus not a dogmatic invention, but a direct expression of the character of the soul and the organism of family and people. It means that the individual acts for the whole, and the whole for the individual, and this is not an abstract or an unnatural claim, but only the substance of normal life. He who keeps the law of love, shows that the soul is sound.'[2] There was only one point in which the Gospel could better this injunction – by adding humanity to family and people. But love itself,

---

[1] Pedersen, loc. cit., pp. 59, 54 and 55.
[2] Pedersen, loc. cit., pp. 309 and 310.

the bond of perfection, as St. Paul calls it in his first Epistle to the Corinthians, is conceived in the Old Testament as it is in the New, and in both there shows, there shines, through the ethical and religious commandment the reality of the clan, constituted as it is as a vital whole.

The revolutionary act by means of which the Christian religion freed itself from, and rose superior to, the national and nationalistic limitations of the Jewish creed, was the expulsion of the physiological element from the definition of community. With the Jews, the social bond was always a bond of blood; descent meant filiation *per ovum et sperma*. For Christianity, the social bond is a bond of the spirit; descent means filiation by discipleship. Sem and Cham started different lines of kindred as did Israel and Ishmael. The offspring of Cham through his son Chanaan are no longer fully identical with the offspring of Sem. Hostility may therefore spring up between them. The physiological principle of unity can turn into a principle of disunity also.

But though the Semites and Israelites could enter into conflict with the Hamites, Canaanites and Ishmaelites, and though they were very conscious of that conflict, so much so indeed that the common descent and the common ancestor higher up the line counted for relatively little in the end, they never gave up the principle of unity and community as their basic form of thought. The Canaanites and the Ishmaelites, and even the more distant nations, also constitute, for the Jews, each of them, a *mishpaha*. When Jeremias curses the outer world, it is upon the 'families' that have not invoked God's name that he calls down the divine wrath (Jeremias x, 25[1]); and Zacharias, where he speaks of those who stubbornly refuse to worship the true Lord, refers to 'the family of Egypt' (Zacharias xiv, 18). Thus, although the world is not, to the Jews, one family of man, it is yet composed of families of man. 'The idea of the *mishpaha* is the basis of all definitions,'[2] and the structure has everything but the coping stone.

Indeed, the Jewish mind was so much given to conceptualization in terms of clanship, that the principle was also used, without misgivings, where it was obviously not applicable. We should never speak of the members of a trade guild as a 'house', the term suggesting, to say the least, a quasi-family; but this is precisely what the Bible does (Nehemia iii, 8). We should never speak of a religious confraternity or sect, formed as it is by the association of the like-minded, not the blood-related, as a house; but, again, this is precisely what the Bible does: the Rechabites constitute a 'house'; they are 'the race' of Jonadab, the Son of Rechab (Jeremias xxxv, 18 and 19). (In fact, they are merely his followers.) In the same spirit Eliseus calls Elias his 'father' (IV Kings ii, 12). Of necessity, the conception of the priesthood is collectivistic, too.

---

[1] The Douai version has 'provinces' instead of 'families', a *constructio ad sensum*. But 'families' is philologically more correct. Cf. Pedersen, p. 49.
[2] Pedersen, ibid.

One man cannot be a priest, or rather if he is, then his kinsmen are priested also. And when a priestly house degenerates, as did that of Eli, it dries off *in toto*, the branches as well as the stem.[1] This is how the Bible thinks and feels.

What all this amounts to is the conviction that wherever there is association and co-operation, albeit on a purely contractual basis, there also is something like friendship, like a family, like an organism integrated in body and soul. The very slaves are not excluded, especially if they are born in the house. They are in quite a number of Bible passages considered as 'sons of the house'[2] and may call their master 'father' (IV Kings v, 13). An ideal is thus sketched out, a vision is given which had its after-effect for many centuries, down to the papal encyclicals on social affairs in our own day. Perhaps it was, where serving men were concerned, no more than an ideal or a vision, but, if so, it was one highly characteristic of the culture which conceived it.

Because community was in this manner so firmly established, both in fact and in thought, two developments which, in other circumstances, would have been apt to lead to the weakening of social coherence, if not indeed to a transition to mere association, did not have that effect in Israel: settlement and urbanization. It is not surprising that the nomad sticks to his kith and kin: they are all on the move together and they all camp together around the same fire or the same water-hole. Their security, if they have any, is collective. Things tend to change, when settlement supervenes, for settlement means as a rule separation. But the farm of Cis (I Kings x) and that of Michas (Judges xvii and xviii) appear to have harboured a wider circle of agnatic kin, and Deuteronomy xxv, 5, begins with the words: 'When brethren dwell together . . .' Obviously, they did dwell together in many cases, if not indeed in all. 'The Israelitic life in caves, in tents and in villages,' Pedersen judges, 'would not dissolve the force of tribal coherence. Even when the invaders conquered walled towns, this would at first agree very well with the tribal conception, seeing that a tribe settled in a couple of towns lying very close to one another, as was done by the tribe of Dan.'[3]

In later times it was indeed the town rather than the cave, the tent or the village which provided the shell in which the life of the Jews could unfold and proceed. The place-names which loom large in Holy Writ are, besides Jerusalem, Megiddo, Jericho, Gezer, Lachich and so forth, all hamlets which could boast the main distinguishing feature of a city, a wall. To the modern sociologist, the town is an archetype of associational society and rightly so, for it is, as he knows it, largely a human existence side by side in severalty, not one of integration and fusion.

[1] Cf. Pedersen, loc. cit., p. 270.
[2] Cf. ibid., p. 64.
[3] Ibid., p. 33.

But the Old Testament town was different. 'The city community is a *mishpaha*,' Pedersen writes, 'and consequently the fellow-citizen becomes a brother.'[1] Abimelech is no brother to Boaz or to the Sichemites, but he is so described because he is a fellow-townsman of Boaz and a kinsman to Sichem's rulers (Ruth IV, 3; Judges IX, 18). The test, of course, here and everywhere, is collective responsibility. The townsmen must stand and fall together like one kin, and one man. The most gruesome illustration of this fact is offered in the First Book of Kings (XXII, 19) which relates how Saul handled a whole settlement: 'And Nobe ... he smote with the edge of his sword, both men and women, children and sucklings and ox and ass and sheep, with the edge of the sword.'

Several details which are highly revealing both singly and collectively demonstrate how consistently this interpretation of the city as a social entity is carried out. The elders are considered as identical with the inhabitants, as the grandfather is with his offspring.[2] Where outlying villages or farms are regarded as belonging to a specific township, they are called its 'daughters':[3] always the same pattern, always the same idea. It should only be mentioned in conclusion that the city, though a *mishpaha*, was not as strong a *mishpaha* as the *mishpaha* properly so called, the kin group. Where clans living within the same walls fell out, the elders could only act as go-betweens between the parties, or at best as arbitrators. A crime remained an offence against the victim and his clansfolk; it failed to become an offence against the town.[4]

If the development of cities was thus unable to dislodge and uproot the principle of community, so was the monarchy when it came. In general, the state drives forward towards a merely associational life, just as the city does. It subjects the people to a distant ruler and moulds it into an anonymous mass. Its whole scheme sees threads running upward from the individual to the king, but not sideways from individual to individual, from kin to kin. 'But conditions in Canaan were not favourable to a development of this kind. The communities were too heterogeneous and their independence too deeply rooted.'[5] Above all, the monarchy did not succeed in transmuting private torts, handled as family feuds, into public crimes, handled by royal courts. It was, so Merz tells us, the concept of family autonomy which had survived from older, nay the oldest, times which made it impossible for the 'kings' of Israel to become real kings.[6]

We have now systematically surveyed the forms and formations which, between them, made up the social life of the Jewish people, and found that all of them, without exception, were conceptualized in terms of clans and communities. And yet, we have still not reached the outer rim of the area which was dominated by this mode of thinking,

[1] Ibid., p. 59; cf. also pp. 50, 34, 275, 407.
[2] Ibid., p. 36.   [3] Ibid., p. 6.   [4] Merz, loc. cit., pp. 36–8.
[5] Pedersen, loc. cit., p. 23.   [6] Merz, loc. cit., pp. 39 and 38.

by this 'realistic' tendency in ontology. The Jews saw communities and clans even in nature, and this shows all the more impressively how deep the foundations were on which Christianity could base its metaphysical conviction that all men fell in the Old Adam, and that all rose again in the New. 'Everything individual is a direct expression of its type,' Pedersen writes in summing up,[1] and there is overwhelming evidence in support of this characterization of Israelite mental modes. In Pedersen's formulation, both the word 'every' and the word 'thing' must receive due emphasis, if his statement is to be correct.

The very language of Scripture shows that it is always a species which is meant when there is talk of animals, never an individual. The Douai version of Amos v, 19 reads as follows: 'If a man should flee from the face of a lion, and a bear should meet him, or enter into the house . . . and a serpent should bite him . . .' This is translation, not only into a modern language, but also into a modern mentality. For the text really refers to *the* lion, *the* bear, *the* serpent. The same applies to I Kings xvIII, 34–7.[2] When we meet the particular, we always meet the general. It is a concomitant of this bracketing together – of this non-distinction – between individuals, that species are all the more anxiously distinguished. They are truly 'defined'. The prohibition to yoke ox and ass together (Deuteronomy xxII, 10), or to sow different seeds together (Leviticus xIx, 19), or to weave wool and linen together (ibid.), are characteristic of a general anxiety to keep *genera* apart; above all, however, was the curse laid on sodomy, the mating of man and beast, an abomination more horrible to the Jew than to modern people (Leviticus xVIII, 23).

Even inanimate things, for instance pieces of the ground, are apprehended as species. There is no individual grave – there is only gravehood, if we may so express it. 'Sheol', Pedersen explains, 'is the entirety into which all graves are merged; but no more than the other entireties which fill the Israelitic world of ideas, it is the result of a summing up of all the single parts, so that Sheol should be the sum of the graves. All graves have certain common characteristics constituting the nature of the grave, and that is Sheol. The "Ur"-grave we might call Sheol; it belongs deep down under the earth, but it manifests itself in every single grave, as *mo'abh* manifests itself in every single Moabite. Where there is grave, there is Sheol, and where there is Sheol, there is grave.'[3]

After all this, we cannot be in the least surprised to hear that the very operation of the Jewish mind is dominated by the concept of totality. The sociologist of knowledge will at this juncture be reminded of Max Scheler's theory of 'functionalization': intuitions or ideas which our intellect habitually handles will in the end penetrate it so deeply that

[1] Pedersen, loc. cit., p. 491. Cf. also pp. 109 and 110.
[2] Ibid., pp. 485 and 486.
[3] Ibid., p. 462; cf. also pp. 460, 461, 466.

they become one with it and turn into its functioning structure.[1] This appears to be a good illustration of the Schelerian thesis. To us, the eye is an organ entirely different from the ear. To the Hebrew they form *one* inlet of knowledge. 'It is characteristic that the word which means to see, *ra'a*, not only means the impression received through the eye, but it also applies to the hearing, to the touch and, upon the whole, to the reception of any mental impression: one "sees" heat, misery, hunger, life and death.' In the same way, no distinction is drawn between sensation and will, a more passive and a decidedly active operation. 'The Israelite has no independent term for will as we understand the word . . . The soul is a totality; its sensations penetrate it entirely and determine its direction; the will is the whole of the tendency of the soul.' Again, 'the peculiarity about the Israelite is that he cannot at all imagine memory, unless at the same time an effect on the totality and its direction of will is taken for granted.' On a different level, thinking is not the progress from premiss to conclusion which it is for us; it is the grasping, *uno actu*, of premiss *and* conclusion. 'The thinking process of the Hebrew consists in forming wholes round certain centres.' Even where the unity of the body or the unity of the mind is not concerned, where two clearly separate (if related) entities are involved, as for instance a man and his appurtenances, the same logic of summation is at work. 'It is not mere chance,' Pedersen remarks, 'when the Hebrew language, in its terms, does not distinguish between the partitive and the possessive: to make part of and to belong to someone.' Truly, we have before us a different *type* of mind from our own. It is the type of mind which fathered Christianity.[2]

A linguistic medium which does not distinguish between a man and his appurtenances or between the many and the one appears to us poor because we consider it inexact. But what is lost on the one side, is gained on the other. When we say 'a Moabite', we mean either an individual from Moab with definite, i.e. limited and enumerable qualities, or simply an inhabitant of the town of that name. There will be no more in it for the typical modern mind, disinclined as it is to generalize. Not so for the Israelite. 'He takes hold of the essential . . . and lets the details subordinate themselves to that, and so his thought is ruled by the general idea. If, for instance, he calls up the image of a Moabite, then it is not an individual person with a number of individual qualities which also include the fact of his coming from Moab. The features which make the specially Moabitic character, create a *type* which is the sum and substance of Moabitic features.'[3] Thus the 'primitive' Hebrew's idea is less 'scientific' than ours because it is less narrowly delimited; but it is at the same time more suggestive and hence richer in content. It

---

[1] Cf. Stark, W., *The Sociology of Knowledge*, as quoted, pp. 329 and 330.
[2] Cf. Pedersen, loc. cit., pp. 100, 103, 107, 120, 228; further pp. 108, 115.
[3] Ibid., p. 109.

makes not only one string vibrate, but many at the same time. One of them or some of them may be specifically religious.

It is not, however, in these more distant mental consequences of the clan constitution of society that the religious implications of it rest; they are to be found, rather, deep in its inner core: in the conviction that all in a community carry a collective responsibility – the conviction most starkly shown up, and acted out, in the blood feud. The classical text is Exodus xx, 5 and 6, i.e. part of the passage conveying the Ten Commandments: 'I am the Lord thy God, mighty, jealous, visiting the iniquity of the fathers upon the children, unto the third and fourth generation of them that hate me, and shewing mercy unto thousands[1] of them that love me and keep my commandments.' Religion is in all societies a matter of suffering and blissfulness, curse and blessing, sin and salvation. The Jewish religion, like the Christian after it, saw both in collectivistic terms. When bliss, blessing and salvation came to David (II Kings vii, 16),[2] he was told by the prophet Nathan: 'Thy house . . . shall be for ever.' And when he had sinned so that curse and suffering were called down upon him, God says to him through the same mouth: 'The sword shall never depart from thy house' (ibid. xii, 10). Both the smile of the sun and the thunderbolt from the skies hit a kin, not a man.

We may fitly speak of blessing first, because it is the basis of everything. The chief blessing is life itself, and that is a never-ending stream stretching back into the dim past and forward into the distant future. We can see here once again, and particularly clearly, the physiological (some religionists might say: carnal) underground of Israelite thinking. When Jacob blessed Ephraim and Manasseh, the sons of Joseph, he said: 'God, in whose sight my fathers Abraham and Isaac walked . . . bless these boys . . . and may they grow into a multitude upon the earth' (Genesis xlviii, 15 and 16). The linking together of the life that was and the life that is to come is manifest here. To be is to be blessed, and to be is to be in a chain of being.[3]

Besides life, a blessing is also the power to make the best of life, to succeed. All that Abraham, Isaac and Jacob undertake, turns out well. And even Joseph, though a wily woman checks his career, rises above his difficulties and in the end reaches a pinnacle of glory. So also David: his wicked son rebels against him, but his luck (if this is the right expression) holds. Is it personal excellence that helps these men on and up? The Jews did not think so. 'Behind the blessing of the individual stand the fathers; from them he has derived it, and its strength depends

[1] The meaning is 'thousands of generations'. Pedersen interprets '(unnumbered) families', and gives corroborative passages. Cf. the appropriate note on p. 521.

[2] Cf., in addition to the Douai version, Pedersen p. 270 for the correct translation.

[3] Concerning other, similar chains of being, e.g. filiation through friendship, through the laying on of hands, etc., all understood by their analogy with physical filiation, cf. Pedersen, p. 165.

on their power . . . The blessing is a mental gift, and as such it has its root in something which partly loses itself in mystery.'[1] The reader can see for himself here how justified we were to ascribe to community in our introductory remarks[2] an inherent tendency towards religiosity which is lacking in associational systems.

The stream of being and of blessing may be interrupted by an incident of evil, the foe of being and the source of accursedness. We speak of an incident, but again, an incident is not a momentary event. It stretches through the centuries and descends to coming generations: it is as if some noisome filth had come to mingle with the pure waters of life that flow from the Godhead. A man called Cham breaks the sacred duty of filial respect and his clan is placed under a hereditary cloud. Characteristically, Noe, when he learns of Cham's behaviour, exclaims: 'Cursed be Chanaan' (Genesis IX, 25). Chanaan the son is mentioned by name, rather than his father, the real culprit, Cham. The reason for this surprising *quid pro quo*, or rather *quis pro quo*, is that the Jews for whom the Holy Scriptures were written were more familiar with, and felt greater enmity towards, the subclan of Chanaan (the Canaanites) than towards the superimposed clan of Cham (the Hamites).[3]

To modern man, the idea is strange, if not indeed revolting. Why punish Chanaan for the deed of Cham? Why involve yet unborn generations? To the Jews, there is no puzzle: who would, who could, make a distinction between those who belong together like one flesh? 'It is a thought with which we are constantly confronted in the prophets: the people bear the blessing of the fathers, but also their guilt.'[4] Both Jeremias and Micheas speak of the sinning Jews as one family (Micheas II, 3, and Jeremias VIII, 3). Even though common or at least widespread misconduct may be the basis of generalization here, a clearly individual fault, too, tarnishes the kindred. The adulterous woman is 'a curse . . . to all the people' (Numbers V, 27), i.e. to all her people. Pharao has involved his whole nation and not only himself in disaster when he personally acts evilly against the House of Israel (Genesis XII, 17).

For the transference of guilt from present culprits to other, and especially future, persons and groupings, direct divine sanction is at times invoked in Holy Writ. Thus Jeremias, who, as we shall see, is already inclined towards individualism,[5] makes God Himself say that, if a man will call his service to the Lord 'a burden', He 'will visit upon that man *and upon his house*' (XXIII, 34). But we must not get the idea that something incomprehensible is to be forced upon men, in the sense in which it is sometimes said: 'God is pleased to punish those that love

---

[1] Pedersen, loc. cit., p. 194.
[2] Cf. above p. 1.
[3] Cf. Stark, W., 'The Sociology of Knowledge and the Problem of Ethics', in *Transactions of the Fourth World Congress of Sociology*, Louvain 1959, vol. IV, pp. 85 et seq.
[4] Pedersen, loc. cit., p. 475.   [5] Cf. below pp. 239 et seq.

Him.' No, the transfer of which we are speaking is entirely natural for the tribal Jew, no outrage, no problem at all. *We* speak of a 'transfer', for to us individualists Cham and Chanaan are two people; *he* does not speak and think in these terms, for to him Cham and Chanaan are *one* person. Perhaps most revealing and convincing is David's prayer after his great sin. 'I have done wickedly. These that are the sheep, what have they done? Let thy hand, I beseech thee, be turned against me, and against my father's house' (II Kings xxiv, 17). The sheep are the king's subjects. A state is but a shadowy formation and so pardon for its members may be requested after their ruler's misdeed. But those of his father's house are so vitally connected with him that they cannot escape. His doom is theirs. There is no injustice involved, for kinsfolk are – to use St. Paul's phrase (Ephesians iv, 25) – literally members of each other. If we punish a thief, we send all of him to jail, and not only the right hand which has done the thieving.

A grim doctrine? Certainly. Yet it is precisely this doctrine of the unity of the many in guilt and punishment which bears in it the promise of salvation. The eighteenth chapter of the Book of Genesis tells the tale of the wicked city of Sodom; of God's sentence of annihilation against it; of Abraham's intercession on its behalf; and of God's readiness to pardon it for the sake of ten just men within the walls. Catholics have always considered this story to be prophetic. Sodom is a symbol of humanity, of the earthly city in St. Augustine's terminology, of Adam's accursed kin and kind; Abraham is a figure of Christ, the intercessor for all our race; the ten just men are the saints conjoined with Him. Hence as some may well destroy all, so also may all be saved by some – indeed, by One. The doctrine of unity and community is thus twosided or invertible. In Jesus it soars above the shadows and assumes the shining image of the Gospel message: salvation has come!

The Eastern Mediterranean

For a very long time, the educated entertained an idea of Greece which was more in accord with their own volitions and valuations, and with their desire to find at least one society in history which had already realized these volitions and valuations, than with the sober historical facts. Greece was to them the country of rationality, democracy and individualism. In so far as these conceptions had any basis in reality at all, it was a narrow one. Rationalism was for a while rampant in some circles; democracy held sway, temporarily, in some cities; individualism made a bid to become the dominant philosophy. But if the attention is directed towards the background and underground against which, and in connection with which, the triad of rationality, democracy and individualism has to be considered, it is found that they were merely the final products – 'the highest achievements', as the modern rationalists, democrats and individualists would say – of a social constitution which was very different in character. It almost comes as a shock when one reads, in the main work of one of the main experts, that, in the primitive period of the history of Hellas, 'the individual did not count in the clan (*genos*); his personality disappeared in a collective existence.'[1] And yet, there should really be no surprise. Plato, the towering central figure, is hardly understandable unless we see him as a scion of clan society. Certainly, that clan society has receded, by Plato's time, before the onslaught of a more associational life. Yet it is still there; it is still decisive. The communism which Plato recommends is clearly based on a low estimation of the principle of private property, and that low estimation in turn is predicated on the surviving conviction that all goods are in a sense belongings of the *genos*, of the group. When, in *The Laws*, the 'Athenian Stranger' says to Clinias of Crete: 'I, as lawgiver, make this ruling – that both you yourself and this your property are not your own, but belong to the whole of your race, both past and future,'[2] the reference is not so much to a state of things yet to come as to a state of things gone by and over. Likewise, and even more undeniably, the fundamental intuition of Plato's epistemology bears the stamp of community life, of clan existence. *Metexis* or participation is the key word. A thing is what it is by dint of its participation in the idea of its kind. A rose is a rose because it participates in the idea of a rose. A cow is a cow because it participates in cowhood. Who would not see here, as Paul Landsberg does,[3] the reflected image of contemporary or yet recent social circumstances? A man is a man only because, and in so far as, he participates in the clan. With Aristotle, this conception wanes, but it cannot be forgotten that he precisely was the chief architect of an organological, totality-centred philosophy of the state. Consistent individualists were only the Sophists; and their name was anathema all over Greece.

We have seen how much the blood feud meant in Greece. But the attitude on which it was based was by no means restricted to inter-family vendettas. 'In primitive civilization,' Glotz points out, 'the unity of the family asserts itself not only in relation to outsiders. It is no momentary accident in social life; it is its permanent ground, its necessary principle. The solidarity of the *genos* acts spontaneously and with unfailing certainty, like a natural force or like a vital instinct . . . The principle of collective responsibility rules . . . all the mutual relationships among the living . . . Absolute devotion to the family, that is the whole morality of these people.'[4]

---

[1] Glotz, loc. cit., p. 168. (Here, and in the sequel, our translation.)
[2] *Laws* XI, 923 A. Plato, *Laws*, transl. Burg, R. G., The Loeb Classical Library ed., New York 1926, vol. II, p. 421.
[3] Cf. Stark, *The Sociology of Knowledge*, as quoted, pp. 40 et seq.
[4] Glotz, loc. cit., pp. 45, 67, 60.

In the first place a descent group, the *genos* is even more than that. 'The members of the primitive *genos* were united, not only through the moral link of an asserted blood relationship, but also by the tangible bond created by neighbourhood. Offsprings of the same forefather, they were inhabitants of the same district or of the same settlement. For a long time, the rural commune . . . was, as Aristotle calls it,[1] a "familial colony", the dwelling place of "those who have sucked the same milk",[2] the abode of the *genos*. In Greece, as in India and in so many other countries, the village was, to start with, the undivided property of a sovereign family.'[3]

This social constitution evoked a mental constitution to match. The Greek language possesses two related terms: *themis*, the right familial order, and *aidos*, the individual's sense of duty. The two are considered to coincide: outer unity expresses itself in inner unity, or rather is identical with it. In the Iliad and the Odyssey, 'the duties which call forth the different modes of *aidos* [the desire to do good or the shame of having done wrong] are those of patriarchal life. All that a man is commanded by *themis* is recommended to him in his own interior by *aidos*. The *themis* has not only an external sanction, *nemesis*, which is an expression of popular and divine consciousness; it has also an inner sanction, *aidos*, the individual conscience which either makes itself obeyed or wreaks vengeance. Charged to bring the laws of *themis* to execution, *aidos* has the very same domain as *themis* itself . . . *Aidos* convinces every one of that which *themis* prescribes for all.'[4] If we may believe Glotz, even the coming of what one might call the age of public opinion did not change much in this respect. Public opinion always meant more in Greece than it does in our world. 'In the soul of that eminently social creature, that *zoon politikon*, which we call the Ancient Greek,' says Glotz, 'preoccupation with what one's neighbours think is an all-powerful spring of action. With the Hellenes, public opinion is not a volatile and sterile abstraction, but a concrete power.'[5]

In view of these facts, Glotz is well justified in asserting that 'the consciousness of the Greeks conceived all relationships of social existence in accordance with the unique and abiding type of patriarchal life'. But this formula does not go far enough. Even nature is pressed into the scheme of thought determined by, and reflective of, the clan. Glotz himself draws attention to this. 'The Hellenes,' he points out, 'went through a period when they regarded the species of animals as alien tribes. To kill an innocent beast appeared as a reprehensible, criminal act [like killing a harmless foreigner]. This idea preserved a singular

---

[1] Cf. *Politics*, I, 1, 7; *Aristotle's Politics*, transl. Jowett, B., ed. Davis, H. W. C., Oxford 1905, p. 27.
[2] Ibid.   [3] Glotz, loc. cit., pp. 193 and 194.
[4] Ibid., pp. 95 and 98.
[5] Ibid., pp. 95, 98, 233.

vitality in the religious traditions of the most civilized and most sceptical cities.'[1]

While the beasts in nature thus belong each to its own clan, in the civilized state they belong to the clan of their owner – so much is the unity of a household emphasized in Greek culture. 'The principle' that prevails 'is that of absolute solidarity, both active and passive, which unites all living beings on the territory of a group. At the beginning, people demanded blood for the wounding of a beast and gave satisfaction with their own blood for a beast guilty of having inflicted a wound. Oinos kills the dog of Hippocoon; the sons of Hippocoon come running and kill Oinos. When, in the contrary case, the dogs of Crotopos tear a small baby to pieces, the victim's father . . . holds the whole town of Argos responsible.' Collectivistic thinking was so strong that it bracketed the beasts of the household together with the sons of the house. But the bond binds not only man and beast, it also binds man and the land. Just as in Israel, the presence of a slain man on the land of a *genos* pollutes that *genos*: it is responsible in its entirety, even if there is no proof that the bloody deed has been done by one of its members.[2]

When we think of Greece, we usually think of her cities, Athens, Sparta, Thebes, Corinth, and so on, just as we think of Bethlehem or Jericho when we think of the Holy Land. But urbanization had relatively little influence on mental modes, because it had relatively little influence on social forms, in either country. Glotz calls the city a *genos agrandi* and the *genos* a *cité rudimentaire* and writes: 'The Greeks have always conceived the bond between the citizens who formed part of a group, a town or even several towns on the model of blood relationships.'[3] Of course, there are progressive changes. A commercial town like Athens must and does become progressively more associational. But the main communitarian conceptualization remains, and it remains particularly in the area with which we are concerned here, religion.

We have only conveyed a small fraction of the evidence, but it will surely have sufficed to show that there was, in Greece, an objective and subjective atmosphere which would allow a doctrine like that of a collective fall of mankind in Adam and a collective redemption of it in and through Christ to enter in. Just how easy this was, can be seen from a study of the legends which, between them, carried the burden of Greek religiosity as the traditions collected in the Bible did that of the Jewish faith. It is universally known that the Greeks did not make as sharp a distinction between the deeds of the divinities and the conduct of men as the Jews did between YHWH and the human race. The immortals mingle with the mortals all the time, and in more respects than one.

[1] Ibid., pp. 103 and 178.
[2] Ibid., pp. 181, 188, 189. Cf. also p. 203.
[3] Ibid., pp. 190 and 90; cf. also 11, 13, 14, 17, 18.

For this reason, human concepts like that of collective responsibility become, without the slightest difficulty, suffused by the religious ethos and gain to all intents and purposes the position of religious dogmas. According to the legend of the gods, Niobe insults Leto. Leto's divine children kill all the offspring of Niobe.

> Six youthful sons, as many blooming maids,
> In one sad day beheld the Stygian shades;
> Those by Apollo's silver bow were slain,
> These Cynthia's arrows stretched upon the plain:
> So was her pride chastised by wrath divine,
> Who matched her own with bright Latona's line.[1]

In the legend of the half-god Heracles, which tells of the murder of the Actorides, the people of Elea, fellow-citizens of the victims, demand reparation from the people of Argos, fellow-citizens of the killer.[2] Fact and fiction could hardly be closer to each other. The guilt of one is the guilt of all on either plane.

But it is particularly the belief that a curse can be transmitted, by generation, to future generations which should occupy us here, for that is the thought-form behind the Judaeo-Christian doctrine of original sin and hence behind all Judaeo-Christian religiosity. The Greeks had that belief, too, and it was deeply rooted in their credal system. A good illustration is the legend of Croesus and Candaules. The tale is this: Candaules, king of Lydia, of the dynasty of the Heraclides, is deposed and killed by one of his bodyguard, Gyges by name, who ascends the throne and founds the royal house of the Mermnadae. The Delphic oracle confirms Gyges in his position. 'The Pythoness, however, [while confirming him] added that, in the fifth generation from Gyges, vengeance should come for the Heraclides.' And this in fact happens. Croesus, descended from Gyges, is defeated by Cyrus, king of Persia. 'It is not possible even for a god to escape the decree of destiny', the Pythoness comments.[3] Gyges is punished in Croesus – Croesus has sinned in Gyges: the two are a community in guilt and punishment as the sons of Adam are in sin, and ultimately in redemption also.

An incidental remark in the Odyssey (XI, 433), brief as it is, provides a particularly striking illustration of what, without apologies, we may call the Greek doctrine of original sin. Clytemnestra has slain

---

[1] *Iliad* XXIV, 602 et seq. Cf. *The Iliad and Odyssey of Homer, translated by Alexander Pope*, ed. Buckley, Th. A., London n.d., pp. 446 and 447. Latona is the Latin form for Leto and Cynthia another name for Artemis.

[2] Glotz, loc. cit., p. 217. For similar cases of collective responsibility involving half-gods or gods, cf. idem, ibid., pp. 165, 166, 167, 168, 557, 558; cf. also pp. 566 and 574.

[3] *Herodotus* I, 13 and 91; cf. also 86. Cf. *The Histories of Herodotus*, transl. Rawlinson, G., ed. Blakeney, E. H., Everyman ed. (printing of 1964), pp. 7 and 47. Cf. also p. 44.

her husband Agamemnon, but her shame is not *her* shame alone. She has infected future generations of women, indeed, all womanhood – even those who are virtuous. As Alexander Pope translates the passage:

> . . . O wife, thy deeds disgrace
> The perjured sex and blacken all the race![1]

'Disgrace' is too weak a term here. 'Involve in disgrace' would come much closer to the proper meaning. But the reference to a perjured *sex* is clear enough.

What we must try to understand is the principle behind all these legends and utterances, and, in seeking it, we may as well entrust ourselves once again to the unfailing guidance of Gustave Glotz. 'For divine justice,' he writes, 'the individual does not exist; the family – that is the being that acts and is responsible. The same man prolongates himself through time and survives himself from generation to generation. The son is tied to the father, and while there are descendants, they are tied to their forefather by a chain which nothing will be able to break. No fault can therefore remain unpunished. The chastisement due always comes at the right time. If it is delayed, it is inescapable; if it does not strike the author of the crime, it is reserved for the offspring born of the crime-infected blood . . . The sins of the parents fall on the children; there is no moral idea which finds expression more often in the literature of the Greeks.'[2]

Confronted with a sentence like the last, the modern observer, including even the modern admirer, of ancient Greece is apt to exclaim: how could they?! The sociologist of knowledge is bound to reply by a counter-question: how could they not, since the *genos* or clan was the primal form of Greek social organization? In any case, the fact is and remains that collective responsibility, especially in its metaphysical and religious formulation, was a dominant conception through much of Hellenic-Hellenistic history. A string of utterances spreading over a thousand years can prove it. There is, indeed, a significant spell of interruption, when associational life had for a time gained the upper hand, and we shall discuss it in its proper place.[3] But though this anticipation of modern ideas may be sympathetic to us, we must beware of giving it undue weight when speaking of antiquity.

Let us begin with Solon (638–568 B.C.), or rather with his early poem, 'A Prayer to the Muses', in which, according to W. Ch. Greene's well-documented report, he was 'setting forth [the] accepted Greek

---

[1] *The Iliad and Odyssey*, as quoted, p. 615. But cf. above all Adkins, A. W. H., *Merit and Responsibility, A Study in Greek Values*, Oxford 1960, p. 45.

[2] Glotz, loc. cit., pp. 560 and 561.

[3] Cf. below, pp. 243 et seq.

views about justice'. There *is* justice in the world, he maintains; if meet reward and punishment do not come to a man, they come to his heirs; come they will. 'Solon accepts this doctrine without criticism.' Indeed, Solon uses a splendid metaphor to make his meaning clear. Sometimes it happens, he says, that the sky of justice is clouded; accumulating vapours cover it from our sight. But Zeus is there all the time, and his thunderbolt will strike when the moment has come.[1] Of Theognis, also of the sixth century of the pre-Christian era, we have conflicting statements,[2] but in one of them, he, 'like Solon, accepts without question the doctrine that the malefactor's innocent children may suffer for his sins'.[3] Pindar (522–448 B.C.) is more emphatic. There is a law of morality at work in life, but to see it we must consider family histories, not detached individuals. If a *genos* complains of injustice, we must either ascend to the forebears to see what guilt they have loaded upon themselves, or descend to the offspring to find the recompense which they receive. But the scales always oscillate around the mean.

Without a doubt, the most important classical text on the subject in hand is Plutarch's essay 'On the Delays of the Divine Vengeance' contained in his great collection, the *Moralia*. We shall look at it presently. At the moment we want to jump ahead to the fifth century of the Christian era, to see what leading thinkers thought of collective responsibility then. They accepted it. From Proclus (A.D. 411–485) we have a treatise *On Providence*. The reference to our theme is brief, but it is clear. Proclus links three generations together. They are one in the flesh, one in life, one in feeling, one in other respects. If Providence visits the third generation and it suffers for the sins of the first, there is therefore no injustice.[4] Hermias, in the same century, writes a *scholium* to Plato's *Phaedrus* which is a good deal stronger. Is there any reason behind the fact that descendants suffer for their ancestors, he asks, and he answers in the affirmative. They inherit the *activa* of their forebears, often ill-gotten and hence guilt-laden; so it is but fair that they should inherit the *passiva*, including condign punishment, also. Nor must it be thought that the children, when they suffer, suffer alone; the souls of the fathers, after all, still exist in another world, and are therefore involved in the children's suffering. This still leaves us with an apparent injustice to the later generation, but Hermias hints, however obscurely, that souls directed into families with an abiding curse on their backs are always souls headed for evil anyway, souls that therefore deserve, for some reason indwelling in themselves, to confront the fate which expects them. Perhaps we come closest to the core of Hermias's argument when we say that he sees successive generations as in a manner

---

[1] Cf. Glotz, loc. cit., pp. 577 and 578.
[2] Cf. below, p. 245.
[3] Greene, loc. cit., pp. 36 and 40. Cf. also Glotz, pp. 560 and 561.
[4] Cf. *Procli Diadochi Tria Opuscula*, Berlin 1960, pp. 98 and 99.

contemporary. Crime and punishment are therefore connected and – over time – well balanced and justly apportioned.[1]

In all this, the Hellenes felt like the Hebrews. Yet there is a difference which should not go unnoticed. In the Old Testament it happens that a man is held responsible for his deeds even though his will, when he committed them, was not free. Thus in Exodus IV, 21, YHWH is supposed to say to Moses concerning Pharao: 'I shall harden his heart.'[2] It looks therefore as if the hapless Egyptian were punished for a crime which he could not help committing. The Greeks avoided this imputation. While asserting the collective responsibility of all (so that the individual's actions appear as fated), they also emphasized each person's personal co-responsibility. In the Odyssey (XXII, 413 et seq.), where the death of Penelope's suitors is discussed, we are told that both destiny *and* their cruel deeds brought them to fall. The form in which this idea appears is invariably theological: men must not blame the gods for their errors; they themselves are the actors and authors of their sins. As Zeus expresses it at the beginning of the Odyssey (I, 32 et seq.):

> Perverse mankind! whose wills created free,
> Charge all their woes on absolute decree.
> All to the dooming gods their guilt translate
> And follies are miscalled the crimes of fate.[3]

But there is a sociological implication as well: the sufferings of later generations are not only the effects, more or less mechanical, of their forefathers' sins; they are also the consequences of their own conduct, which is to a large extent free. In other words, the Greeks were a shade more individualistic than the Jews, which neatly reflects the fact that the associational element was somewhat stronger in their society than in that of Palestine, even if both were classically of the community type. The Protestant shift from the earlier (Catholic) emphasis on the collective character of the fall to their own determined stress on the observable wickedness of each individual is thus foreshadowed in Greek thought, albeit not very clearly.

That the difference between Jews and Greeks in this particular was only small can be seen from Plutarch's important essay to the consideration of which we now turn. Plutarch is well acquainted with the thought of associational-individualistic societies; he knows that the whole idea of collective responsibility can be made to look absurd; yet he defends it. We can pick out only a few strands from his argument. Men do not seem to mind when the children inherit their father's

[1] Cf. *Hermiae Alexandrini in Platonis Phaedrum Scholia*, ed. Couvreur, P., Paris 1901, pp. 96 and 97.
[2] Cf. Merz, loc. cit., p. 125, note.
[3] Cf. the Pope version, as quoted, p. 458. Cf. also Greene, pp. 22, 23, 92, 159.

honours; they object only when they are made to carry their father's burdens – a distinction is made which is entirely illogical (which is ideological, as the sociologist would say today). 'If we preserve in the descendants our gratitude for virtue, we must in reason expect that neither should the punishment of crime flag or falter in its course.' Men also see little that is incomprehensible in the fact that a contagion should spread through space, while they do find it hard to comprehend that it should spread through time – yet again, where is the difference? Surely, 'it is more amazing that a disease which had its origin in Ethiopia should have raged at Athens, killed Pericles, and attacked Thucydides, than that justice, after the crimes of the Delphians and Sybarites, should have found her way to their children'.[1]

These are, to some extent, sophistical arguments, but they constitute merely the outworks of Plutarch's position. Its core and citadel is the assertion that communities *are* unities and *must* share both guilt and merit. 'The visitations of entire cities by divine wrath are readily justified,' Plutarch asserts. 'A city, like a living thing, is a united and continuous whole. This does not cease to be itself as it changes in growing older, nor does it become one thing after another with the lapse of time, but is always at one with its former self in feeling and identity and must take all blame or credit for what it does or has done in its public character, so long as the association that creates it and binds it together ... preserves it as a unity.' If a city in the year 100 must not be blamed for what its citizens have done in the year 50, Plutarch pleads, then a man of the age of 80 must not be blamed for what he did when he was 40 either, for he, too, has changed and is no longer the same. Now nobody would argue like that. We, as persons, are invariably regarded as self-identical through time. 'Yet growing older brings about greater alterations in each of us severally than in a city collectively.'[2]

Needless to say, what lies behind this argument is an organismic theory of society, and that links Plutarch with Paul, Hellenism with Christianity. Soon this ontological and philosophical foundation becomes clearly visible. 'If a city is a single and continuous whole,' we read as we go on, 'surely a family is so too, attached as it is to a single origin which reproduces in the members a certain force and common quality pervading them all; and what has been begotten is not severed from the begetter, as if it were some product of his art; it has been created out of him, not by him, and thus not only contains within itself a portion of what is his, but receives a portion of his due when rightly punished or honoured ... In the ... children of the wicked, the father's principal part is inherent and innate, not quiescent and inert, but by it they live, thrive, are governed, and think: and there is nothing shocking

---

[1] *Moralia*, vol. VII, transl. de Lacy, Ph. H., and Einarson, B., Cambridge, Mass., and London 1959, pp. 241 and 245. Cf. also Glotz, loc. cit., p. 564.
[2] Ibid., pp. 245 and 247.

or absurd that they, who are their father's children, receive their father's due.'[1]

This is a strong assertion of the whole principle of collective responsibility. Yet, like his other fellow-countrymen, Plutarch mitigates the doctrine a little by allotting some room to the contrary principle of personal responsibility. Analysing a few concrete historical cases, he maintains that 'only to those whose nature acquiesced in and espoused the family trait, did punishment, pursuing the vicious resemblance, make its way'. This observation leads to a more general proposition. 'Not all "the sins of parents on the children the gods do visit",[2] but where a good man is born of a bad, as a healthy child may come of a sickly parent, the penalty attached to the family is remitted, and he becomes, as it were, adopted out of vice; whereas if a man's disorder reproduces the traits of a vicious ancestry, it is surely fitting that he should succeed to the punishment of that viciousness as to the debts of an estate.'[3] Thus did a pious Greek of the first century feel about men's sharing of guilt and merit. It was not on this all-important issue that he disagreed with his near-contemporary and near neighbour, Paul of Tarsus.

The similarity of Plutarch's thought with that of, say, Pindar would be inexplicable without the existence of an ongoing tradition linking them together. It should not, however, be assumed that that tradition was unbroken. When the triad associationism-democracy-individualism made its bid for domination, especially in Athens, when, above all, the Sophists appeared and propagated a radical form of nominalism, the belief in collective guilt and collective responsibility had perforce to pass through a period of crisis. That crisis is reflected in one of the most admirable productions of the Greek mind, the *Oresteia* of Aeschylus.

The tale behind this trilogy is quickly told. The wife of Atreus, King of Argus, is seduced by his brother, Thyestes. To avenge himself, Atreus invites Thyestes to supper and serves him the flesh of his own, Thyestes's, infants – a gruesome deed which, according to the Greek ideas which we know, could not possibly be atoned for in one (Atreus's) life. (He who knows his Bible will be reminded here of Deuteronomy XXVIII, 53, where it is said of the wicked man that he shall 'eat the flesh of his sons and daughters, the fruit of the womb'.) As expected, Atreus's son (or grandson) Agamemnon is pursued by evil, and finally he is (in the first play) murdered by his own wife, Clytemnestra, and by Thyestes's son Aegisthus whom she has taken for a lover.

Agamemnon's children, Orestes and Electra, deeply feel the duty to avenge their father, and they do. Clytemnestra falls to Orestes's steel;

---

[1] Ibid., pp. 247 and 249.
[2] This interspersed quotation is from a lost play of Euripides. Cf. the editorial notes on pp. 231 and 266.
[3] Ibid., pp. 269 and 267.

her paramour, too, is dispatched. But then the hereditary curse begins to work against Orestes. There are apparently no relations to take up the cause of Aegisthus and Clytemnestra, now due to be avenged, and so the Erinnyes (Eumenides) enter into the fray. They will secure what no human hand is likely to provide: punishment of the matricide, Orestes. But he is finally saved by his association with Apollo behind whom the power of the High God Zeus is hidden. First, he is cleansed by cultic means; and then he is placed before the Athenian law court of the Areopagus which finds him not guilty; Pallas Athene, tutelary goddess of Athens, herself casts the decisive vote of acquittal when the human judges are deadlocked *pro* and *con*. But she does more. She induces the Furies to give up the whole avocation which the old, fear-inspiring gods had entrusted to them and to align themselves with the new benign gods, like herself and Apollo. The Erinnyes take up their abode at Athens, to live with, and to be a blessing upon, that enlightened city.

One of the greatest experts on Greek literature and culture, Gilbert Murray, has written a commentary on the plays, and this commentary contains passages which are highly relevant to our investigation. It is interesting to realize, Murray writes, 'that the Aeschylean doctrine is in essence an early and less elaborate stage of the theological system which we associate with St. Paul: the suppression of the Law . . . which acts like blind fate . . . by a personal relation to a divine person, the Father who understands . . . Aeschylus would have understood Paul's exhortation to escape beyond the "beggarly elements" to Him who made them, beyond the Creation to the Creator; and Paul would have understood Aeschylus' insistence on the forgiveness of the suppliant, that is, of him who trusts and repents and prays. It is noteworthy, indeed, that Paul made one great concession to primitive thought which Aeschylus had entirely rejected. When Orestes is pardoned by the will of Zeus, the Furies yield; the Law is deemed to be satisfied; there is no talk of its demanding to be paid off with another victim. But in Paul, when man is to be forgiven, the sin still claims punishment, the blood will still have blood; and the only way to appease it is for the Divine King, himself or his son, to "die for the people". Thus the pollution is cleansed and sin duly paid with blood, though it happens to be the blood of the innocent. Aeschylus, as a poet, was familiar with that conception. He knew how Codrus died, and Menoikeus and Macaria, how Agamemnon and Erechtheus and other kings had given their children to die. But for him such practices belonged to that primitive and barbaric world which Hellenic Zeus had swept away, so he hoped, for ever.'[1]

Much depends for our argument on a proper analysis and critique of these lines. Let us notice, first of all, that the trilogy is still full of passages which carry the old conviction that there *is* collective responsibility. To us, Aegisthus is an adulterer and hence despicable. The Hellenes

[1] *The Oresteia, translated by Gilbert Murray*, London 1928, pp. 27–9.

did not see him entirely in this light. Between him and Agamemnon, there is blood; what he, Thyestes's son, does to Agamemnon, the son of Atreus, is above all an incident in a war in which all is fair.[1] The case of Clytemnestra is similar. She has slain her husband, yes, but he was after all not a close kinsman of hers; he was indeed something of a stranger so that her crime appears somewhat less criminal. 'Nowhere in Greek mythology,' writes Greene,[2] 'do the Erinnyes pursue Clytemnestra for the murder of her husband, for he was no blood relation of hers.' Most amazing, however, is the fact that Apollo defends his protégé Orestes precisely with the help of the old philosophy. Orestes has indeed slain his mother, but a mother is little to a man – certainly much less than a father. Descent is from the father's side and through the father's seed; the mother's womb is merely a seedbed for it in which it can get ready for life.

> The mother to the child that men call hers
> Is no true life begetter, but a nurse . . .
> . . . The sower of the seed
> Alone begetteth. Woman comes at need,
> A stranger, to hold safe in trust and love
> That bud . . .[3]

There can hardly be a thought more characteristic of a patrilineal, patrilocal and patripotestal clan society such as Greece was in her early days.

Beyond these detailed passages, there is, however, also a general statement, and we would quote it in E. D. A. Morshead's translation which is particularly clear:

> . . . whensoever the sire
> Breathed forth rebellious fire . . .
> His children's children read the reckoning plain,
> At last, in tears and pain.[4]

It may be urged, of course, that Aeschylus formulated these conceptions merely to lead them *ad absurdum*, as one erects a straw man in order to knock him down. Be this as it may, it is certainly true that the dramatist emphasizes the personal responsibilities of the *dramatis personae*.

[1] Cf. Glotz, loc. cit., p. 168, and the references there (esp. note 4), but esp. pp. 422 and 423.
[2] Cf. loc. cit., p. 17.
[3] *The Oresteia*, as quoted, p. 235. Cf. also Greene, loc. cit., p. 135. Athene, it should be remembered here, had no mother, but sprang full-formed from her father's head. Cf. *The Eumenides*, line 740, *The Oresteia*, Murray version, p. 239.
[4] *Nine Greek Dramas*, New York 1909, p. 19. Murray's text (cf. pp. 50-1) has no corresponding lines.

Clytemnestra's plea—the curse did it!—is not accepted. All that the Chorus will concede is that there is co-responsibility between fate and deed, old, inherited evil and new evil freely done:

> That thou art innocent herein
> What tongue dare boast? It cannot be.
> Yet from the deeps of ancient sin
> The Avenger may have wrought with thee.[1]

Adkins, who has studied the poet's mind closely, writes: 'Aeschylus asserts that even in the extreme case of the accursed family, though some may be predisposed towards evil by supernatural agency, none are so predestined. Though the choice may be harder for some than for others, there is always a choice; and hence no one may escape responsibility for his actions on these grounds.'[2] This is a true summary of Aeschylus's position. Yet how far is he really from more ancient thought? The Odyssey, too, discusses the guilt and non-guilt of Clytemnestra and Aegisthus and has the same ambiguity as later Aeschylus.

> She fell, to lust a voluntary prey,

is one passage, yet in the same breath the poem refers to the adulterous lovers as the objects of the hate of the gods

> Dragged to destruction by the links of fate.[3]

Such passages are sure to show that the 'modernity' of Aeschylus and his mind must not be exaggerated.[4] Yet another consideration is more decisive. Gilbert Murray, in the long quotation which we have given, omits one essential fact: the fact that the final liberation of Orestes is owed to a *human* institution, however god-supported that may appear[5] –

[1] *The Oresteia*, as quoted, p. 103.
[2] Adkins, loc. cit., pp. 123 and 124; cf. also pp. 121, 122, 129, 130.
[3] The Pope version, as quoted, pp. 491 and 490. Pope's translations are correct. Cf. Adkins, loc. cit., pp. 22 and 23. Cf. also pp. 117, 118, 124, 125.
[4] Other points to be mentioned are 1. Orestes, as he kills Clytemnestra, invokes the name of (his father) Agamemnon. This means, as Wilamowitz–Moellendorf emphasizes, that he identifies with him, and that Agamemnon himself avenges himself (cf. *Aischylos Interpretationen*, Berlin 1914, p. 214). 2. The Erinnyes, although a whole group, are addressed in the singular. Murray himself writes to such a passage: 'Greek theology felt the difference between the singular and the plural far less than we do' (*The Oresteia*, as quoted, p. 257). Precisely; therefore an undue modernization of Aeschylus is not permissible.
[5] One must not make too much of the fact that Pallas presides over the court and intervenes when the decision is in balance. Gregory Dix rightly emphasizes that 'the old guardian gods of the cities were little more than their religious embodiments. Athens worshipped Athena and Ephesus Diana of the Ephesians, and almost knew

to the Athenian court of the Areopagus. And on this point hinges the whole interpretation of the *Oresteia*. Far from anticipating the Christian solution of hereditary guilt or even (as Murray asserts) presenting a superior – less 'barbarous' – version of that solution, the Aeschylean trilogy merely helped to bring the metaphysical and religious problem of original sin properly so called more sharply into focus, and thereby to increase the longing for a redemptive deed such as, Christians say, was performed by Jesus on the cross.

Two matters are involved here, not one. One is the blood feud, and with this a legal institution like the Court of the Areopagus could and did deal. We cannot be surprised to find that the Athenians were proud of the inner pacification of their city which they had achieved. By a long and painful development, or rather by long and painful labours, they had succeeded in transmuting private torts into public crimes – crimes avenged, not by irrational hate, but by rational justice. The community was at long last in command. No longer did they have to fear that tragedies like the Capulets *versus* the Montagues or the MacDonalds versus the Campbells would be enacted in their streets. Pallas Athena's children wanted the world to know that, and the *Oresteia* must, at least in part, be understood as a bit of boasting *pro domo*, a pastime in which Aeschylus' fellow citizens liked to indulge. Murray himself admits in a note to the *Eumenides* (line 566 et seq.), though without realizing the important implications of his own remark, that in the play 'the interest lies in the foundation of the Court of the Areopagus, as a tribunal super-seding the blood-feud',[1] i.e. in a purely civic achievement. In the play itself, the attacks of the Erinnyes on the 'younger gods' are indeed couched in general terms;[2] Athena's answer, however, is that she is merely helping to secure the inner peace of the city, to ban for ever

> . . . the blind war
> Within that burneth most where brethren are.[3]

The courts are to deal with new and civic guilt, like that of Orestes himself, and prevent it from becoming hereditary by punishing the culprit and offering due satisfaction to the offended parties. Intra-community strife therefore is to be the Areopagus' field of action. But

[1] *The Oresteia*, as quoted, p. 261. Cf. also Greene, p. 125: 'At last the vicious circle of blood-vengeance is broken by the appearance of a new moral order.'
[2] *The Oresteia*, as quoted, pp. 210 and 241.
[3] Ibid., p. 247. Cf. also p. 250.

that they were worshipping their own best selves.' Cf. *The Shape of the Liturgy*, ed. London 1960, p. 316. On the other hand, Murray overlooks the fact – the salient and essential fact – that the godless, those who offend against, not their fellow-mortals, but the immortals, are, 'as of old', to *remain* under the jurisdiction of the Furies. Cf. The *Eumenides*, Murray version, as quoted, p. 246 (lines 909 and 910).

hereditary guilt towards the gods (like that of Adam) could never be purged by the Areopagus or any other human institution. Aeschylus is not saying that Zeus forgave all sins flowing from men's evil bent when he forgave Orestes' murder of his mother. Far from it. There are in his work the outlines of a doctrine none too different from the Judaeo-Christian dogma of original sin, and other Greek thinkers, nay, all Greek culture, carried the same seed.

We can best see the presence of this doctrine and dogma, which makes nonsense of Murray's statement that Paul reverted to a position which Aeschylus had overcome, by considering a superficially unimportant, but symbolically most significant detail in the first play, the *Agamemnon*. Home from Troy, the hero is hypocritically greeted by his faithless wife. She addresses him as 'head with love and glory crowned', she has her attendants spread a crimson and gold net or tapestry on the soil and invites him to walk over it into the house – the 'red carpet' of our own heroes' welcome. But Agamemnon hesitates, not because he suspects Clytemnestra's wile, but because he does not wish to commit a great sin, the sin of *hybris* or overweening pride.

> 'Tis God that hath
> Such worship; and for mortal man to press
> Rude feet upon this broidered loveliness . . .
> I vow there is danger in it. Let my road
> Be honoured, surely; but as man, not god.

Yet Clytemnestra insists. He is a victor; he must have his triumph. It is then that Agamemnon commits a grave fault: he becomes a victim of his own weakness, of his own vainglory.

> Well, if I needs must . . . Be it as thou hast said! . . .
> Now therefore, seeing I am constrained by thee
> And do thy will, I walk in conqueror's guise
> Beneath my gate, trampling sea-crimson dyes.[1]

Agamemnon, so we may say, using the language of Christianity, has *fallen*. His own sin has laid him low, not only the hate of his enemies. The fate that overtakes him is deserved. Aeschylus knows how to convey this conviction. When the body of the dead king is carried out, after Clytemnestra has slain him, it is seen to be wrapped in the crimson web . . . His sin has recoiled on his own head. But his case is not unique. *Hybris* is a danger to many men, to any man, and he is apt to succumb, whoever he may be. 'We see from the carpet scene in the *Agamemnon*,' writes E. R. Dodds, 'how every manifestation of triumph arouses

[1] *The Oresteia*, as quoted, pp. 72 and 75.

anxious feelings of guilt: *hybris* has become the "primal evil", the sin whose wages is death, which is yet so universal that a Homeric hymn calls it the *themis* or established usage of mankind.'[1] How far is it from this conception to the Judaeo-Christian dogma of original sin? Perhaps a half-step, but no more.

There can in this way be no question of a radical break with the past in Aeschylus' great trilogy. He merely redefines the idea of collective guilt. It is to him, with the eye on the future of a pacified, law-abiding Athens, less an aspect of the blood feud, such as it was in the tragedy of the House of Atreus; it is, or it emerges, more as a quality of man, of all men both individually and collectively, as an indwelling racial trait, a tendency towards *superbia*, as the medieval moralists call it. The hereditary character remains. Greene has soberly and convincingly assessed the content of the essential Aeschylean argument. 'The idea that . . . children may suffer for the sins of their fathers . . . is purified by the tragic poets, as Aeschylus and Sophocles perceive the difference between suffering for another's guilt (a natural, physical fact, verified by all experience) and punishment for another's guilt (the result of an immoral vindictiveness). The latter Aeschylus repudiates, and the hereditary curse now appears as an inherited though not insuperable tendency towards guilt . . . The curse is now conceived . . . to be . . . a terrible hereditary propensity that reappears in successive generations . . . God offers man the occasion for sinning; and, if he yields, and commits the initial sin, God helps him to his ruin.'[2]

The last words indicate the deep connection the Greeks saw between *hybris* and *nemesis*, guilt and punishment. Christianity was to replace it by the concatenation of misdeed and mercy, sin and salvation. What the Gospel brought was less a new form of thought than a new faith and hope. In the long chain of preparatory events which smoothed the path of Christianity, even the *Oresteia* of Aeschylus should find a place.

We have so far concentrated on this one work because it comes closest to the Judaeo-Christian root idea. Aeschylus refers to πρώταρχος ἄτη and Glotz translates this as *faute originaire* – original sin.[3] Aeschylus also emphasizes that we are confronted with a generic trait of the human race; unless he dreads *nemesis*, man will always tend towards *hybris*, 'pride and pride's excess':

> Who that hath no fear at all . . .
> Man or City but shall fall
> From Right somewise?[4]

But the trilogy about the House of Atreus is not the only text that is

---

[1] Dodds, E. R., *The Greeks and the Irrational*, Berkeley and Los Angeles 1951, p. 31.
[2] Greene, loc. cit., pp. 98 and 107.
[3] *Oresteia, Agamemnon*, line 1192, Murray, loc. cit., p. 86; Glotz, loc. cit., p. 409.
[4] *Oresteia*, as quoted, pp. 227 and 228. Cf. also pp. 44, 50, 69, 237.

relevant here. It is essential to realize that the belief in man's dark endowment, in man's urge to self-deification, was very widespread in Greece, indeed, nearly universal. 'The Athenians', for instance, Glotz says, 'were convinced . . . that all men carry by their very nature within themselves that natural root (*fonds*) of hate which sets family against family, states against states, and Greek against barbarian.'[1] All they urged was that Athens had learned, through gaining maturity, the value and virtue of pity also.

To remain for yet another moment with Aeschylus, there is his other play, the *Persae*. We see that once-powerful nation humbled after Salamis. Why are they, why above all is their king Xerxes, down in the dust? Because he and they had got above themselves before. Arrogance was the cause which brought defeat as a consequence. The play, no doubt, greatly exhilarated Greek audiences. It must have given them a feeling of security, relief, release. But, clearly, it was also a warning to them not to commit the same fault as their enemies. For the tendency towards *hybris*, Aeschylus knew, was common to all men and beset his beloved Athenians no less than the nation of Persia. Besides Aeschylus' *Oresteia* and *Persae*, Sophocles' *Oedipus Tyrannus* and Euripides' *Suppliant Women* and *Trojan Women* movingly deal with the problem of *hybris*, the problem of pride.

Many of those whom we have seen asserting and defending the belief in hereditary guilt, also asserted and defended the conviction that *hybris* is the core of that hereditary guilt in its most widespread, nay universal, exemplification. Reference has already been made to Homer. Achilles shows *hybris* when he desecrates the body of Hector; the suitors of Penelope, too, are guilty of it and they receive the just reward for it. *Hybris*, to Homer, is sometimes a sin of wilfulness, and hence culpable; sometimes it is due to temporary madness, and then not culpable; but it is always the cause of *nemesis*. 'During the classical period of Greek thought,' Greene argues, 'Greek equivalents for the English word "sin", and even the idea of sin, are all but absent . . . Sometimes it is said, and with some measure of truth, that Greek ethics is largely intellectual or aesthetic. However true that may be of the classical period, the *Hybris* and still more the *Atasthalie* of Homer represent the idea of sin, with the emphasis not on intellectual error . . . but on innate and growing proneness to mischief, on a deliberate choice of evil. They are the result of an aggravated wilfulness . . .'[2] They are, in other words, due to an original fall or fault.

While the difference between the more ethical thought of the Hebrews and the more aesthetical thought of the Hellenes cannot be overlooked, it should, on the other hand, not be exaggerated. A wicked deed is an ugly deed, and vice versa. We see this when we study such

[1] Glotz, loc. cit., p. 423.
[2] Greene, loc. cit., p. 22.

writers as Solon, Theognis and Pindar. A Solonic poem deals with the plight of Athens: it is the just effect of Athens' injustice, her *hybris*, which calls for retribution. Theognis echoes Solon. If there is any difference, it is a greater emphasis on men's greed for gold, and also on their blameworthiness: the gods must not be blamed for what men bring on themselves. Pindar and Bacchylides carry a similar message; so does Herodotus. The latter's emphasis on the arrogance of Xerxes links him to Aeschylus. The chain does not appear to break off. Most illustrative of the fact that the concept of *hybris* provided a force which propelled the Hellenes towards near-Christian ideas, however, is Pindar. He calls the soul an 'image' of man and asserts that it survives the body. 'This faith in immortality is bound up with ethical conceptions; not only does the soul experience successive incarnations or rebirths, but it is undergoing a probation the result of which, as it chooses well or ill, is to be everlasting bliss or everlasting punishment.'[1] Thus Pindar's world includes the equivalent of a Purgatory, an Inferno, and a Paradiso which are based for the first time wholly on vice or virtue.

Pindar was close to Orphism, and this brings us at long last to this great religious movement which we have already recognized as one of the chief stepping stones to Christianity.[2] It was Orphism which insisted that the reward for good and the punishment for evil are not to be expected (as the typical Greeks expected them) within one life, this life of the body; it was Orphism, too, which summed up the doctrine of a hereditary shadow lying over the human race as nobody else had done before. We are referring to the Zagreus myth whose spread is deeply connected with Orphism. The fantastic detail cannot be unravelled here. Suffice it to say that, according to the legend, man was created from good and bad elements, the good stemming from Zagreus (the infant Dionysus), and the bad from the Titans, the enemies of Zeus. The Titans had torn Dionysus to pieces and devoured him. It was from the ashes of the Titans, destroyed by the Sky-god's lightning, that the human race originated. There is for this reason a Zeus-resisting, a sinful, ingredient in the nature of man.

'By pushing [an older] principle to its logical conclusion,' writes Glotz, 'the Greeks arrived at the doctrine of original sin. As every human being is, by dint of the very fact of his birth, exposed to crime and suffering, it must be assumed that the act of generation, which brings forth one more responsible person, is in itself a taint capable of justifying that new responsibility . . . This doctrine gains precision in the Orphic hymns and occupies a dominant place in the work of Onomacritos . . . Far from being the exclusive property of Judaism and

---

[1] Ibid., p. 79. Cf. on the whole concept of *hybris* also pp. 19, 20, 22, 37, 38, 43, 44, 68, 76, 83, 86, 112, 113, 114, 159, 160.
[2] Cf. our vol. IV, pp. 48, 49, 68.

Christianity, this famous dogma received its final shape in Palestine only after having existed in Greece already for at least four centuries.'[1] Yet to the Orphics, for all their nearness to an anthropology even like that of Calvin, the doctrine of original sin is not a doctrine of total perversion. Human nature is both light and darkness. It bears in it a memory of Dionysus. This good ingredient, this Zagrean soul, is imprisoned in a Titan-derived, evil frame of flesh. It craves liberation and re-union with its divine progenitor. But this is not easy to achieve, for man is in the grip of the original sin of his Titanic half-ancestors; to purge himself from that original sin must be his first and last endeavour.[2]

To achieve this purgation, the Orphics recommended two methods: one cultic, the other moral. The seeker after salvation must have himself initiated into the mysteries where he can gain contact with his god; and he must embrace a life of asceticism which will loosen the grip on him of the tomb-like body which keeps him from soaring aloft. By being initiated, he becomes one of the righteous; by abstaining from evil, he becomes righteous in a deeper sense. The two methods appear to us, made in the mould of Christianity, to demand each other, to be but one. But the Greeks seem to have found it difficult to merge them. If we study the literary evidence, we find that 'the passages which mention a [moral] judgment after death make no mention of the initiated and uninitiated, whereas those which refer to initiation have no mention of a [moral] judgment after death.'[3] The power of synthesis seems to have been lacking. Christianity possessed it to the fullest degree for it taught that those who, through baptism, had joined Christ, and who were at the same time righteous to the end, would gain salvation and blessedness after death. To many Greeks touched by the Orphic tradition, this must have appeared as the final redemption of the pledge and promise of the Orphic faith.

The North of Europe

In the case of the nations of northern Europe, we do not possess a rich literature such as the Bible of the Hebrews or the Homeric poems and the works of the later Hellenic philosophers and dramatists. If we want to know what the mentality of northern Europeans was, we must keep mainly to the evidence afforded by their acts and modes of action: their words will help us far less. We have seen already that collectivism pervaded their deeds, especially in the matter of the blood feud, and also the thoughts and sentiments connected with their deeds. We need hardly more to show how and why they could receive and, so to speak, digest and assimilate a religion which taught that One had fought and

[1] Glotz, loc. cit., pp. 582 and 583.
[2] Cf. Greene, loc. cit., pp. 59–63; Adkins, loc. cit., p. 140.
[3] Adkins, loc. cit., p. 145.

conquered for All. But more concrete formulations of their inherent and essential collectivism do occur in areas divorced from, if still fairly close to, the realm of conduct, for instance in the area of law. I am thinking especially of the legal concept known as 'corruption of blood'. Prior to the English Inheritance Act of 1833, if a man was convicted – the technical term is 'attainted' – for treason or for comparable high felonies, his civil and political rights were forfeited. But that was not all: the person concerned also lost the right to inherit, and to hand on by inheritance, his property and his title. This meant that his descendants were dispossessed and disennobled along with him, even if they were innocent, even if they were still minors, even if they were yet unborn. The existence of this institution of English common law can cause no surprise to a reader of this book. But that it should have remained in the Statute Book to the end of the first third of the nineteenth century is amazing indeed.

We can see how close the culture which produced the concept of 'corruption of blood' was to the mentality of the Jews, by simply setting down here, without comment, a quotation from Pedersen, taken from his chapter on 'Sin and Curse': 'If a deed of blood has been brought into the world, then [according to biblical ideas] the deed persists as a wicked poison, consuming the soul of the man who has committed the deed of blood. And, according to the fundamental law of the soul, the guilt must spread from him and be carried by the whole of his family. The poison follows the blood. If the perpetrator of the deed dies, then it is still in his brothers, passes to his sons and from them into the sons of the sons, until some day it comes out and destroys its victim.'[1] Surely, the subsoil of northern law is the same as that of mid-eastern religiosity. As for the Greeks, they had the self-same concept of corruption of blood as the northerners: 'The penalty for treason . . . was death and confiscation of property: and this . . . penalty . . . was collective and hereditary. No descendant of a traitor could be permitted to live, or to possess property, in the state which condemned him.'[2]

We should not, however, exaggerate the dearth of cultural material even in the case of the northerners, for we have at any rate their sagas, and they will teach us a good deal, if they are properly analysed. There is above all the great complex of traditions around the Nibelungs. Both the Scandinavian and the south-German versions were written down in the thirteenth century, i.e. in a century already fully Christian. Yet parts of the former traditions, the Norwegian songs of Sigfrid, for instance, lead us back into the tenth and eleventh centuries, and the spirit of them is still largely heathen. Furthermore, from the two given variants or versions we may with some justification conclude back to a common

[1] Pedersen, loc. cit., p. 420.
[2] Treston, loc. cit., p. 220.

parent form, to a Burgundian-Frankish saga of the fifth or sixth century.[1] This brings us precisely to the period when the tribes concerned embraced the Christian faith.

However difficult this material may be, the experts have little doubt that they have succeeded in identifying the kernel – the seed, as it were – of the whole saga. 'The basic form is this,' writes Boer. 'Attila has married Hagen's sister Grimhild or Gudrun. He invites his brother-in-law to his house and attacks his guest in the hope of getting possession of his treasure. He kills Hagen. Soon the story is added that Attila's wife avenges her brother.'[2] Around this centre, the imagination, both popular and individual, accumulates in the course of time a vast array of detail. Many are the transpositions that take place. Hagen, in the primal version the victim, becomes the slayer. Attila, in the primal version the slayer, becomes Grimhild's (Kriemhild's) fellow-avenger. Sigfrid enters as the hero who is murdered. But most important is the change in the figure of Grimhild. Originally faithful to her brother, to her clan, she later appears as faithful to her husband, to her love. In the *Nibelungenlied* of Germany *she* sees to it that her treacherous brothers are slaughtered – clear proof of the fact that we are out of the era of clan poetry and into the era of court epos. Yet in all this, the fundamental fact remains: the Nibelungen saga is a saga around the conflict and the killing between in-laws – in-laws who belong to different descent groups, different blood.[3]

The archaic nature of the whole story is well illustrated by some of the gruesome detail. In one version, the *Atlakvida*, we find the terrible Atreus motive: Grimhild (who appears under the name of Gudrun) makes Atli (Attila) eat the flesh of his own children from another marriage, she herself revealing the fact at the feast after the event. All cry; but Gudrun has no tears.[4]

Boer, who knew this whole world of saga, legend and fairy and folk poetry better than any other man, lays the greatest emphasis on the centrality of the treasure motive where he speaks of the first formation, and the enduring substance, of the Nibelungen complex. 'With treasure comes desire. And it is this desire which gives the Nibelungen saga its very own uncanny character . . . From it, the characters in the saga receive their salient traits.' When later the tale becomes more elaborate, two disasters are recounted. One brother-in-law kills the other to get the gold; but the gold does him no good; he himself is killed in the end for the sake of it. 'The very same treasure which induces Hagen to

[1] Cf. Golther, W., *Die sagengeschichtlichen Grundlagen der Ringdichtung Richard Wagners*, Charlottenburg–Berlin 1902, p. 55; Boer, R. C., *Untersuchungen Über den Ursprung und die Entwicklung der Nibelungensage*, vol. II, Halle a.S. 1907, pp. 190–3; vol. III, 1909, p. 132.
[2] Boer, as quoted, vol. I, 1906, p. 1.
[3] Ibid., pp. 7, 8, 9, 56, 129; also pp. 106, 121.
[4] Ibid., vol. III, p. 35.

murder his brother-in-law, also causes his own end . . . If Hagen had not killed Sigfrid, he would not have had his treasure, and Attila would have had no reason to wish for his death . . . We can even speak of a tragic motive in so far as Hagen falls as a victim of his own character, and of an irony of fate in so far as the same passion which drives him to his bloody deed inspires his enemy also. Truly, the idea of the old nordic tradition that a curse rests on the gold is fully prefigured in the raw material.'[1]

We may note in passing that there is a curious shift to be discovered here: the curse is originally in man, more specifically in man's covetousness; it is later connected with the metal which, in a less magical, more rational, view is merely its outer object, its stimulant, as it were. The sociologist must, in his analysis, reverse the process and re-discover the human behind the material aspect. He must deal with this problem of interpretation as Marx did with the phenomenon he called the 'fetishism of the commodity': when things are exchanged, bought or sold, it is not thing that is matched against thing, but man who deals with man: it is not object-relations, but human relations, which form the core of the transaction.

The mention of a curse that lies on the gold brings us from the physical to the metaphysical world, from saga to mythos. It is striking, in taking this step, to find how close, how near-identical, the two realms really are, for the heart of the nordic belief-system about the gods is the assumption and assertion of a clan feud between two sibs of supernal beings for the possession of the supreme treasure, the material universe.

The contending protagonists, figured in the guise of descent-lines, can be most quickly indicated by the following scheme:

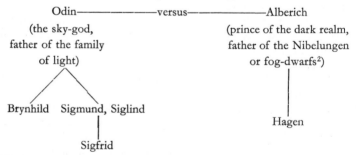

Alberich at first possesses the treasure; it passes into the hands of

[1] Vol. I, pp. 10, and 14. Cf. also pp. 95, 97, 163, 165; vol. II, pp. 34, 36; vol. III, pp. 25, 26, 103.

[2] Nibelung suggests the modern German word *Nebel*, which means fog. *Nifl* in Anglo-Saxon signifies abyss. Sigfrid is a *Waelsung*, son of Waelse. Waelse (literally: shining glory) = Odin, Wotan. Cf. Meinck, E., *Die sagenwissenschaftlichen Grundlagen der Nibelungendichtung Richard Wagners*, Berlin 1892, pp. 97, 161 (note), 177, 192, 307.

Sigfrid; Sigfrid is killed by Hagen; in the end, Hagen, too, is annihilated. The curse ceases to work only when the curse-bearing gold is thrown into the Rhine, to disappear for ever into the depths.

Such hatred is possible only against the background of a clan feud. And, indeed, there is clear indication that a clan feud is involved. The very principle on which Gudrun-Grimhild acts – 'love of kin takes precedence over love of spouse' – is a clan principle:[1] the blood-link is much, the marriage-vow little. In one version, the *Atlamal*, close to the *Atlakvida*, there is a report of a conversation between Gudrun and Atli – an abuse-slinging match one could call it – in which the hostile spouses reproach each other for many evil deeds, killings above all – a typical venting of traditional venom. Atli and Gudrun have married in order to seal an armistice between their respective families, but the bond is too brittle; it snaps.[2] This must have happened not infrequently in tribal history. In the *Beowulf*, Hrothgar, King of the Danes (whose wife is referred to as 'peace-pledge of the folk') gives his daughter, Freawaru, in marriage to Ingeld, Prince of the Heathobards, hoping thereby to end the feud between the two peoples. But the hope proves empty.

> . . . Seldom anywhere . . . even for a little
> Is the deadly spear idle, though virtuous the bride.[3]

It is precisely the saga of the Nibelungs that proves this point. In one version, the Volsungasaga, 'Siggeirr kills his father-in-law Volsungr and eleven brothers-in-law; he himself is then slain by the twelfth; Volsungr's grandfather Sigi is murdered by the brothers of his wife; his son avenges him.'[4]

So far, all we seem to get is merely an artistic reflection of mutual throatcutting, and it might be asked what exactly a sociology of religion may possibly draw from these traditional tales. The answer is: a great deal, and this may be surprising. And yet, the reader has already seen the key-word and encountered the key-fact. We have said, following Richard Boer, that 'Attila . . . attacks his guest in the hope of getting possession of his treasure'.[5] And thereby hangs the religious implication – a truly deep one – of the whole saga complex. The thirst for gold is the original sin of the Germanic tradition. It is the poison that enters the life-stream and muddies it, producing hate after hate and disaster after disaster. Even Shakespeare still carries the same idea. As Romeo

---

[1] Cf. Meinck, loc. cit., pp. 189 and 190.
[2] Boer, loc. cit., vol. III, pp. 52 and 54.
[3] Cf. *Beowulf*, transl. and ed. Crawford, D. H., New York 1966, pp. 156, 157, 77, 78.
[4] Boer, loc. cit., vol. I, p. 3. On the particularly instructive Volsungasaga, which, from the beginning to end, glorifies the principle of clan unity, cf. Golther, loc. cit., pp. 43–6.
[5] Cf. above, p. 57.

buys a dram of 'mortal drug' for forty ducats (*Romeo and Juliet* V, 1), he tells the apothecary:

> There is thy gold, worse poison to men's souls,
> Doing more murders in this loathsome world
> Than these poor compounds that thou mayst not sell:
> I sell thee poison, thou hast sold me none.

Whereas the Jewish tradition concentrates on sexual desire,[1] and the story of Atreus and Thyestes revolves around it, too, the northern nations saw the lust for treasure – Vergil's *auri sacra fames* – as the chief cause of men's fall from grace.

What is this Rhine-gold that all want and that destroys all? The Rhine is not, in northern mythology, the river which runs from the Grisons to Rotterdam, not really a geographical, but rather a mythical concept. The Rhine is the water at the edge of the world, the sea from which the sun rises at daybreak, and into which it returns by nightfall. The Rhine-gold is the reflection of the sun's orb in the world's waters. He who possesses it, controls the source of life and light – indeed, he is the master of light and life. Hence the struggle of the supernal and infernal powers for the treasure of treasures – the 'gold' of the 'Rhine'.[2]

The two most important foreground figures in the tale are Brynhild and Sigfrid. Sigfrid awakens Brynhild from a magic sleep, as the sun in spring-time awakens the earth from her winter-rest and winter-torpor. The whole mythos is calendric, vegetation lore. We can see here a case in which the concepts of the Myth-and-Ritual School, which we have had to criticize in earlier volumes,[3] are fully applicable. Sigfrid and Brynhild are, in the Russian tradition, Ruslan and Ludmila, freed by Ruslan from the hands of the wicked Alberich-like dwarf Czernomor; they are the bewitched Sleeping Beauty and the spell-breaking Prince Charming in the fairy story of world-wide spread.[4] Meinck has well

---

[1] The apple is a sex symbol. Cf. Varagnac, A., *Civilisation Traditionelle et Genres de Vie*, Paris 1948, pp. 154, 156, 231, 244. In Latin, the words for apple and evil are identical (*malum*). One link between the Jewish and the Nordic tradition should be mentioned: it is a woman who, according to one legend, induces her son to steal gold (the first theft of this kind) and thereby brings the golden, property-less age to a close. Cf. Meinck, loc. cit., p. 22 (where the 'primal theft' is called 'the Germanic fall'); cf. also ibid., pp. 15, 16, 20, 39, 42.

[2] Cf. Meinck, loc. cit., pp. 24, 25, 32, 33, 43, 51, 52. The sun and the gold are from early times poetically bracketed together under the image of a golden ring. Cf. also the crown – a gold ring on a king's head which signifies the sun.

[3] Cf. vol. I, pp. 32 et seq., and vol. III, pp. 29, 40, 41.

[4] The relation of Brynhild's father, Wotan, to her mother, Erda or Wala, and of Sigmund to his twin-sister Siglind, who are the father and mother of Sigfrid, is also conceived as a relation between the life-giving sun or sky on the one hand, and the seed-receiving and life-maturing soil on the other. Cf. Meinck, loc. cit., pp. 135, 136, 195, 200, 201.

summed up the meaning of the Nordic theology when he tells us that 'saga experts like Max Rieger, Wilhelm Müller and Wilhelm Hertz have rightly considered Brünnhilde as a telluric divinity, as an earth goddess, who, stung by the cold thorn of winter, sleeps a death-like sleep with the dead in a subterranean realm, until Siegfried, the god of spring and light, arrives and sets her free'.[1] Richard Boer, it is true, has asserted that the core of the Brynhild sagas is a historical personality, the Swedish royal widow Sigridr 'en Storråda' (who lived around the year A.D. 1000),[2] but this takes nothing whatever from the correctness of the opinion of these great scholars. Even if Sigridr was the point, so to speak, around which the multiform mythological material, formerly scattered, began to cluster, the mythological concretions and accretions soon totally overlaid and overwhelmed the thin historical facts. Yet Boer's assertion, otherwise irrelevant for our argument, is interesting for one reason. Sigridr was one of the last champions of Scandinavian heathenism. She rejected the hand of the Norwegian king Olafr Tryggvason because her conversion to Christianity was one of the conditions for the match. Tryggvason's successor was he whom Christians know as St. Olav (995–1030), the confessor and converter of the north. In the sagas which we are considering here, and which received a more settled form in the eleventh century, salvation (or rather non-salvation) on the pattern of the specifically northern sun-mythology confronted salvation by, through and in Jesus Christ – confronted it and lost.

For about a hundred years now, art-lovers at any rate, if not indeed all educated men, have been familiar with the whole legend through Richard Wagner's *Der Ring der Nibelungen* (1869–1876). They know therefore also that the story ends tragically in German lore. The last drama in the great Wagnerian tetralogy is called *Götterdämmerung* – the twilight of the gods, which is the *ragnarök*[3] of Norse mythology. Even the gods are doomed. They must be, for they have shared the original sin of the humans: the lust for domination. According to Wagner, who had and used his poetic licence, but who kept close to his sources and in any case faithfully relayed their message and their mood, the great ash tree (symbol of the world) ceases to grow, loses its leaves and goes into a decay because Wotan-Odin has broken off a branch with which to fashion a magic spear that will secure him dominion over the earth and all it carries. His has been a power-greedy and therefore death-dealing deed. 'The movement of time into the future towards the end of the world received its impulse exclusively from Wotan's guilt.'[4]

---

[1] Meinck, loc. cit., p. 241.

[2] Cf. his vol. III, pp. 147 et seq.

[3] In modern German literally 'Rauch der Recken', a phrase still close to the old Norse form. 'Rauch' is the Scots reek, smoke: the end of the world is envisaged as a great conflagration. 'Recke' is hero.

[4] Meinck, loc. cit., p. 147; cf. also pp. 139, 140, 146.

If the heroes of the secular sagas had to die because of the treasure they held and coveted, so must the heroes of Valhalla, the divine pantheon. If the fall of Adam brought death into the world according to the Judaeo-Christian creed, so did the fall of Wotan according to its Germanic counterpart. We can clearly see why the northern nations could and did welcome the Gospel: it told them of a God who will give, not death, but life, and give it more abundantly.

Where there is the fact of a fall, there also will be the hope of redemption. Both Brynhild and Sigfrid are figures who carry that hope. We must be careful here not to see the legends through Wagner's eyes for he had the whole of the Christian tradition in his mind, however cool his personal attitude to it may have been. Luckily we have the witness of the older Edda at our disposal, and it is unambiguous. Brynhild, the Valkyrie, a higher being, daughter of the Sky-god, learns to feel pity, to commiserate with men, to love. She imparts to Sigurd-Sigmund a knowledge of the magic of the runes, the very secret by dint of which even Odin controls the world.[1] Brynhild, while more than human, learns to be human. We see in this development of the mythos one of the most moving aspects of it.

The case of Sigfrid is far simpler. He is a saviour in so far as – in all extant versions – he fights and kills the dragon who guards the treasure: that gold which symbolizes the life-giving sun as it impinges on the iced-over soil and brings it to life. Killing the dragon (like the snake of *Genesis* a figure of darkness, doom and death) is a necessary preliminary to awakening the Valkyrie (a figure of the good earth). Sigfrid accomplishes both feats which, in a sense, are but one as April, and May are but one period. Sigfrid the high hero of the north has an exact counterpart in the Greek pantheon: Apollo who pursues and slays the python. But he has an exact equivalent in the Germanic pantheon, too. Between him and the god Baldur, there is much in common because both stand for the heavenly orb and for the all-renewing season of spring.[2] The question is only as to why, among the Nordics, a human symbol should have been needed in addition to the divine, Sigfrid beside Baldur. The answer is that redemption could only be expected from one who was not involved in original sin. Yet Baldur was so involved, as all the gods were. To have any hope of salvation, both gods and men had to wait for a pure creature as yet unstained: he alone would be able to break the hereditary curse.[3] Sigfrid is envisaged in precisely this light. Yet the powers of darkness are too strong. They kill him as they kill Baldur. The whole religiosity of the north is of the deepest, darkest hue.

---

[1] Cf. Golther, loc. cit., p. 105; *Götterlieder der älteren Edda*, transl. Simrock, K., ed. Kuhn, H., Stuttgart 1960, p. 62; Meinck, loc. cit., pp. 243–5, 254, 268.

[2] Cf. Meinck, loc. cit., pp. 111 and 305, and Golther, loc. cit., pp. 94 and 95.

[3] Cf. Richard Wagner's *Gesammelte Schriften und Dichtungen*, Leipzig 1872, vol. II, p. 205, cit. Meinck, p. 107.

We have now reached the point where we can finally pose and answer the question as to why Christianity could and did conquer the world. Considering their own sad condition, considering above all suffering and death, men everywhere came to the conclusion that our whole race is under a cloud. In the circumstances in which they found themselves, this feeling, this fact, could not but assume the mental form in which we know it from the Bible – the concept of original collective and hereditary sin. But the very logic of this concept also inspired hope, the hope most poignantly expressed by the great prophets of Israel, Isaias, Jeremias, Ezechiel and Daniel, that a Saviour would come and reconcile all with God, as the Primal Sinner had estranged all from God. 'As by the disobedience of one man, many were made sinners,' writes St. Paul (Romans v, 19), 'so also by the obedience of one, many shall be made just.'[1] Jesus Christ, when He came, was accepted as that One: a very simple but assured historical fact. In His saving deed, mankind saw help, rescue and liberation. Original collective and hereditary sin was blotted out by final collective and hereditary salvation. The Church, which sprang both from the old tradition and from the new inspiration, could not but be deeply imbued with the spirit of unity and community. Unity and community were of her inner essence, and unity and community were also the key-notes of the culture in which that essence tended to incarnate itself and to show itself to the outer world.

THE SELF-INTERPRETATION OF CATHOLICISM AS A COMMUNITY

When the pious Jews thought of their relation to God, they thought of themselves as a unity; and when they thought of themselves as a unity, they had a tendency to express their inner conception on this point in an outer, sensible image. The image, the picture, which they often used, was that of the vine. So Jeremias (xvii, 7 and 8); so Ezechiel (xv and xvii); so the seventy-ninth psalm: 'Give ear, O thou that rulest Israel . . . Shew us thy face, and we shall be saved . . . Thou hast brought a vine out of Egypt: thou hast cast out the Gentiles and planted it . . . Thou plantedst the root thereof, and it filled the land. The shadow of it covered the hills, and the branches thereof the cedars of God. It stretched forth its branches unto the sea and its boughs unto the river . . . Turn again, O God of hosts! Look down from heaven and see and visit this vineyard, and perfect the same which thy right hand hath planted . . . Thou shalt quicken us, and we will call upon thy name.'[2]

[1] Cf. verses 12–21, i.e. the whole coherent passage. There is also a remarkable passage in Irenaeus, *Contra Haereses*, to which attention should be drawn (III, XXI, 10). It is quoted verbatim in Hägglund, B., *History of Theology*, ed. St. Louis and London 1968, p. 49. For the original, see *Patrologia Graeca*, ed. Migne, J. P., vol. VII, Paris 1882, cols 954 and 955.

[2] We have quoted versicles 1, 4, 9–12, 15, 16, 19. And cf. Pedersen, loc. cit., p. 267.

Among the faithful to whom such thinking was familiar, nay, more than that, second nature, was also Jesus of Nazareth, Mary's son. When He addressed His disciples for the last time, He used the simile of the seventy-ninth psalm of which we have just heard the decisive versicles. 'I am the true vine, and my Father is the husbandman. Every branch in me that beareth not fruit, He will take away, and every one that beareth fruit, He will purge it that it may bring forth more fruit . . . Abide in me, and I in you. As the branch cannot bear fruit of itself, unless it abide in the vine, so neither can you, unless you abide in me. I am the vine, you the branches. He that abideth in me, and I in him, the same beareth much fruit: for without me you can do nothing. If any one abide not in me, he shall be cast forth as a branch and shall wither: and they shall gather him up and cast him into the fire, and he burneth . . . You have not chosen me, but I have chosen you and have appointed you that you should go and should bring forth fruit, and your fruit should remain' (St. John xv, 1, 2, 4–6, 16).

The use, by Jesus, of this traditional simile made it a metaphor of sacred undertones and carried it far into the future. The Ecumenical Council of Chalcedon, for instance, describes in the year 451 the contemporary pope, St. Leo the Great, as 'him to whom the custody of the vineyard has been committed by the Saviour . . .'[1] – a characteristic phrasing. St. Paul handles the same manner of speaking[2] most ingeniously where he discusses the relation of the Jewish stem to the Gentile cuttings that came to be conjoined with it: 'If the root be holy, so are the branches. And if some of the branches [meaning the Hebrews who did not accept Christianity] be broken, and thou, being a wild olive, art ingrafted in them and art made partaker of the root and of the fatness of the olive tree: boast not against the [broken] branches. But if thou boast, [remember] thou bearest not the root, but the root thee. Thou wilt say then: the branches were broken off that I might be grafted in. Well: because of unbelief they were broken off. But thou standest by faith. Be not highminded, but fear. For if God hath not spared the natural branches, [take care] lest perhaps also he spare not thee . . . They also, if they abide not still in unbelief, shall be grafted in, for God is able to graft them in again. For if thou wert cut out of the wild olive tree which is natural to thee, and, contrary to nature, wert grafted into the good olive tree, how much more shall they that are the natural branches be grafted into their own olive tree?' (Romans xi, 16–21 and 23–24).

These three passages, connected as they are by strict filiation, introduce us to a whole social philosophy: they convey to us the self-image

---

[1] Cit. Newman, J. H., *An Essay on the Development of Christian Doctrine*, ed. London, etc. 1906, p. 162.
[2] Needless to say, the substitution of the olive tree for the vine makes no difference to the argument.

of the Catholic Church, inherited as it is from the Jewish tradition, confirmed by the *logia* of Christ, and elaborated by Pauline and later usage. The poetry involved, the comparison between a body of men and the body of a plant, is, of course, totally irrelevant: all the more relevant is the point that poetry is designed to make – the assertion that the body of men, though apparently a multiplicity, is in a higher, a religious, a sacred sense a unity, just like the body of a plant. So anxious are the protagonists of this all-important conviction that they sometimes use other, poetically different comparisons, to inculcate the same idea: we get a mixing, or rather a massing, of metaphors. Two of them are particularly appealing: the image of a house built of living stones, and the image of a man composed of cells, the simile of the human organism of flesh and blood.

So far as the former picture is concerned, we need do no more than cast a side-glance at it. St. Paul uses it freely alongside his other picturesque expressions. 'You are no more strangers and foreigners' (to each other), Paul preaches, 'but you are fellow citizens with the saints and the domestics of God, [a house] built upon the foundation of the apostles and prophets, Jesus Christ Himself being the chief corner stone, in whom all the building, being framed together, groweth up into an holy temple in the Lord, in whom you also are built together into an habitation of God in the Spirit' (Ephesians II, 19–22). St. Peter has a parallel passage – so parallel indeed that we desist from placing it here alongside that from St. Paul (I Peter II, 4–8).

The other simile or symbol, whatever we want to call it, the organismic theory, was incomparably more successful, the main reason being in all probability that it had yet greater appeal: nothing could be more convincing than a reference to our own physical self, to our own flesh and blood. St. Paul uses it with great power in I Corinthians XII, 11–27, but we do not have enough space here to quote him *in extenso*; nor do we have the time to track down the other passages which move along the same lines.[1] To give even approximately adequate documentation of the doctrine, we should have to write a work larger than our present one. Even inadequate documentation is out of the question because the progress of the argument must not be unduly delayed. There is, however, an acceptable way out of our quandary. We may, for once, utilize an official document, showing with all desirable clarity that the self-interpretation of Catholicism as a community enjoys the status of a dogmatic, or near-dogmatic, feature: Pope Pius XII's encyclical *Mystici Corporis Christi*, first published on 4 July 1943. In it, we feel ourselves in contact with the first and the last ages of the Church: Pius speaks the language of Paul, as Paul anticipated the language of Pius. And what he, or they, have to say appears to be universally accepted

[1] Cf. Cerfaux, L., *The Church in the Theology of St. Paul*, transl. Webb, G., and Walker, A., ed. New York 1959, pp. 262 et seq.

throughout the Church: no vocal opposition against the content of this document seems to have appeared anywhere in the world.

'The doctrine of the mystical body of Christ, which is the Church,' so the Introduction begins with a reference to Colossians 1, 24, 'a doctrine received originally from the lips of the Redeemer Himself, and making manifest the inestimable boon of our most intimate union with so august a Head, has a surpassing splendour . . .'.[1] This splendour is due to the fact that, to describe the Church, 'there is no name more noble . . . than "the mystical Body of Jesus Christ"', which is 'a name which blossoms like a flower from numerous passages of the Sacred Scriptures and the writings of the Fathers'. Already before this latter passage, the salient idea to the investigation of which, and of whose deep rootings in ancient life, our last section was devoted, the conception of the Church as a descent group, a clan, a community, is introduced: through the Incarnation, we are told, we 'become brethren according to the flesh of the only-begotten Son of God', and we enjoy the fruit of His redemptive sacrifice because He 'merited for us, His kindred, an unspeakable abundance of graces'.[2] The translator's between-title of the preamble of Part I, 'Corporate Fall in Adam – Corporate Redemption in Christ', is not indeed in the papal original, but it is an apt summation of the contents all the same.

Shortly hereafter the proposition 'that the Church is a body' is developed, and three great points are made. Firstly, as a body, the Church is a concrete and visible organization. It is not a hidden kingdom, a ghostly society of saints, but a manifest polity,[3] a material institution of which sinners are an integral part. On the model of St. Augustine, these sinners are interpreted as sickly cells who can be healed as long as they are connected with the healthy organism, but who must finally dry off and die off, if they are severed from it.[4] Secondly, within the Church, all members help each other. 'As in our mortal organism, when one member suffers, the others suffer with it . . . so in the Church the individual members do not live only for themselves: they [are] also co-operating with one another . . .'. These words must not be interpreted in a narrow sense, as if all they implied were that Christians must give economic or social assistance to their fellow-Christians. The true meaning is rather different. The point is essential and we shall have to revert to it.[5] Thirdly, as a concrete and co-operative body, the Church is visibly and organically structured. 'Just as in nature a body does not consist of an indiscriminate heap of members, but must be provided with organs, that is, with members not having the same function yet properly co-ordinated, so the Church

---

[1] Cf. *The Mystical Body of Jesus Christ*, transl. Smith, G. D., London 1944, p. 6.
[2] Ibid., pp. 12 and 11. Cf. also p. 28.
[3] Ibid., pp. 39 and 40. And cf. the next references.
[4] Cf. ibid., pp. 40 and 41 and the next references.   [5] Cf. below, pp. 70, 71.

for this special reason merits to be called a body, because it results from a suitable disposition and coherent union of parts, and is provided with members different from one another but harmoniously compacted.'[1]

Sociologists, and especially experts in the history of theoretical sociology, will recognize in these statements a variant of the organismic theory which was developed in its (supposedly) scientific form by Spencer, Lilienfeld, Schaeffle and many others and was a potent influence even beyond the confines of its proper school.[2] When driven to its extreme, this doctrine is untenable, if not absurd, for it will tend to ascribe reality only to the integral whole and not to the integrated parts; it will, above all, tend to deny the individual's free will. Catholic theorizing about the Catholic Church is preserved from this by its inherent psychological and pneumatological as well as by its equally inherent ethical element.[3] The Church is an organism, but one of the mind rather than one of the body or of bodies; the Church is an organism, but in design rather than in sober fact. *Mystici Corporis* makes this entirely clear: 'Whereas in a physical body the principle of unity joins the parts together in such a way that each of them completely lacks a subsistence of its own,' so we read, 'on the contrary in the mystical Body the cohesive force, intimate though it is, unites the members with one another in such a way that each of them wholly retains his own personality. A further difference is seen if we consider the mutual relation between the whole and each individual member; for in any living physical body the sole final purpose for which each and every individual member exists is the benefit of the whole organism, whereas any social structure of human beings has for its ultimate purpose, in the order of utilitarian finality, the good of each and every member, inasmuch as they are persons.'[4]

The last words, however – and this is essential in our analysis – do not mean that the principle of organicism, which is the mental concomitant of community in real life, is in any way abandoned or even dimmed. For if the Church as a society is not literally like a physical body, it is not like a merely moral body either. There are not only the gathered individuals (to use a phrase dear to the individualistic sects whose sociological thinking is other than organicist),[5] there is also a substantive common life not reducible to (if in the final analysis identical with) the comprised individual lives. The following passage may sound strange to the secular sociologist, yet it is essential to the sacred sociology of Catholicism: 'Comparing now the mystical Body with a moral body, we must notice also between these a difference which

[1] Loc. cit., pp. 12, 17, 13.
[2] Cf. Stark, W., *The Fundamental Forms of Social Thought*, London 1962, esp. pp. 17 et seq.
[3] Cf. *The Mystical Body*, as quoted, pp. 34, 35, 38, 39.
[4] Ibid., p. 37.   [5] Cf. our vol. II, pp. 111 et seq.

is by no means slight but, on the contrary, of the very highest importance. For in a moral body the only principle of unity is a common end,
and a common aspiration of all to that end by means of the social
authority. But in the mystical Body, with which we are concerned,
there is in addition to this common aspiration another internal principle, really existing and operative both in the whole structure and in
each one of its parts, and this principle is of such surpassing excellence
that by itself it immeasurably transcends all the bonds of unity by which
any physical or moral body is knit together. It is . . . something not of
the natural, but of the supernatural order; indeed, in itself it is infinite
and uncreated, namely the divine Spirit, who, in the words of the
Angelic Doctor, "numerically one and the same, fills and unifies the
whole Church".'[1] If the specifically religious content is taken out of this
passage, a perfectly clear sociological assertion remains. It is to the
effect that the Church is not an association in the sense which Tönnies
had given to that term. It is more than merely the sum of its members,
even as the members themselves are more than merely ciphers in a
unity, conceived as independent of them. The ecclesiology of Catholicism is not an extreme organicism; it is somewhat middle of the road;
yet it keeps decidedly closer to the collectivistic than to the individualistic side.

That this is so – a fact which we must emphasize because of the whole
drift of our argument – can be seen from two further pieces of poetizing
which the encyclical contains. The Church is called 'the Bride of
Christ'. Are not bridegroom and bride two different people? By no
means, according to this order of ideas. 'Husband and wife, one body,
one life,' said the Germanic folklore; the Catholic self-interpretation
says so too, thus evincing its deep sociological and philosophical realism,
its conception of any and every society, but above all of ecclesiastical
society, as a real entity. According to Genesis (II, 21 and 22), Eve was
formed of Adam's rib, in other words, formed of bone taken from his
side. This is, if we de-mythologize the statement, essentially the assertion that a married couple are one, a community, not two, an association. Christ and His 'Bride' are similarly conjoined, nay fused: she who
is the Bride of Christ is also the Mystical Body of Christ – identical with
Him. There may be a mixing of metaphors, but there is no missing the
point – the same point; it is made twice over.[2]

The image of a bride, to which must be added that of a mother (the
Church being called by this name, too),[3] refers to the organic realm, the
realm of love and even procreation. So, appearances notwithstanding,
does the second simile which we have to take up here. Baptism appears

[1] *The Mystical Body*, as quoted, pp. 37 and 38. The Aquinas reference is to *De Veri-
tate*, qu. 29, a. 4, c. Cf. St. Thomas Aquinas, *Truth*, vol. III, Chicago 1954, p. 419.
[2] Ibid., pp. 17 and 18.
[3] Ibid. and often, indeed, generally.

at first sight as a symbolic washing, and in a multiple symbolism this meaning may be included alongside several others. But already at the first step there is a reference to an organic happening: it is above all the new-born baby that has to be washed. One step further, and we enter yet deeper into organicism. The water from which the new being emerges is, or suggests, the fruit-water in the mother's womb out of which the birth-act lifts the new separate life. Psychoanalysts are therefore justified if they see this subconscious reference in the baptismal rite. *Mystici Corporis*, while doing nothing to prevent such an interpretation, leads instead back to Pauline language, but – and this is essential – remains within the organismic realm: Christ, it says, 'was prescribing Baptism as the means by which believers would be engrafted into the Body of the Church'.[1] Already St. Augustine had used the very same phrase.[2]

We cannot and will not enter into much of the further detail, for instance into the minutely developed proposition that Christ is the Head of the Church. Only two aspects need emphasizing. The encyclical does not shrink from the conclusion that the Head needs the Body, as (more obviously) the Body needs the Head. 'What Saint Paul says of the human organism is true also of the mystical Body: "The head cannot say . . . to the feet: you are not necessary to me".' For Christ has work to do in the world, and that work is done, under His inspiration, by the limbs.[3] This line of speculation leads to another and no less interesting aspect of the whole organismic-communitarian doctrine. Everyone who is so inspired can do some work, but only all together can do the work of Christ. We are reminded once again of Goethe's great words, already quoted,[4] that 'only all men together are the true man'. In this spirit, Pius XII can write: 'The manifold orders and institutions in the Church show forth Christ in various aspects of His life: contemplating on the mountain, preaching to the people, healing the sick, bringing sinners to repentance, and doing good to all.'[5] Rightly understood, this sentence shows the underlying and overarching organicism of the Catholic Church even more clearly than all the others which we have quoted. Christ is in the many, but only the many *together* are Christ.[6] Protestantism, at least in its more consistent variants, did not, as we shall see, think and feel in quite this way.

As things are illustrated by their opposites, it is indeed a comparison with Protestantism that can serve to bring out the specific characteristics of Catholicism, and that is to say, of the communitarian and organismic form of Christendom. Here belongs above all the doctrine

[1] Ibid., p. 18.
[2] Cf. Stark, W., *Social Theory and Christian Thought*, London 1958/9, pp. 11 and 12.
[3] *The Mystical Body of Christ*, as quoted, pp. 27 and 28. Cf. I Corinthians XII, 21.
[4] Cf. vol. IV, p. 16.
[5] *The Mystical Body*, p. 29; cf. also pp. 27 and 28.
[6] Cf. ibid., pp. 32 and 33.

of the 'cistern of graces in heaven' as it is sometimes called, a doctrine which does not appear reconcilable with Lutheran, Calvinist and Quaker individualism. 'The ministry of the saints to the faithful on earth is not limited to loving intercession,' writes Karl Adam, where he brings the matter up. 'The saints during their mortal life amassed beyond the measure of their duty a store of wealth and of sacrificial values made precious by the blood of Christ. The superabundance of their love and penance forms a rich deposit. United with the superabundance of the merits of Christ, and derived from those merits, this wealth of the saints is that "treasure of the Church" (*thesaurus ecclesiae*), that sacred inheritance, which belongs to all the members of the Body of Christ, and which is at the service especially of its sick and feeble members . . . When a member has not made sufficient reparation for his sins, when after the forgiveness of sin and the remission of its eternal punishment, there yet remains a debt of "temporal" punishment which the just God in His wise ordinance attaches still to forgiven sin, then all the members of the Body help to bear this burden of punishment, and then the Church in virtue of her power of binding and loosing may supplement the poverty of one member out of the wealth of another. And thus she grants "indulgences" . . .'[1] The Lutheran Reformation, as is well known, started with an attack on the sale of indulgences, and the *sale* of them was surely an abuse which was rightly attacked.[2] Yet Luther had, beyond that point, objections of principle to the very idea of indulgences. If we may use a mercantile metaphor (permitted or at least suggested by the term *thesaurus*), we may say that he saw every man's profit and loss account in heaven as a closed *conto corrente* into which no payments could be made from the outside. This is where Catholicism differs because it is thinking in terms of community. Within the conditions so carefully summarized by Adam, every account is, according to Catholic conceptions, entirely open. The merits of others can come to swell the assets, scant as they often must be.

An appealing, nay charming, instance occurs in the *Fioretti di San Francesco*. The thirty-seventh chapter is entitled: 'How St. Francis knew in spirit that Brother Elias[3] was damned . . . for which cause he prayed for him and his prayer was answered.' The misdeeds of the unfortunate Frate are mentioned, and more especially his ganging-up with the Emperor Frederick II who gave the Church such serious trouble. And then it is recorded how Francis is asked to intercede for the sinner. Elia mended his ways, at least half and half, but what really pulled him through was the protection which the Poverello accorded to him, in spite of everything. 'His soul was saved by the merits of St. Francis

[1] Adam, K., *The Spirit of Catholicism*, transl. McCann, J., New York 1937, pp. 137 and 138.
[2] But cf. our vol. III, p. 353.
[3] Cf. our vol. IV, pp. 87 et seq.

and by his prayer in which Brother Elias had placed such great hope.'[1]
'Here, as in no other practice of the Church, do the members of the
Body of Christ co-operate in loving expiation,' writes Adam.[2] 'Co-
operate' is the salient term. We have promised above (cf. p. 66)
that we would explain its meaning when we encountered it in the
encyclical *Mystici Corporis*. We have done so now. The poetry involved
is once again helpful as a mode of expression and explanation. In
The Cathedral, J. K. Huysmans calls a Carmelite nunnery 'a reservoir'
and adds: 'The image is precise for the convent is indeed a reservoir
into which God dips to draw forth the good works of love and tears,
and restore the balance of the scales in which the sins of the world are
so heavy.'[3] It is more usual to speak of a cistern – but the concrete
picture evoked is immaterial so long as the concept of a *sharing* of merit
is conveyed.

How salient the doctrine is, and how much of a dividing line it is
between Catholicism and Protestantism, i.e. community-centred and
individual-centred Christianity, can be seen in the differing attitudes to
the dead. As Catholics have held fast to the Epistle of St. James which
was not to Luther's liking, so they stand by II Macchabees XII, 46, for
which Protestants have less use: 'It is a holy and wholesome thought to
pray for the dead that they may be loosed from sins.' According to an
individualistic theology, a man's account is closed when he dies for he
can no longer add to it and nobody else possibly can. According to its
collectivistic counterpart, things look different. Those in purgatory
are conceived as the 'suffering' church – but though they are in a com-
partment of their own, so to speak, they are still in the Church and can,
do and must partake in her life, a life that floods through all the fibres.
'Having entered into the night "wherein no man can work",' writes
Adam, 'the Suffering Church cannot ripen to its final blessedness by any
efforts of its own, but only through the help of others – through the
intercessory prayers and sacrifices of those living members of the Body
of Christ who being still in this world are able in the grace of Christ to
perform expiatory works.'[4] Hence the mutual support of the strong for
the weak is even greater *post obitum* than even *inter vivos*.

The whole manner of thinking which we have characterized explains
yet another feature which divides the variants of Christianity: the
veneration of the saints. This is one of the points where – surprising as
it may seem – the coherence of Jewish and Christian community-
mindedness can be clearly perceived. The Jews, it is true, had no
formalized canon of saints, but they had the substantial concept of

---

[1] *The Little Flowers of Saint Francis of Assisi*, transl. Franciscan Fathers at Upton, re-
vised by Okey, Th., London n.d., pp. 118–21.
[2] Adam, loc. cit., p. 139.
[3] Transl. Bell, Cl., London 1925, p. 247.
[4] Adam, loc. cit., pp. 140 and 141.

sainthood as a source of blessing for the not-so-saintly. 'Souls . . . must share their contents with each other,' explains Pedersen, in *Israel: Its Life and Culture*, where he speaks about the Jewish philosophy of life. 'The blessed gives to the others because the strength . . . pours from him and up around him. The important thing is to ally oneself closely with the blessed and to get one's share of his gifts. Both Jacob and Joseph, in strange countries, were possessed of the power to spread blessing among their surroundings. Wherever the man who has the blessing in him goes, happiness must spring up and others must get blessing, because he has the mysterious power of the strong soul to inspire them with his strength.'[1]

We clearly see the same idea as before: the linkage of lives, the circulation of fluids through a whole system of interlocked animated channels, the unity of community. As the incarnate Church is in communion with the suffering Church in purgatory to which she can give help, so she is in communion with the triumphant Church in heaven from which she can receive help. Here again, fine theological points must not be forgotten, but the sociological doctrine is the main interest (perhaps even for the theologian). Drawing a clear distinction between the adoration of God (the *cultus latriae*) and the veneration of saints (the *cultus duliae*), Adam explains: 'Adoration belongs to God alone . . . The veneration which we give to . . . saints is essentially different . . . The difference is in fact the whole difference between the creature and the Creator . . . It is God and God only who redeems us and gives us life. Yet . . . saints have the power to accompany the great work of our redemption with their fostering love and by their "intercession" to elevate our prayers for help into the great solitary prayer of the whole Body of Christ . . . For the very reason that Jesus Christ, the God-man, is the Mediator of our redemption, the saints also have a share in it. For they are members of our Redeemer . . . No help comes to us, but that the members of Christ in their manner co-operate with their Head . . . This is the fulfilment of the law of love, the great structural law of the Kingdom of God. God redeems men in such a way that every love-force in the Body of Christ has its proper share in the work. The Body of Christ of its very nature implies communion and co-operation, and so the divine blessing never works without the members, but only in and through their unity. God can help us without the saints; but He will not help us without their co-operation, for it is His nature and will to be communicative love.'[2]

We have now reached the point where we can, with some confidence, move to the study of the 'higher' cultural aspects of Catholic life, i.e. those superstructural aspects which are relatively far removed from the social and organizational substructure. But before we begin to look at

[1] Pedersen, loc. cit., p. 193.
[2] Adam, loc. cit., pp. 133–5.

such phenomena as dogma and ritual, we would cast a brief side-glance at an important book which has not received its due share of attention, especially in the Anglo-Saxon world: Arnold Rademacher's *Die Kirche als Gemeinschaft und Gesellschaft*.[1] As the very title shows, its author has – just like the author of the present work – tried to apply the basic dichotomy of Ferdinand Tönnies to the realities of religion, and there is deep and wide coincidence in basic attitude. In the details, however, there is some divergence, and it is well worth looking at.

Briefly, Rademacher claims that the Catholic Church is both community and association: she is community according to her essence and association according to her appearance. 'The community manifests itself as an association (*Gesellschaft*),' Rademacher writes in one context, and in another he says: 'The community is in its phenomenal form an association. That which objectively and in itself is community, is subjectively and by us experienced as association. The association is the outer aspect of community, as community is the inner side of association.' And again, in a passage which reveals the deeper layers of the author's thought: 'Life is being tamed by form so that it should not dissolve, as form is being kept in motion by life, so that it should not ossify.'[2] Community, then, is the inner core of the Catholic Church, whereas her outer shell is merely associational. Other concepts might still be called in to make Rademacher's meaning clear, for instance 'substance' and 'accidents', but perhaps this is unnecessary and the meaning is clear already.

With this definitional duality Rademacher then links a dynamic one: the realization of community is the end of the association's endeavours. The association 'Church' has as its mission the creation of the community 'Church', i.e. the 'real' Church which coincides with the Kingdom of God and the Communion of Saints. 'The coordination of community and association is . . . a task, in so far as the association may realize the content of the community in a more or less perfect manner. The association can never fall away from the essence of the community whose representation (*Darstellung*) it is, but, as a representation, it can be more or less adequate . . . The association is an educator leading in the direction of the Communion of Saints, and the Communion of Saints is the Mother of the Association of Christians.'[3]

What Rademacher obviously does in these arguments is less to follow the lead of Tönnies, though he uses his terms, than to take his cue from Plato. The community is for him the *noumenon*, the Idea, whereas the ecclesiastical apparatus is the appearance, the *phenomenon*. As there is, in the Divine Mind, an image of the rose in all its glory and perfection to which observable roses may come close, but which, with all their

---

[1] Augsburg 1931.
[2] Loc. cit., pp. 58, 28, 77. Our translations.
[3] Ibid., pp. 60 and 77.

earthy and earthly blemishes, they will never reach, so there is, again in the Divine Mind, the vision of an all-comprehensive human brotherhood which the empirical Church, for all its catholicity and apostolicity, will never implement. The argument of Rademacher is thus a deeply religious one and it deserves our admiration both for its philosophical inspiration and for its descriptive – or perhaps we should say, for its ruthlessly self-critical – realism.

And yet, when we consider this matter soberly, it would appear to be doubtful if it is wise to abandon the dichotomy of Tönnies, and that is what Rademacher in effect does. True, even for Tönnies there is the possibility of a dynamic relationship between association and community, as, for example, when a business firm created by the partners for their individual benefit matures into an institution in its own right, a proper 'we', which, by its long tradition and high standards, absorbs the partners and makes them its organs. All the same, what Tönnies intended was to give us descriptive terms which represent the end points of a continuum, 'ideal types' as Max Weber called them, 'normal concepts' as he himself preferred to say, terms which should serve to characterize and to contrast observable realities, and because of this – because of the typological function of the terms – we should be loath to connect and to confound them.

Rademacher is, of course, only too justified in feeling that the Church as she is, is not the Church as she should be, that the observable Church has the appearance rather than the reality of a brotherhood. But this does not make it necessary for us to abandon the organological simile and theory. For – to use a pair of concepts introduced into the discussion on an earlier occasion[1] – we must in all things distinguish a normative from a positive or positivistic form of organicism. Only the positive or positivistic variant asserts, with Spencer, that 'a society is an organism'; the normative version merely suggests that a society is *ideally* like an organism, that it is quasi-organic in *design*. To fulfil that design, to turn into a form of life not unworthy to be called organic, be it even in a metaphorical sense, it must become what it is – become in fact what it is in promise, and that is by no means easy. *Mystici Corporis* is painfully and penitently aware of this. 'If something is perceived in the Church which points to the infirmity of our human condition,' we read there – to our inability to realize the fullness of the organic pattern, so we may interpose – 'this is not to be attributed to her juridical constitution, but to the lamentable tendency of individuals towards evil, a tendency which her divine Founder suffers to exist even in the higher members of His Mystical Body.'[2] In other words, the inability to live up to the organic principle does not mean that we have to call in another

---

[1] Cf. Stark, W., *The Fundamental Forms of Social Thought*, London 1962, pp. 17 et seq.
[2] *The Mystical Body*, as quoted, p. 40.

principle of interpretation, if organic coherence is *de facto* aimed at and all is judged in terms of it.

On this point, the position of the other, the alternative theory, the individualistic-associational sociology of atomism, is no differently placed: it, too, must face the fact that there can only be approximations to its envisaged pattern, and no more. In his *Kritik der praktischen Vernunft*,[1] Kant sets forth his conception of the ethical man: the strong personality who consciously and willingly accepts submission to the law because he has freely embraced self-discipline and considers it part and parcel of the very essence, of the very definition, of 'man'. Yet Kant candidly concedes that he presents 'an ideal which objectively is represented completely only in reason and which subjectively is only the goal for the person's unceasing endeavours'.[2] Should we therefore cease to speak of ethical men and assert that such do not exist? Even he who merely tries, but truly tries, to be law-abiding is a law-abiding (*recht-schaffener*) man. In the same sense, even a malfunctioning stomach is still a stomach so long as it manages somehow to digest food. But we need not go so far as to call in the image of disease in order to rescue Catholicism's organological ecclesiology, the organismic inspiration which, Rademacher agrees,[3] belongs to its essence. We need only remember the concept of servo-mechanism which we used when we discussed the official Church hierarchy and its proper function.[4] Ideally, every organism is living throughout; in reality it contains less than living tissue, like bone, and even non-living elements, like nails and hair. It is an organism, in spite of this. In so far as bone, nails and hair help our bodies to function, and in so far as *infirmi* and *mortui* (as St. Augustine called them)[5] and the *mechanici* (whom we might add), those whose operation and co-operation is no more than external, without spirit, do the same for the 'Body of Christ', they can still be regarded as belonging to the organisms concerned and as, in a manner, implementing the organical principle. The practical imperfections of essential ordering do not therefore justify our abandonment of the theoretical definition of that ordering itself.

We have cast an interested and even affectionate glance at Rademacher's book; we have taken cognizance of its contents; we are prepared to go so far as to express admiration for it; but we would stick to our acceptance of the Catholic self-image, derived as it is from community in real life, and leading, as it does, to communitarian forms of higher culture, such as dogma, ritual and art. To their investigation we must now turn.

[1] 2. Buch, 1. Hauptstück.
[2] Kant, I., *Critique of Practical Reason*, transl. Beck, L. W., Indianapolis and New York 1956, p. 113.
[3] Cf. esp. his pp. 51 and 52.
[4] Cf. our vol. IV, p. 163.
[5] Cf. Stark, W., *Social Theory and Christian Thought*, as quoted, p. 13.

THE PRINCIPLE OF COMMUNITY IN DOGMA AND RITUAL

Religious dogmas are, ideally and in intention, ultimate answers to ultimate questions. In order to understand how they emerge, it is therefore best to start with a consideration of the ultimate options which appear to be open.

However we may look upon man, however simple or sophisticated our philosophical anthropology may be, it is clear that he is both a creature of reason and a creature of the senses. He can therefore, in his pursuit of religious truth as in all other matters, follow either a more rationalistic or a more experiential line. Once he has made up his mind, once this basic decision has fallen, the sheer logic of thought will lead him forward to very dissimilar and inescapably one-sided results.

If it is the more rationalistic alternative that is chosen, a strictly monotheistic theology will ultimately be formed. The rationalist properly so called prefers to think in mathematical terms; this is entirely natural for him; if he wants to penetrate from the multiplicity of being to the origin of things, he will, on the model of mathematics, be driven towards the number one; in arithmetic and geometry, too, all higher figures are derived from the lowest and simplest, the lowest integer in the one case, the simple point in the other. There is no reason which the rationalist will see and acknowledge for proceeding otherwise in his metaphysical and religious quest. If, on the other hand, it is the more experiential alternative that is embraced, a pantheistic theology will be the end result of the mental effort. The man of the senses will be impressed by the concreteness, and that is to say, the multiformity, of the reality which offers itself to him; he will be loath to exchange its complexity and colourfulness, its riches, for the comparative poverty of a grey concept. He will see Godhood not in One, but in all (pure pantheism) or as an element in all (panentheism).

Yet though it will be entirely natural to come to these final conclusions, be it the one or be it the other, they will, on closer examination, turn out to be untenable as they stand. For if strict (so to speak ruthless) monotheism is considered, not only in its august thesis, but also in its less obvious implications, it will be seen that it is incapable of explaining the act of creation and hence the existence of the multiform world which meets with, and is apprehended by, our senses. Why should the One God have called the universe into being? The religious mind will not be able to envisage Him otherwise than as perfect; but the self-sufficiency, contentment, and happiness which are part of perfection would seem to leave no motive for the act of calling a reality out of the void – a reality moreover which is apt to fall away from its Maker and thus to become the cause of imperfection, of struggle, and of pain. 'Since . . . everlasting and unchangeable quiescence is the simplest and truest notion we can obtain of the Deity,' writes Cardinal Newman, there lies for us a deep problematic in 'the work of creation itself, as opposed to the absolute perfection of the Eternal God, that internal concentration of His Attributes in self-contemplation, which took place on the seventh day when He rested from all the work which He had made'[1] – and which, we must add, also took place before the first day when He had not yet undertaken the work which He decided to do. Clearly, no purely logical, so to speak blind, monotheism would ever still man's craving for knowledge of the Godhead; only a seeing monotheism, a monotheism of complexity would suffice. Without abandoning the monotheistic principle as such, an idea of inner multiformity would have to be added to the concept of the One God. Thus, from the earliest day, there would be laid on a tendency towards the Christian dogma of the Holy One and Undivided Trinity, of a *Deus Unus et Trinus*, as St. Augustine loved to call Him. To the Person of the All-Father would have to be conjoined the Person of the Eternal Son. The 'begetting' of the Son – though, as consubstantial and co-eternal with the Father, He is in no sense part of creation – is yet an indication, an earnest, of the presence of a Dynamical Principle within the Godhead which, in the fullness of time, was to lead to creation. In this sense, Christ – the Logos – was what St. Paul called Him, 'the first-born of every creature' (Colossians I, 15), and what St. John called Him, 'the beginning of the creation' (Apocalypse III, 14). In this way did monotheism, in the hands of the Christian community, become modified – opened up, if we may so express it – to the fact of multiplicity. Monotheism was monotheism still, but one that stressed inner complexity as much as it did outer unity.

While monotheism thus had to struggle free from the over-simplicity, the crudity, of a purely logical conceptualization, which in things sacred will go so far and no further, pantheism, too, was increasingly felt to be incapable of yielding a satisfying theology. If the multiform world apprehended by the senses is taken to be the *ens realissimum*, God must be found in it, an inextricable part of it; but that means that His Selfhood cannot come to be clearly focused. 'What we ourselves witness,' writes Cardinal Newman, 'evidences to us the operation of laws, physical and moral; but it leaves us unsatisfied, whether or not the principle of these be a mere nature or fate, whether the life of all things be a mere *Anima Mundi*, a spirit connatural with the body in which it acts, or an Agent powerful to make or unmake . . . according to His will . . . a Being external to creation and possessed of individuality.'[2] Hence it is possible that God may ultimately disappear behind the matter which He has made; that matter itself may come to be deified; in other words, that pantheism may lose its theism and become pan-materialism. The transition from the one to the other has ever been fatefully easy. Thus

[1] Newman, J. H., *The Arians of the Fourth Century*, ed. London 1895, p. 75.
[2] Ibid., pp. 184 and 185.

while monotheistic cultures like that of the Jews were getting ready to embrace the enriched monotheism that was to come, pantheistic cultures like that of the Greeks were increasingly inclined to reduce their pantheism and to push in the direction of the monotheistic position. Before the Fathers of the Church had begun to elaborate the Nicene theology whose sociological explanation is the object of this section, 'even the heathen had shown a disposition, designedly or from a spontaneous feeling, to trace all their deities up to one Principle or *arche*; as is evident by their Theogonies'.[1] Perhaps the drift of ancient thought in the direction indicated is most clearly discoverable in the philosophy of the Stoic school. Stoicism believed pantheistically that reason (*logos*) was a universal attribute. All men bore a germ of it in themselves – the *logos spermatikos* of which the Stoics loved to speak. From this concept it was a revolutionary and yet a simple step to the idea of a Divine Logos, a Divine Reason indwelling in the One God, the Eternal 'Son' of the Eternal 'Father' – the Christian Creed.

What concerns the sociologist in all this is the fact – the decisive fact – that the theology hammered out in the first centuries of the Church was a *synthesis*, and that in more senses of the word than one. It was first of all a synthesis between the Jewish tradition of monotheism already modified by Judaism's interest in creation, and the Greek tradition of polytheism and near-pantheism already modified by Hellenism's search for a metaphysical or religious centre of unity. But it was not only a junction and fusion of essentially connected, because mutually complementary and mutually corrective, ultimate attitudes. The Church (and we have no hesitation here in using a collective noun in a collective signification) was driven to the conclusion that the proposition that 'God is One' contains the truth; but she was also driven to the conclusion that it is as true to say that 'God is more than one single and simple person'; and when two propositions are equally true, neither can be abandoned, both must be retained and combined. This is what actually happened, because it had to happen. In the Nicene Creed, the struggle between unity and multiplicity was finally laid to rest. Its great formula was the focal point in which the basic alternatives, with all their variants, could meet and merge.

It is the concept of synthesis, then, which gives us the key to the understanding of the thought-process which dominated the religious discussions up to the great points of arrival – the Council of Nicaea in A.D. 325 and the Council of Constantinople in 381. Synthesis, however, or unification, as it might also be called, is essentially the intellectual concomitant of the principle of community in real life. It is, as the Marxists might word it, the superstructural complement of a substructural effort, the effort to overcome disunity and dispersion and to achieve unity and integration. We see once again what we have seen so

[1] Ibid., p. 175.

often before throughout the pages of this work, that Christianity was the product of an *élan vital* which ambitiously attempted to fuse *all* human life or lives, as smaller communities, such as the Jewish *mishpaha* or the Greek *genos* or the Nordic *clan*, had tried to weld their members together into a seamless whole. In this process, the searching mind was forced beyond the borderline of both bookish rationality and sensual experience into the realm of mysticism, for the dual assertion that 'God is Three and God is One' can neither be adequately comprehended nor yet concretely experienced. It must be emphasized, however, that this formally self-contradictory concept of the Deity is in principle neither against reason nor against experience; it is merely against the limitations of both reason and experience; these two great endowments of the human mind, when they struggled for an answer to the ultimate questions, found themselves deadlocked in an apparently final antithesis; and they could only break through this barrier by partially overcoming each other and themselves. The energy which enabled – or perhaps we should say forced – them to achieve the feat was the energy of synthesis, of a search for community so intensive that it carried everything before it, even experience and reason, or rather, not to exaggerate, the poor human measure of these two.[1]

Needless to say, the great synthesis which became the orthodox creed and is still regularly recited in Catholic and other Christian churches was not easy to elaborate. Gnosticism, for instance, was a powerful movement which had to be fought off. This widespread philosophy took the strict monotheistic principle very seriously, or appeared to do so. The true God was far away from reality, deep in the unknown; He had never revealed Himself and there was no reason why He should do so; He was, *a fortiori*, not the Creator of the world. This deed, a highly problematical one, since the world is evil, was performed by a minor divinity, the god of the Old Testament, who knew no better or willed no better than to produce the conditions which we all experience and suffer under. This was the *blasphemia Creatoris* of which the Fathers uniformly complain.[2] What is interesting in our context is that Gnosticism, which began with a consistently monotheistic world-view, was forced, by its very view of the world, to add a second, if lower, divinity to the First or High God, and thus to countermand its own philosophical inspiration and devotional core. In a sense, orthodoxy was a synthesis even of the discordant elements contained in its great adversary, a synthesis made possible by the tremendous thought of a creation indeed fallen away from its benign Creator but ever struggling back

---

[1] Cf. Stark, W., 'The Rational and Social Foundations of Religious Dogma', in *Entwicklung und Fortschritt*, edd. Reimann, H., and Müller, E. W., Tübingen 1969, pp. 303–14.

[2] Cf. Hägglund, B., *History of Theology*, transl. Lund, G. J., St. Louis and London 1968, pp. 36 and 38.

towards Him, a reality in need of, but at the same time capable of, redemption, and waiting for it in longing and travail.

When Gnosticism was out of the way, Monarchianism appeared on the scene. Monarchianism 'elevated God over all material considerations, including change and diversity', and 'was unable to accept the claim that God appeared and acted in this world'. 'Its adherents repudiated the idea of "economy", according to which God, who is certainly one, revealed Himself in such a way that He appeared as the Son and as the Holy Spirit.' Unavoidably, they arrived at a rationalistic position, at an 'abstract idea of God', at Unitarianism.[1] To prise themselves free from it – and they had to do so because rationalism and abstraction cannot content the mind and the man in pursuit of an all-satisfying religious faith – they found themselves driven back towards the Trinitarian, if not indeed towards a tritheistic, theology.

There arose, therefore, again the same tendency which we have observed in Gnosticism: the neglect of the principle, and of the reality, of multiplicity started a dialectical movement which tended to produce the antithesis of the original thesis and cried out for the synthesis which became, at Nicaea, orthodoxy. And this very same phenomenon repeated itself for a third time in the much more ambitious and successful movement of Arianism.[2] According to Arius, God must be conceived as one and indivisible. Christ must therefore be part of creation – perhaps He was created before all other things, before the beginning of time, yet He must have had a beginning and thus is not *in* the Eternal Godhead but merely *of* Him. Many were the honorific appellations which Arius and his friends heaped on Jesus of Nazareth, yet in their rationalistic definition of unity, or of the unit, they found a hard and fast final limit. The counter-stroke was the Semi-Arianism of a figure like Meletius of Antioch who maintained that there were Three Hypostases (or substances) of the Godhead, and who therefore came close to tritheism – the very opposite of Arius' unitarian starting-point.[3]

We cannot possibly follow here, step for step, the effort by which the Church tried to prevent conceptualizations from becoming set and rigid which would have satisfied only part or parts of the human race, and would have ended in irreconcilable religious positions and ecclesiastical societies.[4] Suffice it to emphasize once more that the Athanasian Creed – 'neither dividing the Substance, nor confounding the Persons' – was the synthesis which reconciled the warring opinions and welded the opposing factions into One Body, One Church. We must, however,

[1] Ibid., pp. 69 and 70.
[2] In what follows, we neglect the historically important fact that this heresy enjoyed for a long time the support of the Byzantine court camarilla, because we have already discussed this fact in vol. III, pp. 256 et seq.
[3] Cf. Newman, loc. cit., pp. 368 and 369.
[4] The reader can follow the formation of the orthodox synthesis in Hägglund's very clear survey. Cf. esp. pp. 28, 29, 46, 47, 50, 54, 66, 76–8, 83–5, 86–7.

cast a glance at the second act, so to speak, of the same dramatic development for our thesis should and will find further confirmation there.
After the discussion centring on the vision of the One and Undivided
Trinity came the great Christological debates and they, too, and perhaps
still more clearly, show that the thought-process, like the life-process,
of Catholicism is the elaboration of a *complexio oppositorum*.

Starting, for simplicity's sake, not from the opposing points of
departure, but from the synthesis-providing point of arrival, from the
orthodox doctrine that the Second and Incarnate Person of the Most
Holy Trinity was *both* the Eternal Christ-Logos and the mortal Jesus of
Nazareth, both 'true God and true man', we may conclude that two
antithetic movements must have preceded it, one asserting that He was
God rather than man, and the other that He was man rather than God.
And this is, in fact, what we find. The clarity of the outline, as we
present it, is merely a little dimmed by the successive shifts and
elaborations which took place on the two sides. But there were, properly considered, only two sides. Docetism, Gnosticism, Marcionism,
Patripassionism, Modalism, Sabellianism, Apollinarianism, Eutychianism, Monophysitism and Monotheletism all share the tendency to
exalt the divine Christ over the earthly Jesus, while Adoptionism and
Nestorianism and yet other theologies assert the earthly Jesus as against
the divine Christ. We have before us in history what men of military
science call a ding-dong battle. First the one army advances, then the
other; there is no issue to the fight; or rather there is only one issue –
peace; and that peace costs the price of complexity, of logical self-contradiction even, of 'two are one' – a small price to pay, the believer will
say, as it is only in this way that an apparently ultimate antithesis can be
transmuted into a truly ultimate synthesis. Here again we can discern
behind the foreground of more immediate issues, the background of
final alternatives. We have seen not long ago that, in an environment
far removed from the Judaeo-Grecian one with which we are directly
confronted in the Christological discussions, in the Germanic cultures
of the north of Europe, two ideas of salvation tended to take shape:
salvation through superhuman help, through a heavenly being who
would learn to have mercy on men (Brynhild), and salvation through
human agency, through a representative of the human race who would
lead his fellow-humans back to God, the source of all goodness (Sigfrid). Christian theology, as it developed in the Patristic age, fused these
two ideas into one, thus overcoming a duality which must be overcome
if a lasting doctrine is to be achieved.

It is not impossible that the Gospel according to St. John, one of
Christianity's most sacred sources, was written to refute the theology of
a certain Gnostic, Cerinthus by name. This Cerinthus made a sharp
distinction between the earthly Jesus and the divine Christ. Christ
resided only temporarily in Jesus. Above all, He did not share the

sufferings of Jesus. A God cannot suffer. Christ may at most have appeared to suffer. Perhaps He left the body of the Nazarene before the crucifixion; perhaps it was in fact Simon of Cyrene who was crucified and not He who is usually believed to have died on the cross; perhaps – and this was the preferred assumption – Jesus Christ had only a ghost-like body, a body transparent, immaterial, woven of light. Not many words are needed to prove that this was not a possible variant of Christianity, that it was not Christianity at all, that it was a mythology which, if it had prevailed, would have kept Christianity out. St. John's hammer-like assertion that 'the Word was made flesh' (I, 14) combated and overcame this 'Docetic' doctrine. St. Ignatius, who died his martyr's death in the second decade of the second century, still had to fight on the same front.[1]

If Christ was thus to Cerinthus (and to Marcion and others also) a God, albeit in human shape, He was to Praxeas and Noetus the Eternal Father, the One and Undivided God Himself, an assertion which has been well described as Patripassionism. According to the 'Modalism' of Sabellius, He was merely a form (or *modus*) which the Deity assumed in manifesting Itself to the world. Apollinaris was far from this philosophy, yet he, too, saw Christ as God, and only God, not really as man. 'According to this point of view, Christ did not receive His human nature, His flesh, from the Virgin Mary; He rather brought it with Him, from heaven, a heavenly kind of flesh. The womb of Mary simply served as a passageway.' Though such speculations were one-day-wonders, their essence appeared in a more rational form in powerful figures like Eutyches who was declared a heretic at the Council of Chalcedon in 451. The assertion that even the body of Christ was divine links him to Apollinaris before him; his insistence that there was only one nature even in the incarnate Christ links him to the Monophysites after him. The Monothelites who arose a little later accepted the two-nature theory, yet even they continued the tradition of a Cerinthus and Praxeas, for they taught that Christ had but one will – that of the Divine Logos.[2]

What all these teachings had in common was the tendency to assert that no human being, no *man* was the agent of salvation. Yet, so the vast majority was apt to ask, how could man then be truly redeemed? He had fallen by his own free will – would he not have to make an effort of his own in order to rise up again? A second string of thinkers gave an affirmative answer to this query. There was, for instance, Adoptionism, a late variant of which we have encountered in our volume II.[3] The Ebionites were the earliest representatives of this theology which saw only Jesus, not the Christ, only a man, and not God. They interpreted

[1] Hägglund, loc. cit., pp. 20, 33, 34, 37, 39, 41.
[2] Cf. ibid., pp. 55, 71, 72, 89, 90, 98, 100, 101, 102, 103 (literal quotation on p. 90).
[3] Cf. pp. 103 et seq.

him as one of the prophets, perhaps greater than, but not essentially different from, Moses. He was chosen by God to be the Messiah, adopted as the Son at His baptism but He was not from eternity, not of miraculous birth, not the incarnate Deity. Paul of Samosata, whose influence worked for a very long time, carried this conception forward and developed it strongly. The power or *dynamis* of God came to dwell in Jesus, but Jesus remained like us except that He was equipped with this *dynamis* or power (Dynamic Monarchianism).

Nestorianism is not easily summarized. Its hard core was the conviction that Christ lived, suffered and died only as a man, and this, too, came in the end to a *de facto* denial of His divinity. While moving close to the orthodox doctrine of two natures in One Person, Nestorius 'had a tendency to distinguish between the natures in such a way that there was no actual oneness in the person of Christ'.[1] The diametrical opposition to Eutychianism is strikingly manifest here. Indeed, we may well use Nestorius and Eutyches as summarizers, so to speak, of the opposing currents. 'As Nestorianism presses to the point of heresy the Antiochene theologians' concern for the complete humanity of Christ, so Eutychianism may be described as pushing too far the Alexandrians' insistence on His perfect Godhead.'[2]

The last words are the words of an ecclesiastical author arguing from within the orthodox position. A scholarly observer may be loath to use the value-laden term 'heresy', yet he will welcome such a statement all the same because it is truly revealing. To sum it all up in the simplest possible terms: the Church was pressed on the one hand to say that Christ was true God, and on the other that Jesus was true man; if all were to be embraced, there was no other recourse but to proclaim, the formal difficulties notwithstanding, that Jesus Christ was 'true God *and* true man'. For the Catholic mainstream, the very heart-piece of theology is the conviction that when the Second Person of the Most Holy Trinity became incarnate, He did not lose His divine nature, but He put on His (and our) human nature: *non amittendo quod erat, sed sumendo quod non erat*, as the traditional formula has it.

The modern mind will perhaps ask here, in some puzzlement, why the Church could not, after all, find its rest in some such doctrine as Adoptionism, a mode of thought of high relative rationality, which would have considerably diminished the 'scandal of Christianity' – its unashamed acceptance of, and insistence on, irrational dogmas. Assuming that man had fallen, so to speak, unaided, could he not also rise again unaided, by his – exclusively his own – action? Could there not have appeared, in Jesus of Nazareth, the totally righteous man, acceptable to the Deity above, who, by his righteousness redeemed all humanity, on the principle of 'all for one, one for all' that hovered in

[1] Hägglund, loc. cit., pp. 32, 70, 96, 97 (literal quotation on p. 96).
[2] Butler, B. C., *The Church and Infallibility*, New York 1954, pp. 174 and 175.

the background all the time? The orthodox answer to these queries, given perhaps most clearly at a later date by Anselm of Canterbury, was that man had incurred an infinite guilt which could only be blotted out by an infinite sacrifice of atonement, and such a price could be offered and paid only by One who was Himself part of infinity.

Athanasius made this point very strongly in his polemic against Arius: in Hägglund's summary, his argument was that 'if . . . Christ is just a created being and not of the same substance as the Father, salvation would not be possible. For God alone can save.'[1] Already Irenaeus had written: 'If our salvation is not from God, we cannot be sure that we are saved.'[2] But perhaps we shall get further at this point with a psychological rather than a theological argument. Men experience an apparently inescapable feeling of helplessness when they are confronted with their own situation, the situation of a creature at odds with its Creator and with the higher world. They will not be convinced that they are truly saved unless their Saviour is God as well as man: condemned by God's sternness, they will not believe in their reinstatement in grace, if it is not granted by God's love, the Principle of Love – the Second Person – in God. And that Principle was Christ; that Principle took flesh in Jesus. Hence, as a Nestorian element had to be added to Eutychianism, so an Eutychian element had to be added to Nestorianism, to yield a totally satisfying theology. In other words, there had to be synthesis.

We owe the understanding of this whole history of Catholic orthodoxy mainly to the genius of John Henry (Cardinal) Newman.[3] In his ever-admirable mind (the mind of a man characterized by his capacity for conspectus and integration) there formed the conviction that all the conflicts, indeed, even all the cantankerousness of the factions did not prevent them from forming one coherent pattern. 'These disorders were no interruption to the sustained and steady march of the sacred science from implicit belief to formal statement,' the Cardinal writes. 'The series of ecclesiastical decisions, in which its progress was ever and anon signified, alternate between the one and the other side of the theological dogma especially in question, as if fashioning it into shape by opposite strokes . . . In the long course of the centuries . . . the Church thus wrought out the one and only consistent theory . . .'[4] And, in another volume:[5] 'True religion is the summit and perfection of false religions; it combines in one whatever there is of good and true

[1] Hägglund, loc. cit., p. 80.
[2] Cit. Hägglund, ibid., p. 50. Cf. *Adversus Haereses*, III, XVIII, 7. *Patrologia Graeca*, ed. Migne, J. P., vol. VII, Paris 1882, col. 937.
[3] For a terse overview, cf. *Development of Christian Doctrine*, as quoted, pp. 439 and 440; further for the detail cf. Hägglund, as quoted, esp. pp. 45, 46, 50, 55, 66, 73, 80-2, 92, 97, 98, 104.
[4] *Development*, as quoted, pp. 439 and 440.
[5] *Discussions and Arguments on Various Subjects*, London, etc., 1891, p. 200.

severally remaining in each. And in like manner the Catholic Creed is for the most part the combination of separate truths which heretics have divided among themselves and err in dividing. So that, in matter of fact, if a religious mind were educated in and sincerely attached to some form of heathenism or heresy, and then were brought under the light of truth, it would be drawn off from error into the truth, not by losing what it had, but by gaining what it had not . . . True conversion is ever a positive, not a negative, character.'

The dogma of the two natures conjoined in the one person of Christ, and more specifically of the human nature added on to the divine, offers us yet another opportunity of demonstrating the profoundly, nay decisively, collectivistic character of the thought of the Christian community in the first ages. What was that human nature which was added at the Incarnation to the pre-existent divinity? Was it an individual nature, the kind of nature of which we moderns automatically think when we mention the term 'human nature'? By no means. Among the Fathers who perfected the work of Athanasius and the other pioneers of orthodoxy, one of the most inspired was Gregory of Nyssa, and he leaves us in no doubt about the point which we are discussing: 'He expressly taught that Christ did not assume the nature of an individual man, but, as second Adam, human nature itself, so that . . . *everything* human has blended with the Divinity.' The passage which we have just quoted is from the pen of Adolf von Harnack,[1] and he is a particularly trustworthy witness at this juncture, not only because of his matchless scholarship, but also because he is here speaking against himself. An out-and-out individualist, he saw Christianity in hyper-individualistic terms. His tendency was to find farreaching individualism, not only in the work of the Reformers, but even in that of the original formers. Still, he admits not only that the great Bishop of Nyssa was on the other side of the fence, but even that the Cappadocian's conviction spread throughout the Church. 'The thought that Christ took upon himself humanity as generally conceived,'[2] he admits, 'spread in the East and West and destroyed [better perhaps: inhibited the development of] the idea of a moral union of the Divinity with an individual man.'[3]

But not only the content of the dogma bespeaks a consistent collectivism; the way in which it was elaborated does so, too. Unavoidably, the Christological discussion was carried on by definite and assignable individuals, big individuals whose powerful personalities still talk to us and impress us across the gulf of the centuries. It would be entirely

[1] Harnack, A. von, *Outlines of the History of Dogma*, ed. Rieff, Ph., transl. Mitchell, E. K., Boston 1957, p. 238.
[2] A happier translation would have been: 'generically conceived'. The German text speaks of 'Allgemeinbegriff der Menschheit'. Cf. *Grundriss der Dogmengeschichte*, Freiburg i. Br. 1889, p. 134.
[3] Ibid., pp. 239 and 240.

wrong to belittle the strength of an Arius, a Nestorius or an Eutyches. But they, the opposers of orthodoxy, had a comparatively easy game because they propagated doctrines far closer to untutored common sense than was the orthodoxy of an Athanasius or a Gregory of Nyssa. It is not difficult to believe that Jesus of Nazareth was merely a man; it is not much more difficult to persuade oneself that He was God, or a god, *in human guise*; but that He was God, even though He looked like a man and *was* in all essentials man, is a proposition which, literally, takes some believing. What enabled the majority of Nicaea, the majority of Constantinople, to win in the end? It was the support of the masses of the faithful, of the mind of the masses, if the expression be allowed. The forum in which the two opposing theologies met and, above all, in which they merged, was no parliament, no school, no assignable place. It was the common consciousness of the *plebs Christi*. On this point, too, we must give the word to Cardinal Newman. 'In the first three centuries of the Church,' he writes, 'perhaps there was not one great mind, after the Apostles, to teach and mould her children . . . Rather, in that earliest age, it was simply the living spirit of the myriads of the faithful, none of them known to fame, who received from the disciples of our Lord, and husbanded so well, and circulated so widely, and transmitted so faithfully, generation after generation, the once delivered apostolic faith; who held it with such sharpness of outline and explicitness of detail, as enabled even the unlearned instinctively to discriminate between truth and error . . . We discern . . . a vigorous action of the intellect residing in the [whole] body [social] independent of individuals and giving birth to great men, rather than created by them.' Bengt Hägglund's comment is, compared to this vigour of statement, low-keyed and tame, yet it comes in the end to the same. 'The theology of the Apostolic Fathers cannot be assigned to any particular member of the apostolic band,' he writes. 'It rather reflects the faith of the typical congregation in the first years of Christian history.'[1]

We should, however, be a little more precise; we should insist that what took place within public opinion (to use, for want of a better, a far too colourless term) was the essential achievement – the reconciliation of opposites. Newman points out that the self-same process of development leads first to diversity, to dialectical opposition, and then to unity, to final synthesis. 'When some great enunciation . . . is carried forward into the public throng of men and draws attention, then it is not merely received passively . . . into many minds, but it becomes an active principle within them, leading them to an ever-new contemplation of itself . . . There will be a general agitation of thought and an action of mind upon mind. There will be a time of confusion when conceptions and

[1] Hägglund, loc. cit., p. 16; Newman, J. H., *Historical Sketches,* vol. I, ed. London, etc., 1896, pp. 208 and 209.

misconceptions are in conflict, and it is uncertain whether anything is to come of the idea at all . . . This it is that imparts to the history of both states and of religions its especially turbulent and polemical character. Such is the explanation of the wranglings whether of schools or of parliaments. It is the warfare of ideas under their various aspects striving for the mastery . . . After a while some definite teaching emerges; and, as time proceeds, one view will be modified or expanded by another, and then combined with a third; till the idea to which these various aspects belong, will be to each mind separately what at first it was only to all together . . . This body of thought, thus laboriously gained, will . . . be . . . the proper representative of [that] one idea, being in substance what that idea meant from the first, its complete image as seen in a combination of diversified aspects, with the suggestions and corrections of many minds, and the illustration of many experiences.'[1]

The history of religious thought seemed to Newman a prime example of this general law of the growth of ideas. 'The theology of the Church,' he writes, 'is no random combination of various opinions, but a diligent, patient working out of one doctrine from many materials . . . The doctrines even of the heretical bodies are indices and anticipations of the mind of the Church . . . In the collision, [orthodoxy] broke in pieces its antagonists and divided the spoils . . . Thus Christianity grew in its proportions, gaining aliment and medicine from all that it came near, yet preserving its original type, from its perception and its love of what had been revealed once for all and was no private imagination.'[2]

The Protestant denominations to whom such far-reaching collectivism is unavoidably unsympathetic, have seen, not the life-process of the Christian community, but the text of the Bible, assumed inspired, as the source of all dogma. Yet two facts must not be forgotten, if their point of view is accepted. Firstly, the Scriptures are no text-book. They may enunciate the substance of the faith, but they do not propound it *in terminis*. Its materials have to be assembled, compared, analysed, and that is the task of that sacred science to which the Protestant scholars have made such vast contributions; but before they can be truly used, they must be developed, and that development, Newman would claim, and most Catholics with him, was collective. Secondly, and more incisively, who established the Scripture canon – who, for instance, made some of the Gospels canonical and rejected others as apocryphal? It was the community, and there was no one else who could have done it. What happened is well covered by Newman's theory: a broad agreement emerged as to what belonged to the New Testament and what did not. Already 'Irenaeus referred to a collection of writings as

[1] *Development*, as quoted, pp. 36, 37, 39, 38.
[2] Ibid., pp. 366, 362, 359.

authoritative . . . which was largely the same as our present canon'.[1] Who had formed this collection, who had given canonicity to it? Everybody and nobody. The whole *plebs Christi*.

Still, the difference between Catholicism and Protestantism must remain, even if the historical fact of a developmental-processual formation of the authoritative canon is accepted on all sides, as it ought to be. It lies, and continues to lie, in the contrasting conceptions concerning the seat of Scripture authority. For the Protestant it resides exclusively in its assumed and asserted quality as the Word of God which is accepted in faith. For the Catholic it lies also in its validation by the community. 'Ecclesiastical definition is merely an inventory of the doctrinal possessions of the community,' says Rademacher. But a dogmatic definition upheld by the Church as a whole is infallibly true 'because a divine life is incapable of falsification or degeneracy.' This is where, for Rademacher, a sharp distinction between association and community, and therefore also between the individualistic and the collectivistic variants of Christianity, has its roots. 'In an association, only the general assembly . . . or a majority . . can decide, because . . . the association is no more than the sum of its individuals and has no other life than that of its members. It is otherwise in a community: here the totality decides with binding power . . .'.[2] Rademacher, in fact, speaks literally of legal power (*Rechtskraft*), and this suggests a simile which may be used here with advantage. The Catholic conviction clearly is that there can be no appeal beyond the agreed opinion of the community (even if the agreement is only implicit); the community is the court of last resort – a consistently collectivistic conception.

It is because Catholicism accepts and Protestantism rejects this final arbiter, because Protestantism believes in the supremacy of private, and Catholicism in the supremacy of common, judgment, that the doctrinal ways had ultimately to diverge. A good illustration is the different attitude to the linguistic variants of Scripture. The Vulgate text is authoritative for the Catholic even though it was the work of one man, Saint Jerome. What gives it its authority is not the scholarship or even the sanctity of that one man, but the spontaneous acceptance of his translation by 'the Church' – its validation, so to speak, by all. Protestantism logically cannot come to rest in such a derived version. It must try to push back beyond it, and a far-reaching philologism is the unavoidable result.

Much more momentous, however, than this division *pro* and *con* Saint Jerome is the Catholic evolution of, and the Protestant resistance to, a set of Mariological dogmas. Yet this development was hardly more than an aspect of the Christological debate and its dynamics, and of that orthodox resolution of it which most Protestants devotedly

[1] Cf. Hägglund, loc. cit., p. 44.
[2] Rademacher, loc. cit., pp. 156, 178, 179, 70.

accept. If Christ was truly God as well as truly man, His mother must have been, not only human, but a privileged human. The theologians of Alexandria, the city of Athanasius, the seat of orthodoxy, began to call Mary *Theotokos* – the Mother of God. Nestorius opposed them. She was merely the mother of a son of David, he argued from his essentially Adoptionist position. Surely, Nestorius was but consistent, but so were his orthodox adversaries; so was above all the Council of Ephesus (in the year 431) which accepted the term *Theotokos* as dogmatically correct and could not but do so if the final Christological formula – 'true God and true man' – was to be secure.[1] All the later elaborations of the theme, the doctrines of Mary's immaculate conception and of her assumption into heaven, were but a making explicit of what was implicitly present in the Christian body of thought, and in the Christian body, since the fifth century.

The Ecumenical Council of Chalcedon which met twenty years after the Synod of Ephesus marks the end point of the period of gestation which brought to life the orthodox system of doctrine. That system was, and had to be, and has to remain, a duality-in-unity, a synthesis which still bears the terms of the preceding antithesis in it. Cardinal Newman freely acknowledges this fact: 'Of the two titles ascribed in Scripture to Our Lord, that of the "Word" expresses with peculiar force His co-eternity in the One Almighty Father. On the other hand the title "Son" has more distinct reference to His derivation and ministrative office . . . The terms were received among Catholics; the "Endiathetic" standing for the Word, as hid from everlasting in the bosom of the Father, while the "Prophoric" was the Son sent forth into the world in apparent separation from God . . . The word *Person* which we venture to use in speaking of those three distinct and real modes in which it has pleased Almighty God to reveal to us His being is . . . too wide for our meaning. Its essential signification, as applied to ourselves, is that of an individual intelligent agent, answering the Greek *hypostasis* or *reality*. On the other hand, if we restrict it to its etymological sense of *persona* and *prosopon*, that is *character*, it evidently means less than the Scripture doctrine which we wish to define by means of it . . . The statements of Revelation then lie between these antagonistic senses . . .'[2] But though a tension between the concepts had perforce to remain, they were no longer divided. They were henceforth rather like two poles: at different ends of a continuum, yet still in a continuum, and meaningful only in their connection with each other.

At the end of the Middle Ages, the contrast of the two poles – or, should we say, of the two sides of the coin? – was once again thrown into high relief. Franciscanism and Dominicanism presented and

[1] Cf. Hägglund, loc. cit., pp. 95 and 96. Cf. also Newman, *Development*, as quoted, pp. 145, 294, 295, 403, 426–8, 435.
[2] Newman, *Development*, as quoted, pp. 196, 197, 365, 366.

propagated accentuations unlike each other. Speaking of the most resplendent representatives of either side, Hägglund has well summed up what set them apart: 'Bonaventura referred everything, even natural knowledge, to its divine origins, and he did this in such a way that the natural and the supernatural blended together into a contemplative unity. Thomas, on the other hand, employing a closely related analogy concept, emphasized the lack of similarity and the fundamental distinction between God and the created world.'[1] In this admirably terse statement, the words 'blended together' and 'distinction' are the key terms. Properly interpreted, they reveal to us the continued presence of the duality which is at the basis of all religious speculation and of all religious development.

The philosophy of Bonaventura carried within it possibilities of pantheistic developments: God and creation might come to be 'blended'. The philosophy of Aquinas, on the other hand, was running the risk of declining into a dry scholasticism where distinction-making would be a grand pastime and the colour of reality largely forgotten. Needless to say, neither of these sublime spirits did anything to increase these dangers: both were too securely held in the pattern of synthesis that had been handed down from Nicaea and Constantinople and Ephesus and Chalcedon. Yet the seeds were there. In their missals, Catholics are often offered two prayers, or two kinds of prayer, especially for thanksgiving after communion: one from Bonaventura, the other from Aquinas. The Franciscan urges on the faithful the desire that his soul may 'languish' and 'melt with love' and that it may 'long to be dissolved' and to be with God. Such sentiments point in the direction of that 'oceanic feeling' which has ever been the hallmark of pantheistic mysticism. The kernel of the personality is softened up, so to speak, not hardened and strengthened. Aquinas does not follow this lead. He prays that the soul may be brought to the 'ineffable banquet' of heaven of which the saints partake, where God is to the individual 'fulness of content' and 'eternal joy'.[2] The image is that of host and guest – two persons, united in love indeed, but yet two.

It is proof of the fact that the will to unity still prevailed over a tendency towards polarization that the later generations of the Mendicant Orders moved again close to each other. There is little difference, except in shading and emphasis, between, say, St. Antoninus of Florence and St. Bernardinus of Siena. Yet hardly had the sixteenth century arrived, hardly was the Church broken, when the great credal synthesis threatened to dissolve into the erstwhile antithesis. From Dominic and Thomas there leads, across the gulf of the Reformation, a line to Calvin and thence to the Unitarianism of the Enlightenment; from Francis and Bonaventura to Wesley and thence to the pantheism

---

[1] Hägglund, loc. cit., p. 182.
[2] Cf. e.g. *The Saint Andrew Daily Missal*, Bourges n.d., pp. 958 and 959.

of the Romantics. There appear, in the end, on the horizon, as recent embodiments of the once intermarried and now divorced philosophies, Logical Positivism and Existentialism, two anti-religious attitudes. Such is, and such must be, the final outcome of the abandonment of that will to unity which carried the Church to Nicaea and beyond.

As for Catholicism, it cannot exist, unless it preserves that will to unity. Here and nowhere else lies the heart of Catholic doctrine, as of everything else that is Catholic. This can best be seen from the very nature of Scholasticism – Scholasticism in the historical, the good sense of the word. 'All that mediaeval man could know about divine revelation, and much of what he held to be true in other respects, was transmitted by the authorities (*auctoritates*),' writes Erwin Panofsky, the authorities concerned being the Bible and the Fathers. 'Now, it could not escape notice that these authorities, even passages of Scripture itself, often conflicted with one another. There was no other way out than to accept them just the same and to interpret and reinterpret them over and over again until they could be reconciled. This had been done by theologians from the earliest days. But the problem was not posed as a matter of principle until Abelard wrote his famous *Sic et Non*, wherein he showed the authorities, including Scripture, disagreeing on 158 important points.' This was the challenge. And what was the answer? The answer was that the Scholastics perfected the 'technique of reconciling the seemingly irreconcilable'. 'Every topic (e.g. the content of every *articulus* in the *Summa Theologiae*) had to be formulated as a *quaestio* the discussion of which begins with the alignment of one set of authorities (*videtur quod* . . .) against the other (*sed contra* . . .), proceeds to the solution (*respondeo dicendum* . . .), and is followed by an individual critique of the arguments rejected (*ad primum, ad secundum*, etc.) – rejected, that is, only in so far as the interpretation, not the validity, of the authorities is concerned.'[1] Panofsky then goes on to show that the architects of the Gothic cathedrals were filled by the same spirit as the architects of the Scholastic structure and systems. We cannot follow him into that fascinating area here, but we may and must retain his main point, namely that synthesis is the Scholastic, and hence the Catholic, culture principle *kat exochen*.

Instead of contemplating the heights of artistic creation which it is Panofsky's avocation to understand and to explain, let us rather descend into the depths of human weakness, into misunderstanding, conflict and strife, and see how they were contained and conquered. In a perilous situation of this kind Catholicism has always put its trust in the same technique: the introduction of a *remora* or break in the discussion in order to gain time and give the contending forces a chance to cool off and to move towards a final reconciliation. A concrete example

1 Panofsky, E., *Gothic Architecture and Scholasticism*, Latrobe, Pa., 1951, pp. 65, 66, 68, 69.

will show exactly how the method works. The most dangerous foe Rome ever had to face was Geneva or rather Calvin, whose doctrine of mankind's total perversion packed all the punch typical of an extreme theory. This same harsh dogma raised its head even within Catholicism itself. Its protagonist was Michael Baius, Chancellor of the University of Louvain. This author (condemned in 1567 by Pope Pius V) made a good deal of use of the later writings of St. Augustine, those provoked by the Pelagian heresy which tended to whittle away the doctrine of original sin and became the *pièce de résistance* against which Augustine reacted with vigour and determination. The name of the great Bishop of Hippo thus moved into the centre of interest. Was he not already a Calvinist? Was Calvinism not an old and venerable Christian attitude? Should it not become the Church's official doctrine of man? The debate which started to flare up around these questions was exacerbated by the publication, in 1640, of Cornelius Jansen's *Augustinus*. Hardly had the storm aroused by this weighty tome half blown over, when the struggle was renewed and intensified by the appearance of a great edition of Augustine's works under the aegis of the Benedictine Congregation known as the Maurists. These monks were rightly or wrongly (in all probability wrongly rather than rightly) accused of pro-Calvinist leanings. A veritable war of words ensued; it brought recriminations, insults and hatred. The Jansenists stood by a near-Calvinistic interpretation of the Augustinian position; the so-called Molinists (from the Jesuit Luis Molina, the upholder of a mild and optimistic concept of man) ranged themselves quickly against them. In this confrontation, the Church (even though a large majority favoured the Molinist against the Jansenist interpretation or at least philosophy) merely intervened in order to suspend the campaigning. She acted above all in France, the centre of the fighting, where Bossuet and Fénélon, her two greatest bishops, had taken opposite sides. 'In November [1699], the Archbishop of Paris summoned to his presence the Maurist Superior General and the Jesuit Provincial and communicated to them a . . . mandate strictly ordering them . . . to forbid their subjects to say or write anything more in the controversy and to suppress all that had been written on either side.'[1] There was no authoritative decision; there was rather an authoritative non-decision, a decision not to decide on the basis of authority. Rome then followed suit. In June, 1700, four especially rabid anti-Maurist pamphlets were condemned, but otherwise all that happened was that the disagreement was, so to speak, prorogued. 'Three times during the next thirty years the attack on the edition was renewed, to be promptly suppressed in each case by . . . the Holy See.'[2]

Why this procedure, and not a clear adjudication? The answer is that

[1] Butler, C., *Benedictine Monachism*, London, etc., 1924, p. 344.
[2] Ibid., pp. 344 and 346.

those in formal authority wished to defer to those in real authority – the Christian people, the community at large. There was to be a period of gestation, so to speak, a period of digestion, one might almost say, in which the body social was to find out what it could, and what it could not, assimilate, what it should retain and what it should reject. As anticipated, a compromise began to delineate itself in time. Dom Jean Mabillon gave a lead in his irenic, open-minded introduction to the eleventh and last volume of the embattled edition of St. Augustine. However much a Jansenist like Quesnel or a Molinist like Fénélon might object, a way was now opened out of the impasse and it led to the goal of pacification. The twentieth-century historian, Dom Cuthbert Butler, is clearly on the side of his fellow-Benedictines. Yet even he gives praise to an authority which would not act in an authoritarian manner – an authority which would give time and its healing power a chance to do what was needed. 'The whole story shows,' he writes, 'how the Holy See discerned the truth amidst all the dust of controversy and did not allow itself to be carried away from the golden mean between the contending parties.'[1] Whether the term 'golden mean' is justified here or not, might need further investigation; it is not necessarily justified, nor would it seem to have been the aim pursued in this and similar situations; what was pursued was rather synthesis, a richer doctrine which would do justice both to the fact of the fall (which the Jansenists emphasized) and to the possibility of man's rise out of the depths into which he had fallen (which the Molinists had close to their hearts).

This is merely one illustration which might be complemented by a good many others. The conflict between the Jesuit scholars known as the Bollandists and the Carmelites which erupted after the publication of the April volume of the *Acta Sanctorum* containing the day of St. Albert would have provided us with another good case in point.[2] In this instance, too, a papal brief of 25 November 1698 imposed silence on the parties, with the same result which we have observed before: the emergence of a final situation with which both the Bollandists and the Carmelites could manage to live.

With this side-glance at conflict we have brought to a close our analysis of the great subject of doctrinal development and should perhaps offer a simple formula as a convenient summing-up of the insights which we have gained. Dogmas, we might say, are a visible growth from an invisible fund of life, explicit expressions of implicit states of thought and feeling. But the very same might be said, and must be said, of ritual also. That is the reason why we have bracketed the two aspects together. Just as the Church sought, in a collective process, for stable –

[1] Ibid., p. 345.
[2] Cf. Stark, W., 'The Sociology of Catholicism', *Blackfriars*, September, 1954, pp. 365 et seq.

indeed, final – forms of belief, so did she also look for stable – indeed, final – forms of worship. Differently expressed: just as she is a community of creed, so she is also a community of cult. Prayer and sacrifice are both communal, in a deeper sense of the word than the one which might conceivably be applied to Protestant, especially radically Protestant, denominations and their ways.

When, a little earlier, we considered the issues of Christology, we saw that, according to the admirably clear conceptions of Gregory of Nyssa, which are those of all true Catholics, Christ put on, not so much the nature of man, as the nature of mankind; He incarnated at the same time both the human race and the Second Person of the Divine Trinity. This doctrinal conviction has direct and inescapable consequences for the practice of worship. Men must pray, not only with Christ, but also, and much rather, *in* Him, for only so can their prayer be truly collective. Yet what applies to prayer applies with even stronger force to sacrifice. Men cannot offer more, and they must not offer less, to God than themselves. But if they are to offer themselves together, as a collectivity – and this is a demand, nay a necessity, which flows with cogency from the basic self-conception and self-definition of Catholic Christianity – they must offer themselves as 'the Body of Christ'; in other words, they must offer to the Eternal Father Christ the Son, constantly renewed by the dying of old and the entry of new members, yet constantly also the same with Him who suffered and died on the mount of Golgatha. The supreme act of worship can therefore be nothing else but a cultic representation and repetition of Jesus' life.

We have just, for brevity's sake, spoken of the relationship between dogma and ritual as if it were one of logical concatenation, and this is permissible, nay advisable, in order to demonstrate the strain of consistency which runs through the whole of religious existence. Yet such brevity, such conciseness, though it elucidates one aspect, is in danger of obscuring others. The cult is not, of course, a consequence drawn from doctrinal antecedents as a logical conclusion is the upshot of a set of pre-existent premises. The coherence of thought-forms and prayer-forms is in reality not direct, not lateral, though it may be depicted as such; it is much rather a community of derivation, a kinship in genesis, due to the emergence of both teaching and worship from the same parent reality – the inclusive Christian life. After duly emphasizing the co-ordination, nay the identity, of the community's intellectual and cultic effort, it is our task to point to their difference, their otherness-in-unity. Whereas thought leads to the abstract, cult tends towards the concrete. Indeed, it drives towards the pictorial. Religious societies which have set their face against this divergent evolution, have invariably found that their prayer becomes dry and dead, colourless and arid like textbook propositions. If it is the mission of theology within the common life to see to it that prayer remains 'correct', it is the concomitant task of prayer to ensure that ratiocination does not lead to rationalism and – to use Max Weber's famous formula – to 'routinization' and routine.

A certain writer has described the Mass as a kind of 'sacred dance',[1] and though there is little doubt that this sobriquet was meant to deride and to wound, it need not be totally rejected by the serious and unprejudiced interpreter. The Mass is not a sacred dance, but it is a sacred drama. It brings to mind the tragedy and triumph of Him who, to the believer, was both the Son of God and the Son of Man. It begins with the priest's and the people's bowing down when, after a few opening words, they recite the confession of sins: so was Jesus bent to the earth on the Mount of Olives when, in a dread experience, He felt upon Him the whole load of the sins of mankind. It ends with the priest's gesture of blessing as he dismisses the worshipping community before it disperses: and this recalls the last actions of Christ at the Ascension before He sent His disciples out to the ends of the earth to disseminate the Gospel. It has at its climax the elevation of the Host – the symbolic representation and repetition of the Crucifixion, the high point of Christ's story and of the history of mankind. And what is true of the daily and weekly worship is no less true of the yearly circle or cycle of the cult. It begins with the Advent or Annunciation; it closes with the prophecy of the Second Coming. It is a repetition and re-creation of the whole *cursus* of salvation.

The liturgy, therefore, and especially the Eucharist, is 'primarily an action',[2] in contrast to dogma which is primarily thought, abstract thought. For the Christian believer, and probably for the independent historian as well, it goes back to the last supper of Jesus with His disciples. St. Luke's Gospel records the essential action on the part of Jesus on this occasion, in which we must see the religious institution as well as the temporal beginning of the *ritus* of the Mass: 'And taking bread, He gave thanks and brake and gave to them saying: This is my body which is given for you. Do this,' i.e. repeat this, 'for a commemoration of Me' (xxii, 19). The operative words are clearly: *do* this, and this command has provided the kernel of the liturgy. The rest of the sentence, for a commemoration of me, has determined all the manifold embellishments which, in the course of time, have clustered around this kernel and gradually led from a simple gesture to a complex work of art.[3]

There is, of course, unavoidably, quite a distance between an actual, unique agapeic meal on the one hand, and a repeatable rite recalling it

---

[1] 'A ritual dance by sacred persons', Burns C. Delisle, Art. 'Ceremony, Historical', *Encyclopaedia of the Social Sciences*, edd. Seligman, E. R., and Johnson, A., vol. III, New York 1937, p. 315.

[2] Cf. Dix, G., *The Shape of the Liturgy*, ed. London 1960, p. 156. It may be as well to mention and even to emphasize that the author of this massive piece of scholarship is an Anglican (though of the Romanizing wing of that Church).

[3] Cf. ibid., p. 237.

centuries later on the other, a distance which is due to, and measures, the contrast between an event symbolized and a symbolic re-enacting of it. Yet the two have never broken asunder. The question has often been raised as to why it was the Roman form which came to be the general model, and not any of the other, parallel yet also deviating, versions which we know to have existed and to have been regularly enacted in other parts of the Christian *oikumene*. Various theories have been proposed; chief among them was a socio-political and even socio-economic one which pointed to the administrative position of the city of Rome in ancient times which must have given a particular prestige to the Roman congregation of Christians as well, and to the relative riches of the town on the Tiber which probably enabled the believers there to send material support to the smaller and weaker clusters of brethren in the provinces.[1] We need not deny that these non-religious factors may have helped to spread the Roman Mass across the face of the earth: there is, after all, a lot of common sense in Gabriel Tarde's 'laws of imitation', one of which would seem to cover, very comfortably, precisely what has happened. Yet Gregory Dix, an expert without peer, has given a different explanation: 'The Roman rite,' he says, 'has about it still an archaic angularity and abruptness, a concentration on the performance of the Eucharistic action rather than talking about it, which is no longer found in any other rite.' And in another context, when he discusses the introduction of hymns into the service, he speaks of a Roman 'reluctance to amplify the rite on all occasions with purely decorative additions' and a 'Roman concentration on the main purpose and end of the liturgy and the sense of its form which comes out in the directness and brevity of the Roman prayers'. According to him, it was this 'repugnance to the Roman liturgical instinct of all additions to the rite which play no clear logical part in the performance of the Eucharistic action, and so may confuse the bare simplicity of its outline, even while adorning it', which made the *Missale Romanum* into a *Missale Urbis et Orbis*. 'One reason at least why the Roman rite was so largely adopted in the West without compulsion and by the gradual acceptance of so many local churches in the seventh–tenth centuries lies precisely in this, that on the whole it was a simpler and more expressive rite. The old local rites were redolent of the soil on which they arose, and rightly dear to those who used them from ancestral tradition. But rite for rite and prayer for prayer the Roman was apt to be both more practical and better thought out; and those who compared them carefully could hardly fail to notice it. Hence the growing voluntary adoption of Roman prayers and pieces and chants, and ultimately of the Roman Shape of the Liturgy as a whole, which is so marked a feature of liturgical history in the territories of the Gallican and Mozarabic rites during the seventh and

[1] Prof. Ludwig Wahrmund pressed this opinion on his students in the University of Prague.

eighth centuries, when the Popes were in no position to bring pressure to bear on anyone to adopt their rite.'[1]

These words should be noted and pondered by all those who think in terms of a 'routinization of charisma', i.e. of a progressive abandonment of the original inspiration. In this important area of the cult, what we find is the exact opposite – a stubborn clinging both to its outer form and to its inner meaning. What actually took place was a positive rather than a negative development. From the welter of incipient, semi-evolved or even fully evolved alternatives, the Church, in a collective process, selected one particular concrete form of the Mass, and this then became the agreed pattern the wide world over. Not imitation but appreciation – choice, if largely semi-conscious choice – explains the direction in which the evolution of worship (essentially a history of confluence) has moved: not Tarde, but Sumner – or rather his folkway theory – offers the key to the understanding of it. Other variants have managed to survive beside the Roman, even inside the Catholic Church, a community much more multiform than many outsiders suspect, and much more tolerant of deviation than many detractors allow. Yet these variants, too, are like the Roman norm, so far as essentials are concerned. 'The main structure of the liturgy,' Dix insists, 'is always and everywhere the same, however much it be overlaid with local ways and decorations, because the Eucharist is always identically the same action – "Do this" – with the same meaning – "for the *anamnesis* of Me". In so far as the Christian Syrian and Byzantine and Copt and Englishman and Frenchman and Roman are all Christians and so partakers in the one Eucharistic action and experience of the one Body of Christ, the Shape of the Liturgy by which that action is performed is bound to be the same in all essentials for them all.'[2]

Yet even Dix speaks of an involution besides this evolution, and we must ponder what he has to say. His assertion briefly is that the action element has decayed in so far as, in the beginning, it was the whole congregation which acted, while in the end it is only the priest – one man, as he implies, instead of all. This is over and above the loss of concreteness which is unavoidable if a symbolic event is to take the place of a real one. The attenuation of action due to the last-named *quid pro quo* need not be regretted, nay must be acknowledged as necessary: the one historical meal on the eve of Christ's passion is to the later generations perforce no longer an ordinary supper and thus *had* to be transposed into a symbolistic-artistic key. But it is different with the question who is to enact the symbol and to perform the work of art. Christ died for all; He *was* all. Should not *all* 'do this' for a commemoration of Him, rather than one person?

To prove his point, Dix refers us to the changes that have taken place

---

[1] Dix, loc. cit., pp. 433, 457, 497.
[2] Ibid., p. 433.

in linguistic usage – always a good argument, as nothing is a better indication of collective attitudes than language, the prime product of the folkways. The Greeks spoke of performing the mysteries (*mysteria telein*); the Romans of doing the Eucharist (*eucharistiam facere*); the modern believer, on the other hand, says that he *hears* Mass, while the priest *says* it. So universal and so strong was the feeling here evinced by the learned author that the Second Vatican Council decided to transfer the bulk of prayer recitation back to the whole congregation. It is now once again the *plebs Christi* in the nave which says the Mass, rather than the priest in the sanctuary who did it before, and this reform is widely considered as a re-collectivization of the rite, undoing the destructive work of a century-long de-collectivization. In so far as collectivism is the ground-base of all Catholic life, thought and worship, this re-emphasis of it is all to the good. The question is only whether the Catholic Church had really fallen away from the original form of collective worshipping. Dix asserts it, and we are not inclined to take an assertion on his part lightly. While he admits that it was 'the Reformers of the sixteenth century who regarded the Eucharist primarily as something "said" by the clergy,' he also asserts, almost in the same breath, that 'the change made by regarding the rite as something "said" and not something "done" . . . is essentially the work of the Latin Middle Ages and not of the Reformers', and so even Catholicism made the essential step which led to the virtual exclusion of the people at large from the performance of the ritual drama. On another page Dix refers expressly to 'Western devotion as a whole, Catholic and Protestant alike', and charges against modern language generally that it 'implies a certain difference between the functions of the clergy and the laity, as between active and passive'. This, however, is the salient reason 'that makes it difficult for modern Western Christians, Protestant and Catholic alike, to enter immediately into the mind of the early Church'.[1] Thus there would seem to be, after all, a loss of contact with the base, a falling away from the true worship of the first days.

The reader of the present pages knows already what we are going to urge against these considerations, against these strictures. Surely they make sense only if and where the priest is seen as a man who stands over against all others, so that what he does is done by one person, and exclusively one person. They do not make sense, however, and they carry no conviction, indeed, they do not apply, if and where the priest is conceived as the incarnation of the parish, as identical with its population, as functioning in the role of their collective self, for then what he does is, by definition, what they do. We must remember here the great word of St. Cyprian of Carthage which we discussed so fully in volume IV: 'the Church is in the Bishop'.[2] The pope, the ordinary

[1] Ibid., pp. 397, 398, 12.
[2] Cf. p. 246, and also p. 158.

and the *parroco*, we might say, act vicariously for the world, the diocese and the local community respectively, and community-type societies will not understand the term 'vicariously' as implying two – the representer and the represented – but rather as implying *one* only, one hand, for the representer and the represented are, according to this manner of acting and thinking, truly one.

What we must not forget in this context, be it even for a single moment, is the fact that the many are in any case vicariously represented in, and acting through, One, that One being Jesus Christ. Dix himself has emphasized this as strongly as it needs to be emphasized. 'In the idea of Ignatius, and of the primitive writers generally,' he says, meaning, of course, St. Ignatius of Antioch, like Cyprian of Carthage one of the clearest voices of the common body and mind, 'it is the *Church as a whole*, and not any one order in it, which not so much "represents" as "is" Christ on earth . . . The primitive church took this conception with its fullest force, and pressed it with a rigour which is quite foreign to our weakened notions. The *whole Church* prayed in the Person of Christ; the *whole Church* was charged with "proclaiming" the revelation of Christ; the *whole Church* offered the Eucharist as the "recalling" before God and man of the offering of Christ. All that which He has done once for all as the Priest and Proclaimer of the kingship of God, the Church which is "the fulfilment of Him" enters into and fulfills.'[1] There is thus at the very root of Christianity a collectivistic summing-up of many in one, and it is but logical to see it repeated on all levels of the structure, even on so low a level and on so narrow a scene as that of a simple parish at prayer. If Dix can write, concerning the apostolic and primitive Church, 'that it had a clear and unhesitating grasp of the fact that [the Eucharistic] action was *corporate*, the united joint action of the whole Church and not of the celebrant only,'[2] then he makes a statement which is fully applicable to the Roman communion of later ages also, for in this respect – that of collectivistic conceptions and convictions – there is, as this whole book demonstrates, no difference between orthodoxy in the second and orthodoxy in the twentieth century. In the early days St. Ignatius of Antioch wrote to the laity at Magnesia: 'As the Lord did nothing without the Father . . . so neither do you anything without the bishop and presbyters . . . Let there be one prayer, one supplication, one mind, one hope . . .'.[3] It would hardly be necessary to repeat this plea to Catholics of today.

This does not necessarily mean that Dix does not have a point to make and that the recent reform (one might fitly write here: the recent re-forming) of the service which shifted the major part of prayer

---

[1] Dix, loc. cit., p. 29. Author's emphasis. The definition of the Church as the 'fulfilment' of Christ is from St. Paul (Ephesians 1, 23).

[2] Ibid., p. 15.

[3] Cit. ibid., p. 21. Cf. *Patrologia Graeca*, as quoted, vol. V, Paris 1894, cols 763–6.

recitation back to the body of believers was anything but desirable. If the priest alone speaks, be it even on behalf of all, be it even as the one who *is* all, there is a danger that the bystanders, unoccupied as they are, will let their minds wander, and if this happens that very integration of the praying community which Catholicism at any rate presupposes and commands is lost. Indeed, worse abuses may develop. Somebody may begin to say prayers different from those recited by the priest; he or she may, for instance, begin to say the beads of the rosary; and if something like that comes to pass, the circle is broken, the unity, so meaningful, so precious, so essential to the liturgy, is finally gone. Giving the laity once again larger duties was therefore a way of safeguarding the oneness of the many, of securing anew the true joining of voices in a common prayer. But a 'saying of the Mass' by all rather than by one is only psychologically-didactically different from the saying of it by one with and for all, or by one as the mouth of all; sociologically-symbolically there is no difference.

We have brought this matter up, not only because we wanted to get a misunderstanding out of the way, but also because we wished to lay a firm foundation for the analysis of the rite which we have now to undertake. The Mass of the Faithful, which is the true liturgy, in contradistinction to the Mass of the Catechumens which precedes it and is merely instructional, consists of three parts: the Offertory, the Canon (with the Eucharistic prayer *kat exochen* as its core), and the Communion. (In the East, this tripartite division is even clearer than in the West, as the Offertory, called 'the Great Entrance', and the Communion take place in front of the *iconostasis*, or screen, while the Canon is hidden behind it.) What we are interested in is the sociological meaning of it all, and this is best grasped if one symbolic detail is constantly kept in mind: the symbol of bread. The Offertory is the collection and offering of the flour from which the bread will be fashioned; the Canon is the raising of the bread so fashioned, in which the many grains have become one wafer, up to Heaven and its Transsubstantiation into the Body of Christ; the Communion is the breaking of the bread (intended from the beginning to be shared) into parts, the distribution of the particles to the faithful and their consumption by them. Thus the rite advances from multiplicity (the numberless loose grains of the flour) to unity (the One Host that means all) back to multiplicity (the broken pieces which are handed out). In I Corinthians x, 17, St. Paul expresses all this by saying: 'We, being many, are one bread, one body: all that partake of one bread.' There could hardly be a more transparent 'shape of the liturgy'. And this transparency is made even more transparent by the allotment of roles which is traditional and universal whenever and wherever the rite is celebrated. The Offertory and Communion involve the many; they are the *liturgia*, or work, of the people; the Canon is in the hands of one; it is the *liturgia*, or work, of the priest – but clearly not of the priest as himself, as a private person, but of the priest as all, as the person of the community. Dix is mistaken when he calls the Eucharistic prayer 'essentially the celebrant's own individual contribution to the corporate act'.[1] Like the bread which he handles, the celebrant who handles it is the many who have become one, the dust of the flour that has been transmuted into the coherent Body of Christ. The Eucharistic prayer proper is not now, and never has been, recited by several voices (unless there be concelebration in which case, too, there is really only one voice as the concelebrants count, by definition, as one priest, and hence as one voice). Any change at this point (which, surely, is not contemplated by anybody) would dim the meaning of the Mass: that meaning can be tersely defined by saying that it is, in its inmost nature, collective prayer. Aquinas, for this reason, calls the Eucharist *sacramentum totius ecclesiae unitatis*.[2]

The symbol of the bread, explained as we have explained it, is sufficient for us to demonstrate this collectivity of the rite of the Mass. To the Jews it was not quite sufficient, for they broke bread at every meal, public or private: it accompanied the blessing – the grace before meat – which their religion prescribed for them. But it was different with the wine. The 'cup of blessing' was traditionally a hallmark of a communal meal, the *chaburah* meeting, or meeting in friendship. It had deep collective undertones. One man said it for all; all said it through one mouth, just as the Eucharistic prayer in the Mass was later to be said. Hence Dix judges that Jesus '*could not* have been understood to be giving . . . a corporate meaning to the bread-breaking alone *without associating the breaking of the bread in some way with the cup of blessing*'.[3] The point is mainly historical. Yet it should not be lost sight of, for it throws the intention to make the ritual collectivistic into high relief.

Needless to say, what the faithful are offering in the *Offertorium* is not a material substance like flour, but an immaterial one: their selves, their souls; and what they receive back in the *Communio* is not (according to their faith) another material substance, a disk of bread, but God's own body and blood under the appearance of tangible signs and things. This, of course, belongs to theology rather than sociology, yet sociology is involved too, since the Mass, however we consider it, is and remains the making, as well as the action, of a community. We are setting down here, without further comment, a few more lines from Dix's book in order to round off our account. Speaking of St. Irenaeus and his age, Dix writes as follows: 'Each communicant from the bishop to the newly confirmed gave *himself* under the forms of bread

[1] Ibid., p. 442.
[2] *Summa Theologiae*, III, qu. 73, art. 2. Cf. *The Summa Theologica of St. Thomas Aquinas*, transl. Fathers of the English Dominican Province, vol. XVII, London 1923, p. 235. 'The Eucharist is the sacrament of the Church's unity'.
[3] Dix, loc. cit., p. 62; cf. also pp. 59 and 78. Author's emphasis.

THE AGE OF COMMUNITY AND ITS RELIGIOUS CULTURE

and wine to God, as God gives Himself to them under the same forms. In the united oblations of all her members, the Body of Christ, the Church, gave herself to *become* the Body of Christ, the sacrament, in order that receiving again the symbol of herself now transformed and hallowed, she might be truly that which by nature she is, the Body of Christ, and each of her members members of Christ . . . The layman brought the sacrifice of himself, of which he is the priest . . . The high-priest, the bishop, "offered" all together, for he alone can speak for the whole Body. In Christ, as His Body, the Church is "accepted" by God "in the Beloved". Its sacrifice of itself is taken up into His sacrifice of Himself . . . She, too, took bread and a cup and gave thanks and brake and distributed, entering into, not merely repeating, His own act . . . The whole rite was a true corporate offering by the Church in its hierarchic completeness of the Church in its organic unity.'[1]

A sociologist who knows a little of the history of his subject will, on reading the preceding paragraphs, have come to a definite conclusion and conviction – the conclusion and conviction that there is truth in Emile Durkheim's assertion that religious rites are socializing experiences. In the Mass, the many become one, and when they disperse, i.e. when they once again turn into the many, they carry within themselves something of the community which, in the form of a sacrament, they have just received. What takes place is, if we may so express it, a re-charging of the individual soul with a content which is more than individual, a content coming from, and bringing in, a higher life. So far there is not, and there cannot be, conflict between a full-fledged Catholic and an orthodox Durkheimian. The only question which remains is whether Durkheim and his school are justified in going a big step further and maintaining that the Mass is *only* and *exclusively* a socializing experience, that the metaphysical meaning which is asserted to inhere in the rite is in fact a purely secular, or, more precisely, sociological meaning which has come to present itself in a phantasmagoric form, differently expressed, that 'God' or 'Christ' are poetic representations behind which there hides the real entity, Society. At this point, two faiths present themselves and confront each other: religion and positivism, and the choice between them cannot be scientific, but must be personal. If the Durkheimians are free to assume that what looks religious is in reality but sociological, and even physical, the Christians must be allowed to believe that what looks like an empty form is in truth filled with a metaphysically real content. The problem raised by Durkheimian positivism is the problem of reduction: is it permissible to reduce one set of facts to another, or rather to dissolve one set of facts in another, to conjure away a whole realm of phenomena by making them appear as merely masked pieces of other phenomena

[1] Ibid., pp. 117 and 393. Author's emphasis.

which alone are said to be real? All his life, Durkheim denied the legitimacy of such a procedure. He argued, for instance, and with considerable passion, that sociological phenomena must not be reduced to psychological ones, that nothing but error can result if the realm of sociality is not acknowledged to have a factuality of its own. Yet when it came to the religious sphere, he followed the very path of reductionism which, in matters closer to his heart, he had so incisively and decisively condemned.

However that may be, and however one may resolve the conflict between the orthodox and the positivist position, the fact remains that, so far as ritual is concerned, Durkheim's collectivistic interpretation is incomparably more correct than, for instance, Max Weber's, who saw in the Mass no more than a survival of primitive magical practices.[1] Many are the passages in Gregory Dix's great work which bear out Durkheim. The whole difference between heathen and Christian worship seems to Dix to hinge on this its communal character. While the heathen rituals try to impress, to stimulate, to excite the individual, indeed to chase him into, and through, exalted and ecstatic states, the Christian liturgy is, by comparison, 'unemotional to a degree', 'bare and unimpressive to the point of dullness'. What then brought the faithful every Lord's Day to the holy table, even when attending Mass was a crime that might lead one finally to the Colosseum, or to some provincial arena, to be devoured, for the amusement of the populace, by the lions? Dix's answer is that it was – if it was any experience at all – the experience of collective unity. 'At the Eucharist,' Dix says of the earliest days, 'the individual is perfectly integrated in society, for there the individual Christian only exists as a Christian individual inasmuch as he is fully exercising his own function in the Christian society . . . There the eternal and absolute value of each individual is affirmed by setting him in the most direct of all earthly relations with the eternal and absolute Being of God,' but 'it is thus affirmed and established only through his membership of the perfect society'. 'Literally, scores of . . . illustrations from contemporary documents of unimpeachable historical authority are available of the fact that it was not so much the personal reception of Holy Communion as the corporate Eucharistic action as a whole (which included Communion) which was then regarded as the very essence of the life of the Church, and through that of the individual soul,' Dix writes on another page. 'There was, indeed, a rather striking absence from the primitive Eucharistic rite of any devotional practice which was calculated to arouse or feed a subjective piety – no confession of sins or devotions in preparation for communion, no corporate thanksgiving even, nothing but the bare requisites for the sacramental *act*. It was a burning faith in the vital importance of that Eucharist *action* as

[1] Cf. Stark, W., 'The Place of Catholicism in Max Weber's Sociology of Religion', *Sociological Analysis*, 1968, pp. 202 et seq., esp. p. 204.

such ... which made the Christians cling to the rite of the Eucharist ... the corporate celebration of the liturgy ... against all odds.'[1]

At this point, however, there clearly appears the possibility of an undue exaggeration of the collectivist, or merely the social, element of which Durkheim has been so often, and so rightly, accused – of that 'sociologism' or 'agelecism' which vitiates his work. Dix avoids it to some extent where he says that what brought the believer to the communal service even in penal times, even at the risk of his life, 'was the conviction that there rested on each of the redeemed an absolute necessity to take his own part in the self-offering of Christ, a necessity more binding even than the instinct of self-preservation.'[2] We would go a good deal further and assert, even for the early days – which were, after all, days set in the matrix of a society by no means free of individualistic tendencies – the presence of a decidedly personal element in the community's liturgical worship. In *The Fundamental Forms of Social Thought*, we have argued that an element of individualism, a dash of Weber, has always to be added to a thought-pattern of organicism, a thought-pattern *à la* Durkheim, if a true sociology is to emerge.[3] We must remember this general insight here. Prayer is always a help to individual action, to a religiously and ethically correct conduct of life, though it is never only that, as Weber was inclined to believe. Perhaps it is Friedrich Heiler who offers us the best formulation which can bring out the relation of the individual worshipper to the collective worship. In the liturgical experience, Heiler asserts, and we are with him, 'the infinitely rich life of Christendom as a whole flows over into the piety of the separate souls'.[4]

So also it is in social life generally. All create a language, a system of norms, a state of feeling, and these, once created, enter into individual minds, action-centres and hearts, filling them in, filling them out, and making them what they are. There can be no doubt (as we have emphasized in our vol. III[5]) that the general turn of society towards individualism, which is the last explanation of the great revolt known as the Reformation, brought a strengthening of the individualistic-experiential element even in the Mass; but a strengthening of this kind is merely the accentuation of an already existing ingredient, the development of a germ which lay in the soil from the very beginning. The Mass has always been both worship by all and worship by each. And how could it have been otherwise in a Church which conceived herself as a *societas perfecta*?

The individual and even individualistic element was not totally swamped by the admittedly predominating collectivistic character of the liturgy because of the very collectivism which predominated. We

---

[1] Dix, loc. cit., pp. XVIII, 153, 151.   [2] Ibid., p. 153.
[3] Cf. esp. p. 249.   [4] *Der Katholizismus*, München 1923, p. 394.
[5] Cf. pp. 30 and 381.

are saying this not in order to peddle a spurious paradox, but in order to bring out a sober sociological truth. The liturgy as it developed, mainly under Roman guidance, into the Catholic Mass, was collectivistic not only in its content, but also in and through its process of formation. Who created these ritual forms? Everybody and nobody. They were a *growth* – the precipitate of the anonymous forces of the Christian societies and society of the formative period. We see once again, what we have repeatedly seen before, for instance not long ago in our analysis of the emergence of an agreed credal system, that the process of folkway-formation, so splendidly elucidated by William Graham Sumner, affords us a golden key to the understanding of the sociology of religion in general and of Catholicism in particular. Indeed, it may unlock the mystery of the creation of the liturgical patterns of action even more easily and more fully than that of the formulation of theological patterns of thought, for, as Dix rightly emphasizes, 'theology is a progressive technical science and remains therefore always the professional preserve of the clergy and the interest of a comparatively small educated *élite* of the laity,' while 'liturgy, on the contrary, is a universal Christian activity, and so a *popular* interest'.[1] Now if the making of the Mass was indeed a process comparable to the formation of folkways, then individual needs must have been both active and effective in it. They always are in such processes, as Sumner has shown. There is a searching for, and striving after, forms which will satisfy all the longings of and in the society concerned, be they collective or individual, and the end result will be an institutional arrangement which will subserve all the vital desires which were present in the place and at the time of gestation. For this general reason alone we are justified in assuming that the developing rites of the Christian congregations catered to the individual need to pray and to be physically, morally and metaphysically strengthened (which, surely, existed then as it does now and always has done) – catered to it no less than to the collective wish to be associated with Christ's saving sacrifice and thus to be both socialized and sanctified.

In a way, the development of the Mass began already before there were Christians to develop it. Every pious Jew broke bread before every meal; every circle of Jewish friends offered a cup of blessing after every meal through the hands and mouth of its *praeses*. The liturgy moved these two actions towards the centre of the rite and anchored them there, combining them at the same time. What was new was the religious and specifically Christian belief that the bread and wine signified and became Christ Himself, His body and His blood. 'What our Lord did at the last supper,' writes Dix, 'was not to establish any new rite. He attached to the two corporate acts which were sure to be done when His disciples met in the future – *the only two things which He could be sure they would do together regularly in any case* – a quite new

[1] Dix, loc. cit., p. 7. Author's emphasis.

meaning which had a special connection with His own impending death.'[1]

A certain amount of discussion has developed around Dix's assumption contained in these words (an assumption shared by all Christian believers) that the Eucharistic rite was instituted by Christ Himself. Not only atheists but even liberal Protestants have asserted that the last supper was an ordinary meal and therefore would not, or even could not, be used by Jesus for legislation concerning acts of worship in the future, let alone the distant future, e.g. the twentieth century.[2] The whole argument is characteristic of that narrow individualism which simply will not work when it comes to the study of a strictly and strongly collectivistic movement such as primitive Christianity. Whatever Christ did, or did not do, as a historical personality, that surely He could and might do as a historical community: is not the Church the Body of Christ, His other self? How the Christian significance came to be connected with the breaking of the bread and the offering of the cup is therefore both religiously and sociologically irrelevant. Whether there was an express command on the part of the historical Jesus (and there is no reason why there should not have been one), or whether there was an implied desire on the part of the faithful, welling up from the very depths of that society, to 'do this in commemoration of Him', in either case it was the collective will to worship in this form which shaped and carried the great prayer-action of the Mass.

But the liberal–atheist thrust is not only negative, denying an assumed historical fact, the institution of the Eucharist by Christ Himself, it is also positive – asserting an alternative historical fact, the formation of the Christian ritual by semi-pagan, if not indeed semi-savage, forces, forces which streamed into the Church as soon as mass-conversions, or rather half-conversions, began. Dix is trying to show that there was no such infiltration of primitive forms. 'The carrying and exhibition of symbolic objects in processions and liturgical rites,' he says, 'was a notable feature of the [pagan] mysteries in so far as they were public cults, and indeed of classical pagan worship generally. But what emerges from the evidence is that the Christian Church made *no* ceremonial use of such things . . . It seems quite impossible [therefore] to bring home to the fourth-century Church any imitation of the pagan mysteries.'[3] Later, it is true, lights made their appearance in the Christian liturgy,[4] and these were taken over from some court ceremonials connected with emperor worship. But quite apart from the fact that these embellishments did not touch the core of the rite, we have already seen in this work[5] why they were introduced in the first place – to deny to an old idol any honour which might be lavished on the true God, an unexceptional desire. Yet, here again, it would be easy to exaggerate things and

[1] Ibid., p. 58. Author's emphasis.   [2] Ibid., pp. 70–2.
[3] Ibid., p. 416.   [4] Ibid., p. 417.   [5] Cf. vol. III, p. 50.

to miss a sociologically important point. Pre-Christian, even primitive, rituals were part and parcel of the scene within which Christian worship developed. The Christian community watched and weighed them in order to see whether they might not be made to accept a Christian meaning. If the answer were positive, if it were found that for once new wine might be poured into an old bottle, then they were accepted, even though they were re-interpreted and transmuted into a new key. After all, the old bottle might be beautiful and worth keeping. Less metaphorically expressed, the traditional heathen (e.g. Orphic) patterns might be useful, pious, inspiring – why discard them?[1] To a community so tradition-centred as early Christendom was, there seemed to be no good reason for getting rid of what was good, if it could be made better. 'Primitive' forms were often deeply religious; it could not be irreligious, with the proper adjustments, of course, to carry them into the future. Friedrich Heiler understood this matter well. 'The continued existence of such [archaic] elements,' he writes, 'secures for religious life a certain naturalness and freshness; what is tangible and material in the cult protects, like a strong shell, the tender mystery of what is irrational and makes it impossible for rationalistic dogmatism to emaciate living piety.'[2] We are saying all this for a definite reason – because we wish to bring out the true centre of the atheist–liberal argument. It is in essence rationalistic. The Mass is rejected because it is action and not argument, drama and not discussion, a symbolic performance and not a sober sermon. Argument, discussion and sermonizing, no doubt, have their place in religious life, but it can only be an auxiliary one. In worship men wish to experience the inexpressible, and that is what a rational rite – the phrase is almost a contradiction in terms – can never provide. So, at any rate, felt the God- and salvation-hungry men in whose hearts the ritual of the Mass had its pregnant seed and has its abiding root.

It was these men, these multitudes, who dominated and steered the development which in the fullness of time yielded the Missal and all it contains. And they not only determined the ground plan of the rite, they also provided its elaboration or rather improvement. For improved it was in the course of time, by a largely, not to say totally, collective process. What happened in practice was that local details, if they were generally appealing, travelled from place to place and were in the end universally accepted. Rome certainly gave much to the provinces; but there was two-way traffic; the provinces on their part gave much to Rome. One point which needs emphasizing is the relatively small part which authoritative and hence conscious intervention played in the collective effort and achievement. Historians tell us that the revision

---

[1] Cf. Chateaubriand, F. R., *Génie du Christianisme*, paperback ed., Paris 1966, vol. II, pp. 46 and 50. Cf. also our vol. III, pp. 256 et seq.
[2] Heiler, loc. cit., p. 235. Cf. also p. 236 ad finem.

of the local Roman rite, in A.D. 595 or thereabouts, carried out by Pope (St.) Gregory the Great, was of surpassing importance. Yet 'Pope Gregory himself [did not have] any idea of setting up his own text as a standard necessarily to be accepted elsewhere. He advised Augustine at Canterbury to take what seemed best out of both the Gallican and Roman rites and form a new mixed rite for the Anglo-Saxon church; he advised the Bishop of Milan to continue old Milanese customs; he recognized without *arrière pensée* that the customs of Ravenna are in some things not those of Rome and insists that they shall be maintained.'[1] If the Gregorian Sacramentary became none the less the universal model, this was due, not to pushing from above, but to welcome from below. It was its inherent excellence that won all hearts for it, especially Gregory's 'delicate sense of the music of words', not exterior constraint. And the same applies to the tidying up under the aegis of Charlemagne which in effect produced the modern Mass. Not that Emperor's mighty command, but his co-operator's, Alcuin of York's, ability and religiousness secured that unification which Charlemagne, in his curious preoccupation with cultic forms, so ardently desired. 'Even in the first century the use of the liturgical Eucharist . . must have spread by mere borrowing from church to church . . . And after that in every century every liturgy borrowed where it chose, without the intervention of "authority" in the matter at all, till we come to the edicts of . . . Charlemagne. It is true that in every church the rite was from time to time codified in a revision by the local bishop – a Serapion, a Basil, a Gregory. But it is also true that their work never endures as they leave it. The same process of unauthorized alteration and addition and borrowing begins again, as it began again within fifty years of the imposition of Alcuin's authorized rite.'[2] The intervention, by Pope Pius V, after Trent, merely said a final 'so be it' to the forms which the centuries had anonymously evolved; and the adjustments, under Pope Paul VI, after the Second Vatican Council, which met the needs of a more hurried and less liturgical-minded generation, did not touch the essential shape of the Mass either – let alone its sacred core. Gregory Dix's final judgment on the development of the liturgy fits in well with the tenor and with the upshot of our over-all analysis of Catholicism as a culture: 'the comparative freedom in which the churches were left to achieve the process in the West results in *a real synthesis*, in which the old local rites each contribute a good deal to the final result and lose themselves in it.'[3]

We cannot, unfortunately, say even a single word about the daily, weekly and yearly round of liturgical services, with their double – sea-

---

[1] Dix, loc. cit., pp. 570 and 571.

[2] Ibid., p. 587. Cf. also p. 208.

[3] Ibid., p. 546. Our emphasis. Cf. also pp. 8, 10, 435, 474, 575, 578, 581, 582, 584, 586, 588, 589.

sonal and sanctorial – cycle, nor yet about the climax of the Christian year in the Easter Vigil, painful though it must be to pass such a subject by. But we must, before turning to new matters, recall to the reader's mind two aspects which are as relevant here as where they were first considered. One is the strong philosophical realism in which the Mass is, so to speak, drenched. All earthly phenomena are manifestations of heavenly noumena; every single and concrete rose is a manifestation of the divine idea of a rose. So also is the action of the Mass a manifestation of divine actions – a showing-forth of the God-man's path through life and His final deed of salvation. Words must be used with extreme caution here. We are speaking of a 'showing forth' and not of a 'recalling' because you recall what is over, while you show forth what is at hand. 'We have to take account of the clear understanding then general,' Dix says, 'of the word *anamnesis* as meaning a "re-calling" of a thing in such a way that it is not so much regarded as being absent, as itself *presently operative* by its effects.'[1] The doctrine of the 'real presence' which characterizes Catholic, and even, if in an attenuated form, Lutheran belief, has here its philosophical – indeed, we might say, its rational – basis. The Mass is more than a repetition of the drama of redemption, it is that drama itself, in so far as it is what it is by dint of its participation in its eternal archetype, just as the rose is what it is by dint of the self-same *metexis* or participation – just as a clansman is what he is by dint of his re-incarnation or re-doubling of his founder-father's self. We are led back, once again, to community and its ways of thought.[2]

Our second point concerns, not the past, but the future. Sociologists have (not surprisingly in view of their *métier*) emphasized (and perhaps over-emphasized) the sectarian and eschatological character of the early Christian groupings. We are, on the whole, with them; the end of the world *was* regarded as close. Yet it is an undue secularization of the whole movement to assume that nothing mattered but the impending revolution, the divine wrath that was to come – what mattered was also, and at least as much, the revolution which had already been, the accomplished Incarnation, the divine love that had come and become manifest in Jesus Christ. Differently expressed, to the early Christians, their religion revealed not only the conclusion, the *end*, but also the climax, the *meaning* of history, which is salvation and sanctification through contact with the Divine. The advent of the Kingdom of God was connected, not only with Christ's Second Coming, but with His First Coming as well. For the First Coming had brought at least some men to the Father so that they are, here and now, and apart from any cataclysm that may yet take place, *His* holy people. Perhaps we may also say that Christianity offered the prospect of two fresh beginnings: one a breakthrough to a new outer life, the other a breakthrough to a new

[1] Ibid., p. 245; cf. also pp. 243, 244, 246, 247.
[2] Cf. our vol. IV, p. 14.

inner life, a life through, with and in God as it is possible in the form and with the aid of the sacred rites. If these are, in rationalistic fashion, considered as empty show, as hocus-pocus, then, indeed, they cannot have meant much to men longing for a new deal. But they were not so considered; they did mean much; and that is why such men found ful-filment, not only in their participation in eschatological hopes, but also in their participation in communal worship, in the Mass, which lifted them (psychologically and experientially speaking) as effectively out of their depressing rut as any destruction of the world could possibly have done.[1]

We have, on an earlier occasion, pointed out that the Reformers, after initially moving towards the Quaker conception of the congregation as merely a society of friends, retraced their steps and travelled again towards the Catholic definition of the Church as the Body of Christ.[2] Their second thoughts were due above all to a fear of outer anarchy of which Luther had seen ominous signs in the Peasants' War and Calvin had seen in the millenarian experiment at Münster. But though Luther and Calvin in this way re-emphasized order, they did not re-embrace collectivism. And this precisely is seen most clearly in the shape of their worship, or rather in the cultic developments, such as they were, within Calvinism, which demonstrated the underlying trend much more clearly than Lutheranism ever did. We may once again allow Gregory Dix to define the salient contrast for us. 'What is striking about the [Catholic] liturgy,' he writes, 'is . . . its intense concentration and insistence upon the external sacramental *action* . . . This is a type of worship the very re-verse of the Puritan, for which the subjective experience, not the ex-ternal action, is always the important thing . . . Briefly, the Puritan theory is that worship is a purely *mental* activity, to be exercised by a strictly psychological "attention" to a subjective . . . experience. For the Puritan, this is the essence of worship, and all external things which might impair this strictly mental attention have no rightful place in it. At most, they are to be admitted grudgingly and with suspicion . . .'. In practice, Dix concludes, this leads to 'verbalism'. 'That is the Puritan theory of worship in a nutshell – to "admit only words".'[3] Perhaps we should be more fair here and reformulate Dix's dictum by saying that Puritan worship admitted only the Word.

Many important, nay all-important, consequences flowed from this switch-over from collective action to individual experience, or rather from the primacy of the one to the primacy of the other, but at this point, where we want to drive the analysis of Catholic culture forward, only one needs emphasizing: the presence, in Catholicism, of a strongly

---

[1] Cf. ibid., p. 151. Apposite passages in Dix which should be consulted are on pp. 261, 262, 263, 265, 266.
[2] Cf. our vol. IV, pp. 20 et seq.
[3] Dix, loc. cit., pp. 312 and 495.

symbolistic tendency which is alien to modern mentalities. Bread and wine are symbols. So are altars and vestments, incense and candles, and all other paraphernalia of the Roman cult. Indeed, we encounter yet again, unavoidably, the massing of symbolisms which we have observed before.[1] To give but one example: for the early Christians, the flour which they offered so that it could be baked into the Host, recalled *inter alia* the cleansing of the lepers prescribed in the Old Testament. 'This is the rite of a leper when he is to be cleansed . . . He shall take two lambs without blemish and an ewe of a year old . . . and three-tenths of flour tempered with oil for a sacrifice . . . And he shall offer them on the eighth day of his purification to the priest at the door of the tabernacle . . .' (Leviticus, XIV, 2, 10, 23). Were not the faithful, as they entered the church from the outside world, also unclean? And were they not made clean in the church, by their participation in the rite which reconciled mankind to God and thus blotted out sin – the stain of sin? In his *Dialogus cum Tryphone Judaeo*, St. Justin Martyr expressed precisely this idea: 'The offering of flour prescribed for those who were cleansed of leprosy was a figure of the Eucharistic bread which Our Lord Jesus Christ ordered to be provided for the commemoration of the passion He had undergone for the sake of those who are being purged of all wickedness.'[2] By the multiplication of meanings which we see exemplified in this passage, the ritual was made richer and richer, more and more powerful and gripping. And yet, even this concentration of many inner significations in one outer symbol[3] is insufficient to explain the whole depth of the liturgy and its forms, and its appeal to the believer. For the conviction of the believer was that the sacred symbols of his Church were more than merely symbols: they were symbols which – unlike others – effected what they symbolized. In other words, they were sacraments. Needless to say, the subject of sacramentalism belongs pre-eminently to theology – pre-eminently, yet not exclusively. There is a sociological side even to these forms of faith which it is our duty to investigate.

THE SACRAMENTAL SYSTEM: SYMBOLISM AND FAITH

Among the great students of the human psyche who can lead us to a proper understanding of those symbols which are more than signs, i.e. more than merely shorthand descriptions of assignable realities, none can do more for the sociologist (or, indeed, for any analyst) of religion

---

[1] Cf. above, p. 68.

[2] Paragraph 41. Cf. *Patrologia Graeca*, as quoted, vol. VI, Paris 1857, cols 563 and 564.

[3] To St. Ambrose, the baptismal waters recalled no fewer than seven scriptural pre-figurations: the creation (the world's emergence from the primal deep), the flood, the Jews' passage through the Red Sea, the cloud, the wells of Mara (Exodus xv, 23–5), the cleansing of Naaman (IV Kings v), and the pool of Bethsaida (or Bethesda: John v). Cf. Chateaubriand, as quoted, vol. I, p. 76.

than Carl Gustav Jung. Freudianism, for instance, has only little to contribute, if anything at all. Freud saw in things of a symbolical character and function essentially representations of, and references to, certain physical features, especially those of the reproductive tract: a pillar was the outer male, a door the outer female, sex organ, and so on. Clearly, such interpretations cannot reasonably be driven beyond a certain borderline. They may well shed light on the mental life of deranged persons, especially if the derangement is rooted in sexual difficulties, but they cannot be legitimately applied to the spiritual quest of mankind. Attempts so to apply them have regularly ended in artificialities and absurdities. Jung split from Freud mainly because he wished to have a depth-psychology which would not follow a one-track route, but would find for every department of psychic activity its own appropriate key. The area of religious symbolism aroused and engaged Jung's attention more than any other set of phenomena, and his teachings ultimately contained an attempted explanation of the sacramental system which, whether it be accepted or not, deserves the fullest consideration.

It is an unfortunate fact that the sciences of psychology and sociology have not yet found that point-for-point adjustment and agreement which is demanded both by the general principles of scientific knowledge and by the similarity and near-coincidence of their fields of observation. Yet Jung's starting point cannot possibly arouse misgivings in the mind of a theoretical sociologist. It is the concept of the collective consciousness. 'Under the concept of "collective consciousness",' so a particularly clear summarizer of the Jungian system has explained, 'we understand the totality of the traditions, conventions, rules, prejudices and norms in a human collective that are followed consciously but unreflectively by the individual, or that give the consciousness of the group as a whole its direction.'[1] It should be immediately obvious that this definition not only coincides with Freud's super-ego, but also that it tallies very largely, if not indeed totally, with Sumner's folkway-complex, or (as he also calls it) ethos – those basic customs which constitute an inclusive culture and enter, by way of internalization, into every normal, not alienated personality and lead to his successful socialization.

It is not, however, Jung's concept of the collective conscious, but rather his co-ordinated concept of the *collective unconscious* that can guide us at this particular juncture. Today it is almost a banality to say that the conscious sector is not the whole of our mental lives but only a part of it – that part which (to use a hackneyed phrase) is above the water line, whereas the greater half of it is (as with an iceberg) below it. The unconscious, so all psychologists agree, shows itself *inter alia* in dreams,

[1] Jacobi, J., *The Psychology of C. G. Jung*, transl. Bash, K. W., ed. New Haven 1951, p. 26.

phantasies and visions, and the individualists among them have considered it mainly as a relict, a repository, of individual experiences. It
is not so to Jung. While he knows, of course, a personal subconscious-
ness also, he knows above all of a collective one. 'The unconscious',
Jolande Jacobi explains, 'consists of contents that are entirely undiff-
erentiated, representing the precipitate of humanity's typical forms of
reaction since the earliest beginnings in situations of general human
character, e.g. such situations as those of fear, danger, struggle against
superior force, the relations of the sexes, of children to parents, to the
father- and mother-imago, of reaction to hate and love, to birth and
death, to the power of the bright and dark principle, etc.'[1] Jung has, in
his own words, expressed himself as follows: 'The collective unconscious is the tremendous mental inheritance of human evolution, re-
born in every individual . . . structure,'[2] or rather in every individual
mentality. He sees the relation of the two layers of the psyche (which
only together constitute the full, the true, man) as one of complemen-
tarity: he asserts that 'a basic capacity' – perhaps even the basic capacity – 'of the unconscious is that of acting compensatively and of setting
up in contrast to consciousness'.[3] Whereas the consciousness adjusts
to the outer conditions of existence, and that in a purposive-rational
manner, the subconscious tends to bring about an inner emotional-
vital adjustment and thereby secures a balance in and for the mental
self. This reference to an 'inner adjustment' must be closely watched,
for in it lurks the danger at least of a *petitio principii*. If religion is seen
in relation to the unconscious life – and Jung sees it in this manner, as
do most of us – it might easily be concluded that it is 'only' something
psychological, which is half the way to saying that it is in essence delusionary. We must urge therefore, if for no other reason than in order to
avoid an automatic prejudgment of the main issue, that the adjustment
which the unconscious effects is both an inner and an outer one. It
certainly gives to man wholeness, equilibrium, health (and this is
meant by inner adjustment); but it also gives him an outer adjustment,
a viable relationship to the mystery of existence which, by definition,
and even more according to experience, cannot be successfully handled
by the conscious or rational self alone. Of course, this mystery, as a
feeling of puzzlement, awe, and anxiety, is inside man, indeed, in his
very depths; but it is inside him only because it is outside him as well,
surrounding him, encompassing him, pressing on him from all sides.
Mystery is part and parcel of the world, not only of the mind. What the
unconscious does is to enable man to come to grips with, and to
achieve some sort of peace with, that part of objective reality which
he cannot scientifically understand and technically dominate – that part

[1] Ibid., p. 12.
[2] *Seelenprobleme der Gegenwart*, Zürich 1931, p. 175. My translation.
[3] Jacobi, loc. cit., p. 12. Cf. also p. 44.

of reality which is bigger than he is, in front of which he is servant and not master. That coming-to-grips with reality, *ultimate* reality, that achieving-some-sort-of-peace with it, is precisely what we call religion.

It would obviously have been easy for Jung to slip, at this point, into some sort of psychological reductionism which would have been parallel to Durkheim's sociological 'explanation', or rather dissolution, of religiosity. But he resists the temptation. Indeed, as he builds up his theory, he moves it still closer to the core-facts of religious life. He develops his concept of *archetypes*. The very word smacks of religious philosophy, and Jung himself informs us that it is an outstanding philosopher-saint to whom he owes the term: he quotes St. Augustine's *Liber de Diversis Quaestionibus* where the great Bishop of Hippo speaks of *ideae principales . . . quae in divina intelligentia continentur*, and which the human mind (and, of all creatures, man alone) can intuit.[1] We do not stay to investigate further the religious derivation of the word and of the idea behind it; a proper study would lead us back to that *fons et origo* of later religiosity, Plato – perhaps, borrowing a Renaissance conceit, we might write here: *Plato Christianus*.[2] (It is in fact of him that Augustine speaks in the context quoted.) We will ask instead, what Jung means by an archetype and how this concept can help us to elucidate the existence, and above all the power, of the sacramental system. In trying to answer this question, we are meeting with difficulty. That an archetype is a content of the collective, and, through it, of every individual, unconscious, is clear enough, but what kind of content? Critics have found an unwelcome ambiguity in Jung's texts. Sometimes, says Raymond Hostie, 'he speaks . . . of archetypes as collective representations . . . and then a little later goes on to say . . . in even the same essay, that these archetypes are only "dominants" of the collective unconscious or *"a priori"* forms,'[3] in which latter case they are not representations, i.e. images, indeed, not concretized at all. What are we to make of this?

Perhaps an example will help to clear up the difficulty which, if the truth is told, is more apparent than real. Mankind has, from its earliest days, known of evil – experienced it both as a fact of objective reality and as a tendency in every subjective self. A whole welter of deep feelings has clustered around this double – external and internal – intuition: fear and anxiety, but also fascination and attraction, shame, repentance and many other emotive tendencies both positive and

[1] 'Root ideas . . . contained in the divine mind.' *Liber di Diversis Quaestionibus*, XLVI, 2, *Patrologia Latina*, as quoted, vol. XL, Paris 1887, col. 30. Cf. Jacobi, as quoted, p. 53 note 6.
[2] Cf. Jacobi, p. 56: 'The archetypes are akin to what Plato called the "idea".' Re Aristotle, cf. p. 58.
[3] Hostie, R., *Religion and the Psychology of Jung*, transl. Lamb, G. R., New York 1957, p. 58. Cf. ibid., notes 3–5 for references to Jung's writings.

negative. There is an inchoate mass of psychic contents which cannot be reduced to a rational concept, even as the experience of happiness can never be caught by, and adequately conveyed in, a definition of it. This inchoate mass of psychic contents, as we call it, has no face. It is, if we may so express it, darkness, in accordance with Ibsen's saying that

> Life is a ceaseless struggle
> Against the darkness within . . .[1]

The reference to original sin is obvious. Neither original sin nor evil (Protean as they are) can be gripped, held, nailed down. Yet there is a tendency in us to bring them to mind in a concrete, tangible, pictorial fashion, for only by so bringing them to mind can we hope to deal with them. Thus there arises (among others) the image of the serpent, cause of original sin, symbol of evil. Henceforth the inchoate mass has received a shape, a face, a name, and we can confront it on the plane of consciousness. 'The snake', says Jung somewhere in an aside, 'is symbol and expression . . . of the dangers of the drives waiting their chance for seduction in the dark of the unconscious.'[2] We see from all this that the archetype is both a psychic content without representation or image and at the same time a representation or image of that psychic content – both the inchoate cluster itself and the form under which it is apprehended. Hostie quotes Jung to the effect that the archetype is not a case of representations, but of dispositions which produce representations – representations which, as the sociologist must be quick to emphasize, are collective, common to all men. Jung speaks of 'the psyche having identical, universal structures' and of 'a disposition to produce over and over again the same, or similar, mythical conceptions'. Hostie, in an excellent summing up, indicates that 'the archetype is therefore an energic centre of the collective unconscious . . . The archetype', he adds, and thereby stresses a salient point, 'is not a dormant disposition peacefully awaiting its activation . . . It is a dynamic disposition tending towards its own realization.'[3] From it – from the psyche's 'deepest layers'[4] – have sprung all truly religious symbols, and among them above all the sacraments. In them, there meet men's inner longing for salvation and (as the believer has to insist) God's outer bringing of salvation. They are (for faith) nodal points between soul and grace.

A sociology of religion need hardly take this analysis further than we

---

[1] This is an occasional verse. Cf. Puntsch, E., *Zitatenhandbuch*, München 1965, p. 954. The translation is mine.

[2] Cit. Jacobi, loc. cit., p. 160, the reference being to *Two Essays on Analytical Psychology*, transl. Baynes, H. G. and C. F., London 1928, p. 230. Cf. also Jacobi, p. 117.

[3] Cf. Hostie, loc. cit., p. 60. References in notes 2 and 3.

[4] Jacobi, as quoted, p. 53.

have done. Only its implications have to be brought out. First among them is the fact that the sacraments have a harmonizing, peace-providing function. The psychologist will, quite naturally, think above all of harmony within the self and inner peace: 'The symbol unifies the conscious and the unconscious. It likewise totalizes the rational and the irrational in man . . . The symbol which unifies both conscious and unconscious, rational and irrational, is simply the expression of the psychic totality as manifested spontaneously at any particular moment.'[1] The sociologist will add to this that harmony with other selves, with society, hence outer peace, will be achieved by the same means. The need for the sacred symbols is in all, as it is in each; the acceptance of the sacred symbols therefore brings everyone into line with his neighbours. This is merely a consequence of the collectivity of the unconscious, its connection with the life experience of the whole race rather than with the life experience of the individual. Finally, the man of religion will complete the picture by asserting that the sacraments can also mediate a still wider harmony than that in and with society – harmony with all existence, and above all with the mysterious-metaphysical realm of or above it. The soul who, under the urging of something deep down within, longs for rebirth into a higher, more-than-fleshly life (according to religion) is granted that rebirth through descending into and arising from the baptismal font: the rite – a sacramental one – achieves what it symbolizes. 'Baptism', writes Jung, 'exalts man out of archaic identity with the world and transforms him into a transcendent being. The fact that mankind has reached the height of this idea signifies in the deepest sense the birth and baptism of the spiritual, no longer merely natural man.'[2]

The second implication concerns the possibility, or rather the impossibility, of a totally rational life. We are touching here on Max Weber's thesis of the growing 'disenchantment' of the world, a process which he thought inevitable though it did not precisely fill him with enthusiasm. For depth-psychology (and it does not matter too much of which concrete author one is thinking when using this word), this assumed involution of mysteriousness and irrationality is impossible. True, science and technology advance, and often with seven-league boots. But they are, unavoidably and by definition, restricted to matter and manipulation; they cannot say anything about the meaning of life. Locke somewhere speaks of a candlelight which we hold and which illumines the area around our feet. Assuming that we may come to hold an arc-lamp of whatever voltage, there will still be an exterior and interior darkness with which we shall have to live, and of which we shall have to take cognizance, and that we can do only with the help of symbols, not by direct apprehension – faith and not knowledge. 'In

[1] Hostie, loc. cit., p. 42.
[2] Cit. Jacobi, loc. cit., p. 177. *Modern Man in Search of a Soul,* London 1934, p. 166.

the mirror of the human psyche,' writes Jolande Jacobi, echoing Jung, 'we can divine the Absolute only as it is "refracted" through our own mortal limitations and never can know it in its true essence. This capacity is immanent in the psyche; but it can clothe its notion of the Absolute only in an image that can be expressed and envisioned, and such an image always can give evidence only for the mortal part alone, never for the immortal, which it is never granted the psyche fully to express.'[1] An even greater thinker than Jung knew this, and said this, before – Hegel. 'The symbol in the proper sense of the word,' he writes in his *Aesthetic*,[2] 'is enigmatic in itself. The external thing through which a general meaning is to be made visible, remains different from the significance which it is supposed to depict. It therefore is for ever doubtful in what manner the material sign is to be accepted and conceived.'

Pure and simple logic should be sufficient to show that a satisfactory science and an unfailing manipulation of the unconscious within and the mysterious without are unimaginable, just as it is impossible for us to think of anything outside space and time. If the unconscious is unconscious, its content cannot become an object of consciousness, i.e. knowledge. We certainly know that we have one, but we cannot know what it is or what it contains. That precisely breaks into consciousness only in the form of images, not propositions, of images moreover which suggest more than they convey, in other words, which still carry the mysteriousness of their origin around with them.[3] Unlike mathematical symbols which we posit, the symbols of religion are given to us. The image is not 'produced'; it 'arises'; in fact, it 'is already there in the dark where it has lain from the time when it first enhanced the psychic store of mankind as a typical fundamental experience'. 'The creative process, as far as we are able to follow it at all, consists of an activation of the timeless symbols of humanity resting in the unconscious and in the development and refinement of them into the completed work of art.'[4] Trying totally to disenchant the world, to expel the unconscious out of subjective, and mystery out of objective, reality would be tantamount to the attempt to jump over one's own shadow. Neither is possible for man. The intensified and often frightening irrationality which has recently raised its head, for instance in fancy flights on the wings of drug addiction, is merely the inescapable consequence, the reverse side, of the growing rationalization of life in other aspects. 'Archetypes,' Jung writes in one of his finest efforts, *Das göttliche*

---

[1] Jacobi, loc. cit., p. 197.
[2] Ed. Lukács, G., Berlin 1955, pp. 391 and 392. My translation.
[3] This is also the reason why symbols, too, are only of partial help to us. No *one* symbol exhausts, or even adequately represents, any archetypal mind content. Hence the tendency towards the massing of metaphors which we have noticed twice before (cf. pp. iii and 68.).
[4] Jacobi, loc. cit., pp. 57 and 35. Cf. also pp. 61, 62, 75, 76, 127, 129 (note 3).

Kind,[1] 'were and are vital powers of the psyche which demand to be taken seriously and see to it, in the most amazing manner, that they receive their due. They have always been bringers of protection and salvation; their neglect leads to perils of the soul.' *Caveat homo rationalis*: beware, O Man, who would be nothing but reason!

The sociologist of knowledge, confronted with Jung's depth-psychology, will be inclined to suggest that different societies tend to activate different parts of the unconscious and therefore generate and choose different symbols, and empirical observation bears out this suggestion. How else could we explain the contrasts between the world's great religions? Not only Jung but many thinkers, including even some who were tied to concrete religious traditions, have been under the impression that the visions of all the religious geniuses who have deeply moved human kind were similar, if not identical, and that only their modes of expressing the inexpressible were irreconcilable, verbal modes being even more irreconcilable with each other than pictorial ones. We are not concerned in this work with the non-Christian world. But even within the orbit of Christianity, the over-all change in sociality has tended to bring new archetype-symbols to the fore. One such, which comes immediately to mind, is Doctor Faustus. Since the Renaissance, this figure has been the focus of a kind of interest which is more than merely biographical or historical. Deep down in man there is a desire to create; not only the artist and the author but even the economic entrepreneur is in its grip and much more strongly activated by it than by any prospect of material gain. (A great economist like Alfred Marshall fully realized this fact.) This vital craving for achievement strove to incarnate itself in modern times in the symbolic Faustus, as it had in antiquity in the symbolic Prometheus. There even appeared rudiments of a Gospel of work. Goethe's hero finds final satisfaction only in service to society – in the draining of swamps, in the creation of new land. A quasi-religious edge surrounds this whole mythology.

> Whoever strives with all his strength
> Shall work his self's salvation,

writes Goethe.[2] In the Puritan, as above all Max Weber has depicted him to us, this ideal found far-reaching realization. He is the active, economically creative type *par excellence*; and though he may not have dared to think (let alone to say) so, this drive for a purposive re-model-

---

[1] Ed. Amsterdam 1949, p. 112. My translation. A profound book, in which sentiments like those displayed in the text are impressively developed, is Hermann Broch's *Der Tod des Vergil*. Cf. ed. Zürich 1958, pp. 391, 393, 394. Even the collectivistic aspect is not forgotten, cf. p. 424. Engl. ed., *The Death of Vergil*, New York 1945, pp. 355, 356, 357, 358, 384, 385.

[2] *Faust*, part II, V. Cf. *Goethes Werke*, ed. Heinemann, K., Leipzig und Wien, n.d., vol. V, p. 467.

ling of matter was felt by him to be divine, or at least a reflection of divine creativity, of the Old Testament's Father God and of His making and shaping of the material universe. Yet strong as this sentiment was, it did not mature into a new symbolism. Outside of mentalities akin to Calvinism, like that of Thomas Carlyle, the question as to whether Faustus was truly saved, and whether his means of salvation – sacramental work, as we might call it – was sufficient for the task, remained open. By the side of Goethe's optimistic *magnum opus*, there appeared negative and pessimistic versions of the legend, such as Lenau's poignant poem, *Faust*, and Berlioz's powerful symphonic cantata, *The Damnation of Faust*. Even Goethe ascribes Faust's acceptance by the higher powers in the end, not to his creative effort, but to love – Gretchen's and God's. Indeed, the end of his Part II is brimful of medieval-Catholic symbolism, a circumstance which has greatly puzzled some of his admirers and scandalized others. But perhaps the great poet's turning back to pre-Renaissance imagery was, on the deepest level, unavoidable. The post-Renaissance world has found it difficult to provide appropriate symbols for the clothing of archetypes. (Attempts like those of the Freemasons or the Rosicrucians have remained marginal.) Above all Calvinism, surely the most significant religious effort of Western man since the Church's disruption by Martin Luther, has remained almost totally barren in this regard. The reason for this failure was partly the rationalistic trend which, from the beginning, inhered in the Genevan's thought, and which in the end led to the development of Unitarianism – that latter-day Arianism – out of Calvinism; but partly, or rather mainly, the reason for the failure was the nominalistic philosophy with which Calvinism was loaded and to which it was chained, and this is the point which the sociologist of knowledge has to stress before and above all others. Symbols make sense only for a mentality which does not have its attention glued to the concrete and singular instance. Symbols are by their inmost nature social, and entirely so. And thus the arrival of an individualistic society with its indwelling nominalistic world-view robbed religiousness – that religiousness which lives in the depths of the soul, in the true anchorground of all faith worthy of the name – of its appropriate means of expression, indeed, of the very possibility of appropriate expression, with consequences which can only be called catastrophic.

There is, of course, as everyone knows, a widespread opinion which runs counter to the one on which the analysis of the foregoing pages was based. It asserts, not only that religion can well live without the pictorial element which, following Jung, we have described as vital for it, but that it can live best if it gets rid of that pictorial element which is described and condemned as primitive, popular and materialistic. The term 'spiritualization' is often used to sum up the ideas and the ideal of that movement. Nobody in our century has thought more deeply about this 'spiritualization' than Ernst Cassirer, and he is a totally unsuspect witness for he was involved with neither of the parties dividing Christendom and stood for a strictly and stringently idealistic philosophy – that of Neo-Kantianism, of the Marburg School. Yet it was precisely Ernst Cassirer who, more than anybody else, insisted that, if the pictorial element be taken out of religion, nothing will remain. The second volume of *Die Philosophie der symbolischen Formen*, which deals with man's apprehension of mystery, ends with the assertion that the contradictory tendencies towards pictorial expression and away from it (towards spiritualization) are both essential ingredients in man's religious quest: though mutually irreconcilable, they are also mutually corrective and hence co-operative. This is what Cassirer writes: 'The striving beyond the mythical image world and an indissoluble attachment to this same world constitute a basic factor of the religious process itself. Even the highest spiritual sublimation of religion does not cause this opposition to disappear but only makes it increasingly clear and understands it in its immanent necessity . . . A reconciliation between these two extremes is continuously sought but never fully achieved.' And, on the penultimate page of this volume, he writes: 'The movement of the religious spirit . . . consists in a living oscillation between those two fundamental views,' between 'meaning and image'. 'On the one hand, the very lowest, most primitive mythical configuration proves to be a vehicle of meaning, for already it stands in the sign of that primordial division which raises the world of the sacred from the world of the profane and delimits the one from the other. But on the other hand, even the highest religious truth remains attached to sensuous existence, to the world of images as well as things. It must continuously immerse and submerge itself in this existence which its intelligible purpose strives to cast off and reject – because only in this existence does religious truth possess its expressive form and hence its concrete reality and efficacy.'[1]

This is precisely what, with the help of Jung, we have been urging. But Cassirer's sentences so far quoted do not yet say enough. Spiritualization occurs not only when the pictorial element is decreased; it occurs also when it is increased. For what is it that happens when a symbol is set, when, for instance, the pom-pom on a priest's biretta becomes a symbol of Christ, the apex of reality, as the top of the biretta is the top point of a given man? What happens above all when a sacrament emerges from the stream of collective life, when, for instance, the water in the baptismal font becomes (as it did in the earliest years of Christianity) a means of cleansing the soul, of metaphysically removing the stain of sin? What happens is that a material object ceases to be merely a material object, that it becomes the sign of a spiritual reality, and hence, as a total phenomenon, spiritualized. As the symbolistic

[1] *The Philosophy of Symbolic Forms*, as quoted, vol. II, pp. 252 and 260.

world-view is driven forward towards perfection, fewer and fewer things are merely things, more and more become pointers to the beyond, and if this is not spiritualization, nothing is. 'What appears to the common, profane world view as the immediately given reality of "things",' Cassirer writes, 'is transformed by the religious view into a world of "signs". The specifically religious point of view is indeed determined by this reversal.

'All physical and material things, every substance and every action, now become metaphoric, the corporeal, imaged expression of a spiritual meaning.' Medieval thought especially was so largely pictorial because it was so deeply religious and vice versa. Cassirer sends us in this context to the man who has so often figured in our five volumes as the representative of the archetypal Catholic world-view – to Dante and his *Convivio*. Both Dante's theology and poetics are drenched in allegories, in the attempt to see the material world, not as religiously meaningless, but, on the contrary, as religiously supremely meaningful.[1] We shall return to these conceptions in our final remarks about the culture of Catholicism.

Cassirer leads us into these paths by the lamp of philosophy, but faith is a second light which can at this point guide our feet in the quest for understanding. What the great Kantian explains to us is the fact that the religious consciousness introduces meaning into matter – the symbolic meaning which is added on to materiality, to things. But is this not parallel to the corner-fact of the Christian faith, the fact of faith that 'the Word was made flesh and dwelt among us'? Is the entry of Christ into a secular and sinful sphere not the entry of meaning into it? Cassirer, thinking for a moment with a mind not quite his own, answers this question in the affirmative. The religious hermeneutic which transforms all physical reality into a metaphor 'can be . . . applied only if there is *one* point at which the world of spiritual, transcendent meaning and that of empirical-temporal reality come into contact, despite their inner divergence and antagonism, and if at this point they directly permeate each other'.[2] That point is the Incarnation. It is, intellectually, the very point of the symbolistic world-view which, some would tell us, is inherently pre- and anti-Christian, primitive, popular and materialistic.

We can now pull together the strands of our analysis. The contents of the collective unconscious can enter our consciousness only in the form of images, and these images are provided by a spontaneous psychic process in which the conscious and the unconscious co-operate, the unconscious providing the tendency, the energy, towards image-formation, and the conscious providing the image itself, or at least the

---

[1] Ibid., p. 252. Cf. also p. 256; *re* Dante, *Convivio*, II, 1, cf. *Dante's Convivio translated into English by William Walrond Jackson, D.D.*, Oxford 1909, pp. 73–5.

[2] Cassirer, loc. cit., p. 257.

apprehension of it. Once in the light of consciousness, the contents of the collective unconscious can be handled and dealt with by us – handled and dealt with in and by the symbols in which they have become visible and, so to speak, manageable. In the Christian religion which, especially in its Catholic form, has allowed the process of image-formation freely to proceed, the sacraments are the prime means of achieving a pacification of the unconscious and its tendencies. The dark urge towards cleansing from primal involvement in evil and death – or in the evil of death – for instance, is achieved through the rite of baptism which, as a sacrament, effects, in the firm conviction of the individual believer and of the believing community, what it symbolizes. But the sacraments are only specific, so to speak privileged, symbols: they are set within a whole world of symbolisms, all of which arise – like the sacraments themselves – from the unconscious, from the depths of our hidden life. Seven ritual symbols, or rather seven symbolical actions, operating as they are at the crisis points of our existence, may – if they are underlaid and carried by an adequate measure of faith – suffice to still the most vital desires of our souls; they can never suffice to body forth all the contents of our unconscious and to bring it into the light of day. The religious culture, therefore, which, in the seven sacraments, has given itself the chief means of salvation, will have the tendency to lay itself out, to realize itself, in a wider, nay encompassing, pictorial and artistic array of self-expression. With this unfolding of a consistently symbolistic world-view we have to deal next.

Concluding note: In view of the fact that we have very largely followed Carl Gustav Jung in our analysis of the sacred symbols of Catholicism, it is our duty to explain in what points it is impossible for us to accept his opinion. There is first of all his doctrine of *engrams*. The word archetype has in it the word type, and type may mean printer's type, a hard object which is impressed on, and leaves its mark in, a softer material. The archetypes were originally conceived as imprints physically stamped on the matter of the brain, as engravings so to speak (hence *engrams*). This materialism is a metaphysical (or anti-metaphysical) judgment which nobody is obliged to accept. Luckily Jung thought better of this in later life. He did, however, develop another curious idea which seems highly problematic: he attempted to re-interpret the traditional Christian dogmas so as to make them quaternitarian, either by including Evil, or by including the Virgin, in the Trinity. This tendency is less irrational than might be thought at first sight. It is a (well-nigh unavoidable) consequence of that psychologism which Jung never completely outgrew. As he believed that the self had four basic elements, he was driven to assume that the Divinity – as the self's pendant – had to have also four constituent features. With the rejection of psychologism, the necessity to think in these terms falls to the ground.

Serious though the theological conflict between Jung's quaternitarian and Christianity's trinitarian creed must be, it is not there that his deepest disagreement with Catholicism lies. It is rooted, rather, in his basic philosophical conceptions; perhaps we may say, in his abiding individualism – and this is the reason why the sociologist must concern himself with it. Jung tries to mediate between philosophical universalism and nominalism (cf. Hostie, pp. 90 and 91). His final conclusion is that the universal and objective 'idea' – the Platonic idea, the Augustinian *idea principalis* – is only subjectively realized (or realizable). Catholicism, on the other hand, takes its

THE UNFOLDING OF A SYMBOLISTIC WORLD-VIEW

There is, as has appeared already, a sharp distinction between symbols which are, and symbols which are not, sacramental in character. If water is applied to the forehead in the baptismal rite, the soul becomes Christian; in the eye of the faithful, a real change of status is brought about, not so much in time as in eternity. But if water is applied to the forehead by taking a drop from the stoup at the church door, no such transformation is assumed to take place. The gesture, though pious and meaningful, is merely physical, not metaphysical. Yet in a sociological and cultural view, symbol is symbol, whatever effects faith may, or may not, ascribe to it. A religious society and culture which has drawn from its collective unconscious, or rather from the collective unconscious of mankind, a sacramental system will be, as we have already asserted, spontaneously led to develop a wider and wider range of symbolisms and may well end up by considering all things less as things than as signs, as pointers to a higher, more than material reality. This precisely is the case of classical Catholicism. It is with the development of symbolism as it is with the development of the social division of labour:[1] both were given free rein in Rome; both were kept down by Wittenberg and especially by Geneva. The great poet Jorris Karl Huysmans, to whom in the sequel we shall have to refer very often, calls symbolism a 'great science of the Middle Ages' and 'a language peculiar to the Church, expressing by images . . . what the Liturgy expresses in words'. This sentence seems to set up a distinction between symbolism and liturgy which does not, in fact, exist, and so Huysmans at once corrects himself. The contrast, such as it is, obtains only between pictorial symbolism and verbal prayer, and not really between symbolism

[1] Cf. our vol. IV, the passages assembled in the Index *sub verbo* Labour, Division of.

stand squarely in the universalist camp. As one of its greatest representatives in the twentieth century has said: 'It is before all else the realism of its sacramental thought which gives the sacramental worship of the Church its religious and moral value. The Church does not attenuate the sacrament into an empty symbol or into a sign of grace which obtains all its efficacy from subjective faith. On the contrary, it is a real . . . sign of Christ and as such it already ensures the presence of His grace through itself, through its actual performance. That is a fundamental point of Catholic sacramental doctrine . . . In the Sacrifice of the Mass we are not merely reminded of the Sacrifice of the Cross in a symbolical form. On the contrary, the Sacrifice of Calvary, as a great supra-temporal reality, enters into the immediate present. Space and time are abolished' (Adam, loc. cit., p. 214). To say the very least, Jung, in spite of all his boldness, hesitates to think in properly metaphysical – and that means also in properly religious – terms. His ontology and that of Christianity, or generally that of theism, are not the same. God is indeed a reality to him, but more one of the mind than of the world. This is where Jung's limitation as an analyst of religion lies. He remains enclosed in a psychologism which cannot but be reductionist in tendency and hence, in tendency, inimical to faith.

as such and liturgical action. 'That part of the liturgy,' Huysmans emphasizes, 'which relates to forms and injunctions as to worship, is itself symbolism; symbolism is the soul of it. In fact, the limit-line of the two branches is not always easy to trace, so often are they grafted together; they inspire each other, intertwine, and at last are almost one.'[1] This is well said. Indeed, it is doubtful whether the assumed contrast between picture and word does not have to be further reduced. For are not even the words of the Mass largely symbolical?

When we move from the sacramental centre outward towards other phenomena which still belong to the core of religiosity, we encounter at once the Holy Scriptures, and on investigation we find very soon that the specifically Catholic understanding and use of them is in line with Catholicism's total mentality. Two principles appear to determine the way in which they are handled – the connected, mutually supportive principles of integration and allegorical interpretation.

There is, then, first of all, the desire to see the whole vast mass of biblical matter, from Genesis to Apocalypse, as one system. To the modern mind, there is a long, long chain of discrete events: to the ancient and medieval mind, which present-day Catholicism continues, there is one coherent revelation. The sociology of knowledge can be applied at this point with particular ease: the fact and the ideal of organic integration which dominated the societies which brought Christianity forth, and which laid down the groundwork for the Church's organization as well, demands as its intellectual concomitant and completion an organic, i.e. systemic, penetration and ordering of the sacred traditions. In thought as in life, multiplicity must give way to unity. How this is done can best be seen by looking at some works of art which depict the biblical incidents, for instance the choir stalls of Roskilde Cathedral, south of Copenhagen, or the 'Verdun altar' in the abbey church of Klosterneuburg, before the gates of Vienna. The basic idea is that the New Testament is contained – hidden as it were – in the Old, and that the Old Testament is made manifest in the New. An example will quickly elucidate the method applied. At Roskilde, Moses and St. John stand opposite, facing each other. Moses is the herald of God's law, St. John the herald of God's love. While the one lived later than the other and incarnates a subsequent phase in the story of salvation, they are yet systematically, rather than historically, co-ordinated. Law and love are one like legs and arms or body and soul. In the same spirit, a carving of the Crucifixion is made to face, across the aisle, a carving of the Brazen Serpent: both are the tenth panel within their series. Let us look at the Scripture passages involved. Numbers xxi, 5–8, relates how the Jews murmured against their fate, 'wherefore the Lord sent among the people fiery serpents which bit them and killed many of them . . . And Moses prayed for the people. And the Lord said to him: make a

[1] *The Cathedral*, as quoted, p. 328.

brazen serpent and set it up for a sign. Whosoever being struck shall look on it, shall live'. The meaning of this record must be a puzzle to modern man, for, as the product of an associational society, and as the carrier of an individualist outlook, he will take it as it stands. It was no puzzle to medieval man and is no puzzle to the Catholic Scripture scholar for he finds it explained by John III, 14 and 15, where Christ says to Nicodemus: 'As Moses lifted up the serpent in the desert, so must the Son of Man be lifted up: that whosoever believeth in him may not perish, but may have life everlasting.' Thus Numbers XXI, 5–8, and John III, 14–15, correspond, and the word correspondence, as here used, is a technical term, indicating the key with the help of which the meaning of the Bible is unlocked.

But the inner co-ordination of Bible passages which we behold in this juxtaposition of two sculptured panels goes much further. The Crucifixion scene has incorporated in it a long scroll which carries, not Numbers XXI, 5–8 – this 'correspondence' is too obvious to need pointing out – but four further quotations: Psalm XXI, 17 ('They have dug my hands and feet'); Ecclesiasticus II, 4 ('In thy sorrow endure, and in thy humiliation keep patience'); Isaias LIII, 7 ('He was offered because it was His own will, and He opened not His mouth'); and Job XVI, 18 ('These things have I suffered without the iniquity of my hand').[1] The whole array of (originally) forty-eight stalls is fascinating, but we cannot linger over its height of beauty and depth of meaning. Nor can we bring anything but a line, anything but one detail, about the Minster of Strasbourg, more enchanting even than the Cathedral at Roskilde. At the south portal, two groups of women are placed in juxtaposition: the two mothers, one true, one false, who contended before the king for an infant son (III Kings III, 16 et seq.), and the two brides of the Lord, one faithless and one faithful, the Synagogue and the Church. Over the scene presides Solomon; yet above him, even higher up, appears Christ, of whom Solomon was but an adumbration.[2] We must be satisfied with these two illustrations of how the medieval-Catholic mind works.[3] It fits the scattered fragments together like the pieces of a puzzle and does not come to rest unless and until it has forced them into the frame of one all-inclusive and more or less flawless picture.

The method applied (and predominant since the Epistle of Barnabas written around A.D. 130)[4] is clear: the feat of co-ordination and

<hr/>

[1] Cf. Kürstein, P., *Korstolene i Roskilde Domkirke og deres Billeder*, Kobenhavn 1966, passim, but esp. pp. 56, 57, 112, 113.
[2] Cf. Sauer, J., *Symbolik des Kirchengebäudes*, ed. Freiburg i. Br. 1924, p. 359.
[3] To mention just one more: IV Kings IV, 42–4 is likened to, and linked with, John VI, 5–13 (the feeding of the five thousand).
[4] Cf. Hägglund, loc. cit., p. 19; cf. also pp. 64 and 65 (*re* Origines) and 79 and 80 (*re* Athanasius). The typological-symbolistic interpretation of the Bible was one of Alexandria's gifts to Christendom. Cf. Sauer, loc. cit., p. 382.

integration is achieved by interpreting the earlier events as symbolical prefigurings of the later; or perhaps we had better say, by interpreting merely human happenings as symbolical prefigurings of more than merely human happenings, happenings in which God Himself was involved and which therefore have noumenal rather than phenomenal character. Either way: the interpretation given is allegorical, not literal, and this brings us back to the theme of symbolism. To illustrate this aspect (which is, of course, the obverse side of the coin of which the converse is collectivism), we may turn to St. Augustine's great work on *The City of God*. God commands Noe to build an ark in which he and his family ride out the storms of the flood and are saved (Genesis VI, 12 et seq.). 'This', says Augustine, 'is certainly a figure of the city of God ... which sojourns in this wicked world as in a deluge [of sin]; that is to say, of the Church, which is rescued by the wood on which hung the mediator of God and men, the man Christ Jesus.' And then the philosopher-saint goes into the detail: the ark's 'having a door made in the side of it certainly signified the wound which was made when the side of the Crucified was pierced with the spear: for by this those who come to him enter; for thence flowed the sacraments by which those who believed are initiated.[1] And the fact that it was ordered to be made of squared timbers, signifies the immovable steadiness of the life of the saints; for however you turn a cube, it still stands. And the other peculiarities of the ark's construction are [likewise] signs of features of the Church.'

After the flood, Noe plants a vineyard and makes wine; he becomes drunk and lies incapacitated in his tent; his son Cham derides him, while his other two sons, Sem and Japheth (the oldest and the youngest) treat him with respect (Genesis IX, 20 et seq.). 'The planting of the vine by Noah, and his intoxication by its fruit, and his nakedness while he slept, and the other things done at this time, and recorded, are all of them pregnant with prophetic meanings and veiled in mysteries,' Augustine comments. But we can understand what is implied. 'It is Christ ... who planted the vine of which the prophet says, "The vine of the Lord of Hosts is the House of Israel" [Isaias v, 7].' It is Christ, too, who drinks of the wine after having prayed, according to Matthew XXVI, 39: 'My father, if it is possible, let this chalice pass from me.' It is also Christ, finally, who is exposed to nakedness, for nakedly He hung on the cross. Noe is therefore not only Noe, the patriarch; he is at the same time, and that more significantly, a figure of Jesus Christ.[2] 'The object of the writer of these sacred books, or rather of the Spirit of

---

[1] The water flowing from Christ's side is here added to St. Ambrose's seven Scripture references mentioned on p. iii, footnote 3.

[2] Concerning the pre-figurations of the Virgin in the Old Testament, cf. the splendid passage in Huysmans, loc. cit., pp. 227 and 228; concerning the pre-figuration of the Cross, cf. Sauer, loc. cit., p. 223.

God in him,' Augustine concludes, 'is not only to record the past, but to depict the future, so far as it regards the City of God.'[1]

It is this identification of Noe and Christ that allows us to understand Sem, Cham and Japheth. 'Shem and Japheth, that is to say, the circumcision and uncircumcision, or, as the Apostle otherwise calls them, the Jews and Greeks . . . having somehow discovered the nakedness of their father (which signifies the Saviour's passion), took a garment and laid it upon their backs, and entered backwards and covered their father's nakedness without their seeing what their reverence hid . . . The garment signifies the sacrament, their backs the memory of things past; for the Church celebrates the passion of Christ as already accomplished . . . And Ham, who was the middle son of Noah, and, as it were, separated himself from both [his brethren] and remained between them, neither belonging to the first-fruits of Israel nor to the fullness of the Gentiles, what does he signify but the tribe of heretics,'[2] those who have no respect for the sacred mysteries? Augustine has no doubt whatever that we have to read the Old Testament with the eyes of the New: what is promised in the one, is fulfilled in the other; what is but symbol in the one, in the other is the reality symbolized.

Much could still be said in illustration of the Saint's style of thought; there are thrilling examples like the discussion of Agar and Ismael (who represent 'the carnal people of the old covenant') and Cetura and her sons (who represent 'the carnal people who think they belong to the new covenant'),[3] but we must forbear lest we overload our text. Instead, we want to look at Augustine's general attitude towards the historical record, and we find that he accepted it in a dual capacity, both as factually true and as symbolically significant. 'No one ought to suppose,' he says, 'that these things were written for no purpose, or that we should study only the historical truth, apart from any allegorical meanings; or, on the contrary, that they are only allegories, and that there were no such facts at all.'[4] The words are unambiguous: there was to be no undue allegorizing of the biblical text. Yet if we descend to the deeper layers of Augustine's (and his fellow-Catholics') mind, we see that the symbolical interpretation easily outstrips any historical understanding. For in that mind, the main contrast is between the noumenal and the phenomenal, God's doings and men's, appearance and essence. The history of the chosen people, as depicted in the Old Testament, conveys – God's gracious intervention on behalf of Israel notwithstanding – in contrast to the New, more of the phenomenal and human, and not only the noumenal and divine – not the pure reality (if we may

---

[1] St. Augustine, *The City of God*, transl. Dods, M., New York 1950, pp. 516, 521, 523, 524.
[2] St. Augustine, as quoted, pp. 522 and 523.
[3] Ibid., p. 556. Cf. Genesis, XVI, XXI, 1–21, XXV, 1–6.
[4] Ibid., p. 517; cf. also p. 519.

so word it) which is really real. For this reason, the historical critique of the Bible did not mean to Catholics what it did to Protestants. An attack, like that of Colenso, on the scientific credibility of Genesis was bound to have destructive consequences for a predominantly fact-related world-view; it did not, and did not need, to shock those who, more interested in meanings, intimations, and allegories, saw in Genesis mainly a collection of highly educational stories whose purpose it is to attune the spirit to holy thoughts and draw its attention to the *unum necessarium* – Christ's redemptive deed.

We are not concerned here with the relation of religion to science, but we may mention, simply in passing, that it was also the consistently allegorical interpretation of Scripture which enabled Catholicism to find a *modus vivendi*, for instance, with the new cosmology of the Renaissance. The first versicle of Psalm XCII says: 'He hath established the world which shall not be moved,' but this did not rivet Rome to the Ptolomaean system. Indeed, Copernicus, by whose name the newer system has come to be known, dedicated his work, *De Revolutionibus Orbium Coelestium* (1543), to the contemporary pope, Paul III. This fact should not be forgotten over the passing difficulties which Galileo Galilei experienced with the Curia.

What is true of the Bible, is true of later legendary growths also. One story which appears again and again tells of a saintly hero who slays a dragon. Usually it is St. George who is credited with the feat, but other names, too, are mentioned in this context, for instance St. Julian and St. Servatius. Even a female personality is, sometimes and at some places, connected with the tale: St. Margaretha. 'We may say without hesitation that in most cases the dragon is to be considered as a symbol of pernicious disbelief, of that heathenism which, according to popular conceptions, is the cause of all temporal and moral evil. The Old and New Testament, too, regard the dragon in this manner as the terrible spirit of darkness who incessantly works against the earthly and eternal welfare of mankind (Psalm LXXIII, 14; CIII, 26; Isaias LI, 9; Apocalypse XII, 3 et seq., XIII, 2 et seq. and repeatedly).'[1]

We have, on several occasions, notably in connection with our discussion of the Christological debates up to the Council of Constantinople described the fully formed Catholic positions as syntheses between antithetic movements which preceded them.[2] Here we can do the same in reverse, so to speak. We can show that, once the unity of Christendom was broken, antithetic movements appeared which succeeded the Catholic position in which they were, in a fashion, reconciled. Protestantism has generated, on the one hand, Fundamentalism, the assertion that Holy Writ is totally inspired and hence must be accepted as literally true, sentence for sentence and word for word; it has generated, on the

[1] Sauer, loc. cit., pp. 215 and 370.
[2] Cf. above, pp. 78 et seq.

other hand, the so-called Higher Criticism, a scholarly technique which handles the sacred text like any other historical document and which has ended up by largely shattering the belief in its credibility. Both tendencies stem from something deep down in the Protestant mind. When Luther broke with Rome, he repudiated the authority which had guided wayward humanity for many centuries. There appeared a vacuum which had to be filled, and the Bible, as the Word of God, was used to fill it. Hence it was but logical if some set it up as the one sheet-anchor to which men can cling and without which they would founder and drown. But it is also understandable if others tried to go back, from the written record, to the facts, and especially to the sayings, of Christ which it brings to us. The New Testament is in Greek; Jesus spoke Aramaic; therefore the authority of the Scriptures could only be preliminary; the final certainty was to be expected from something which lay behind them. The philologism of the great Reformers has its roots in these considerations. But philologism leads to textual criticism, and textual criticism to historical criticism – to that very Higher Criticism which created such havoc in the Protestant camp. In comparison to these attitudes of which the one (Fundamentalism) is unavoidably unacceptable to modern, i.e. scientific man, and the other (Higher Criticism) is as unavoidably unacceptable to the man of faith, at whatever period he may live, the Catholic conception of the Bible as true, but as symbolically rather than literally true, constitutes a *tertium quid* which avoids the pitfalls into which the other two were dragged and from which they can hardly hope to extricate themselves.

So much about the Scriptures. From them, we turn to a consideration of the church as a building, and here it might appear that we are making an abrupt transition which, to say the least, is unpleasing in an author. But the transition is not really abrupt. For if the Old Testament, no less than the New, is Christological in meaning, so is the church building, its very stone, wood and glass, from floor to roof. Sauer calls it a 'pictorial catechism' in one context, and a 'summa theologica' in another.[1] Both expressions are entirely correct. The very door carries a deep significance: it symbolizes Christ through whom alone we can enter into heaven. He Himself had described Himself as a door (John x, 7), i.e. the gateway to blessedness, and said 'No man cometh to the Father but by me' (ibid., xiv, 6). The church, therefore, as a building, is an earthly anticipation of the abode of the blessed, the Jerusalem above. Surveying a number of inscriptions which adorn church lintels, Sauer sums up their message by saying that 'the material church appears . . . clearly as the House of God, the image of paradise, the entry into which stands open, through Christ, for all Christians who are truly devoted and honour the Church'.[2] But the symbolism of

[1] Loc. cit., pp. 7 and 308.
[2] Ibid., p. 309.

the door is only the beginning of a far wider and richer, indeed, of a comprehensive symbolism. Its classical exponent was Gulielmus Durandus or Durandi whose *Rationale Divinorum Officiorum* (before 1296) lovingly collected the speculation of the centuries into one large pool. 'Durandus gives the structural parts of the mystical temple of God and grace as follows: the foundation is faith which is directed towards what is invisible; the roof is love which covers a multitude of sins (I Peter IV, 8); the door is obedience of which it is said: "If thou wilt enter into life, keep the commandments" (Matthew XIX, 17); the floor is humility which, in the Psalmist's words, forces the soul to ground (Psalm CXVIII, 25); the four walls are the four cardinal virtues: justice, fortitude, prudence and temperance; they recall the four equal sides of the celestial city (Apocalypse XXI, 16).'[1] Such interpretations are extremely archaic. Already the proto-Christian *Testamentum Domini Nostri Jesu Christi* described the Church structure with its three doors as a symbol of the Most Holy Trinity.[2]

The Middle Ages continued where the earlier Christians, an Origen, a Clement, an Augustine, a Gregory had left off. The later symbolists stress the fact that the ground plan of typical church buildings has two aspects: it is cruciform and it is centred. 'In the former layout they see the admonition that . . . we must follow the Crucified One; in the other feature [the ideal] that the Church must spread outward towards the circumference of the earth, according to the Psalmist's word: "Their sound has gone forth . . . unto the ends of the world" (XVIII, 5), or that we must rise from the circle of men to the dome of heaven.'[3] The last-named symbolism, already present in pre-Gothic days, proliferates in post-Gothic days and creates the cupola of Renaissance and Baroque. The cruciform plan was also used to stress the living character of the apparently dead structure: it recalls man, man alive (and therefore also the God-man, He in whom all men are summed up), for the sanctuary is the head, the transept the arms, and the nave to the westward the rest of the body. The eastward position of the altar end symbolizes the community's directedness towards Christ: Christ is symbolized by this particular point of the compass, for it is from the east that the light comes. The east was determined by the point of sunrise at the equinox. As the world is then between summer and winter, so the Church must ever be between joy and suffering.[4]

The stones from which the building is fashioned are the individuals; the mortar is the love which keeps them together. Men, like the stones, support each other; together they constitute the Kingdom of God as the stones do the church. The foundation-stone, of course, is Christ,

[1] Ibid., p. 122.
[2] Ibid., p. 4. Once again it is Alexandria, the city of Athanasius, which leads the way.
[3] Ibid., p. 110.
[4] Ibid., pp. 111 and 112.

according to the Apostle's words: 'Other foundation no man can lay but that which is laid: which is Christ Jesus' (I Corinthians II, 11). It is the rock upon which the Church is built (Matthew VII, 24, and XVI, 18). Christ, is, however, not only in the depths of the Church: He is also at its height. The cock who crowns as a rule the top of the highest spire is a symbol of Him, too. And how could He, the East, from which the day comes, not also be the chanticleer, the harbinger of the day? Is it not He who conquers the power and the powers of the dark and calls us into the marvellous light, the morning of salvation?[1]

We see from all this that at the root of the multiform symbolism concerning the House of God as a physical structure, there lies an equation between the Church in the spiritual sense (a society built of living stones) and the church in the material sense (an edifice made of hewn blocks), and this identification explains also why only one word is used to describe them both. Another such linguistic-symbolistic connection is indicated by the word nave. Nave means the body of the church; it also means a boat, a sea-vessel. Those who are in the nave of the church are also in Christ's boat, in the vessel of salvation – the boat or vessel prefigured in Noe's ark (Genesis VI et seq.) and in Peter's bark (Matthew VIII, 23). Yet, here again we get that massing of metaphors which we have encountered everywhere. Those in the nave are the Body of Christ; the nave therefore stands for Christ as well, like foundation-stone and highest pinnacle. In a sense, the church walls are an outer shell which surrounds a precious inner core. Therefore they are like the ribs which protect the heart, or like the whole frame of flesh which contains the human soul. The nave is the ark; the ark is for this reason a symbol of the soul also, as Leo the Great pointed out in one of his sermons.[2] From what we have said, the reader can infer two facts: that the symbolism proliferates, and that it tends to develop into a system, that there is *manifestatio*, a laying out of meanings, and at the same time *concordantia*, a pulling together of them and weaving into one. The salient phenomena which we encountered in our study of the Bible are here repeated and reduplicated. 'In its imagery', writes Erwin Panofsky, 'the High Gothic cathedral sought to embody the whole of Christian knowledge, theological, moral, natural and historical.' It was pan-symbolic. And 'like the High Scholastic *Summa*, the High Gothic cathedral aimed . . . at "totality"'. It was pan-systemic. The aim of both was 'to establish the unity of truth'.[3]

We cannot, unfortunately, go further into detail. We cannot, for

---

[1] Ibid., pp. 112, 114, 143.

[2] *Patrologia Latina*, as quoted, vol. LIV, Paris 1881, col. 344. Cf. Sauer, loc. cit., pp. 100–05. In our references, we have kept to the scholarly Sauer and avoided the poetical Huysmans. Yet Huysmans' book is truly illuminating. The reader will find all of it relevant, but more especially the following pages: 43–5, 79–80, 82–6, 107, 108, 115, 337, 338.

[3] Panofsky, loc. cit., pp. 64, 44, 28.

instance, speak of the special symbolism of the Virgin (the rose window which lets the light into the church, as her womb brought Christ into the world, is her main emblem), nor yet of Chartres where that symbolism reached its highest point, a realization of well-nigh incredible splendour. We have sent the reader to Huysmans' *La Cathédrale*; we would send him also to Henry Adams' *Mont-Saint-Michel and Chartres*. We only beg leave to quote a few lines from the latter book, in order to show that the symbolism of the church building, and the great enthusiasm and effort which went into the elaboration of it, stemmed in the final analysis from the very depths of religious experience: 'Like all great churches,' Adams writes,[1] 'Chartres expressed, besides whatever else it meant, an emotion, the deepest man ever felt – the struggle of his own littleness to grasp the infinite. You may, if you like, figure it in a mathematical formula of infinity – the broken arch, our finite idea of space; the spire, pointing, with its converging lines, to unity beyond space; the sleepless, restless thrust of the vaults, telling the unsatisfied, incomplete, over-strained effort of man to rival the energy, intelligence and purpose of God.' The words may seem exaggerated; they are not. The last petty ascription of meaning to the last small nook or corner or mould or cornice, playful as it may at times appear, is yet essentially an evidence, tiny and yet important and revealing in its way, of man's wish and will to express the inexpressible, to hold mystery in his hands.

What is true of the house, is true of the furnishings also. 'Every material object used in divine worship is representative of some theological truth'; in this particular 'script', 'everything is a reminiscence, an echo, a reflection, and every part is connected to form a whole'.[2] Out of a very long list, we can only take two items for closer study: bells and censers, both carriers of a deep symbolism which might almost be called affectionate.

So far as the bell is concerned, the fundamental allegory, later luxuriantly developed, depends on the fact that it has a voice. Because it has a voice, it is almost human. Bells have always been given names, and their solemn dedication shows more than merely one parallel to the baptismal rite. Bells also age, as men do: their sound, as is well known, becomes more sonorous as time elapses; they mature. More specifically, the voice of the bell is the voice of a preacher. As the man in the pulpit addresses those who are in the church building, so the metal tongue in the tower addresses those who are outside. 'According to Hugh of Saint Victor, the tongue of the bell is the sacerdotal tongue which, striking on both sides of the body, declares the truth of both Testaments . . . Durand of Mende compares the hardness of the metal to the power of the preacher and thinks that the blows of the tongue against

[1] Paperback ed., Garden City, N.Y. 1959, p. 115.
[2] Huysmans, loc. cit., p. 110.

the side aim at showing the orator that he should punish himself and correct his own vices before he blames those of others. The wooden crossbeam to which the bell is suspended resembles in form the Cross of Christ and the rope pulled by the ringer to set the bell going, is allegorical of the knowledge of the Scripture which depends on the Cross itself.'[1] Around the rope which, mechanically, is of little consequence, a whole rich web of meanings has been woven – a symbolism of its own within the wider symbolism of bell and belfry. The rope is made of three strands or strings, a fact of obvious implications. It is pulled down and then again rises upward, a multiple symbolism which the symbolists lovingly explore and exploit. The downward movement, for instance, betokens the literal interpretation of God's word of which we are sometimes guilty, the upward swing its inspired exposition which we achieve when we aspire to the heights. The coming down also signifies our work-a-day entry into active life, the rising up our festive turning towards the contemplation of divine things. The bell calls the faithful to church, but it also goes out to those who cannot come, notably the sick and the dying. It is the messenger of the community. In the Scriptures, it has its figure in Psalm XVIII, verse 5: 'Their sound hath gone forth into all the earth', and in I Corinthians XIII, 1: 'If I speak with the tongues of men and of angels . . .'. But the deepest meaning of the ringing of the bells is that it signifies Christ's resurrection. In the Easter Mass, the intoning of the Gloria marks the moment, and at that moment the bells raise their voice after their sorrowful lenten silence – both the silver bells at the altar and the bronze bells in the steeples. The sound of the bells is therefore ever one of joy, even when they are heard at an interment, for what they say is above all that death is conquered, that death has lost its sting.[2]

The interpretation of the bell thus leads in the end to a Christological core of meaning, and, needless to say, it is the same with the censer. The censer signifies Christ's physical body and hence the Word that was made flesh, the incense itself His soul and divinity, the fire the Holy Spirit. If there are four chains, Honorius of Autun says, 'they represent the four cardinal virtues of the Lord, and the chain by which the cover is lifted from the vessel answers to the Soul of Christ quitting His body. If, on the other hand, there are but three chains, it is because the Person of the Saviour includes three elements: a human organism, a soul, and the Godhead of the Word. And Honorius adds: "the ring through which the chains run represents the Infinite in which all these things are included".'[3] The fragrance rising up is, of course, the prayer sent to

---

[1] Ibid., p. 268.
[2] Cf. Sauer, loc. cit., pp. 141, 147–9, 153, 154; and, in addition to Huysmans' La Cathédrale, also his Là-Bas, Engl. transl. by Wallis, K., Down There, ed. New Hyde Park, N.Y. 1958, pp. 38 and 39; cf. also pp. 204 and 205.
[3] Huysmans, The Cathedral, as quoted, pp. 88 and 89.

heaven; its reflection by the roof is the coming down of divine grace in response to the supplication. Parallel to it lie the flames of the candles, another symbol of human devotion and aspiration. The candle itself is once again Christ. Pierre d'Esquilin explains: 'The wax . . . is the spotless body of the Saviour born of the Virgin; the wick enclosed in the wax is His most holy Soul hidden in the veil of flesh; and the light . . . is emblematic of His Godhead.' In this context, even the snuffers used to clean candles and lamps bear a secret, or rather reveal a secret. According to Durand of Mende, they are 'the divine words of which we cut the letter of the law and by so doing reveal the Spirit which giveth light'. The two blades of which these scissors consist, and which work so closely together, are the Old and the New Testament, and, in the final analysis, God the Father and God the Son, hence once again a symbol of Divinity Itself.[1] Thus in the least significant the Most Significant is for ever mirrored and contained.

While discussing these matters, we have, almost without noticing it, changed over to the consideration of a substantial new subject – the subject of art and its relationship to religion. To modern man, who, in all his typical incarnations, is devoted to other than aesthetic and metaphysical values, art is no more than a marginal interest, an embellishment, a luxury, something he can at a pinch do without, and he is inclined to apply this conviction to religious as well as to all other forms of artistic creation. The downright hostility to beauty which characterized the Reformation and more especially Calvinism which, in sharp revulsion from the one-sided aestheticism of the Renaissance, considered and condemned art as inescapably sensuous and heathen, has perhaps diminished, but a largely negative attitude has remained. Certainly there are few today, even among Catholics, who would say that the fate of religion is linked with that of art, and that they will rise and sink together. And yet this is a conviction deeply built into classical Catholicism. Its rationale is as simple as, from a religious point of view, it is convincing.

Religion, like all other vital phenomena, must be able to express itself, if it is to survive; if it cannot express itself, if it is deprived of the medium and the means in which and by which it can express itself, it must languish. A general law of life is involved here: a muscle or an organ which is never used, atrophies; animals which take to an underground existence, turn blind. But only art offers an appropriate language to religious sentiment, the word language taken in its widest connotation. Words can express a creed, i.e. the rationalistic aspect of faith; they can convey the contents of a moral code, i.e. the ethical aspect of faith; they

[1] Ibid., p. 89. Cf. also, Sauer, loc. cit., pp. 205, 206, 191. We have said nothing of the symbolism of the priestly vestments because they are explained in many Missals. Generally speaking, we have not even scratched the surface of the whole subject of symbolism anyway.

can render auxiliary service even beyond these limitations; but it is difficult to imagine that (pure poetry apart) all that is in religion, above all the religious experience as such, can be pressed into verbal moulds.

The unspeakable, so a wise writer of our day has said, escapes the concept, but not the image. An absolute that is beyond words cannot become the object of perception or of knowledge, but it can be divined. (The very term divining is deep and revealing: the divine is that which can be divined, and that which can only be divined.) 'Any excessive emphasis on the power of the reasoning faculty, any cerebral hybris which absolutizes the intellect, i.e. any habit which "hypostasizes" the importance of the intellect which is [in fact] only functional, and which thereby wrenches the spirit from its metaphysical, mystical or religious ties, leads to a loss of human breadth, to a loss of human totality.'[1] These words are true, but perhaps it is better to stress the positive side rather than the negative: to emphasize what art *can* do rather than what reason can*not* do. When Anton Bruckner was given his honorary doctorate in the University of Vienna, the Rector of that institution made a statement in his *laudatio* which conveys precisely what should be said here: 'Where science has to call a halt, where unsurmountable barriers bar its progress, there the realm of art begins which is capable of expressing those experiences from which knowledge remains excluded.'[2] We may well take the great musician who was honoured on that occasion as a first exemplification of the truth of these words.

Even at the most primitive level, words fail the truly religious person, the saint (and Anton Bruckner, if he was not technically a saint, came very close to being one). For how is he adequately to express his belief, if he has only words at his disposal? He can say, of course, 'I believe' – but saying, with the Creed, 'I believe in one God' is linguistically not different from saying, 'I believe it is twelve noon.' He can try to mass words: 'I believe, I assure you I do believe, I have no doubt at all, etc.', but the result would be unconvincing at best and absurd at the worst. All is changed, if music is brought in. In Beethoven's *Missa Solemnis*, the word 'Credo' at the beginning of every sentence of the Creed is repeated, and we can hint at the effect achieved, if we translate: 'I am a man of faith. I believe . . .' Yet how inadequate is this mode of expression, compared to the tremendous power of sound! Sound, music, orchestration put a new dimension at the disposal of the *homo religiosus*, a dimension moreover which works with a scale of intensity, which allows a statement to become ever more strong, ever more winged, ever more convincing. Mere word-magic (if there is such a thing) is left far behind.

[1] Hocke, G. R., *Die Welt als Labyrinth*, Hamburg 1957, ed. 1966, pp. 108, 110, 160, 161.
[2] Cit. Redlich, H. F., *Bruckner and Mahler*, London 1955, p. 23.

There are, of course, many tremendous examples from the history of music – Hector Berlioz's *The Childhood of Christ* which achieves a tenderness even poetry cannot possibly communicate, Antonin Dvořák's *Stabat Mater* which tells us of a sorrow with depths upon depths, César Franck's *Panis Angelicus* which reveals a mystical love the mystical writers were unable to put into their books, to mention only a few which come to one man's mind in the fleeting moment when this page is being written. But no composition is a better object of demonstration at this point than Anton Bruckner's *Te Deum*. At first (from 1842 or so to 1867–68), this simple, yet great man, wrote masses, i.e. he set liturgical words to music; then, from 1862–63 onward, he composed symphonies, i.e. he explored the great realm of wordlessness; and finally he returned to the verbal mode of expression – but how much did he bring with himself, how much had he learned! The *Te Deum*, given final form in 1883–84, is more than a text set to music and more than a symphony that can do without a text: it is a massing of means, an outstripping of all measure, a titanic outburst. It sweeps the hearer along like a torrent which nobody and nothing can arrest.

We have just used superlatives and thereby in all probability aroused the resistance of rationalistic readers who mistrust such words, if they do not indeed hate them. Yet all the authors who have discussed this tremendous confession of faith have used similar terms; what else could they do – apart, of course, from saying (what Max Scheler regarded as the last resort of all religious conversation[1]): Go and hear for yourself! Referring more especially to Bruckner's Masses in D minor and F minor, Fritz Grüninger writes this in his searching study of the composer: 'The musical stream breaking from this soul merged with the prayers of the holy liturgy, but with the difference that the power of music to convince sheds a new light on the convincingness which dwells in the words as such. It is because of this that the pious master, if only we know how to understand him, says even more to us than the words which he set to music, that his expressiveness grows beyond the words, that . . . we can no longer pray when we hear Bruckner's church music because our soul is, on the wings of sound, lifted up and brought much closer to God than words could carry it.' Yet when the two Masses in D minor and F minor were composed, Bruckner had the better part of his symphonic apprenticeship still before him: he had learned his lesson by 1881 when he worked on the *Te Deum*. And therefore the *Te Deum* exhibits the same strengths as the two masses, only raised to an even higher pitch. 'This majestic work,' writes the musicologist whom we have quoted, 'is one of those powerful outpourings of Bruckner's genius in which the soul soars above all earthly barriers in order to float higher and higher . . . Drunk with the

[1] Cf. Stark, W., Introduction to Max Scheler, *The Nature of Sympathy*, London 1954, p. XXII.

divine splendour, . . . it proclaims the praises of God in a roar of jubilation.'[1]

More soberly, we can say that Bruckner leads the hearer from *pianissimo* to *fortissimo*, using the words as symbols of religious emotion rather than as technical terms. Grüninger says in this sense that the chorus 'Sanctus, sanctus, sanctus, Dominus Deus Sabaoth' ascends 'from the *pianissimo* of the awe-struck soul to a *fortissimo* of divine enthusiasm which leaves all limitations behind'. This statement applies not only to one movement of the composition, but to all. It is built on an antithesis caught up in a synthesis: the antithesis between humble prayer and jubilant thanksgiving, yielding, as its synthesis, the mood of confidence which informs the whole piece. Nowhere is this confidence – this hope which is more than hope, which is certainty – more convincingly expressed than in the final part built on the words: 'In Te, Domine, speravi; non confundar in aeternum.' 'How Bruckner makes this motive rise up from a sombre, anxiety-filled F minor to a flaming B major, and how he lifts this B major, in a world-shaking struggle, to an ocean of light in the C major which floods the final passage belongs to the most magnificent feats that music has ever achieved.'[2]

Even those who dislike and distrust Grüninger's enthusiasm – an enthusiasm shared by most musicologists who have written about Bruckner[3] – will have gathered at least one thing from his exposition, namely that Bruckner's *Te Deum* mediates, for those who are attuned to his intensely religious spirit, a powerful religious experience. It is by such experiences that faith flourishes, nay lives: without them, dryness sooner or later supervenes, a fact which the history of Christianity has amply demonstrated. But music is not the only medium through which experiences of this kind can be evoked: the pictorial arts can do it also, for the eye, no less than the ear, is an inlet through which a man may receive religious stimulation. We therefore add to the example which we have just presented another taken from the world of painting: Matthias Grünewald's *Crucifixion* at present in the great gallery (Kunsthalle) at Karlsruhe. We shall try to see this tremendous work of art through the eyes of Joris Karl Huysmans.[4]

Huysmans says, and one must agree with him, that this picture is without its equivalent in literature.[5] Yet his own description of it is strong enough to convey something at least of the power of the

---

[1] Grüninger, F., *Anton Bruckner*, Augsburg 1949, pp. 167, 168, 170. My translation.
[2] Ibid., pp. 171–9. Literal quotations from pp. 171 and 178.
[3] Cf. e.g. Auer, M., *Anton Bruckner: Sein Leben und Werk*, ed. Wien 1947, pp. 364 et seq., and especially Griesbacher, P., *Bruckners Tedeum, Führer und Studie*, Regensburg 1919.
[4] Huysmans, *Down There* (as quoted, p. 6) ascribed this work to the Gallery at Kassel. How it got from the one place to the other can be read in Lauts, J., *Katalog der Staatlichen Kunsthalle Karlsruhe, Alte Mesiter bis 1800*, Karlsruhe 1966, p. 131.
[5] *Down There*, as quoted, p. 10.

original. Jesus is presented on a rude cross of barky wood, with the horizontal beam bending under His Body's weight. 'Dislocated, almost ripped out of their sockets, the arms of Christ seemed trammelled by the knotty cords of the straining muscles. The laboured tendons of the armpits seemed ready to snap. The fingers, wide apart, were contorted in an arrested gesture in which were supplication and reproach but also benediction. The trembling thighs were greasy with sweat. The ribs were like staves, or like the bars of a cage, the flesh swollen blue . . . specked as with pin-pricks by spines broken off from the rods of the scourging and now festering beneath the skin where they had pene-trated . . . The knees had been forced together and the rotulae touched, but the lower legs were held wide apart, though the feet were placed one on top of the other. These, beginning to putrefy, were turning green beneath a river of blood. Spongy and blistered, they were hor-rible, the flesh tumified, swollen over the head of the spike, and the gripping toes, with the horny blue nails, contradicted the imploring gesture of the hands, turning that benediction into a curse; and as the hands pointed heavenward, so the feet seemed to cling to earth . . .'[1]

Critics have called Bruckner's *Te Deum* the 'peasant Te Deum', and, indeed, it is not a piece aimed at the people of the *salons*. The same is true – even more true, if possible – of Grünewald's *Crucifixion*. 'This lockjaw Christ was not the Christ of the rich, the Adonis of Galilee, the exquisite dandy, the handsome youth with the curly brown tresses, divided beard and insipid, doll-like features whom the faithful have adored for four centuries. This was the Christ of Justin, Basil, Cyril, Tertullian, the Christ of the apostolic Church, the vulgar Christ, ugly with the assumption of the whole burden of our sins and clothed, through humanity, in the most abject of forms. It was the Christ of the poor, the Christ incarnate in the image of the most miserable of us He came to save; the Christ of the afflicted, of the beggar, of all those on whose indigence and helplessness the greed of their brother battens, the human Christ frail of flesh . . . Thus, dying like a thief, like a dog, basely, vilely, physically, He had sunk himself to the deepest depth of fallen humanity and had not spared Himself the last ignominy of putrefac-tion.' And yet – 'a divine light played about that ulcerated head, a superhuman expression illuminated the fermenting skin of the epileptic features. This crucified corpse was a very God, and, without aureole, without nimbus, with none of the stock accoutrements except the blood-sprinkled crown of thorns, Jesus appeared in His celestial super-essence, between the stunned, grief-torn Virgin and a Saint John whose calcined eyes were beyond the shedding of tears.'[2]

'Grünewald had passed all measure,' Huysmans writes, and Grüninger has said much the same of Bruckner. The term 'magnificent exaltation'

[1] Ibid., p. 7.
[2] Ibid., pp. 8, 9, 10.

is also applicable to both these truly inspired artists.[1] It is to be feared that modern man, anxiously enclosing himself in his own petty self-made world, in his own time-serving security, such as it is, will be repelled rather than attracted by these fierce, burning and almost brutal men. Yet if religion is to be more than an adjunct of bourgeois respectability, if it is to open our minds both to the horrors of hell and to the glories of heaven, it needs such all-out appeals; it needs to activate the slumbering potentialities of our souls, their capacity to shiver and to freeze, to be on fire and to be consumed, to descend to the depths of anxiety and to climb the heights of assurance. A reasonable Christianity, that abortive concept of the eighteenth century, is no more than a contradiction in terms.

Of course, not all religious art is tending towards the colossal; Mozart's *Ave, ave, verum corpus* is not like Bruckner's *Te Deum*, nor is Altdorfer's *Birth of the Virgin* like Grünewald's *Crucifixion*. Yet they are religious art all the same. They evoke and confirm other strands in the texture of faith: the one a mystical seriousness, the other an over-brimming joy. Thus they come from the same depths beyond the reach of reason from which all religion arises, and they leave the religious spirit stimulated and enriched as all art does which is not finally divorced from metaphysics and has reduced itself to a mere depiction of reality. In any case – and this is the point we have to make as strongly as we can in this volume which is devoted to a study of the types of religious culture – there is a common root to Catholic religiosity and artistic creation, a common subsoil, too, namely the collective unconscious from which both religious and aesthetic values draw their sustenance. We are confronted here – to stress this once again – with a situation parallel to that which we encountered and analysed in volume IV:[2] as there is (if we may say so) a natural tendency towards a division of labour and Catholicism allows it to proliferate and to produce the contrast between layman and priest, parish priest and bishop, and so on, while Calvinism opposes this tendency, so there is a natural tendency towards a creation of symbols and other artistic expressions which Rome has fostered and Geneva has fettered. Calvinists would not deny this, and we cannot accuse them of failure in this field. Nobody can be criticized for not doing what he does not want to do. It is all a matter of one's values. Calvinism based its world-view on ethical, not aesthetic values: it preferred a narrowly moral to a widely unfolded man. It saw beauty as a seducer, as heathen, as a stimulator of the senses, not as a revealer of the glory of creation, as a help to god-ward motion, as profoundly Christian. To each his own. The question is only whether the inhibition of the mind's symbol-setting activity (of which art is a consequence, indeed, a branch) does not deprive religiosity of its most convincing language and reduce

[1] Ibid., pp. 9 and 10.
[2] Cf. the passages adduced in the Index *sub verbo* Labour, Division of.

it to the use of a language which is less than satisfactory and sufficient –
words. The great Protestant predicants did not think so; a psychology
like Jung's which knows about the unconscious and its elementary
urge to express itself in images must judge otherwise.

We have, in the last paragraph, mentioned the division of labour, not
only because we wanted to draw the parallel which we did draw, and
because we wanted to show that there is in cultures an inherent strain
towards consistency, but also because this concept allows us to make a
further move in our effort to understand the essence of Catholicism.
Catholicism is inclined towards hierarchy, as Protestantism is towards
democracy. There is no 'supremacy of private judgment'; there are
some who lead and others who follow. Those who lead must be able to
speak to those who follow – speak not only in everyday language, as
when they issue administrative commands, but also in the sacred language of symbols, as when they induce others to pray or simply to contemplate the higher things. And this is what religious artists do. It is difficult to hear Bruckner's *Te Deum* (or Mozart's *Ave*, or a host of other
compositions) and not to take one step, however small, out of the
secular rut and towards, if not indeed into, the sacred realm; it is also
difficult to see Grünewald's *Crucifixion* (or Altdorfer's *Birth of the Virgin*, or a host of other paintings) and not to feel the same compelling
lift. Art, no less than rational theology, and perhaps even more than
rational theology, is part and parcel of the spontaneous, uninhibited
self-constitution of religious systems. If Calvinism did not recognize
this, this was too bad for Calvinism. Perhaps it would not have
declined so quickly into a new Arianism, that is, essentially a form of
rationalism, if it had not nipped the counterbalancing aesthetic and
experiential tendencies in the bud.

One more secondary facet has to be mentioned in this analysis, and it
is very close to the social core of Catholicism. Among the Catholic sacraments there is, and among the Calvinist sacraments there is not, the
sacrament of penance. One of the sharpest dividing lines between the
confessions lies there. Calvinism imagined that a man's final fate was
fixed from eternity. God predestined, before the foundations of the world
were laid, some for blessedness and others for perdition, and the decree
was absolute. Catholicism left the dread question open, and if it argued
for God's foreknowledge, it did not accept His predestination: man
himself was responsible for what was to befall him. He could, above all,
re-instate himself in grace by a good confession and due sorrow for sin,
by contrition or even by attrition. The consequence was, and still is,
that the Catholic tends to swing to and fro between two poles: oppression
by the sense of sin and a feeling of liberation from guilt, between a dark
mood and a light one, depression and joy, Lent and Easter. This alterna-
tion is strongly stimulating for art. It is as strengthening for emotional
life as physical exercise is for the body and its muscular equipment. Its

one phase can inspire a humble *Kyrie*, its other an exultant *Credo*, as in Beethoven's *Missa Solemnis*. Its one phase can also inspire a serious symphony like Beethoven's third or fifth, the other a jolly and joyful one like his fourth, sixth, seventh and eighth. Calvinism tended to fix man between the extremes, a little left of centre towards the pole of depression, the sense of sin, and thereby it further reduced the urge towards artistic creation, making it even more difficult to develop those symbolisms which are religion's most effective mode of expression.

We shall do well, at this point, to remember a passage from Heiler's *Der Katholizismus* which we have quoted already in volume IV:[1] Catholics, the great Lutheran scholar writes there, are, so long as they truly adhere to their religion, 'in the last resort Platonists. They see in the phenomenal world imperfect mirrorings of perfect divine originals.' This is true, and it explains why and how the Catholic countries could become the chief homes of art. Just as there is a Protestant ethic averse to aesthetics which has (*pace* Max Weber) inspired the spirit of capitalism, i.e. released economic productivity, so there is a Catholic ethic akin to aesthetics, and it has created a taste, a longing, for beauty and released artistic productivity. The Platonism of which Heiler speaks is, somewhat playfully, reflected in one of Petrarca's sonnets written under the impact of Simone Memmi's portrait of his beloved Laura:

> The painter must have been in paradise
> From whence this noble lady has descended.
> He saw her there, and what he apprehended,
> His earthly art reveals to our eyes.[2]

But the greatest representative of this religious philosophy of art was Michelangelo. The well-known story which Condivi tells of him[3] shows how deeply he could, not only feel, but even think about Christianity. The *Pietà* is the work which is involved. This is what Condivi writes: 'This figure of our Lady, which is seated on the stone where the cross was set up, with her Son dead in her lap, is of so great and so rare a beauty, that no one sees it who is not thereby moved to pity; an image truly worthy of that humanity, which is proper to the Son of God, and to such a mother: nevertheless, there are some who censure the figure of the Virgin as being too young in comparison to that of her Son. One day as I was discoursing of this with Michelagnolo, he replied to me, "Do you not know that chaste women maintain their freshness much longer than those who are not chaste? How much more so would this be in a virgin, into whom never entered the least lascivious desire,

---

[1] Cf. p. 105.
[2] The sonnet is usually numbered LXXVII. Cf. *Le Rime di Francesco Petrarca*, edd. Carducci, G., and Ferrari, S., Firenze 1937, pp. 120 and 121. My translation.
[3] Cf. Condivi, A., *The Life of Michelagnolo Buonarotti* (1553), transl. Horne, H. P., Boston 1904, pp. 19 and 20.

that might work change in her body? Aye, and I would tell you, it is, moreover, credible that this freshness and flower of youth, besides being maintained in her by such natural means, were fostered by the work of God, in order to give proof to the world of the virginity and perpetual purity of that mother. But this was not necessary in the Son: indeed, rather the contrary: inasmuch as, in order to show that the Son might verily take on, as he took, a human body, and be subjected to all that an ordinary man undergoes, excepting sin, there was no occasion to restrain what was human in him, by what was divine, but rather to leave it in its course and order, so that time might show exactly how many years he had lived. Therefore you need not marvel if, out of that regard, I made the most holy Virgin and Mother of God seem, in comparison to her Son, much younger than women of that age ordinarily appear to be; whilst I left the Son in his own proper age" . . .'

John Addington Symonds has, in his classical *Life of Michelangelo Buonarotti*, called the great genius 'a soul which has recognized deity made manifest in one of its main attributes, beauty',[1] and the sonnets bear him out. To quote but one:

> Nor hath God deigned to show Himself elsewhere
> More clearly than in human forms sublime,
> Which, since they image Him, alone I love.[2]

It is a comment on passages such as this when Symonds writes: 'It was not . . . to this or that young man, to this or that woman, that Michelangelo paid homage, but to the eternal beauty revealed in the mortal image of divinity before his eyes . . . In the very large number of his [poetic] compositions which are devoted to love, this one idea predominates: that physical beauty is a direct beam sent from the eternal source of all reality, in order to elevate the lover's soul and lead him on the upward path toward heaven. Carnal passion he regards with the aversion of an aesthetic.'[3]

The last sentence must be stressed because the truly religious nature of a predominantly aesthetic culture has to be established. Calvinism has ever found it difficult clearly to distinguish between aestheticism and eroticism. Michelangelo makes this distinction with all desirable energy.

> The love of that whereof I speak ascends:
> Woman is different far; the love of her
> But ill befits a heart manly and wise.

[1] Ed. New York, n.d., p. 411.
[2] Ibid., p. 404. Symonds quotes his own translations which we are using because they are excellent. Cf. *The Sonnets of Michael* [sic] *Angelo Buonarotti*, ed. New York 1948, pp. 44, 41, 63.
[3] Ibid., pp. 410 and 411.

> The one love soars, the other earthward tends;
> The soul lights this, while that the senses stir;
> And still lust's arrow at base quarry flies.[1]

Such 'base quarry' Michelangelo rejects like any Puritan:

> Sense is not love, but lawlessness accurst:
> This kills the soul . . .
> Nay, things that die cannot assuage the thirst
> Of souls undying; nor Eternity
> Serves time, when all must fade that flourisheth.

But the possibility that the love of beauty may become affixed to comparatively worthless things instead of soaring towards the Value of Values does not mean that love and beauty cannot help us in our religious quest.

> Love is not always harsh and deadly sin
> When love for boundless beauty makes us pine;
> The heart by love left soft and infantine,
> Will let the shafts of God's grace enter in.[2]

These last words bare the core of Michelangelo's creed. He sums it up in seven tremendous words:

> Beauty alone lifts man to heaven's spheres.[3]

Beauty alone . . . This, surely, is exaggeration. Not only Calvinists, but all believers must protest. In the Catholic camp, no less a saint, no less a protagonist of divine love than St. Bernard of Clairvaux did protest against such sentiments as we shall soon see.[4] A onesided aestheticism, however exalted, however religious, is no less objectionable than any other onesidedness. Yet the fact remains that the path of beauty is one of the broad avenues, if not indeed the broadest, by which we can approach the Summit of Perfection, and Michelangelo was justified to walk it and to invite others to it. By doing so, he revealed himself to be a true Catholic. Perhaps we should in this matter, as in so many others, give the last word to Thomas Aquinas, as ever sober and sane as well as saintly. He wished to see art in churches, for it was serviceable there *ad quamdam significationem* – 'for the purpose of signification', as the translators have it, perhaps better: for a reference beyond itself (to higher things); and *ut per hujusmodi imagines mentibus hominum imprimatur et confidetur fides* – 'in order that belief . . . may be impressed and confirmed in the mind of man'.[5]

---

[1] Ibid., p. 406.   [2] Ibid., pp. 415, 416, 405.
[3] Ibid., p. 406.   [4] Cf. below, pp. 156 et seq.
[5] *Summa Theologica*, IIa, IIae, qu. 94, art. 2 ad 1. Cf. *The 'Summa Theologica'*, as quoted, vol. XI, London 1922, p. 184.

It is a far cry indeed from the form-finding art of Michelangelo and his age to the form-bursting experimentation of the twentieth-century surrealists, yet much of the old impetus and insight has survived. Hugo Ball was one of the founding-fathers of the literary movement known as Dadaism, and his Diaries contain deep musings even on the pictorial arts, especially those efforts which ran parallel to his own. On 8 April 1917, he noted this after attending a lecture on Kandinsky: 'The painter [is] a trustee [*Sachverwalter*] of the *vita contemplativa*. As the herald of a supernatural language of signs, he exerts influence on the imagery of the poets also ... Is the language of signs the true [*eigentliche*] language of paradise?' The idea is formulated in the form of a question, but an affirmative answer is implied. Painting is to Ball, as it was to Michelangelo, as it was to Plato, a speaking of the unspeakable, a bodying forth of truths which are too great and too mysterious to be caught and conveyed by words. Gustav René Hocke, who quotes Ball's *aperçu*, writes in another context of *Die Welt als Labyrinth*: 'Light and colour, line play and music are for the "Mannerists" of Europe, as for Plato, ... the media for [the expression of] the vital rhythms of an Absolute which cannot be ontologically described, but which can be ontologically experienced – for [the expression of] that "Idea" which remains the idea of God or of the divine, i.e. the primal mystery, even if it is "secularized".'[1] Because this is profoundly true, it was possible for one of the great surrealists, Salvador Dali, to change back to an art like that of Michelangelo, to achieve (in his own words)[2] a 'reactualization of the Catholic tradition', to paint his *Sacrament of the Last Supper* which is now one of the most splendid exhibits in the modern collection of the National Gallery of Art in Washington. Like Bernini's two rows of columns in front of St. Peter's, which Dali sees as symbolical arms stretching out to embrace all humanity, this deeply religious painting opens up towards the spectators standing before it, as if it wanted to draw them, and all men, into the Eucharistic feast.

We cannot, unfortunately, do much more for the further elucidation of this topic, even though it is central to the subject-matter of this volume, religious culture.[3] To complete our argument as best we may within the narrow – alas, all too narrow! – confines of this book, we propose to take a bird's eye view of the history of music which will bring out some of the sociologically most relevant features, and then append a short discussion of painting in order to show that the same, or parallel, principles obtain in the pictorial art also.

[1] Cf. loc. cit., pp. 54 and 139; cf. also p. 177 (Jacques Maritain's positive judgment of surrealism).
[2] Cf. *The Secret Life of Salvador Dali*, New York 1942, p. 395.
[3] We can only give a marginal mention to Hans Urs von Balthasar's great work, *Herrlichkeit: Eine theologische Ästhetik*, Einsiedeln 1961–67 (eight volumes with approximately four thousand pages). The author wishes to add to the theologies developed *sub apecstu veri* and *sub aspectu boni*, a pendant developed *sub aspectu pulchri*.

Why liturgical music should have arisen in the first place, cannot possibly be a puzzle to anybody. Even if we set aside the theories going back to Vico that singing historically preceded ordinary speech and is in a manner more natural than speech, it is true that the two are at least coeval, co-ordinated and equally natural. It all depends on our mood. When it is even, when we go about our humdrum everyday duties, we shall but speak; but when our spirits rise, we shall spontaneously heighten our voices and ultimately break into song (unless, of course, the culture around us discourages us, as Calvinism did in its early days). Religious life, however, is a particularly intense life, and for this reason alone it will have the tendency to foster that intensified use of our vocal cords which we call singing. How do Christians feel on Easter morning? Gerard Manley Hopkins has caught their spirit to admiration:

> Beauty now for ashes wear,
> Perfumes for the garb of woe;
> Chaplets for dishevelled hair,
> Dances for sad footsteps slow.
> Open wide your hearts that they
> Let in joy this Easter Day.
>
> Seek God's house in happy throng;
> Crowded let His table be;
> Mingle praises, prayer and song,
> Singing to the Trinity.
> Henceforth let your souls alway
> Make each morn an Easter Day.[1]

Who would not sing if such sentiments fill him? And so long as Christianity is alive, they will fill every Christian heart. Even the Requiem Mass will be no different. For is earthly death not, to the man in a state of grace, a resurrection of a kind, a new birth to life everlasting?

Emile Durkheim has taught us sociologists that the sacred and the secular are essentially divorced, nay contrasted – contrasted like the work day and the Sunday. We need not fall for his sociologism according to which the difference – if not the only difference, then at least the salient difference – lies in the dispersed nature of ordinary life and the foregathering at the hour of worship; we are free to give due weight to other factors, especially the religious factor properly so called, also. The fact remains that the secular sphere is the sphere of drabness, of *grisaille*, while the sacred sphere is that of colour, of solemnity, of excitement.

[1] We have quoted the last two stanzas; cf. Lahey, G. F., *Gerard Manley Hopkins*, London 1930, p. 27.

If that is so, then there will be a tendency to distinguish the language of the one from the language of the other. This may happen in different degrees of intensity. Church language may simply be differently pronounced ordinary language as in the Puritan's pulpit tone; it may be an archaic language as in the Anglican churches; it may be a classical language as Latin was down the centuries in Catholicism. But the main discrimination will be the setting of the words to music. Discussing the *Agnus Dei* of a rather early Mass, Thrasybulos Georgiades writes: 'This text is not being enunciated in the natural tone of voice. Varying vocal levels are being used. From the point of view of everyday speech, this intonation has something unreal about it. But everyday speech would not be proper, for the action is not an everyday action which serves utilitarian purposes. Hence even the word is here not a mere means of communication. By connecting it with musical sound, another aspect of it, the sacred aspect, is given expression.'[1] This explanation applies, as it stands, only to one concrete sentence in one concrete Mass; but it is fully applicable to all liturgical music and, indeed, a good key to the understanding of its development. 'The tendency towards a combination of speech and music,' Georgiades also writes, 'is present already in the primitive Christian liturgy. The linguistic form is prose, but there is a need to speak in a cultic manner, a need for a communal language of sacredness. The word must sound. For a community, the word exists only as something that sounds ... but as a sacral word it cannot sound like ordinary language, like subjective speech. It demands a musically fixed intonation.'[2] Thus liturgical music arises not only from the heightened mood of the religiously hallowed time, but also from the fact of communal worship. Strongly collectivistic churches, like the Catholic, will therefore have a particularly strongly developed bent for the development of ecclesiastical music.

The words of Georgiades which we have quoted not only introduce us to an understanding of the origin of religious song and sound, they reveal also, if we interpret them aright, its problematic and its evolution, which was an attempt to conquer that problematic. Two tasks were before the community: to reconcile word and music, and to reconcile mood and action – liturgical action must proceed and be accomplished in a reasonable time, while moods would linger and abide. The first synthesis was sought and achieved before and by Palestrina; the second in and after him.

What the liturgy needed was the imparting of a musical character to language and a concomitant imparting of a linguistic character to music[3] – in simple words, a balance between the two. But such a balance is not easy to secure. We cannot go here into the technical ques-

[1] Georgiades, Thr., *Musik und Sprache*, Berlin, Göttingen, Heidelberg 1954, p. 11. Cf. also p. 9. Our translation.
[2] Ibid., p. 7.   [3] Cf. ibid., p. 30.

tions involved, the use and the abuse of *cantus firmus*, etc. Suffice it to say that at the end of the Middle Ages, the musical element had, so to speak, got out of hand. The often secular melodies used were no longer in keeping with the sacred words which they were supposed to heighten. Profane music had entered into the religious world, with deplorable results.[1] It was the great genius Giovanni Pierluigi, called after his birthplace Palestrina, who set matters right. He caught, if we may so express it, the runaway horse and got it again to accept the harness: in his masses, music and language run harmoniously side by side. In Georgiades' words, he made music into a mirror of language. He was 'able to combine sounds, so to order them, so to set them into motion, that immanent musical development and spoken sentence totally coincide'.[2] So great was the feat, and so splendid the performance of it, that Palestrina has in a sense become *the* Catholic church musician as Aristotle was once *the* Philosopher.

In a sense, but in what sense? What about the other Catholic composers whose name is legion? What about Mozart and Haydn, Gounod and Bruckner, what about Bach's Mass in B minor and Beethoven's 'Solemnis' in D? Is Palestrina not dwarfed by the tremendous quantity and quality of his successors? Was it not simply a whim of the Church authorities to set him up as a model and an injustice to the others not to give them the same place? Was this not a flagrant case of reprehensible interference, on the part of authority, in what is, and must be, a free activity?

The fact of the matter is that the post-Palestrinian composers did not provide what he provided – a setting of the liturgical text which could be used – comfortably used, one might say – on a Sunday morning. What they did provide was something very different, namely, an exploration, in the medium of sound, of the intellectual, spiritual and emotional contents of the Mass and its component parts. Every sentence of the *Gloria* and the *Credo*, for instance, has a different tone in meaning and feeling and suggests, and can be represented in, a different musical shape. Sometimes it is the glory and the power of the Father that must be extolled, sometimes the love and mercy of the Son. Sometimes, indeed, the power and the sternness of the Son, as in the words: *el iterum venturus est judicare vivos et mortuos*. Once the religious and refined mind begins to ponder and to penetrate a text so pregnant in significance as the Mass, it will discover innumerable inflections in both idea and emotion, and a highly complex musical picture will be the end result.

But this will no longer be easily co-ordinated with the needs of a cultic action which has to proceed at a steady pace, to show itself to be a unit, and which must be over in half an hour or so since men cannot (as many observers have felt – St. Ignatius Loyola among them) concentrate

[1] Cf. ibid., pp. 39 and 40.
[2] Ibid., pp. 48 and 45; also p. 47 and especially p. 44.

on the business of prayer for much more than that space of time. Unlike Palestrina (and those akin to him, like Tomas Luis de Vittoria or Victoria), the later composers have the habit of breaking the various parts of the Mass up into sentences or even smaller sections, and this is both right and unavoidable if every nook and cranny, as it were, of the structure is to be explored. Beethoven, for instance, takes the statement of the Creed, *et incarnatus est de spiritu sancto ex Maria Virgine, et homo factus est*, and cuts it in two. He distinguishes sharply between the words which circle around the mystery of the God-Man and the words which announce a definite this-worldly and historical event.[1] The result is both artistically and religiously (there is hardly any distinction between the two aspects), tremendous, but the liturgical action is left far behind. Mozart loves to embroider the words *et homo factus est*, because he feels we should linger over them, but the liturgical practice of his day simply prescribed a rapid genuflection, over as soon as it has arrived. The truth is that the Mass music of the great composers is much more akin to religious meditation than to cultic action and therefore these twain have remained and must remain separated. Beethoven's *Missa Solemnis* is simply too much for parish use. Mozart, Haydn and Schubert have written masses intended for use, as is Stravinsky's in more recent times, but they all are meditative and explorative rather than action-centred and action-supporting, and have therefore met with but occasional performance in actual Sunday services.

In view of what we have said, the Motu Proprio of Pope Pius X (in 1903) on sacred music which ordains that the organ must not drown the singing, that long preludes or interludes are to be avoided, that *Kyrie*, *Gloria* and *Credo* are not to be divided into separate movements, etc., is therefore entirely understandable and justified. Yet it must not be thought that the religious value of the type of musical Mass not easily usable in ordinary worship was thereby denied or meant to be diminished. Church music is of two kinds. In the narrower sense it is Mass-action-music, if we may so call it, like that of Palestrina or Victoria; in the wider sense, it is Mass-exploration-music, music of meditation, and, above all, music of education. Any and every hearing of the Bach Mass in B minor or the Beethoven Mass in D leaves the hearer more understanding of the meaning of the Mass in general, the meaning hidden behind the words; and if he hears the words again, be they carried by melodies *à la* Palestrina or be they unaccompanied as in 'Low Mass', they will strike a deeper chord in him than before. We have pointed out in vol. III[1] that the more subjective piety which came with the Jesuits was made, out of a spirit of synthesis, to merge with the more objective forms which had been inherited, that new wine was added to the contents (already rich) of the old bottles. We have something very

[1] Cf. Georgiades, p. 101.
[2] Cf. esp. p. 381.

similar here. Palestrina and Bach or Beethoven may be different because they fulfil different functions; but they fulfil different functions
within the same organism. It is only a slight exaggeration to say that
Bach and Beethoven and all the others have added a new depth dimension to Palestrina, as Palestrina himself did to the words of the liturgy.

In the case of painting, there was no practical, no, so to speak, operational, interest which would single out one particular style as a (limited)
standard, and so no standard in the hard and fast sense of the word has
ever emerged. (Only certain lapses from taste, such as the symbolizing
of the Holy Trinity as a three-headed man, have been censured.) But if
it is true, as we have asserted all along, that Catholicism has an inherent
tendency towards synthesis because it is the surviving product of the
ages of community, because it is in its abiding sociological essence
community, then we must assume that in this art, too, something like
an ideal summarizer must have emerged. And this is in fact so. Sometimes Giotto is singled out as the man who came closest to this position,
sometimes Fra Angelico whose style can be characterized as a *Neo-
Giottismo*.[1] Glib statements to this effect are over-simplifications which
must be received with appropriate caution. There is no total synthesis,
even in the greatest. But there is a tendency towards synthesis, and this
needs stressing.

Before even possible synthesis, there is antithesis, and the terms of
the antithesis are found respectively in the Florentine and Sienese
schools of painting. 'The Florentines clearly anticipated what was to be
the most typical characteristic of the Renaissance: rationalism, self-
control, the struggle of reason against feeling, even at the risk of . . .
giving rise to an intellectualism which in the end largely discredited itself . . . [Their] object was to reduce the multiplicity of appearances to
their ideal principles. The Sienese, on the other hand, worshipped God
in the very multiplicity of phenomena . . . In every object and living
thing they recognized a value, rightfully conferred on it by the very fact
of its existence, and they made no distinctions of hierarchy, between
individual and individual, object and object.' The art historian Eugenio
Battisti, to whom we owe this remarkable analysis, adds that the Sienese style 'may be defined as candidly Franciscan', whereas that of
Florence, with its evidence of rationality such as abstractionism and
geometricism, was much rather Dominican.[2]

We have, in what has gone before, the terms of the great antithesis
clearly before us, and we are setting them out in the form of a table
which will be useful for the sociology of knowledge:

[1] Cf. Argan, G. C., *Fra Angelico*, transl. Emmons, J., Geneva(?) 1955, pp. 25, 27,
also 26. Reporting on the deep studies of Luigi Lanzi, Argan says: 'Giotto seemed to
him an incarnation of Thomist thought', and Angelico 'a return to the fundamentals of a vital religious art such as . . . found . . . in Giotto'.

[2] Cf. Battisti, E., *Giotto*, transl. Emmons, J., Geneva(?) 1960, p. 26; cf. also pp. 31–
35, 36, 106.

Florence	*Siena*
Dominicanism	Franciscanism
Rationalism	Emotionalism
Hierarchical Structuring	Co-ordination
Unity	Multiplicity

While the Florentine style appealed more to a relatively upper stratum of the bourgeoisie, the Sienese art addressed all classes of society,[1] and especially the lowest, as it was right and meet for a Franciscan-inspired effort.

Giotto was a 'Florentine' rather than a 'Sienese', while Duccio was a 'Sienese' rather than a 'Florentine'. But – and this is decisive – neither are they far apart to start with, nor do they strive for anything but a close approach to each other. There was more than accident, there was symbolical meaning to the fact that the masterpieces of both, Giotto's great *Crucifix* and Duccio's *Madonna Enthroned* were under the same roof in Florence's Santa Maria Novella. 'Duccio was a few years older than Giotto . . . In his hands the sacred figures of the past were humanized . . . In Giotto, the process was reversed. With him, the human was deified . . .' Therefore, 'the contrast which undoubtedly existed between Florentines and Sienese must not be pressed too far . . . The truth is that in many ways the Sienese school developed under the influence of Giotto and his followers. Some of the Sienese masters, the Lorenzetti, for instance, and even Duccio in his "Virgin and Child" at Badia ad Isola, often come very close to Giotto.'[2] In this sense, then, and with these provisos, Giotto does emerge as the great creator of synthesis and hence as a supreme incarnation of the dominant communitarian and Catholic cultural tendency, the tendency towards integration: 'The great problem he set himself to solve in his paintings,' writes Battisti, on his last page,[3] was 'that of reconciling mind and matter, sacred and profane, idea and action, geometrical structure and nature'. And this it was which raised him to the pinnacle: 'It must be acknowledged that he worked out pictorial solutions which for centuries set the standard of Western art whose visual categories he virtually created.'

I hope I am not unduly bold in saying that Giotto was the Palestrina of painting, as Palestrina was the Giotto of music. The reader who has followed the text will know what is meant. He who reconciles words and music reconciles rationalism (for the word is always relatively rational) and emotionalism (for music is always relatively emotional); he is therefore like the painter who unites a Dominican with a Franciscan ingredient. But, to press the analogy, painting must also have had its explorers-in-depth, its Bachs and Beethovens, its Mozarts and Haydns, as music did. To demonstrate that exploration in depth

[1] Ibid., p. 26.　　[2] Ibid., pp. 34, 26, 27.　　[3] p. 30.

went on in every age, we can only pick one strand in a broad and rich texture and give it a passing glance: the representation of Christ in the visual arts.

To compress the subject, however painful that may be, we can say in a summary fashion that four avenues or aspects were investigated. To the first Christians, Jesus is above all the Good Shepherd; then, in response particularly to Byzantine moods, He is transformed into the dread Pantocrator, the Eternal Judge, looking down sternly from the basilical apses; in the West, He appears at the same time, and deep into the Middle Ages, as the conquering hero, the victor over pain and death; but concomitantly there forms the image which has, for a good reason, remained predominant ever since, the image of the Man of Sorrows, the Christ of the Passion, not to say the Passionist Christ. Christ is all these and more. The later representations do not cancel the earlier. The Good Shepherd is also the Judge of the World, and Judge of the World is also the broken and mangled body on the Cross. We may use here a technical term which Max Scheler has contributed to the sociology of knowledge: the term 'aspectual truth'.[1] Each artistic style takes one limited feature and displays it, opening our minds to it. It is only together that they lead us a little closer to the *Tremendum Mysterium* of One who was both God and man. Thus synthesis is once again seen to be laid on in antithesis, unity in multiplicity; Truth itself is found in aspectual truths.

The image of the Good Shepherd reflects the period when the Christian community was still turned in upon itself; or, as we could also say, turned towards the essential. The Good Shepherd is He who rescues his sheep, according to St. John's Gospel, x, 7 and 9: 'I am the door of the sheep . . . By me, if any man enter in, he shall be saved.' The symbol, not surprisingly, appears above all in burial places: 129 times in the catacombs, 184 times on sarcophagi, and so on.[2] The latest and greatest of these burial places is the mausoleum of Galla Placidia, half-sister of the Emperor Honorius, at Ravenna. But here Christ is shown in a new light. Still the good shepherd, He is attired in gorgeous robes: His tunic is golden, His mantle purple. He sits on a rock that looks uncommonly like a throne. Before long He is transmuted into the Lord of the Universe, a symbol of power rather than of solicitude. 'The round youthful head becomes oblong, the whole face more manly and firm, the nose powerfully emphasized, the eyes are more deeply embedded and become larger . . . In the end a beard frames chin, lips and cheeks . . . Indeed, in time art takes further steps. After the sixth century some pictures of Christ assume a sombre and menacing character. Like a stern, uncanny old man, the Lord looks at us from the high apsidal

[1] Cf. Stark, W., *The Sociology of Knowledge*, London 1958, pp. 328 et seq. The statement in the text is based on the whole of chapter 8.
[2] Cf. Preuss, H., *Das Bild Christi im Wandel der Zeiten*, Leipzig 1932, p. 6.

vaults and impresses us today almost like a misrepresentation.'[1] Byzantinism, with its ruler deification,[2] could hardly present Christ differently. If already the emperor was a divinity, how else could they depict Him who was the Emperor's Emperor? The West, as we have shown earlier on, thought differently,[3] yet there, too, the conceptions of the upper classes dominated both taste and artistic effort for a long time. The Carolingian and Ottonian periods love to present, not the suffering and dying, but the conquering and commanding Saviour. Often He wears the crown, even on the cross. Indeed, there are crucifixes which show Him alive, standing upright on the footrest, weary perhaps, but not suffering. 'The whole breathes mildness, but it is the mildness of majesty.'[4]

Underneath these imperial and aristocratic representations, there must always have been a different image, the image of the suffering Christ, the Christ of the poor, even if it was not carved in stone or painted on canvas. It is present, in Giotto's art, alongside the older and more upper-class conceptions, and so we see again that the great Giotto is indeed the man of synthesis. 'This master,' writes Hans Preuss, 'has created, in his magnificent cycle of frescoes in the Arena Chapel at Padua, a type of Christ which still fills us with admiration even today ... This Christ arouses compassion and indeed terror, and yet He gives at the same time consolation drawn from a divine plenitude of power ... Here is One who reminds us of our sin and who can yet help us to stand erect. It has been said with justice that Giotto has come as close to a clarification of the very concept of Christ as it is possible for the pictorial arts.'[5] Preuss allows only one associate for Giotto: Fra Angelico of Fiesole.[6] We may, somewhat poetically, sum up their achievement by saying that to the normal eye a royal crown and a crown of thorns are two different objects. But Giotto and Angelico know how to merge them, how to make them look like one thing – a crown of glory.

After Giotto and Angelico, there is less synthesis, but more exploration, with the ideal of synthesis always both behind and before the artists. The crown of thorns is, on the whole, more in evidence than the royal crown. Grünewald, Dürer, Holbein, Rembrandt, Velasquez and many, many others show us the Man of Sorrows, not the Ruler of the Universe. Guido Reni's *Ecce Homo*, widely distributed in different techniques of reproduction (often, alas! very bad ones), became something like a must for many believing households. Even the nineteenth and the twentieth centuries prefer this aspect which has a special appeal to the 'sorrowful and heavily laden' – a proof of the fact that Christianity and Catholicism are still essentially the religion of the poor. What

[1] Ibid.   [2] Cf. our vol. I, pp. 35 et seq.
[3] Ibid., p. 37, and vol. III, p. 54.   [4] Preuss, loc. cit., pp. 8 and 42.
[5] Ibid., p. 8.   [6] Ibid., p. 9.

has happened, in contrast to earlier centuries, is merely – in response to the individualism of modern society – that a loss of stylistic unity has taken place. At an exhibition, in 1898, of contemporary paintings of Christ, depth of feeling was indeed encountered, but a common conception was seen to be absent. There was still contemplation, meditation and exploration, but every artist went his own way.[1]

We are stressing this difference, which illustrates the close connection between social substructure and artistic superstructure, but we must urge that its importance be not unduly exaggerated. For not only the *history* of art is a step-for-step exploration and revelation of religious mystery. The art of *every* age is the same: the modern period has merely increased the degree of diversity, increased it strongly, some would say painfully, but *some* diversity has, of course, always existed. Just as successive generations of painters differ in presenting different aspects of the *one* sacred archetype, so do the members of the same generation, those who stand side by side. We shall try to exemplify this fact by a short glance at the late sixteenth century, the period when Christianity, and more especially Catholicism, endeavoured to regain its balance after the earthquake of the Reformation.

Two men, so E. H. Gombrich tells us in *The Story of Art*,[2] represent the main currents in painting at this juncture, Annibale Carracci (who died in 1609) and Michelangelo de Caravaggio (who died in 1610). Carracci was deeply in love with Raphael and Perugino, Correggio and Parmigianino, the gentle painters, if we may call them so. 'The battle-cry of his party among the cliques of Rome was the cultivation of classical beauty.' Even his altar-painting of *The Virgin mourning Christ*, now in the National Museum at Naples, eschews both the horrors of death and the agonies of pain. It shows us instead the repose of Christ after the *consummatum est* and the dignity of Mary, the Mother of Sorrows. Among his disciples, Guido Reni stands out as a true heir of his style. If we accept his ideal, Gombrich tells us, we may well 'admire the way in which Reni carried out his programme of beauty, how he deliberately discarded anything in nature that he considered low and ugly or unsuitable for his lofty ideas, and how his quest for forms more perfect and more ideal than reality were rewarded with success'.[3] Here we have an art idealistic and idealizing, an art that raises its eyes (and our hearts) to heaven, an art that thinks little of the accidental and ephemeral and much of the essential and eternal.

It was different with Caravaggio and his school, for he and they were, by comparison at least, realists. 'To be afraid of ugliness seemed to Caravaggio a contemptible weakness. What he wanted was truth. Truth as he saw it. He had no liking for classical models, nor any respect for "ideal beauty" ... He was one of the great artists like Giotto [or Grüne-wald] and Dürer before him, who wanted to see the holy events before

[1] Ibid., p. 17.   [2] Ed. London 1956, pp. 290 et seq.   [3] Ibid., pp. 291, 293, 294.

his own eyes as if they had been happening in his neighbour's house. And he did everything possible to make the figures of the ancient texts look more real and tangible.' If this meant showing the Apostles, for instance, not as dignified old men, but as 'common labourers with weathered faces and wrinkled brows', Caravaggio and his followers, who included above all the great Spaniards, for instance Ribera and Zurbaran, were unconcerned.[1] Had God not become man for the sake of common labourers? Had He not Himself accepted the ugliness of the flesh? 'Christ had preached to the poor, the hungry and the sad, and poverty, hunger and tears are not beautiful.'[2] If Carracci and his group based themselves on Psalm XLIV, 3: 'Thou art beautiful above the sons of men,' Caravaggio and the Caravaggeschi pointed to the passage on the man of sorrows in Isaias LIII, 2 and 3: 'His [true] look was as it were hidden . . . There is no beauty in him . . .'. Even St. Alphonso of Liguori felt like these men.[3]

The difference between the two schools is truly striking. It came to a head through Caravaggio's great canvas, *The Death of the Virgin*, now in the Louvre, but originally painted for Santa Maria della Scala, the church of the Discalced Carmelites in the Roman suburb of Trastevere. The good fathers were scandalized and got rid of the picture. 'Ecclesiastical circles accused Caravaggio of having made the Virgin a commonplace type of woman. Some claimed that he had modelled her on a swollen corpse fished out of the Tiber.' The accusation was unjust, for the name of the model is known; she was 'a poor but respectable woman'.[4] Yet it is understandable that some were shocked – some who surely included part at least of the working-class population of Trastevere. An aristocratic Madonna like Carracci's, or like Parmigianino's *Madonna with the Long Neck*,[5] with a graceful figure, a gentle bearing, long fingers and tiny feet, has an attractiveness all her own, and, as experience proves, particularly for those condemned to live in a world of crudeness and coarseness and dismal depression.

The contrast in depicting Christ's Mother is also noticeable in the depicting of Christ Himself, as a look at Caravaggio's *Deposizione* can teach,[6] though here the difference between the two schools seems somewhat attenuated. In comparing and evaluating the divergent traditions, Gombrich confesses to a certain predilection for what Huysmans has finely called 'mystical realism',[7] and this preference is based

[1] Ibid., pp. 291 and 292. Cf. also p. 306 *re* Velasquez. Cf. further Lassaigne, J. *Spanish Painting*, Geneva 1952, esp. pp. 24 and 26.
[2] Gombrich, loc. cit., p. 318.
[3] Cf. The Sixth Station of his 'Way of the Cross'.
[4] Bazin, G., *The Louvre*, ed. London 1959, p. 174.
[5] Gombrich, loc. cit., p. 268, illustration 226.
[6] Cf. e.g. *Caravaggio*, in the series *Maestri del Colore*, Bergamo 1958, plate X. The work is in the Vatican.
[7] *The Cathedral*, as quoted, p. 260.

on religious rather than on artistic considerations: 'Caravaggio's "naturalism",' he says, 'was perhaps more devout than Carracci's emphasis on beauty.'[1] The judgment is understandable. Many of us will value the strong colours of Caravaggio more than the subtle ones of Carracci.[2] Yet to rank the one decidedly above the other would be tantamount to praising the upper blade of a pair of scissors to the detriment of the lower, or the higher millstone to the detriment of the nether. These dissimilar artists need each other as the two terms of an antithesis do, if they are to lead to a synthesis. Just as Christ is not only the mighty Pantocrator of the Byzantines and the conquering hero of the Lombards and Goths, but also the Good Shepherd of the early and the humble sufferer of the later Christians, so He is both Carracci's heavenly apparition and Caravaggio's earthly figure of flesh and bone. Behind Carracci and his school there arises here, in the distance, the memory of those who, like the Eutychians, could see the God-Man only as God, and behind Caravaggio and his disciples the memory of those who, like the Nestorians, could see Him only as man. But Christ, as the creed insists so strongly, is for the Christian both God and man. The striving of the artists, like that of the theologians, must ever be for a *complexio oppositorum*. None has fully achieved it, though the most gifted and most inspired, a Giotto and a Beato Angelico, a Murillo perhaps, or a Velasquez,[3] have come close to it. But in this endeavour as in all others – notably in theology – to arrive is little, to be on the way is all. Men cannot reach the absolute. To stretch towards it, be it in thought, be it in art, be it in prayer, is the best effort that can be theirs.

EXCURSUS: THE CALVINIST ATTITUDE TO SYMBOLISM AND ART

All that has gone before conspires to show that a symbolistic and aestheticizing element is built deeply into the foundations of the Catholic culture. But perhaps no specious proof is needed: any visit to a typical Catholic country, be it Italy or Spain or Austria or France, will be a sufficient *ad oculos demonstratio* of the fact. It must not be thought, however, that this tendency, strong as it appears to be, was ever unopposed. All art bears within itself a little trace of playfulness, and those whose mind is, in matters religious, attuned to earnestness, to rigorism, are apt to take exception to it. There is a whole history of Puritanism before the Puritans, a history of Catholic Puritanism, and, to balance the picture, we must look at some of its heights and highlights.

[1] Gombrich, loc. cit., p. 292.
[2] Personally, I, too, admit a special liking for Caravaggio and the Spaniards, more particularly Zurbaran (my favourite painter), but it would be nothing short of narrowmindedness to remain blind to the excellencies of a Correggio, Carracci, or Reni, not to speak of Perugino and Raphael.
[3] Cf. Lassaigne, loc. cit., pp. 43 and 59.

The origins of this counter-tendency, not to say counter-cultural tendency, are lost in the darkness of the first ages. 'Though the ceremonious tradition of Catholic worship . . . goes back uninterruptedly to the fourth century and can be shown to have a fair half or more of its roots in the third and second and even in the New Testament itself,' writes Gregory Dix, 'I do not know that it is fair to call it outright an older tradition of Christian worship than its Puritan rival. The monks and hermits of the fourth century were Catholics in doctrine, but many of them had much of the Puritan theory of worship.'[1] No less a figure than the great St. Augustine had misgivings about the symbolistic-aesthetic appeal to ear and eye. He tells us that church music often beguiles him so much that 'physical sense does not attend on reason', i.e. that he pays more heed to the melodies than to the meaning of the words. This, he says, is bad. 'When it happens that I am more moved by the singing than by what is sung, I confess myself to have sinned wickedly, and then I would rather not have heard the singing . . . Sometimes,' Augustine adds, 'I go to the point of wishing that all the melodies of the pleasant songs to which David's Psalter is adapted should be banished both from my ears and from those of the Church itself.' Even Calvin was not to feel quite so strongly. Psalmody at least has survived in the communities that have descended from him.

'The delights of the eye,' too, belong for Augustine to 'the list of the temptations of carnal appetite' which still assail him. 'The eyes delight in fair and varied forms and bright and pleasing colours. Let these not take possession of my soul! . . . I resist the seductions of my eyes lest my feet be entangled as I go forward.' The danger is indeed great, for 'corporeal light . . . seasons the life of the world for her blind lovers with a tempting and fatal sweetness'. The Church authorities are, at least by implication, blamed for their aestheticism, for 'such things as pictures and statuary' exist 'beyond the necessary and moderate use of them or their significance for the life of piety'.[2]

Some four centuries later, the legitimacy of the use of art in worship became the subject of a public controversy. Bishop Claudius of Turin showed himself, in his *Apologeticum adversus Theutmirum Abbatem*, to be a true iconoclast and had to be severely reprimanded, on behalf of the majority, by Dungal of Saint-Denis in his *Responsa contra Perversas Claudii Sententias*.[3] But the most telling voice – more telling, perhaps, in this context, than even the voice of St. Augustine – was that of St. Bernard of Clairvaux. This is what he writes to William, Abbot of Thierry, with an eye on the artistry and love of art on the part of the Cluniacs: 'I say naught of the vast height of your churches, their

---

[1] Dix, loc. cit., p. 316.
[2] *Confessions* X, 33 and 34. Cf. Augustine, *Confessions and Enchiridion*, transl. Butler, A. C., *The Library of Christian Classics*, vol. VII, Philadelphia 1955, pp. 230-3.
[3] Sauer, loc. cit., p. 277.

immoderate length, their superfluous breadth, the costly polishings, the curious carvings and paintings which attract the worshipper's gaze and hinder his attention, and seem to me in some sort a revival of the ancient Jewish rites. Let this pass, however: say that this is done for God's honour. But ... what profit is there in those ridiculous monsters [seen inside and outside of churches], in that marvellous and deformed comeliness, that comely deformity? To what purpose are those unclean apes, those fierce lions, those monstrous centaurs, those halfmen, those striped tigers, those fighting knights, those hunters winding their horns? Many bodies are there seen under one head, or again, many heads to a single body. Here is a four-footed beast with a serpent's tail; there, a fish with a beast's head. Here again the forepart of a horse trails half a goat behind it, or a horned beast bears the hinder quarters of a horse. In short so many and so marvellous are the varieties of divers shapes on every hand, that we are more tempted to read in the marble than in our books, and to spend the whole day in wondering at these things rather than in meditating the law of God ... What, think you, is the purpose of all this? The compunction of penitents, or the admiration of beholders? O vanity of vanities, yet no more vain than insane!'[1]

Another four hundred years on, we find one more abbot, Rumpler of Formbach, expressing himself in very similar terms.[2] Though a minor figure, his appearance proved, if nothing else, the uninterrupted continuation of Puritan sentiments in the Catholic Church. Even in the nineteenth century, a great prince of the Church like Cardinal Manning had no hesitation in publicly condemning the theatre and all it stood for.[3] By this time, the aesthetic tendency has surely fought its last battle and won its final victory, but the protest against its predominance had not yet been stilled.

What was it that deprived this protest of its power, even though its protagonists included some of the most influential figures in the Church's history? The answer is simple: though the protest was genuine and came from considerable depths, it was not radical, it did not go to the real roots. Augustine and Bernard disliked, nay hated, some of the excrescences of symbolism and aestheticism, but their own thinking was, to say the least, completely symbolistic, and where symbolism is present, aestheticism, too, cannot fail to appear and re-appear, for it is symbolism's spontaneous adjunct and product, not to say its *alter ego*, its twin. Augustine sternly weighed the pros and cons of the use of music in worship; he had his doubts about it; but in the end he came,

[1] Cit. Coulton, C. G., *Life in the Middle Ages*, vol. IV, Cambridge 1930, pp. 172, 174, 173.
[2] Sauer, loc. cit., p. 280; cf. esp. footnote 3.
[3] de la Gorce, A., *Francis Thompson*, transl. Kynaston-Snell, H. F., London 1933, p. 105.

as he tells us, 'to acknowledge the great utility of this custom'. Utility, of course, is a weak word, but it does not stand alone. The Saint recalls, as he sets it down, how deeply he had been moved when he had heard the Church's songs while he stood on her threshold, 'at the outset of my recovered faith'. Music had given him much then, and so he confesses that he is 'inclined to approve of the use of singing in the church, so that by the delights of the ear the weaker minds may be stimulated to a devotional mood'.[1]

Much more interesting than this hesitant approval of music are the Saint's considerations of the pictorial arts, for in them we find, not only a positive attitude to beauty, but even an inkling of that Platonic concept of it which we have encountered, for instance, in Michelangelo,[2] and which is very close to the core of the Catholic culture complex. Augustine gives thanks for the delights of ear and eye though he feels that an undue attention to them may imperil the soul: 'O my God and my Joy, I raise a hymn to thee for all these things, and offer a sacrifice of praise to my Sanctifier, because those beautiful forms which pass through the medium of the human soul into the artist's hands come from that beauty which is above our minds, which my soul sighs for day and night. The craftsmen and devotees of these outward beauties discover the norm by which they judge them from that higher beauty . . . Even if they do not see it, it is there nevertheless . . .'[3] God, then, is in the beautiful things wrought by human hands, as He is in the things that His own hands have wrought. Augustine sees art, as he sees nature, *in lumine Dei*. There is no essential anti-aestheticism in his thought.

It was not so with St. Bernard. He does, indeed, remember the twenty-fifth psalm in this context: 'I have loved, O Lord, the beauty of thy house, and the place where thy glory dwelleth' (verse 9). But its implied injunction to adorn the temple does not take him far towards a positive estimation of art: 'I grant it, then, let us suffer even this to be done in the church; for, though it is harmful to vain . . . folk, yet not so to the simple and devout.'[4] The hard fact remains that the great Cistercian saw little value in earthly beauty. Yet if aestheticism had no hold on him, symbolism did so all the more. Bernard's main literary work was his *Sermones in Cantica Canticorum*. And how else could a man of God handle this book of the Old Testament than in the spirit of allegorical interpretation? Literally understood, even the first sentence would be devoid of spiritual meaning: 'Let him kiss me with the kiss of his mouth, for thy breasts are better than wine.' Indeed, it is not too much to say that the whole poem comes close to love literature, not to say pornographic literature, unless a deeper meaning is discovered underneath its eroticism. Bernard, of course, dug for that meaning and

---

[1] *Confessions and Enchiridion*, as quoted, p. 231.   [2] Cf. above, p. 141.
[3] *Confessions and Enchiridion*, p. 233.   [4] Cit. Coulton, as quoted, p. 174.

brought it out; every page and every paragraph of his work shows that his is the typical medieval-Catholic mind, the mind of a symbol-seeker and symbol-setter. And so even this Puritan before the age of Puritanism[1] is in the final analysis not a Puritan. He may not have fostered art, but he cultivated the spirit from which art takes its rise and draws its strength. Even if there had been more St. Bernards than one, Catholicism would not have been turned away from its deeply laid aesthetic predilections.

The great change came only with the Reformation when the tendencies evinced by Augustine and Bernard and Abbot Rumpler were broken out of the system of checks and balances within which they had been contained and gained the freedom fully to unfold. What in Augustine and Rumpler had been a scruple and in Bernard a worry, became in Calvin a point of his programme, not to say a hate and an obsession. Beauty was heathen and worse. He was prepared to appreciate Seneca. He did not appreciate Praxiteles.

It could hardly be otherwise. For Protestantism in all its forms was a turning away from the older symbolistic world-view and a turning towards the newer realistic one. The change is nowhere more easily and more clearly discernible than at the core. Religious movements which could and did reduce the sacramental element could not be like the Church which had developed and maintained it, and their culture could not be like the culture of that Church. After the weakening of the heart-symbols, a weakening of the outer symbolisms was virtually unavoidable. And in the natural course of events, the outer symbolisms, too, were bound to droop and to drop off, to disappear altogether. Lutheranism was still close to Catholicism; its dogma of consubstantiation was still similar to Rome's faith in transubstantiation; in consequence, Lutheranism still had a friendly attitude to art.[2] Calvinism was already far away from Catholicism; its interpretation of the central sacrament of the Lord's Supper as a mere meal of remembrance was the expression of a new philosophy, of that nominalism which always goes with an all-round hard-headed realism; in consequence Calvinism had a hostile attitude towards art. The religious movements arising yet further to the left felt in much the same way and had (if possible) still greater aversion to man-made beauty. The Quakers knew no sacraments, and they cared nothing about art.

The difference between Lutheranism and Calvinism, so far as symbolicism and art are concerned, consisted, however, not only in the fact that the one Protestant grouping was in its whole attitude nearer to the Middle Ages than the other. The time factor, it is true, played a significant part, but another circumstance was at least as

---

[1] Coulton calls him so, loc. cit., p. 169 (between-title).
[2] Cf. Nettl, P., *Luther and Music*, transl. Wood, F. B., and R., ed. New York 1967, p. 72.

important. Lutheranism, because it was still tied to the past, carried a good deal of ancient art forward, for instance the beautiful hymns which the local German congregations had sung since time immemorial. But this would only have meant conservation; it would not have stimulated creation. What stimulated creation was the appearance of a new cultural centre, not only in the Lutheran areas, but in all caesaropapist countries – the monarch, surrounded as he was by a religious aura, a supernal light. In music, we may think, as an example, of Georg Friedrich Handel's Dettingen *Te Deum*, written after the battle near that township under the aegis, and for the honour, of the victors; in painting, of Holbein's portraits which give us even today a vivid impression of the personalities of Henry VIII's court, and of Henry VIII himself. There are plenty of other illustrations, some remarkable ones (including the château of Versailles) from France which, as we have seen in our first volume, was, before the great Revolution, as close to Caesaropapism as to Catholicism. Indeed, this development of a caesaropapist art, almost a caesaropapist style, influenced the situation even in Calvinist Holland. One reason why the Stadtholder, Prince Frederick Henry, did not support Rembrandt more than in fact he did, was that he felt him to be too far from the monarchical and courtly taste of the day.[1] But the Netherlands are a very special case at which we shall look more closely later on.[2]

What Protestantism, advancing from Luther to Zwingli and from Zwingli to Calvin and beyond, did to art can quickly be gathered from the history of music. Luther was still fond of both its vocal and its instrumental form, and because of his compositions (whose authenticity is, however, a matter of controversy) a place has been claimed for him in the annals of the art. In any case, he wrote, as a young man, an *Encomium Musices*. And he praised music not only because it was beautiful, but also because it was godly. 'The Devil, the source of all unhappiness and worries, flees music as much as he does theology,' he writes to his friend Ludwig Senfl, and in his Table Talk, the same conviction makes its appearance: this 'winsome art' is called 'one of the fairest and most glorious gifts of God, to which Satan is hostile since it drives away temptation and evil thoughts. The Devil does not care for music.'[3]

Can one say more? And yet it is with Luther that a definite involution of music begins. If there are passages which extol it, there are others which condemn it. For instance: 'As in the time of King Manasseh the cries of the burning children were drowned out by music and drums, so now church music drowns out the ruin of souls.'[4] But we must not think that the fate of the art was dependent on Luther's moods. Rather was it dependent on his, and his fellow-Protestants', thought, and this

---

[1] Cf. Gerson, H., *Rembrandt Paintings*, Amsterdam 1968, pp. 46, 161, 122, 124; also p. 90. [2] Cf. below, pp. 170 et seq.
[3] Cit. Nettl, as quoted, pp. 24 and 17. [4] Ibid., p. 99.

was – mainly because of its indwelling rationalism – tied to the texts, tied to the words of the texts. Catholicism had no objection to polyphony, believing as it did, and still does, that you could speak to the soul by sounds; Lutheranism preferred homophony because it doubted that anything could convey religious contents but language. Homophonic 'simplicity . . . which made the text more comprehensible to the listener . . . was particularly suited to express the idea of Protestantism. Luther desired that the believer approach his God personally, and this could [in his opinion] only be accomplished by simplicity of speech and tone.'[1] Thus an inhibition was introduced into the art which could not but lead to its limitation, indeed, involution. But there is an even deeper cause of musical decline laid on in Luther's mind. 'Psalms and music exist to stimulate the fear of the Lord,' he said in his first lecture on the Psalms.[2] But it is not fear that inspires music; it is joy. And a religion which brings little joy, brings little or no music. It is true that the doctrine of free grace and salvation by faith alone had an uplifting element, an element of gladness, in it, and rightly does Paul Nettl insist that Luther's own music-making was connected with, and fed by, it.[3] But we cannot forget his deep pessimism concerning man which comes to the fore in such considered statements as *De Servo Arbitrio*; and neither could he forget it, nor could his followers. The net influence of Lutheranism on music, if we consider, not only such comparatively naïve forms as hymn-singing, but also the more sophisticated creations of polyphony, was therefore, on the whole, negative. Of Johann Sebastian Bach we shall speak later on.[4]

With Zwingli and Calvin the joyful side of religion, as is well known, practically disappeared, and for this reason alone the voices became muted, while orchestras and organs were permanently stilled. Calvin once protested that 'we are nowhere forbidden to laugh, or to be delighted with music, or to drink wine'.[5] But he always insisted that to drink wine was dangerous, and he had the same feeling about any inordinate addiction to music. As for laughter, it was not in line with so serious and severe a view of the world as Calvinism. If there had been more of it in this camp, it would have been different from what we know it to have been. And – let this be said with all emphasis – it would have been smaller than it was. It was precisely the greatness of the Genevan's creed that it reminded man of his abysmal weakness and wickedness and of the overwhelming power and glory of Almighty God. The restriction of music to the minor key (if we may so express it), to mournfulness and melancholy, was therefore a natural concomitant of this theology. Zwingli tells us that music 'was given to man to moderate and

[1] Ibid., p. 86. [2] Ibid., p. 99.
[3] Ibid., pp. 2, 18, 45, 64, 132.
[4] Cf. below, pp. 205 et seq.
[5] Harkness, G., *John Calvin*, New York 1931, p. 27.

soothe savage passions',[1] i.e. that it has a negative function only, and Milton, while recommending the use of it in education, puts the emphasis entirely on 'solemn harmonies' and 'grave descant'.[2]

Huldreich Zwingli had a natural love of music, if ever a man did. Indeed, he almost missed the appointment to Zürich's main pulpit at the *Grossmünster* because of it. "There are some whom your ready talent for music offends,' writes his friend Oswald Myconius on 3 December 1518. His adversaries (who finally acquiesced in his induction) need not have worried. It was none other than the suspect himself who, in 1523, insisted that music be completely prohibited in public worship.[3]

Biographers give as the reason for Zwingli's changed attitude his experience of the plague with which he was mortally sick in the fall of 1519. The sociologist will be more interested in another facet. Zwingli had become an out-and-out individualist. He went so far as to assert that 'worship is corrupted and vitiated by the many'.[4] But if the isolated individual worships, he will, of course, not sing; his prayer will be mute. In contrast to this true prayer, public ceremonies are but a false show, and choir-chant in particular is hypocritical and ostentatious. 'Zwingli will not tolerate even an unaccompanied unison singing in the vernacular by the congregation.'[5] 'Do not bellow the prayer in public as the dumb [cattle] do,' he gruffly says. 'Go and do it in private!'[6] Given such a conviction, the reduction of public worship to predication is virtually unavoidable, and so it makes little difference if a psalm is allowed to be sung, for that singing, too, is only to inculcate the meaning and the words. Music in the proper sense of the word is simply eliminated. The Genevan prophet substantially agreed with his precursor at Zürich. Between them, they shaped a liturgy which was, in substance, verbal. What is surprising in all this is the scant regard paid to the Old Testament and its injunctions to praise God 'on all manner of instruments . . . on harps and lutes and timbrels and cornets and cymbals' (II Kings VI, 5).[7] It did not suit these men, who yet saw themselves as the New Israel, to remember this and similar passages in the Holy Book.

What Zwingli and his followers started in June 1524, they completed

---

[1] Cit. Garside, Ch., *Zwingli and the Arts*, New Haven 1966, p. 74. Cf. *Huldreich Zwinglis Sämtliche Werke*, vol. XIV, Zürich 1959, p. 163.

[2] *Of Education*, cf. *The Works of John Milton*, ed. New York 1931, vol. IV, p. 288.

[3] Garside, loc. cit., pp. 14, 16, 17, 26.

[4] Ibid., p. 43; *Werke*, vol. II, Leipzig 1908, p. 349.

[5] Garside, loc. cit., p. 47. Cf. also pp. 43–6.

[6] Ibid., p. 48. *Werke*, as quoted, vol. II, p. 351. I have amended Garside's otherwise reliable translation. He refers to 'dumb harlots', thinking that *bule* is the standard German *Buhle*. It links, however, with *Bulle* (steer).

[7] Cf. also Paralipomenon I, XIII, 8, and Psalms XCVII, 4 and 5; CXLIX, 3; and especially CL (*in toto*). Cf. further Dix, loc. cit., pp. 330 and 331.

in December 1527. Until then – to quote Charles Garside, whose book, published in 1966, still echoes sixteenth-century convictions – 'the organs, although unused, still remained as visible witness to the musical violations committed by the old Church against the Word of God'.[1] What happened in Zürich, happened elsewhere as well. 'Fanatics in Switzerland stormed the churches and monasteries and destroyed the altar paintings, statues and organs. The famous organist Hans Kotter in Berne was forced to give up his profession and become a schoolmaster.' There started then, in Nettl's words, 'that vacuum in music . . . which countries like Switzerland have never quite overcome'. In another context, the music historian whom we are following brackets Holland and even England with Switzerland; he might well have thrown in Scotland (where a church organ is, to this day, contemptuously known as a 'kist o' whistles') at the same time. And while he is doing his best to show that the Lutheran tradition was different, in this respect, from the Calvinic, he has yet to admit that it had to undergo, at least for a while, the influence of the stronger movement. Referring to the Calvinists, he writes: 'Their Puritan conception of worship as a period of instruction, their merely symbolical [i.e. non-sacramental] understanding of the Lord's Supper, and their moral and pedagogic philosophy and theology brought about a growing antagonism to . . . organ playing.' And then he continues: 'The Lutherans were gradually influenced by these views. Music as an art was only tolerated and, as time went on, it came to be regarded as a papist horror and abomination . . . The hymn alone remained the unquestioned requisite of the Lutheran service, whereas the Calvinists . . . rejected even that.'[2] The hymn remained, and that was a great thing. From it there could arise, in the fullness of time, a marvellous new flourishing of music – that reawakening which we connect with the name of Johann Sebastian Bach. But, to bring it about, more was needed than the appearance of a supreme genius. What was needed was also a definite religious revolution. Of that we shall speak in its due place.[3]

The fate of music overtook the pictorial arts at the same time, and it would have been strange if it had been otherwise. The mobs which destroyed the organs made bonfires of the paintings on the walls and smashed the statuary wherever they could lay their hands on it. A look into the Lady Chapel of Ely Cathedral even today is enough to break an art-lover's heart, and the experience can be repeated all over the once-Calvinist and still-Calvinist world. Even France did not escape.[4] But we are not concerned with the excesses of the masses; we must understand, as dispassionately as we can, what happened, and why it did. The Calvinists who did not remember the last psalm: 'Praise ye

[1] Garside, loc. cit., p. 61.
[2] Nettl, loc. cit., pp. 5, 7, 162, 106, 107.
[3] Cf. below, p. 207.   [4] Cf. Sauer, loc. cit., p. 344.

the Lord in his holy places, . . . praise him with psaltery and harp,' never forgot the second commandment:[1] 'Thou shalt not make to thyself a graven thing,' and they did not restrict this order to idols, but included all art without exception. The conversion of Huldreich Zwingli is once again typical. In his early days he declared more than once: 'There is no one who is a greater admirer of paintings, statues and images than I.' Yet in 1525 he condemned what he had valued so highly: 'God has not told us to teach from pictures, but from His word.'[2] The rank and file understood these apparently mild words in their own fashion, with results which are reflected in Walter Hugelshofer's study, *Die Zürcher Malerei bis zum Anfang der Spätgotik*: 'Any accurate assessment of the visual arts in pre-Reformation Zürich is difficult because so much was destroyed by Protestant iconoclasm . . . Nothing whatsoever is known of Zürich sculpture, and scarcely a tenth of the pre-Reformation painting has been preserved.'[3] No wonder that Garside, who, throughout his book, has sided with the Reformer, closes it with the following words: 'The liturgy of Zürich in 1598, just as that of 1525, was open witness that the Zwinglian reformation had shattered the unity of art and religion which for centuries had been the greatest single source of higher culture in Western Europe. The great wheel of the Church encompassing and enriching all artistic activity, inspiring it and encouraging it to contribute to the liturgy of the Mass at its center, had been broken.'

What Garside has studied on the stage of one town, Gombrich has considered on a universal scale, but the results are largely identical. He speaks of a 'great crisis . . . brought about by the Reformation' and writes: 'In the north [of Europe] the question soon became whether painting could and should continue at all.' As an example, he cites the case of the younger Hans Holbein who, in self-defence, had to move from Switzerland to England[4] in 1526: 'When Holbein had left the German-speaking countries, painting there began to decline to a frightening extent', a condition which contrasts vividly with 'the splendid panorama of painting in the countries adhering to Roman Catholicism'. Particularly interesting in this context is what Gombrich has to say about English architecture in the seventeenth century. In England, the court carried art forward into the future, yet the Protestant element in the country acted as a great damper to its *élan*. A comparison between St. Paul's Cathedral in London with the smaller, but otherwise rather similar church of Sant' Agnese in Piazza Navona in Rome proves how

[1] While Catholics and Lutherans include the words quoted in the text in the first commandment, the Reformed Churches of whom we are speaking here traditionally count them as the second.

[2] Garside, loc. cit., pp. 76 and 173. *Werke*, as quoted, vol. III, Leipzig 1914, p. 906, and vol. IV, Leipzig 1927, p. 122.

[3] Garside's summary, p. 80. Cf. also ibid., pp. 159 and 160.

[4] Cf. above, p. 160.

things in Britain had slipped into the minor key. 'Compared with the exuberance of Borromini . . . Wren impresses us as being restrained and sober.' This is characteristic. 'The contrast between Protestant and Catholic architecture is even more marked when we consider the interior of Wren's churches, for instance that of St. Stephen in London . . . Its aim is not to conjure up a vision of another world, but rather to allow us to collect our thoughts . . . A church like this is designed mainly as a hall where the faithful meet for common worship.' In Quaker language, even this 'steeple-house' was not too different from the Quaker 'meeting-house'. The spirit which stood sponsor at its conception was similar. Thus even in England 'the victory of Protestantism . . . had dealt the tradition of art . . . a severe blow'.[1]

The contrast, obvious for all to see, between Catholic productiveness and Calvinist unproductiveness in art is not, however, restricted to a difference in the mass or volume of artistic creation. It reached down into the foundations, into the theory of art. We have seen that Michelangelo professed a Platonizing philosophy: earthly beauty shown on a canvas or in stone is a replica, a reflection, of the beauty of a higher sphere, and in the last resort of the perfection of the ideas contained in the Divine Mind. This whole conception was repudiated by Calvinism. 'Suppose . . . with thyself thou hadst been that Apostle's [i.e. St. John's] fellow traveller into the celestial kingdom,' writes Richard Baxter in that great Puritan classic, *The Saints' Everlasting Rest*,[2] 'and that thou hadst seen all the saints in their white robes, with palms in their hands; suppose thou hadst heard those songs of Moses and of the Lamb; or didst even now hear them praising and glorifying the living God . . . I would not have thee, as the Papists, draw them in pictures, nor use such ways to represent them. This . . . would but seduce and draw down thy heart.' Whether it would seduce the heart is a matter of judgment and opinion about which it is impossible to quarrel; but whether it would draw down the heart is more a matter of fact. There can surely be very few whose heart was, or could be, 'drawn down' by the contemplation of the frescoes in St. Petronio in Bologna or Dürer's *Feast of all Saints*.

The contrast, then, was total, embracing theory as well as practice or production. What concerns us, as sociologists of culture, is, however, not so much the fact itself as the aetiology of the fact, its 'real substructure', as Marx would have expressed it. Why did the Calvinists extend the meaning of the second commandment so much that it became a ban on all art? The final answer must be sought in the total transformation of contemporary society, its set towards the capitalist dispensation which, as Max Weber has so convincingly shown, is genetically connected with the coming of Calvinism. There was a total turning away

[1] Gombrich, loc. cit., pp. 274, 279, 292, 344, 346.
[2] IV, 11, 2. Ed. London 1688, pp. 709 and 710.

from contemplation to action, from aestheticism which is an adjunct of contemplation, to ethics which is a helpmate to action. There was also a total turning away from playfulness which is an ingredient in all art, to a serious conception and conduct of life which has to condemn all play. There was, at the same time, and for reasons which are not mysterious, a far-reaching turning towards rationalism – that rationalism which, in modern society's preferred fields of endeavour, economics and technology, is the dominant principle. But if rationalism advances, emotion must recoil; and art is as much the child of emotion, as it is its mother. In a rationalistic society, such as capitalism, factualness will flourish, not imagination; science will flourish, not art; and, ultimately at least, a mechanistic view of the universe will win out which will drive the religious *visio mundi* into a deep crisis.

Besides, or, so to speak, above these basic reasons there is one which fits particularly well into the over-all account of socio-intellectual and socio-religious development which this book is trying to present. Catholicism was and is largely collectivistic, Calvinism largely individualistic and atomistic. The individualistic and atomistic mind, however, tends to be fixed to the detail. It will stand helpless before works of art where many small features are to be integrated into one total impression. It is a well-known fact that Englishmen dislike Baroque; it is 'too rich', as they complain; there are too many angels, great and small, to be taken in before a façade or a wall or an altar can be appreciated. This is precisely where the Catholic mind – we might even say: the Catholic eye – is different. It has no difficulty in appreciating a multiplicity (in art as in philosophy and sociology) it has learned to see them as a unity. The Jesuit Church in Tepozotlan or the Dominican Chapel of the Rosary in Puebla do not overwhelm or worry them; they get a unitary impression which may be denied to men of another culture. The Catholic art of the Counter-Reformation makes sense only if it is approached in a spirit of integration. Rubens, for instance, demands of us that 'having looked at the details, we . . . once more consider the whole and admire the grand sweep with which [he] has contrived all the figures together'.[1] Even a great aesthete like John Ruskin found this difficult because of the Calvinist element that was in him. 'When he observed, he liked to observe details; but he always found it difficult, and in later life he found it impossible, to relate and co-ordinate his observations,' Wilenski says of him. And in another part of his book, he refers to Ruskin's 'visual hyper-reaction to detail'.[2] The medieval-Catholic mind is different. It perceives the composition rather than the component parts. Henry Adams, who stresses this throughout *Mont-Saint-Michel and Chartres*, points to the roses of medieval cathedrals, and more especially to the great west rose at Chartres as an

[1] Gombrich, loc. cit., p. 299.
[2] Wilenski, R. H., *John Ruskin*, New York, n.d., pp. 33 and 188.

illustration. There are countless colours, but there is only one light, complex certainly, but unitary at the same time.[1]

Connected with this fixation to detail is a certain addiction to quantity. In more senses than one, Calvinist and modern man sees reality in terms of numbers, whereas medieval and Catholic man is more interested in, and attuned to, quality. The detail cannot be pursued here, but one point may be made which will allow the reader to form at least an inkling of this factor. Protestants know no cult of the saints. They fear that any honour given to the saints will be subtracted from the honour given to Almighty God. They conceive the love of God as a quantity, and a fixed one at that. The Catholic veneration of the saints rests on an entirely different intuition. It assumes that the honour given to God's friends will enrich the honour given to God Himself. If we give *dulia* to St. John or to St. Francis, and if we give *hyperdulia* to Mary, we learn how to love. There is a specific relationship to each individual saint, and hence a special colour or quality to each such relationship; they all make us more feeling, more devoted, more loving. And they all enter into the *latria* which we give to God. This *latria* profits from every one of the *duliae* which we develop. The love of God should be like good wine: good wine combines many tastes which are often impossible to separate out and to identify. It should be like the white colour which contains all the shades of the spectrum. It should be the love of loves, carrying within itself something of all we have learned in the field of loving devotion. It must surely be clear that a quantity-centred mentality will lead to achievements different from those which spring from a quality-centred mentality. It will gain its triumphs in the sphere of economics and technology, and not in that of music and painting.

In a bitter aside on 'tourists of English blood and American training', Henry Adams complains that they find it difficult to appreciate the glories of Chartres. And he gives a reason which follows from the two which we have just considered and is perhaps greater than either of them: 'The scientific mind is atrophied ... we have lost many senses.' 'We can only study'; but most of us, unless they be artists at heart, 'cannot feel'.[2] Of all the after-effects of Calvinism, this involution of the world of sentiment (so different from the sentimentality with which the Calvinist-descended mind invariably confuses it)[3] is the one most damaging to artistic creation and even to art appreciation. The capacity to feel has to be renewed, if artistic production or understanding for art are to be achieved. But that means running counter to the Calvinist tradition, indeed, conquering it, throwing it off. An interesting –

[1] Cf. Adams, loc. cit., esp. pp. 151, 152, 155, 156.
[2] Adams, loc. cit., pp. 215, 141, 142.
[3] There is deep emotion in Schubert's Ninth Symphony, or in Beethoven's Ninth Symphony, but there is no sentimentality.

indeed, we should say, moving – illustration of recent years is the case of the incomparable alto, Kathleen Ferrier, still lovingly remembered by many of us. Neville Cardus writes in his memoir: 'She was always ready gratefully to acknowledge her debt to Bruno Walter, who revealed to her the "tone-world" of Mahler. Also, she would say, he removed those inhibitions which in English singers frequently "keep them shy of letting themselves go"; emotionally she meant. She would say things like this with a full Lancashire flavour. It was at a performance of *Das Lied von der Erde*, during the Edinburgh Festival of 1947, that I heard her sing for the first time. I had been told by a mutual friend to get in touch with her on my return from Australia. During this performance she could scarcely finish the last two repetitions of the word "Ewig" at the end. She was in tears. Afterwards in the artists' room I met her and, as though she had known me a lifetime, she said: "What a fool I've made of myself. And what will Dr. Walter think of me?" I told her she needn't worry, for I was certain that Bruno Walter would reply, taking both her hands in his: "My dear child, if we had all been artists great as you we should all have wept – myself, orchestra, audience, everybody . . ." '[1] What led this uniquely gifted singer to the heights of artistic excellence which she did attain, was her capacity to rise superior to the confining atmosphere in which she had been born and bred.

Societies which do not achieve this liberation, do and must find their fulfilment outside the arts, outside music and painting. A case in point is Scotland. That great Calvinistic country has given many gifts to mankind; it has above all enriched intellectual culture in a generous measure. The name of David Hume alone is a token of Scots philosophical sophistication. But in the realm of beauty, the record is not equally distinguished. In 1947, there appeared, under the editorship of H. W. Meikle, a volume which tried to assess the country's culture and its contents,[2] and the chapters on music and painting prove what we are saying. Stewart Deas's survey of music is even more revealing than Stanley Cursiter's chapter on the pictorial arts. In other lands, Deas points out, the great heritage of folk music has released great individual music-making: Austria had her Haydn and Mozart, Bohemia her Dvořák and Smetana, Russia her Glinka and Borodin; even Finland had her Sibelius and Norway her Grieg. Scotland, too, had her inherited treasure, but, says Deas, 'it may be readily admitted that few of our composers until quite recently have known how to use it'. By 'our composers' Deas means mainly 'the three Macs' – Mackenzie, MacCann and McEwen – hardly figures of world importance. Their failure, and the failure of other and greater composers to come forward, is ascribed by our informant to the absence of 'magnificent secular and church

[1] *Kathleen Ferrier: A Memoir*, ed. Cardus, N., London 1954, p. 32.
[2] *Scotland: A Description of Scotland and Scottish Life*, London, etc., 1947.

music'.[1] This is correct, though the real causes lie a good deal deeper, as our own analysis has shown. As for painting, the Reformation squashed whatever hopeful beginnings there were in the country. 'Towards the end of the seventeenth century, art in Scotland had sunk to a low level,' writes Cursiter. Things had become so bad that outside help was clearly needed, and 'in 1688, John de Medina, an artist of Flemish-Spanish extraction, was persuaded to settle in Scotland'.[2] He started an upward movement which in one field, that of portrait painting, led to a considerable height, Allan Ramsay and Henry Raeburn being the commanding peaks. Why it was possible for this particular branch to flourish, though all others did not, will immediately be explained. For the moment, let us only add that the Scots people themselves, equipped as they are with the great Calvinist virtue of veracity and candour, accept the judgment of their contribution to artistic culture which we have set forth. Few would deny that the Caledonian contribution to architecture and poetry has been far from negligible. Yet the reviewer of Dr. Meikle's volume in the *Weekly Scotsman* could comment on 3 July 1947: 'In architecture as in food the Caledonian tradition is distinguished more by simplicity and solidity and dignity than by brilliance and opulence', and, in the book itself, H. Harvey Wood has this to say in the chapter on literature: 'In many of the qualities that are central in the poetry of England, Spain and Italy, Scots literature is singularly poor. There is little sensuous love of beauty, little mysticism, little philosophy, and little high imaginative creation in our poetry . . . The Scots poets have cultivated the lower slopes of Mount Parnassus.'[3]

Generally speaking, then, Calvinism turned away from the arts, and especially the pictorial arts, but there is no rule without its confirming exception, and we must give it the attention it deserves. 'There was . . . one Protestant country in Europe where art fully survived the crisis of the Reformation,' writes Gombrich, and 'that was the Netherlands,' better: the northern Netherlands, Holland.[4] The reasons may be manifold and devious, but the most manifest, and, in all probability, the most potent, was the existence of a powerful artistic tradition in the country. This was so vital and so strong that it could not be simply switched off. It took a century for it to run out, and in that time it produced ever-admirable painters, such as Frans Hals, Jan Steen, and Jan Vermeer, not to speak of Rembrandt who, as a special case, will find special treatment.[5] A study of these men will be particularly enlightening for the sociologist of religious cultures for they can show us what kind of art was akin to the life principles of Calvinism and could

---

[1] Ibid., p. 211.   [2] Ibid., p. 195.
[3] Pp. 153 and 154.
[4] Gombrich, loc. cit., p. 279. Gombrich in fact writes: 'only one Protestant country'.
[5] Cf. below, pp. 197 et seq.

be fitted into its frame. If Calvinism had not decayed, if it had shown greater stamina, it would in the end everywhere have produced its own art; the amount of energy allotted to this pursuit would assuredly have remained comparatively small, but, small or large, it would have tended to develop a style of its own. We can see this style in those northern provinces of the Netherlands which broke away from the Catholic culture complex in the sixteenth century.

In one word, that style was realistic, descriptive, one might even say, tending to be photographic. 'Since the early days of Van Eyck,' Gombrich explains, 'the artists of the Netherlands had been recognized as perfect masters in the imitation of nature. While the Italians prided themselves on being unrivalled in the representation of the beautiful human figure . . . they were ready to recognize that, for sheer patience and accuracy in depicting a flower, a tree, a barn or a flock of sheep, the "Flemings"[1] were apt to outstrip them . . . The Dutchmen . . . needed nothing dramatic or striking to make their pictures interesting. They simply represented a piece of the world as it appeared to them . . .' Vermeer was in his way the most realistic of them all, and that is why he is the most beloved of his fellow-countrymen to this day. 'His paintings are really still lives with human beings . . . They make us see the quiet beauty of a simple scene with fresh eyes and give us an idea of what the artist felt when he watched the light flooding through the window and heightening the colour of a piece of cloth.'[2] Vermeer,we read in one fine study of Dutch painting, 'would paint a woman in some ordinary room at an unimportant moment – pouring milk, reading a note, making lace, quietly busy with a small task – for only then did he see the essential . . . His art was a matter of choice, of seizing on the characteristic and intimate moments of everyday life in Delft.'[3] Here, then, we have Calvinism's inherent artistic possibilities unfolded and at their best. When de Tocqueville said that in democratic societies 'the imagination is not extinct; but its chief function is to devise what may be useful, and to represent what is real', he hit the nail on the head; we would only urge that he is speaking, not so much of democracy in general, as of democracy in a basically Calvinist country, as indeed he is.[4]

Among the possible objects of a realistic art were, of course, the human figure and especially the human face, and that is the reason why Calvinist Scotland could excel in this particular *genre* while it did not do

---

[1] The word must be written in inverted commas as the real Flemings, i.e. the inhabitants of Flanders, remained Catholic and became Belgians.

[2] Gombrich, loc. cit., pp. 279, 312, 324.

[3] Hammacher, A. M., and Hammacher Vandenbrande, R., *Flemish and Dutch Art*, New York 1965, p. 12.

[4] Cf. *Democracy in America*, ed. Bradley, Ph., paperback ed., New York 1954, vol. II, p. 76. Our analysis is further confirmed by what Garside says about Switzerland, cf. loc. cit., pp. 181 and 182.

so in most others.[1] Holland, too, developed this speciality on a grand scale. Properly understood, Dutch portrait painting represents an epitome of the evolution and involution of Calvinism. This stern religion made man a problem unto himself. He was for ever brooding about his whence and whereto, and above all about his destiny in the beyond. The great series of self-representations which came from the brush of Rembrandt illustrate this implication of the Reformed theology, and to that extent Rembrandt was influenced by his sombre environment though in other respects, as we shall see, he was opposed to it.[2] But soon another psychological motive took over: self-satisfaction, even vanity. As the money-bags filled and life became more pleasant, as respectability removed self-doubt and replaced it with self-assurance, the portrait became simply a piece of pride, a treasured possession, a status symbol. Frans Hals's rotund sitters do not look as if they had worried very much about the doctrine of predestination, nor do Rembrandt's Staalmeesters though they were of sterner stuff. But, of course, portrait painting had another propulsive force behind it. Deprived of churchly and courtly patronage, the poor painters had to find new patrons, and there was only the bourgeoisie. And their orders could best be secured by promising to paint them as they were.

In the end it was this factor – the shrinkage of the market to one close-fisted class – which brought about the doom of Dutch painting. Rembrandt ended as a declared and condemned bankrupt. Hals was often in debt to the baker and shoe-repairer. Steen could not make a living as an artist and had to become an inn-keeper. Vermeer was never out of financial straits and left many debts when he died.[3] Their fate contrasts most unfavourably with that of the Antwerp painters, Rubens and Van Dyck, whom the Roman Church and the English Court helped to honour and affluence.

In view of all that we have said, it should surprise nobody to hear that Margaret Ruskin, an Evangelical if ever there was one, had dark shades drawn every Sabbath day over the pictures with which her aesthete son, John, had adorned the walls.[4] Such enjoyments could be suffered at ordinary times; in hallowed hours they were out of the question. But this raises the problem as to what the position of an art-lover can be in a Calvinist-type society, and we must investigate it, because it will shed further light on Calvinism as a principle of culture.

John Ruskin had a strict Calvinistic-Evangelical upbringing. He knew the Apocalypse by heart before he was twelve years old, and its grim message remained with him all his life. So did all the other tenets

---

[1] Cf. above, pp. 169.   [2] Cf. below, pp. 199 et seq.
[3] Cf. Gombrich, loc. cit., pp. 314, 310, 319; Hammacher, loc. cit., pp. 110 and 119.
[4] Quennell, P., *John Ruskin: The Portrait of a Prophet*, New York 1949, p. 239. R. H. Wilenski, *John Ruskin*, as quoted, p. 42, calls Ruskin's mother 'an Evangelical Protestant, a stupid bigot bully'.

of the Genevan theology. No wonder that 'he early conceived the notion that the taking of any kind of pleasure was a sin'. Fortunately for the world, but unfortunately for him, there was one pleasure which, in spite of this conviction, he could not live without – the contemplation of beauty. Of course, he indulged in it, as a hungry man will in bread and meat. But what a price did he have to pay! 'To Ruskin his drawing and his intermittent studies of the past . . . were forms of play, and he could never pursue these activities without a sense of guilt . . . When he was sketching at Abbéville, or drawing the monuments at Verona, or copying a corner of a picture by Giotto or Botticelli, or pottering among the archives of Venice,' a triple shadow was lying over his soul: that of his disapproving mother, behind whom there was a disapproving Calvin, behind whom there was a disapproving Puritan Jehova. 'He believed from the outset that art, science and scholarship, pursued for themselves, were really drugs . . . and when he lost himself in drawing, or writing, or study, he was always haunted . . .'[1].

The device, *l'art pour l'art*, was part and parcel of Ruskin's most intimate creed, and in his heart of hearts he believed that the contemplation of beauty was a value in itself. But because of the Puritanism which he had imbibed, he rejected this adage and this philosophy on the conscious level – or tried to do so. 'As you may neither eat, nor read, for the pleasure of eating or reading, so you may do *nothing else* for the pleasure of it, but for the use,' he writes in *Fors Clavigera*.[2] 'The moral difference between a man and a beast is that the one acts primarily for use, the other for pleasure . . .' The self-condemnation contained in these sentences stands well out for all to see. To justify himself, he tended to develop a theory of art according to which art was in essence a moralizing force. This is typical of Calvinism: the primacy of the ethical over the aesthetic values is part of this creed, as we have already seen, and shall see again. As for his own person, Ruskin built a parallel ideology: 'he persuaded himself that – in cultivating his own happiness and contentment by accepting his agreeable life in London and in Venice, by making drawings and notes of sculpture and mosaics, by dipping into archives and producing expensive and elegant illustrated volumes – he was really cultivating his power of service'.[3] Needless to say, he never believed a word of what he said, even though he said it to himself. When, on 7 June 1880, he wrote to the Oxford University Herald: 'The theology I teach is not mine, but St. Bernard's and St. Francis's: the philosophy I teach is Plato's and Bacon's; the art, Phidias' and John Bellini's,' he was merely putting into words what he had not dared to put into words before.

Indeed, the art-for-use theory which he pretended for so long, had to

---

[1] Wilenski, loc. cit., pp. 364, 38, 39, 49.
[2] Letter 61. Cf. *The Works of John Ruskin*, edd. Cook, E. T., and Wedderburn, A., vol. XXVIII, London 1907, p. 502.   [3] Wilenski, loc. cit., p. 217.

coexist, in his mind, with – to say the least – elements of that metaphysical art theory which, Platonic in origin, was Michelangelo's, and is Catholicism's basic aesthetic conviction. In *Modern Painters* he offers a double definition of beauty: there is vital beauty, and there is typical beauty. Vital beauty is based on 'the appearance of felicitous fulfilment of function in living things', a definition not necessarily religious in implication, but in so far as it is so, it is close to that organicism which has ever been Catholicism's preferred philosophy of nature. As for typical beauty, it is so called because it 'may be shown to be in some sort typical of the divine attributes'.[1] The artist's function, and his – Ruskin's own – was therefore to apprehend and to communicate something from the supernal, metaphysical world – an utterly un-Calvinic conception since, according to Calvin, *nothing* in this fallen nether sphere could possibly reveal *anything* of the divine reality. 'He believed that a great work of art is the conscious revelation of aspects of God,' so Wilenski sums up his thinking.[2] It would have been hazardous to voice such an opinion at Geneva in the days of Calvin's dictatorship.

Once established in his mind, this religious rather than utilitarian – this Platonizing – art theory started to proliferate. It tended to draw Ruskin towards symbolicism. 'He was led to the study of abstraction in art, to the consideration . . . of art as a formative activity by means of which the artist's experience of phenomena is symbolised.'[3] Looked at from this point of view, the kind of painting closest to Calvinism's potentialities – representational art – appeared to Ruskin mean and low. 'The pleasure resulting from imitation [is] the most contemptible that can be derived from art.'[4]

In these passages we see Ruskin pathetically reaching out for a world whose mentality would not be Puritan, and Catholicism would have suited him, as it has always suited those of his artistic preoccupations. But he was reaching out through the bars of a prison, of a cage. He could not go where he needed to go. He remained a divided man. Peter Quennell has brought this out even more strongly than Reginald Wilenski. He ends his study with a passage which sums up the great art-lover's tragedy: 'Ruskin was not fortunate. He could neither accept the evangelical creed of Denmark Hill . . . nor succumb to . . . Brompton Oratory . . . He was still an Anglican who mocked at Protestantism [and] a Catholic sympathizer who declined to take his final vows.'[5]

There was a period when it looked as if Ruskin would manage to break through the bars. Once, in Turin, he walked out of a Waldensian chapel and declared that he was done with this sort of religion. He

[1] *Modern Painters*, vol. II, III, I, III, 16. *Works*, as quoted, vol. IV, London 1903, p. 64.
[2] Loc. cit., p. 212. [3] Ibid., p. 235.
[4] *Modern Painters*, vol. I, I, I, IV, 4. *Works*, as quoted, vol. III, London 1903, p. 101.
[5] Quennell, loc. cit., p. 287. Denmark Hill was Ruskin's childhood home, the scene of his Evangelical indoctrination.

openly said on the occasion that he had contemplated such a step for a long time. We get an explanation in a simple but revealing diary entry of the time. 'Is this mighty Paul Veronese . . . a servant of the devil? and is the poor little wretch in a tidy black tie, to whom I have been listening this Sunday morning expounding Nothing with a Twang – is he a servant of God?'[1] Nearly twenty years later, the episode is recounted in *Fors Clavigera*.[2] 'In 1858 . . . one Sunday morning, at Turin . . . from before Paul Veronese's "Queen of Sheba", and under quite overwhelmed sense of his God-given power, I went away to a Waldensian chapel,' where the minister 'was preaching . . . that all the people in Turin outside the chapel . . . would be damned. I came out of the chapel, in sum of twenty years of thought, a conclusively *un-*converted man . . . "Here is an end to my Mother-Law of Protestantism".' In *Praeterita*[3] the end of the event is then described: 'I walked back into the condemned city and up into the gallery where Paul Veronese's "Solomon and the Queen of Sheba" glowed in full afternoon light. The gallery windows being open, there came in with the warm air floating swells and falls of military music from the courtyard before the palace which seemed to me more devotional, in their perfect art, tune, and discipline, than anything I remembered of evangelical hymns . . . That day, my evangelical beliefs were put away, to be debated no more.'

Having left one haven, did Ruskin head for another? He wanted to, at least at the subconscious level, yet he was too deeply in thrall to his childhood, when he had learned to consider even 'Papist art', let alone Papist religion, as 'naturally evil', to accomplish the new landing. He remained at sea for the rest of his life. But there is pathetic proof of the shore for which he yearned. In 1871, as he lay sick and delirious in Matlock, he dreamed that he was 'a brother of St. Francis'. In 1874, sane and sober, he wrote to Joan Severn from Rome: 'I quite begin to understand the power of this place over the most noble class of English religious mind . . . The intense reality of the past becomes to them an irresistible claim on their submission and affection . . . I verily believe that were I a Christian at all, Rome would make a Romanist of me in a fortnight.' When Ruskin, a little later, donated a stained glass window to a Catholic church near Coniston, the hour of conversion seemed at hand and Cardinal Manning tried to effect it. But he failed. In a letter to the *Morning Post*, on 7 April 1887, the great art-lover declared that, though he was indeed 'a Christian Catholic in the wide and eternal sense', he was 'no more likely to become a Roman Catholic than a Quaker, Evangelical or Turk'.[4]

---

[1] Wilenski, loc. cit., p. 338. Cf. also p. 66.
[2] Letter 76. *Works*, as quoted, vol. XXIX, London 1907, pp. 89 and 90.
[3] III, I, 23. Cf. *Works*, as quoted, vol. XXXV, London 1908, pp. 495 and 496.
[4] For documentation, cf. Wilenski, loc. cit., pp. 352–4.

In a sense, this was Ruskin's last word; but in a sense, it was not. For the battle between the two selves which confronted each other in his tortured mind became more intense now, not less so. He had already had spells of madness in 1878, 1881, 1882, 1885 and 1886; now his sanity was finally at an end. There is complete agreement among his biographers as to the reasons for his final collapse. It was the unresolved and unresolvable irreconcilability, laid on in his youth, between his love of beauty and his fear of hellfire which, his mother had taught him, was the condign punishment of such wicked preoccupations. Time had done little to mitigate the problem – Puritanism had bitten too deeply into his soul. Quennell is once again right when he says: 'A conviction of sinfulness, imbibed in youth and childhood, not infrequently survives the religious beliefs that first of all impressed it . . . It was natural enough that the effects of his early training should have left a mark upon Ruskin's mind that even his own loss of faith and many years of adventurous speculation could not wholly charm away.'[1]

When Ruskin found that he could not, after all, finally free himself from his Evangelical prison house, he had forfeited his sanity for ever. But he continued to long for integration in another, more sympathetic communion. One of the most characteristic features of his mental illness was his delusionary self-identification with Saint Francis.[2] That is who he wanted to be; and that shows where he wished to be, and where he would have been, if only he would have been a free man. And there is yet another trait in the picture of his alienated mind which is equally revealing: his fascination with, and fear of, lights, especially lights in the dusk and darkness. 'About eighteen months before the collapse into admitted madness . . . Ruskin went to the Grosvenor Gallery and saw Whistler's picture called "Nocturne in Black and Gold: The Falling Rocket", which represented fireworks watched by masqueraders in Cremorne Gardens; and he experienced . . . a rush of subconscious anger as he looked at this cascade of glittering light spots surrounded with the black gloom of the night sky.' Why this curious reaction which was, as it turned out, a harbinger of mental collapse? 'It is . . . possible,' Wilenski cautiously says, 'that the fear was really connected by his early fear of being attracted by Roman Catholic ritual associated with images of grouped candles flickering in dark cathedral chapels.' Our biographer is rightly cautious and speaks of a possibility only, for who knows what destroyed this great man? Yet in another part of his book, Wilenski firmly accepts what he here only hesitatingly suggests. Ruskin, he writes, 'was the victim of some curious and personal obsessions. In the days when he was writing the second volume of *Modern Painters* and the *Seven Lamps of Architecture* and *The Stones of Venice*, he

---

[1] Quennell, loc. cit., pp. 202 and 203.
[2] Wilenski, loc. cit., pp. 352 and 356. He had identified himself with Dante in earlier difficulties, cf. ibid., p. 133.

was haunted by the fear of being seduced to Roman Catholicism by the aesthetic appeal of the Roman Catholic ritual which he encountered in the cathedrals of Italy and France – a fear which lay beneath his diatribes against Roman Catholicism in those books.'[1] Poor man! It is a hard fate to have to hate and to fear what you love – but that precisely was Ruskin's lot and it ruined his mind. An analysis of this unhappy life story thus leads to a confirmation of the thesis which we have argued all along – namely that Calvinism and art are antithetic and cannot peacefully abide under one roof.

If we had more space at our disposal and could present a second English example,[2] we would discuss Oscar Wilde, another aesthete of the purest water. He was from early years attracted to Catholicism,[3] but while his frivolity lasted, any positive step towards religion was out of the question. When, as a sobered and stricken man, he emerged from Reading Gaol, his first step was to try to go to Brompton Oratory for an extended retreat,[4] but what religious house could accept a man, be it only for six months, who had just become notorious as a homosexual? Yet the desire to convert to Rome remained. What held him back was in all probability merely the necessity to face the ordeal of confession; Wilde may have been too ashamed to do that; at any rate, friends urged on him that he could not, and should not, expose his self and his sins, be it only in the privacy of a confessional box. He gave in to such voices. But he implored those around him not to let him die outside the Church, and, in accordance with this his expressed and deeply felt heart-wish, he was received *in articulo mortis* on 29 November 1900, baptism and extreme unction being administered at the same time. He died less than twenty-four hours later and was buried with a rosary around his neck and a medal of St. Francis on his breast.[5]

What created havoc in Wilde's life, as it did in that of Ruskin, was over-mothering, for Lady Wilde was not much less formidable than Mrs. Ruskin. Our American example, Henry Adams, was much more fortunate in those who stood around his cradle. Yet his conflict with the surrounding civilization was similar to that of Ruskin and Wilde. He found it difficult to breathe in a country 'where passion and poetry

[1] Ibid., pp. 143 and 32; but cf. the whole chapter on 'Ruskin's Religion', pp. 329 et seq. In a lecture on 'Cistercian Architecture', delivered on 4 December 1882, Ruskin himself refers to 'dread of ritualist devotion' as a source of error in his earlier books on art. Cf. ibid., p. 335, note 3.

[2] Further interesting possibilities from the same period would have been the poet Coventry Patmore, the painter Aubrey Beardsley, and, a little later, the sculptor Eric Gill whose autobiography is particularly instructive. And who would not think of Gerard Manley Hopkins? But there are too many cases even to mention.

[3] Cf. Winwar, F., *Oscar Wilde and the Yellow Nineties*, New York and London 1940, pp. 28, 30–4, 110, 154, 231, 232, 332.

[4] Ibid., p. 338.

[5] Ibid., pp. 341, 359, 362, 363. Concerning the difficulties about the confessional, cf. Pearson, H., *Oscar Wilde, His Life and Wit*, New York and London 1946, p. 332.

were eccentricities' and whose President, Ulysses Grant, had gone on record with the remark 'that Venice would be a fine city if it were drained'.[1]

Born and bred in the atmosphere of Boston's Beacon Hill, whose religious traditions showed a definite family likeness to those of London's Denmark Hill, Henry Adams was exposed to much the same childhood influences as John Ruskin; but if the *quale* was similar, the *quantum* was different. Still, looking back from the vantage point of maturity, he judged that he was made into 'a quintessence of Boston', and that meant that his 'instinct [for art] was blighted from babyhood'.[2] All the stronger was the revolution in his soul and his revulsion from Bostonianism when he met with surpassing beauty. The autobiography mentions two particular encounters which were decisive: hearing Beethoven's music and seeing Santa Maria in Ara Coeli, the church perched on top of Rome's Capitol Hill. Writing in the third person, Adams recalls how in Berlin he had shocked a friend by saying 'that he loathed Beethoven', and that in his opinion 'every one thought Beethoven a bore'. But this prejudice bred in a 'Pullman civilization' melted away when it came face to face with the real Beethoven. Adams, sitting one day in a common beer-garden, 'was surprised to notice that his mind followed the movement of a *Sinfonie*. He could not have been more astonished had he suddenly read a new language. Among the marvels of education, this was the most marvellous. A prison-wall that barred his senses on one great side of life suddenly fell of its own accord without so much as his knowing when it happened ... A new sense burst out like a flower in his life, so superior to the old senses, so bewildering, so astonished at its own existence, that he could not credit it and watched it as something apart, accidental and not to be trusted.' Not much later, sitting 'at sunset on the steps of the church of Santa Maria di Ara Coeli', Adams felt that his whole inherited world view was bursting asunder. Rome simply 'could not be fitted into an orderly, middle class, Bostonian ... scheme of evolution'. The moment was one of grace. During the dry years at Washington when, to refresh himself, he went for rambles in the surrounding woods and saw the dome of the Capitol in the distance, its outline reminded him not only of St. Peter's, but, characteristically, also of 'the steps of Ara Coeli'.[3]

Even later in life, from about 1891 onward, Adams became the devoted student, and ultimately the passionate lover, of Gothic art. This made him the author of American literature's aesthetic masterpiece, the incomparable book on *Mont-Saint-Michel and Chartres*. In it, there are two passages which show that yet one more art-loving soul was breaking loose from art-condemning Puritanism. 'To the Virgin and

[1] *The Education of Henry Adams*, ed. Boston and New York 1946, pp. 221 and 265.
[2] Ibid., p. 387.
[3] Ibid., pp. 245, 80, 91, 282.

to her suppliants,' we read in one context, 'as to us who, though out-casts in other churches, can still hope in hers, the Last Judgment was not a symbol of God's justice or man's corruption, but of her own infinite mercy.' A man who could set down this remarkable sentence was no longer a true Protestant, for it is imbued with that *hyperdulia* which in the West is exclusively Catholic, with Mariolatry, and that has always been Protestantism's chief abomination. But the other passage is, if possible, even clearer: 'We, although utter strangers to her, are not far from getting down on our knees and praying to her still.'[1] These words carry something like a contradiction in terms, for how can he who is prepared to invoke the Virgin, be a stranger, an utter stranger, to her? No, Henry Adams who penned these pages was a man moving away from his father's tents.

In his attitude towards abstract speculation, something of Henry Adams' Calvinist upbringing remained, for he could confess that he was 'rigidly denying himself the amusement of philosophy which consists chiefly in suggesting unintelligible answers to insoluble problems'. But his ideas on art were turned inside out and upside down. Not Thomas Aquinas brought him round, but Chartres; not Thomas Aquinas, but Francis, 'whose solution of historical riddles seemed [increasingly] the most satisfactory – or sufficient – ever offered'. Trying to formulate the difference between the two cultures with which he felt himself con-fronted, and between which he considered himself constrained to choose, Adams began to picture them as divided by irreconcilable concepts of power. Among the men of English stock 'a railway train' is felt 'as power'. 'The attitude was so American that, for at least forty years, Adams had never realized that any other could be in sound taste ... but he knew that ... since 1895 [he] had ... begun to feel the Virgin or Venus as force.' 'All the steam in the world could not, like the Virgin, build Chartres,' Adams writes on the same page. 'Symbol or energy, the Virgin had acted as the greatest force the Western world ever felt, and had drawn man's activities to herself more strongly than any other power, natural or supernatural, had ever done.'[2] The male world of post-Reformation religiosity, so we may formulate the conviction which shaped in Adams' mind, was filled with a love of power – material power; the female world of pre-Reformation faith, on the other hand, with a power of love; for it was love which forced stone into form, which erected towers, and, above all, which filled the windows at Chartres with that incomparable glass on which the Virgin is depicted more than seven hundred times.

Apart from this contrasting of two forms of power, Adams charac-terized the hostile cultures also as different mainly in socio-cultural integration. This is particularly gratifying to the sociologist of know-

[1] Paperback ed., Garden City, New York 1959, pp. 158 and 307.
[2] *The Education*, as quoted, pp. 377, 367, 368, 388, 389.

ledge, and fits in perfectly with the fundamental thesis of the present book. At the end of the twenty-ninth chapter of his autobiography, Adams speaks about his two literary projects: the one, on himself, a modern person, he suggests, might be subtitled: 'a study of twentieth century multiplicity', the other, on medieval art, he says, could be described as 'a study of thirteenth century unity'. In itself, these labels are not revealing; but they are revealing – indeed, they are a striking proof of Adams' conversion and of the depth, nay violence, of it – if they are connected with another passage in which he declares that God is unity and Satan complexity.[1]

Among the influences which helped Adams on his way was that of his close friend John La Farge, an artist and a Catholic. 'The question how much he owed to La Farge,' Adams writes of himself, hiding behind the pseudonym 'he', 'could be answered only by admitting that he had no standard to measure it by. Of all his friends La Farge alone owned a mind complex enough to contrast against the commonplaces of American uniformity . . . The American mind – the Bostonian as well as the southern or western – likes to walk straight up to its object and assert or deny something that it takes for a fact; it has a conventional approach, a conventional analysis and a conventional conclusion as well as a conventional expression, all the time loudly asserting its unconventionality. The most disconcerting tract of La Farge was his reversal of the process . . . He moved round an object and never separated it from its surroundings . . . Even a contradiction was to him only a shade of difference, a complementary color . . .'[2] In one word, La Farge was to Adams an incarnation of that spirit of synthesis which he was to see so splendidly realized at Chartres – of that synthesis which, as the readers of the present work and volume have so often been told – is the very culture-principle of Catholicism.

The Education of Henry Adams stops with the year 1905, and the question arises as to whether the journey from Boston to Rome continued in the remaining thirteen years of Adams' life. Fortunately for the scholar, where one book of retrospect ceases, another continues. A second John La Farge, son of the first, better known as Father La Farge, published in 1954 a volume entitled *The Manner is Ordinary*, and in it, the name of his paternal friend – 'Uncle Henry' – looms very large. The young man who became a priest on 5 August 1905, and a Jesuit on 12 November of the same year, would have loved to know how Adams stood or progressed, but he was reluctant to raise what appeared to him as too personal a matter. Yet if there were no direct indications, there were indirect ones, and they are clear. 'On one occasion, a feast of the Blessed Virgin,' *The Manner is Ordinary* recalls for us, Adams 'upbraided [his friend] Monsignor [Sigourney Fay] for casually remarking

[1] Ibid., pp. 435 and 397.
[2] Ibid., pp. 369 and 370.

that he would put off reciting his daily breviary office until they had returned from their afternoon drive. "Our Blessed Lady," said Adams, "will not tolerate that sort of thing. Today is her feast and she wants her office said in time. Please go up to your room and finish it, and then we can take our drive." As Father Fay left to fulfil this imperative command, Adams added, in a grave manner: "She is my *only* hope".[1]

Did Adams ever formally become a Catholic? A clear answer is not possible. 'He spoke of himself as a Catholic. To a friend who asked him what particular "church" he meant when he talked of "the Church", Adams scornfully replied that the question was pointless since there could be and was but one Church.' Yet the influence of Beacon Hill was not easy to shake off. 'Not unlike Simone Weil, child of a later generation, Adams seems to have rationalized, as it were, his own inner hesitation – or refusal,' Father La Farge says in closing his account. '"Uncle Henry" may have found his way before the end into the Catholic faith, if not by explicit profession, at least implicitly by a true spirit of penance and genuine desire.'[2] In our context, the question as to whether the great aesthete and art-historian ever became legally a Catholic, is of little interest; what matters is whether he became culturally one, and of that there is no shadow of a doubt.

In addition to the study of biographies, such as those of John Ruskin and Henry Adams, a look at some relevant novels is also apt to confirm our basic contention. There is a regrettable banausic tendency on the part of a few to claim that literary material must not be used in scholarly investigations, for are not novels 'fiction' which is diametrically opposed to that 'fact' with which science is concerned? The truth is, of course, that a great deal of so-called fiction is as much of an attempt to interpret and to understand experience as scholarship is or can be, only that the form taken by the exploration is different. Yet, however that may be, in our context attention to some novels must be unexceptionable by any standard, for the sociology of knowledge which we are applying here is concerned with prevailing modes of thought and feeling, and these are faithfully reflected in the pieces of literary writing to which we shall presently turn. The subject of 'Catholic and Calvinist culture in the mirror of literature' is far too vast to be adequately discussed in this chapter; even individual novelists cannot be considered *in toto*; but we may cast a glance at two outstanding books which are directly concerned with our theme – Henry James' *The Ambassadors* and E. M. Forster's *Where Angels Fear to Tread*.

Henry James' upbringing was not altogether different from that of John Ruskin. His father, Henry James senior, had indeed broken away from the strict Calvinism of his grandfather, William James senior, had rejected the 'infection of religion with the commercial spirit' which

---

[1] La Farge, J., *The Manner is Ordinary*, New York 1954, p. 175. Cf. also p. 174.
[2] Ibid., pp. 176 and 177.

maintained that God kept 'a debtor and creditor account' with man, had rejected, too, the tendency to 'bring hell into the parlour' and to enforce a 'paralytic Sunday routine', and had ended up as a Swedenborgian; but his anti-Catholicism had remained.[1] 'A horror of Rome as the capital of superstitious orthodoxy was strong in the elder James, and in 1873, when William and Henry (the philosopher and the novelist) were there together, they made a frightening moonlight visit to the Colosseum which William described as "that damned blood-soaked soil", remarking of Italy in general that "the weight of the past here is fatal".'[2]

Such memories left their mark. Yet Henry James, like John Ruskin, was too much of an aesthete to be for ever prejudiced against the predominantly aesthetic cultures. A visit to France opened his eyes wide. 'It was Paris, he says, that first awoke him to the greatness of Europe, a greatness that transcended its treasures of painting and architecture, but to which those treasures were a major clue. With its mythical name and its fabled rows of canvases, the *Galerie d'Apollon* in the Louvre breathed "a general sense of glory".' So deep was the impression the youngster received there, that he dreamt of the place many years later, a fact which is reflected in *A Small Boy and Others* (1912). A 'sense deep within me,' he says, had kept the memory of 'the wondrous place . . . whole.'[3] The desire to live in such an atmosphere was henceforth strong and led to his ultimate settlement in England. In England, not in France, simply because the crude, proletarian France of the late nineteenth century, with its coarse naturalistic novel, dismayed and repelled him. 'The Paris of which he wrote home that the passions of the Commune still worked below the surface – this Paris vexed and grieved a James to whom history considered as clash and change was ever a nightmare.' But 'there was a kind of eternal France which he continued to love . . . The congregated evidences of its great history and genius for enjoyment still attached him to Paris as they were always to do; and that city was never to become the scene of one of his stories without its taking on a preternatural glitter. That . . . was the Paris of his memories and desires, the ideal antithesis of his ideally uncivilized America.'[4]

Henry James was not popular in Boston, and this is far from surprising. 'Beginning with his first tale, his sharply allusive pictures of New England and New Englanders were to represent a personal animus raised to the level of a general observation. His father's old half-serious feud with the mind of the region' and his own 'distrust of the Calvinist strain in himself – these supplied the animus. The general observation was to the effect that New England constituted the dead hand; that America's future, that "life" itself, lay elsewhere.'[5] When he discussed Hawthorne, he deplored the 'wintry' atmosphere in which this great

[1] Cf. Dupee, F. W., *Henry James*, New York 1951, pp. 6 et seq.
[2] Ibid., p. 110.   [3] Ibid., pp. 34 and 35. Cf. also p. 67.
[4] Ibid., p. 90. Cf. also pp. 94 and 95.   [5] Ibid., p. 71.

romantic had to live and work; and when he assessed Turgenev's achievement, it was one way of expressing his admiration for the gifted Russian to say that 'our Anglo-Saxon, Protestant, moralistic, conventional standards were far away from him'.[1]

In his personal philosophy, James settled before long on the principle of *l'art pour l'art*.[2] How close did this bring him to Catholic culture? The answer is given, at least obliquely, in a late story, 'The Altar of the Dead'. The central figure, Stransom, is deeply caught up in the memory of his departed friends, above all his fiancée whom he lost before she could be finally joined to him. His abiding pain 'has paralysed a part of his nature . . . till at last he hits on the idea of maintaining in a Catholic church a private altar to his dead, a candle for each of them'. 'There is a great deal of the late James . . . in "The Altar of the Dead",' judges Dupee in his study of the novelist. 'Stransom tending his private altar in a Catholic church is an emblem of James' mind, late as well as early.'[3]

In *The Ambassadors* the two cultures in which we are interested are contrasted in two persons – Mrs. Newsome and Madame de Vionnet, and two cities – Woollett, Massachusetts, and Paris, France.[4] They fight for a young man, Mrs. Newsome's son and Madame de Vionnet's lover. An emissary sent to fetch him back, Lambert Strether, arrives with the typical Woollett conviction that Mme. de Vionnet must be a low and abandoned creature who is the ruin of Chadwick Newsome. He finds in fact the exact opposite. She is the height of culture and refinement, and she has turned a raw youth into a polished man – polished in the best sense of the word. Slowly, the truth dawns on Strether: human relations cannot only be righteous and correct; they can also be beautiful; and if they are so, they are totally admirable. Mrs. Newsome and Woollett, he now sees, are 'all cold thought' and 'no imagination'; as for Mme. de Vionnet she has, like France, 'the sense of a fine harmony of things': 'As she presented things, the ugliness – goodness knew why – went out of them.' Strether had come from America with an 'odious ascetic suspicion of any form of beauty'; but he is touched by 'the aesthetic torch, lighting that wondrous world forever'; so much so that, on considering his return to Mrs. Newsome's world, 'he saw himself recommitted, under her direction, to Woollett, as juvenile offenders are committed to reformatories'.[5]

In his introduction, M. W. Sampson informs us that Lambert Strether is 'a man of James' own type',[6] and this is obviously true. He emerges as the liberated, not to say, converted man, whereas a second envoy,

[1] Ibid., pp. 106 and 93.   [2] Cf. ibid., p. 28.
[3] Ibid., pp. 179 and 186.
[4] Woollett suggests Worcester, Mass. Cf. Dupee, loc. cit., p. 239.
[5] *The Ambassadors*, edd. Sampson, M. W., and Gerber, J. C., New York 1930, pp. 368, 371, 376, 398, 133, 136, 244.
[6] P. XII.

Mrs. Sarah Pocock, née Newsome, sent to fetch home the errant Strether as well as the errant Chadwick, appears as the eternal prisoner of the Calvinist narrowness of Woollett. Sarah Pocock is the product of an activistic civilization, not of an aesthetic culture: she is 'as prompt to act as the scrape of a safety-match', but she has no charm.[1] She appals Strether. Yet he cannot in the end forsake Woollett for Paris. Woollett righteousness is as important as Parisian refinement. The awakened man must be, and must remain, a wanderer between two worlds.

In one of his later books, E. M. Forster refers to 'Paris's healing, civilizing power',[2] and he sums up, in this short phrase, precisely what Henry James wants to tell us about the city on the Seine. In general, the similarity between the two novelists is surprising. In *Where Angels Fear to Tread* we have the same confrontation as in *The Ambassadors*; Sawston, England, stands for the one mentality,[3] Monteriano in central Italy for the other. The struggle is again for the possession of a son, this time the baby of an Italian father and an English mother who had died in childbirth. There are again ambassadors, two of whom are converted: Caroline Abbott and Philip Herriton, whereas the third, Harriet Herriton, proves incapable of conversion. Filled with the righteousness which alone her upbringing, and above all her religion, has laid into her, she is the fool who rushed in where angels fear to tread. The death of the hapless child is the result of her brutal intervention.

Perhaps the title of the novel is not quite fair to Harriet Herriton. She is no fool in the ordinary sense of the word. Her trouble is much better expressed in a passage contained in Forster's 'Notes on the English Character': when Anglo-Saxons go out into the world, we read there, 'they go forth into it with well-developed bodies, fairly developed minds, and undeveloped hearts. And it is this undeveloped heart that is largely responsible for the difficulties of Englishmen abroad. An undeveloped heart – not a cold one.'[4] Our novel may be said to be a dissertation on this theme; indeed, all Forster's novels are.[5] Lionel Trilling considers the chief point of the greatest of them, *A Passage to India*, to be 'that by reason of the undeveloped heart the English have thrown away the possibility of holding India. For want of a smile, an empire is to be lost —'[6] or rather has been lost by now.

Caroline Abbott, on whom, to the exclusion of the rather weak Philip Herriton, we may concentrate in our discussion, also has an undeveloped heart, but it is not dead yet, it can still be developed. She comes to Monteriano as Strether does to Paris, convinced that Signor Carella, like Mme de Vionnet, is totally immoral and low. But a very

---

[1] Pp. 252 and 281.
[2] *Marianne Thornton, A Domestic Biography*, New York 1956, p. 286.
[3] As Woollett may be Worcester, Mass., so Sawston may be Tonbridge. Cf. Trilling, L., *E. M. Forster*, paperback ed., New York 1964, p. 26.
[4] *Abinger Harvest*, paperback ed., London 1967, p. 15.
[5] Cf. Trilling, loc. cit., p. 28.   [6] Ibid., p. 150.

simple thing shakes her to the depths: she sees this man Gino give a bath to his baby son and she recognizes in a flash of lightning that he has something to offer which is lacking in Sawston: true, uninhibited, simple human affection. 'The horrible truth that wicked people are capable of love, stood naked before her, and her moral being was abashed.'[1] This sentence is the core of the tale; its moral, its message. Using a phrase which Forster himself does not always shun, we can say that Caroline Abbott is now saved.[2]

In stark contrast to her, Harriet Herriton is beyond reclaim. Her own brother says of her that she had 'bolted all the cardinal virtues and couldn't digest them'.[3] The remark is easily understandable, but it is not quite correct. In a sense, she has digested such virtues as were offered to her only too well: they have become flesh and bone with her, so much so that she cannot regard them, or anything else, as problematic. The typical product of an activistic civilization, her whole being, like that of Sarah Pocock in *The Ambassadors*, is geared to action. She will not stop to consider: she must rush in and on. 'Forster will not let us forget that it is her Low-Church fervour, her insensitivity to all distinctions save moral ones, that blinds her.'[4] After she has set out on her ill-advised expedition to steal the baby, the Bible is found in her room open at the one hundred and forty-fourth psalm which begins: 'Blessed be the Lord my God who teacheth my hands to war and my fingers to fight.'[5] But it is not a godly deed which she accomplishes.

Harriet is thus the condemned character in the book, not to say the villainess, and with her the atmosphere which has bred her stands condemned, too. She is not the only unlovely character in the tale. Forster does not represent Gino Carella as lovable; in fact, he does not spare him at all. He is depicted as feckless, vain, loud, inconstant, and, above all, too easily moved to anger. When he learns of his baby-son's death, he nearly kills the blameless Philip and tortures him in order to abreact his emotion which a civilized man would, in spite of everything, have controlled. But Gino's weaknesses are human and, taken as a man, they do not make him unsympathetic. Harriet's strengths, on the other hand, bespeak a lack of humanity and therefore they disgust and repel.

We have now given the content of the novel and do not have to add a single word by way of commentary: it speaks for itself. But the contrast between the Anglo-Saxon-Protestant and the Italian-Catholic mentality shows itself in yet another way and that aspect, or rather Forster's discussion of it, is particularly interesting for the sociologist and must be brought out. The Calvinist countries are countries in which wholeness is not achieved. This is stressed especially in Forster's last

[1] *Where Angels Fear to Tread*, paperback ed., New York 1958, p. 136.
[2] Ibid., p. 173.   [3] Ibid., p. 13.
[4] Crews, F. C., *E. M. Forster: The Perils of Humanism*, Princeton 1962, p. 78.
[5] In the Vulgate this is, of course, the one hundred and forty-third psalm.

novel. 'The theme of separateness, of fences and barriers, . . . which runs through all Forster's novels, is, in *A Passage to India*, hugely expanded and everywhere dominant. The separation of race from race, sex from sex, culture from culture, even of man from himself, is what underlies every relationship,' even among the English themselves. Their 'separation . . . from the Indians is merely the most dramatic of the chasms in this novel'.[1] But wholeness is what Forster longs for. The words which he puts, as a motto, on the title page of his penultimate great piece of fiction, *Howards End*, is like a sigh of longing: 'Only connect . . .' Margaret Schlegel (characteristically she is only half English) is the heroine of the story. Her 'redeeming virtue, the ability to "connect", operates on every level of action in *Howards End*'. It shows itself above all in her marrying the lonely and all too businesslike Henry Wilcox, for by accepting him 'she not only bridges the perilous gap between male and female, but symbolically marries her civilizing force to the power of modern England'.[2]

In so far as integration, synthesis and organicism are the chief values, not only of the mediterranean cultures, but also of the Catholic Church connected with them, Forster's philosophy of life comes rather close to hers. On occasion he can therefore feel near to her. Thus he writes as follows in a passage in which he condemns Henry Wilcox as he had condemned Harriet Herriton: 'Whether as boy, husband, or widower, he had always the sneaking belief that bodily passion is bad, a belief that is desirable only when held passionately. Religion [*his* religion] had confirmed him. The words that were read aloud on Sunday to him and to other respectable men were the words that had once kindled the souls of St. Catherine and St. Francis into a white-hot hatred of the carnal. He could not be as the saints and love the Infinite with a seraphic ardour, but he could be a little ashamed of loving a wife.'[3] These words, however, though significant, do not indicate any openness to the Catholic culture. Forster does indeed write, in *The Longest Journey*, with his eye on the Catholic church at Cambridge (as it happens, a proof that even fake Gothic can, on occasions, be beautiful): it asserts, 'however wildly, that here is eternity, stability, and bubbles unbreakable upon a windless sea',[4] but the symbol does not mean much to him. 'It is in Wiltshire, where man's life is properly related to the earth that the most convincing monuments stand,' especially those heathen relics, the Cadbury Rings.[5] Forster is not really a Christian; he condemns asceticism as – in his passionate individualism – he rejects organized religion in any shape or form. He, too, wishes to connect; he, too, fails to

[1] Trilling, loc. cit., p. 151.
[2] Crews, loc. cit., p. 121. Crews' whole analysis on this page is relevant and enlightening.
[3] *Howards End*, ed. New York 1921, p. 186.
[4] *The Longest Journey*, ed. Norfolk, Conn., 1922, p. 71.
[5] Crews, loc. cit., p. 66.

achieve connection. He is a humanist with sadness at the knowledge that humanism's values – life's values – are shadowy and problematical. But this does not diminish his stature as an explorer of man and culture, or rather of men and cultures, and what he has to say, especially about the setting which has born and bred him, is truly profound and truly the truth.

In spite of all the evidence which has now been amassed, it is possible that one more argument might be advanced against our contention that, as the eighteenth century would have expressed it, Calvinism had 'no genius' for art. It might be said that Calvinist countries have, after all, produced great art, some of the greatest art even. What about Milton? What about Rembrandt? And what about Johann Sebastian Bach who, if he was a Lutheran and not a Calvinist, was yet born into a period when Lutheranism had, just like Calvinism, undergone considerable rationalization, considerable cooling-down and cooling-out? We shall now, to conclude this section, look at these three cases. The reference to them is somewhat too simple to begin with; to live within the area of Calvinism does not necessarily mean to be an adherent of Calvinism, especially not in a world of complexity and flux; but even a superficial question deserves a well-considered and well-documented reply.

First, then, to John Milton, the author of *Paradise Lost*. He was a Puritan, no doubt of that; but he was not only a Puritan. If he had not been more than a Puritan, he would not have become a great poet. He was a complex, not to say an inwardly broken man. This comes out even in statements about him which are summaries of summaries. Thus the *Schweizer Lexikon* writes: 'Milton reconciled in his work the Renaissance ideal of sensuous beauty with the seriousness of Puritanism.'[1] In this sentence, which gets close to the truth, only the word 'reconcile' is problematic, for how can two largely contradictory tendencies be 'reconciled'? But if they cannot be reconciled, they can coexist, at any rate in the form of latent conflict, and this precisely is the case of the man we wish to consider here.

Dates are important at this point. Milton was born in 1608, eight years before Shakespeare's death; and he died in 1674, when John Locke was already forty-two years old. Thus he came into a world which was still permeated by the Renaissance spirit, and he left a world which was rapidly moving towards latitudinarianism in religion, not to say towards scepticism and secularization. The great crisis of the Civil War, which brought English Calvinism to its acme, appears, when seen within this historical framework, as merely an interlude. True, it was much more than an interlude for the bourgeois classes who received an abiding imprint from it. But so far as culture is concerned, higher culture, if we may say so without bringing in an adverse value judgment, it jumped from one anti-Calvinic constellation to another. Neither the

[1] Vol. V, Zürich 1947, p. 569.

court of Elizabeth and James I, nor that of Charles II was touched by the sterner spirit of middle-class Protestantism; neither Shakespeare nor Dryden was a Puritan. To what extent was Milton, *in his culture,* a Puritan, he who stands between the Caroline and the Elizabethan efflorescences?

One answer that has been given to this query – given by a good many of the leading Milton scholars – is to the effect that his life, too, just like the wider world, falls into three periods. Let us hear one of the experts. 'Milton's life is a drama in three acts,' writes Mark Pattison. 'The first discovers him in the calm retirement of Horton, of which *L'Allegro, Il Penseroso* and *Lycidas* are the expression. In the second act he is breathing the foul and heated atmosphere of party passion and religious hate, generating the lurid fires which glare in the battailous canticles of his prose pamphlets. The three great poems, *Paradise Lost, Paradise Regained,* and *Samson Agonistes,* are the utterance of his final period of solitary Promethean grandeur, when, blind, destitute, friendless, he testified of righteousness, temperance, and judgment to come, alone before a fallen world.'[1] This is well said; it must only be emphasized that the Milton of declining years moved away from Calvinistic, and with it from Christian, theology, into a new Arianism which was even more rationalistic than the old.

Some students of Milton have felt that the historizing three-tier theory of the poet's mind is an unjustifiable cutting up of a unitary life. Thus Bush thinks of an abiding psychological condition when he refers to a 'conflict between the sensuous and the ethical impulses in his nature'.[2] But what have these authors tended to substitute for Pattison's view? They have substituted for it the picture of a man permanently divided against himself. Even Pattison comes, in one context, close to this opinion. 'The fanaticism of the covenanter and the sad grace of Petrarch seem to meet in Milton's monody,' he writes. 'The conflict between the old cavalier world, the years of gaiety and festivity of a splendid and pleasure-loving court, and the new puritan world into which love and pleasure were not to enter – this conflict which was commencing in the social life of England is also begun in Milton's own breast and is reflected in *Lycidas*.'[3] The point here is that the chief characteristic of the first period, attunement to Renaissance values, spills over and maintains itself in the second period, the period of Puritanism. This is entirely correct, and all the experts are agreed that it is so. One context in which we can, so to speak, touch – almost bodily touch

[1] Pattison, M., *Milton,* ed. London 1926, pp. 14 and 15. Cf. also Bush, D., *The Renaissance and English Humanism,* Toronto 1939, pp. 108, 124–6; Hanford, J. H., *John Milton, Poet and Humanist,* Cleveland 1966, pp. 32, 38, 48; Nelson, J. G., *The Sublime Puritan,* Madison 1963, pp. 96, 100–03; Belloc, H., *Milton,* Philadelphia and London 1935, pp. 15, 41, 287.
[2] Bush, loc. cit., p. 108.
[3] Pattison, loc. cit., p. 30.

– the two souls which together dwell in Milton's breast, occurs in *Paradise Regained*.[1] He praises there 'Athens, the eye of Greece, mother of arts', and immediately afterwards, in one breath, condemns her as a place of vacuity and vanity.

The two opinions which we have outlined – a three-phase life versus a life split from end to end – are not necessarily irreconcilable. Progress and persistence are mutually exclusive only in their textbook definitions. In reality they coexist, if not without difficulties. Let us say, then, that there was a shift in Milton's prevailing mood, but never a total conversion; and let us take this sober assessment as the basis of our further disquisition.

The thesis which we wish to argue here is that Milton's poetry is of Renaissance origin and character, but that the artistic forms which he owed to pre-Reformation culture and creativity are later filled by Reformation contents. A good illustration of this fact is his much admired sonnet, 'On the Late Massacre in Piedmont'. It is a sonnet, that typical Renaissance conceit and convention, which Petrarca had brought to high perfection, and Milton is his disciple. But, unlike Petrarca, he does not speak of a noble lady descended from paradise;[2] he speaks of brutal men murdering their brothers down here on earth. A playful form is made to accept a political content. It is as if a crystal goblet were filled, not with sweet wine, but with some bitter potion. And if this simile is correct, as we are sure it is, then it shows forth the duality of John Milton in general. He was a Renaissance poet turned Puritan politician. But as a poet, as an artist, as a man of culture, he belongs to Francesco Petrarca rather than to Jehan Calvin.

In view of what we have said, we are anxious to show how much of Puritanism did in our opinion enter into Milton's poetry, even though it was pre-Puritan in origin, character, form and even substance. A man may be divided, but (setting aside the case of split personality) he is yet always one. There were no watertight compartments in Milton's mind; the mental fluids mingled – which does not mean that the artistic mode of the mind's expression may not have been the work of one of the tendencies within it rather than of the other. To do justice to Milton's Puritanism, let us for once use the technique of enumeration, notwithstanding the fact that it is somewhat pedantic. Better to be pedantic than to be accused of underplaying a truth.

Milton's Puritanism, then, is seen in his literary work (1) in that it is didactic. No *l'art pour l'art* here: we have poetry for use. A poetic writer of a later day felt this rather acutely. Francis Thompson speaks of 'a certain strain of exalted declamation' and continues: 'Always he seems perorating to some august assembly, like his own Satan in Pandemonium: the very rhythm seems designed to swell through resounding

[1] IV, 240 et seq. Cf. *Works*, as quoted, vol. II/2, New York 1931, pp. 467 et seq.
[2] Cf. above, p. 141.

distances and reverberate above the multitudinous murmur of frequent congregations . . . It is in such mood and at such opportunities, therefore, that his great and entirely personal style is most completely under his control, can deploy its full resources and rejoice unafraid in its own power.'[1] With this desire to teach is connected (2) a certain coolness or coldness, a certain lack of emotion which, needless to say, is thoroughly Calvinist. Speaking of the ode 'On the Morning of Christ's Nativity', James Holly Hanford comments: 'He contemplates the event, not at all with the loving surrender of a Catholic poet to its human sweetness, but with an austere intellectualized emotion stirred in him by the idea of its moral significance.'[2] The prevalence of the ethical over the aesthetic and even over the religious values thus springs into sharp relief. Francis Thompson made the same point when he called Milton 'a poet for the accomplishment not equalled in our language . . . yet in youth or age without humaneness or heart-blood in his greatness . . . a poet to whom all must bow the knee, few or none the heart . . . who had gone near to being the first, if his grandeurs, his majesties, his splendours, his august solemnities, had been humid with a tear or a smile.'[3]

Connected with the lack of emotion is (3) a concomitant lack of humour. Puritans rarely laughed, and in his way he was, in this particular, one of them. 'In Milton humour was so lacking that when he attempted attack in this form he is himself the object of our ridicule, and not the opponent whom he would have made our laughing stock,' Hilaire Belloc writes. 'And indeed all through Milton's work this incapacity for laughter appears . . . But when he attempts the sublime, . . . he triumphs.'[4] Belloc also exposes yet another Calvinistic trait: (4) his greater interest in nature than in people. 'With Milton, persons and their contrasts were vague,' he states, 'or for the most part non-existent; contrariwise, he was intoxicated by landscape, and there again he was national.'[5]

While the last point may appear to some over-drawn, all are apparently agreed on the next. By common consent, *Paradise Lost* is a much more powerful poem than *Paradise Regained*. It is hardly necessary here to bring an expert witness into court, so general – so notorious – is the conviction of the later work's decided inferiority. There are in all probability several reasons for this fact: simple exhaustion is sure to be

---

[1] *Literary Criticisms by Francis Thompson*, ed. Connolly, T. L., New York 1948, p. 87. Cf. also Hanford, loc. cit., pp. 18 and 184; also pp. 69 and 70; and Dowden, E., *Puritan and Anglican*, London 1900, p. 33: 'God the Father and His Son discuss the scheme of salvation too much in the manner of school-divines . . . We cannot assert that Milton entirely succeeded in finding an imaginative vehicle to convey his Puritan conceptions.'

[2] Hanford, loc. cit., p. 35.

[3] *The Works of Francis Thompson*, vol. III, London 1913, pp. 201 and 202.

[4] Belloc, loc. cit., p. 56. Cf. also p. 90.

[5] Ibid., p. 54.

one. But (5) the presence of a near-Calvinist theology in Milton's mind must also be remembered at this juncture. The God of the Puritans was the God of the Old Testament. Difficult though it may be to understand it, the image of Jehova was much more concrete for these men than the image of Jesus. And because of this, it is not overly surprising that an epic-poetic rendering of the Old Testament should have turned out better than one of the New; not overly surprising either that a man like Milton should in the end have abandoned Trinitarianism and embraced Unitarianism, as in effect he did.

(6) Finally, there remains a somewhat subtle and elusive aspect which is, however, of surpassing interest to the sociologist. We have seen all along that Catholicism tends in all things towards unity, whereas Calvinism's set is towards multiplicity. And this, as Thomas Babington Macaulay assures us, is visible in Milton also, not only in his general individualism, but also in the finer and more formal characteristics of his poetry. This is what the great historian writes: 'The comparisons of . . . Milton are magnificent digressions. It scarcely injures their effect to detach them from the work. Those of Dante are very different. They derive their beauty from the context, and reflect beauty upon it. His embroidery cannot be taken out without spoiling the whole web.'[1]

All this goes to show that Milton's poetry and his Puritanism are not separate entities, and that the latter largely enters into the former. But – and this is the main point – it merely enters into it, as the waters of one river enter into those of another: indistinguishable in the end, they are yet distinct in the beginning. The source of Milton's art is his Renaissance humanism, and it is almost justifiable to say that his Puritanism was something of a contaminating influence on it and in it.

That Renaissance humanism was indeed the well-spring and fountainhead of Milton's art can be seen from the models which he followed, and admitted he followed. To begin with, it was Ovid, *Ars Amatoria* and all. Indeed, Milton psychologically identified himself with the Roman: his rustication from Cambridge was experienced as parallel to Ovid's banishment from Rome. Then 'purer' – i.e. morally purer – types are substituted for the teacher of physical love. But who are they? Again 'Romans', Neo-Romans – Dante and Petrarca. And, finally, Milton moves away from elegy altogether because it is not sufficiently serious, not sufficiently godly, we may perhaps already say. But that only brings yet another Roman into the centre of the stage – Virgil. The inspiration of *Paradise Lost* is, artistically speaking, the *Aeneid*;[2] Ariosto and Spenser also were influential, but they, too, are products of the Renaissance and hence ultimately of Antiquity. 'The art of the Romans he still, like a

[1] Macaulay, T. B., 'Milton', in *Critical, Historical and Miscellaneous Essays*, ed. New York 1893, pp. 71 and 72.
[2] Cf. esp. Hanford, loc. cit., pp. 21, 31, 38, 48.

good humanist, judges superior, the men themselves far lower in a spiritual scale. His own path is clear. He will continue to rival the pagans in their perfection of outward form, but he will follow the Christians in the purity and elevation of their conceptions. This is the formula for Milton's youthful poetic aspirations. It was later transformed to suit with a more mature idea of his true objects, but it was never abandoned.'[1]

To prove that it was in fact never abandoned, it would be necessary to work with the tools of literary history and criticism, and these do not belong to the equipment of one who is in essence a social theorist. Hence references to Milton scholarship must suffice.[2] But we can reinforce and perhaps clinch our argument by showing that even the biblical dramas are presented, by Milton, in a classical garb. There is, first of all, Eden itself, the primal setting as it were. Milton describes it in an early Latin piece, *In Obitum Praesulis Wintoniensis*. 'With its flowers, its silver streams playing over golden sands, its bejewelled angelic presence, its fanfare of celestial music, the passage anticipates both *Lycidas* and the *Epitaphium Damonis* and is the first of a series of Paradisiac pictures elaborated from antique models and enriched by the more luxuriant poetic tradition of the Renaissance – a series which culminates in the account of Eden in *Paradise Lost*.'[3] There are, further, the main protagonists, and they again owe at least as much to pagan mythology as to Christian belief. 'We recognize in Eve the enchantress Circe and the enchanter Comus,' and what is demanded of Adam is more in line with Platonic moderation than with Pauline asceticism: 'We perceive that what is exacted of Adam is the control of his instinct, not its denial.'[4] As with the human personages, so with the superhuman: 'Perhaps the gods and daemons of Aeschylus may best bear a comparison with the angels and devils of Milton . . . Prometheus bears undoubtedly a considerable resemblance to the Satan of Milton. In both we find the same impatience of control, the same ferocity, the same unconquerable pride. In both characters also are mingled, though in very different proportions, some kind and generous feelings.'[5] Some have felt that even the Christ of Milton is not the Christ of the Gospels. Thus Sir John Seeley asserts that what we encounter in *Paradise Regained* is merely 'a more gifted and energetic Marcus Aurelius'.[6] Edward Dowden, who disagrees with Seeley in many respects, agrees with him here: 'How could the Puritan Milton,' he asks, 'present . . . a Messiah, who, seated in His chariot,

---

[1] Ibid., p. 32.
[2] Cf. esp. Hanford's essay, 'Milton and the Return to Humanism', loc. cit., pp. 161 et seq. and more particularly pp. 163–5 and 178–83, with the literature cited in the footnotes.
[3] Hanford, loc. cit., p. 11.
[4] Ibid., p. 72. Cf. also Bush, loc. cit., p. 119.
[5] Macaulay, loc. cit., pp. 228 and 229.
[6] Dowden, loc. cit., p. 191; Seeley, J. R., *Lectures and Essays*, London 1870, p. 145.

bears upon His side a bow and quiver, as though He were some far-shooting Apollo? Are we reading a Pagan or a Christian poem?'[1]

Seeley, in pronouncing his judgment, has also suggested that the whole ethos of Milton is Grecian rather than Christian, for his moral ideal is based on the concept of self-respect, not self-sacrifice. Dowden has protested against this interpretation.[2] But however that may be, there is a conflict of the kind Seeley has in mind on a far deeper level. Milton is a believer in free will. There is nothing of Luther's *De Servo Arbitrio* in him; there is therefore even less of Calvin's *Institutio*. 'When we survey Milton's whole body of writing in prose and verse,' says one who knows him well, 'we see that his various ideas and principles start from a passionate belief in the freedom of the will. There, of course, he breaks utterly with Calvinistic doctrine. Over a century earlier Erasmus had challenged Luther on just that ground. No humanist who had learned from the ancients the dignity of human reason could accept predestination and the depravity of man.'[3] The words of God in *Paradise Lost* are unambiguous:

> So without least impulse or shadow of fate
> Or ought by me immutably foreseen,
> They trespass, authors to themselves in all
> Both what they judge and what they choose; for so
> I formed them free and free they must remain
> Till they enthrall themselves; I else must change
> Their nature, and revoke the high decree,
> Unchangeable, eternal, which ordained
> Their freedom; they themselves ordained their fall.[4]

A man who could express himself in this way would hardly have passed muster in a strictly Calvinic school of theology. 'Lutheran and Calvinist dogmas were incompatible with the humanistic doctrine of the self-governing reason and dignity of man,' writes Bush,[5] and he is right. But Milton adheres to the latter concepts. He 'insists on the freedom of the human will', Dowden tells us, and adds: 'It was a faith difficult to reconcile with the Calvinistic dogma of Divine decrees. But [in this particular] Milton was not a Calvinist.'[6]

How just is Seeley's accusation and assessment? Was the poet in Milton truly a heathen? That he was not, as a poet, a Puritan, is true enough, for Puritanism simply was not a possible basis for poetry. But Puritanism was Christian, and Christianity in the wider sense could well

---

[1] Dowden, loc. cit., p. 178.   [2] Ibid., pp. 191 and 192.
[3] Bush, loc. cit., p. 114; cf. also pp. 101 and 103.
[4] III, 120 et seq., *Works*, as quoted, vol. II/1, New York 1931, pp. 81 and 82; cf. also V, 524 et seq., ibid., pp. 162 and 163.
[5] Bush, loc. cit., p. 83.   [6] Dowden, loc. cit., p. 182.

have determined Milton's attitude to beauty even if narrow Calvinism did not. This is the decisive question about Milton which we have to raise and to lay to rest.

Perhaps we can best cut through to the core of the problem if we consider, not this detail or that, but the basic philosophical position from which everything else had to follow. What, we should ask above all, was Milton's view of that Platonic art theory which, deeply religious, considered all beauty as a showing-forth – as, at least, a shadowing-forth – of divine archetypes, divine ideas? – that art theory which Catholicism has ever made its own? If we could find a clear statement on this aesthetic, an assured insight into Milton's mind on matters of art could easily be gained. Luckily we have such a statement from Milton's pen. It occurs in one of the most precious biographical sources which we possess, the widely self-revelatory letter to his friend Charles Diodati, dated 23 September 1637. The whole effusion is steeped, as it were, in Platonism; and the Platonic-Catholic art theory is expressly accepted, accepted without reservation. 'Whatever the Deity may have bestowed on me in other respects,' Milton declares, 'He has certainly inspired me, if any were ever inspired, with a passion for the good and fair. Nor did Ceres, according to the fable, ever seek her daughter Proserpine with such unceasing solicitude as I have sought this idea of the beautiful in all the forms and appearances of things, for many are the forms of the divine.' Hanford, in quoting this document, remarks that 'it reflects as in a mirror a whole phase of the Renaissance – the attempt of high souls to make the spiritual discipline of Platonic philosophy a reality . . . [Milton's] idealism harks back to the days of Ficino and Pico and the Platonic academy of Lorenzo dei Medici.'[1] It harks back, so we should add, to men like Petrarca and Michelangelo who were Christians and Catholics.

The Platonist theory of art which is so clearly expressed in the letter to Diodati does not fail to make its appearance even in *Paradise Lost*.[2] It is not so positively formulated there, but it is none the less accepted. Milton asks through Raphael's mouth:

> . . . what if earth
> Be but the shadow of heaven, and things therein
> Each to other like, more than on earth is thought?

We may take the last words to mean 'more than is assumed in my (Puritanical) environment', for, to the Puritans, the higher realm and the lower were ever sundered, while to the Platonists they were ever joined – joined as a dark mirror is to the lighted objects which it reflects. Milton, it clearly appears, was not disinclined, even while he wrote *Paradise*

[1] Hanford, loc. cit., pp. 58 and 57.
[2] V, 574 et seq. Cf. *Works*, vol. II/1, as quoted, p. 164.

Lost, to assert – 'by likening spiritual and corporal forms'[1] – that the things of earth and the things of heaven are 'each to the other like'.

To come to a conclusion: in what sense, then, was Milton a Puritan; in what sense was he not? The answer can be precise: in poetry he was not, as we have seen; in theology he was not either, as we shall yet see; in politics he was. We can recognize the primacy of politics in Milton's mind by casting a side-glance at a fact which has puzzled all his readers and scandalized many: his obvious sympathy with Satan. Walter Bagehot has convincingly explained this trait. 'There is no wonder,' he says, 'that Milton's hell is better than his heaven for he hated officials and he loved rebels . . . Though the theme of *Paradise Lost* obliged Milton to side with the monarchical element in the universe, his old habits are often too much for him; and his real sympathy – the impetus and energy of his nature – side with the rebellious element.'[2] In view of this, we would make the following words of Macaulay our own, for they are in this as in so many other matters a safe guide: 'Hating tyranny with a perfect hatred, he had nevertheless all the estimable and ornamental qualities which were almost entirely monopolized by the party of the tyrant. There was none who had a stronger sense of the values of literature, a finer relish for every elegant amusement, or a more chivalrous delicacy of honour and love. Though his opinions were democratic, his tastes and his associations were such as harmonize best with monarchy and aristocracy. He was under the influence of all the feelings by which the gallant Cavaliers were misled.' As for the Puritans, Macaulay tersely says that he was not one of them. 'Not the coolest sceptic or the most profane scoffer was more perfectly free from the contagion of their frantic delusions, their savage manners, their ludicrous jargon, their scorn of science, and their aversion to pleasure.'[3]

'Any person who will contrast the sentiments expressed in his treatises on Prelacy with the exquisite lines on ecclesiastical architecture and music in the *Penseroso*, which was published at the same time, will understand our meaning,' writes Macaulay.[4] There was, in this way, an aesthete underneath the politician, and the question is of what nature his aestheticism was. Sir John Seeley asserted, as we have already seen when we considered ethics rather than poetics, that it was essentially Pre-Christian, Greek. 'How strange an inconsistency lies in the construction of *Paradise Lost*,' he writes. 'A Puritan has rebelled against

[1] Ibid., line 573.
[2] Bagehot, W., *Literary Studies*, vol. II, ed. London 1944, pp. 322, 321.
[3] Macaulay, loc. cit., pp. 260 and 259. It must not be inferred from the quoted lines that Macaulay was hostile to the Puritans. He understood them and did them full justice. While 'they were not men of letters'; while they did 'their utmost to decry and ruin literature', they had virtues of their own, the virtues of action: 'Those had little reason to laugh [about them] who encountered them in the hall of debate or on the field of battle.' Ibid., pp. 253, 234, 256.
[4] Ibid., p. 261.

sensuous worship. He has risen in indignation against a scheme of religion which was too material, too sensuous, which degraded invisible and awful realities by too near an association with what was visible and familiar. But in the meanwhile a poet, who is the same person, having a mind inveterately plastic and creative, is quite unable to think, even on religious subjects, without forms distinctly conceived. And, therefore, while with one hand he throws down forms, with the other he raises them up. The iconoclast is at the same time an idolater.'[1] Seeley concludes by comparing Milton with Dante; both, he considers, are mythological, but whereas the mythology of Dante is Christian, that of Milton is otherwise.

This, however, is going far too far. Just because Milton was a Renaissance man, Plato was to him, as to so many of his persuasion, a Plato Christianus, and his attitude to art therefore, to say the least, potentially Christian. The decisive and intriguing question can only be as to whether Milton may after all find his place in the line which leads from Plato to Dante, Michelangelo, Petrarca and beyond, and in answer to it we have to point to certain passages where he seems to join the cultural mainstream in spite of his political adherence to Puritanism. His tractate *Of Education* was written in the forties, when Puritanism had reached its height and Milton's adherence to it was of the firmest. Yet Dowden[2] can sum up his teaching as follows: 'If "to know God aright" be the first end of education, the Puritan Milton does not suppose that this knowledge is to be gained solely or chiefly from churches or creeds or catechisms or even from Holy Scripture. Through the visible world, through the nature of man, through the laws of human society we make acquaintance with what is divine. Through sense we ascend to spirit.' This is rank Platonism, even Thomism. Nor is this the only context where such an opinion lies concealed, or rather half-concealed. Hanford, for instance, sees in the closing passage of the *Epitaphium Damonis* 'an imaginative and religious rapture which allies him for the moment with the tradition of Catholic Christianity'. But, he adds, and thereby points in the direction where we shall find a final answer to the problem raised by Seeley, 'it does so only outwardly, for there is fundamental disparity between the essentially humanistic attitude and the devout asceticism of the Middle Ages. He belongs by temper and inheritance to the Renaissance,' and the Renaissance – or rather *his* Renaissance – Hanford implies, coming down on the side of Seeley, is not fully Christian. 'The Christian meaning is transfused with the spirit, as it is assimilated to the language, of Pagan poetry.'[3] Compared to Dante, compared even to Michelangelo and Petrarca, Milton appears, from the

---

[1] Seeley, loc. cit., p. 136.
[2] Dowden, loc. cit., p. 148. Cf. *Works*, as quoted, vol. IV, New York 1931, pp. 275 et seq., esp. p. 277.
[3] Hanford, loc. cit., p. 65.

point of view of Christianity, almost as a throw-back. He did, in a sense, belong to the Christian Platonists, but he belonged to a Platonism which was decreasingly Christian.

This does not mean, of course, that *Paradise Lost* is pagan poetry; it would be absurd to claim that. It was and is and remains one of the world's supreme Christian classics, but it owes its sublimity to a unique marriage of Puritanism with Platonism, to a union in which Platonism provided all the vision and even some of the substance while Christianity provided merely the raw material, the tale told. As Milton passed from his earliest to his last phase, he went through a period in which, under the whip of political passion, the pre-Reformation element in him was temporarily stemmed back and Hebraic influences could for a while overshadow Grecian ones – overshadow them completely on the level of consciousness. But in the depths they were still there, they were still a driving force, and in the end they could come powerfully to the fore, to the extent even of undermining that Puritanism and that Christianity with which they had been so fruitfully – so blessedly – allied. What distinguished the Platonizing aestheticism of Milton from that of Catholicism was Milton's insistence, characteristic in many ways of the modern age to which he belonged as well as that of antiquity to which he harked back, that only the beauty of nature carries and reflects perfection, whereas human creations do not or do so in a lesser manner. Hence he rejects, for instance, ritual and everything connected with it. But with this onesided emphasis on nature came an involution, not only of his sympathy for such arts as sculpture and painting, but also for those religious conceptions with which these arts were traditionally connected – indeed for all Christian conceptions without distinction. He who looks to nature rather than to man, will look to the Creator God rather than to the Redeemer God, to Jehova rather than to Jesus, and he will be on the best way to becoming a Unitarian. Milton was a Unitarian in the end. And he who looks to nature as the value of values, will tend to demote even the Creator God who will increasingly appear as an adjunct to nature rather than as its Master and Maker. Milton finally defined God more as the great form-giver of a realm of matter connatural with Him than as the One who had called that matter out of the void and was thus the true origin of things. Hence Milton was a full Puritan neither in youth nor in age, simply because in the one period he was a Platonist and in the other a Deist rather than a right-thinking Protestant Christian. He *was* a Puritan in his middle years, but even then his poetry was not fed exclusively by his Calvinistic religiousness, but rather, subterraneously, by that flow of un-Calvinic aestheticism which led from an old heathenism towards a new.[1]

[1] On Milton's abandonment of Trinitarianism and full personalistic theism, and his advance towards pantheism, cf. his *De Doctrina Christiana*. Cf. also the excellent summary of Dowden, loc. cit., pp. 178 et seq.

Compared to the complexities of Milton, the case of Rembrandt, to which we now turn, is relatively simple. To begin with, he was not, like the English poet, at any time of his life formally linked to a Calvinistic church organization. On the contrary, he belonged to that pool of anti-Calvinist dissent to which various Baptist or near-Baptist groupings, like the Doopers and the Collegiants, had contributed and were in his day still contributing. The matter became most obvious in the year 1654, when the Consistory of Amsterdam decided to take steps against his companion or common-law wife, Hendrickje Stoffels, for unlawful cohabitation. She was summoned and censured, while Rembrandt was not. The ecclesiastical authorities were powerless against him, for he was not on their register and hence outside their reach and jurisdiction. Baldinucci says that he was one of the *Menisti*,[1] and we can take it that he means Mennonite. The description cannot be far wrong for the Mennonites, placed somewhere between the Anabaptists and the Quakers, had little or no church organization, and if you belonged to them, you belonged to them, not organizationally, but 'by the spirit'. Carl Neumann who (as Max Weber testifies[2]) knew as much about these matters as any man, brings Rembrandt close to Jakob Böhme.[3] But Böhme was a mystic, and mysticism was not kindred to, but different from, Calvinism.

Formal affiliation, however, or the lack of it, does not mean too much. The atmosphere of contemporary Holland was permeated by Calvinism, and the question is as to how much of it entered into the painter's mind and soul. One apparently near-Calvinistic trait is Rembrandt's manifest disinterest in, perhaps we may even say, contempt of, physical beauty. Preoccupation with it was generally condemned as heathenism, as creature-divinization, as idolatry of the flesh, and it was urged that before the Creator even the finest face was but a mask of death, even the fullest body but dust and ashes. Rembrandt seems to have felt the same way. It makes no difference to him, says Neumann, whether he painted a naked Diana in her bath or the corpse of a hanged man. If the latter is repulsive, the model of the former was 'arch-ugly'. Rembrandt was, in the opinion of this great art historian, 'no painter of ladies', and he quotes another aesthetic critic (Michel) who says that the legs of Rembrandt's Bathseba are of *grande vulgarité* and her midriff is marred by *déformations*. The facts are beyond doubt. There is a downright 'cult of ugliness'.[4] But it would be quite wrong to consider this characteristic

---

[1] Baldinucci, F., *Cominciamento e Progresso de l'Arte dell'Intagliare in Rame, Opere*, vol. I, ed. Milano 1808, pp. 194 and 195: 'Professava la religione dei Menisti...contraria a quella di Calvino.'
[2] *The Protestant Ethic and the Spirit of Capitalism*, transl. Parsons, T., ed. New York 1958, p. 273.
[3] Neumann, C., *Rembrandt*, ed. München 1924, p. 549. Cf. also p. 692. The translations from Neumann are our own.
[4] Neumann, loc. cit., pp. 76, 442, 392, 209; cf. also pp. 362, 363, 461.

as a specific property or privilege of Calvinism. So far as coarseness is concerned, it would be difficult to find a more coarse-looking set of human beings than St. John, St. Mary and even Christ in *The Crucifixion with the Virgin and St. John* by Hendrick Terbrugghen in the Metropolitan Museum of Art (New York). But Terbrugghen was not a Calvinist; he was a Catholic who was born and bred in a family devoted to the traditional Catholic values[1] and spent a good deal of time in Rome. We must see Rembrandt and Terbrugghen together; and we may see them together, for they were both *Caravaggeschi*, disciples of Caravaggio,[2] whose rejection of the concept of ideal beauty we have already discussed.

That the brutal exposure of the ugliness of the flesh is no onesidedly Calvinistic trait can perhaps best be seen if we place the one of Caravaggio's greatest followers, Rembrandt, side by side with the other – Velasquez. Neumann does this for us. 'Holland must be compared to Spain,' he writes. 'The obvious interest of Velasquez for what is ugly corresponds to the inclinations of Dutch art.'[3] The real division, Neumann explains – and the sociologist of knowledge will not contradict him – lies not between the countries and the confessions, but between the classes. Aristocratic art is inclined to subtle idealization, democratic art to brutal realism. A figure like the Catholic Jusepe de Ribera shows it no less than any Protestant. Even the saints of Murillo are, according to Neumann, 'plebeian in feature'.[4] 'Letting himself go,' writes Benesch about one of the Dutchman's greatest canvases *(The Blinding of Samson)*, 'Rembrandt achieves all the *terribilità* of Caravaggio himself'.[5] As can be seen, the experts always tend to take us back to this *fons et origo* of seventeenth-century realism. But that *fons et origo* was on Italian soil, and it came to Catholic Spain no less than to Calvinist Holland.[6]

The second matter which we have to raise still concerns realism, but

[1] Cf. *Kindlers Malerei Lexikon*, Zürich 1964, vol. I, p. 562.
[2] Cf. esp. Benesch, O., *Rembrandt*, transl. Emmons, J., Geneva (?) 1957, p. 26.
[3] Neumann, loc. cit., p. 209. [4] Ibid.
[5] Benesch, loc. cit., p. 55.
[6] Max Weber makes a remark on this subject which we cannot pass over in silence. He ascribes Holland's 'uncouthly realistic art' to the Renaissance of the Old Testament, and then adds: 'In the Roman Church quite different (demagogic) motives led to outwardly similar effects.' (*Prot. Ethic*, as quoted, pp. 168 and 273). There is, first of all, an incomprehensible confusion of dates. Caravaggio died when Rembrandt was not even one year old (in 1610). But there is, next to it – and this matters much more – an equally incomprehensible, or at least a reprehensible, slur on the motives of great and integer artists like Terbrugghen, Murillo and Velasquez. Does Weber suggest they painted the way they did because they were ordered to imitate the Protestants and thus to keep the proletariat in subjection to the Church? The idea is ludicrous; it is also totally unsupported and unsupportable by facts. If this is Max Weber's much vaunted 'objectivity', then it is no more than a sham. Cf. on this subject, Stark, W., 'The Place of Catholicism in Max Weber's Sociology of Religion', *Sociological Analysis*, 1968, pp. 202 et seq.

realism in general, and not only ugliness. Was Rembrandt not typically Calvinist at least in that he painted things as they were, and not as fond delusion would have them? Two points can be made, in a preliminary fashion, in support of a possible answer to this query. One can be given in the words of a very great sociologist, Georg Simmel, who published several studies on the great Dutchman and had a deep and sympathetic understanding of him. 'Rembrandt's artistic nature,' he says, 'is characterized by the absence of all symbolism, by a direct apprehension of life.'[1] We shall see before long, to what extent this judgment is true. Here we hasten to add a second fact pointing in the same direction, i.e. in the direction of a deep Calvinist influence on the painter: the relative absence, from his work, of emotionalism. There is one particularly impressive proof of this trait: a sketch, dated 1635, which copies Leonardo da Vinci's *Last Supper*. It is not a simple, but a corrected replica, and the correction consists, most characteristically, in a reduction of the gestures – a reduction of 'rhetoric', as Neumann has it. The last apostle on the right, for instance, does not stretch out his hands, he lets them quietly rest on the table. This is good Calvinistic conduct: the avoidance of all violent emotions, or at least of a 'theatrical' demonstration of them.[2]

The two references given – references to the absence of symbolism and to the restraint of emotion – do go some way towards proving that Rembrandt was influenced by Calvinism, but not all the way. In other words, he was only partially influenced by it. To speak of the emotions first. How many paintings are there which do not rouse them? Weber reminds us of *Saul and David* in the Mauritshuis[3] and writes: 'Standing before [this canvas], one seems directly to feel the powerful influence of Puritan emotions.'[4] Of this remark, that much is true that one does feel 'the powerful influence of emotions'. Whether they are Puritan or not, is another matter. Weber had the unfortunate habit of lumping all 'ascetic' movements together, of bracketing emotional Methodism with unemotional Calvinism.[5] Due distinctions must be made; they are essential at this point. It is precisely one of the proofs of the fact that Rembrandt was not a Calvinist but a man close to the *Doopgezinde* or the Mennonites that he can paint so painfully emotional a picture. Saul is overcome. He cannot contain his tears. He dries them on the next thing to hand, a curtain. The whole pathos of ageing streams

[1] Simmel, G., *Rembrandt: Ein kunstphilosophischer Versuch*, ed. Leipzig 1919, pp. 103 and 104. Our translation.
[2] Cf. Neumann, loc. cit., pp. 469–71.
[3] The painting (usually called *David Harping before Saul*) is not to be confused with a different conception of the theme displayed by a canvas at Frankfurt. Cf. Bredius, A., *The Paintings of Rembrandt*, London n.d., illustration 526 (as against 490).
[4] *Prot. Ethic*, as quoted, p. 273.
[5] Cf. on this point, Stark, W., 'Die Sektenethiken und der Geist des Kapitalismus', *Revista Internacional de Sociologia*, 1967, pp. 5 et seq.

from the depicted scene into our hearts and lacerates them. An unemotional picture? One might as well call Schubert's Unfinished Symphony unemotional! And there are many examples like this one. To one of them, perhaps the greatest, we shall turn in a little while.[1]

As for the absence of symbolicism (by far the more important aspect), we can also best consider it with the help of a concrete canvas. Otto Benesch describes *The Holy Family with Angels* (in the Hermitage, Leningrad) as a scene of 'daily life in a workaday world', and says that 'there results a deeply human directness and immediacy'. 'Joseph bends over his carpentry work in the faint, red-golden glow of the fire burning in the hearth. Mary is a young girl, hardly more than a child, the image of a purity and innocence befitting the "handmaid of the Lord". She turns for a moment from the Bible to the cradle . . .' We get the picture: a photograph of domesticity and domestic bliss. That, and no more? Certainly not. That and much more. For this is what Benesch really writes: 'She turns for a moment from the Bible to the cradle, unaware of the celestial light softly streaming down upon her . . . An idyll of love and solicitude, unwitting in its grandeur, blends with the tidings from a higher world to form a unified whole of the simplest, tenderest kind . . . Once again Rembrandt stresses local colors, but they remain vehicles of light.'[2] The very last words are decisive. Understood as they should be, they prove that Rembrandt, far from being no symbolist, was in fact one of the greatest of them. True, he did not have many symbols, and to that extent Simmel is right. But there is one which he explored and displayed with a depth of truth and artistry which hardly had its equal in the annals of art: the symbolism of light. Our interpretation of Rembrandt, our understanding of his attitude to the competing culture-currents of his day, must start from, and stand on, this fact. We shall revert to it in the next pages. Art critics have always been conscious and convinced that in the final analysis Rembrandt was not simply a realist. Thus Sandrart wrote of him that he 'did not hesitate to oppose and contradict our rules of art, such as anatomy and the proportions of the human body, perspective and . . . judicious pictorial disposition . . . As circumstances demanded, he approved in a picture light and shade and the outline of objects, even if in contradiction with the simple fact of the horizon, as long as in his opinion they were successful and apposite.'[3]

If there was realism in Rembrandt, it was realism with a difference. And the same is true of his individualism. He was an individualist, to be sure; why else would he have painted himself again and again? But his individualism was not that of the Calvinists. And it is easy to say wherein precisely the difference consisted. The realistic portraitists

[1] Cf. below, p. 205.
[2] Benesch, loc. cit., pp. 73 and 75.
[3] Cit. White, Chr., *Rembrandt and His World*, New York 1964, p. 91.

tried to present the outer surface of their sitters, to show how they really looked. Not so Rembrandt. Apart from a few pictures painted more for the fee to be received than for interest's sake, his portrayals of the human face always seek something beneath the skin, the essential self behind its accidental appearance, in one word, the soul. This applies particularly to the self-portraits. They show a brooding mind. Who am I? What am I like? Will I reveal my inmost secret even to myself? Simmel very rightly shows that this is not Calvinistic individualism.[1] For Calvinism tended to take man away from contemplation, to lead him into action so that he may not brood, not speculate over secrets that are God's alone (Max Weber's main point). We see here very clearly that Rembrandt belonged to an introspective tradition of religiosity and Neumann's reference to Jakob Böhme appears in this light as particularly felicitous. Calvinists, on the other hand, were typical, nay extreme extroverts, and if they had not been, they would not have helped to create the modern world of business. Weber would have seen this very well, if his categories had not been so mixed up. The insight would have strengthened his main thesis, but it would also have taught him a lesson about Rembrandt.

The searching nature of Rembrandt's eye puts, incidentally, a different complexion even on his so-called cult of ugliness. 'Beautiful and ugly,' writes Neumann, 'are percepts which belong to the outer shell and to the sensuous surface of the world. When eye and art turn towards the kernel of things, they lose their importance and their contrast. He who believes that the path of artistry always leads more from the outside to the inside and from the body to the soul will be convinced that Rembrandt has been one of the most powerful pathbreakers in this quest. Before his glance, the sensuous becomes the gate of the supra-sensuous which opens itself more and more.'[2] How far is it from this statement to the assertion, or rather to the truth, that Rembrandt reached out for the noumenal behind the phenomenal, for the divine idea behind the less than divine disguise of it, that he was in philosophy an idealist, a downright Platonist?

That it was indeed in the final analysis a Platonizing view of the world which guided Rembrandt in his artistic creativity can be seen by a continuation of our comparison between him and the other incomparable follower of Caravaggio, Diego Velasquez. 'All his resources are directed to a single end,' Benesch says of Rembrandt,[3] and that end is 'the expression of spiritual essences'. But Velasquez, too, searched for an inner substance, an intimate soul, and wanted to fix it for ever by paint and

---

[1] Simmel, loc. cit., pp. 163–6. Simmel's main point is that Calvinism tied man to a hard and fast, tangible world whereas Rembrandt's religiosity allowed him, or even induced him, to thrust into the depths of being. Hence Rembrandt was a mystic. This is entirely correct.

[2] Neumann, loc. cit., p. 461. Cf. also pp. 536–8, and Benesch, loc. cit., pp. 85 and 92.

[3] Benesch, loc. cit., p. 102.

brush, to make it visible in time and posterity, not to say, time and eternity. He left us, not a series of self-portraits as Rembrandt did, but a series of portrayals of his master and friend,[1] Philip IV. If the reader will turn to our volume III, p. 171, he will find there an art-historian's assessment of the Spaniard's achievement which will show him that Velasquez penetrated as deeply into the inner self of his sitter as Rembrandt did. But we need no mentor to tell us that: we can see it for ourselves. Nor did Velasquez show us the depth-dimension of one man only, of an exalted man: his portraits of dwarfs are as incredibly successful as those of kings and princes. His image of the Court Jester Calabacillas (in the Prado), for instance, ranks with the best that Rembrandt has left.[2] The man from Leiden and the man from Seville were truly brothers under the skin.

All this takes nothing from the fact that Rembrandt was an individualist, and that individualism linked him with the Protestant world. The whole thinking of Velasquez, on the other hand, is Catholic in that it is integrational. His greatest achievement was, by common consent, the canvas known as *Las Meninas* (*The Maids of Honour* – not a very good name). One of its excellencies is the organic unity which is imparted to the scene, even though it is anything but simple and static. Velasquez himself is present in the picture, working at his easel, obviously portraying the king and queen whom we do not see for they are outside – are, in fact, where we are, we the beholders. A little princess and her attendants come to visit the parents, a quiet sitting is livened up, interrupted even, but the integration of the picture is not broken for the king and queen, though not seen, for we, who now occupy their place, draw all eyes and thereby secure harmony and order – an ingenious arrangement. Typical Dutch paintings do not show such unity. In group paintings, for instance, which are so substantial a proportion of the output, the individuals depicted are regularly side by side, each looking at us on his own, a typically individualist, and hence Protestant, layout. Yet Rembrandt – and this is essential – is much closer in this to Velasquez than to his countrymen. The *Night Watch*, Rembrandt's most fought-over work, has a lively scene, a group of militia-men marshalling for a parade, but in spite of all the excitement and shooting to and fro, there is yet, as all analysts agree, an admirable integration of the rich detail into one harmonious whole. 'Rembrandt', writes Otto Benesch, echoing Alois Riegl,[3] 'carried the Italian principle of subordinating secondary elements to the point of doing violence to the Dutch principle of coordinating all parts of the picture.' In other words,

[1] Philip bestowed one of Spain's highest honours (a Knighthood of the Order of Santiago) on Velasquez and deeply mourned him, when he died. Cf. Troutman, Ph., *Velasquez*, London 1965, p. 21.
[2] Cf. the beautiful words of Philip Troutman on 'the most splendid single portrait series produced in the Baroque age', loc. cit., p. 19. Cf. also pp. 14 and 41.
[3] Benesch, loc. cit., pp. 69 and 70.

he was, not like Hals or Pickenoy, but like Caravaggio and Velasquez, son to the one and brother to the other.

This kinship reaches down into the very core of Rembrandt's artistic passion, his passion for light, and for the symbolism of light. It is not surprising to encounter this symbol in the Catholic Velasquez for he lived in a symbolistic church and world. It may be surprising to find it in the Mennonite (or Dooper or Collegiant) Rembrandt for he lived in an atmosphere turned towards reality. But it is there all the same. Superficially it comes from Caravaggio, the common master; fundamentally it comes from the fact that all great artists are in the final analysis Platonists, whether they know it or not.

In a passage which is perhaps a little too technical, but which will serve us splendidly all the same, Troutman tells us that 'Velasquez does not first draw the outlines of the objects he knows to be there and then model the forms by the imposition of a light and shade he has not observed, but he observes the forms and records them through the medium of light, allowing the light to reveal the forms . . . This approach gives a reality to the light, and a heightened reality to the objects.'[1] A heightened reality to the objects: that is the main point. Essentially, this is Caravaggio's *maniera*. His *Basket of Fruit* in the Ambrosiana, for instance, is authentic fruit, real apples and grapes and figs, to the extent even of showing a spot of decay on one of the apples. But the glowing light lifts them up into a higher sphere, still a sphere of reality, to be sure, but one that is essential rather than accidental, noumenal rather than phenomenal, God's vision (if we may say so) rather than men's. This precisely is the Platonism, the religiosity, of art. This precisely is the Platonism, the religiosity, of Rembrandt. He has left the realism of his Dutch, Calvinist-bred contemporaries far behind.

Nothing but a weighty tome could do justice to the subject 'Rembrandt and the Light' (if justice can be done to it at all by one who is restricted to words). All the Rembrandt literature together can hardly be said to have fathomed this unfathomable theme. Carl Neumann, however, comes close to the salient truth when he writes: 'The mystical feeling that all which is corporeal is but a mask of divine potencies, that we can everywhere sense the presence of deity, and that light is its messenger, dominates [in Rembrandt] everything.'[2] Hammacher and Vandenbrande, too, are on the right track when they declare: 'In Rembrandt the light is a varying scale of twilights in which man participates spiritually as well as physically . . . His *chiaroscuro* is essentially an expression of a metaphysical concept of light and shade.'[3] And Benesch: 'The extraordinary thing . . . is the way in which Rembrandt uses the dramatic play of light to deepen the religious import' of his pictures. 'Even his

[1] Troutman, loc. cit., p. 12.
[2] Neumann, loc. cit., p. 691.
[3] Hammacher and Vandenbrande, loc. cit., p. 11.

own mother becomes an apparition from the ancestral past when he portrays her as a prophetess or sybil, in the spellbinding painting (1631, Amsterdam) where we see her bending over the Bible whose shining pages reflect a soft golden glow upon her shadowed face . . . By some miracle of color this visionary presence arises out of shadow into light, and a mood of awed suspense descends on the beholder, as if he had crossed the threshold of a sanctuary . . . The "Supper at Emmaus" in the Musée Jacquemart-André . . . shows to what degree mastery in the handling of light can transform and spiritualize matter, can effect a "transsubstantiation" – which is in fact the esoteric theme of this small panel,'[1] and, so we may add, of many others, too.

We can touch the tremendous subject of the symbolism of light in Rembrandt van Rijn only tangentially and must once again ask our readers to be satisfied with references to the literature, especially Carl Neumann's great, seven-hundred-page study.[2] Consciously descending to a level which is a little lower than most of the literature, we may, however, pick out two aspects which will help us to bring our account of the great Dutch painter to a close. Rembrandt uses light as a symbol in a double way. Where holy personages are present in a picture, it is they who spread light in the darkness, not the candles on the wall or the fire in the hearth. A good example is the *Supper at Emmaus* in the Louvre. 'Faintly tinted with gold, red and green, the moldering walls seem to palpitate in the radiance emanating from Christ, and become a transparent medium through which we perceive depths of space.' The famous *Hundred Guilder Print* is like that, too. The other way of using the light is to show it breaking into the heavy gloom from outside. So it is in the splendid etching of Dr. Faustus. He is in his sombre study surrounded by the shadows, but a shining disk appears above him, harbinger of a greater light and life. *The Holy Family with Angels* in the Hermitage at Leningrad, of which we have already spoken, is conceived along similar lines. Mary's face is caught by a 'celestial light softly streaming down upon her,' bringing 'tidings from a higher world'.[3] It is not difficult to see that Rembrandt wishes to express a deep conviction in these paintings, and that this conviction is to the effect that the divine love is constantly breaking into our world and spreading its radiance over it, in spite of everything that divides our nether sphere from the supernal realm. This faith of the heart is not Calvinistic. It is the very opposite. In Rembrandt, part of the Protestant world regained the Catholic confidence that God is not angry for ever, nor ever far away – that He is Love rather than Power, as the Calvinists believed.

[1] Benesch, loc. cit., pp. 39 and 31.
[2] Cf. esp. pp. 192, 210, 211, 214, 408, 691; cf. also (more on colour) pp. 616, 618, 619, 622–5.
[3] Benesch, loc. cit., pp. 78, 73, 75.

That this is indeed Rembrandt's personal faith, can be seen from the fact that, unlike other Dutch painters of his day, he prefers subjects from the New Testament to those from the Old. His eyes are turned towards Jesus, not towards Jehova, towards the forgiving rather than towards the condemning God. But of all the parables of the Gospel one was particularly close to Rembrandt's heart, and it is the most un-Calvinistic of them all: the story of the Prodigal Son (Luke xv, 11 et seq.). There is no predestination which would either throw a man off for ever or automatically excuse his misdeeds, whatever they may be: sin and forgiveness are and remain linked, and sin may lead to forgiveness as well as to perdition, if only repentance reaches the sinner's soul. Rembrandt loved to rest on this theme. There is, for instance, his *Reconciliation of David and Absalom*, in the Hermitage, a great work of art, but there is above all *The Return of the Prodigal Son* in the same collection, a true *chef d'oeuvre*. Neumann calls it 'the miracle above all miracles'; he also calls it 'Rembrandt's last word' which is 'the expression of mercy'.[1] It lays bare the whole character of this incomparable artist and especially his deep religiosity: his belief in a loving God and in a humanity that is capable of loving, too, loving in a puny measure, to be sure, but loving all the same; his belief also in the power of the emotions to cleanse the heart and to bind it to others. In painting this canvas, Rembrandt reached his journey's end. 'Physical substance is now no more than the outward manifestation of an ultimate spiritual essence. With infinite love, like an image of the Heavenly Father, the old man embraces the kneeling penitent and draws him to his bosom . . . The prodigal's face is turned away, but we are made aware of the powerful uprush of tears that convulses his whole being. His tattered clothing flares in the light like the costliest attire, for it is the garb of his humility.'[2]

We may now, finally, turn to Johann Sebastian Bach, and we can start our discussion of him by asserting that, as Rembrandt's case was more transparent than that of Milton, so Bach's case is more transparent than that of Rembrandt. That Rembrandt was an adversary of Calvinism is true beyond the shadow of a doubt; yet the fact has to be laboriously established and documented. Not so for Bach: his divorce from, nay enmity to, the Calvinist culture is quite conscious and comes at times to the surface, openly for all to see. When he composed for his second wife, Anna Magdalena, a small *Klavierbüchlein*, or piano instruction, he noted on it, by way of recommendation, two books, Dr. August Pfeiffer's *Anticalvinismus* and *Antimelancholicus*. The titles alone indicate the contents, but the former text reveals its message even more clearly in its last sentence: 'We have demonstrated that the Reformed doctrine overturns the foundations of the faith and is therefore to be condemned.'

[1] Neumann, loc. cit., pp. 619 and 624. Cf. generally, pp. 619 et seq.
[2] Benesch, loc. cit., pp. 132 and 134.

Even more conclusive than Bach's reading is, however, his mode of action. When he lived in a Calvinist territory, he did not send his children to the government schools, but to a private (Lutheran) establishment. He would not have them exposed to the ideas of the Genevan *Melancholicus*.[1]

Bach experienced the atmosphere of Calvinism at the court of Köthen where he served from 1717 to 1723. He was not personally unhappy there: the Prince, Leopold of Anhalt-Köthen, was interested in music and appreciated the qualities of his *Kapellmeister und Kammermusikdirektor*. But, of course, there was no church music to be composed or to be performed, and this must have been keenly felt by a man who, as no other, was uniquely gifted for, and destined for, the cultivation of just this field. When Leopold married Friederike Henriette of Anhalt-Bernburg, a strong influence inimical to all music came to the court. She exerted constant pressure on her husband to give up what had been his favourite pastime and was obviously a wicked waste of time to her, and, in Bach's judgment, she was not entirely unsuccessful. He began to look around for another home.

Where was he to go? We know where he did go: he went to the Lutheran city of Leipzig where he remained, or rather was forced to remain, to his death. But we know also where he wanted to go: to a Catholic court, the court of Friedrich August II of Saxony at Dresden. We possess the most direct and convincing of all possible pieces of evidence: a letter, dated 27 July 1733, applying for a position. Unfortunately, he did not receive a paid position; he received instead – cold comfort, we can be sure – merely the honorific title of *Hofkomponist* (19 November 1736). What interests us most at this point is Bach's expressed willingness to write Catholic church music. 'I shall,' he assures the Elector, 'with the most dutiful obedience and unflagging diligence, show myself ready to fulfill your Majesty's commands to compose *musique* for church.'[2] As a sign of the earnest of his intentions, he enclosed a Kyrie and a Gloria – 'those towering products of his genius which in the last years of [his] life were extended to encompass the whole ordinary of [the Roman] mass, a sublime work known today as the Mass in B Minor'.[3] True, these movements were at first not formally Catholic. They represent fragments which the truncated Lutheran Mass had retained. But they became Catholic by their final inclusion in what was even technically Catholic music, and they were – as we shall see – destined to be just that from the very beginning. For Bach did not find it difficult to immerse himself in Catholic religiosity and to draw from it works of surpassing splendour and beauty.

[1] Cf. Besch, H., *Johann Sebastian Bach, Frömmigkeit und Glaube*, Gütersloh 1938, p. 9.
[2] Cit. Geiringer, K., *Johann Sebastian Bach: The Culmination of an Era*, New York 1966, p. 82. Cf. also Neumann, W., *Bach: A Pictorial Biography*, New York 1961, esp. p. 133.
[3] Geiringer, loc. cit., p. 81.

Still, Bach's place in life was half-way between Calvinism and Catholicism; he was and remained a faithful Lutheran. Yet the salient question is as to what kind of Lutheran, for in his day there were two varieties: Orthodoxy and Pietism. These were not simply church parties, nor yet theological coteries. What set them off from each other was something of far deeper import. It was the fact that Orthodoxy and Pietism had dwelling in them different culture-principles. The one tended towards a rationalistic culture and thus was kindred to Calvinism (and, if we may go further back, to Dominicanism); the other tended towards an emotional dispensation and thus anticipated Methodism (and was in the final analysis derived from Franciscanism). If we are to understand Bach, we must know where he stood in relation to these two movements. A genius may surpass the cadres of his time; he may be independent, lonely, unique; but in spite of everything he is not, and cannot be, an island.

Was Johann Sebastian Bach a Pietist? Without displaying a long list of quotations,[1] let us report that the literature is about equally divided on this question. This is a sure indication that the great composer was, and at the same time was not, a Pietist. Both parties to the dispute have good arguments on their side; they cannot, either of them, be entirely wrong; they must be, both of them, in a sense right. But how can this be? Can $+a$ and $-a$ ever be combined without becoming zero, i.e. without vanishing altogether?

The solution of the apparently insoluble puzzle can be found in the fact that Pietism operated on two levels; indeed, it might be justifiable to say that it was two things, not one. It was a narrow near-sectarian movement producing a series of *ecclesiolae in* [the Lutheran] *ecclesia*;[2] it was also a wide and deep dislocation in the subsoil of European culture. The first phenomenon was only a superficial and marginal manifestation of the second. As we have seen in volume III,[3] Catholicism, too, experienced the strength of the seismic shocks and reacted to them by giving birth to the great religious orders of the Passionists and Redemptorists; Pietism was thus bigger than Protestantism. But it was bigger than all religious organization and organizations. It created a new mental condition in the world, and one of its fruits was the music of Johann Sebastian Bach.

So far as the Pietist conventicles were concerned, Bach's attitude to them was totally negative. Early in life, he had earned his bread as organist at the *Blasiuskirche* in Mühlhausen (Thuringia), and there the Superintendent, Johann Adolph Frohne, had thrown in his lot with the Pietists, indeed, become one of the more extreme among them. In accordance with the narrow views of his likes, he opposed the use of

[1] Cf. Besch,l .oc. cit., pp. 177–81 for a survey.
[2] Cf. our vol II, p. 82.
[3] Cf. our vol. III, pp. 302 et seq., esp. 311 et seq.

musical compositions in the divine services, and it can easily be imagined what this meant to Bach for he was the composer's immediate superior. When the Orthodox incumbent of the local *Marienkirche* stood up to the Superintendent, Bach's place was by his side. It could not be anywhere else. The result was inevitable: Bach had to go, and go he did. The experience remained with him. Pietists, he continued to feel, are bigots. They despise the God-given gift of music-making. What could a musician have in common with them?[1] To the observer of another century, things look a little different. The undoubted enmity of men like Frohne to art was not necessarily a proper Pietist trait. True, Pietism was to some extent influenced by Calvinism whose sternness appeared to many as a convincing sign of religious earnestness, in contrast to the lukewarmness of so many of the Orthodox. But this was hardly decisive. What was decisive was that the Pietists recruited themselves from the lower classes, and their attitude to culture was unavoidably somewhat negative as they saw it as an adjunct to power and riches. Thus Pietism had an accidental, but not an essential connection with social forces inimical to art. It could spread its message – which was to the effect that the heart of man is as important as the head and must be given its due – to art-loving circles as well. Indeed, it was these circles which could profit most from its high valuation of the emotions, despised and starved and laid to rest by the Calvinist tradition and only half-awakened by sentimentalizing, but not really deep-feeling petty-bourgeois believers.

In Bach, this awakening went all the way. Or – to change our metaphor – the soul-shaking around him made the streams of emotion flow in him, too, and rise into a flood, releasing the creativity which, for reasons which we cannot fathom, was laid on in his privileged mind. That Bach was indeed a Pietist in the non-sectarian sense of the word, can be seen, not only in his life's work in general, but also in some of the emotional-artistic detail. The Pietists developed, for instance, a curious attitude to death, half terror-stricken, half hope-informed, an attitude totally incomprehensible to rational, and above all to hedonistic man. Bach shared it to a large extent. 'His whole thought was transfigured by a wonderful, serene longing for death,' writes Albert Schweitzer, who knew him very well. 'Again and again, whenever the text affords the least pretext for it, he gives voice to this longing in his music; and nowhere is his speech so moving as in the cantatas in which he discourses on the release from the body . . . Sometimes it is a sorrowful and weary longing that the music expresses; at others, a glad, serene desire, finding voice in one of those lulling cradle-songs that only he could write; then again a passionate, ecstatic longing that calls death to it jubilantly and goes forth in rapture to meet it.'[2] Arias like *Ach schlage*

[1] Cf. Neumann, loc. cit., pp. 28 and 136.
[2] Schweitzer, A., *J. S. Bach*, transl. Newman, E., vol. I, London 1945, pp. 169 and 170.

doch bald, sel'ge Stunde – 'Strike, strike soon, O blessed hour' – from the cantata *Christus, der ist mein Leben*, are among the best things Bach ever wrote, and they belong in feeling-tone entirely to the Pietist and Passionist mood and style.

We must take care, however, that, by pointing up this closeness of Bach to Pietism, we do not oversimplify what in life was multiform and complex. It is and remains true that Bach was carried by the stream of emotionalism which was welling up so strongly in his day and brought verdure to the fields which Calvinist aridity had dried out. We must see him together with Schütz and Handel: all three were nourished by the same life-giving waters. But all three also had in them a rationalistic element. 'Schütz is . . . wavering between orthodoxy and rationalism on one side, and mysticism and emotionalism on the other, and very often fusing one with the other,' writes the musicologist Nettl, and he says the same about Bach: 'His organ music . . . is fundamentally of an orthodox nature, but it also expresses the pietistic feeling and striving for an inner spirituality . . . Thus, in the St. John and St. Matthew Passions, the two phases of Lutheranism of that age are represented. In the Passion of St. John it is orthodoxy, and in the St. Matthew Passion pietism which is typified . . . It is the synthesis of orthodoxy and pietism – these two tendencies which so bitterly opposed each other in writing and from the pulpit . . . which blossomed forth in Bach's music in . . . wondrous beauty and unity.'[1]

As for rationalism in general, which, to all intents and purposes, constituted the spirit of the age, Bach grew up in its penumbra, and his mind was deeply influenced, indeed, penetrated, by it. It is well known that his compositions are mathematical in structure: their architectonic, like that of any building, seems to rest on a, or on the, science of statics. Yet mathematics was neither subjectively nor objectively the dominant trait of his music: it was merely the dead skeleton in and under it, not its living matter. Subjectively, Bach was, in his day, generally known to be 'little . . . troubled about the mathematical basis of the fundamental laws of harmony'.[2] Objectively, numerical proportion was not used to construct the scores, it was merely discovered in them, after they had been conceived and composed. Mathematics provided at best the form; the content came, not from reason, but from experience. One of the first, and one of the greatest, analysts of Bach was Johann Friedrich Rochlitz (1769–1842), and he already pointed out that the *ratio* which was alive in Bach, was not the abstract intellect, but concrete and concretizing reason – the 'active, inflammable and penetrating representative reason', as he expressed himself.[3] By 'representative rea-

[1] Nettl, loc. cit., pp. 122, 151, 144; cf. also pp. 147 and 148.
[2] Schweitzer, vol. I, p. 189.
[3] Cit. ibid., p. 238.

son'[1] is meant, in this context, pictorial reason, that is, the reasoning faculty when it is turned towards, and in the service of, the imagination, not the calculating mind, the producer of definitions and deductions. Bach's music has indeed a pictorial quality:[2] he who wrote it thought in images, not in numbers. Rationalism did indeed enter into Bach's artistic creativity, but only as an organizing, so to speak disciplining, principle, and that principle had to meet and to merge with quite another, indeed, richer and stronger principle: the principle of experience, emotion and inner vision.

Bach's music, therefore, is a *complexio oppositorum*, and this fact accounts for its tremendous riches and richness. We are describing it by this medieval term which we have used a short time ago in connection with painting,[3] because it brings out the essential fact; but we are also describing it in this way because we want to, and have to, trace the roots of this master musician further back, beyond the period of both Lutheran Orthodoxy and Lutheran Pietism, to those medieval sources from which it also stemmed – from which it ultimately stemmed. Not only Lutheranism, but all Christianity is (as we have emphasized more than once) split between a rationalizing and a sentimentalizing wing. In the thirteenth century Dominicanism taught men how to think, Franciscanism how to feel. The mind of the Church has ever been a compound of the two endowments and tendencies. Bach was like the Church – which is to say that he was like Giotto: a man of logic and a man of emotion at the same time. If it is true that he was a summarizer of Lutheranism, as indeed he was, it is no less true that he was also a summarizer of Christianity, including Catholic Christianity, in general. He belonged and belongs and will ever belong to all except the Calvinists who have, in their pure form, no organ for his art, no organ for music.

Bach was a Lutheran, and nobody should try to rob Lutheranism of this most precious jewel. Yet one of the greatest Lutherans of this century, Albert Schweitzer, could write: 'In the last resort, Bach's real religion was not . . . Lutheranism, but mysticism.'[4] What Schweitzer does, in this sentence, is to invite us, in our attempt to understand Bach's greatness in so far as it can be understood, to go back beyond that parting of the ways which we call the Reformation to the days of unity – to the days, for instance, of Thomas à Kempis whose great

[1] The German original has 'vorstellende Vernunft'. Cf. Schweitzer, ed. Leipzig 1947, p. 220.
[2] Cf. the passages adduced in Schweitzer's index, *J. S. Bach*, as quoted, vol. II, p. 472, *sub* Bach, Johann Sebastian; as artist; pictorial quality of his music. Cf. above all, ibid., vol. I, p. 247, and vol. II, pp. 41 et seq., and chapters XXII and XXIII.
[3] Cf. above, p. 155.
[4] Schweitzer, loc. cit., p. 169. In this sense also Hashagen, Fr., *J. S. Bach als Sänger und Musiker des Evangeliums*, Wiemar 1909, p. 15, and Pirro, A., *L'Esthétique de Jean-Sebastien Bach*. Paris 1907, p. 450.

vademecum, the *Imitatio Christi,* is neither Catholic nor Protestant, but both; to the days of the Brethren of the Common Life from where there issued two streamlets, one leading to Luther, the other to Loyola;[1] indeed, to the days of Johannes Tauler whose sermons were found among Bach's books after his death – to that Tauler who, born in the year 1300, when Dominicanism and Franciscanism had come so close to each other that one can almost speak of a spiritual merger, was rationalist and visionary at the same time. Bach also was both. Once again we can see that the secret and the substance of greatness is synthesis.

That Bach was indeed the universal Christian can best be gathered from his Mass in B minor. We have noted already that it was formally Catholic; we must emphasize now – what is much more important – that it was also Catholic in fact and in truth, materially as it were. Albert Schweitzer's comments are to the point and unambiguous: 'The salient quality of the B minor Mass is its wonderful sublimity. The first chord of the *Kyrie* takes us into the world of great and profound emotions; we do not leave it until the final cadence of the *Dona nobis pacem.* It is as if Bach had here tried to write a really *Catholic* Mass;[2] he endeavours to present faith under its larger and more objective aspects. Some of the splendid and brilliant chief choruses have quite a "Catholic" tinge. Yet in the other movements we get the same subjective, intimate spirit as in the cantatas which we may regard as the Protestant element in Bach's religion. The sublime and the intimate do not interpenetrate; they co-exist side by side; they are separable from each other like the objective and the subjective in Bach's piety; and so the B minor Mass is at once Catholic and Protestant, and in addition as enigmatic and unfathomable as the religious consciousness of its creator.'[3]

In a sense we have, in the foregoing disquisition, overstepped the borderline of the area of discussion determined by our basic thesis. That thesis was a negative one, namely, that Calvinism has no tendency to produce great art. We did not assert the same of Lutheranism, and we could have left it at that, omitting even mention of Johann Sebastian Bach. Yet our analysis of him was, we hope, enlightening. For it has taught us that, in so far as Lutheranism was typologically similar to Calvinism, it was relatively barren in the field of music, and in so far as it was typologically similar to Catholicism, it was fertile – a confirmation of our strategic assertion. There cannot have been in history many

---

[1] Wilhelm Dilthey, in an analysis similar to Schweitzer's and to our own, links Bach both with the Lutheran poet Gerhardt and the Jesuit poet Spee. Cf. *Von Deutscher Dichtung und Musik,* ed. Stuttgart und Göttingen 1957, p. 245. Gerhardt's most famous hymn, *O Haupt voll Blut und Wunden,* is, incidentally, derived from St. Bernard's *Salve, Caput Cruentatum.* For Dilthey's view of the close relation between Bach's personal, and Catholicism's typical, religiosity, cf. pp. 207–9.

[2] Schweitzer's emphasis.

[3] Schweitzer, *J. S. Bach,* as quoted, vol. II, London 1947, p. 314.

Lutherans who were further from Calvinism and closer to contemporary Catholicism than Johann Sebastian Bach; and this is true particularly with regard to his artistic creed. Calvinism saw the senses as part of man's animal outfit, not to be 'titillated' because they were prone to evil and useless unto good. For Bach, on the other hand, tongue and ear were instruments of spirituality – the diametrically opposed conception. If it is true to say, as Schweitzer does, that Luther 'regarded artistic music as one of the most perfect manifestations of the Deity',[1] then this is doubly and trebly true of the *Thomas-Kantor*, the author of the Mass in B minor.[2] He *lived* the Platonic-Thomist doctrine of beauty, according to which pure art is an adumbration of the divine realities, part of the light which pierces our darkness and which the darkness cannot overwhelm, a revelation which links us with, and leads us to, the Deity who *is* Beauty, just as He is Justice and the Truth.

THE CLOSURE OF THE SYMBOLISTIC WORLD-VIEW

The culture-principles which we have considered in the preceding pages are essentially culture-tendencies and no more. Within societies which are deeply influenced by Catholicism we can, as a rule, observe a drift towards a metaphysical, symbolistic, and, ultimately, artistic world-view, and this drift will carry the cultures concerned some way in the predetermined direction. Some way, but not all the way. For there are resistances, and there are contrary winds as well, and so the development, however strong it may inherently be, will be arrested somewhere in mid-stream. But what would happen, we may ask, if only to satisfy an idle curiosity, if it were not arrested, if it could run its whole course? Principle comes from *principium*, which means beginning. Where would be the logical end of these beginnings, these principles? What would a consistently Catholic culture look like?

We have given the answer to this question already on an earlier page.[3] We have asserted that an archetypically Catholic culture, driven to its logical conclusion, would evolve a totally symbolistic world-view. The meaning of things would be determined, less by their physical qualities, than by their symbolical import. Things would be – to express it with some exaggeration – not so much what they are as what they point to, not so much what they appear to be as what there hides behind them, not so much phenomena as noumena, incarnations of divine ideas. And this interpretation would engulf all observable reality.

How powerful the thrust in this direction in fact was, can best be seen by a survey of the principal realms of that reality. Let us look at

[1] Schweitzer, vol. I, as quoted, p. 29.
[2] Cf. ibid., p. 167: 'Bach includes religion in the definition of art in general. All great art, even secular, is in itself religious in his eyes.'
[3] Cf. above, p. 123.

animals, plants and minerals, and try to find out what the deeply religious mind has made of them. A lamb may be a product of agriculture or a means of consumption, and it may be the Lamb of God, a sacred symbol of considerable significance. In Christian cultures it is pre-eminently the latter. By Christian culture we need not mean here exclusively Catholicism: Pietism, too – Count Zinzendorf, for instance – made far-reaching use of this mystical sign and enveloped it with meaning and with love.

But the Lamb of God is only one thing that points beyond itself, and our assertion is that a whole network of such interpretations was spun out and cast over the animal realm and most, if not indeed all, of what it contains. To be somewhat systematic, let us say that creatures can signify, or stand for, virtues and vices, and that they can signify, and stand for, persons who have embodied these virtues or vices. The persons again can be superhuman or human – more than saints or saints.

Joris Karl Huysmans, who has studied such matters profoundly, has this to say about beasts symbolizing evil and hell: 'They are almost without number; the whole creation of monsters is to be found there. Then among real animals we find: the serpent – the aspic of Scripture, the scorpion, the wolf as mentioned by Jesus Himself, the leopard, noted by Saint Melito as being allied to Antichrist, the she-tiger representing the sins of arrogance, the hyena, the jackal, the bear, the wild boar which, in the Psalms, is said to destroy the vineyard of the Lord, the fox . . . All beasts of prey; and the hog, the toad, . . . the he-goat . . . the leech . . . the spider . . .' The lizard and the viper, too, are emblems of evil. But we cannot give the whole list; our samples must suffice. 'As to the virtues antithetical to these vices, humility may be typified by the ox and the ass; . . . chastity by the dove . . . charity by the lark . . . temperance by the camel . . . vigilance by the lion, the peacock, the ant . . . and especially by the cock.'[1]

The cock – the cock on the weathervanes – we have encountered before.[2] We have seen there that he is a symbol of Christ the Light-Bringer. But this is not the only heraldic animal of the Saviour. The pelican who opens his breast in order to feed his young with his own blood is another, according to the hymn's[3] words:

> Pie pelicane, Jesu Domine,
> Me immundum munda Tuo sanguine . . .

The owl in its nest, the sparrow alone on the house-top, the hart thirsting for the running waters are likewise symbols of the God-Man. As

---

[1] Huysmans, *The Cathedral*, as quoted, pp. 288, 289, 296, 304, 305. On the very interesting symbolism of the ostrich (which stands for sinning humanity), cf. Sauer, loc. cit., p. 212.

[2] Cf. above, p. 131.

[3] St. Thomas Aquinas, *Adoro Te*.

for the Virgin, she is above all represented by the dove; sometimes also by the bee. The dove further symbolizes the Holy Spirit, the Paraclete. Different variants of the pigeon are distinguished. The turtle dove personifies the contemplative life, whereas the ring dove shows forth the active life, and especially the preacher's, whose voice is – like the bird's cooing – frequently heard.[1]

While various animals thus signify virtues and supernal personages, they may also remind the beholder of saints: St. Hubertus' attribute is the stag; St. Benedict's the raven; the doe St. Giles'; the swan St. Cuthbert's; 'and the list might be indefinitely extended', says Huysmans, after giving a much longer one than we have given.[2] Whenever, in the Middle Ages, a pious man saw a pigeon, he saw not only a member of the scientific species *Columbae* (as does modern man), but many strings were touched in his soul: he was reminded of St. Gregory the Great, St. Ambrose, St. Hilary, St. Ursula, St. Scholastica; he was reminded of the Arc of Noe (cf. Genesis VIII, 8–12); he was reminded of the Virgin; he was reminded of simplicity, quietude, contemplation, purity, and a host of other persons and virtues as well. Perhaps a shadow of a shadow of this reaction has survived to the present day, though it would appear to be as nothing compared to what it once was.

One curious trait of this symbolism which, so to speak, spiritualized nature, was its frequent ambiguity. Thus the serpent could signify both Christ and the Devil, in connection with Genesis III, 1 (Eve's seduction) and Numbers XXI, 8 (the Brazen Serpent set up – like the Cross – for a sign); and the same is true of the lion and the eagle. Medieval rationalism tried to clear up this confusion by making definitional distinctions: the serpent signifies God in so far as it symbolizes wisdom; it signifies the Devil in so far as it is poisonous.[3] Rationalism will always make for neat, univocal concepts and even words or signs. But medieval life in general, and especially religious life, hardly saw a problem. For it thought in terms, not of individual images, but of total compositions or *Gestalten*. It would always be clear from the context whether an animal carried a supernal or an infernal connotation.

It would be tempting, at this point, to enter into a discussion of the rich symbolism of plants and stones – to speak, for instance, about the deep meaning of buckthorn and bracken or amethyst, jasper, and sapphire, but what concerns us here is merely *one* fact, namely the culturally all-important fact that the plants and stones mentioned, and scores of others, *did* have such a deep meaning and thus served as references beyond themselves to hidden and mystic significations. 'All that does not tend to Heaven is vain on earth,' Huysmans makes one of his

---

[1] *The Cathedral*, as quoted, pp. 287, 288, 305.
[2] Ibid., p. 306.
[3] Cf. Sauer, loc. cit., p. 60; esp. the texts given in the footnotes. Cf. also Huysmans, as quoted, pp. 131, 132, 289, 290, 291.

characters say.[1] The sentence is strong and sums up an essential religious conviction of the religiously convicted of all ages.

But not only what the world contains – the very framework of the world was religiously-symbolically conceived: even the categories of thought, such as space and time, were not merely empty receptacles embracing sense-provided contents, but carriers of metaphysical meanings. There was an elaborate symbolism, not to say mysticism, of the points of the compass, and we must briefly indicate its bearings. Summarizing the speculations of the Fathers, and referring more particularly to Origen, Athanasius, Basil and Jerome, Sauer characterizes the varied feelings connected with the four quarters in the following passage: 'In the East lies our homeland, the lost paradise, towards which we turn, in painfully-sad remembrance, when we pray; in the East, on the other hand, the light of day rises above the horizon and reminds us of Him who is called the Sun of Justice. In the West is situated the end of time, the great evening of the world, or, from a moral point of view, the kingdom of unbelief and darkness ... The South, with its fullness of light, is the place from whence the Lord comes. The cold North, short on sunshine, is [already] in the Old Testament the breeding place of mischance, terror and demonic assault, the locality where the Evil Fiend has erected his royal throne.'[2] These basic moods are not specifically Christian although they entered into Christianity. They might almost be called natural since our very bodies prefer warmth to coldness, light to night. But they were Christianized by being connected with – indeed, blended into – the theology of the Cross. 'At a later time,' Sauer reports, 'the symbolism of the form of the Cross was linked with that of the points of the compass and there arose the whole deeply spiritual conception of the House of God as the Body of Christ resting on the wood of the Cross: the head laid towards the east, where there dwell light and hope and salvation; the right hand stretched towards the south, the kingdom of grace, the left towards the north, the sombre precinct of sin and unbelief, the eyes directed towards the west into which the light of grace is to penetrate and where at some future date the end of all existence is to be initiated on the Day of Judgment.'[3] On Calvary, the Cross faced west, the back of the Crucified being turned towards Jerusalem in the east – a symbolic expression of the fact that the future of Christianity lay with a new people of God to be recruited from the ranks of the heathens, rather than with the old people of God, the Jewish nation. Such mystical speculations are often to be encountered in the literature. A particularly fine expression of them is the poem *De Laudibus Sanctae Crucis* by Rabanus Maurus (who died in the year 856 as Archbishop of Mayence).[4]

---

[1] *The Cathedral*, as quoted, p. 243.
[2] Sauer, loc. cit., pp. 97 and 88. For documentation, cf. the footnotes ibid.
[3] Ibid., p. 292.   [4] Ibid., pp. 91 and 92.

With the symbolism of north and south was also connected a symbolism of right and left. These were not simply colourless concepts of no value-content or of equal value among themselves, but right received a higher valuation than left and was the side of honour. The right hand is the half betokening salvation and the life to come, the left the half symbolizing earthly and even unredeemed existence, mortality, and sin. The wound in the side of Christ from which there flowed the water of life was on the right; on the right was the repentant thief, and on the left the hardened sinner. On the dread day when the wheat will finally be separated from the chaff, those elected for eternal blessedness will take their places on the Judge's right, while those rejected and condemned will be ranged on the left.[1]

Right is still the side of more honorific connotations, but with advancing rationalization and secularization the whole matter has lost much of its meaning, not to say all of it. It was different in earlier societies. When Prince Charles Edward marshalled his host before the Battle of Culloden Moor, he placed Lord George Murray's men on the right, the Clan MacDonald on the left – with dire consequences. 'By this division a formal slight of the gravest kind had been given to the Mac-Donalds. They sulked . . . When the clash came, they delayed the charge, or even, according to some observers, charged half-heartedly.'[2] The day may have been lost for other reasons – who knows? But that the difference between right and left was more to the Highland Scots of 1745 than it is to a modern geographer or engineer is obvious enough.

What is true of space, is equally true of time. Indeed, in this area, more of the one-time symbolical and religious content has survived than in the other. The division of the epochs into B.C. and A.D. is itself revealing: our years are all years of grace, however little this may signify for modern man. On another plane, authority over the calendar is one of the pope's remaining privileges. So far as the inner life of the Church is concerned, the valuational discrimination between the four points of the compass is closely paralleled by a valuational discrimination between the four seasons of the year. Sauer's account is perhaps a little involved, but we are quoting it all the same because it is authoritative: 'Winter is the seed-time – the time of mankind's turning away from God, dominated by spiritual death; in the history of salvation it reaches from Adam to Moses, and liturgically it is represented by the period of Septuagesima to Easter; "a time of aberration, punishment, guilt and despair" (readings from the Pentateuch). Spring signifies the awakening of nature – the time of the recall of humanity from Egypt and its remodelling; from Moses to Christ: "a time which has some light in it,

---

[1] Ibid., p. 95.
[2] Cole, G. D. H., and Postgate, R., *The British People, 1746–1946*, ed. London and New York 1961, p. 4.

but much darkness, a time of teaching and prophecy" (the Law and the Prophets); liturgically it is commemorated during Advent until Christmas (readings from the Prophets, especially Isaias). The summer is the time of ripening and harvesting – of visitation and reconciliation; from the Birth of Christ to the Ascension; liturgically from Easter to the Octave of Pentecost: "a time of freedom, grace, joy and clarity" (readings from the Apocalypse, the Acts of the Apostles and the canonical Epistles). The fall, finally, is the time of the separation of the good fruits from the waste . . . a time of pilgrimage; from Christ's Ascension to the Day of Judgment; liturgically from the Octave of Pentecost to Advent: "a time which has much light in it, but also some darkness, a time of labour and excitement" (readings from the Books of Kings, of Wisdom, the deuterocanonical books, the Macchabees and the Prophets).' Durandus, much of whose thought is behind Sauer's summing-up (the inserted quotations are from him), connects the four seasons with the four main happenings in the Saviour's life: birth, passion, resurrection, and coming in judgment.[1] Thus every period has its colour and its tone of feeling: none is merely an empty stretch.

The symbolism of the twelve months has not been equally evolved, yet it exists. Each month has its proper note. May, for instance, is devoted to the Virgin, November to the Holy Souls. The linking of the twelve months with the twelve apostles is basically somewhat formal, but a deeper thought is expressed in the representations, frequently to be found, which show the year as a twelve-spiked wheel, with Christ as the hub and centre, and the disciples as the spikes.[2] Everything turns: but One remains 'hieri, et hodie, et in saecula saeculorum'. A special development, which we can but mention in passing, is the Benedictine method of time-keeping with its glorification of the day and rejection of the night and variant lengths of hours – a symbolism and mysticism of its own.[3]

The days of the week receive their colour and tone mainly from the events of Holy Week; individual days also from the saints whose earthly death and heavenly birth occurred on them. Friday as the day of the Crucifixion bears a sombre hue, Sunday as the day of the Resurrection strikes a joyful note. As for the hours, their symbolism is less elaborate, but there is enough in the sacred traditions to stamp on each of them some religious and symbolical mark. The monks, at any rate, had an incentive to speculate about this matter, for the division of their day was a preoccupation and a problem for them. We cannot go deeper into this matter. Suffice it to give one example of their style of speculation. 'At the sixth hour,' writes Cassian, the Abbot, 'the immaculate victim, our Lord and Saviour, was offered to the Father . . . (Matthew

---

[1] Sauer, loc. cit., p. 263.
[2] Ibid., pp. 263, 271, 272, 276. Cf. also Huysmans, loc. cit., p. 161.
[3] Cf. Steidle, B., *Die Regel St. Benedikts,* Beuron 1952, pp. 145 et seq.

XXVIII, 45) ... At the sixth hour, too, St. Peter receives, in a trance, the revelation that all the nations are called (Acts X, 10).' Thus the sixth hour of the Roman computation – our three o'clock p.m. – has a significance all its own, and so have other hours theirs.[1] In the St. Annen-Museum at Lübeck, there is an altarpiece with the canonical times of the day which show the events of the Passion in an hour-for-hour account and characterize the moods of the successive periods by appropriate inscriptions on scrolls, culled from hymns.[2]

The filling of the empty spaces of time, and of the equally empty spaces of space, with a concrete and religious symbolical meaning is very similar to the treatment of numbers: they, too, are colourless indicators which receive a colour, waiting receptacles into which a content is poured which comes to dominate them. 'The natural and realistic value of a figure,' writes Sauer with reference to the Fathers of the Church such as St. Augustine, 'is for them of far smaller significance than the higher spiritual sense which attached to each number by virtue of God's command. Thus the number six does not symbolize perfection because God created the universe in six days, but God remained, in the act of creation, within this period of time, because the number six is a priori a perfect number.'[3] Sociologists who know their Pareto will remember how he handles such ideas:[4] the whole, world-wide contrast between the scientific and technological mentality on the one hand, the religious and mystical on the other, thus springs into high relief.

According to the mystical theory of numbers,[5] *one* represents, in sharp contrast to the rational multiplication table, the highest of all values: one stands for God, the Undivided Unity. Any other reference, such as a reference to the human soul, is in comparison so weak and so pale that it cannot enter into the concept or influence its feeling-tone. Visually one is symbolized less by the point than by the circle or ring because this shows better that to the One there is neither beginning nor end.

Two has, of course, also high and holy referents, such as the two natures united in Christ or the twofold law of love (to God and men). Yet there is a definitely negative undercurrent to this concept. For the very idea of duality implies the fact of dividedness, if not indeed that of contrast and conflict. The two Testaments are in a sense antithetical to each other; so are the Synagogue and the Church, this world and the

---

[1] Ibid., pp. 169–71. The reference would better have been to Acts X, 9–16.
[2] Cf. *Lübecker Museumsführer*, vol. I, Sankt Annen-Museum, Hasse, M., *Die Sakralen Werke des Mittelalters*, Lübeck 1964, pp. 94 and 95 (exhibit 32).
[3] Sauer, loc. cit., p. 85.
[4] Cf. *The Mind and Society (Trattato di Sociologia Generale)*, transl. Bongiorno, A., and Livingston, A., New York 1935, vol. II, pp. 585 and 586.
[5] For what follows, cf. Sauer, loc. cit., pp. 69–85, 62–6, 242–3, 260–1, and Huysmans, loc. cit., pp. 86 and 87. Sauer gives in his footnotes many revealing references.

next, secular and spiritual power, mind and matter, priesthood and laity, *via activa* and *via contemplativa*, Martha and Mary. Perhaps we may say that the meaning of two is itself twofold: good in so far as it indicates that the two are united, are really one, bad in so far as it demonstrates that duality is at times irreducible to unity, that there remains a point beyond which it is impossible for us to advance towards reconciliation and fusion. Two may thus be the emblem of imperfection and mortality. The two 'great lights', sun and moon, often symbolize it in art.

If two is problematic, three is not, for it is dominated by the vision of the Holy One and Undivided Trinity. It betokens – we might almost say, it incarnates and glorifies – synthesis. Indeed, three is the sacred number *kat exochen*, and is handled as such, for instance, by St. Augustine. '*Quo numero,*' he says in his comment on the Sermon on the Mount (I, XIX, 61), '*significatur perfectio.*'[1] Wherever there is a triad – three persons, three things, or whatever else it may be – in the scriptures or in the liturgy or anywhere else, the symbolistic-religious mind is inclined to look for an extraordinary depth of meaning. Analysis has shown that many religious paintings are constructed to the pattern of the triangle, and this is design rather than accident. Nor is it accident that Christianity's most inspired poem, Dante's *Divina Commedia*, consists of three parts with thirty-three cantos to each.[2]

Much, much more could still be said under this heading; but we must desist. Just to show that the later and larger numbers receive the same kind of interpretation, let us emphasize that eleven contrasts unfavourably both with ten and with twelve. As ten embraces in a manner all the other figures, it is, like one and three, a symbol of unity; it is also a symbol of perfection in so far as the Ten Commandments give us the terms of perfection, or at least of perfectibility. Eleven is by comparison an emblem of exaggeration, transgression and sin. It also reminds us of the reduced number of apostles after the defection of Ischariot. Twelve is the full number of the apostolic circle, and for that reason alone it has a positive implication, a pleasant hue. But there are many other reasons for this as well. There are not only twelve apostles, but also twelve patriarchs, twelve minor prophets, twelve fruits of the Holy Spirit, twelve virtues, twelve articles in the Apostles' Creed. Pope Innocent III, in *De Sacro Altaris Mysterio*, has even more to say in praise of the dozen than this.[3] Many paleo-Christian works of art show the faithful in the form of twelve sheep, with a clear reference to the twelve tribes of Israel. The Apocalypse (chapter VII) likewise

---

[1] Cf. *Patrologia Latina*, as quoted, vol. XXXIV, Paris 1887, col. 1261.

[2] Modern editions give the *Inferno* thirty-four cantos, but there is no doubt that the first is meant to be a mere *proemium*. Cf. Panofsky, *Gothic Architecture and Scholasticism*, as quoted, pp. 36 and 98.

[3] II, 50. Cf. *Patrologia Latina*, as quoted, vol. CCXVII, Paris 1890, cols. 828 and 829.

follows this lead. Twelve times twelve thousand are sealed with the sign of salvation.

Letters and colours also have their hermetic meaning. T stands for the Cross. V and D were at one time particularly important for the art of book illustration because of the words *Vere dignum* which open the Preface of the Mass and regularly receive loving elaboration. V symbolizes the human nature of Christ. It has a sharp point below and is open on top, signifying that the Saviour emerged from Mary's womb, but came to embrace all men. D on the other hand symbolizes Christ's divine nature. It is a letter closed in itself and close to ring or circle, the emblem, as we have seen, of the uncreate and eternal.[1]

The symbolism of colours is relatively well known, at least to Catholic church-goers, because it determines the priest's vestments of the day, and, through them, indicates the day's prevailing mood. Thus the celebrant is clad in white and gold on the joyful feasts of Christmas and Easter, in red at Pentecost when the Holy Spirit, in the form of fiery tongues, descended on the Apostles, in black on Good Friday, to signify pain and death, in purple during the penitential season, in green when the emphasis is on quietude and waiting, in light blue when the Virgin is to be honoured. A particularly appealing detail is the hue to be seen twice a year, on the third Sunday of Advent and on the fourth Sunday of Lent – 'the shade called "old rose", a medium between violet and crimson, between grief and joy'. It expresses 'the idea of the spiritual dawn rising on the night of the soul'; it gives 'promise, in the penitential season that [is] ending, of a beginning of gladness'[2] – of the white and gold to come.

In Huysmans' *La Cathédrale*, there is inserted[3] a special paper entitled 'The Coronation of the Virgin' which discusses Fra Beato Angelico's painting of that name and subject.[4] This most pious of all painters, who, it is said, would never work on a Crucifixion other than on his knees, developed the religious symbolism of colours in a determined and systematic manner, employing some with joy, but eschewing others, and thereby giving his canvases a particularly radiant quality which has won him many hearts in every age. His 'good' palette contained white, blue, red, rose-pink and green; his 'bad' one black, brown, grey, yellow, orange, dead-leaf and violet. White is the hallmark of the Supreme Being and of Absolute Truth; it also suggests virginity and goodness; blue symbolizes chastity, innocence and guilelessness; red is the garb of charity, suffering (or martyrdom) and love; rose-pink is wisdom; the meaning of green is freshness, humility and hope. Black, on the other hand, is 'the colour of error and the void, the seal of death'; brown is the antitype of green – dryness and barrenness; so, in another sense, is

[1] Cf. Sauer, loc. cit., pp. 178–80.
[2] Huysmans, loc. cit., p. 133.   [3] Pp. 120 et seq.
[4] Cf. our vol. IV, p. 13.

grey, the hue of ashes, together with sackcloth the emblem of penance; yellow betokens envy and treason; it is the colour of Judas Ischariot; orange suggests the idea of falsehood, dead-leaf of moral degradation, violet of mourning. These latter shades Fra Beato Angelico would only use in so far as they were specially redeemed. Thus the specific grey of the habit of St. Francis and his Grey Friars was acceptable: sanctity would change a colour's significance. So far as other painters are concerned, the ambiguity which we noted in connection with animals and plants made its appearance in this area also. There is, Huysmans tells us, a law of antagonism and a rule of inversion 'allowing the use of the hues which are appropriated to certain virtues to indicate the vices opposed to them'. Thus green can (in the appropriate context) mean despair as well as hope; on the other hand, black may mean renunciation and mortification – virtues which lead away from the death of the soul, while otherwise it is the colour of death. Yet one more complication is the mixed nature of some shades. Grey is composed of black and white, and so may signify light breaking through, and conquering, darkness; it is therefore at times promoted to the position of an emblem of the Resurrection.[1]

In a bitter aside on unbelieving man, Chateaubriand says that the coming of the light of day appeared to the ancients as no more than the effect of a *machine d'opéra*, while it recalls to the Christian mind each morning the miracle of creation.[2] This taunt can be directed with even more justification to the modern heathen whose world-view is pan-mechanistic, with every element of mystery screened and drained out. For this reason, he does not even see what the believer sees. A scion of the twentieth century, confronted with Jan van Eyck's picture, *Giovanni Arnolfini and his Wife*, will discover little in the frame except a young couple side by side. Yet how much more did the artist have to say! 'The painter's aim, it seems, was to celebrate the climax of the marriage ceremony when the couple link hands. Though light is flooding in from the window, a candle is alight in the chandelier: symbol of Christ, Light of the World, unseen witness of the pledge expressed by the bridegroom's lifted hand. As Panofsky points out, every detail here has its significance, and there are similar details in van Eyck's religious works. Thus the necklace of beads and the flawless mirror, whose frame is decorated with scenes of the Passion, symbolize purity and innocence; the fruit in the window, the delights of man's lost paradise; the small griffin terrier, fidelity.'[3] It is no different with paint-

---

[1] Huysmans, pp. 123–5, 130, 132–3. On the use of colour by Rogier van der Weyden, cf. pp. 130 and 131.

[2] *Génie du Christianisme*, as quoted, vol. I, p. 315.

[3] Lassaigne, J., and Argan, G. C., *The Great Centuries of Painting: The Fifteenth Century*, Cleveland n.d., p. 27. The reference is to Panofsky, *Early Netherlandish Painting*, Cambridge, Mass., 1953, chapters VII and VIII.

ings of landscapes, or indeed with landscapes themselves.[1] God is reflected everywhere. As more particularly St. Francis has taught us, we see Him, when we see them.

In the great work of Goethe's old age, *Westöstlicher Divan*, there is one poem[2] which expresses this conviction in a manner both charming and profound.

> Suleika speaks.
> The mirror tells me, I am fair.
> You say: my bloom must fade away.
> But before God all stands for ever still.
> Love Him, in me, then, on this passing day.

How wonderfully well these lines convey the essential vision of the believer's eye! But Goethe, his formal Protestantism and his leaning towards Pantheism notwithstanding, expressed the same idea even more magnificently in the closing chorus of his *Faust*, in the climactic scene which he filled so brimful with Catholic imagery:

> All that's ephemeral
> Is but a symbol.

All, all. Goethe manifestly thought like Thomas à Kempis who says in his *Imitatio Christi* (II, 4) that, if our heart is right, every created thing is to us 'a looking-glass of life and a book of holy doctrine'.

The social system called community then, – this is our final conclusion – leads to the religion of Catholicism, and the religion of Catholicism in turn leads to a pansymbolic conception of the world. The only value of things visible, writes Huysmans where he draws all his analyses together, lies, for the man of faith, in the fact that they correspond to things invisible.[3] It is not so that the modern mind works and feels. Things are today what they are, not what they portend. The contrast is as sharp as noon and night, and as wide as heaven and earth. How did the human race get from the one world-view to the other? This is what we have to discover next.

[1] For a revealing explanation of how much even a simple piece of ground could suggest, cf. H. Friedmann's excellent article in the *Bulletin* of the Metropolitan Museum of Art, Summer 1969, pp. 1–17.

[2] *Goethe's Werke*, ed. Heinemann, K., vol. IV, Leipzig und Wien n.d., p. 239. My translation.

[3] Cf. Huysmans, p. 330, and also p. 331. In the same sense also Sauer, loc. cit., pp. 376 and 377.

2 · THE TRANSITION FROM COMMUNITY TO ASSOCIATION

Saint Thomas Aquinas is universally considered as the most authoritative spokesman of the Catholic tradition, and although it is hardly reasonable to see a tradition so broad and so rich as adequately summed up in one man, there is far-reaching justification for this view. Yet it is precisely an investigation of the Aquinate's thought which can reveal to us the difficulties into which Catholicism, and with it all Christianity, was bound to drift when society went over from community to association, from a life and thought which stressed unity as against multiplicity to a condition which re-evaluated the values and placed multiplicity above unity, the individual person above the social whole.

Up to the thirteenth century, community was the substructure of culture, including religious culture, and so the decisive text – the twelfth versicle of the fifth chapter of St. Paul's Epistle to the Romans – found open ears and open minds everywhere: 'By one man sin entered into this world, and by sin, death; and so death passed upon all men [through one] *in whom all have sinned.*' All that had to be done by the Christian thinkers was to elaborate this last clause, and for this task a commodious instrument was at hand: Plato's philosophy, and especially his doctrine of *metexis* or participation. According to this epistemology, a thing is what it is by dint of its participation in its archetype or 'idea': a rose is a rose because, and in so far as, it participates in the archetype or idea of a rose, in rose-hood, as it were. In a parallel manner, a man is a man, if and in so far as he participates in the archetype of mankind. That archetype, so it could be, and so it was, argued, was Adam: we are men through our descent from – through our participation in – Adam. Therefore when he fell, we also fell. Logic alone demands this conclusion. The doctrines of original sin and redemption were safe in a world which thought along these lines.

St. Augustine was originally, and remained all his life, something of a disciple of Plato, and so the conception which we have briefly and crudely sketched entered the stream of orthodoxy and remained there for more than seven hundred years.[1] Let us look, by way of illustration, only at one major author, Bishop Odo of Cambrai, though others, like John (Scotus) Erigena or Anselm of Canterbury, would serve equally

---

[1] Cf. Kors, J. B., *La Justice Primitive et le Péché Original d'après S. Thomas*, Paris 1930, pp. 17 et seq., and the copious quotations and references given there.

well. 'Odo of Cambrai,' writes a great student of these matters, 'found a very clear-cut solution to the vexing problem: why did all men sin in Adam? Human nature, he supposes, is the numerically one and invariable Platonic form and idea. Instead, however, of finding the place of this idea in a Platonic heaven, he located it in paradise. Adam, then, is human nature in the very substantial and realistic Platonic sense. He is *homo species*, substantially identical with all further copies of the original. When Adam sinned, there was no other man to be found anywhere. In him, therefore, the person sinned in such a way that at the same time the total human substance, i.e. that Platonic metaphysical reality, was sinfully vitiated.'[1] 'Odo's theory,' the same writer says a few lines later, 'is that of the real, substantial identity of Adam and all men.' In other words, it is the theory of the real, substantial identity of all MacDonalds with the eponymous original Donald. It is a theory born and bred of community. Peter Lombard, the greatest preceptor of the Schools, who died in *c.* 1164, about half a century after Odo, though he laid greater emphasis on the physical link between the progenitor and his progeny, still had a similar opinion of the inception and perpetuation of original sin.[2] Yet the age of association was now approaching, and its facts were entering into men's minds and creating a new condition there which we can discern in St. Thomas Aquinas' texts.

Already in St. Augustine there is a second current, or at least undercurrent though the centuries of community chose to disregard it. It stands out most clearly in one of his letters. A young bishop, Auxilius by name, had excommunicated one Classicianus, together with all his household. Augustine writes to his colleague and remonstrates with him: on what grounds does he involve the innocent in the guilt of the guilty? To Augustine there appear to be no such grounds. 'For although the son of Classicianus derived through his father, from our first parent, guilt which behoved to be washed away by the sacred waters of baptism, who hesitates for a moment to say that he is in no way responsible for any sin which his father may have committed, since he was born, without his participation?'[3] In this crucial passage, the collective character of original sin is indeed unambiguously asserted, but it is represented, not as something natural and normal, but as something unique and exceptional, and hence incomprehensible and problematic. In another text, the collectivity of guilt and punishment is said to be characteristic of, and restricted to, pagan society: 'Whoever lives a good life within Holy Church, is not hurt by the sins of others, for in her every one has

[1] Eschmann, I. Th., 'Studies on the Notion of Society in St. Thomas Aquinas', Part II, *Mediaeval Studies*, vol. IX, 1947, p. 40.

[2] Kors, loc. cit., pp. 56 and 58.

[3] Cit. Eschmann, I. Th., 'Studies on the Notion of Society in St. Thomas Aquinas', Part I, *Mediaeval Studies*, vol. VIII, 1946, p. 21. Cf. *Patrologia Latina*, vol. XXXIII, Paris 1902, col. 1067. The translation used is that given in *The Works of Aurelius Augustine*, ed. Dods, M., vol. XIII/2, Edinburgh 1875, p. 456.

to carry his own burden, as the Apostle says.'[1] The Apostle meant is Paul, and the passage Galatians VI, 5: 'Every one shall bear his own burden.'

Modern associational man will feel that Augustine is simply 'talking sense' in these statements, that 'reason' is breaking through in them; but the sociologist of knowledge may well be puzzled. Whence comes this division in Augustine's mind, whence his occasional individualism? The answer is not difficult to find. Though a disciple of Plato and, through him, of the old culture of community, he was also a disciple of the Roman lawyers and through them influenced by associational modes of thought and life. Rome at the time of Gaius and Ulpian was a market society, a society of associated self-seekers. The jurisprudence which it produced was therefore necessarily shot through by individualistic sentiments and attitudes. Criminal responsibility, for instance, could only attach to a man, never to a multiplicity, and this heritage weighed as heavily with the Bishop of Hippo as the Platonic philosophy which he carried at the same time. A Roman in still primitive Africa, he belonged to two worlds: one supported his belief in the credibility of the doctrine of original sin, the other his conviction that, apart from Adam's, sin was the failing of one soul only, and never of many.

There is yet a third passage from Augustine's pen which points and presses in the same direction. In his *Contra Epistolam Parmeniani*, he comments on Matthew XIII, 29, and the gist of his discussion was received into the *Glossa Ordinaria*, that important medieval handbook of biblical knowledge. The formulation of the *Glossa Ordinaria* is a terse compression of the Saint's argument, but it is none the less supremely interesting in our context. It reads: *multitudo non est excommunicanda*.[2] The salient word is *multitudo*, a multitude. The text does not read: *universitas non est excommunicanda*. All that the medieval, still collectivistic mind conceded was that a stray multitude, an unorganized crowd, should not be held collectively responsible for the deeds of one individual within it, but it was decidedly reluctant to extend this mode of thinking to coherent and abiding groupings, to organized society. The great lawyer Bartholomew of Brescia, for instance, was not, like his Roman predecessors, unwilling to see a collectivity as collectively responsible, where the facts warranted it, though he was careful about it.[3] Yet the question must always be: what is a society generally

[1] Cit. Eschmann, loc. cit., pp. 21 and 22, referring to the *Decretum Gratiani*, Distinction IV, chapter 129, 'De consecratione'. (The title of this chapter runs: 'Baptized infants are not prejudiced by the sin of their parents'.) Cf. *Corpus Iuris Canonici*, edd. Richter, E. L., and Friedberg, E., Leipzig 1879, vol. I, cols 1402–4, and *Patrologia Latina*, vol. XXXIII, as quoted, col. 359–64; cf. also cols 579 and 580. My translation.
[2] Cf. Eschmann, loc. cit., p. 16, and *Patrologia Latina*, vol. CXIV, Paris 1879, col. 132.
[3] Cf. Eschmann, op. cit., Part II, as quoted, p. 54.

speaking? Is it a *multitudo* or an *universitas*, a collection of persons or itself a person? Is it an association or a community? The universal shift was decidedly in the direction of the definition of society as a multiplicity rather than as a unity, and because it carried St. Thomas Aquinas some way with it, the traditional doctrine of original sin became problematic under his hands.

Father Eschmann, in a study so thorough that it can hardly be imagined more reliable,[1] has asserted that we shall do well to distinguish three stages in St. Thomas' thought on our subject: the first is reflected in his *Scriptum super Libros Sententiarum*; the second in his *Contra Gentiles* and *De Malo*; the third especially in his *Compendium Theologiae*, usually considered as of late date, and also in the great *Summa Theologiae*. Only in the middle period, Father Eschmann tells us, did Aquinas approach the old position presented by Odo and Anselm, the mode of thought characteristic of community in the full and consistent sense of the word. Before that and in his closing years, he saw society as less of a unity and more of a multiplicity. Not that he ever doubted the collective character of Adam's fault and fall; but, like Augustine, only more so, he made it appear an isolated phenomenon, a phenomenon out of keeping with the rest of reality, and to that extent profoundly puzzling, perhaps even difficult to accept.

The *Scriptum super Libros Sententiarum* is concerned with the problem which the *Glossa Ordinaria* had not even raised: whether an *universitas*, a true and truly integrated society, could by rights be collectively excommunicated because it might be guilty like one man. A constitution of Pope Innocent IV called *Romana Ecclesia* (chapter *Ceterum*) had just forbidden the excommunication of a whole community, and St. Thomas is providing a rationale for this decretal with the spirit of which he heartily agrees. 'Excommunication,' so Eschmann sums up the essential argument, 'is only to be inflicted when one has committed a mortal sin. Now a sin consists in an act. Yet, in most cases, an act is not done by the whole community but by some persons. Hence these persons from among the community may be excommunicated, but not the community itself. And even if it be that sometimes an act pertain to a whole multitude – for instance: several men pull a ship which no one is able to pull – yet it is not probable that a community consent so entirely to evil that some people do not disagree ... Therefore the Church ... has, very wisely indeed, enacted the statute that "a whole community be not excommunicated", lest, when gathering up the tares, the wheat be rooted out with them.'[2] Thomas, as can be seen, refers back to the same Gospel passage from which Augustine had started out – the twenty-ninth versicle of Matthew XIII.

'When dealing with Innocent IV's decretal,' Eschmann sums up, 'St.

[1] Cf. footnotes on pp. 224 and 225.
[2] Eschmann, as quoted, Part I, p. 11.

Thomas knows of only one notion of the *delictum universitatis*: it is the delict of *all* its members, a misdeed actually committed by *all* . . .'[1] Yet this is, properly speaking, imprecise language. It would be more correct to say that, in this *opusculum*, and so far as it goes, St. Thomas knows of *no* notion of the *delictum universitatis*: such a *delictum* is merely the sum of the misdeeds of the associated individuals; the fact of association neither adds to, nor detracts anything from, it. The sociology in the background here is clearly atomistic and nominalistic, hence a bad companion-piece to the doctrine of original sin. All this is different in the second group of writings, and especially in the *Quaestiones Disputatae de Malo*. Eschmann, himself the product of modern atomistic-nominalistic society, would wish to see the Saint close to his own atomistic-nominalistic position. Yet he has to admit: 'There is no getting away from the fact that in *De Malo* the Angelic Doctor, knowing exactly what he did and meaning it, found formal unity in humanity and proposed to consider all men as a social organism.'[2] There is indeed no possibility of getting around this admission, for in his usual discussion of objections (*In contrarium*, point 18) Aquinas leaves no doubt whatever where he stands. Adam might be called by an objector a *causa particularis*, a *homo particularis* he might even say. But a *particular cause* cannot have a universal effect. The main assumption here is wrong, Thomas answers. 'Adam, in so far as (*in quantum*) he was the beginning of human nature, had the character (*rationem*) of a universal cause. And so all human nature, which is derived from him, was corrupted by his action.'[3]

The sociology behind *De Malo* 'which designates original sin as a kind of collective guilt',[4] is thus clearly organismic in the full sense of the word. The technical term 'formal unity' or 'unitas per se' describes a *real* unity, an *essential* oneness. From this extreme position, Eschmann assures us, St. Thomas retreated in his closing years. Mankind becomes to him a merely material unity or 'unitas per accidens'; the term 'body social' turns into more of a metaphor. The consequences are far-reaching. Fathers and sons are indeed connected, indeed in a sense one, even according to this second opinion, but only through their physical bond. They are not one in a moral sense. The generations appear now as a loosely connected chain, as something vague and indefinite, not, like an organism, as something manifestly and firmly and indissolubly coherent. If there is any comparison behind the later texts, it is not that between society and a body physical, but rather that between society and a body politic. We suffer for Adam's guilt, not because we are one with him, as a thieving hand is one with the person to whom it

---

[1] Ibid., p. 7. Emphasis added. Cf. also pp. 13 and 41–2. For the far-reaching sociological nominalism of Innocent IV himself, cf. ibid., p. 31 (*sub* 80), and p. 33.
[2] Eschmann, Part II, p. 32.   [3] Cit. ibid., p. 35. Our translation.
[4] Ibid.

belongs and for whom it steals, but rather because subjects always suffer with their rulers, especially for the blunders which these rulers commit. It is amply obvious that this mode of thinking (whether or not it was indeed St. Thomas' own) must weaken the credibility and acceptability of the doctrine of original sin. That doctrine, so easily understood and embraced on the basis of community life and 'realistic' epistemology, becomes part and parcel of impenetrable mystery, a dogma in the hard sense of the word.

Still, in spite of these threatening implications, Father Eschmann can write in his last sentence: 'Our conclusion. . . . is that in his final teaching Aquinas did not admit the possibility of collective guilt.'[1] Other equally learned Thomists have taken a different line. Father Rogatien Bernard, for instance, in his authoritative commentary on the *Summa Theologica*,[2] refuses to see the distinction between the successive stages of the Saint's thought which his fellow-Dominican Eschmann asserts to have discovered, and considers the Thomas of *De Malo* as the veritable and abiding Aquinas. 'This is the essential point,' he writes. 'We are not only bound to suffer the punishment for the fault of our first forefather, we have really part in that fault; our nature is not only punished for the fault of its chief, it is in its entirety guilty of that same fault.' As for Aquinas, whatever avenues he may explore, 'he comes always back to his great argument which is drawn from our incorporation in the first man.'[3] There are many more passages, and indeed arguments, in Bernard's work which might be quoted here, but this is hardly necessary. Suffice it to say that Bernard sees a more community-minded and Platonist (one might almost say: a more Catholic) St. Thomas.

For our purposes it is not imperative to inquire which interpretation of the Master of the Schools is more correct. Eschmann has at least established this much – that there are shifting nuances in the Thomist doctrine, even if these nuances are variants of the same shade rather than contrasting colours. Their appearance is a first and ominous sign of difficulties to come. The day was to dawn when people would fail to see how and why they were involved in Adam's fall; but with the sense of collective sin, the longing for collective redemption in Christ would, as if by a reflex, also be weakened; and Christianity would tend to lose its grip on mankind. With Aquinas and other believers down the centuries, this would and could not happen. For he and they would hold fast to the belief in the incorporation of all redeemed mankind in Jesus Christ, the New Adam, whatever they may or may not have thought about the incorporation of unredeemed mankind in the Old Adam. We may not

<hr />

[1] Ibid., p. 55.

[2] Cf. esp. *Le Péché*, vol. II, *Saint Thomas d'Aquin, Somme Théologique*, transl. R. Bernard, O.P., Paris, Tournai, Rome 1931.

[3] Ibid., pp. 327, 339, 340. My translation. Cf. also pp. 334–7.

have been to Aquinas, as Eschmann insists, the *corpus Adae* (though even in the late *Compendium Theologiae* he uses the expression *quasi quaedam membra eius* – 'so to speak, members of Adam' – to describe men),[1] but the Church was certainly to him the *corpus Christi mysticum*, a rock-bottom conviction which left the essential collectivism of original Christianity standing in his mind.

Yet it was not only one traditional Christian dogma, or even the whole number of such dogmas, that was left standing in the Aquinate's mind; that mind was totally permeated by the archetypal Catholic *mode* of thinking, which means that it was in all things tending towards reconciliation and synthesis. For this reason Thomas tried, quite spontaneously, to develop intermediate and overarching opinions which would close the gap that was beginning to open in his philosophy and was soon painfully to broaden in the wider world. Adam, he speculated, may not have been the head of humanity (as Christ was and is of the mystical body), but he was certainly its beginning. What he had, he handed on to succeeding generations. Nobody, however, can hand on more than he has; but Adam had, after his fall, only a vitiated – a stained and wounded – nature, and this, this alone, could be received, and in turn bequeathed, by his offspring. In that way, original sin attaches to the whole human race. The 'whole' meant in this formula is not a definite community or unity comparable to a physical organism; its outline and circumference, for one thing, is quite indefinite, since it is still open and moves on into an unpredictable future. But that makes very little difference so far as the universality of original sin is concerned.[2] By such ingenious theorizing, Thomas succeeded in sidestepping any possible clash between realism and nominalism in the theology of the fall and its consequences. The realists could stick to the assumptions, to the Platonism, of Odo and Anselm; budding nominalism could continue to carry the same doctrine, even though these assumptions and this way of philosophizing appeared unacceptable to its representatives.

We cannot follow this matter deeper into Thomas' technical philosophy. Merely to wind up our discussion, let us hint as to how it is handled there. As always, Aquinas uses his two chief tools, distinction and analogy. Once actual sin (*peccatum personae*) and original sin (*peccatum naturae*) are distinguished, they can be brought together again by seeing them in terms of an analogy. If this is done, a set of propositions can be worked out which should (so it may be hoped) be acceptable to all. Eschmann formulates 'the basic solution' in the following way:

[1] Eschmann, loc. cit., Part II, p. 47.
[2] Cf. ibid., p. 39. See, however, what Bernard (pp. 332 and 333) has to say on this point: original sin is not like an heirloom which can hardly be said really to connect the testator and the heir; it does create a bond – a community – between them, and Thomas realized this very well.

'Even as the actual sin of a member of the person, e.g. the hand, stands to the first moving principle of the acting person, viz. the will, so, analogically speaking, the original sin in each and every member of human nature stands to the first moving principle of that nature, viz., the first parent . . . Original sin in this or that man is a sin in the proper, but analogical, meaning of the term because, and in so far as, this man is moved by the first man, i.e. receives human nature, through genera-tion, from the protoparent.'[1]

Will a formula of this kind in fact be found acceptable, and by whom? The answer to this question must surely be that it will be accepted by all who live in a society of the community type, or at least long to live in such a society; in other words, by all for whom social unity is the supreme value. It will not be accepted by those who live in a merely associational society or rank individual independence higher than social coherence. The towns in which St. Thomas' life was set – Naples, Paris, Cologne – were already well on the way towards becoming associational; hence associational modes of thinking appeared in his mind and demanded their due. But his heart was still turned towards the old (Catholic) idea, indeed, indissolubly tied to it. The complex con-victions which we have studied are the outcome of an inner struggle in which the idea and ideal of mankind's incorporation in its Redeemer and with it a certain all-round organicism or sociological realism gained the upper hand. Even if Eschmann's analysis is entirely correct, Thomas remains in full accord with the orthodox position as later defined by the Council of Trent in its fifth session on 17 June 1546: Adam fell, body and soul, and the whole race fell with and in him, by a participation not only in his punishment, but also in his sin (canons 1 and 2)[2] – a credal proposition which was enunciated without deciding in any way in what precise manner Adam was connected with his progeny, and which left wide latitude for speculation and theorizing on this point. Others, whose faith was less complete, were prepared, without compunction, to move away from the tradition of the fathers. Peter Abelard, for instance,[3] taught, in accordance with his basic con-viction that the individual alone is real while the species is not, that there is only one kind of sin – actual sin, sin due to a concrete act of sinning. Children under the age of reason and responsibility are not, therefore, properly speaking, under the grip of sin. Yet Abelard, seeing around him the all too obvious misery of the human race, did not doubt that all humans were odious to God and punished by Him. Why punished? First of all because of a quality of God rather than of men: His omni-

---

[1] Eschmann, Part II, p. 27. Cf. *Summa Theologiae*, Ia IIae 81, 1 and 3, *The Summa Theo-logica*, as quoted, vol. VII, ed. London 1927, pp. 405 and 409.
[2] Denzinger, H., *Enchyridion Symbolorum &c*, Barcelona, Freiburg i. Br., Rome 1957, pp. 281 and 282.
[3] Cf. our vol. IV, p. 17.

potence. 'God, who can treat His creatures as He sees fit without being unjust, has condemned Adam and, with him, all his posterity without its having deserved it.'[1] Yet there is after all a quality of men which makes God's hard sentence appear less incomprehensible and more justifiable: 'It is the concupiscence of the conjugal act which makes the sons of men into sons of wrath.'[2] With such opinions, we are already close to the Reformers, Luther laying stronger emphasis on men's concupiscence, Calvin on God's omnipotence. In either case, the old Christian collectivism is sensibly diminished. Concupiscence roots in our bodies, and these bodies being *höchstpersönlich*[3] our own, are the very *principium individuationis*. God's free will (one might almost say: His irresponsibility) is again a Person's personal prerogative. Indeed, Calvin pursues and underlines this factor further by teaching that God redeems and rescues only selected individuals whom He plucks out of the *massa damnationis* as a stick here or there may be plucked from a burning fire. Here, then, a more individualistic variant of Christianity makes its appearance. By inviting individuals to associate themselves with God, and especially with God-made-man, Jesus Christ, it appealed powerfully to the new type of personality bred in associational society. But even while it spread and established itself, developments were set in motion which made wide circles doubt both the culpability of concupiscence, which is, after all, natural, and the incomprehensibility of God, who is, after all, Reason, and when that happened, the trying and testing time of traditional Christianity had arrived.

THE COMING OF ASSOCIATIONAL SOCIETY
AND ITS MENTALITY

The appearance of an individualistic element in the thought of St. Thomas Aquinas is but one of the indications, one of the proofs, of the fact that society was in his day undergoing a radical transformation: it was beginning to change into a consistently associational system, an order within which the individual would be strong and social coherence weak – in short, into that condition which, following Karl Marx, we have come to call capitalism. The partial readjustment of the old religious culture and the development of a new one parallel and opposed to it are essentially incidents in this vast, all-embracing process and must be understood as such. Yet it was not for the first time in history that the principle of association made a bid for supremacy and control: it was only for the first time that that bid was totally

---

[1] Cf. our vol. III, p. 87. In fairness to Abelard it should be added that a reference to the hidden ways of God is also to be found in Aquinas. Cf. Eschmann, Part II, pp. 52 et seq.
[2] Kors, loc. cit., pp. 37 and 38, where ample corroborative quotations are given.
[3] Cf. our vol. IV, p. 2.

successful. Already earlier on, associationism, with its necessary adjunct, individualism, had several times tried to raise its head, and brought forth certain cultural consequences which it is instructive, not to say imperative, for us to study. Paralleling the first part of this volume, we shall present two: one from Hebrew, the other from Hellenic culture. They will both show us tendencies which are not easy to reconcile with the Christian core-conception of the solidarity of all men in guilt and merit.

Even a slight acquaintance with the Bible is sufficient to prove that there was a great difference between Saul and David on the one hand and Solomon on the other. Saul and David are herders in the hills; Solomon is a nabob, a Croesus, with a luxurious court in the foreground and a wealthy city to the back of it. 'We are able to distinguish two main types,' writes Pedersen. 'The old Israel of the small communities and the remodelled Israel of the great towns.' Little happened in and to the former circles: 'People who had their abodes in the small towns and on the steppes ... stand out in sharp contrast to the doings of the kingdom and the large cities. Their life and ideals [continued to be] as they were before the immigration ... The most important change in the monarchic period took place in the larger cities, the centres of international trade and politics. Here new classes sprang up, appropriated the whole of the property and thus obtained complete control ... The remainder of the population, above all the small landed proprietors, degenerated and became a proletariat, living in poverty and misery.'[1] They held fast to the old communitarian conceptions; they produced the prophets; they produced, in the fullness of time, Jesus Christ. But new-fangled ideas appeared where the fresh semi- and quasi-capitalist reality tended to become predominant.

We see the clash between the two ways of life and the two modes of thinking implied in them very clearly in the simple, but supremely moving story of Naboth's vineyard, told in the third Book of Kings (chapter xxi). Naboth possessed some land close to the royal city of Samaria, and Achab, the ruler of Israel who resided there, had his eyes on it. He therefore made a business proposition: let me have your vineyard and I will either pay for it in cash or exchange it for another (even better) piece of ground somewhere else, whichever you prefer. According to the ethos of the new, proto-capitalist civilization, there could be nothing wrong with the suggestion of such a deal. Land was to Achab simply what it is to us, a piece of property only loosely connected with its owner and therefore alienable, nay, easily alienated. But Naboth felt differently. The land was not really his, for he was merely a link in a long chain of owners; and it was not to be parted with for there was a mystical link between it and the family which had held it since time immemorial and was destined to hold it for ages yet to come.

[1] Pedersen, loc. cit., pp. 25, 24, 23.

Naboth's thinking was on two levels, or, let us say, in two widening circles, determined by the principles of unity and community. There was a unity and community between the generations of yesteryear and those of tomorrow and the day after; and that familial body social in its entirety formed a wider unity and community with its appurtenances, above all, of course, with its soil. Such ideas of symbiosis were no longer understandable for Achab; in his eyes Naboth cannot have been more than a quaint anachronism.

Achab's conception of property, comparable as it is to that of the Roman lawyers and of their modern imitators, had not, however, sprung up in the field of agriculture; it had merely spilled over into it from the area in which it had first developed and in which it had, so to speak, its proper home: the sphere of trade. A place like Samaria was not, like the older townships of Israel, merely the hub and centre of an agricultural district, a country settlement or hamlet, it was essentially a market, and that is something sociologically different. We get the picture of that kind of city best in the twenty-seventh chapter of Ezechiel. He speaks, it is true, of Tyre, a town beyond the frontiers, but what he says is applicable to a number of Israelite places as well, even if they were perhaps somewhat less magnificent than she who was 'situate in the heart of the sea'. Ezechiel's account is indeed glowing, but it mixes admiration with disgust. Tyre will come to nought – and so will her Jewish sisters for the same reason (Ezechiel XXII). Sin proliferates within her walls. The two harlots of whom the Prophet speaks, and for whom he predicts a heart-rending end (chapter XXIII), Oolla and Ooliba, are, as is openly indicated, none other than Samaria and Jerusalem.

Isaias shared Ezechiel's observations, and he was puzzled by what he saw. 'How is the faithful city,' he asks concerning Jerusalem, 'become a harlot? Justice dwelt in it, but now murderers' (I, 21). Yet he gives the answer himself: 'Their land is filled with silver and gold' (II, 7). Where there is buying and selling, there man stands against man, interest against interest, selfishness against selfishness. Even so vital and so fundamental an institution as the family is apt to be weakened. 'Monarchy and the development of the great towns did not have a favourable effect on the old-fashioned type of marriage,' says Pedersen. 'The pact became looser . . .'.[1] It was a far cry from the total solidarity of the Jewish tribal past to these conditions of the prophetic present, and they could not reconcile themselves to the new forms of human conduct.[2] Yet these had, in the cities at least, become legitimate. What Ezechiel and Isaias (and Osee and Amos and others, too) experienced and decried as the decay of morality was in fact (as the modern sociologist has to see things) the advent of a new ethos, the ethos of associational

[1] Pedersen, loc. cit., p. 70.
[2] Cf. also the Psalms, e.g. XII, XXXI and XLI; Pedersen, pp. 264 and 265; also 450.

and individualistic life, the ethos of an 'achieving' society. It was sooner or later bound to bring with it at least the rudiments of a new ethico-religious outlook.

One point of detail is worth noticing before we move on. To the conflict between buyer and seller is inexorably added that between borrower and lender, and ultimately that between rich and poor. Tribal Jewry had condemned and tried to keep down the whole phenomenon of interest. Now that prime pump of capitalism was working and having its usual, near-unavoidable result: the development of strife, and hence of lasting alienation between men. Where Ezechiel chides Jerusalem, one of his bitterest accusations concerns this point: 'Thou hast taken usury and increase and hast covetously oppressed thy neighbours'; therefore, says the Lord, 'I will disperse thee in the nations and will scatter thee among the countries, and I will put an end to thy uncleanness in thee . . . and thou shalt know that I am the Lord' (XXII, 12 and 15).

We must not, however, assume – even in face of the evidence given – that this near-capitalism was to gain a total victory. It was, first of all, of very tardy growth. The minting of money belongs only to post-exilic times. The Book of Deuteronomy, written shortly before the exile, talks always of silver, never of coin.[1] Furthermore, the greatest and for a long time only great trader was the king himself. One might go so far as to speak of a royal trading monopoly and even of a royal capitalism. Such a capitalism was, however, too dependent on govern-mental support to gain a substantial existence of its own and to last. Even if it had not been saddled with a thieving and extortionist bureaucracy, as it was (a decidedly pre- and anti-capitalist feature), it could never have hoped to outlive the political set-up with which it was connected and had perforce to disappear along with it. Thus while the efflorescence of associational life under and after Solomon led to the remarkable individualistic pleas which we shall presently encounter, Israel returned in the end to the time-hallowed collectivism of its pristine days and so could engender the organicism which we find in the Gospels, in Paul and in the whole history of Christian and Catholic thought.

The upsurge of a commercial and near-capitalist civilization in Israel which we have just investigated was repeated later on on Greek soil, with Athens playing the leading part. The main difference between the two otherwise parallel developments consisted in the fact that the peak reached in Attica lay decidedly higher than any ever achieved in Jerusalem or Samaria. Above all, the monetary system was fully unfolded. 'As early as during the Persian Wars,' writes F. M.

[1] Lurje, M., *Studien zur Geschichte der wirtschaftlichen und sozialen Verhältnisse im israe-litisch-jüdischen Reiche*, Giessen 1927, pp. 9, 25, 28; de Vaux, R., *Ancient Israel: its Life and Institutions*, New York, Toronto, London 1961, pp. 78 and 79.

Heichelheim in *An Ancient Economic History*,[1] 'there were very few *poleis* or tribal states inhabited by Greeks in which coined money was not used,' yet 'all other mints pale in importance for the fifth century B.C. when they are compared with the contemporary Athenian output ... More than that, during the fifth century B.C. the Attic currency was almost the principal system of valuation for the more highly developed countries of the period from the age of Cimon to that of Nicias, only occasionally supplemented by the competition with the Persian gold, the Corinthian silver, and the Cyzicene electrum.' Athens, side by side with Corinth, was simply the world mint.[2] Hoards of Attic coins, dating from this period of economic advancement, have been found everywhere in the ancient *orbis terrarum*, from Egypt in the south-east to Anatolia in the north and Iberia far to the west. Confidence in the strength of this currency seems to have been widespread, not to say universal.

It is a fact which may at first surprise the reader that no hoards of Attic coins of the fifth century have been found on Attic soil itself,[3] but a little reflection will show that this is entirely natural and indeed another proof of the flourishing state of the Greek economy and of Greek life generally in this their golden age. Athens, having fought off the Persians and enhanced, nay perfected, her security by the building of a powerful navy, was secure. The free pursuit of material welfare and the rise of a specific culture connected with it, a culture which means much to modern man because he feels its life-style to be a-kindred to his own, were the fruit of this, alas only transient, security.

So great was this security that men did not hesitate to save and to invest, in other words, to form capital and to apply it. 'In the time from *c.* 560 to 330 B.C.,' says Heichelheim, 'we observe a steady increase of working capital in Hellas. This emerges in fact quite clearly from the ... decline in the rate of interest during these centuries.'[4] There was no merely royal capitalism here, as there had been in Israel, there was a real capitalism comparable with that which we know ourselves. Large private fortunes can be found like those of the mining magnates Callias and Nicias and of the banker Pasion.[5] Most importantly, the taking of interest was no longer simply winked at, but was fully accepted and approved of, a sure sign that a form of capitalism had arisen and even established itself. 'Quite different from Rome and Israel, the usurers had almost complete freedom in the Hellas of our period,' Heichelheim writes. 'With very few exceptions, the earlier Hellenic experiments to abolish all legal restrictions in connection with taking interest were imitated generally during the period from the accession of Pisistratus to the reign of Alexander the Great and became the normal practice

[1] Vol. II, Leiden 1964, p. 8. [2] Ibid., pp. 15, 9, 10, 15.
[3] Ibid., pp. 13 and 14. [4] Ibid., p. 28; cf. also p. 29.
[5] Ibid., p. 35.

throughout Greece.'[1] The usual consequences did not fail to appear: 'Wages were gradually depressed.'[2]

With this aspect we are less concerned here. What truly interests us is the influence of the economic developments just described on the character of social coherence, and in this detail too, capitalism showed itself in its proper colours. Up to the fifth century, a loan was called *chreos*, a term which retained in its meaning a reference to 'the Homeric and early Greek moral and ethical obligation to help one's neighbour ... similarly found in the Bible'. Then, in the fifth century, there arises a new word, *daneion*, 'a business-like loan', a purely economic, profit-directed transaction without a trace of the older sentiment[3] – a truly eloquent linguistic innovation.

Many traits, among them some of the most salient traits, of modern capitalism were in this way present in the Athenian economy of the fifth century B.C. And yet it would be an unjustifiable exaggeration to say that modern capitalism was present. For, just as in Israel, there were assignable limits beyond which the development of Attica did not go. To remain for a moment with the philological aspect: while it is certainly significant that a word appeared which described the pure business loan bereft of any human implication, there were, to the end of antiquity, no words for competition or, on the other hand, for business partnership.[4] Even the unfolding of the currency system which we have duly emphasized failed to leave its imprint on everyday speech: 'One of the most usual words for money, *chremata*, ... has always kept its original meaning (objects for daily use); in some passages we cannot make out whether money or goods are meant. And the circumstance that objects of art or precious metal as cups, dishes and such like were considered and treated at the same time as coinage, indicates that money was never counted exclusively as a medium of exchange in the same degree as nowadays.'[5]

One measure of the length to which an economy evolves towards the condition of a capitalist society is the presence, and the relative perfection, of banking within it. Classical Greece had banking, even banking resembling modern banking enterprise. Speaking of the end of the fifth century, Heichelheim expresses the opinion that the '*trapezitai* were large capitalistic enterprises'; yet on the very same page he informs us that the term *trapeza* was taken from 'table of exchange', and this relatively pre- and uncapitalistic branch of the business – exchanging Athenian coins for Corinthian or vice versa – remained the determining element in the meaning of the word.[6] 'Recent research demonstrates quite clearly,' we read on another page,[7] 'that the struc-

---

[1] Ibid., pp. 27 and 24.   [2] Ibid., p. 31.   [3] Ibid., p. 30.
[4] Bolkestein, H., *Economic Life in Greece's Golden Age*, Leiden 1958, pp. 67 and 115–17.
[5] Ibid., p. 123.   [6] Heichelheim, loc. cit., p. 74.   [7] Ibid., p. 84. Cf. also p. 85.

tural level reached by Greek banking between the sixth and fourth centuries B.C. cannot be estimated as high.'

If this seems to be a somewhat vague statement, it is possible to render it much more concrete and hence convincing. A capitalist bank is not so much a money-changer's shop as a credit institution, and this precisely is what the Athenian banks did not become. 'There is,' says Heichelheim, 'one significant omission in our evidence. Practically no mention is made of business credit advanced for individual workshops of craftsmen. The few instances on record seem to have been nothing else except agreements between close friends without that the creditor expected proper business gains.'[1] On this most important point, Bolkestein bears out his colleague: 'Unproductive loans,' he says very simply, 'predominate'; and later he explains that we are, even in Attica, confronted with a world 'where borrowing in need was a rule and borrowing to do business belonged to the exceptions'.[2]

But even this is not finally decisive; finally decisive is the fact that, whatever capitalist developments there were, no *industrial* capitalism made its appearance. For this reason a realistic comparison of the classical picture with modern conditions is out of the question. 'A status of industrial entrepreneur was . . . lacking,' Bolkestein maintains. 'The Greek language did not know a word resembling our "factory-owner". It is still more significant that Aristotle in his *Politics* never mentions entrepreneurs in general or industrial entrepreneurs, viz. factory owners, in particular, when enumerating the different stations in life.' He knows, on the one hand, craftsmen, he knows on the other traders (literally: those who go to market – a somewhat primitive term); he knows no captain of industry. Even the rich Demosthenes (the like-named father of the famous orator) was a money-lender, not an entrepreneur.[3]

It was because of this fact, because the principles of capitalism – of a modernism before its day – did not prove strong enough to break through into the sphere of production, that the forms of life characteristic of it failed to gain consistency and permanence in the Hellenic world. Yet even a weakly struck chord will reverberate and evoke an echo. The Sophists may have been a marginal group in Athens, not comparable in position and prestige to the Platonic and Aristotelian schools. Yet they were there. They made themselves heard. And they brought on a crisis in religious culture which must deeply concern us because it was in many respects similar to that which racks Christianity at the present time.

However passing a phase associationism may have been in the ancient world, there is no gainsaying its significance, no denying its

[1] Ibid., p. 81.
[2] Bolkestein, loc. cit., pp. 65 and 132.
[3] Ibid., pp. 64 and 60 et seq. Cf. also p. 111.

237

intellectual punch and power. What precisely was its message? We have seen its 'material substructure' in Hebrew and Hellenic society; let us now outline the 'mental superstructure' which it erected on the bases of this its concrete historical reality.

TWO HISTORICAL EXAMPLES

The case of Israel

The point at which we should logically expect the primal and primeval concept of kin solidarity to weaken first, is the institution of the blood feud. The symbiosis and solidarity within a wandering desert tribe is so great that its members can hardly imagine a conflict of interest within their own ranks: trouble comes on the grazing grounds or near the water holes, and so it is always another tribe, another collectivity, that is its cause, rarely an individual. It is radically different in a city. Walled as it is, it is normally not concerned with outsiders. Conflicts of interest develop between neighbours, especially in connection with buying and selling, and then brother stands against brother rather than stranger against stranger. Hence a new idea of justice must spring up, and it is bound to develop in the direction of an individualistic concept of responsibility. Not only the laws of contract, but even the criminal laws will receive the imprint of this individualism – this associationism, as we should say in the sociologist's lingo. The law of talion[1] is very old, yet it is a full step beyond tribal collectivism. 'An eye for an eye, a tooth for a tooth' means, or at least may mean, the culprit's eye or the culprit's tooth, with nobody else involved. '*He* that giveth a blemish to any of his neighbours,' so we may read, 'as *he* hath done, so shall it be done to *him*.'[2]

Among the sacred codes of Judaism, it is the Book of Deuteronomy which draws out the individualistic implications of the principle of talion. 'The fathers shall not be put to death for the children,' so the chief pronouncement runs, 'nor the children for the fathers; but every one shall die for his own sin' (xxiv, 16). According to the Book of Kings, obedience to this behest is essential to, and enters into, the image of the good, God-fearing ruler: 'In the second year of Joas son of Joachaz, king of Israel, reigned Amazias son of Joas king of Juda . . . He did that which was right before the Lord . . . And when he had possession of the kingdom, he put his servants to death that had slain the king his father. But the children of the murderers he did not put to death, according to that which is written in the book of the law of Moses, wherein the Lord commanded, saying: The fathers shall not be put to death for the children, neither shall the children be put to death for the fathers: but every man shall die for his own sins' (IV

[1] Cf. Leviticus xxiv, 19 and 20.　　[2] Ibid.

Kings XIV, 1–6).[1] Pedersen calls this a norm apt 'to annul the unity of the family and make the family crumble away into individuals', and he derives it directly from the existence and the influence of the associational sector inside Hebrew society: 'It follows,' he says, 'currents which made themselves felt through the metropolitan life developing in Jerusalem.'[2]

The probable date of Deuteronomy coincides in all likelihood with the life span of the Prophet Jeremias,[3] and so it is less than surprising that we should find very similar ideas in his mind. Disgusted by the miserable present, this seer throws his eyes forward to a better future for his people, and he envisages it as a new dispensation under which the principle of individual responsibility and individualistic justice will reign supreme. Though he is dismayed by the first fruits of the associational society around him, he is yet too much a product of it not to expect salvation from an idealistic development and application of the basic tendencies dwelling within it, rather than from a return to the collectivism of the fathers. 'Behold,' he exclaims, 'the days come, saith the Lord: and I will sow the house of Israel and the house of Juda with the seed of men and with the seed of beasts. And as I have watched over them, to pluck up and to throw down and to scatter and destroy and afflict: so will I watch over them, to build up and to plant them, saith the Lord. In those days they shall say no more: the fathers have eaten a sour grape, and the teeth of the children are set on edge. But every one shall die for his own iniquity: every man that shall eat the sour grape, his teeth shall be set on edge' (Jeremias XXXI, 27–30).

From Jeremias there is historically only a short step to Ezechiel, even though most of the former's life was lived before the deportation of the Jews to Babylon, most of the latter's after that event. Ezechiel's is the clearest voice of the individualistic-associational mode of thinking within the canon of the sacred scriptures; his eighteenth chapter is its *locus classicus*. His words are strong: 'And the word of the Lord came to me saying: what is the meaning that you use among you this parable as a proverb in the land of Israel, saying: the fathers have eaten sour grapes and the teeth of the children are set on edge? As I live, saith the Lord God, this parable shall be no more to you a proverb in Israel. Behold, all souls are mine: as the soul of the father, so also the soul of the son is mine: the soul that sinneth, the same shall die . . . But if he beget a son who, seeing all his father's sins . . . is afraid and shall not do the like . . . but hath executed my judgments and hath walked in my commandments: this man shall not die for the inquity of his father, but living he shall live. As for his father, because he oppressed and offered violence to his brother and wrought evil in the midst of his

[1] Cf. also II Paralipomenon XXV, 1–4.
[2] Pedersen, loc. cit., p. 398.
[3] Cf. de Vaux, loc. cit., p. 75.

people, behold, he is dead in his own iniquity. And you say: why hath not the son borne the iniquity of his father? Verily, because the son hath wrought judgment and justice, hath kept all my commandments and done them, living he shall live. The soul that sinneth, the same shall die: the son shall not bear the iniquity of the father, and the father shall not bear the iniquity of the son. The justice of the just shall be upon him [i.e. upon him alone], and the wickedness of the wicked shall be upon him [i.e. upon him alone] ... Therefore will I judge every man according to his [own] ways, O house of Israel, saith the Lord God' (Ezechiel xviii, 1–4, 14, 17–20, 30).

In addition to this eighteenth chapter, the fourteenth, too, is significant in this context. It foreshadows in a manner the later conflict between Catholics and Protestants concerning the role of saints in the economy of salvation. 'And the word of the Lord came to me, saying: Son of man, when a land shall sin against me, so as to transgress grievously, I will stretch forth my hand upon it and will break the staff of the bread thereof: and I will send famine upon it and will destroy man and beast out of it. And if these three men, Noe, Daniel and Job, shall be in it: they shall deliver their own souls by their justice, saith the Lord of hosts.' But (and this is the way in which Luther and Calvin, too, were to feel in their day), 'if these three men shall be in it, as I live, saith the Lord, they shall deliver neither sons nor daughters: but they only shall be delivered and the land shall be made desolate' (Ezechiel xiv, 12–14, 16). The very last words are repeated once again on the same page (verse 20), lest their teaching should be underestimated or lost.

This predication of an associational and individualistic ethic is, surely, loud and unambiguous enough. And yet, Johannes Pedersen can assert that such 'attempts to set up man as an isolated individual are quite sporadic and nowhere carried out fully'.[1] Strange though this may sound, in view of what we have heard from Ezechiel's own mouth, this judgment is entirely correct. Ezechiel himself does not always feel as he seems to assert that all men should. In his sixteenth chapter – one of the most dramatic and impressive of them all – he speaks of the impending humiliation of Jerusalem, the 'unfaithful wife', and of the mercy which God will show her in the end, in spite of her transgressions. Both in cursing and in blessing, no distinction is drawn between individual inhabitants. It is the community of the holy city that is threatened, and it is the community that is comforted. Indeed, Ezechiel quotes here an adage of the very kind which we have seen him reject so sharply: 'Behold, every one that useth a common proverb shall use this against thee, saying: as the mother was, so also is her daughter' (xvi, 44). And there is even stronger proof of the deep collectivism in the Prophet's mind. Both the Jews before him and the Christians after

[1] Pedersen, loc. cit., p. 376.

him compared the community to a vine, to symbolize its unity.[1] Ezechiel uses the same phrase, and we see quite clearly that the implications in his case are no different from earlier and later usage: 'Thus saith the Lord God: as the vine tree among the trees of the forests which I have given to the fire to be consumed, so will I deliver up the inhabitants of Jerusalem' (xv, 6).

Furthermore, this collectivism was not confined merely to the words of the Prophet: it lived in his sentiments, too: it is a subjective feeling in his heart as well as an objective concept in his head. 'He experiences himself as a representative of Israel. The guilt of his nation falls upon him like a heavy load and fells him to the ground,' writes Walther Eichrodt in his great commentary,[2] and Pedersen asserts: 'Ezechiel is sure that he bears the inqiuity of the Israelites'.[3] The chief passage concerned is less than clear for modern man because modern man has lost the key to the understanding of the symbolism used; yet the point which we have to make in our context emerges with sufficient clarity. God is represented as saying to Ezechiel: 'Thou shalt sleep upon thy left side and shalt lay the iniquities of the house of Israel upon it . . . and thou shalt take upon thee their iniquity . . . And when thou hast accomplished this, thou shalt sleep again upon thy right side, and thou shalt take upon thee the iniquity of the house of Juda . . .' (IV, 4 and 6). Like the symbolism of the vine, this self-interpretation of the Prophet's role fits faultlessly into the unbroken chain of passages betokening Judaeo-Christian collectivism: it points back to the sacrificial beast of the Old Covenant (Leviticus XVI, 22), and it points forward to the atoning Lamb of God in the New (John I, 29). In all three cases, one suffers for all and all suffer in one.

A first reading and a superficial comparison of the passages which we have given is apt to leave one with the impression that Ezechiel's mind was hopelessly split, that he was a man at odds with himself. Yet, on closer consideration, it appears that this conclusion is by no means inescapable. Bible scholars tell us that the sermon, in chapter XVIII, enjoining individual rectitude and insisting on individual responsibility was addressed to the Jewish exiles in Babylon. If this is indeed true, a totally different interpretation of the salient passages becomes possible. The deportees were murmuring against their fate and even against their God who had sent that fate. *All* Jews had incurred the guilt of ingratitude to YHWH and of sin against *Him*, but collective punishment had *not* been meted out. They were weeping and wailing by the waters of Babylon, while others, no less guilty than they and perhaps more so, were safe at home. Ezechiel's aim was to remove this bitterness

---

[1] Cf. Psalm LXXIX, 9 et seq., and *The Gospel according to St. John*, xv, 1 et seq.
[2] *Das Alte Testament Deutsch*, vol. XXII/1, *Der Prophet Hesekiel, Kapitel 1–18*, Göttingen 1959, p. 29.
[3] Pedersen, loc. cit., p. 436.

and to bring a new ray of hope into the broken lives of these deeply afflicted men. As they are out of Israel, out of the body of their nation, broken men comparable to broken-off branches, they must embrace a mode of morality which is suitable for them. They stand alone, true, but even he who stands alone, he who must, because of his whole situation, turn away from the collectivist ethos of the past, can act rightfully and regain the favour of his God. He can walk in purity, and if he does so, YHWH may yet show mercy to him and accept him as His child.[1]

Such an analysis pushes Ezechiel's individualistic passages out of the cadres of Jewish life and out of the canons of Jewish thought. What, then, about Jeremias? Here a textual solution has been tried. Pedersen considers that the saying about the fathers who have eaten sour grapes and the sons whose teeth are set on edge 'does not at all belong' to the speeches of Jeremias,[2] that it is an interpolation of later days. Eichrodt is not disinclined to agree.[3] Artur Weiser, in his authoritative exegesis of Jeremias, takes a different view.[4] Yet he stresses at the same time, what we would also stress, that the advent of an individualistic ethos is only predicted (Behold, the days come ... In those days ...); it is not asserted that it is already the prevalent and positive norm. And in all probability we shall have to take Deuteronomy xxiv, 16, in the same sense: it enunciates a programme; it does not state an accomplished fact. Of course, for our purposes, this is enough. It shows a *tendency* towards individualism within religious culture, paralleling the tendency towards an associational society in substructural life. Whether this tendency was strong or weak, is relatively unimportant in the present context. It was in any case strong enough to leave some traces in the Holy Book.

One further consideration must be appended here, though, admittedly, it only presents an *argumentum e silentio*. Wherever the associational principle of social life develops, and, more importantly, wherever it prevails, sociological thinking in the broadest sense of the word turns towards contractualism.[5] The individuals are first, and they only *make* a society by acting and compacting together. Religious affiliation, too, tends then to become a matter of personal decision. 'You must take Christ for your Saviour', as some of the more consistent

---

[1] We have given a free summary of Eichrodt's argument; cf. his commentary, as quoted, pp. 143 et seq., esp. pp. 150 and 151. Cf. also p. 148 on Ezechiel's abiding collectivism, and Eichrodt's analysis in *Die Krisis der Gemeinschaft in Israel*, Basel 1953.

[2] Pedersen, loc. cit., p. 436.

[3] Eichrodt, loc. cit., p. 147, referring to Rudolph, W., *Jeremia*, Tübingen 1947.

[4] Weiser, A., *Das Alte Testament Deutsch*, vol. XXI/2, *Das Buch des Propheten Jeremia, Kapitel 25, 15–52, 34*, Göttingen 1955, pp. 292 and 293. Cf. also Pedersen, loc. cit., p. 398.

[5] Cf. Stark, W., *The Fundamental Forms of Social Life*, London 1962, pp. 184 et seq.

Protestant sects are wont to say today. 'You must contract into the sect,' so we might also, more soberly, formulate the same concept. From this idea of a sacred contract it is not too far to the covenant idea of the Old Testament. Yet – and this is decisive – the covenants of Hebrew history and religion are always collective.[1] Whether it is the marriage between Jacob and Lia or Rachel (really a treaty between Jacob's people and Laban's), or between YHWH and the Israelites under Moses, or even between YHWH and Abraham, the contracting party at the human end or ends is invariably 'a house'. That the step from this mode of thinking to the *solus cum solo* doctrine of fully unfolded Protestantism – a step none too difficult to make, as the Calvinic and post-Calvinic age was to show – was not taken by the Jews of biblical times proves that the appearance of an associational ethic and philosophy in their midst was no more than a momentary deviation from their otherwise settled ways.

The Eastern Mediterranean

In Israel, the contrast between the alternative forms of social organization, association and community, showed itself mainly in the tension between the larger cities and the smaller settlements: it was Jerusalem and Samaria versus the rest. In Greece the same distinction existed and persisted; but it was of even greater consequence that the larger cities themselves were internally divided. In all typical cases there was, on the one hand, an upper class, land-owning and slave-holding, which conserved the old clan constitution and continued to think in terms of it: there was, on the other, a lower, but upward-thrusting class which monopolized the mobile property and especially the monetary wealth, and which cared little for family ties and other collective forms of life. An appreciable fraction of them (Heichelheim speaks of 70 to 80 per cent.) had indeed started as incomers from other places and hence as men outside the established cadres of society. They became the breeding ground of new – individualistic – conceptions. Class struggles, and especially power struggles, soon developed and put a sharp edge on the confrontation between the two strata and their respective philosophies.[2]

In the great contest between community and association, the associational principle progressively gained the upper hand as the cities matured and, so to speak, modernized themselves, until catastrophe overtook Greek life as a whole. 'During the Middle Ages of Hellas, that is to say, from the eighth to the sixth century,' writes Glotz, 'the *genos*, broken up into families, is stripped of its sovereignty. The state progressively strengthens its jurisdiction until it becomes binding and

[1] Cf. Pedersen, pp. 292, 293, 357, 358, 481, 487, 489; also p. 342.
[2] Glotz, loc. cit., pp. 238, 239, 406, 407; Bolkestein, loc. cit., pp. 48 and 51; Heichelheim, loc. cit., pp. 126–8.

destroys, step by step, the solidarity of the families until it retains only those fragments of it which it can use for the increase of its own power.'[1] But the state, when fully developed, knows no clans: it knows only individuals. Collective responsibility is dead so far as practical life is concerned. Indeed, it becomes simply unthinkable.

This is not the place to follow the successive stages of the process. The blood feud gives way to composition-payments. The acceptance of a sum of money, the *poiné*, in lieu of the infliction of vengeance is characteristic of the deep penetration of Greek society by a monetary economy: the Jews never agreed to this *quid pro quo*. But this transition from bloodshed to bloodwit betokens not only a 'softening of manners', to use an old phrase: it lays bare basic social transformations. He on whom you wreak vengeance is the member of another *genos*; he from whom you accept a composition payment is a citizen of the same town. At first, the individual culprit is singled out while the prosecuting clan still acts *in corpore*; then both the party hurt and the offender appear as persons before the tribunals.[2] When this stage is reached, the scene is set for the development of new, associational forms of thought and feeling.

A document in which the breakthrough of these forms is openly visible is a bronze tablet found at Olympia with an inscription whose content is likened, by Glotz, to the tenor of the Deuteronomic code with which it is roughly contemporary.[3] The main injunction of the text (a legal one) is that if somebody has recourse to violence against a man who is accused in a court of law, he shall be liable to a fine of ten *minae*, provided he acted as he did, knowing that the case was pending. This is clearly a stipulation meant to discourage the blood feud: it is for the tribunal, not the individual or grouping involved, to see to it that justice is done. But most important is the first sentence of the inscription. An expert has translated it as follows: 'If one should utter imprecations against a male Elean, no harm shall come to his [i.e. the latter's] clan or family or property.'[4] Philologically, the passage is most difficult; the dialect in which it is expressed is not too well known; but assuming that this rendering is correct, as it is in all probability, we have here, near the dividing line between the seventh and the sixth century, an effort to end the age of collective responsibility and usher in that of its opposite, the exclusive responsibility of the individual.

Glotz, winding up his discussion of this historical source, or rather of this piece of legislation, waxes lyrical and exclaims: 'The *rhetra* of Elis forms, with the Deuteronomium, a double link in the golden chain

---

[1] Glotz, loc. cit., p. 225.
[2] Cf. ibid., pp. 109–11, 134, 192, 272.
[3] Ibid., pp. 247, 258, 259.
[4] Roberts, E. S., *An Introduction to Greek Epigraphy, Part I*, Cambridge 1887, p. 364; cf. Glotz, pp. 247 et seq.

which ends with the Declaration of the Rights of Man.'[1] There is some sober truth in this less than sober formulation, yet, taking scholarly soberness one step further, we must ask, how much a declaration like this may really have meant in contemporary Greece. And if we widen our purview and try to form some sort of general impression, we see that the Hellenes did not go over, with flying colours, to the new position. Theognis indeed complains that a system is unfair under which the criminal escapes punishment while it falls on somebody else later on. Yet there are passages of diametrically opposite import in the poems which go by his name. It is simply the way of the gods to visit the iniquity of the fathers on their offspring, and this decree of the higher powers must be accepted because it is built into the foundations of being. An obvious inference from this crude self-contradiction within the Theognid corpus seems to be that it cannot really have been from one pen, but must have had two or more authors who felt differently about the problem which interests us here. Yet this makes little difference, for the possible fellow-authors would in any case be close contemporaries. If there is no division in one mind, therefore, there is certainly division within one period, a *Zeitgeist* in conflict with itself.[2]

To give another example, an intermediate position must also have built up in the thought of Aeschylus. The divine law of collective responsibility forms the firm background of his dramas, yet two supplementary and modifying convictions seem to struggle upward all the time. One is that the gods do not really strike the innocent, only the apparently innocent. Sons are in fact like their fathers; they share their character; they could have done what their progenitor did; hence it is not, or it is not only, he who is punished in his offspring: they are punished for their own criminal bent. The other budding belief is of the same tendency, only that it leads further. There is salvation for the truly innocent, at least through the agency of the newer, milder, more understanding gods, such as Apollo and Athene. Orestes is personally without guilt, and for that reason they see to it that he should be freed from his sufferings. There is thus no break, on the part of Aeschylus, with the time-hallowed concept of familial solidarity; there is merely a modification. Where Glotz explains all this, he most interestingly refers also to a piece of legislation on the part of Athens which evinces the same attitude. The *Oresteia* was first performed in 458 B.C. But some time between 464 and 457, the Athenian authorities gave a law to the Erytraeans which condemned traitors and their children to death, excepting, however, the case in which these children had given proof of their loyalty to Athens and Erytraea. 'The legislation hints that this exception should become the rule: it has the same aspirations, it follows the same aim as the poet,' as Aeschylus.[3]

[1] Ibid., p. 259.   [2] Cf. Adkins, loc. cit., pp. 68, 69, 76.
[3] Glotz, pp. 409-13; cf. also p. 579.

Plato, too, appears to have had the same aim. If a man has committed the capital crime of sacrilege and is to die for it, his descendants are not to suffer with him if they have known how to keep clear of the noxious parental influences impinging on them. So teach *The Laws*.[1] But Plato insists at the same time that there are cases in which evil must indeed be considered as hereditary and collective. If a father, grandfather and great-grandfather have been guilty of treason, the fourth generation cannot escape scot-free. It is manifestly caught in a curse, engulfed in a comprehensive fault. Still, in spite of this proviso, Plato appears in this particular to make large concessions to the concept of exclusive personal responsibility. Yet in his epistemology, i.e. in the very centre of his system, his aim is clearly to reconcile the old style of thought and the new, rather than to opt for the one or the other. According to the principle inherent in community life, only the species is real, the concrete copy of it is not; according to the principle dominant in associational life, only the concrete is real, the universal, the species is not. Plato overcomes this contrast by offering his theory of *metexis*. The individual is indeed real, but it is what it is only by dint of its *participation* in the species, and in the divine idea behind both species and individual.[2]

Writing in the first century of the Christian era, after much of the dust raised by the Greek discussions about personal and collective responsibility had settled, Plutarch still reflects, in his own way, the basic tendency visible in Aeschylus and Plato. 'Where a good man is born of a bad,' he writes, 'as a healthy child may come of a sickly parent, the penalty attached to the family is remitted, and he becomes, as it were, adopted out of vice; whereas if a man's disorder reproduces the traits of a vicious ancestry, it is surely fitting that he should succeed to the punishment of that viciousness as to the debts of an estate.'[3] Plutarch took this view, even so late in the day, partly because associational society had undergone a considerable involution since the heyday of Athenian capitalism, and partly because, as a religious man, he held fast to the basic conceptions of the traditional creed. We can see in him and through him the truth of the following words of Gustave Glotz: 'It is undeniable that the dogmas of Greek theology have preserved the primitive principles of family solidarity and transmissible responsibility: among the nations of antiquity, the doctrine of hereditary punishment has always had the upper hand over the doctrine of personal retribution in another world.'[4]

In winding up this analysis, we should not, however, restrict our-

[1] IX, 855 and 856. Cf. Glotz, p. 417, and *The Laws of Plato*, transl. Taylor, A. E., London 1934, pp. 242 and 244.
[2] Cf. Landsberg's analysis, as summarized in Stark, W., *The Sociology of Knowledge*, London 1958, pp. 37 et seq.
[3] 'On the Delays of the Divine Vengeance', as quoted (cf. p. 45 above), p. 267.
[4] Glotz, loc. cit., p. 607.

selves to a characterization of Plutarch's own opinion, even though it is indicative of a widespread attitude and shows that, by and large, the classical mind became arrested somewhere half-way between the ethos of archaic and clan society on the one hand, capitalist and modern society on the other.[1] We should also use his essay for the identification of the consistently individualistic mentality which certain periods and certain strata carried to considerable lengths, and in some cases even to its logical conclusion. Plutarch quotes Bion of Borysthenes, a philosopher of the third century B.C.,[2] as saying that in punishing the son for his father's misdeed God is more ridiculous than a physician who administers medicine to a child in order to cure the sickness of his elders. Here, indeed, the end of the road is reached. To the contemporary Greek, a statement of this kind was in the first place an act of impiety; to the modern observer it is the ripest product of that revolutionary leaven in Greek society which is known as Sophism and whose rejection by the Greek majority is still recognizable in the pejorative undertone with which that name is even now associated. The Sophists and their two subschools, the Cynics and the Cyrenaics, knew only man and mankind; they knew nothing in between, above all no *genos* and no *polis*. The very idea of collective responsibility was therefore alien to them. They were indeed a power to be reckoned with, but they did not succeed in making their radical individualism into the unconscious metaphysics of a whole age. That feat remained reserved for modern society.

THE SELF-INTERPRETATION OF CALVINISM AS A COVENANT-SOCIETY

The connection, explored in these pages, between Christianity and especially Catholicism on the one hand, community and collectivistic thinking on the other, is no accident, historical or otherwise, but belongs to the very essence of these ever-conjoined phenomena. Perhaps we can best prove that this is indeed so by using an *argumentum e contrario*. If a consistently associational and individualistic system of life and thought should ever achieve complete control, Christianity would have to shrivel up and fade away. For such a system would have to see men, in the style of Leibniz's *jeu d'esprit*, as monads, and monads have, in his parlance, no windows: nothing can possibly come out of them, and nothing can possibly enter into them. They are simply self-enclosed souls. In consequence, there would be no way in which the merits of Christ could come to their assistance and rescue them from sin. Neither could they be, as Catholic philosophy asserts, integral parts in an integrated whole, cells in the Body of Christ, nor

[1] Cf. ibid., pp. 589, 590, 592, 593, 597.
[2] Plutarch, as quoted, p. 259.

yet could they be regarded, as Protestant doctrine suggests, as associated with Christ in the way one friend may be with another. They would have to find their salvation by their own unaided efforts.

While a fusion between Christianity and total associationism-individualism is thus out of the question, a mutual adjustment and accommodation may be achieved. And this is what modern Protestantism has brought about; even modern Catholicism, under the guidance of the Jesuit inspiration, has made half of a move in this direction.[1] If we may for a moment disregard the weighty political factors (in the widest sense of the word), if we may for that moment concentrate on the social and spiritual aspects of the story, we may say that the Church split in the sixteenth century because the willingness to meet modernity was not the same in all her children: some rejected any abandonment of traditional collectivism, others were prepared to embrace the new individualism. That was the parting of the ways. It is one thing to say that the saved sinner is 'in' Christ and thus partakes of His Grace: it is another to argue that Christ's righteousness is 'imputed' to him, that Christ, as it were, stands before him and covers him so that his sores cannot be seen. In the first case, there is one being, a multiplicity made into a unity; in the second, there are two, a number not further reducible. Both confessions may be modes of Christianity, but they are different modes, variants of a common theme perhaps, but yet each set in another key. Even if they have been or can be united, they will at best yield a contrapuntally complex sound and not strike a simple, unsophisticated chord.

Our whole investigation, throughout its five volumes, has proved, if it has proved anything, that Christianity has sprung from, and remains rooted in, community. The bulk of its tradition is dominated by the fact of synthesis and the desire for it. And yet there was, from the beginning, an element in the Judaeo-Christian system which made a transition to more personalistic attitudes possible and lent it the mantle of legitimacy. Its core-concept is that of the covenant. A covenant, whatever its *differentia specifica*, is a kind of contract; but every contract presupposes, by definition, two parties who meet, two wills that come to agreement. Such an agreement, when reached, will create only a bipolar relationship; indeed, regularly and in principle, it will create only a concrete and specific – one might say, only an *ad-hoc* – act of co-operation, a *point* of order and no more. But out of points are formed lines, out of lines, planes, out of planes, three-dimensional bodies. In the same manner, contracts may generate chains of contracts and ongoing lines of co-operation, and these in turn may structure themselves into social systems, into bodies social. In this way, an inclusive mode of social thinking may be drawn from the concept of covenanting, and it may succeed in permeating and in informing the whole of culture.

[1] Cf. our vol. III, pp. 365 et seq.

The culture which thus arises must, of necessity, be totally different from a culture of community. It is one thing to go from the whole to the part, to be an organicist; it is a very different thing to go from the part to the whole, to be a contractualist. It is therefore one thing to be a Catholic and a very different thing to be a Calvinist. Even though, for reasons which we have given, something of collectivism remained, and had to remain, in Calvinist thinking, there was yet a radically new mental condition in the Protestant camp, once it had condemned the 'realistic' and embraced a nominalistic philosophy of social and religious life. Ever since Kant used, in the Introduction to the *Critique of Pure Reason*, the term 'Copernican revolution' to describe the transition from the older modes of thought to his own subjectivist epistemology, the phrase has been repeated again and again, with unavoidably decreasing effect. We hesitate, therefore, to apply it; yet it would not be inappropriate. Indeed, as a change-over to relative subjectivism characterizes both the great Protestants and Kant (a fact which has often been noted), it would be particularly appropriate in our context.

The concept of the covenant makes its first appearance (a very powerful one) in the biblical account of God's dealings with Abraham.[1] Like every desert tribesman, the Patriarch is concerned about two things: the survival of his descent group and the conquest of land sufficient to sustain his progeny. On both points, YHWH reassures him. A son will be born to Abraham, even though he is already well on in years; and a rich country will fall to him and his clan, even though he is as yet only a wandering nomad. 'The word of the Lord came to Abram in a vision, saying, Fear not, Abram, I am thy protector . . . And He brought him forth abroad, and said to him: Look up to heaven, and number the stars, if thou canst. And He said to him: so shall thy seed be. Abram believed God, and it was reputed to him unto justice. And He said to him: I am the Lord who brought thee out from Ur of the Chaldees, to give thee this land, and that thou mightest possess it.' 'That day,' says the Scripture a little later, as if to explain what had taken place, 'God made a covenant with Abram' (Genesis xv, 1, 5, 6, 7, 18).

Two chapters later, this concept is taken up again and more fully developed. 'And after he [Abram] began to be ninety and nine years old, the Lord appeared to him and said unto him: I am the Almighty God; walk before me and be perfect . . . I will establish my covenant between me and thee, and between thy seed after thee in their generations, by a perpetual covenant: to be a God to thee and to thy seed after

[1] Genesis III, 15, is, in the Calvinist literature, sometimes adduced as well, as incorporating a promise of God to Adam, but this must be taken together with the admission, in the same literature, that the sacred concepts appear at first only in vague guises, or rather in disguises. Cf. esp. Calvin, J., *Institutes of the Christian Religion*, transl. Battles, F. L., ed. McNeill, J. T., vol. I (*The Library of Christian Classics, vol. XX*), Philadelphia n.d., p. 446 (II, X, 20).

thee. And I will give to thee and to thy seed the land of thy sojourn-
ment, all the land of Chanaan, for a perpetual possession; and I will be
their God. And again God said to Abraham: And thou therefore shall
keep my covenant and thy seed after thee in their generations' (XVII,
1, 7, 8, 9). The contractual pattern is clearly visible in this passage:
there is a mutual agreement between two parties, involving rights and
duties on either side; there is a meeting and matching of promises,
creating a bond of obligations. We can hardly blame either the Jewish
lawyers of later days or the modern Calvinists, if they looked at the two
chapters of Genesis concerned somewhat from the juridical point of
view. Yet one later and especially modern idea cannot, in a sound
exegesis, be interpreted into the text: the assertion that Abraham was
but an isolated person, that God and the Patriarch met *Solus cum solo*.
It is true that a further covenant and contract is envisaged between God
and Abraham's first free-born manchild: 'And God said to Abraham:
Sara, thy wife, shall bear thee a son, and thou shalt call his name Isaac.
And I will establish my covenant with him for a perpetual covenant,
and with his seed after him' (ibid. 19). But, from all we know of primitive, including primitive Hebrew, thought we can be sure that no such
re-tying of the cord was really necessary. Isaac was a party to the
'perpetual covenant' (cf. versicle 7) along with, or rather 'in', his father
Abraham; and, in the same manner, Isaac's 'seed', though yet unborn,
is to be a party to the same perpetual covenant along with, or rather 'in',
their forebear. The very last words of verse 19 make this sufficiently
clear.

This covenantal theme is sounded on several occasions in the sacred
canon, sometimes more loudly, sometimes less. Calvin, for instance, was
inclined to remember Leviticus XXVI, 3 and 12: 'If you walk in my
precepts and keep my commandments and do them ... I will walk
among you and will be your God, and you shall be my people.' From
the sociological point of view it is, however, most significant that the
strongest passages appear in the books conceived at the time when the
development of associational society was at its peak: Deuteronomy and
Jeremias. In Deuteronomy the supposition is that the agreement is
being implemented: 'When thou hast made an end of tithing all thy
fruits, in the third year of tithes thou shalt give it to the Levite, and to
the stranger, and to the fatherless, and to the widow, that they may eat
within thy gates and be filled. And thou shalt speak thus in the sight of
the Lord thy God ... I have not transgressed thy commandments nor
forgotten thy precepts ... I have obeyed the voice of the Lord my
God and have done all things ... commanded me.' After this assertion,
a voice of praise is raised: 'Thou hast chosen the Lord this day to be thy
God and to walk in His ways and keep His ceremonies and precepts and
judgments and obey His command. And the Lord hath chosen thee this
day to be His peculiar people ... and to make thee higher than all

nations which He hath created to His own praise and name and glory'
(Deuteronomy XXVI, 12–14 and 17–19). The principle, basic to any
contract, which the Romans called *do ut des* and the English *tit for tat*,
stands well out in these sentences. Israel is the nation of and in and
under the covenant.

The mood of Jeremias is very different, but his thought is rather
similar. The original compact has not been honoured; things have gone
awry. But, being the child of an at least partially associational and
individualistic society, this Prophet expects Israel's salvation from a
new and firmer contractual tie between God and man. 'Behold, the
days shall come, saith the Lord, and I will make a new covenant with
the house of Israel and with the house of Juda: not according to the
covenant which I made with their fathers . . . the covenant which they
made void . . . But this shall be the covenant that I will make with the
house of Israel after those days, saith the Lord: I will give my law in
their bowels and I will write it in their heart, and I will be their God,
and they shall be my people . . . I will forgive their iniquity and I will
remember their sin no more' (Jeremias XXXI, 31–34).

So far there is very little that would allow an individualistic mentality
to enter in. Yet later on we get an application of the covenantal conception to the more concrete circumstances in which the Jewish people
found themselves at this juncture, and there we behold a thought-
pattern which Calvinism was to repeat and to unfold. 'Thus saith the
Lord, the God of Israel, to this city, whereof you say that it shall be
delivered into the hands of the king of Babylon by the sword and by
famine and by pestilence: Behold, I will gather them together out of all
the lands to which I have cast them out in my anger and in my wrath and
in my great indignation, and I will bring them again into this place and
will cause them to dwell securely. And they shall be my people and I
will be their God . . . And I will make an everlasting covenant with
them and will not cease to do them good, and I will give my fear in
their heart that they may not revolt from me [again] . . . For thus saith
the Lord: as I have brought upon this people all this great evil, so will
I bring upon them all the good that I now speak to thee' (XXXII, 36–38,
40, 42; cf. also Deuteronomy XXX).

The decisive words in this chain of verses occur in the thirty-seventh
versicle: 'Behold, I will gather them out of all lands!' The sanctified
society, so it may be concluded from this line, is not an ongoing stream
of life, something that already exists: it is, on the contrary, something
which has yet to be created. It is not a womb out of which individuals
emerge and a body in which they remain: it is a collection into which
these individuals are gathered and inducted. In any case – and this is the
decisive sociological ontology which may be discovered in, or interpreted from, this text – the individuals are first, society is only a
secondary formation, a derivative, an artefact. To get into the covenant,

the individual has to contract in; he has to give his assent to member-ship; the place where the die is cast is his personal will. This is socio-logical nominalism: behind Jehan Calvin who developed the germs which we have just tried to lay bare we behold already, in the not too distant future, Jean-Jacques Rousseau and his *Contrat Social*.

But between the death of Jeremias and the birth of Jean-Jacques, there lie some two thousand three hundred years, and much did happen in them. To the Jews, the idea that the individual was prior to the community was – if we disregard the Deuteronomic-Jeremian inter-lude – largely alien. For them, the prophecy of Jeremias was a promise of collective redemption. It was the claim of Jesus when He came that He was the fulfiller of this promise, the bringer of redemption, the Messiah. Therefore He said, on the occasion of His last supper, according to St. Mark (XIV, 24), when raising the cup: 'This is the blood of the new covenant', words which St. Luke records as: 'This is the chalice, the new covenant in my blood' (XXII, 20).[1] Henceforth, the covenant conception had a place in the very citadel of Christianity.

No wonder, then, that St. Paul made incisive use of it. What had come down to him, as he read the Scriptures (including, of course, the Gospel, whether already down on parchment or as yet an oral tradition), was the theology of two covenants, one voided and one valid. The voided one was the covenant mediated by Moses under which the Israelites received the Law and undertook to obey it;[2] the valid one was the covenant mediated by Christ under which the Christians obtain mercy and open their hearts to the divine voice. To drive home the contrast between the two dispensations, Paul used as symbols the figures of Abraham's spouses, Agar, the bondwoman, and Sara, the free. The old covenant must remind one of Agar, for it means bondage – bondage to the fear of sin and damnation. The new covenant is shining like Sara for it brings liberation – the freedom of those forgiven and finally converted. As for the Abrahamic covenant, it is the adumbration of either and both.

The Epistle in which Paul dwells on this elaboration of the covenant conception is that to the Galatians, and in it there occurs a passage which seems to invite a new, individualistic interpretation of the whole tradition. It is the sixteenth verse in chapter III: 'To Abraham were the promises made and to his seed. He [i.e. God] saith not: and to his seeds, as of many. But as of one: and to thy seed, which is Christ'. It was, at least in part, because they remembered this passage, that a consistently individualistic sect such as the Quakers liked to call themselves 'the seed'.[3] They were, each one of them, a Christ. If they still remembered

---

[1] The Douai version which we are using has in fact 'testament' instead of 'covenant', but the terms are synonymous.
[2] Cf. Exodus XXIV.
[3] Cf. our vol. II, p. 106.

the covenant conception, they imagined one partner in heaven and many on earth. Or, even better expressed: they imagined not one compact, but many – as many as there were Friends. In their case, the turn-around from community to association, social unity to irreducible multiplicity, was complete.

Needless to say, no such idea entered St. Paul's mind. Indeed, the versicle which we are considering is not even a half-turn towards sociological nominalism. The whole theme of the Epistle is different. It is concerned with the tendency of the earliest Judaeo-Christians to push Christianity back into Judaism, a desire which Paul abhorred and defeated.[1] Do you not realize, he says to those he calls the 'senseless Galatians' (III, 1), that you are new men since you have received 'the Spirit'? Do you not appreciate that you are no longer under the law, but in a state of grace? Your mediator is not Moses, but Christ! This does not mean, Paul adds, that you are not children of the original, or Abrahamic, covenant. You are: you are descended from him through Sara and Isaac. But your derivation from him is not by physical genera-tion, by carnal means: it is due to the oneness with him in faith, to a common godliness. Such faith and such godliness, however, are not restricted to the Jews. 'Know ye, therefore, that they who are of faith' – they who are 'of the faith', as we should say today – 'the same are the children of Abraham' (III, 7). They may be Israelites according to the flesh, but they may also be of different extraction: 'For as many . . . as have been baptized in Christ, have put on Christ. There is neither Jew nor Greek, there is neither bond nor free, there is neither male nor female. For you are all one in Christ Jesus' (ibid. 27 and 28). And Paul concludes: 'If you be Christ's, then you are the seed of Abraham, heirs according to the promise' (29).

The point which Paul desires to drive home, then, is that 'the blessing of Abraham' has 'come to the Gentiles through Christ Jesus' (III, 14). This doctrine is entirely devoid of individualistic content. Does the Apostle not say, *expressis verbis*, in verse 28, that all Christians are 'one in Christ Jesus'? Does he not insist on this – an entirely organismic – idea in his other Epistles? And are we not told that the Master said to him, at the gate of Damascus, 'Saul, Saul, why persecutest thou me' (Acts IX, 4) – *me*, not 'my disciples' or 'the many who follow me'? Paul's was indeed a revolutionary mind, but his attacks were not directed against collectivism. They were directed against the old idea that physical descent makes a social community and little else does. No, Paul preaches, the new formation founded by Jesus Christ, the Church, is a social community and a total unity, not by means of physical birth, but by means of spiritual rebirth, not by means of a fact, but by means of a faith. The promise given to Abraham was indeed fulfilled by One, Christ, but that One was destined to become many, 'the Body of

[1] Cf. our vol. IV, pp. 82 et seq.

Christ', the Church, with all who find salvation in her. Paul used the covenantal conception with great effect, but not in order to overturn the realistic tradition in Judaeo-Christian social speculation.

If further proof were required of the assertion that contractualism was, for fifteen hundred years, alien to the Christian Church – alien to the mainstream, and almost to the whole, of it – it can surely be found in the absence of all traces of it in the literature, broad as it was. 'It is a remarkable fact,' writes F. W. Dillistone, 'that only one pre-Reformation writer makes any extended use of the covenant-idea in developing his theological teaching. This one is Irenaeus.'[1] But even Irenaeus used this concept only for the purpose of polemics and not in a positive sense, as a foundation stone in the building of his system. Anticipating one of Calvin's later preoccupations, he asserted, against Marcion, that the old and the new dispensation are in truth one: there is *one* God who covenants with men, once through the mediation of Moses, and after that through the mediation of Christ. It is therefore wrong to speak of the Lord of the Old Testament as an inferior deity.[2] Where, on the other hand, he has no apologetic end in mind, Irenaeus is as organismic as the rest of the Fathers. Indeed, the unity of the saints of Judaism, the precursor-saints, with the saints of Christianity, the disciples, consists for him precisely in this that they, too, were 'members of Christ', exhibiting 'the working of the whole body.'[3]

The unfolding of the contractual theory is in this way a typically modern phenomenon. And there can be, for the reader of these pages, little in this that is surprising. For modern society was prefigured in the medieval city, and that medieval city was in its turn prefigured in the urban growths of antiquity repeating, *mutatis mutandis*, both their socio-organizational substructure and their philosophico-religious superstructure. Geneva started, so to speak, where Jerusalem or Samaria and Athens stopped. But the medieval city was far more conscious of its own associational and contractual nature than were her predecessors. The bond uniting the citizens was conceived as a *conjuratio*,[4] and often it had in fact begun by a compacting together of the neighbours within the walls. But even where this was a historical fiction rather than a historical fact, the reception of a new townsman was in any case a contracting-in, followed by a solemn asseveration of loyalty, assuring the co-contractants of a *will* to associate with them and to share their duties and rights. Thus a tendency towards nominalistic thinking in matters social and political was endemic in these societies. If, as has often been asserted and re-asserted, *nemine contradicente*, the Reformation was the deed of the free cities,[5] then we must expect, what we in fact find, that it ushers in an age of individualistic mentality.

[1] *The Structure of the Divine Society*, London 1951, p. 117.
[2] Cf. ibid.   [3] Cit. Dillistone, ibid., p. 89.
[4] Möller, B., *Reichsstadt und Reformation*, Gütersloh 1962, p. 11.   [5] Ibid., passim.

We must, however, be careful here and not overshoot the mark. As there was a great difference between Samaria and, say, Gezer or Lachish, so there was a great difference between Geneva and Wittenberg or Erfurt, or even Leipzig and Halle. The latter cities were small, by any standards which we may apply. They had still much of the face-to-face character about them which constitutes the true community, and – as importantly – they were firmly integrated in the surrounding territory and in the territorial state in which that territory had found its political form. Small towns like those in which Luther grew up, worked and lived, evinced therefore only a limited drive towards nominalism. It was there, as we shall see; it bore its fruit.[1] But it was not all-encompassing or all-consistent. And later, when the state had become the master of the church, had, so to speak, absorbed it, organicism could survive and revive, for it provided a convenient ideology for the budding power-state which tried, might and main, to become a closed unity, a big Leviathan. Characteristically, the thought form which came to prevail in Lutheran lands cohered around the concept of the prince as *Landesvater* – 'the father of the country'.[2] The father of a country is no longer quite the head of a body; to that extent there was a retreat from erstwhile organicism; but the relation between progenitor and offspring is still an organic one. The family, used here as the guiding metaphor, is a figure taken from nature, not an artefact like a *contrat social*. There is, then, a half-way house, and this suited Lutheranism, in theory and practice, very well. The greater caesaropapist reality that emerged at the time, the reality of England, bred the same sociopolitical philosophy. We need only mention Sir Robert Filmer's *Patriarcha, or, the Natural Power of Kings* (London 1680) in order to show that a similar doctrine satisfied the Anglican establishment and the Tory party associated with it. Rightly does Troeltsch therefore bracket Luther and Filmer together, as men of parallel mentalities in matters politic and in political philosophy.[3]

Things were very different in a place like Geneva (or, for that matter, Zürich or Berne or even Strasbourg). Situated on the great trade routes between the north and the south of Europe, the Swiss cities had advanced much further on the road towards modern capitalism than a petty agricultural township like Wittenberg or Marburg. They nourished a rich upper stratum living by commerce, and a broader petty bourgeoisie basing itself on the crafts, and these two elements together offered a firm substructure on which an associational-individualistic superstructure could well be erected. Indeed, it was called for, and the local Reformers heard, and responded to, the call. In

---

[1] Cf. below, pp. 275 et seq.
[2] Cf. *D. Martin Luthers Werke*, vol. XXX/1, Weimar 1910, pp. 70 and 153.
[3] Cf. Troeltsch, E., *The Social Teaching of the Christian Churches*, transl. Wyon, O., ed. New York 1960, vol. II, p. 637.

Calvin's work, the covenantal concept is central. 'The Lord,' he says in an often-quoted passage, 'always covenanted with his servants thus: "I will be your God, and you shall be my people". As the Prophets have explained, life and salvation and the whole of blessedness are embraced in these words.'[1]

Yet even in Calvin's mind, contractualism still met with considerable obstacles which set limits to its development. As St. Thomas Aquinas had halted in his retreat from sociological realism because he firmly believed that all men are one in Christ Jesus, the Redeemer, so Calvin came up against a last barrier in his advance towards sociological nominalism because he was quite sure that all men had fallen in Adam, the Primal Progenitor. What some will call Renaissance splendour and others riotous living had brought on a violent reaction. The stirring forces of the revolutionary bourgeoisie embraced, and prided themselves on, their self-discipline, godly continence and moral superiority – those qualities which, on the hour of fulfilment, were to shine forth so impressively in Maximilien Robespierre. From Calvin to Robespierre and vice versa, there is a straight road. There is an indwelling moralism which, in its Christian representatives, triggered a self-interpretation in terms of ethical élitism. The mass of mankind was corrupt. Only the converted are cleansed and cleared. It took the deeper revolution of Antinomianism (with its greatest product, Quakerism) to produce the idea that man is born good, and thereby to undermine the collectivistic doctrine, to which Calvin clung most energetically, that a common catastrophe had overtaken the human race when Adam defied the Lord's command and was condignly punished for this defiance.

Yet the élitism of which we have just spoken was a two-edged sword. It kept alive some sociological realism in Calvin's thought, and we see it in a few passages even about the Church, so for instance in the assertion that 'there is no other way to enter into life unless this mother conceive us in her womb, give us birth, nourish us at her breast and . . . keep us under her care and guidance until, putting off mortal flesh, we become like angels'.[2] But a powerful counter-tendency towards the covenantal-nominalistic position emanates from the same source. The wheat has to be separated from the chaff; the saints have to be called out from the mass of sinners. They have to enter into the Church, and how else can they do this than by an act kindred to the contracting into other societies, secular as well as sacred? Sometimes, in a clever, but merely verbal bridging of the gap between the two sociologies, Calvin says that they are 'engrafted', that the many 'grow together' into one body.[3] But often the other opinion comes to the surface. In one context, the Church is called 'the multitude of those whom God gathers into the

---

[1] *Institutes*, II, X, 8, cf. ed. quoted, vol. I, pp. 434 and 435.
[2] Loc. cit., IV, I, 4; vol. II, p. 1016.
[3] Ibid., IV, I, 2; vol. II, p. 1014.

communion of His Church from all peoples', and in another we read even more clearly: 'All men adopted by God into the company of His people since the beginning of the world were covenanted to Him . . .'.[1] The latter quotation is particularly important because Calvin gives it as a summary of his opinion, and it shows a rather radical individualism. For it implies that the covenant of the elect is concluded with each of them personally.

Should we accuse Calvin of inconsistency? By no means. There are, in him, two ways of looking at the Church, or, better, two states of the Church which he is looking at: the constituted Church and the Church in the process of being constituted – the Church already grown together and the Church as yet recruiting. Where the organismic simile is used – in the passage which we have adduced above and in the material which we presented in vol. IV[2] – Calvin talks of the end product, and he is closer to sociological realism. However, where the covenantal scheme is emphasized the image before his mind is that of the collecting together of the individual elect, the massing of the grains of wheat into a contiguous heap. So may a man be legitimately inclined towards sociological realism when he considers an elderly married couple who have become one life, and towards sociological nominalism when he directs his attention to a young bride and groom ready to exchange their marriage vows.

Still, the question remains which thought-pattern is closer to the centre of Calvin's system, and the answer is undoubtedly that, all talk in the traditional terms of organicism notwithstanding, it is the contractual pattern. The editor of the *Institutes* appends a footnote to the passage about the mother who must 'conceive us in her womb' etc. which lays bare a decisive fact: the 'mother', he says, who is meant here, is only the *visible* Church.[3] But the visible Church is not the real Church. It contains, as Calvin expresses it, quoting a phrase from St. Augustine, many wolves, while many sheep remain outside her.[4] The true Church is the invisible Church whose members are known to God alone, and that true Church is a contractual whole, a community of the covenant. Yet is this a specifically Calvinist conception? Does not the reference to St. Augustine reveal that we have here a conviction which is common to Calvinists and Catholics? Indeed we do have such a common conviction; and yet this very similarity between the one tradition and the other reveals, when it is properly pursued and analysed, the deep distinction between the collectivistic and the individualistic variants of Christianity. Augustine calls the unredeemed sinners inside the Church *infirmi* and *mortui* – sick or dead cells.[5] Though

---

[1] Ibid., II, X, 1 and II, XI, 8; vol. I, pp. 428 and 457.
[2] Cf. pp. 24 et seq.   [3] p. 1016, note 10.   [4] IV, I, 8, p. 1022.
[5] Cf. Stark, W., *Social Theory and Christian Thought*, London 1959, p. 13, and the references given there.

sick or dead, and bringing sickness and possibly even death to the body to which they belong, they are yet *in* that body – the body metaphor is never abandoned. According to Calvin, they are *not* in the body, for God does not invite them and admit them into the Covenant. Hence his ecclesiology is basically and consistently associational and contractualist. When he says[1] that the true Church or 'Church universal is a *multitude* gathered from all nations ... divided and dispersed in different places,' though agreeing 'on the one truth of divine doctrine', he shows with sufficient clarity that ontologically it is not to him a *communio totius vitae*.

That this is indeed so, that the Church, according to Jehan Calvin, fulfils in the individuals' life only *one* function, albeit an essential one, that it is not therefore an organism enclosing him and carrying him as a body physical encloses and carries its constituent cells, can be seen from a wider study of his whole ecclesiological discussion. We have so far considered this matter under the tacit assumption that the great Genevan literally means what he says when he calls the Church a mother who has conceived us in her womb. But this assumption is not necessarily justified. A man may be excused if he indulges now and then in a little poetizing. If we fix our attention, not on a stray word, but on the true substance of the exposition, we see that the Church is to Calvin men's schoolteacher rather than their genitrix. 'The Church is built up solely by outward preaching,' he writes, and 'the saints are held together by one bond only: that with common accord, through learning and advancement, they keep the Church order established by God ... God, who could in a moment perfect His own, nevertheless desires them to grow up into manhood solely under the education of the Church.'[2] Dillistone, in commenting on such passages, remarks that Calvin 'finally abandons the mother-conception and concentrates his whole attention upon the Church as a school of doctrine, a place where men may learn true knowledge and be instructed in the way of the Lord'. Somewhat pungently he adds: 'One is inclined to suspect that Calvin regarded even a mother as most usefully employed when seeking to impart some rudiments of knowledge to her lazy and refractory children.'[3]

That the definition of the Church as a schoolteacher was indeed one of the decisive germinal ideas of early Calvinism can be seen in the full development of this conviction in later Calvinism. We have encountered George Salmon earlier on as one of the more recent spokesmen of the tradition.[4] This is how he justifies the very existence of the Church: 'In the institution of His Church, Christ has provided for the instruction of those who, either from youth or lack of time or of

---

[1] IV, 1, 9; vol. II, p. 1023. Our emphasis.
[2] IV, 1, 5; vol. II, pp. 1019 and 1017.
[3] Dillistone, loc. cit., p.126.   [4] Cf. our vol. IV, pp. 6 et seq.

knowledge, might be unable or unlikely to study His word for them-selves.'[1] For such a way of thinking, the Church is essentially a tool in the service of the individual: the individual occupies the centre of the picture. Calvin's thought is at this point very close to that of Locke and other sociological nominalists: the state is a public utility, created by the people to make *their* life better than it otherwise would be, and justified, if and in so far as it fulfils that subservient function.

In moving from Calvin to Salmon, we made a long jump forward, but it was justified because, according to the Gospel (Matthew VII, 16), we know men by the fruit which they bear. One of the reasons why we may with confidence assert that Calvin's thinking was essentially contractual lies in the undeniable fact that the Calvinists after him thought in this style and manner. The master was still brought up in Catholic schools and moved forward wearily; the disciples had no such hang-over from medieval times and could step out boldly. They did. The self-interpretation of Calvinism as a covenant-society was laid on in the leader; the followers brought it to fruition. And they could do so because they lived in a world where such centripetal tendencies as loyalty to one's town, still strong in sixteenth-century Geneva, had waned and such centrifugal tendencies as preoccupation with one's own fate in eternity, but also in this life, waxed strong, as in seventeenth-century America. It was in the Anglo-Saxon countries and above all in New England, the modern society *kat exochen*, the society unencumbered by the heritage of the collectivistic ages, that Calvinism could most freely and most fully develop into Catholicism's individualistic counterpart, the associational variant of the Christian faith.

Just how far contractualism could advance in this uninhibited setting can be seen from a concept which, being essentially theological, does not otherwise concern us: the 'covenant of redemption'. All Christians agree that the Incarnation was decided on by the Holy Trinity even before Adam's fall. Man's disgrace was foreseen, and God's mercy was granted straight away. What the Calvinists did was to cast this credal conviction into a covenantal form, a development which would in all probability have shocked Calvin himself rather severely. There was, these theologians speculated, an agreement between the First Person of the Trinity and its Second Person to the effect that the Second Person would be allowed to pay the undischarged debt of Adam and his progeny and thus secure their reconciliation with the First Person, the Father-God. 'Not content with resting salvation upon a compact between man and God,' writes Perry Miller in *The New England Mind*,[2] 'the federal theologians were soon reinforcing the justice, the rationality, and the permanence of the "covenant of grace" with the hypothesis of

---

[1] Salmon, G., *The Infallibility of the Church*, abridged ed. Woodhouse, H. F., London 1952, p. 39.
[2] New York 1939, p. 405. Cf. also Dillistone, loc. cit., pp. 136, 137, 141, 142.

another and a previous covenant between God and Christ, so that they made God not merely bound by His pledge to the creature, but still more firmly tied by a compact with Himself.' 'God covenanted with Christ,' writes Thomas Hooker in an illustrative passage which Miller adduces,[1] 'that if He would pay the full price for the redemption of believers, they should be discharged.' 'To the curious historian,' so runs Miller's comment, 'this audacious intrusion into the holy sanctuary of the Trinity seems one of the more shocking exhibitions of Puritan effrontery, a conformation of the supreme irrationality of Christianity to the prosaic cadences of common sense, blasphemous degradation of the tripartite divinity into a joint stock company.'[2] The outrage is understandable; thinking along these lines had in the end to strip the mysterious of its mystery and thereby destroy it, making it easy for the forces of unbelief to prevail; yet every generation will translate the ideas it has inherited into the language of its own experience, and the life experience of seventeenth-century America was one of an associational society, a society living in and through contract, or rather in and through contracts, great and small.

The 'covenant of redemption' was essentially a flanking and confirming conception of the 'covenant of grace' which is of truly central importance, both from the theological *and* sociological points of view. If the 'covenant of redemption' was thought to be before it and holds little interest for the social scientist because it is remote from ongoing and observable reality, the 'church covenant' follows after it and holds much interest for the social scientist because it enters into, and is basic to, ongoing and observable reality, creating, as it does, the ecclesiastical organizations in which the friends of God are supposed to be associated and assembled. Departing from Calvin's own conceptions according to which there was only one everlasting tie into which the saints of all ages were invited, the later Calvinists went back to Paul and distinguished between the 'covenant of works' and the 'covenant of grace', Agar and Sara, Sinai and Golgatha, law and mercy. 'You must understand,' John Preston wrote in *The Breast-Plate of Faith and Love* (ed. London 1634), 'that there are two ways or covenants whereby God offers salvation to men. One is the covenant of works and that was that righteousness by which Adam had been saved [i.e. in modern English, would have been saved], if he had stood in his innocency: for it was the way that God appointed for him, *Do this and live*. But Adam performed not the condition of that covenant and therefore now there is another covenant, that is, the covenant of grace, a board given as against shipwreck ... Christ has provided a righteousness and salvation; that is His work that He has done already. Now if you will believe and take

---

[1] Cit. Miller, p. 406. Cf. Hooker, T., *The Saints Dignitie and Dutie*, London 1651, p. 33.
[2] Miller, loc. cit., p. 407.

him upon those terms that He is offered, you shall be saved.'[1] We may, within the confines of our interest, as well forget about the 'covenant of works'. Yet the 'covenant of grace' is just like it in the sociologically salient sense: it is a proper contract, a two-sided and in-one-setting system of obligations. 'A covenant has two parts: if God do this for you, you must do somewhat on your own part, you must love Him and obey Him. As in a marriage, the husband does not only take the wife, but the wife also takes the husband.'[2] There is thus true mutuality, a typical tit for tat. The two are first and ontologically primary; the one – the association – arises only afterwards and is a pure derivate, a secondary phenomenon.

The problem which concerns us here in the first place is of course the question as to who precisely was the contractual partner at the human end of the 'covenant of grace'? Was it a collectivity or a person? Was Christ, as the incarnation of the race, the only and sufficient contractant, or was He a third party, a mediator in the sense of a middleman, who only brought the parties together so that they, the parties, were the principals to the agreement? In the former case, there is still closeness to Catholicism; in the latter, opposition to it. Peter de Jong, in his study, *The Covenant Idea in New England Theology*,[3] has emphasized that the Reformed theologians 'were not altogether clear' on this specific point.[4] We have no reason to be surprised when we hear a statement of this kind, for the intellectuals among the Calvinists were clearly impaled on the horns of a dilemma. On the one hand, there was the massive organological tradition of Christianity from whose original spirit they did not wish to depart, indeed, to whose original spirit they were claiming to return. On the other hand, there was the obvious contractual condition of the society or societies around them with whose inner structure they strove to associate themselves and to conform. A really searching study of this particular aspect of the Protestant history of ideas is not yet at our disposal so that it remains uncertain. Yet de Jong suggests a solution. He gives as his opinion that the Calvinists were still collectivists and that individualism appeared only with the sects. We would agree that radical – so to speak uninhibited – individualism did indeed appear only with the sects. But this says nothing against the existence of a creeping individualism in the Puritan mind, an individualism which was in fact stronger than the official formulations, which seem to point the other way.

This, verbatim, is what de Jong writes where he analyses 'the leading confessions of the several Reformed churches': 'In every one of these symbols the human race was regarded not as an aggregate of individuals, each responsible solely for his own personal spiritual welfare. The organic relationship of all to Adam as well as the relation

---

[1] Op. cit., pp. 31 and 32. Spelling modernized. Author's italics.
[2] Ibid., p. 201.   [3] Grand Rapids 1945.   [4] Op. cit., p. 27.

of children severally to their parents was maintained instead ... The Anabaptists on the contrary seemed to lose sight of these organic relations in their effort to stress the need of personal surrender to the will of God. Thus they never could carry out the covenant idea completely in their construction of Christian Theology. Whereas the Reformed made it basic to their whole presentation of God's dealings with man in the state of rectitude as well as in the state of sin, these others preferred to speak of it as an oath of allegiance on the part of the individual to God.'[1]

Several things are wrong with this statement, and a study of them will teach us a good deal. It was, surely, the Anabaptists who carried out the covenant idea completely, and not the Calvinists, if indeed they stuck to the older conceptions. A covenant, like any contract, presupposes in law assignable, concrete, so to speak hard and fast, partners. This is why the New England Puritans, who were rather legalistic in their mental modes, found it easier to envisage the 'covenant of redemption' than the 'covenant of grace', in so far as the latter was open-ended on the human side, involving a vague multiplicity and uncountable generations. But this is a minor point. The major error of the author is to base the supposed collectivism of the Puritans on the organic relationship of all men to Adam and the equally organic relationship (a parallel one) of children to their parents. But the salient question is posed by the 'covenant of grace'. There is no organic relationship between the redeemed sinner, the 'elect', and Christ. This tie – and it is the truly material one because on it hangs the whole hope of salvation – is merely associational, unless an integral and metaphysical organicism is upheld, as it is by Catholicism. Calvinism upheld no such integral and metaphysical organicism. On the contrary, it entertained, as we have seen already, a tendency to depart from it.

In another part of his study, de Jong himself clears the matter up for us. By such early authors as Heinrich Bullinger and Kaspar Olevianus, he explains, 'original guilt was considered transmitted to all men purely because of the natural relationship in which Adam stood to the race, thus in much the same manner as original pollution'. 'Some time later,' however, in the seventeenth century, 'the idea of his legal and representative relationship was stressed as distinct from the physical.'[2] This, however, is, from the sociological point of view a radically new departure. And if Adam – who, after all, was our father according to the flesh – is seen as our representative only, and not as one in whom we were seminally present, not as one who was the sum and substance of ourselves, then Christ can *a fortiori* be no more than our advocate, our agent, our protector. We are not, then, one with Him, but there are two, He and us, or rather He and each one of us, and individualism is rampant, nay, victorious.

[1] Ibid., pp. 47 and 48.   [2] Ibid., p. 27. Cf. also p. 51.

Of course, since many, or at least some, conclude the same covenant (Joshua Moody called Abraham 'the great pattern believer'),[1] there does in the end, by reflex, so to speak, arise an association of the redeemed – but this not a collectivity, it is merely a collection. It is not like a body with one soul, it is merely like a heap of sand with adjacent grains. Miller, where he gives an over-all characterization of seventeenth-century political writing in Massachusetts and Connecticut, has, by way of summary, this to say: 'The "covenant of grace" is first propounded in Scripture to Abraham as an inward and personal bond, but from the very beginning it includes Abraham's "seed", upon whom is to be continuously devolved his ability to take up the covenant and who will successively stand to the identical engagement. The children of Israel are chosen first as individuals, but since all, or almost all of them, are in covenant with the God of Israel, bound by their own consent to discharge His law, it becomes apparent that the "covenant of grace" is a covenant for the group as well as for individuals.'[2] Yes, indeed. But it is a covenant for individuals before it is a covenant for the group. In Aristotle's parlance, the part is prior to the whole. Thought has thus well settled into the mould of sociological nominalism.

That this was indeed so, notwithstanding all that Peter de Jong, and all that the official creeds, may say to the contrary, can be seen from several utterances straight from the foremost ranks of the seventeenth-century Calvinists. One which leaves nothing to be desired on the score of clarity and directness, runs as follows: 'God conveys His salvation by way of covenant, and He does it to those only that are in covenant with Him. ... This covenant must every soul enter into; every particular soul must enter into a particular covenant with God; out of this way there is no life.'[3] In the same sense Thomas Hooker asserts that the covenant of the Gospel 'in the narrowest acceptation' is a compact 'betwixt God and the soul only' and does not necessarily have social implications or consequences.[4] Richard Mather follows suit. The 'covenant of grace', he says, is in the first place 'personal, private and particular, between God and one particular soul'. A 'Church covenant may flow from it, but such a church covenant, such a *contrat social*' 'differs not in substance of the things promised from that which is between the Lord and every particular soul'.[5]

Sometimes the statements we get are not as direct, but that does not necessarily mean that they are less clear. Indeed, they may, through their very indirectness, give us a precious glimpse of the depth to which individualism had penetrated the Puritan mind. Of all the writers who

[1] Cit. Miller, p. 378. Moody, J., *Souldiery Spiritualized*, Cambridge 1674, p. 31.
[2] Ibid., p. 414.
[3] Cit. ibid., p 378. Cf. Bulkeley, P., *The Gospel Covenant*, London 1651, p. 47.
[4] Cit. ibid., p. 446.
[5] Cit. ibid., p. 447. Cf. Mather, R., *An Apologie of the Churches*, London 1643, p. 3.

developed the convenant theology, John Preston was the most pioneering. When he speaks of the torturing question in a man's heart as to whether he be elect or not, i.e. whether he be fore-ordained to eternal bliss and blessedness in heaven or forecondemned to eternal shame and misery in hell, he advises the searcher to think of *his own* part in the 'covenant of grace': 'When thou findest this act on thine own part; when thou sayest, I have resolved to take Him (for a man may know what he hath done) – I have resolved to take Him for my husband, I have resolved to prefer Him before all things in the world, to be divorced from all things in the world and to cleave to Him: this I know . . . when thou findest this wrought in thyself, be assured there is faith wrought in thee . . .'[1] This piece of advice may have brought comfort to many, but it was hardly orthodox Calvinism, for according to the tenets of this creed, the names of the elect were for ever locked in God's bosom and therefore unknowable to men. How then can men gain assurance that they are numbered among the elect simply by looking into their own memories and minds? But no matter: the passage from Preston which we have quoted proves what we desire to prove here, namely that the 'covenant of grace' was to the Puritans basically an agreement between two persons, God and the sinner, God and the 'saint'.

Let us add, for good measure, a *locus classicus* from outside the Anglo-American orbit, in order to show that even continental European Calvinism thought in the same terms. Hermannus Witsius (or Hermann Wits), a Dutchman of high renown as a theologian, offers the following definition: 'The covenant of grace is an agreement between God and the elect sinner, God declaring His free goodwill concerning eternal salvation and everything relative thereto, freely to be given to those in covenant by and for the sake of the Mediator Christ; and man consenting to that goodwill by a sincere faith.'[2]

The time has now come to call a temporary halt and to invite the reader to compare the picture of the Calvinist mentality as it has emerged from the foregoing pages with the portrait of the Catholic culture which we presented in the first part of this volume. Unbelievers like Vilfredo Pareto have often asserted that there is little difference between the variants of Christianity, but this is merely a way of declaring that they appear to them all equally fatuous. A sociologist should know better. A society which may be called 'the Body of Christ' approaches one pole of the sociological continuum, the pole of community and unity and fusion; a society which appears to be made up of

---

[1] *The Breast-Plate of Faith and Love*, as quoted, p. 199. We have slightly modernized the text.

[2] Cit. Murray, J., *The Covenant of Grace*, ed. London 1956, p. 7, from *De Oeconomia Foederum Dei cum Hominibus*, Leeuwarden 1677, II, 1, 5. Cf. *The Oeconomy of the Covenants between God and Man*, vol. I, New York 1798, p. 226.

innumerable contracts (even if they are all initiated and mediated and guaranteed by One) approaches the opposite pole, the pole of association and abiding multiplicity. For the second social philosophy, there are direct lines between God and each man; they pass through one focal point, Jesus Christ; but this fact only makes them into a bundle, not into a body.

In all this – as the sociologist of knowledge has to point out and to insist, even at the risk of repetition – it is not so much the ideas that are different (though they *are* different) as the life from which they have sprung. Look with X-ray eyes through Catholicism and you see the clan; do the same for Calvinism and you behold the market. The very language in which Calvinist literature is couched is revealing. Perry Miller tells us of Thomas Hooker that he constantly employs commercial metaphors in preaching the covenantal doctrine, and refers a little later, with momentary annoyance, to 'this spiritual commercialism'.[1] As an illustration of exactly what he has in mind we may adduce Samuel Willard's remark that the 'covenant of grace is like any other covenant, and therefore arises from, or is grounded upon, the occasions of dealing or trading between one and another' so that 'each party may be secured from suffering any damage by the other, but may be able to claim and recover the performance'.[2] In the same spirit another Puritan author declares: 'In a covenant [of any kind], first there must be conditions and articles of agreement between the parties offered and consented unto, and secondly a binding one another to the performance thereof by bond, perhaps a pair of indentures are drawn between them wherein is declared that they mutually agree ... It is just so here [in religion]. Mark the agreement between us and the Lord. He propounds the Law and says that, if we will keep the Law, He will bless us abundantly in all things, house and land ... Then the people, they agree, and say, content, Lord, whatever thou sayest, we will do.'[3]

This style of exposition does not suit everybody, and Perry Miller's negative reaction to it is understandable. Yet so appropriate is the language used, that Miller himself falls into it on several occasions. 'The covenant theory,' he says, for instance, 'permitted man to conceive of divine grace as an opportunity to strike a bargain, to do himself a good turn, to make sure profit ...'[4] Then, at the end of his chapter on 'The Covenant of Grace', he draws the final conclusions from his whole analysis in a statement which will please any devotee of the sociology of knowledge. 'Perhaps it would not be amiss to say,' he writes cautiously, 'that though the covenant doctrine was elaborated by orthodox

[1] Miller, loc. cit., pp. 384 and 389.
[2] Cit. ibid., p. 380. Cf. Willard, S., *Covenant-Keeping the Way to Blessedness*, Boston 1682, pp. 8 and 9.
[3] Cit. ibid., p. 388. Cf. Hooker, Th., *The Faithful Covenanter*, London 1644, pp. 18 and 19.
[4] Ibid., p. 394.

Puritans against Arminianism and Antinomianism, yet in their attempt to fend off these heresies, the orthodox took up many ideas not so much for theological as for social and economic reasons. When the federal theologians are viewed historically, they seem to have served not so much the cause of their creed as of their party[1] ... If we are to seek ultimate causes for the federal doctrine in historical terms, we must undoubtedly resort to such considerations . . .'.[2]

But covenantal thinking not only arose from contemporary circumstances, it also returned to them and inserted itself into their very context. The nations which tended to organize themselves at this time, had, if and in so far as they belonged to the orbit of Calvinism, the tendency to conceive of themselves as covenanted nations. The prime example here is Scotland. The 'First Scots Confession' of 1560, of which Dillistone says that in it 'the true voice of the Reformation rings out with more joyful assurance' than from any other document,[3] described the Kirk as constituted by those who have embraced God's promises, and thus lays the foundation for a further and stronger development of the federal conception. By 1580, great strides had been made, for the 'Second Scots Confession' adopted in that year was officially described as 'The National Covenant'. The crucial passage runs as follows: 'We, noblemen, barons, gentlemen, burgesses, ministers and commons underwritten . . . do hereby profess, and before God, His angels and the world solemnly declare that with our whole hearts we agree and resolve all the days of our life constantly to adhere unto and to defend the ... true religion ...'[4] This resolution was renewed in 1590, 1596 and above all in 1638 when crisis conditions were once again developing. The Civil War in England then evoked the 'Solemn League and Covenant' of September 1643, a document formally adopted by the Edinburgh Parliament, which the Scots forced Charles I to accept in 1647 and Charles II in 1650. All these conjurations were in the first place defensive leagues with the aim of forestalling and warding off the attempts to dislodge Presbyterianism that were threatening from Episcopacy, and to some extent even from Catholicism. But with this negative and political aim, a positive aim went hand in hand, and it was double: religious and social. Religiously, the Scots covenants were contracts of service with Almighty God, or rather offers of such a contract of service, of which the covenanters had no doubt that it had been accepted in heaven. Socially, there was implied a whole system of social control, a regimen at which it is necessary for us to glance briefly.

What precisely did the Scots have in mind when they called them-

---

[1] On p. 399 Miller even refers to 'the interest of their class of merchants and capitalists'.

[2] Ibid., pp. 397–9.   [3] Dillistone, loc. cit., p. 130.

[4] Cf. Burrage, Ch., *The Church Covenant Idea*, Philadelphia 1904, p. 30.

selves a 'covenanted nation'? The answer to this question has to be sought in the firm Calvinistic conviction that *all* men, whether elect or reprobate, are obliged to obey the divine behests, e.g. to fulfil the Ten Commandments. True, the reprobate would gain nothing by so obeying, but they would have to be prevented from giving scandal. True also, they would not, in their fallen condition, be able to worship God as He should be worshipped, but they would in any case have to be constrained to pay Him formal and external respect. Thus the Scots Presbyterians saw themselves as the supremely disciplined nation, the discipline embracing everybody from the Tweed to John o'Groats. As Gregory VII had dreamt of a state which would be subject to the Church, i.e. to the spiritual values, conceived to be supreme, entrusted to the Church, so did Knox and Melville and the Presbyteries who succeeded to their power. This is the reason why we could, in our third volume, place Catholicism and Calvinism in parallel: both avoided the association of the Church with the State which is characteristic of established religion and the opposition of the Church to the State which is characteristic of sectarianism. Sociologically, the salient point is the all-inclusiveness of the scheme. Already the earliest protagonists of the Reform had laid the foundations of this socio-political system. 'In determining the boundary of the "covenant of grace", Olevianus advocated the position that it was made by God with the elect in Christ. In this he was followed by such prominent men as Musculus, Polanus and Martinus of Bremen.' However, this did not involve a rejection of the idea that the non-elect who are in the visible Church – or, we may interject, in the covenanted state – 'sustain some relationship to the covenant . . . Rather, they . . . sought to show that the essence of the covenant was realized in the lives of the elect alone.'[1] The last idea was much more pungently expressed by a Swiss Confession of Faith, that of 1675. 'Although more than the elect are included in the temporal administration of this covenant,' so de Jong sums up the decisive passage, 'only the elect are saved in it'.[2]

Where the Scots led, the New Englanders followed. 'Of all Protestant groups coming to America,' says de Jong, whom we would quote once again, 'the Congregationalists showed the greatest degree of willingness, if not eagerness, to pattern their ecclesiastical and civil life according to the system inherent in their cherished ideals. Among these, and the most comprehensive of them all, was the idea of the covenant by which *all* life was to be related to, and regulated by, the revealed will of God. The ambition of these early pioneers was to establish in the wilderness a holy commonwealth in which the theocratic ideals would be realized as never before in the history of Christ's Church.'[3]

[1] De Jong, loc. cit., p. 25.
[2] Ibid., p. 47.
[3] Ibid., pp. 77 and 78. Emphasis added. Cf. also p. 80.

Thus the sacred purpose of transatlantic and cisatlantic Calvinism seems to have been the same. But there was one important difference. The Scots were Presbyterians, the Americans Congregationalists. The Scots thought in terms of a national Church (singular), the Americans in terms of local Churches (plural). Yet the distinction had less to do with geographical and/or organizational matters than might appear at first sight. What contrasts the two religious cultures above all else, at least from the sociological point of view, is the greater degree of individualism which typifies the American experiment. In spite of everything, the Church was, to the Scots, an institution with a life of its own. To the Thirteen Colonies, on the other hand, the Church was much more of a multiplicity, much more of a frame in which the individuals could pursue parallel purposes. In their case, the retreat from collectivism or the advance to individualism had gone one big step further. What was implicit in Calvinism from the beginning became explicit on the shores of Massachusetts Bay.

The first Puritan Church to be founded on American soil was that of Salem in Massachusetts. It happened in 1629. In 1636, the original covenant was renewed and much extended. The sacred passage invoked on the occasion was from the Psalms: 'The Lord hath spoken . . . Gather ye together His saints . . . who set His covenant before sacrifices' (XLIX, 1 and 5[1]). The contractual form was used as a matter of course. For our analysis, the relationship of such 'Church covenants' to the 'covenants of grace' will be of crucial importance. It will finally clinch the argument of this chapter and demonstrate as clearly as can be desired that the Calvinist tradition is also, and ever-increasingly, a tradition of sociological nominalism, regarding social formations as merely secondary phenomena.

Briefly expressed, the 'Church Covenant' is in every case a consequence of a number of 'covenants of grace': to express the fundamental fact in a fashion which would have pleased the Puritans themselves, their coming together in an ecclesiastical grouping was a reflex of their coming together with God in their souls. Yet differently worded: what came to be in the outer world, was essentially a manifestation of what had come about in some inner worlds. There can be no doubt where, according to such a culture, the primacy of being is situated.

Following the lead of a New England writer of the period, Perry Miller defined a New England Church of the seventeenth century very clearly as 'a company of people combined together by holy covenant with God, and one with another'.[2] In this brief sentence, the comma is no purely typographical device; it has a deeper meaning, for it sets apart

---

[1] The number given is that of the Vulgate. Protestant Bibles consider this the fiftieth psalm.
[2] Miller, p. 435. Cf. Mather, R., *Church-Government and Church-Covenant Discussed* London 1643, p. 14.

what is ontologically prior and what is posterior. 'The heart of the Church theory was the Church covenant,' Miller writes. 'Regenerate men, the theory ran, acquire a liberty to observe God's commanding will, and when a company of them are met together and can satisfy each other that they are men of faith, they covenant together, and out of their compact create a Church ... The numbers from whom the Church originates, perpetuate it by receiving into the fellowship those whom they judge, as far as one man can judge another, to be within the "covenant of grace", and also protect the society by expelling those in whom they have been deceived and who violate the compact.'[1] 'In tne "covenant of grace",' Miller explains in another part of his great work, 'God requires as a condition of salvation that men perform duties to other men as well as to Himself; in the Church covenant they undertake to perform social duties; *ergo* the saints must undertake the Church covenant... Having subscribed the covenant of heaven, they must seek admission to the covenant of fraternity... The ultimate triumph of the New England mind was, to use the language in which it conversed, the discovery that the "covenant of grace" included and generated the covenant of the Churches.'[2]

A few passages from the sources will further confirm that the social contract is essentially seen as a consequence to an individual contract, or even to an individual condition. 'Watchfulness and duties of edification one towards another are but branches of the Lord's covenant, being duties commanded by the Law,' writes Richard Mather, and in another context he comments that the compact of the congregation 'is not another covenant contrary to the covenant of grace which every believer is brought into at his first conversion, but an open profession of a man's subjection to that very covenant . . .'.[3] Clearest, however, is a third passage from his pen: a Church covenant, he says, 'differs not in substance of the things promised from that which is between the Lord and every particular soul, but only in some other respects, as first, the one is of one Christian in particular, the other of a company jointly together. Secondly, if right order is observed, a man ought not to enter into Church-covenant till he be in covenant with God before, in respect of his personal estate. Thirdly, the one is usually done in private, as in a man's closet between the Lord and his soul, and the other in some public assembly. Fourthly, the one in these days is of such duties as the Gospel requires of every Christian as a Christian, the other of such duties as the Gospel requires of every Church and the members thereof'.[4] In this passage, the second distinction is the most important, and in the sentence concerned the word 'before' is the most significant: 'till he be in covenant with God *before*'. The Church is a

---

[1] Miller, p. 435. [2] Ibid., pp. 445 and 444.
[3] Cit. ibid., pp. 445 and 446. Cf. *Apologie*, as quoted, pp. 7 and 26.
[4] Cit. ibid., p. 447. Cf. *Apologie*, as quoted, p. 3.

derived phenomenon: men's offspring, not to say artefact, rather than their maternal womb.

In all this the congregational principle is basic and presupposed: the Church is not an inclusive framework, but a face-to-face group, and each petty grouping of this kind is independent and autonomous. A sociologist must therefore raise the question as to why Calvinism descended from the wider vision of Calvin himself and of his Scottish disciples to the realities of New England of which narrowness was the key fact. One answer has been given by Ernst Troeltsch. The New England Congregationalists, he argues, were descended, not only from Calvinism, but also from Anabaptism.[1] This may well be historically true, at least to some extent; but the matter cannot be allowed to rest there. Troeltsch's statement is analytically unsatisfying, even if it is historically correct. It suggests, nay, forces on us, the further question as to how a fundamentally Calvinist movement could become amenable to Anabaptist influences, and only a study of Anglo-Saxon Calvinism, or rather its sociology, can provide the key to a proper understanding here.

That key lies, not so much in Calvinist individualism *per se*, as in that intensified form of individualism which we have, a little while ago, described as élitism.[2] Calvinism knew a definite élite, separated from the common herd in the divine mind and by a divine decree before the foundations of the world were laid: God's elect, those 'in the covenant'. But these could not be assigned. Their names were known to God alone. 'Because a small and contemptible number are hidden in a huge multitude and a few grains of wheat are covered by a pile of chaff,' we read in Calvin's *Institutes* (IV, 1, 2),[3] 'we must leave to God alone the knowledge of His Church, whose foundation is His secret election.' We have seen already, in an earlier volume, that Calvin himself found it psychologically impossible to live with this doctrine.[4] Others, understandably, found it no easier. There was a hunger and thirst for an assurance of salvation, that *certitudo salutis* which looms so large in the contemporary literature. Max Weber's famous theory of the origin of capitalism, which we shall soon encounter once again,[5] takes this as its starting-point. Capital and capitalism began to be formed, when enrichment came to be regarded as a sign of acceptance, poverty of rejection. There is truth in this analysis, but it focuses unduly on just one point. Other indices of divine favour were sought beside the cash-box and the balance-sheet. One was the ability to live the godly life. God, it was said, aids the elect to obey His commandments and to walk in soberness before Him and among men. Once this idea was abroad (and who can wonder that it spread?), it was only the tiniest of steps to

[1] Troeltsch, loc. cit., vol. II, p. 664.　　[2] Cf. above, p. 256.
[3] Op. cit., vol. II, p. 1013.　　[4] Cf. our vol. III, p. 427.
[5] Cf. below, pp. 315 et seq.

identifying the church-goers with the elect – to saying that those who had been admitted to a local Church-covenant were also those whom the Father had invited from the beginning into a 'covenant of grace'.

While this development undoubtedly moved Congregationalism closer to Anabaptism and approximated a basically universal Church to the sectarian type,[1] the remaining differences between the two should not be forgotten. They were, and continued to be, decisive. 'From some points of view the New England way, as against English Presbyterianism, seems to have more in common with the sectaries' enthusiasm,' says Perry Miller, our prime expert, 'but as against the sectaries themselves, it remained solid and orthodox, . . . condemning all proposals for a Church ruled by an inner light.'[2] 'The sectarians desired to form self-contained societies apart from the heathen world,' writes Dillistone in the same sense in a very clear passage, and he might have quoted Robert Browne, the 'Father of Congregationalism', who said: 'The kingdom of God was not to be begun by whole parishes, but rather of the worthiest, were they never so few.' 'The New England Puritans wished to make their societies in every case the living centre of the unregenerate world.'[3] They were, like the Anabaptists, a minority in society, but unlike them they continued to feel that they were the appointed rulers of the country. Nothing is more characteristic of them than the electoral law of Massachusetts passed in 1631 which limited the franchise to covenanted Church members and thereby disenfranchised a considerable proportion of inhabitants.[4] The original Calvinic vision of a sanctified – and in this way 'covenanted' – commonwealth was thus retained.[5]

But in our context another issue between Congregationalism and Anabaptism is of still greater consequence. All the Congregationalists' tests of election were objective. Society could see the wealth that was accumulating in a man's hands and house; society could judge his conduct and pronounce it Christian-like or otherwise. Man's *inner* self was not as yet decisive. True, the fissiparous tendency was at work and broke down the larger units, a fact of which contemporaries, and especially the contemporary Presbyterians, were painfully aware. 'Much of the dispute between Congregationalists and Presbyterians was conducted in the jargon of dialectic, the great points contested between Thomas Hooker and Samuel Stone on the one side and Samuel Hudson on the other being whether individual Churches were primary artificial arguments or *argumenta a primo orta*, whether the Churches together were a *totum universale* (in which the parts give being to the whole) or a

---

[1] Cf. Troeltsch, loc. cit.   [2] Miller, loc. cit., p. 460.
[3] Dillistone, loc. cit., p. 144, and de Jong, loc. cit., p. 68. Cf. ibid., p. 233, note 15, for the Browne reference.
[4] De Jong, loc. cit., p. 103.
[5] Cf. Miller, loc. cit., p. 415.

totum integrale (in which the whole gives being to the parts).'[1] But even
if the whole of Christ's Church was regarded as merely a *totum universale*
and not a *totum integrale*, a body in its unity comparable to man's body,
the emphasis lay still on the unity, a whole, an *objective* whole, the local
congregation. In this the Anabaptists, the proper sectarians, differed.
'Here the idea of the Church as a society of experiential believers instead
of a divinely chosen group of believers . . . was dominant . . . The difference between the two resolved itself quite largely into this that whereas
the [Congregationalists] made the objective aspect of Christ's saving
work the more basic, the [Anabaptists] stressed the subjective application of it.'[2] This is certainly true, but what it shows above all else is
that the Anabaptists were merely one step further on on the road to
individualism which all Protestantism was destined to travel. 'The
doctrine of election,' says de Jong, 'strongly emphasized in all historic
Calvinistic Churches, tended towards individualization.' And he adds:
'There was among the Puritans both in England and America far more
intense individualism . . . than was characteristic of those who followed
Calvin more closely.'[3]

Thus we find, in the end, that the cleavage between Congregationalism and Anabaptism was not as sharp in their philosophy as in their
politics. Both are links in a chain which stretches from Calvin onward
towards a far horizon, the horizon of modern super-individualism. The
linking idea – that nominalism which teaches that the individual is
first, the society afterwards – is present in the master himself. A reading
of the twentieth section in the first chapter of book IV of the *Institutes
of the Christian Religion* soon shows this to be so. 'Entrance into God's
family is not open to us unless we first are cleansed of our filth by His
goodness,' we read there.[4] There must, in other words, be *first* a
personal quality, that of electedness, before a step can be made towards
the church. There is not, therefore, as there is for Catholics, first a Holy
Church, in which salvation comes to the individual soul, a church which
pre-exists and, as a spiritual mother, bestows a new life. Characteristically, baptism is for Calvin merely a seal that *attests to* and *confirms* a
fact and not a sacrament that, *ex opere operato*, *effects* what it signifies.

We would see, then, the Calvinism of Calvin, the Presbyterianism of
the Scots, the Congregationalism of the Americans and the Sectarianism of the Baptists (most of whom are Calvinists in their theology and
philosophy) as linked together in a common progressive pattern. But
the rush towards consistent individualism did not stop with the
formation of the last-named group. It went on inside it. We can see that
from the changing form in which the covenanting was carried out. The
first important Independent Church on English soil was organized by
one Henry Jacob in 1616 and this is how it was done: 'Standing

[1] Ibid., pp. 438 and 439.   [2] De Jong, loc. cit., pp. 56 and 58.
[3] Ibid., pp. 52 and 63.   [4] *Institutes*, as quoted, vol. II, p. 1034.

together, they joined hands and solemnly covenanted with each other in the presence of Almighty God, to walk together in all God's ways and ordinances, according as he had already revealed or should further make them known to them.'[1] The Brownist, i.e. Baptist, Churches seem in general to have followed this or a similar ritual. There was *one* act of compacting, and the oneness of it was expressed by the joining of hands. But there was an advanced group which broke away from the form common to Independents, i.e. Congregationalists, and Brownists, i.e. Baptists, and symbolized in its procedure its own, more pronounced individualism. We hear of it through a critical mind, John Murton. 'John Murton, in his "A Description [of what God hath predestinated concerning Man]", has preserved for us an account of the manner in which John Robinson's Church, probably at Scrooby in 1606, was formed. He says [on p. 170]: "Is this so strange to John Robinson? do we not know the beginnings of his Church? that there was first one stood up and made a covenant, and then another, and these two joined together, and so a third, and these became a Church, say they?"' Champlin Burrage, after transcribing this report, remarks: 'This method of covenanting was . . . different from that of earlier Brownist Churches, excepting possibly Smyth's original Gainsborough Church [in all likelihood formed in 1602] from which Robinson is said to have come. In fact, this quotation may indicate the way in which the so-called Mayflower covenant was first used.'[2] If this last surmise is correct, then Troeltsch is indeed right when he sees Anabaptist influences on American Congregationalism. But however that may be, the thread of filiation between Calvinism on the one hand, Congregationalism and Anabaptism on the other, remains intact.

Throughout this work, and especially in its third volume, Calvinism has been held up as one of the great variants of Christianity in the West, and so it was, for it taught that nobody can be saved who does not covenant with the Father, and that nobody can covenant with the Father who is not associated with Jesus Christ, the Son, who alone can pay for him the debt that he, a natural bankrupt, is unable to discharge. But by being the product of an increasingly individualistic age, by not sufficiently resisting the spirit of that age, by in fact fostering and further developing that spirit, it helped to bring about a condition of society in which Christianity is reduced to fighting for its life. It was from the pen of a citizen of the Calvinist heartland, from the founder of Springfield in Massachusetts, that there issued William Pynchon's challenging book, *The Meritorious Price of our Redemption* (published in London in the year 1650). In it, the whole concept of vicarious or substitutionary atonement is rejected. There can be no imputation of Adam's guilt to all men, says the author, nor yet an imputation of

[1] Cf. Burrage, loc. cit., p. 79.
[2] Ibid., pp. 211 and 212.

Christ's merit to the elect. 'He championed the theory that every man faced the problem of sin and obedience to God personally.'[1] This is indeed the end of the road. Naturally, the good Congregationalists of New England were scandalized, and they severed the offending limb. William Pynchon died an exile. But his name remained a menacing omen. We are, however, anticipating. Our analysis of Protestant culture has still to be presented, and we are turning to this further task.

THE PRINCIPLE OF INDIVIDUALISM IN DOGMA AND CONDUCT

Historians are agreed that what is called the Reformation started on 31 October 1517, the Saturday before All Saints, at about noon, when Martin Luther affixed his 'Ninety-five Theses' to the north portal of the Castle Church at Wittenberg, for these 'Theses' contained a challenge to the ecclesiastical authorities which was bound to develop into a major confrontation and finally into that open split which has left Western Christendom divided and distressed.[2]

The problem which loomed largest in this poster was the sale of indulgences, and so our first task at this point is to make clear wherein indulgences consist. Basing ourselves on the definition given in the *Codex Juris Canonici*,[3] we can say that they are grants to a sinner whose guilt has been, in principle, forgiven, whereby the temporal punishment still hanging over him is remitted, be it in whole ('plenary indulgence'), be it in part ('partial indulgence'). How can the Church make such a grant? How can the Church help the sinner? She can make such a grant and she can help the sinner because she has a treasury, a fund of assets, at her disposal on which she can draw. This treasury is filled by the merits of Christ and by the merit of Christ's saints in so far as these latter go beyond the due satisfaction which they on their part have to make for their own personal, i.e. actual, sins.

If this institution is considered, it is immediately apparent that it is yet another implication of that collectivism which we have seen all along to be the hallmark of Catholic life and thought. The stronger parts of the Body of Christ come to the aid of the weaker ones. The principle of solidarity is at work. 'The body cannot rejoice over the misery of one of its members,' Tertullian writes in *De Poenitentia* (X). 'No, the body as a whole is made to suffer, and the body as a whole must work for a cure.'[4] It is a Christian imperative that those who

[1] De Jong, loc. cit., pp. 98 and 99.
[2] Cf. Boehmer, H., *Der Junge Luther*, Gotha 1925, p. 174.
[3] Canons 911 et seq., esp. 911 and 925; ed. Gasparri, Card. P., Westminster, Maryland 1951, pp. 305 et seq., esp. 305 and 309.
[4] Cf. *Patrologia Latina*, as quoted, vol. I, Paris 1878, col. 1356.

have more than enough should sustain those who have less than enough. Superfluity should be fluid; the excess should be drained and directed to the places of insufficiency.

A good illustration of what is involved in an indulgence is an 'indulgenced prayer'. The sinner who is yet to suffer for a sin (though forgiven, for reparation has still to be made), the sinner who has to expect that he is headed for purgatory to be cleansed there from the remnants of dross still sticking to him, can shorten his penance by praying, and if he prays in the form of an indulgenced prayer, he secures additional relief *ex merito Christi et sanctorum Ejus*. But the benefits of an indulgence could for a long time be gained in other ways as well. They could be gained by a material sacrifice. And this opened the door to the abuse which rightly raised Martin Luther's ire. It could be said that anyone who gives a sum of money, for instance towards the cost of building Saint Peter's at Rome, would get his reward out of the Church's treasury, out of the fund of merits accumulated by the saints who had done more in their lives than was required to cover and counterbalance their own failings. Since 1567, such a transaction is no longer possible for in that year Pope Pius V (St. Pius V) banned all indulgences which are in any way connected with the *facultas quaestuandi*, or right of taking up collections.[1] But before 1567, before 1517, the date of Luther's protest, such offerings of bits of mercy for sums of money were in vogue and had assumed scandalous proportions, especially as banking houses like the Fuggers had inserted themselves into the business.

If Luther had concerned himself only with the abuse of indulgences, not with their use, if he had called for an end to the sale of them, and not for an end to their proper acquisition through worthy, i.e. truly religious, acts, the schism would assuredly not have come about. True, for reasons which we have given,[2] the Curia needed money and was loath to let go of any source of income. But the desire for reform was widespread in the Church, even in her innermost and most orthodox circles, and it would have brought about the necessary adjustments – as, in fact, it did under a saintly pontiff – even if the 'Ninety-five Theses' had never been posted. What led to the parting of the ways was the condemnation of the *principle* behind the institution, the principle of solidarity. And that the Church of Rome could not let go without losing her very heart.

In the 'Ninety-five Theses' there are two groups of propositions in which the momentous character of the whole issue becomes apparent. The one (numbers 56–68) is concerned with the concept of the 'treasure

---

[1] Cf. *Bullarum . . . Editio* (often quoted as *Bullarium Romanum*), ed. Gaude, F., vol. VII, Augusta Taurinorum (Naples) 1862, pp. 535 et seq.

[2] Cf. our vol. III, p. 285.

of the Church'. 'The true treasure of the Church is the most holy Gospel of the glory and grace of God,' Luther says (62).[1] No Catholic would have denied that the Gospel is *a* treasure of the Church, but to say that it is *the* treasure of the Church would be a different matter, for the implication of such a formulation is that there is no other. Yet this precisely is Luther's meaning. The form of words which he carefully, cautiously and cleverly chose is intended to get across a negative rather than a positive point: apart from Christ's infinite, yet personal merit there is no cistern of graces in heaven on which the sinners can draw, or (what is not very different), if there is such a cistern of graces in heaven, the sinners cannot draw on it. The other group of incisive propositions (numbers 8–29) deals with a specific sub-problem: the application of indulgences to souls in purgatory. For Catholics this was no issue. They had always believed that the living can help the 'dead', or rather the yet-to-be-cleansed souls of the departed on their passage through penance to glory, and this was simply another application of the principle which underlay the whole institution of indulgences and of Catholic culture in general, the principle of solidarity. Luther, with a new way of thinking dominating his mind, feels differently. He asserts, though in a somewhat veiled way, that the power of the keys does not extend to purgatory.[2]

Later on, this special problem of the 'holy souls' was to loom even larger, indeed, so large that it almost became a formal dividing line between the contending confessions. If the Luther Bible is compared with, say, the Douai version, one point where the texts sharply deviate from each other is II Macchabees XII, 46. Douai reads: 'It is a holy and wholesome thought to pray for the dead that they may be loosed from sins.' Luther reads otherwise.[3] Where Douai presents a general precept, Luther gives a concrete historical incident: when Judas Macchabeus came with his men to bury some of their dead – dead on whom heathen idols had been discovered – he sent money to Jerusalem to have a sacrifice offered up on their behalf and in reparation for their sin, and *that* had been a good and holy intention (*Meinung*). This reduction of the chapter by one versicle not only shows Luther's general tendency towards the concrete and unique, it represents also an attempt to get rid of a passage traditionally considered as scriptural which did not fit into his theological system. In this matter Luther, and Calvin after him, fell away, not only from Catholicism, but even from Augustine whom they regarded as their very own, their master and their mentor.[4] 'It is not to be denied,' Augustine writes in his *Enchiridion* (*De Fide, Spe et*

[1] *Selected Writings of Martin Luther*, ed. Tappert, Th. G., Philadelphia 1967, p. 57.
[2] Cf. ibid., p. 53, note 7. The proposition concerned is number 26.
[3] It is not our duty to investigate what nineteenth- and twentieth-century scholarship has to say about the textual question as such. We are speaking of the sixteenth century.
[4] Cf. Hägglund, loc. cit., p. 214.

Charitate, CX) 'that the souls of the departed are relieved by the pity of their living friends.'[1]

The counter-positions to Luther's assertions were most brilliantly formulated by the great theologian Thomas de Vio, better known as Cardinal Cajetan, 'the man from Gaeta'. Between 25 September and 29 October 1518, Cajetan drafted a number of papers, two of which are the most interesting in our context: number 9, 'whether the indulgences are made from the treasury of the merits of Christ and of the saints', and number 13, 'whether the pope, by the power of the keys, may give an indulgence to souls in purgatory'.[2] Both questions are, of course, answered in the affirmative. Cajetan was at the time papal legate in Germany, and he was asked to interview the *fraterculus* or little friar from Wittenberg. They met at Augsburg, but failed to remove the disagreements which had come out in the open in the 'Ninety-five Theses'. We should not be surprised when we hear that the result of the encounter was negative. It is not easy to reconcile sociological realism and sociological nominalism. It was nominalism, deeply nominalistic conceptions which determined Luther's convictions, as some would say, or caused his stubbornness, as others would formulate it. It is certainly no accident that the first, most brilliant and most unyielding adversary of the institution of indulgences was the man whom we have already met, and that more than once,[3] as the greatest representative of a consistent individualism in sacred philosophy, Peter Abelard.[4] Luther, *via* Ockham and Biel, was his distant disciple.[5]

We must be grateful that the days at Augsburg confronted Luther with Cajetan and not with any other possible legate, because in their tussle extraneous matters, such as the corrupt sale of indulgences, could not and did not occupy the prime place: principle had to be at the centre of discussion. Cajetan was as much of a reformer (the word written with a small 'r') as Luther.[6] He was a man of the profoundest personal religiosity, on whom no shadow of unworthiness could be said to lie. But he was firmly convinced that any antipapal reconstruction of the Church would lead to Babel, the city of confusion, not to Jerusalem, the abode of peace; and when he set about reforming his own order, that of the Friars Preachers, he did it by taking it back to the most deeply Catholic practice, that of the common life.[7]

When the spirit, the whole mode of thinking, of the two antagonists is studied, rather than this argument or that, we see that they were very distant from each other, almost diametrically opposed. According to

[1] Cf. *Patrologia Latina*, as quoted, vol. XL, Paris 1887, col. 283. My translation.
[2] Cf. Hennig, G., *Gajetan und Luther*, Stuttgart 1966, p. 47. My translation.
[3] Cf. above, p. 230, and our vol. IV, p. 17.
[4] Boehmer, loc. cit., p. 164.
[5] Cf. Hägglund, as quoted, pp. 197–219 passim
[6] Cf. Hennig, loc. cit., pp. 98, 135, 137.
[7] Cf. ibid., pp. 34 and 39–40.

the Cardinal's mind, the Church was indeed composed of three divisions, the triumphant Church in heaven, the struggling Church on earth and the suffering Church in purgatory, but these three were distinguished rather than distinct, one rather than three. Above all, there were open conduits of grace leading from the higher to the lower areas, as the blood circulates through unblocked veins and arteries in the human bodies even to the outermost limbs. That the merits of those above could reach those below was a matter of course to a man with a vision of this kind. For Luther, on the other hand, there was discontinuity rather than continuity; hard lines of separation cut and kept asunder what de Vio saw as organically interconnected. No grace could flow from the triumphant Church to her militant part on earth, and even less could any relief from the triumphant and militant Church be expected to filter through to the suffering souls, or rather to the Church's suffering self, below. When faced with a transitional thinker such as Martin Luther, in whose world-view there was still much that is medieval, including even a good deal of genuine organicism, one must be careful what one says. Yet a Rubicon had been crossed; nominalism had come to stay, and it had taught the man from Wittenberg, the disciple of Abelard, Ockham and Biel, to think in terms of units, not of unities, of individuals and not of communities. A big step towards Leibniz – 'monads have no windows' – had been taken, and that it was which kept the protagonists at Augsburg from coming closer to each other than they did, that it was which was presently to divide the circles for which Cajetan and Luther respectively stood, and certainly not a miserable, petty abuse which both wanted to see abolished.

The conversation between the Legate and Luther soon passed on to another plane, that of authority, and it is hardly surprising that this happened. When Cajetan demanded retraction and submission, Luther, sounding one of the main themes of his life, declared that he would not comply because the doctrine of the 'cistern of graces in heaven', on which the institution of indulgences rested, was not 'scriptural'. It had indeed been formulated by Clement VI in his 'extravagans' *Unigenitus Dei Filius*[1] of 27 January 1343, but what was the word of a pope in comparison with the Word of God? Where, Luther asked, was there a passage in the biblical canon to justify the whole idea? Cajetan, great Bible scholar that he was, was ready. He pointed to Colossians, I 24. 1, 'an Apostle of Jesus Christ,' says Paul, 'now rejoice in my sufferings for you and fill up . . . in my flesh . . . those things that are wanting of the sufferings of Christ . . . for His body, which is the Church'. This

---

[1] Cf. *Corpus Iuris Canonici*, edd. Richter and Friedberg, as quoted, vol. II, cols 1304-6. An 'extravagans' is a papal pronouncement which was not included in the original frame of the *Decretum Gratiani*, but 'wandering around outside' it – hence a kind of appendix.

quotation, however, made little impression on Luther; he turned away from it as he was to turn away from II Maccabees xii, 46, and from the Epistle of James which did not fit into his theological system either.

In having a Scripture passage ready and bringing it up, Cajetan can hardly be said to have done more than score a debating point. The taproots of the impugned institution lay deeper than even the Bible; they led down into the very life, into the very subsoil, of Christendom. Christians had thought so long in terms of organicism, that this mode of thinking had (as Scheler would have said[1]) undergone 'functionalization', i.e. that the very functioning of their minds had come to be determined by the category of totality. As they looked at the scene of Golgatha, they saw not only the God-Man bleeding on the cross, they also saw His Mother and His Beloved Disciple standing underneath it. Their sorrow was not, for them, separate or even separable from His. There was *one* great act of suffering and satisfaction, and in it Christ's companions had their place as well. These were the sufferings of which St. Paul speaks in his letter to the Colossians and which made the cup, already filled to the brim by the self-sacrifice of the Saviour, over-full and overflowing. When, more than eighteen centuries later, the composer Antonín Dvořák lost a baby daughter, his sorrow led him immediately to the foot of the Cross. He began the *Stabat Mater*, one of his most deeply felt, nay heart-rending compositions.[2] He identified himself with Mary who, too, had lost a child; and, through Mary he identified himself with Christ, for he, Dvořák, too, wished to offer the pain he was suffering to God in reparation for the innumerable sins which men commit and by which their Heavenly Father is offended and outraged. This is a typical Catholic reaction. It shows where the institution of indulgences comes from. That Luther could no longer feel in this way goes to show how far his nominalism had already taken him from Catholicism.

The conversations at Augsburg came to a close by Luther's precipitous flight from the city, and the conflict then entered another phase. Its political aspects, as they developed, are not of interest to us here. We would emphasize only one point before we move on, namely that Cajetan saw in Luther's nominalism rather than in his anti-authoritarianism the real problem. After the earlier exchanges, two issues stand out and come to tower above the rest. 'Cardinal Cajetan,' writes a historian, 'after making vain representations to Luther, finally demanded the withdrawal of two propositions which he had plainly taught and acknowledged as his. The first was his denial that the treasure of the merits of Christ and the saints was the foundation of indulgences; the second was the statement . . . that the sacraments of the Church owed

---

[1] Cf. above, pp. 33 and 34.
[2] Cf. Stefan, P., *Anton Dvořák*, transl. Vance, Y. W., New York 1941, pp. 69 et seq.

their efficacy only to faith.'[1] Read the literature on and around Luther, and you will find that the latter doctrine, justification by faith alone, is represented as far more decisive than the first. Yet Cajetan, a shrewd man, thought otherwise. He realized that at the root of the whole trouble sat the fact that Luther had abandoned the Catholic core-principle of community. When the rebel had already closed the door behind him, there was still a meeting between the Cardinal and Luther's friend Wenzel Link, to see whether anything more could possibly be done. Cajetan is reported to have said on this occasion that he was prepared to put the question, whether faith alone could justify, aside, if only Luther would withdraw his statement about the treasure of the Church.[2]

After Augsburg, the rift became in fact irreparable, but twelve or thirteen years later there was for a short while a transient revival of hope, not unconnected with the rising importance of the irenic Melanchthon, that the quarrel might after all be brought to a peaceful conclusion. Cajetan, whose interest in the new religious movements was still very much alive, started to think about the question what Catholics could conceivably concede to the Protestants, and what they could not. He drafted and published a little investigation, *De Quattuor Luteranorum Erroribus*[3] (Rome 1531), which in turn led a year later to his *De Fide et Operibus adversus Lutheranos Tractatus*, a text which is of great importance for our analysis. Since the 'Ninety-five Theses', the face of Protestantism had become a good deal more profiled and one of the features of it which was now clearly discernible was the contempt it carried for fallen man. This bitter bias was to become much more extreme in Jehan Calvin, but there was enough of it even in Martin Luther to give his readers pause. The connection between this attitude – this anti-humanism, as we might call it – and the doctrine of indulgences is obvious. If men can have no merits at all, how can they add anything to a treasury of merits? A query of this nature had not been contained in the original 'Ninety-five Theses' but it had been raised shortly afterwards, in 1518, in Luther's explanation of these theses entitled *Resolutiones Disputationum de Indulgentiarum Virtute*. The treasure of the Church, he says there, is Christ alone. There are no 'merits of the saints', for no saint has ever fully complied with the divine commandments, let alone done more than that.[4] This assertion might almost be called the ninety-sixth thesis. It was certainly firmly established in Luther's mind when he met the Legate in Augsburg. Concerning this

[1] Grisar, H., *Luther*, transl. Lamond, E. M., ed. Cappadelta, L., St. Louis and London 1916, vol. I, p. 357. The theses mainly involved were numbers 58 and 7, the latter amplified in the *Resolutiones* presently to be mentioned. Cf. Boehmer, loc. cit., p. 218.
[2] Boehmer, loc. cit., p. 222.
[3] Luteranorum (without the 'h') is correct.
[4] Cf. Boehmer, loc. cit., p. 183; *Luther's Works*, ed. Lehmann, H. T., vol. XXXI, ed. Grimm, H. J., Philadelphia 1957, p. 213.

subject, Cajetan may therefore have felt a permanent challenge to himself; but whether he did or not, he decided in 1531-2 to have his say in the matter. It is truly fascinating to see how he handled it.

The starting-point is, of course, the conviction, which unites all Christians, that men are saved through the merits acquired by Christ. But Cajetan adds – and this is where the paths of Catholicism and Protestantism diverge – that men are also saved through the merits acquired *in* Christ, i.e. in the Body of Christ, the Church. A hand, in the well-integrated physical organism, acts at the behest of, and in the sense of, the head. It carries out the commands it receives from the head, so much so that it is correct to say that the head acts through the hand and in the hand. In that higher type of organism which we call a society, for instance in the society of Christians, the Church, the will of the 'organ' enters as a complicating factor. The peripheral part can, in self-will, deviate from the pattern of conduct which would keep it in harmony with the centre of life. But this is not necessarily so. If and when the 'hand' decides to remain at one with the 'Head', if and when the human will does not deviate from the divine will, there is only One Will, and that is the Will of God. Men merging their wills with Christ's can therefore be said to acquire true merit. It is almost a logical necessity for the Christian – any Christian – to admit that this is so, for if they were to deny it, they would at the same time deny that Christ Himself acquired true merit. This is the theory of 'co-operationalism' formulated in St. Thomas Aquinas' *Summa Theologiae* (Ia IIae, quaestio 114).[1] Cajetan who was called, even in his life-time, '*quasi vivens Aquinatis imago*'[2], developed it further. This is what he writes: 'To those adults who advance in grace, eternal life is due in two ways. Firstly, out of the title of Christ's merit, [that merit] which He gained in His own person; and then out of the title of Christ's merit, [the merit] which Christ the Head gains by working in the adult and through the adult.'[3] Remembering that he was at grips with men to whom the Bible meant much, if not everything, Cajetan draws attention to Galatians II, 20, perhaps the most strongly supportive text for his exposition. 'I live now not I,' Paul says there, 'but Christ liveth in me.' The Apostle may have been a rare man, but he was *a man*, and what is possible in one man is possible in others also. Therefore, the Cardinal concludes, against Luther, and, by anticipation, even against Calvin, men can acquire saving merit which may be added to Christ's. In a sense, indeed, it is Christ's; but in another sense it is men's, and, as it flows from their freely Godward and God-tied personal wills, it is properly theirs.

---

[1] Cf. *The Summa Theologica*, as quoted, vol. VIII, London 1915, pp. 403 et seq., esp. pp. 408 and 409.

[2] 'A living image, so to speak, of the Aquinate', Bartholomaeus Spina in 1518. Cf. Hennig, loc. cit., p. 10.

[3] Cit. Hennig, p. 175. Our translation.

We may sum all this up with the help of two syllogisms, one expressing the Catholic, the other the Lutheran and Calvinist positions. The former may be worded as follows:

Man separated from God cannot acquire merit conducive to salvation;
Christian man is not separated from God;
Therefore Christian man may acquire merit conducive to salvation.

That merit may, indeed, not be sufficient if it is left unsupplemented, if vicarious satisfaction does not come to give it sufficiency; but that changes little in the principle; co-operation remains. The latter syllogism looks like this:

Man separated from God cannot acquire merit conducive to salvation;
All men are separated from God;
Therefore no man may acquire merit conducive to salvation.

This does not mean that all men are damned, for Christ may rescue them in spite of their beggarliness through His own power. But it does mean that grace becomes a totally free gift. The contrast is tremendous. It carries all the difference between optimism and pessimism, humanism and anti-humanism. It is so great that it must affect all theology, all culture. But the point with which we are immediately concerned here is the narrower fact that the difference between the confessions is mainly due to their disparate sociologies. The major in the above syllogisms is, as we have seen, the same; only the minors are different; and the clash of the conclusions is due to these irreconcilable minors. But the minors embody (or reject) the concept of the Body of Christ, the organical conception of the Church. What we have seen so often, especially in volume II, namely that it is, as much as anything, the social factor which divides the forms of Christianity from each other, becomes at this juncture once again manifest. This may be emphasized even by one who is ever anxious not to claim too much for his speciality.[1]

What we have done so far in this section is to consider one move of one man, together, of course, with its aftermath, and we have proceeded in this manner for obvious historical reasons. This one move of this one man was the beginning of a religious, or at least an ecclesiastical, revolution, and it has left Christendom in a painfully changed condition. But there was more to the concentration on one single individual than probably meets the eye. We would hesitate to give it as a universally valid proposition that socio-centric religions and churches arise from the operation of anonymous and popular forces, whereas individualistic churches and religions arise from the assertion of one personal will; yet there would be at least some truth in such an asser-

[1] For the raw materials of the above analysis, cf. Hennig, loc. cit., pp. 174 et seq.

tion, and it is certainly applicable to the matter we have in hand, the inception and the character of Protestantism and its specific culture. Friend and foe are agreed that the new faith came into being in and through the travail in one man's soul. Among the foes we may quote Jacques Maritain: 'Lutheranism', he writes, 'is not a system worked out by Luther; it is the overflow of Luther's individuality ... a universalization of his self, a projection of himself into the world of eternal truths ... His doctrine, clearly, is born chiefly of his own inward experience ... What Luther's doctrine especially expresses is Luther's interior states, spiritual adventures, and individual history.' Lutherans may well protest, if Maritain at this point continues: 'Unable to conquer himself, he transforms his necessities into theological truths and his own actual case into a universal law.'[1] Such a formulation appears value-laden and is neither binding on Luther's admirers nor inviting for the scholarly analyst. Yet subtract the negative element that has crept into the exposition, and what remains is a clear fact which the scholarly analyst will eagerly grasp and the admirers of Luther willingly accept. Indeed, Maritain, in what he says here, is essentially the disciple of the Lutheran historians. It is their custom to begin their presentation of the Reformation with a searching account of the inner developments of Luther himself. When the outstanding Lutheran historian, Justus Hashagen, in the early thirties introduced his students to 'The History of the Reformation', a course which led right to the onset of the Catholic Counter-Reformation, i.e. in practice to the appearance of the Jesuit movement, he devoted about half of his time to Luther himself, in spite of the masses of material which he had still to present. This was assuredly not due to simple drifting; it was very definitely the implication and consequence of a conscious decision which, for its part, stemmed from the fundamental conviction that Lutheranism was one soul's gift to the world, however much the objective circumstances of the times may have made men in general willing to listen to that one man's message.

This basic individualism was certainly apparent in the drama's first act, the protest, not against the abuses of the institution of indulgences, but against the institution itself, or rather against the social philosophy behind it. But we must look for it elsewhere as well, and especially in the theological ground conceptions of original sin and justification, i.e. final salvation. We have already given it as our opinion that the element of medieval collectivism surviving in Protestant thought is to be seen most clearly in the Protestant doctrine of the fall.[2] Both Luther and Calvin are convinced that *all* fell from grace in *one*, Adam, and there seems to be little here that betokens a philosophy of 'every man for

---

[1] Cf. Maritain, J., *Three Reformers: Luther, Descartes, Rousseau*, New York 1932, pp. 10, 11, 15.
[2] Cf. above, p. 256.

himself'. Yet if we look at the Reformers' opinions more closely under the microscope, we discover traces of a drift towards individualism even in this admittedly still largely collectivistic concept.

What, at least on the surface, distinguishes the Catholic, e.g. Thomist, version of the doctrine of original sin from the shape which the same doctrine received at the hands of Luther and Calvin, is the mildness of the earlier and the strictness, nay fierceness, of the later formulations. Thomas would never have thought or spoken in terms of a 'total corruption' of human nature; Luther and Calvin most certainly did. 'Original sin, as Luther understood it,' Bengt Hägglund explains in his *History of Theology*,[1] 'is not merely the lack of original Godlikeness; it is a real form of corruption, which has set its mark on the whole man. In concrete terms it is not only . . . a negative disposition of the lower powers of the soul, but an evil which afflicts man in his entirety, including (and indeed above all) the higher powers of the soul.' It is easy to adduce corroborative passages from Luther's own pen. To the most pungent belong the following two which are none the less impressive for being so brief: 'A just man sins in all his good works,' and 'A good deed, done in the very best way, is yet a . . . sin.'[2] What more can even the greatest misanthropist say? Even the best are still corrupt in the best they do! We forbear to give further documentation; the point is surely made.

Whence, so we must ask, this extremism? Three answers may be given to this query. One which has sometimes been made in inter-confessional mudslingings is to the effect that Catholics have low moral standards and therefore are easily pleased with man, even if he is truly wicked, while Protestants have high moral standards and therefore are easily displeased with man, even if he is truly decent. This argument belongs in the same category as the suggestion that Protestants are habitually sadists and only Catholics know what the word mercy really means. All this is off the right track. So far as moral standards in the abstract are concerned (we are not speaking here of educational strategy as practised in the confessional box), there is little or no contrast between the variants of Christianity. Cajetan did not judge differently from Luther, not to speak of St. Raymund of Peñafort. A better line to follow is a reference to contemporary circumstances, more concretely expressed, to the contemporary revulsion from the excesses of the Renaissance, which were considerable and therefore shocking to awakened consciences. We have used this argument ourselves[3] and believe it to be important and convincing. We must not forget that Luther lived at exactly the same time as Machiavelli; the latter was born in 1469, the former in 1483. Who would not recoil in horror when faced

[1] As quoted, p. 229.
[2] Cf. *Werke*, as quoted, vol. VII, Weimar 1897, pp. 136 and 138. Our translation.
[3] Cf. above, p. 256.

with the stark portrait of human, and especially political, behaviour which is presented to us in *The Prince* and even in the *Discourses on Livy*? Luther had been in Renaissance Rome on an errand on behalf of his Order; he had not liked what he had seen. Bad memories remained with him all his life. They counted for much in the image which he formed of human nature.

But even the explanation just given of Luther's grim picture of fallen man, true as it is, does not, by itself, reveal all the roots of this character-istic Protestant conception. If disgust with the riotous living of the Renaissance princelings had been the only reason behind the definition of mankind as a *massa damnationis*, a milder attitude would soon have appeared and prevailed. But seventeenth-century Lutherans thought exactly like their master. There were indeed protests against Lutheran, and generally Protestant, pessimism with regard to man, from the near-contemporary Quakers to the pervading Pelagianism of the twentieth century, but they were all outside the fold: inside the fold the stern judgment of the founders stood; witness Methodism, Calvinistic and even Arminian; witness Evangelicalism. We must therefore look for an abiding feature which inspired (if this is the correct word) the convic-tion that even the just can do but one thing, and that is sin.

This abiding feature was once again the basic individualism of Protestant philosophy, the human isolation of Protestant man. Even Catholic man, like any *homo religiosus*, had at times felt the horror of the human condition. The medieval Church sang at every requiem the deeply disturbing hymn of Thomas of Celano: *Dies irae* – The Day of Judgment, the Day of Wrath. The soul of the sinner must meet its appointed judge – how shall it fare then?

> What shall I, a wretch, then say,
> Who for me can plead and pray,
> If the just must dread that day?[1]

But the horror of medieval and Catholic man was not a permanent sentiment on his part. The mood of depression would soon change, not indeed to assurance (assurance there could not be, as Cajetan, for instance, insisted),[2] but to quiet confidence, or at least to hope. And that confidence, that hope, was founded and grounded on one belief, the conviction that the weaknesses of sinners (unless their sins were unforgivable) could be compensated for by the strength of the saints. The fearful knew well enough *quem patronum rogaturus* – whom he should ask to be his defender. There were saints enough in the calendar. And if every other intercessor should fail, there would yet be God's very own Mother, *advocata nostra*, she who had carried the Judge

---

[1] My translation.
[2] Cf. Hennig, loc. cit., esp. pp. 100 et seq.

Himself in her womb and fed Him at her breast. To her, surely, He would not say no. The Love of the Virgin flourishing at the height of the Middle Ages, on which Henry Adams laid so much stress, as we have seen,[1] that love which built the great cathedrals of France, such as Notre-Dame de Paris and Chartres, had its roots in the intense confidence that her mantle was going to cover a lot of sins, that it would rescue those who otherwise would have no chance to escape.

Luther, in one quick move, took this shelter away. There *are* no saints, he had said in so many words;[2] hence they cannot intercede for us. The wind was therefore no longer tempered to the shorn lamb, or rather the naked ape: man was now fully exposed to the icy blast of divine displeasure. There remained, of course, the possibility of a gratuitous pardon. The Judge could decide to squash a case rather than to carry it through to its damning conclusion. Protestants could hope in Christ and Christ alone, and their sentiments in this respect belong to the most moving evidences of true religiosity which the world history of religion has provided. Protestants could pray in the words of Thomas of Celano, as their forebears had prayed, and as their Catholic contemporaries were still praying:

> King of awesome majesty,
> Whose best gift is granted free,
> Fount of mercy, save Thou me.

But there was a difficulty. It was necessary now to conceive of Christ as an intercessor as well as of a judge, and it could not be known which role He would, in a given instance, implement. Justice or mercy – which would it be? Of course, for the Catholic believer, this question also existed, but it was by far not so sharp-edged. Mercy could be preferred, not for one's own sake, one had no right to demand it, but for the sake of one's sainted patrons who were worthy to ask for it. This was no longer so. And therefore there arose, in the Protestant camp, the plaguing problem of the *certitudo salutis* which Max Weber has so fully discussed and so amply elucidated in *The Protestant Ethic and the Spirit of Capitalism*.[3] Anxiety was ripe in many Lutheran and Calvinist hearts; Luther himself suffered atrociously from it. But anxiety generated, by the operation of psychological mechanisms which it is not our avocation to investigate, the feeling of deep unworthiness which is one of the hallmarks of the Protestant faiths, and not the least impressive of them.

We have, in this analysis, based ourselves on one of the ideas which stood at the cradle, so to speak, of the whole science of sociology. What

[1] Cf. above, p. 178.
[2] Cf. above, p. 280.
[3] See index, *sub verbo*.

gave Auguste Comte the hope that his suggested 'Religion of Humanity' would sweep the world and be able to fulfil the function which out-moded creeds could no longer fulfil? It was a fact, an undeniable fact – Comte was a positivist, a scientist – the fact that humanity was shielding the individual from woe and the threat of destruction. Society, he argued, is like a mother to us, her babies: what we have, we owe to her, including the chance of survival and happiness. Take society away, and we are all doomed to death and despair. This was still a character-istically Catholic thought, showing how right Thomas Huxley was when, in a much repeated joke, he called Comteanism 'Catholicism *minus* Christianity'. The difference between the Comtean and the Catholic position was merely that they singled out different societies as the sheltering, salvation-promising and salvation-providing reality: for Comte it was the race, the scientifically definable genus *homo sapiens*; for Catholicism it was the Church, the Body of Christ; it was an organic unity in either case. Protestantism was opposed to both because it was and is individualistic.

Thus even the doctrine of original sin, though it was a take-over from collectivistic life and thought, shows, in its Lutheran form, when it is more closely considered, the imprint of associational society and culture. But there are still other aspects of it which reveal the same background. Both the older and the newer thought-system centred the attention on two concepts or rather realities: the human body and the human will. The human body with its animal drives prevented the human will from concentrating on the supernal realm, from 'seeking first the Kingdom of God and His righteousness': it was the seat of original sin, an ever-present cause of spiritual entropy. So far, there is no disagreement. But the emphasis was differently placed, and to such a degree that different anthropologies and theologies had to spring up. For Luther, *concupiscentia*, the desire, the lust which we feel in our physical bodies, is the besetting evil. The weakness of the will is merely a consequence. Luther himself was much preoccupied with this, the unruliness of our flesh: compare, for instance, his letter to Melanchthon from the Wartburg, dated 13 July 1521.[1] Why this preoccupation? We must avoid an apodictic and simplistic answer, but one element in the aetiology of this emphasis on the animalic side of man is the relative devaluation of sociality and isolation on the individual. After all, that which, more than anything else, sets us up as independent selves, is the possession of a body exclusively our own. Our thought, our will is different. Even those who are not Durkheimians must admit that there is such a thing as an 'internalization of values' which makes our wills to some extent social, and which washes into us traces at least of altruism,

---

[1] Cf. *Works*, ed. Lehmann, as quoted, vol. XLVIII, ed. Krodel, G. G., Philadelphia 1963, pp. 256 et seq., esp. 257. On the Catholic conception concerning concupis-cence, cf. Maritain, loc. cit., pp. 247, 256, 286, 288.

norms of conduct which are more than beastly. Hence the greater optimism of the older variant of Christianity; but hence also, by a reverse operation of the chain of causes and effects, its greater sociality: by starting from the picture of a concrete society, the clan, in which men did acknowledge communal values and pursue them, it was inspired with a comparatively sociologistic view of human coexistence which an associational dispensation, with increasing emphasis on the legitimacy of competition and the free pursuit of personal happiness, could not possibly generate.

Concentration on the body, as the most concrete demonstration of the uniqueness of the self, is therefore another proof that individualism had, with Luther, entered into the dogma of original sin, even though that doctrine was, remained, and had to remain, largely collectivistic. But no society is simply made up of individuals; it is made up of individuals who are interrelated, and that is something else and something more. We must pursue the matter at hand into the realm of interrelatedness also and see whether the mental picture of Lutheranism shows the same characteristics in this particular as it does in others. Let us look at Hägglund's very clear summary; it will give us the clues which we need. 'If man is judged only in his relationship to other men, and on the basis of his observable conduct,' Hägglund writes, 'the import of original sin may not be apparent . . . The judgment which says that man is a sinner involves his entire person, *such as he is before God* . . . What the *totus homo* view means, therefore, is that man is seen from the theological point of view in his relationship to God (*coram Deo*).'[1] This *coram Deo* is a revealing formula, for what it teaches is that man is a sinner within a bipolar relationship. We have a pendant here to that *solus cum solo* conception which we shall soon recognize as the heart of Luther's doctrine of redemption. An I-and-Thou relationship, however, is the most attenuated form of sociality that can be imagined, even though, we must add, it can gain on the score of intensity what it has lost in the matter of extension. For the Catholic, the sinner is, of course, also a sinner before God, but, as the Church is the Body of Christ, in a manner identical with Him, he is a sinner before Sacred Society as well; the whole institute of sacramental confession and penance rests on this view. No wonder that it disappeared under Luther's grip. But we should compare Luther at this point not only with those who went before him, we should see him also in connection with those who came after him. Unlike Calvin, he does not make much of the idea of the covenant; outer circumstances were against developing a basically democratic or at least aristocratic idea in a world dominated by the conviction, still rampant in Luther's political environment, that the state, under the prince, under the Leviathan, was one. Yet if the concept of *foedus* or contract is left implicit, the world-view in which it is contained and

[1] Hägglund, loc. cit., p. 230. Our emphasis.

from which it could be drawn so as to become explicit, is already present: it is a world-view in which bipolarity, face-to-face confrontation, occupies the focus, not community – a world-view of I and Thou, rather than of We.

In the last section, we have come to the conviction that the covenantal theology is kindred to, or even identical with, nominalism in sociology: society is only a secondary phenomenon. If the analysis we have just presented is correct, Luther's conception of the social whole must at least tend to the same conclusion. It does. In spite of occasional inroads of traditional organicism into his texts, his fundamental category of bipolarity leads him in the end – quite logically, it would seem – to the idea that the social bond is merely a reflex of other and deeper realities. 'That men belong together,' writes Werner Betcke in an important study, 'stems basically from the fact that they all stand before God in the same condition of corruption. Luther does not know the modern concept of a collective sense of guilt, and he would have rejected such a concept in so far as it implies a diminution of personal responsibility. He would never have said "everybody is guilty of everything", but rather "all are equally guilty".'[1] This is correct. We may reword Betcke's statement a little to bring its essential content out even more clearly than do the lines as they stand. 'All stand before God in the same condition of corruption,' he writes. He might have written – and this is plainly his meaning – 'all stand before God in a parallel condition', in a parallel plight. Sinfulness is the state of each rather than the state of all. A leper's encampment may be a community, but it has formed, and it is held together, only as a result of the fact that each inmate has personally contracted the same disease.

It is in line with all that has gone before that Luther places the struggle between Heaven and Hell as much in the individual breast, the *forum internum*, as in world history, the outer scene. 'The combat between God and the devil,' writes Wingren, 'takes place within every single human being . . . God wishes man to be saved from the power of sin, and the devil wants man kept in it. Out of that invisible combat . . . come all the agony and anxiety that enter into human life. A creature must know suffering when two powers lay hold of it, struggling to win and possess it.' The proper word here to use might well be 'frustration', for the individual is dragged hither and thither without being able to do much about it. 'Between these two man stands, like an animal to be ridden,' writes Luther in his most pessimistic book, *De Servo Arbitrio*. 'If God be the rider, the creature goes where God wills . . . If Satan be the rider, he goes where Satan directs. Man cannot freely choose to leap to the side of one or the other of these riders, or to seek

---

[1] Betcke, W., *Luthers Sozialethik: Ein Beitrag zu Luthers Verhältnis zum Individualismus*, Gütersloh 1934, pp. 47 and 48. On Luther's individualism in general, cf. ibid., pp. 41–3 and the quotations given there.

one out. It is the riders themselves who contend to win and possess man.'[1]

In this passage, we see once again that Luther's thinking is in thraldom to the category of bipolarity. Two are matched in combat; the third, man, is merely the object of the fight. The aim is to drive the devil from the field so that the road is free for an association between God and the individual, a new bipolarity better than the old, the bipolarity of redemption. In this blessed relationship, God is very much the giver and man the receiver. But man can at any rate invite the gift, and he does that by opening himself up in an attitude of faith.[2] This is the Lutheran doctrine of *justificatio per fidem*, justification by faith *alone*. If in his exposition of the other basic Christian belief, the fact of the fall, Luther displayed relatively much collectivism and relatively little individualism (though, in fact, enough of it), here the proportions are reversed. Barring one point to which we shall turn before long, Luther's dogma of justification is a substantial piece of individualism. It does not appear that this judgment has ever been impugned by anybody. We need not therefore say too many words about it. We can also easily link the theological concept now taken up with the one which we have already discussed, original sin. As there is original sin only in a bipolarity, so there is justification only in that same bipolarity: 'The righteousness of faith refers to man in his relation to God (*coram Deo*).'[3]

The heart of Luther's religiosity can be laid bare, and its character as a form of thought in keeping with an associational society and culture can be revealed, by considering its negative as well as its positive implications, by seeing what he excludes as well as what he includes. What he excludes is the institution, the communal factor. The passage in Matthew xvi, 18: 'Upon this rock I will build my church,' is understood to refer to Peter's personal faith, not to his social function. But exclusion is the fate not only of collective organs with their objectivity, not only of reifications, so to speak, it is the fate also of what Durkheim calls 'collective representations', interior, intra-mental ideas which are common to 'the Body of Christ'. To the Catholic, to have faith means to participate in the faith of the Church. But the collectivity is bypassed in Luther's system. According to him, 'a man participates in the spirit from the time that he appropriates the merits of Christ to himself by faith'. There is no mediating collectivity; there is a direct confrontation

---

[1] Wingren, G., *Luther on Vocation*, transl. Rasmussen, C. C., Philadelphia 1957, pp. 86, 80, 78. Cf. also p. 122, note 76, and *Werke*, as quoted, vol. XVIII, Weimar 1908, p. 635.

[2] In this formulation we disregard those occasional passages in Luther in which he ascribes even the attitude of faith entirely to divine action and makes man himself totally passive. This belief is fully unfolded only in Calvin. Cf. Maritain, loc. cit., p. 272, and the texts quoted there.

[3] Hägglund, loc. cit., p. 228. Cf. above, p. 288.

of persons; there is again pure bipolarity. Sometimes this comes out very clearly, as in the following passage which is none the worse for being polemical. 'The acquired faith as well as the infused faith of the Sophists [i.e. of the Scholastics] says of Christ, "I believe in the Son of God, who suffered and was awakened", and there it leaves off. But the true faith says, "I certainly believe in God's Son, who suffered and was resurrected; I am sure he did all this for me . . .".'[1]

Shall we let one of the 'Sophists' reply? This will be useful because things are illustrated by their opposites. 'What is the Lutheran dogma of the certainty of salvation,' Jacques Maritain asks, in his essay on Luther,[2] 'but the transference to the human individual and his subjective state of that absolute assurance in the divine promises which was formerly the privilege of the Church and her mission? . . . Without perfect certainty of her state of grace the [Protestant] soul could not exist without breaking for agony because she has become the centre and seeks her salvation in the justice with which she covers herself, not in the abyss in the mercies of Another Who made her.'

Two theologies – two sociologically distinct theologies – are thus presented to us, and what concerns us is merely the fact that they are *sociologically* distinct, that – in Maritain's words – 'the [individual] soul . . . has become the centre' in Lutheran theology. We should be unduly and to little purpose prolonging the present section if we were to offer detailed proof of this assertion, especially as there is not likely to be any dissent from it. Just one passage or two will suffice: in his comment on the *Magnificat* Luther asserts that 'each is alone before God. Before God the individual is as alone as if there were only God and he in heaven and earth'. The same idea is expressed more poetically in the Reformer's musings on the one hundred and second psalm.[3] Verses 2 and 8 run: 'Hear, O Lord, my prayer, and let my cry come to thee . . . I . . . am become a sparrow all alone on the housetop.'[4] Man, redeemed man, says Luther, is that sparrow. He hovers 'alone in faith' between heaven and earth.

Like all Christian societies, the Lutheran Churches have, in the course of the centuries, loomed large in service to their more unfortunate brothers: names like Amalie Sieveking and Friedrich von Bodelschwingh come to mind at once. Their charitable effort puts before us the question as to in what way faith and works are connected in the Lutheran world-view, more concretely expressed, how works fit into the framework totally dominated by the concept of

---

[1] Hägglund, pp. 245, 251, 227. *Werke*, as quoted, vol. XXXIX/1, Weimar 1926, p. 45.

[2] Maritain, loc. cit., pp. 16 and 17.

[3] In the Vulgate (or Douai version) this is Psalm CI.

[4] Wingren, loc. cit., pp. 13 and 39. Cf. *Werke*, as quoted, vol. VII, Weimar 1897, p. 566, and vol. I, Weimar 1883, p. 198.

faith. Basically, the Lutheran thought-pattern is similar to that characteristic of Catholicism: God demands both faith *and* works. But the
weights are again very differently distributed: for Rome, works are
what saves a man; faith is simply presupposed; for Wittenberg, faith
is what saves a man; works are merely a consequence of faith. Once
more, a difference in emphasis comes close to being a difference in
essence.

But a comparison with Catholicism can offer us only a picture *ab
extra*. We must enter into Lutheranism itself in order to understand the
relationship there obtaining between works and faith, and on this topic
we shall quote only carefully selected writers, to be quite sure that the
analysis remains fair. Some of these writers have doubted that there is
an organic, or even a logical, connection between *fides* and *opera* in
Luther. Karl Eger, for instance, has maintained that there is a bare
'assertion that the one cannot be without the other'. He has judged that
'serious consequences followed from the theoretical lack of a systematic
relationship between justifying faith and the fulfilment of vocation in
the service of love'. In the same vein, P. H. Schifferdecker suggested a
generation later that 'the necessary inner unity between faith and the
power proceeding therefrom for action . . . Luther has not been able to
establish'.[1] E. A. Berger argued that Luther's ethic remains 'an individual ethic even in its application to social life', that it is not directed
towards 'the realization of definitely communal purposes'.[2] But most
arresting are the opinions of Franz Lau. 'Franz Lau . . . presses the
thesis . . . that according to Luther Christian living is only faith, not
works at all, not even works in love. In Lau's presentation we see faith
as flight from earth, upreach to heaven, aloneness before God, waiting
for death. All this,' Wingren admits, where he quotes these assertions,
'is purely Lutheran'.[3]

In an age like ours, when there is a strong tendency to reduce
religion to an agency for social reform and the Churches to political
pressure groups, Lau's characterization of Luther's attitude might
arouse resentments, and some exaggeration of the truth may in any case
be charged against it. But if religion is seen strictly as religion, that is,
as the soul's endeavour to re-unite itself with God, implied blame may
be turned into implied praise. 'Upreach to heaven', to use Lau's phrase,
was the one thing necessary to Luther, compared with which works on
earth were decidedly secondary. In a sermon delivered on 20 March
1530, Luther defined what he meant by a Christian, and he did it in the

[1] Both Eger's *Die Anschauungen Luthers vom Beruf*, Giessen 1900, and Schifferdecker's
Der Berufsgedanke bei Luther, Heidelberg Dissertation 1932, are quoted in Wingren,
loc. cit., p. 40.
[2] Cit. from the preface of the Luther edition of the *Bibliographisches Institut*, Leipzig
und Berlin 1917, vol. I, p. 38, by Betcke, loc. cit., p. 70.
[3] Wingren, loc. cit., pp. 44 and 45. (No closer reference to Lau's concrete publication
given.) On the 'waiting for death', cf. above, p. 208.

following words: 'He is a Christian who, first of all, is aware of himself (*sich selbst erkennt*), who, secondly, holds fast to Christ, and who, in the third place, does good deeds.'[1] The order of exposition is clearly an order of values and value preferences: self – faith – works. Works are mentioned last.

If Luther himself is studied, rather than his interpreters, who are sometimes a little too subtle, a fairly simple idea of the connection between faith and works is seen to be identifiable: works are a proof of our gratitude to God. We do social work 'for Christ's sake'. Thus in his *Commentary on Galatians*, Luther writes: 'Christ is not the Law, nor one who exacts [obedience to] the Law or [the performance of] works, but He is the Lamb of God who takes away the sins of the world. This is what pure faith apprehends, and not charity, which ought indeed to follow upon faith but as a kind of thanksgiving (*gratitudo*).'[2] We can sum up the salient idea behind this passage by saying that service to one's fellow men is secondary, a reflex of a bipolar relationship. It is not indistinguishable from the love of God, as it is for Catholics.

Needless to say, social work may be none the less effective or meritorious for having this place in the intellectual scheme of things. To an epileptic cared for in Bodelschwingh's institution at Bethel, it would make little difference whether the religious philosophy behind the doctors and nurses ranked charity above or below belief. Yet individualism did enter into the practice of social work as well. There was a tendency (present also in such English figures as Sir Charles Loch of the Charity Organization Society, a man with an attitude akin to that of German Evangelicalism) to understand the charitable effort in terms of bipolarity. The helper and his client were, once again and consistently, *solus cum solo*. The *social* aspect of social work was relatively understressed. It was a work of individual support for an individual that was undertaken. The aim was all the time to make the poor man or the sick man independent as soon as possible (often, in harmony with the identification of original sin and concupiscence, by teaching him how to be more sober, more self-controlled, more provident). This style of charitable help reflected deep Christian values: at its best, it embodied an attempt to bridge a social gap by means of a personal tie, a personal friendship. But even two friends remain two separate personalities, and in his individualism, Luther was not certain how far the one could really aid the other. Basing himself more especially on an analysis of the *Kirchenpostille*, Wingren formulates one of the Reformer's more basic convictions as follows: 'The only saint who could in any sense be the proper object of my imitation would be one who had precisely the same neighbour as I and stood in the same relation to him as I do. But no saint has ever stood precisely where I stand. Only I stand

[1] *Werke*, as quoted, vol. XXXII, Weimar 1906, p. 20. My translation.
[2] *Werke*, as quoted, vol. XL/1, Weimar 1911, p. 241.

there.'[1] Thus in the end everything comes down again to the person, his uniqueness and isolation.

We have now laid all the necessary emphasis on the individualism of the great individualist with whom we are dealing, but it remains for us to draw attention to the collectivistic element which, as we have hinted,[2] remains in Luther's thought even on the subject of salvation. We see it in his handling of the sacrament of baptism. The efficacy of the sacrament is not dependent on the presence of faith on the part of the *baptisandus*. 'As a result of this, Luther did not consider it an important question whether a baptized child can be said to have faith. He accepted the traditional answer that the faith of the sponsors takes the place of the child's faith . . .'[3] It should, however, be emphasized, that faith is expected to develop later on and, in a manner, to validate the rite. If our quotation from Hägglund brings out the still medieval-collectivistic implication of the Lutheran doctrine of baptism, the latter conception which must also be stressed shows him again well on the way to modern personalistic convictions.

A word must still be said on Luther's Biblicalism because it has been asserted that 'Luther was saved from subjectivism by his unshakeable belief in the authority of the Bible'.[4] If, for 'subjectivism' we could read here 'anarchism', the statement would be correct. Luther had no sympathy with people who claimed personal inspirations, visions, the gift of tongues and so on, and he made that more than clear in his dealings with the 'saints', or rather the sectarians, of Zwickau and of Münster who had drifted into their troubles, so Luther shouted from the rooftops, because they had written off the Scriptures as a 'dead word', far inferior to the 'living word within'. But if we compare him, not with Nikolaus Storch and Thomas Müntzer, but with Aquinas and Cajetan, we see once again how deeply individualistic was his whole attitude. The Word of God is addressed to man, *each* man (singular). 'The Bible can be understood out of itself, each person acting as his own interpreter,' says Hägglund where he discusses 'Luther's view of Scripture'.[5] Tradition is expressly rejected as a guide. Let popes and councils teach what they will, Luther proclaimed in a sermon on 10 August 1522, 'it is up to me to judge whether I want to accept it or not'. And again: 'If I am to identify an erroneous doctrine, the decision rests with me.'[6]

But, personal interpretation or no, the insistence on the sacred authority of Holy Writ brings us – or rather brings Luther – up against a painful problem. What about those passages in the Bible which

[1] Wingren, loc. cit., p. 182; cf. the references given there. Cf. also p. 184. Cf. further, Betcke, loc. cit., p. 68.

[2] Cf. above, p. 255.   [3] Hägglund, loc. cit., p. 241.

[4] Betcke, loc. cit, p. 53. Cf. also p. 56.

[5] Op. cit., p. 222.

[6] *Werke*, as quoted, vol. X/3, Weimar 1905, pp. 259 and 258.

preach collective responsibility, above all the Commandment (Exodus xx, 5), where God is heard to say that He will be 'visiting the iniquity of the fathers upon the children'? How would this conflict between the objective Word and the subjective individualism of the Reformer be resolved? The *Greater Catechism* gives us the answer: God's Word must stand. 'These words had to be proved true, because God can neither lie nor deceive,' Luther writes. And they were proved true. 'Saul was a great king, chosen by God, and a pious man, but when he was firmly seated on his throne, he turned his heart from God . . . and he perished, with all he had, so that even of his children none remained.'[1]

These lines are clear enough; and yet Luther could not live happily with them. God, he insinuates, is after all aiming His whip only at the backs of those who have sinned – sinned in person. 'Because . . . obstinate minds think that, since He looks on and lets them go their way unhindered, He knows not what they do or does not heed it,' Luther writes, 'He must therefore strike in and punish, and He cannot forget it, and visits their sins on their children, so that each may be impressed by it and see that He is in earnest. For it is these whom He means when He says, [*unto the third and fourth generation*] *of those who hate Me* . . .'.[2] It is the sinners themselves whom He means, the obstinate ones, 'those who keep up their defiance and pride'. The hapless children are therefore the victims of another one's guilt.

That this is indeed the opinion of Luther – an opinion implying a kind of rejection of collective responsibility, even though the principle is laid down in the Bible – can be seen from yet another decisive passage. In his *Commentary on Genesis* the Reformer had to deal with Noe's curse, a curse which, as we know, was hurled at the head of Chanaan, the son, not at that of Cham, the father, who had deserved it by his wickedness.[3] This is how he handles the versicle (Genesis IX, 25): 'The Holy Spirit is moved to such great wrath against [Cham], the disobedient and contemptuous son [of Noe], that He even refuses to call him by his own name, but designates him as Canaan, after his son [Noe's grandson] . . . Nevertheless, the curse upon the son recoils upon the father, who deserved it. Hence the name Ham disappears at this point because the Holy Spirit hates it, and this is indeed an ominous hatred.'[4] It is not too much to say that, in this exegesis, the individualism of Luther overlays and blots out the collectivism of the Bible which was, after all, the holy book of a nation organized in clans, the holy book of a 'we' society.

We have now reached the point where we must take leave of Luther.

[1] *Luther's Primary Works*, edd. Wace, H., and Buchheim, C. A., London 1895, p. 41.
[2] Ibid., p. 39.
[3] Cf. above, p. 36.
[4] *Luther's Works*, ed. Pelikan, J., vol. II, ed. Poellot, D. E., St. Louis 1960, p. 174. (This edition later becomes the Lehmann ed. published at Philadelphia and quoted above.)

He was one of those great historical figures in whom tendencies arising from life find conscious expression in order to return them to life once again, but made firmer and stronger by passing through an individual mind and mould. Luther is the nodal point in the development of an individualistic culture. Herbert Schöffler, in his important work, *Deutsches Geistesleben zwischen Reformation und Aufklärung*,[1] has clearly recognized that 'the meaning of the Lutheran Reformation was a subjectivation of the truths of salvation, an emphasizing of the self, indeed, a centrality of the self, which did not agree with the character of the older structure of Catholicism', and has followed the effects of this 'subjectivation' into many, often remote fields and corners. To give but one example: 'In the Catholic drama glorifying martyrdom, the protagonist is more than an individual; he is the representative of an idea. The Protestant pendant in Silesia knows only individuals as antagonists.'[2]

But we cannot follow this informing culture-principle to all the nooks and crannies into which it penetrated. It must be sufficient to adduce its main achievement, and that was the ever-admirable philosophical school of German idealism from Kant to Hegel and beyond. It was a consistently subjectivist school, as can best be seen from the man who stands, in time, half-way between Kant and Hegel, Johann Gottlieb Fichte[3] – as can also be seen from the man in whom it ran itself, so to speak, to death, Max Stirner, whose work, *Der Einzige und sein Eigentum*, led individualism to its *acme*, and also *ad absurdum*. The characteristically speculative form which the whole development assumed in Luther's own country of Germany was due to the divorce of the bourgeoisie from practical-political life which had been pre-empted by the authoritarian state. In the Anglo-Saxon West, where the kindred religiosity of Calvinism came to prevail, the self-same inspiration could much more freely unfold. Important cultural contrasts could therefore spring up in the Protestant world. But there was, in the final analysis, the self-same individualistic inspiration.

If there is a difference which deserves to be called decisive between the basic philosophy of Lutheranism and that of Calvinism, it would seem to relate to a purely theological matter, the interpretation of the sacrament of the Lord's Supper.[4] For Luther, who formulated the dogma of consubstantiation,[5] the consecrated particles of bread and wine contained Christ *realiter* and not only symbolically: he held fast to the medieval and Catholic belief in a 'real presence'. Calvin, on the

---

[1] Frankfurt a. M. 1956.
[2] Ibid., pp. 108 and 94. (Schöffler is a Lutheran.)
[3] Cf. our vol. IV, pp. 1 and 2.
[4] Cf. Niesel, W., *The Theology of Calvin*, transl. Knight, H., Philadelphia 1956, p. 15: 'In the last resort, his [Calvin's] chief concern was that Luther held wrong views on the question of the Eucharist.'
[5] Cf. above, p. 159.

other hand, dubbed the rite a 'memorial meal': there could be no question of a real presence. Christ's sacrifice was an historical event that was over and could at best be recalled, but not, as Catholics and Lutherans think, repeated. The modern observer, unless he has freed himself from his native *naïveté*, will see here merely descending degrees of irrationality. Calvin, he will say, was not as credulous as Luther and the Catholics. But on closer analysis it will be found that behind the theological front there hides once again a sociological shift – the same shift away from community and community-type thinking towards associational society and associational thinking which we have identified all along, and which is the fundamental theme of this whole volume. Calvinism is in essence a higher, more fully unfolded form of nominalism than Luther's philosophy.

Luther, too, was a nominalist: we do not have to cancel what we have asserted before. But he knew limits: disciple of Biel, Ockham and Abelard though he was, he did not introduce his nominalism into the sacred precinct but made it stop at the threshold and stairway. The sacramental teaching of Lutheranism was still indebted to Plato. Christ's immolation on Calvary was, even to Luther, a universal, a noumenon, which incorporated itself in many concrete copies or phenomena. These latter were, through their participation in the archetype, one with it. The sacrifice of the Mass (even Luther's truncated Mass) was therefore one with the God-Man's self-sacrifice on Calvary which it repeated in an unbloody form. The very term 'consubstantiation' expresses this in its fashion very neatly. Calvin shed this remnant of philosophical realism mainly because (as the sociologist of knowledge will argue) he lived in a world in which sociological realism was no longer acceptable – a world in which the individual was the *ens realissimum*, the really real, and archetypes, human or super-human, were merely abstractions, figures, definitions, nothing certainly that could claim actual presence in actual life. For the mind of Calvin – much more modernized than that of his cousin at Wittenberg – there was only the concrete: this man, this action, this event. And therefore the sacrament could only be a reference back, no more. We see, then, what Calvinism is: a more consistent elaboration of the Lutheran world-view, a Lutheranism raised to a higher potency.[1]

We feel the hot breath of Calvin very vividly, not to say painfully, in his discussion of the institution of indulgences which we take up first to show the parallelism with Martin Luther and the increase of polemical intensity under the Genevan's pen. The monies collected by the pardoners are not used for the building of the new St. Peter's in Rome, as Luther always indicated, but they are 'filthily spent on whores, pimps and drunken revelries'. Indulgences, according to the Papalists 'supply what our powers lack'. This doctrine is 'mad'. Its upholders should be

[1] Cf. in the same sense, Niesel, loc. cit., p. 12.

treated with 'hellebore' (a drug supposed to cure insanity). They should not be argued with.[1]

Luckily, Calvin *does* discuss the matter, and his argumentation is instructive, if it is presented coolly and rationally. Perhaps the most revealing passage is the following two sentences: 'Indulgences lodge satisfaction of sins in the blood of martyrs. Paul proclaimed and testified to the Corinthians that Christ alone was crucified and died for them.'[2] We hold here in our hands a master-key, so to speak, to the understanding of the contrast between the Catholic and Calvinist religions. For in Calvin's view, there is an inescapable either-or: we are saved *either* through the blood of Christ, *or* through the blood of martyrs; and since the Romanists bring the blood of martyrs in as an agent of salvation, they do, they must, *uno actu* reject the blood of Christ as all-sufficient – at least as all-sufficient, if they do not, in effect, reject it altogether. This conviction gives Calvin all his ire, all his passion, all his invective, and, once his basic conviction is accepted, his aggressiveness becomes a necessary and understandable consequence. But the older variants of Christianity did not accept his basic conviction because their whole philosophical and sociological substructure was different. For them, there was no either-or but, on the contrary, a one-and-the-other. Where sociality and synthesis is the bedrock of thought, the blood of Christ and the blood of the martyrs simply *cannot* be divided and divorced. Christ was the archetype of the martyrs; the martyrs were the imitators of Christ, nay, more: other Christs, so far as their martyrdom went. The Catholic attitude is, in the narrowest sense of the word, diametrically opposed to the Calvinist. Rejecting the blood of the martyrs is according to it a rejection of the blood of Christ. For it is ever Christ's blood that is being shed, even if physically it comes out of the veins of Ignatius of Antioch, or, for that matter, of Thomas More or John Fisher.

In the next section, Calvin tries to convict his opponents by their own tongues. A Romanist is called to the bar to overthrow Romanism: St. Leo the Great. In his letter to the Palestinian Monks this Pope appears to reject the concept of vicarious satisfaction, in so far as not Christ, but the saints are concerned. 'The righteous have received, not given crowns,' Leo writes. 'Each one surely died his own death, not paying by his end the debt of another, since one Lord Christ exists, in whom all are crucified, all are dead, buried, raised.'[3] Push an individualistic and somatic meaning underneath these words, and you have indeed ammunition against indulgences. Product of an associational society with its appropriate implied metaphysics, Calvin could hardly take the

---

[1] *Institutes*, as quoted, III, V, 1; loc. cit., vol. I, p. 670.
[2] Ibid., III, V, 2; p. 672. Cf. First Epistle to the Corinthians 1, 13.
[3] Cit. ibid., III, V, 2, p. 672. Cf. *Patrologia Latina*, as quoted, vol. LIV, Paris 1881, cols 1064 and 1065.

passage he is quoting in any other sense. Yet it reads rather differently if it is held against a collectivistic background. To earlier centuries and to the Catholic spirit, Leo's words must be taken to mean: 'Each one surely dies his own [personal] death, not paying by his end the [personal] debt of another, since our Lord Christ exists, in whom [as in one integral body] all are crucified, all are dead, buried, raised [and in whom all have gained merit, establishing a collective treasury of grace which is at the disposal of the abiding Body of the Lord Christ].' When Calvin then proceeds to take bits of Augustine to use them to the same purpose, he is a little disingenuous. For Augustine is pre-eminently the theologian of the 'Body of Christ' which he even conceives along rather strictly 'realistic', organismic, near-physiological lines.[1]

Calvin, of course, like Luther before him, had to face Colossians 1, 24, quoted above on p. 278, and he added, of his own free will, another Scripture passage of similar import, II Corinthians 1, 6: my tribulations, says the Apostle there, are for the salvation of my friends, of my flock at Corinth. Yet Calvin can cry: 'Away with the notion that Paul . . . meant to add anything' to the sufferings of Christ! Calvin's innuendo is all the time that it is blasphemous to suggest that Christ's sufferings need supplementation; yet no such blasphemy had been committed anywhere in the older theological literature. One wonders why Calvin did not remember, at this point, St. Anselm and his book, *Cur Deus Homo*, an entirely orthodox text, where what he insists on, is insisted on with equal conviction: Christ's merits are infinite. But the point is that to the Catholic mind, merit, like love, is not a quantity at all, and that for this reason alone it cannot be said to be in need of, or even capable of, addition. Rather it is a quality, and the more participate in it, the richer it will be: not necessarily the greater in extension, but the deeper in intensity. The modern, quantifying mind, the mind that would, by hook or by crook, quantify even that which is not quantifiable, announces itself in such passages from Calvin's pen. But, to remain with his overt argument: Paul's martyrdom, and the martyrdom of other saints, was accepted and endured in order to glorify God, to show contempt for life, and to strengthen the faith of fellow-believers. Only in this sense, says Calvin, does Paul assert that he is filling up those things that are wanting in the sufferings of Christ 'for His body, which is the Church'. Again we have before us Calvin's either-or: the saints work for the building-up of an earthly structure, therefore they cannot be co-workers in eternal salvation. To Catholic theology this can be no more than a simple *non sequitur*. Calvin shows his hand very clearly when he writes, in the paragraph which we have just discussed, that Christ *alone* should be preached; that He *alone* should be set forth;

---

[1] Cf. Stark, W., *Social Theory and Christian Thought*, London 1959, pp. 8 et seq. Even in the passage which Calvin quotes (*Patrologia Latina*, vol. XXXV, Paris 1902, col. 1847) there stand the words: 'We, as brethren, die for our brethren'.

that He *alone* should be named, etc. The small word 'alone' carries in the Calvinic text a very large – a metaphysical – meaning.[1] For Catholics, Christ is as little alone as those whom He calls his own. Of course, those whom Christ calls his own are not alone even according to Calvin. On the very next page he asserts that 'believers know the value of the fellowship of Christ'; but even this takes us only so far as Luther found it possible to advance: to bipolarity. What Maritain said of Luther, is true of Calvin also: God is to them 'only an ally, a co-operator, a powerful partner'.[4]

What then of the collectivistic passages in the Bible? Calvin's insistence on the binding character of the Holy Book is certainly no smaller and no greater than that of Luther, and yet the challenge which these passages offered must have been a good deal more excruciating for the Genevan, for they are mainly Old Testament texts, such as Genesis ix, 25, and Exodus xx, 5, and Calvinism set much more store by the Hebrew Scriptures than Lutheranism did.

Calvin faced up to his problems when, in his *Commentaries*, he came to Genesis ix, 25; or rather, he faced half up to them. For when he is directly confronted with the text, he takes refuge behind his conviction that God is unknowable, and that therefore a satisfactory solution of the riddle – why Chanaan, the innocent son, was cursed instead of the guilty father – is unavailable. 'Here we must not allow too much range to our curiosity,' he writes. 'We should keep in mind, it is not without reason that the judgments of God are called an unfathomable abyss. It is not fitting that God, before whose tribunal we must all finally stand, be subjected to our judgment – or rather to our foolish temerity. God chooses as He pleases some, to make them examples of His grace and long-suffering; He destines others for a different purpose, to be proofs of His anger and severity. Here human minds are blind . . .'.[3] The passage is truly intriguing. Man must not accuse God, Calvin says; and yet he intimates, as clearly as can be, that there would be a cause for accusation: the injustice inflicted on blameless Chanaan. And this injustice was inflicted by God, not Noe; for Noe, Calvin emphasizes, 'spoke as the Spirit directed his tongue'.[2]

In the quotations which we have given, Calvin forbids himself to speculate about this divine mystery, to peer into the abyss. Yet he finds it impossible really to stop his brain. And as he turns the matter over in his mind, he is increasingly driven to an individualistic interpretation of the crucial verse, even though he intimates – even though, with characteristic perspicacity, he sees – that 'the whole seed of Ham', and above all all Canaanites, are involved in the curse. 'I am sure that the

---

[1] III, V, 4 and 3; pp. 674 and 673. [2] *Three Reformers*, as quoted, p. 37.
[3] *The Library of Christian Classics*, vol. XXIII, *Calvin: Commentaries*, transl. and edd. Haroutunian, J., and Smith, L. P., London 1958, p. 275.
[4] Ibid.

punishment was transferred to posterity to make its severity all the more obvious,' Calvin writes,[1] 'for God was giving clear testimony that He did not consider the punishment of one man to be sufficient, and that therefore the curse had to include his descendants and continue in force through the ages. Meanwhile Ham himself was certainly not exempted; God made his judgment heavier by including his son with him.' As the reader can see, the 'solution' – very much a solution in quotation marks! – is the same as with Luther. God really wants to get at the true culprit, all appearances to the contrary notwithstanding. For God, even the God of Abraham, of Isaac and of Israel, is, like Luther and Calvin, an individualist.

But is the God of Abraham, of Isaac and of Israel an individualist? He spoke on Mount Sinai, and there He announced that, in blessing and in malediction, He would deal with lineages, not with lonely souls. Calvin takes this subject up in his *Institutes*, and the pages concerned are of crucial importance for our analysis. In the twentieth section of the eighth chapter of book II,[2] the question is raised as to whether the visitation of the sins of the fathers upon the children, threatened in Exodus xx, 5, does not run counter to God's justice, and an answer is attempted which cuts very deep. Apart from those whom God freely pardons, i.e. apart from those whom Calvinists call the elect, 'the whole nature of men ... is condemnable ... They perish by their own iniquity, not by any unjust hatred on God's part'.[3] God, therefore, is not to be blamed. This looks at first sight like the Augustinian doctrine which, though sensibly mitigated by St. Thomas Aquinas, and even more reduced by later theologians, is yet orthodoxly Catholic. But appearances are deceptive. Calvin's is not a dogma of collective responsibility.

Already the general way in which he handles the passages in which malediction is said to involve three or four and blessing a thousand generations shows the individualistic approach characteristic of Calvin. 'If after death the memory both of righteousness and of wickedness has such value in God's sight that the blessing of the one and the curse of the other redound to their posterity, much more will it rest on the heads of the doers themselves.' The posterity is merely like Chanaan through whom YHWH wanted to get at Cham: the targets are the sinning fathers, not the children as yet unborn. Why, then, are they involved at all? To serve as an *objectum demonstrationis*, Calvin says, as a threat to evildoers in the case of the curse, and a promise of favour in the case of righteousness. 'The temporal punishments, inflicted upon a few scoundrels, are testimonies of the divine wrath against sin, and of the judgment some day coming to all sinners, though many go unpunished till the end of this life. Thus, when the Lord gives one example of this blessing to show His mercy and kindness to the son for the father's sake, He gives proof of his constant and perpetual favour towards those

[1] Ibid.   [2] Loc. cit., p. 386.   [3] Ibid.

who worship Him. When once he pursues the iniquity of the father in the son, He teaches what sort of judgment awaits all the wicked for their own offences. In this passage, He was particularly concerned with the certainty of the latter.'[1]

'For *their own* offences . . .': the words must be fully appreciated. They show two traits of Calvin – firstly, his individualism, and secondly, his preoccupation with evil. The curse receives far more emphasis in this context than the possible blessing. Nothing can be more surprising, yet at the same time nothing can be more significant, than the fact that Calvin introduces Ezechiel xviii, 20 into his argument according to which 'the punishment of the father's sin will not pass on to the child'. Does this not look like a restriction of God's wrath to the immediately guilty? Calvin argues that the exact opposite is intended, or is at least derivable from the Prophet's dictum. The Jews of Ezechiel's day had complained that they were being unfairly victimized for deeds not their own. 'The Prophet announces to them that this is not so; for they are punished for their own offences.' *All* fallen men are guilty *all the time*; all fallen men are all the time liable to be punished, and if they *are* punished, this is right and meet. In a sense, Calvin seems to concede, 'the children . . . bear God's curses for their father's evil deeds. But' – and this is the decisive proviso – 'but the fact that they are also subjected to temporal miseries and at last to eternal destruction is the punishment inflicted by God's righteous judgment, not for another's sins, but for their own wickedness'.[2]

These words bring us close to the core of Calvin's anthropology and theology. Men are condemned sinners, not because *one* of them incurred condemnation, but because *all* do so. Adam is dethroned, so to speak, and each one – Jack Everyman – takes his place. To the layman, this may well look like hairsplitting. What difference does it make if we go to perdition because of Adam's sin or because of our own sins, if we are headed for hell in any case? The sociologist cannot argue like this. For him there is a theoretical contrast of the greatest consequence between the two positions. In the one, society is a unity, for the other a multiplicity, in the one it is a body, in the other a bundle; in the one a collectivity, in the other a collection; in the one men have a common fate, in the other fates that lie parallel. The culture which will emanate from the one parent conception will be very different from the culture which will derive from the other.

But even the layman will soon see that there is a difference, and a vital one to boot. For in the Christian's mind, the concept of sin, original or otherwise, never stands alone; it is always linked to the concept of salvation. If all fell in one, then all can rise up through One; some, many, may indeed come to grief later through personal misconduct, but in

[1] II, VIII, 21; pp. 387 and 388.
[2] II, VIII, 20; pp. 386 and 387.

principle all are redeemed together. If each one falls separately, then those to be rescued must be rescued separately, one by one. Here the doctrine – all-important within the Calvinist system – of election has its root and its place. Calvin himself gives it precedence even over Holy Writ. In saying that He will visit the iniquity of the fathers on the children unto the third and fourth generation, God has not bound Himself to leave them all in the natural state of damnation; in saying that He will be showing mercy unto a thousand or thousands of generations, He has not bound Himself to pluck them all out of the fire that will engulf the wicked. 'The Lawgiver desired here to frame no such perpetual rule as might detract from His election,'[1] Calvin writes, and though these words may give scant insight into the mind of the Almighty, they certainly do open a broad access road to the thought of Jehan Calvin. For him, salvation depended on being *personally* selected for the privilege by God's inscrutable decree, His *consilium arcanum*.

So deep is this doctrine of personal election in Calvin that he appears to make, under the impact of the Bible, one exception to it, but then withdraws this concession to collectivism almost immediately. The exception, needless to say, is in favour of Israel, the 'chosen race'. 'We call predestination,' the *Institutes* teach, 'God's eternal decree, by which He determined with Himself what He willed to become of each man. For all are not created in equal condition; rather, eternal life is fore-ordained for some, eternal damnation for others . . . God has attested this not only in individual persons, but has given us an example of it in the whole offspring of Abraham . . . In the person of Abraham, as in a dry tree trunk, one people is peculiarly chosen . . .'.[2] 'That adoption of Abraham's seed in common was a visible image of the greater benefit that God bestowed on some out of the many.'[3] But was it really an 'adoption in common'? Calvin himself cancels the whole idea by pointing out that even within Israel some were called and others rejected. He speaks of a 'second, more limited degree of election': 'Ishmael had at first obtained equal rank with his brother Isaac, for in him the spiritual covenant had been equally sealed by the sign of circumcision. Ishmael is cut off; then Esau; afterwards, a countless multitude, and well-nigh all Israel.' Thus individualism receives the last word. 'God freely chooses whom He pleases,' Calvin writes with all desirable clarity. 'His free election has been only half explained *until we come to individual persons* . . .'[4]

Among the readers of the last pages, there may well have been some who may have demurred at the individualistic interpretation of Calvinism given there, and, if so, they did not belong to the least instructed. Scattered throughout Calvin's writings there are passages, not too few

---

[1] II, VIII, 21; p. 387.
[2] III, XXI, 5; pp. 926 and 927.   [3] III, XXI, 7; p. 931.
[4] III, XXI, 6 and 7; pp. 929 and 930. My emphasis. Cf. also IV, XVI, 14; p. 1336.

in number, in which he appears to state and restate the traditional position on original sin, to argue, not only like Luther, but even like the Catholic writers. For instance: 'All of us, who have descended from impure seed, are born infected with the contagion of sin. In fact, before we saw the light of this life, we were soiled and spotted in God's sight. "For who can bring a clean thing from an unclean? There is not one" – as the Book of Job says.'[1] It is anything but surprising that there should be such statements. Calvin's veneration for the Bible as well as for the Jewish people, and his belief that the Reformation was going back to the origins, made him more than chary of dissent. Besides, formulations like 'all men are fallen creatures' were capable of an interpretation which suited him ('each man is a fallen creature on his own account') as well as of one which did not really suit him ('all men are fallen creatures because one of them fell'), and there was no need always to append a detailed explanation. This, however, raises the question as to whether we can be in fact sure of our ground if we describe him as an individualist and even as a greater individualist than Martin Luther. Luckily, a fine book, Hans Engelland's *Gott und Mensch bei Calvin* (München 1934), has splendidly solved this problem for us.

When the more sophisticated analyses of Luther and Melanchthon are studied, it appears that they consider us connected with Adam in two ways: firstly, because we participate in the sin which he has left to his descendants, and secondly, because we participate in the sin which he himself committed before God. So far as the first point is concerned, the properly hereditary character of original sin, we know already how Calvin deals with it: by not dealing with it. There is an impenetrable mystery here, and we should be both foolish and impertinent if we tried to solve it: 'The guilt of one man could not concern us at all if our Heavenly Judge had not delivered us over to eternal ruin.'[2] He *has* done so. *Sapienti sat.* 'We are too weak and stupid to understand the judgments of God which are so high.'[3] The second point is fully as important as the first. If we are really *one* with Adam, we are one even with his personal act, the act of disobedience which brought him down. This is what Luther and Melanchthon believed, and to that extent they clearly were traditionalists and collectivists, philosophical 'realists' in theology. Calvin, however, did not go along with his fellow-Reformers. Or rather, he has left them behind. Calvin accepts only one half of the Lutheran-Melanchthonian definition of original sin. 'Luther's and Melanchthon's doctrine that we are responsible, not only for the sin inherited from Adam, but for Adam's personal sin before God as well,

---

[1] *Institutes*, II, I, 5; p. 248. The quotation is from Job xiv, 4.
[2] Cit. Niesel, p. 83. Cf. *Corpus Reformatorum*, vol. XXXVII (*Calvini Opera*, vol. IX), edd. Baum, W., Cunitz, E., and Reuss, E., Braunschweig 1870, col. 289.
[3] Cit. Niesel, p. 86. Cf. *Corpus Reformatorum*, vol. LVI (*Calvini Opera*, vol. XXVIII), as quoted, col. 192. (Niesel incorrectly quotes vol. XXVII.)

seemed to him unbearable . . . We are guilty of our own sin, but not for that of another. He knows no community of fate on the part of mankind in the sense that "all are guilty of everything". He seems, in the final analysis, to know only the monadological relationship of men to each other, according to which everybody is responsible only for himself.'[1] It does not seem necessary for us to add a single syllable to this very clear exposition.

If we were writing a historical and descriptive, instead of a typological and analytical book, and if we had time and space *ad libitum* at our disposal, we might show in detail how the associational mode of thinking contained in, and developed by, the great Reformers, spread in certain countries through all society and came to dominate the inclusive culture. As it is, we must bring our discussion to a close. Only one vehicle can be mentioned which helped to transport the Reformation outlook, and especially the Calvinic version, to the masses: John Bunyan's *The Pilgrim's Progress*, one of the greatest best-sellers of all time. Roger Sharrock, the leading expert on this important, if naïve, literary figure, calls the classic a 'drama of the individual soul' and remarks: 'The first poignant words of [the hero] Christian, "What shall I do to be saved", set the tone for the whole work'.[2] What shall I do to be saved? What Bunyan himself did is explained in his autobiography, *Grace Abounding*, and of this work Sharrock says that 'it is typical in its concentration on the inner life of grace'.[3]

Max Weber has thrown the essence of Bunyan's allegory into high relief. 'In spite of the necessity of membership in the true Church for salvation,' he writes, 'the Calvinist's intercourse with God was carried on in deep spiritual isolation. To see the specific results of this peculiar atmosphere, it is only necessary to read Bunyan's *The Pilgrim's Progress*, by far the most widely read book of the Puritan literature. In the description of Christian's attitude after he had realized that he was living in the City of Destruction and he had received the call to take up his pilgrimage to the celestial city, wife and children cling to him, but stopping his ears with his fingers and crying, "life, eternal life", he staggers forth across the fields. No refinement could surpass the naïve feeling of the tinker who, writing in his prison cell, earned the applause of a believing world in expressing the emotions of the faithful Puritan thinking only of his own salvation.'[4]

[1] Engelland, loc. cit., pp. 52 and 53. Our translation. Concerning Melanchthon's statement which served as Calvin's *pièce de résistance*, cf. his *Loci Theologici, Corpus Reformatorum*, vol. XXI, edd. Bretschneider, K. G., and Bindseil, H. E., Braunschweig 1854, col. 668.
[2] Bunyan, J., *Grace Abounding to the Chief of Sinners and The Pilgrim's Progress*, ed. Sharrock, R., London 1966, p. X.
[3] Ibid., p. IX. Cf. also Perry Miller, loc. cit., p. 297.
[4] Weber, M., *The Protestant Ethic and the Spirit of Capitalism*, as quoted, pp. 106 and 107.

Weber might have made his point much more forcefully by adducing a few characteristic incidents from the narrative. Perhaps the most characteristic is Christian's encounter with Faithful beyond the Valley of the Shadow of Death, when he is already rather close to his destination. Both regret that they have not been able to share more of the journey; but they agree that this could not be. For each must set out for the celestial city by himself.[1]

Another interesting moment is Christian's meeting with Mr. Worldly-Wiseman while he is yet groaning under the load of his sins. Worldly-Wiseman asks him if he has a wife and children, and he answers: 'Yes, but I am so laden with this burden that I cannot take that pleasure in them as formerly; methinks, I am as if I had none.'[2] This sentiment sat somewhat more lightly on the fictitious Christian than on the real Bunyan. 'The parting with my wife and poor children,' he confesses in *Grace Abounding*, 'has oft been to me . . . as the pulling the flesh from my bones.' But he insists before himself that this is an improper weakness. 'I am somewhat too fond of these great mercies . . . Yet thought I, I must do it, I must do it: and now I thought of those two milche kine that were to carry the Ark of God into another country and to leave their calves behind them, I Samuel vi, 10, 11, 12.'[3]

We see from Bunyan very clearly in which direction the Protestant soul developed. Accepting the imprint of an associational society, it tended, like all moderns, towards selfhood rather than sociality, but this tendency was not, as in the Catholic cultures, inhibited; it was, on the contrary, favoured and fostered by the religious forces which made explicit, and thereby magnified, what was contained in contemporary life. To be the relatively lonely man has ever been the glory and the sorrow of the Protestant. Any meeting of the cultures is apt to release this insight. When a young Frenchman (André Maurois) served, in World War I, as an interpreter with a Scottish army brigade, he laid down his experiences in a book revealingly called, *Les Silences du Colonel Bramble* (1918); and when a young Englishwoman (Charlotte Brontë) was sent, in Victorian days, to Belgium to receive her education there, she unburdened herself in a merciless – indeed, hate-filled – novel, *The Professor* (1857). The 'British English', as she quaintly says, were not a bit like the French Walloons. 'A general air of native propriety and decency: by this last circumstance alone I could at a glance distinguish the daughter of Albion and nursling of Protestantism from the foster-child of Rome, the protégée of Jesuitry. Proud, too, was the aspect of these British girls; at once envied and ridiculed by their Continental associates, they warded off insult with austere civility and met hate with mute disdain. They eschewed company-keeping and in the midst of numbers seemed to dwell isolated.'[4] The last sentence is the most

[1] Cf. ed. Sharrock, as quoted, p. 193.   [2] Ibid., p. 153.
[3] Ibid., p. 100.   [4] Nelson Classics ed., London n.d., p. 95.

instructive. Independence is not only a fact, it is an ideal; not only a source of suffering, but also a hallmark of Godliness. Already John Milton had felt like this:

> ... Wisdom's self
> Oft seeks to sweet retired solitude,
> Where ... she plumes her feathers and lets grow her wings,
> That in the various bustle of resort
> Were all too ruffled, and sometimes impaired.[1]

To be alone is better than to be merged in a crowd.

Like John Milton, Charlotte Brontë and Colonel Bramble, or rather the real person hidden behind this fanciful pseudonym, were products of a basically Calvinist culture, and the loneliness of the Calvinist has ever been harder, if also more heroic, than the loneliness of even the Lutheran. We have given the reason already in the remarks which opened our discussion of Jehan Calvin: Calvinism was in this respect, as in most others, an intensified version of the religious system which is also confronted in Lutheranism. Between Luther and Calvin, the associational principle of social organization had achieved great strides: Geneva was much closer to modern capitalism, individualism, and all the rest of it, than Wittenberg. With greater human isolation came greater anxiety; with greater anxiety, greater self-laceration; with greater self-laceration, a harsher doctrine of man; with a harsher doctrine of man again greater – even greater – human isolation; and so the circle of causes and effects was closed. The Genevan's doctrine of 'total perversion' was darker than the German's doctrine of the 'bondage of the will'. It left a feeling that nothing good could come out of man, not even if it was good in appearance. Hence the Calvinistic ban on the emotions. Were they anything but the stirrings of the Old Adam, a subtle form of wickedness which had made God rue that He had ever created man? (Genesis VI, 5). But, as E. M. Forster has said,[2] 'emotion ... is the only final path to intimacy'. That path was therefore blocked. Yet the Lutheran could help himself in his quandary. Was he – the man of faith – not *solus cum solo*, a soul in direct personal contact with God? Where other feelings could be deceptive, was not at least the feeling of grace, of acceptedness, as the promised divine response to genuine faith, reliable? Calvin doubted even that. He pointed out, with some brutality, that the reprobate could have the same inner experiences, or nearly the same experiences, as the elect.[3] Who, then, could say that

---

[1] *The Works of John Milton*, Columbia ed., New York 1931, vol. I, p. 99. Spelling slightly modernized.
[2] *The Longest Journey*, ed. New York 1953, p. 193. Cf. also *Marianne Thornton: A Domestic Biography*, London 1956, p. 128.
[3] Cf. Engelland, loc. cit., pp. 108 and 109 and the documentation given there.

he was a true believer? Indeed, was there such a thing as a true believer? 'It is dangerous to speak of faith with too much emphasis,' writes Niesel where he paraphrases Calvin's thought.[1] And Calvin, in a rare aside aimed at Luther, as well as at Osiander who is mentioned by name, asserts: 'Faith of itself does not possess the power of justifying . . . For if faith justified of itself . . . as it is always weak and imperfect, it would effect this only in part. Thus the righteousness that conferred a fragment of salvation upon us would be defective.'[2] What this amounts to is the terrible conviction that closeness to God is as unavailable to man as intimacy with other souls. Max Weber has brought out this contrast between the two variants of Protestantism very well: 'The highest religious experience which the Lutheran faith strives to attain . . . is the *unio mystica* with the deity. As the name itself, which is unknown to the Reformed faith in this form, suggests, it is a feeling . . . of a real entrance of the divine into the soul of the believer . . . The typical religion of the Reformed Church, on the other hand, has from the beginning repudiated . . . this purely inward emotional piety . . . A real penetration of the human soul by the divine was made impossible by the absolute transcendality of God compared to the flesh.'[3]

Thus the Calvinist is the lonely man *kat exochen*. He is the powerless man *kat exochen* also. He is the one because he is the other. If he understands the Bible, it is really God who understands; if he prays, it is really God who prays; if he is obedient to God, it is really God who is obedient to God.[4] Is it possible that social isolation alone can have brought on this feeling of total annihilation? Hardly. To be sure, it must have pushed in this direction for to be isolated from other men *is* to be powerless. But a new and more potent factor entered about this time into men's outlook on the world, and it made a great difference. It was nature. The discouragement so poignantly felt by the Calvinists was in part, in great and growing part, we would venture to say, due to men's incipient discovery of the fact that the whole universe is bound by iron laws, is a quasi-mechanical system in which everything is as it has to be – inexorably, inevitably, irremediably, eternally. Scientific determinism and religious predestination are locked by stronger ties than those of linguistics. Where medieval man had seen a chain connecting man with society and society with the deity; where Lutheran man had seen a chainlet connecting, without intermediate realities, the single soul with God; there Calvinist man learned to place a logic that led from man to nature and from nature to the Almighty – to that Almighty who, in time, was to be reduced to the Creator alone (Unitarianism) and thereafter to the Unknown and Unknowable (Deism),

---

[1] Niesel, loc. cit., p. 136.
[2] III, XI, 7; p. 733.   [3] Weber, loc. cit., pp. 112 and 113.
[4] Cf. Niesel, loc. cit., pp. 24, 37, 38, 153–8, 103, 123, 124. Cf. esp. p. 154: 'The possibility of prayer does not really lie within our grasp.'

so that finally the prevailing philosophy was to centre on man's relation to nature, with results both good and evil which all of us know. In any case – and this brings us to the threshold of a new subject – nature was now beginning to be a greater preoccupation than sociality. The aim of the Catholic ages had been to build a good society; the aim of the Calvinist centuries was to be to achieve domination over our physical habitat. A new type of culture was in the making – an activistic culture, a culture of science and technology.

THE UNFOLDING OF AN ACTIVISTIC WORLD-VIEW

The change of society from community to association, and, concomitantly or consequently, from collectivism to individualism, was the most momentous revolution that ever took place in the sphere which Karl Marx has called 'the substructure' of culture, 'the real basis' on which a superstructure of ideas is placed and reared. Where there had been a desire to apprehend wholes before, there was now a desire to make distinctions; where there had been a tendency towards synthesis, there was now a tendency towards antithesis or rather antitheses (plural); where there had been an ontology of unity, there was now an ontology of multiplicity and individuality. As if by a miracle, the flow of thought was reversed. The new variants of Christianity were the effect of the great turn of the tide of which we are speaking; they became in due course also one of its causes. A new type of man had called for and shaped them; they for their part were calling for and shaping a new type of man.

Of all the antitheses which were increasingly emphasized and elaborated, that between man and nature was by far the most important. Johannes Pedersen has pointed out that animals were to the Jew of tribal days a kind of kin rather than a category of things; but to a later generation, a generation urbanized and rationalized, they became a category of things rather than a kind of kin. Pedersen speaks of a 'narrowing of the world' – the world of brotherhood, the world of life.[1] The very same process was to be repeated at the end of the Middle Ages. A subject-and-object relationship was springing up between man and nature, to replace the feeling of mutual belonging which had dominated before. This was the inception of that consistent and comprehensive manipulation of matter which is the *unum necessarium* to modern capitalist society, the *hic Rhodus, hic salta*, of modern man.

When St. Francis felt that his life was declining, he decided to leave Mount Alverna, one of his most beloved retreats, and as he did so, he dismounted from his donkey and took leave of the landscape. 'May God keep you, mountain of God,' he is reported to have said, 'holy mountain, *mons coagulatus* . . . May God Keep you, mons Alverna! May

[1] Pedersen, loc. cit., p. 484. Cf. pp. 481–6.

God the Father, and the Son, and the Holy Spirit, bless you. Remain in peace. We shall never see each other again.'[1] It is thus that one says normally good-bye to a living person, not to a pile of rock and earth. St. Francis was a poet, and it was in part, no doubt, the poetical vein in him that made him address the mountain in the way we are told he did. But St. Francis was also a man of the Middle Ages, and in the Middle Ages his action was in the eyes of ordinary people much less strange than it appears in our day. Man and nature, animate and inanimate creation, were not as yet so sharply divided as they are now. Communication between them was an idea far less absurd than it must seem at present.

Max Scheler, in his analysis of the origins of modern society, has depicted St. Francis as a harbinger of things to come. His love of the objects of nature, expressed above all in his 'Canticle of the Creatures', was the first serious form of preoccupation with them, and it opened the door and paved the way for other forms of the same preoccupation, decreasingly poetical and increasingly scientific. Francis found that 'our sister, the water', as she gushes from a rocky surface, is 'refreshing and chaste'. Others were to find that our object, the water, is matter in a liquid, i.e. droppable, state and consists of hydrogen and oxygen in a relation of 2 : 1. There may be a long way from the former insight to the latter, but it is, according to Scheler, a straight road all the same. He is right. Francis was above all a man of the eye. His apprehension of nature was not only loving, but also living. Albrecht Dürer's nature studies, for instance his paintings of a piece of grassy surface or of a rhinoceros or a squirrel, owe something, nay, quite a lot, to the Franciscan spirit, and in their meticulously descriptive character they are indeed a step nearer to the technically different, but in its decisive intention rather similar, descriptivism of botany and zoology.[2]

But every man, however progressive he may be – and Francis of Assisi was not the most progressive – is beholden to the past, and in his ties to nature there still lies a good deal of early man's desire to be inside of nature rather than stand over against it. The best-known legends about the Poverello attest this: his sermon to the birds at the Carceri, his friendship with the wolf of Gubbio. A dove was not to him an exemplar of the species *Columbidae* or a wolf an exemplar of the species *Canis lupus*: a dove was still a real sister and a wolf a brother, at least a potential brother. There is, in history, a sharp dividing line between early humanity still hankering after inclusion in the framework of nature, and late humanity finally reconciled to its exclusion from that framework, expulsion from the maternal womb, alienation from the rest of creation. Francis had not crossed that Rubicon. Medieval man never crossed it. The splendid research of André Varganac in his

[1] Thode, H., *Franz von Assisi*, ed. Wien 1934, p. 64.
[2] Cf. Stark, W., *The Sociology of Knowledge*, London 1958, pp. 114 and 115.

incomparable book, *Civilisation Traditionelle et Genres de Vie* (1948), has proved how persistently, how toughly, man has stuck to his place inside physical reality, and how painful, how excruciatingly difficult, it was for him to step outside and be on his own. Only a man reconciled to being lonely and strong enough to stand alone could cut the umbilical cord. The Protestant was that man. For the Calvinist in the proper sense of the word, a figure like Francis could be little more than a sentimentalist and little less than a fool, bating of course occasional effusions which cannot be taken quite seriously. To face up to the facts – that was the essential desire of the scions of Jehan Calvin. Everything else was damnable delusion. But soberness has its reward. He who knows the laws of nature will learn how to use the laws of nature: from *savoir* comes *pouvoir*. If the Calvinist was, as we have explained a short time ago, the man who reached the depths of despair because he saw us, naked so to speak, exposed to the inexorable necessities of nature, he was also the man, as we have to explain now, who leads us out of our enslavement to necessities not understood to that elevated vantage point from which we can overlook the universal mechanism, insert our will into it and come to manipulate its wheels and springs. Calvinism must be understood as a catalyst in history which brought on a dialectical development. In the beginning, it gave mankind the conviction that man was nothing in the face of nature and nature's God; in the end it generated the conviction that man is everything in the realm of nature, a minor god, if not indeed god himself. That conviction is no more than a delusion; he who can build and operate machines, however complex and efficient, is still far from being the lord of the universe. But, from the point of view of an operative ideology, which is all that most men want, this makes little difference. The whole of modern humanity lives by dint of an over-compensated inferiority complex. Calvinism gave it that complex when it taught that man is less before creation and the Creator than the dung-beetle is before man; it also helped to overcompensate that complex when it led man to study the facts and to learn a few useful tricks as to how to manipulate them, how to develop science and technology, which would allow him to feel that *he* was the master of reality.

From anxiety to confidence, or rather from over-anxiety to over-confidence – that is the historical road of humanity from the sixteenth to the twentieth century. Let us see how Protestantism helped to cover the distance.

Already in Martin Luther there appear elements of the solution which was later to emerge more fully from the work of Jehan Calvin, although Max Weber is inclined to deny this. Yet in his main work, *Wirtschaft und Gesellschaft*, it is precisely Weber who draws a very sharp dividing line between innerworldly asceticism, mainly represented by the

Calvinist religion, an attitude which fosters activity in the workaday world, and innerworldly mysticism, a diametrically opposed attitude which takes no interest in the world and therefore leads to quietude rather than to activism.[1] The Founder of Christianity belonged to the latter category; indeed, He is its most consistent representative. 'Why are you solicitous?', He asked His followers. 'Consider the lilies of the field, how they grow: they labour not, neither do they spin. But I say to you that not even Solomon in all his glory was arrayed as one of these ... Be not solicitous, therefore, saying, What shall we eat, or, What shall we drink, or, Wherewith shall we be clothed? For after all these things do the heathens seek ... Be not therefore solicitous for tomorrow: for the morrow will be solicitous for itself. Sufficient for the day is the evil thereof' (Matthew VI, 28–29, 31–32, 34). We are confronted with the very same life-policy in the account of Jesus' stay in the house of Mary and Martha. Martha, 'troubled about many things', is depicted for us as an activistic type; Mary, on the other hand, as a contemplative. Christ did not hesitate to show His preference: 'Mary hath chosen the best part,' He said, 'which shall not be taken away from her' (Luke X, 41 and 42). Clearly, from such a mentality a civilization like that of capitalism could not have sprung. The Christianity of Christ was too indifferent to material values to generate the feverish pursuit of the material values which we call capitalism. The first historical presupposition of such a society was a transvaluation of values which would place Martha above Mary. This is what Calvinism did. And this is what Lutheranism started to do. By starting to do it, Lutheranism was, on Weber's own premises, an important pathbreaker of modern activism.

One illustration must suffice here in order to show how hostile Martin Luther was to the contemplative attitude. This is what he writes in his Commentary on Galatians: 'Under the papacy it was regarded as an act of the greatest spirituality when the monks sat in their cells and meditated about God and His works, or when their fervent devotions so inflamed them as they genuflected, prayed, and contemplated heavenly things, that they wept for sheer pleasure and joy. There was no thinking here about women or about any other creature, but only about the Creator and His marvellous works. And yet this action, which reason regards as eminently spiritual, is a "work of the flesh" ... The more spiritual and holy it appears to be, the more dangerous and destructive it is ...'[2]

Rejecting contemplation does not, of course, in and by itself, mean accepting a hectically active life, but there is, in Lutheranism, a strain

[1] Cf. Weber, M., *Economy and Society*, edd. Roth, G., and Wittich, Cl., New York 1968, vol. II, pp. 544 et seq. and 633.
[2] *Werke*, as quoted, vol. XL/II, Weimar 1914, p. 110. Translation by Hansen, W. A., *Luther's Works*, ed. Pelikan, J., vol. XXVII, St. Louis 1964, pp. 87 and 88.

at least of that electrifying current which Weber ascribed to Calvinism. The truly pious man, above all the man who had achieved the *unio mystica*, could come to rest in what he had achieved, but who had achieved the *unio mystica*, who could claim that he was the truly pious man? Lutheranism denied that there are other-than-psychological, other-than-internal marks of divine grace, but where outer, i.e. visible proofs of acceptedness, of justification, are missing,[1] nobody can ever be sure. A measure of anxiety must remain and this may be abreacted in an active, Martha-like conduct. Luther himself is here the best exemplification of Lutheran man. The bitter realization that concupiscence is unconquerable plunges him into a deep crisis, into despair. 'What does he do? . . . Does he cast himself on God?' No. 'He gave up praying and threw himself into activity to escape. He tried to drown his anguish in a sea of toil. "I need two secretaries," he writes in 1516 to Lang, prior of Erfurt. "I do practically nothing all day long but write letters . . . I am Preacher of the Convent and in the Refectory; I am called daily to preach in the parish; I am Director of Studies and Vicar of the district, and thereby elevenfold Prior; I am responsible for the fish-ponds at Leitzkau; I am agent at Torgau in the suit for Herzberg parish church; I give lectures on St. Paul, I am collecting notes on the Psalter. I rarely have time to recite my Office and say Mass".[2] In 1516, Jehan Calvin was about seven years old; he was not yet an example of Calvinist man; but Martin Luther was, so far as feverish activity in order to escape from the dreadful question of personal acceptedness or damnation was concerned.

In spite of this, it is, however, understandable that Max Weber should not have attributed to Lutheranism a great role in the preparation of modern capitalist society. For Lutheranism was part and parcel of an authoritarian world in which the burgher was trained to obey, not to develop ideas and activities of his own, in which he was destined to become and to remain a subject rather than an entrepreneur. Briefly expressed, what the Lutheran ethos demanded was that the Christian should fulfil his vocational duties, not that he should necessarily have success in them. 'Even today,' writes Alfred Müller-Armack in his important book, *Religion und Wirtschaft*,[3] 'the work ethos of the Calvinist countries is decisively different from the specifically German vocational ethic and shows its Calvinist origin in the fact that it values labour exclusively from the side of its success, but does not see perseverance in a given profession in a positive light. The appreciation of man under the aspect of the *fulfilment* of his vocation is as Lutheran in its inspiration as high valuation because of *success* in one's vocation is

---

[1] Cf. Betcke, loc. cit., p. 57.
[2] Maritain, loc. cit., p. 8. For the letter to Johann Lang, dated 26 October 1516, cf. *Werke,* as quoted, *Briefwechsel,* vol. I, Weimar 1930, p. 72.
[3] Stuttgart 1959.

Calvinistic.'[1] Another expert, Klara Vontobel, has collected passages from later Lutheran literature which show how deeply conservative this particular form of Protestantism was. Thus Gottlob Cober wrote in *Der aufrichtige Cabinet-Prediger* (1715): 'The main thing is that man should labour hard (*sich abmüht*); it is less important whether or not the result of the effort and the objective achievement is considerable.' And G. J. Zollikofer expressed himself in *Andachtsübungen und Gebete* (3 vols, 1798–1801) as follows: 'If I should labour altogether in vain, so far as success is concerned, should I not have exerted my forces? . . . Work will be dear to me simply as work, even if I should effect little by it that is good.'[2]

Thus Lutheranism was not the powerful modernizer Calvinism proved to be, and to that extent Weber is certainly correct. But it achieved more than he was prepared to allow. Sometimes we must look a little under the surface to find out what really happened, and if we do so, we may be surprised at what we find there. Most late medieval towns in Germany possessed somewhere on the outskirts a 'Way of the Cross' showing the journey of Jesus from Pilate's Court to Mount Calvary. The relation of the successive 'stations' to the true locations in Jerusalem was envisaged, in the usual Platonic fashion, as the connection between noumenon and phenomenon, the 'real' and the pictorial or symbolic, with the pictorial and symbolic receiving something, and carrying something, of the real. The people of Nuremberg – a city presently to become largely Lutheran – also built themselves a 'Way of the Cross', but they did so in a curiously new-fangled spirit. What that spirit was, and why we can call it new-fangled, may be seen from the columns which were erected to mark the successive stages on the progress towards Golgatha. On one, for instance, we read: 'Here Simon [of Cyrene] was forced to help Christ to carry His cross. 295 paces from Pilate's house.' And, on the next: 'Here Jesus said, You daughters of Jerusalem, do not cry over me, but over yourselves and your children. 380 paces from Pilate's house.' The distances are meticulously marked. The idea behind these indications, which cannot but appear irrelevant, if not indeed ridiculous, to the religious consciousness, was to demonstrate that care had been taken to make the *via dolorosa* of Nuremberg agree, even in circumstantial detail, with the *via dolorosa* at Jerusalem. 'Pilate's house' in Jerusalem was Pilate's house; 'Pilate's house' in Nuremberg was Martin Ketzel's house at the Thiergärtnerthorplatz. From there the successive 'stations' led, to Mount Calvary in the one place, to the Johanneskirchhof in the other. The *via*

---

[1] Ibid., p. 112. Author's italics. Our translation. Cf. also pp. 122 and 140–1.
[2] Cit. Vontobel, K., *Das Arbeitsethos des deutschen Protestantismus*, Bern 1946, pp. 26 and 52. Our translation. For Weber's decided antipathy to this aspect of Lutheranism, cf. Mitzman, A., *The Iron Cage: An Historical Interpretation of Max Weber*, New York 1970, pp. 65, 194, 195, 218, 241, 242.

dolorosa of Nuremberg was to reflect the 'true' distances between them, yard for yard.[1] It was in this way to be a physical rather than a symbolic representation of the sacred places – a very different matter. Our example is perhaps petty, but it is eye-opening at the same time. The Nurembergers were already modern people. They had a touch of the factual, the mathematical, the scientific spirit. That core-piece of Catholicism – a symbolistic attitude – had decayed with them, not to say disappeared. Its place had been taken by modern factualness. And they were very close in this to Martin Luther. Luther's understanding of the Bible was anti-symbolistic. 'As far as he was concerned, Scripture has but one original and proper meaning, the grammatical or historical. He ... recognized, as a matter of course, the figurative interpretation which is to be found in the Bible itself, as for example in the parallels drawn between Christ and certain Old Testament figures (typology). Luther also spoke (especially in his early sermons) of a *sensus spiritualis* or *mysticus* which points to a direct allegory. But this point of view was given a subordinate position ... In later years, Luther forsook this kind of Bible interpretation more and more.[2]

As can be seen, Lutheranism too was an agent of modernization, but one which cannot be ascribed great reality-transforming power. Calvinism was different. It produced a radically new type of man who had enough inner dynamism to transform the world. Max Weber has to some extent, to a large extent even, explained how and why. His theory is, in spite of all the attacks that have been levelled against it, substantially correct. Tortured, like Luther, by the uncertainty of salvation, but unlike Luther incapable of receiving assurance from within, the Calvinist believer was forced to seek and find the signs of his predestination to eternal blessedness in the outer world. In his quandary, and in his Biblicism, he remembered how God had dealt with His saints of the Old Dispensation, with His chosen ones, Abraham, Isaac and Jacob: He had filled their byres and their barns. And this was no accident for He was the Dispenser of All Things. If wealth came to a man, or power for that matter, it came through God's gracious contrivance. If one's business prospered, if one's till was filling, if one's balance sheet showed a gratifying result, this was an indication of divine favour. 'The providential interpretation of profit-making,' writes Weber in what is perhaps the best summing-up of his whole essay, 'justified the activities of the business man.'[3] 'Rare indeed is the mind that is not repeatedly struck with this thought: whence comes our salvation but from God's election?' Calvin asks in a passage

---

[1] Cf. Rettberg, R. von, *Nürnbergs Kunstleben in seinen Denkmalen dargestellt*, Stuttgart 1854, pp. 83 and 84. Cf. also Kusch, E., *The Immortal Nuremberg*, Nuremberg 1959, p. 24.

[2] Hägglund, loc. cit., p. 222.

[3] *The Protestant Ethic*, as quoted, p. 163.

which Weber could have and should have quoted. 'Now, what revelation do you have of your election? This thought, if it has impressed itself upon him, either continually strikes him in his misery with harsh torments or utterly overwhelms him.' Yet there appears to be no help: God's will is an unfathomable abyss. 'Still,' Calvin adds, and here he opens the escape-hatch on which the Weberian theory is built, 'this does not prevent believers from feeling that the benefits they receive daily from God's hand are derived from [their] secret adoption ... since God wills to confirm to us by this, as by a token, as much as we may lawfully know of His plan.'[1] Wealth is such a token. Here was a grand message for the budding bourgeoisie, and they did not miss it. They received it eagerly. And so it was that what was to medieval folk merely a humdrum activity far inferior in interest to almost any other, became overnight a most interesting, meaningful and rewarding line of endeavour. It is as if an electric wire which, up to that time, had only carried low voltage currents, was all of a sudden made the conveyor of a truly powerful stream of energy.

By concentrating his whole analysis on one point, the *certitudo*, or rather *incertitudo, salutis*, the Calvinists' desperate search for outer hallmarks of sanctoral status, Weber gave to his now classical book a certain narrowness which has to be overcome.[2] In point of fact, Calvinism fostered capitalism in more ways than one. Weber knew this very well for in his closing remarks he indicated that his effort needed supplementation. 'The next task would be,' he writes, 'to show the significance of ascetic rationalism ... for the content of practical social ethics ... Then its relations to humanistic rationalism, its ideals of life and cultural influence; further to the development of philosophical and scientific empiricism, to technical development and to spiritual ideals would have to be analysed.'[3] Needless to say, this vast programme cannot be carried out within the covers of the present book. But where an exploration in breadth is quite impossible, one in depth may perhaps be confidently attempted.

Our confidence in this respect stems from the fact that the essence of Calvinism is neither a secret to anyone nor yet a matter of doubt and disagreement. It is, on the one hand, the insistence on the unspeakable power and majesty of God, and, on the other hand, on the nothingness and misery of man since he forfeited God's friendship in the fall. When the doors of Paradise were shut behind him, Adam with his whole progeny (who are all, only too obviously, exiles from Eden) lost (as the great Neo-Calvinist of the twentieth century, Karl Barth, an enemy to all 'natural theology', has so strongly insisted) the capacity of thinking

---

[1] *Institutes*, III, XXIV, 4; ed. cit., p. 969.
[2] Cf. our attempt to correct Weber's undue concentration on Calvinism and underestimation of the influence of sectarianism, in vol. II, pp. 276 et seq.
[3] Weber, loc. cit. pp. 182 and 183.

holy thoughts: they could not know the truths of religion, apart, of course, from such revelations as God might vouchsafe. 'Whatever, by ourselves, we think concerning [God] is foolish, and whatever we speak, absurd,' Calvin pronounces in his *Institutes*.[1] Man also lost the capacity of constructively exploring the realm of metaphysics, quite apart from its theological domain; he became a creature of the senses pure and simple, with an intellect capable of successful work within material – i.e. lower – creation, but no more. This had to be recognized by any realistic view of the human condition. There were certain things which God had put beyond our ken – which it was not only temerarious to pursue, but above all useless, as we can never hope to be successful in such a quest. There were, on the other hand, things which God had allowed to remain within our capacity – which it was not only permissible to pursue, but above all useful, as we can obviously be assured of progress in these fields. The fields concerned are agriculture and the mechanical arts and, more generally, all those areas which are, so to speak, beneath us, below our feet and before our eyes. Man could never become a great metaphysician; he *could* become a great scientist. Such speculations on the part of the Calvinist worthies are every bit as important for the understanding of the world-historical role of Calvinism as those to which Weber has drawn our attention. Capitalism is, after all, as Marx did not fail to emphasize in a purple passage of his *Communist Manifesto*,[2] as much a scientific and techno-logical as a profit-producing civilization. Calvinism spurred both developments: not only the drive for gain (because gain was a sign of salvation), but also the search for scientific insights (for going all out in quest of them was a falling in with God's design for our race, a fulfilment of the Godhead's most sacred plan on our behalf).

The Biblical passages which served as a foundation to this philosophy were Genesis I, 26–30, and IX, 1–3: the 'divine donation', as it has been called. God blessed those whom He had created male and female, and invited them to subdue the earth. They were to 'rule over the fishes of the sea and the fowls of the air and all living creatures that move upon the earth', as well as over every herb and tree. This gracious gift was not lost by the otherwise grace-destroying rebellion on the part of Eve and Adam. On the contrary, it was confirmed to Noe when he left the ark. As Noe's children we are, all of us, rightful owners of the lower creation (a fact on which John Locke was still to lay very strong emphasis);[3] exploring it and controlling it is a God-given task, not a greed-inspired madness. Thus the successful scientist, no less than the successful entrepreneur, is a man after God's own heart.

We have now made an important point and might leave the matter as

[1] I, XIII, 3; ed. cit., p. 124.
[2] Cf. ed. Taylor, A. J. P., Baltimore 1969, p. 85.
[3] Cf. Stark, W., *The Ideal Foundations of Economic Thought*, London 1943, p. 15.

it stands. We would, however, like to append a further suggestion which is a little more daring, but may not, for that reason, be any less true. The Calvinist believer, though in his consciousness convinced that he was nothing, was yet subconsciously striving to be something, and indeed to be much. How could he be something? How could he be much? By being a little like God. What was certainly unthinkable to him, was yet the matter of a subliminal wish: nothing is more understandable. But God was to this basically Old Testament theology above all the form-giver of matter. He found *tohu wabohu*, 'darkness upon the face of the deep', chaos: He made of it an ordered, law-obeying, systematic totality. It is not surprising that Calvin's less orthodox disciples, from John Milton to Max Weber, thought of the Almighty less as the Creator than as the Organizer of the Universe.[1] But man, too, could give form to raw materials and organize some area of the realm of matter: he, too, could be a demiurge in his own little way. And if he was so, if he achieved these ends, then he continued the chief divine activity on his own level, in however petty and humble a fashion. Then he was a little god himself. We have emphasized and we repeat it: no Calvinist believer would have dared, or would have dreamt, to say this, not even to think it. But the springs of human action lie deep in the soul's nether regions and its unavowed desires: they do not directly erupt into the light of consciousness, the door of entry being too securely guarded; yet they can and do work themselves out in the strivings of men, and not least in their economic and scientific endeavours which are never totally dominated by utilitarian considerations.

Yet another way in which the coming of Calvinism helped the functioning and the widening of the capitalist sector in the contemporary economy was the favourable influence it had on the fulfilment of contractual obligations. Perhaps the Quakers contributed most in this area,[2] but in any case Presbyterians and Congregationalists made their contribution, too. In opposition to the old feudal world, the young capitalist order, because of its greatly enhanced division of labour, depended vitally on the smoothness of buying and selling. Obligations had therefore to be carefully weighed and meticulously carried out. Medieval man had hardly been a precisionist in this respect. Even today, travellers to pre-capitalist areas have their tale to tell about the delays they had to experience and the generally nonchalant fashion in which they were treated by the tradesmen with whom they had to deal. The Calvinist-bred bourgeoisie was different. The fulfilment of contractual obligations, however petty in themselves, was a duty with definite religious undertones. This aspect of the 'spirit of capitalism' came from the sanctification of the concept of covenanting whose importance for the Calvinist movement we so fully discussed in the

[1] Cf. above, p. 196.
[2] Cf. our vol. II, p. 277.

section entitled 'The Self-Interpretation of Calvinism as a Covenant-Society'. In the Puritan's mouth, the three words *pacta sunt servanda* had a serious and solemn ring. We realize the world-historical importance of this detail when we remember Niccolò Machiavelli on the one hand and Hugo de Groot, or Grotius, on the other. Machiavelli, in the *Principe*, came close to saying *pacta non sunt servanda*; and if this is an unfair assertion, he certainly pressed the *rebus sic stantibus* subterfuge very far: contracts are to be carried out, if and in so far as the circumstances are still the same as at the time of contracting. Grotius, in *De Jure Belli et Pacis*, allowed no such escape route. A statesman must keep his word. So, said his fellow-Calvinists, must a tradesman or a merchant; and this greatly promoted the vitality of the society of tradesmen and merchants which was just then in the process of formation.

In what I have said so far, I have followed the Weberian model, i.e. I have put the culture-content of the two classical versions of Protestantism into the foreground and talked as if *it* were the *causa causans* of all the rest. I have done this, however, only for heuristic reasons for – if I may echo Weber once again – 'it is not my aim to substitute for a one-sided materialistic an equally one-sided spiritualistic causal interpretation of culture and of history'.[1] What we must therefore do now is to re-insert the doctrinal systems and psychological implications of both Luther and Calvin into the framework of contemporary life and see how they interfunctioned with it. The result is relatively simple. Both operated within a society whose compass was set in the direction of oncoming capitalism. But there were important differences so far as the developmental stages reached were concerned. Lutheranism was still the product of a largely pre-capitalist, not to say semi-medieval society. It lacked above all the makings of a broad-based entrepreneurial class. If there was to be economic progress in this world, it had to come from the political centre, the state. The Calvinist countries, on the other hand, though also as yet mainly or merely petty-bourgeois, had all that was needed for a more decisive entrepreneurial class to form and to assert itself. There could be economic progress in these parts, and it did not have to come from the prince. The market, free enterprise, could be its agent. The Germany of Luther was two hundred years or so behind the Geneva of Calvin and the Holland of his disciples. As for the British Isles, their case was rather more complicated. Scotland, especially, saddled with the pre-capitalist and still largely Catholic highlands, had a hard time following her continental co-religionists' lead. The union with England and her geographical position on the outermost rim of Europe also worked against her. In England, the civil war between Cavalier and Puritan was largely the conflict between rural-conservative and urban-progressive and proto-capitalist strata. The thrust towards modernity clearly came from the latter who, in the

[1] *The Protestant Ethic*, as quoted, p. 183.

'Glorious Revolution', created for themselves a state which they could use for their purposes. That William III was a Dutchman is significant and symbolic of the fact that here, too, it was Calvinism which pressed forward towards a properly capitalist dispensation, a market society.

Both the similarity and the dissimilarity between Lutheran and Calvinist attitudes and activities come to clear expression in the economic and technological literatures of the seventeenth and early eighteenth centuries. Historians of ideas have, without exception, distinguished between cameralism and mercantilism, and the labels which they are traditionally using are very informative. Cameralism reflects the convictions and the recommendations of those who were in and around the *camera*, or treasury, of a prince; mercantilism, on the other hand, enshrines the world-view and the programme of the merchants, those who were in or around a national market. There was considerable agreement on central issues. Both cameralism and mercantilism, for instance, recognized that a developing capitalist economy demanded, nay presupposed, a developed monetary system without which an adequate volume of market transactions could not be managed. Both therefore wished for, and pressed for, export surpluses, so that the trade partners would have to pay the balance in cash, thereby making a widened circulation of specie possible. But the cameralists wanted to see the stream of gold flow into the prince's coffers, the mercantilists wanted to see it enter into the national circulation. Cameralism was greatly concerned about the governmental budget and taken up with finance, especially the financing of a powerful army, while mercantilism, the much more modern, already fully capitalist variant, shed these preoccupations and concentrated on the level of production and consumption, i.e. on the purely economic aspects of life. Again, both desired an increased population, but whereas cameralists were thinking in the first place of more soldiers, mercantilists were thinking above all of more proletarians, more 'hands'.

What interests the sociologist of religion in these matters is the fact, meticulously proved by Müller-Armack in his great work,[1] *Religion und Wirtschaft*, that Lutheran lands produced the cameralist, while Calvinist areas produced the mercantilist literature. We do not have to reproduce here the lists of names which Müller-Armack adduces, but it is significant that thirteen of the most important cameralists were the sons of Lutheran clergymen: J. J. Becher, Becmann, Boxhorn, Büsch, Conring, Darjes, Hertius, Kosegarten, Pufendorf, Rau, Sartorius, von Schlözer, and Zincke.[2] Müller-Armack described the whole phenomenon of cameralism as a product of the spiritual condition (*Seelenlage*) of Lutheranism, and judges that, owing to the development of established

[1] Cf. esp. pp. 177, 183, 190.
[2] Cf. ibid., p. 191.

Churches, all thinking became imprisoned in a politico-administrative cage. In sharp contrast to later German speculation, when it was carried on by the private citizen, this early economic science was indeed almost exclusively pragmatic. Written mainly by officials, in whose number the academic teachers of the day have also to be included, it was concerned with day-to-day problems. There is even descent to questions such as where water pails should be placed in public buildings so as to be quickly available in case of fire. Of true theory, there is very little. A definite after-effect of this beginning in Lutheranism is the historical and discursively descriptive bent of the social sciences in Germany, negatively expressed, their longtime coolness to exact investigations. Even Achenwall's so-called 'statistics' was in fact a comparative study of state forms.[1]

While the Lutheran-cameralist literature thus sprang from the minds and pens of officials, the Calvinist-mercantilist output was fathered by free merchants and dissenting ministers. They see the state not from the inside, as a bureaucratic apparatus which they have to help make efficient, but from the outside. Their point of view is that of the sharp observer and testing critic. Not that theirs was an 'objective point of view'. They, too, were advocates, but what they defended was the interest of the citizen, not that of the ruler. Daniel Defoe was one of them, and his Robinson Crusoe showed what a man can do, a free man without a government to boss him. Adam Smith still reflects their philosophy.[2] Even in Germany, the universities which were more deeply influenced by Calvinism, such as Heidelberg, show a different tendency from their orthodoxly Lutheran neighbours.[3] 'In the Calvinist territories,' writes Müller-Armack, 'the State was not the all-inclusive interest . . . Foreign trade, the enhancement and measurement of civic welfare, questions of money and credit and problems of banking and insurance moved into the foreground.'[4] But what also moved into the foreground was, most significantly, the mathematical method.[5] English, and later Anglo-American, Calvinism was leading on this front, with consequences which are still with us.[6] Sir William Petty, with his Political Arithmetic of 1690, is archetypal. His programme was to investigate social reality with the help of the categories of 'number, weight and measure'.[7]

We are thus seeing again what we have seen repeatedly before, and what Max Weber has so strongly emphasized, that it was not the Reformation as such, but rather Calvinism which overcame the pre-capitalist condition of the economy and ushered in the modern age.

[1] Ibid., pp. 195, 196, 227, 228.   [2] Ibid., pp. 179, 180, 186.   [3] Ibid., p. 179.
[4] Ibid., p. 191.   [5] Ibid., p. 197.
[6] Cf. Stark, W., 'The Protestant Ethic and the Spirit of Sociology', Social Compass, 1966, pp. 373 et seq.
[7] Müller-Armack, pp. 227 and 228.

But it is easy here to miss an important point. Granted that capitalist society needs above all entrepreneurs, a fact so obvious that it is almost unjustifiable to put it down in black and white, it also needs an appropriate bureaucracy, and that is by no means equally manifest. Without judges who will see to it that the necessary legal frame of market transactions is provided and maintained, without officials who will so administrate the State that industry can do its business unharassed and unhampered, without educators who will deliver the right kind of workman and clerk and even manager, a modern economy simply could not function. The existence of such services is by no means a matter of course. The kadi with his unpredictable decisions, the vezir with his drive for personal enrichment, the imam who hands on a dead lore and nothing else, were not confined to the Ottoman Empire. They had their parallels in the West as well. It was Lutheranism which created that admirable, if also confined, class of devoted men – the German *Beamte*. It was Prussia which first developed, and led to considerable heights, the institution and the institutions of a reliable bureaucracy, and Prussia (though her rulers were Calvinist)[1] was a Lutheran country.

There is something for the sociologist of religion to explain here, but he will not find it difficult to explain it. The explanation can run parallel to Max Weber's celebrated analysis. What he says (to use once more our own simile) is that Calvinism, by ascribing to enrichment a metaphysical and religious significance, shot stronger currents of energy into one particular channel, that of commercial enterprise. What we have to add here amounts to the suggestion that Lutheranism, by ascribing to the state a metaphysical and religious significance, by clothing it, as Müller-Armack says, with the 'dignity of the absolute',[2] shot stronger currents of energy into another, if partly connected channel, that of bureaucratic service. It is one thing to serve a secular ruler; it is another thing to serve a sacred or near-sacred king. That tremendous devotion to duty which is the classical attribute of the Prussian official, above all that incorruptibility in the face of bribery and other temptations which was for centuries its finest hallmark, would have been impossible, not only without the Reformation, but more especially without that specific form of it which we call Lutheranism.

At this juncture, it is highly advisable, not to say downright necessary, to throw a side-glance at the case of England for the Anglican and

[1] We cannot fully discuss here why Johann Sigismund converted in 1613 to the Reformed Creed, but his step seems to have had something to do with his desire to take his state out of its isolation in the East and to gain for it association with the West, especially with Holland.

[2] *Religion und Wirtschaft*, as quoted, p. 121. Cf. also pp. 37, 41, 122, 125. On the intellectual bases of the Lutheran attitude to officialdom, cf. Hägglund, op. cit., pp. 235 and 236.

Lutheran Reformations lie parallel so far as the fact which interests us here is concerned: both ended in the investment of the secular ruler with a sacred role. Yet the case of England turns out, on closer inspection, to be something of a negative instance (and this makes its discussion all the more desirable or necessary).

In an important book, *The Tudor Revolution in Government*,[1] G. R. Elton has shown that the age of Henry VIII was one of great transformations in administration: the very title of the volume indicates this fact. There was modernization. What is modernization in this particular area? 'Where we find administration in and through the [royal] household, there we have medieval government; where there are plentiful signs of emancipation from the household, however mingled they may be with survivals from the past, we must justly suspect the beginnings of a new attitude to government which for want of a better word we call modern.' Cardinal Wolsey was, in this sense, the last medieval administrator; his successor, Thomas Cromwell, was, by the same token, the first modern one. But Cromwell was an enemy of Rome: the breakaway of England from the papacy was to a considerable extent his work. Thus there seems to be a close connection between religious reformation and bureaucratic reconstruction, and this impression is apt to be strengthened when we learn that the Court of Augmentations, introduced in 1536 to deal with the take-over of monastic lands, was one of the first truly modern governmental agencies in the realm. 'This setting up of a court for monastic lands,' Elton writes, 'announced that from now on "household" government in the finances was to be at an end, and that a national bureaucracy would take over.'[2]

But this last phrase – 'a national bureaucracy' – must not be taken *au pied de la lettre*, as Dr. Elton himself amply explains. The sociologist, especially the sociological theorist, even more than the historian, will have to insist that such modernization as was achieved under the Tudor monarchs did not really overcome the feudal pattern of public administration. In the very heart of his book, where 'the new civil service' is illustrated, Elton speaks of '*one* fundamental change', and that was 'the change from a bureaucracy trained in the Church or the king's household to a bureaucracy trained in a minister's household and then employed in the service of the State. As a rule,' he adds, and this is all-important for our analysis, 'these new civil servants obtained preferment under the crown, but they depended on the favour of the great ministers of State, that is, in the main, on the secretaries. The system is known as the clientage system.'[3] The very name is characteristic: clientage is a feudal term. The king's right-hand man, for instance,

---

[1] Cambridge 1962.
[2] Ibid., pp. 19, 20, 42, 37, 40, 211, 212.
[3] Ibid., p. 308. Our emphasis.

Thomas Cromwell, was the *patronus*: *his* right-hand men, a John Gostwick or a Richard Riche, were his *manni*. No wonder that Elton, in summing up, while reiterating that 'a revolution took place in government', has immediately thereafter to refer to 'survivals of the medieval system' which were 'allowed to continue ... for some three hundred years'.[1]

The clientage system did indeed survive. Other experts bear Geoffrey Elton out, for instance David Mathew and Gerald Aylmer. Mathew, speaking of the seventeenth century, indeed emphasizes that both patron and client served the state, but, referring to the higher ranks of the bureaucratic class in general he says that 'in the formation of this official grouping we can [still] trace both the cool thought and the lucid calculating practice of Thomas Cromwell. Not only was he the father of modern bureaucracy, but he also gave a clear expression to the patron-client relationship', and this 'involved an intermediate loyalty' such as the late medieval nexus under which 'a soldier conceived himself as a sworn man to another of the queen's subjects'.[2] Aylmer, in a wider survey, has shown that this system (which, he says, lasted to the age of the younger Pitt) was in contrast both to the absolutist conceptions of the more energetic kings and to the liberal convictions of the more determined reformers. This, surely, amounts once again to saying that it was a semi-feudalism. 'It was the successive victories of oligarchy ... in 1660, 1688–89, and in 1714, and later the wars against France and the reaction against the French Revolution (1793–1815), which shored the system up and then enabled it to survive – even if uneasily – into the nineteenth century.'[3]

In the quotation which we have given from David Mathew, there was only talk of the higher, i.e. central, bureaucracy. To complete the picture, we must also show what his judgment is of the local conditions. 'By the early years of the seventeenth century,' he writes, 'the county officials throughout England and Wales provided the fulcrum for administrative action. It is true that these appointments depended sometimes upon London, but more often upon a knot of gentry wielding local influence. It was, of course, the strength of the squires that they parcelled out among their own number both the administrative and judicial posts ... In the counties, therefore, the official world ... was composed of the members of that body of the squires which itself was the expression, in terms of rural life, of ... the great Whig oligarchy.'[4] This amounts to saying that the circumstances at the bottom

[1] Ibid., p. 424. On Cromwell's (still semi-feudal) relation to Henry VIII, cf. pp. 81 and 82; on Cromwell's relation to John Gostwick, pp. 157, 192, 193, 198, 199; to Richard Riche, p. 213; cf. also pp. 113, 149, 115, 388, 422.
[2] Mathew, D., *The Social Structure in Caroline England*, Oxford 1948, pp. 4 and 2.
[3] Aylmer, G. E., *The King's Servants: The Civil Service of Charles I*, London 1961, esp. chapter VII, I, pp. 429, 430, 433, 436, 438.
[4] Mathew, loc. cit., p. 3. Cf. also p. 1.

of the bureaucratic system were roughly identical with those at the top. Neither up above nor down below was there that concentration of loyalty upon king and crown which, starting from a religious conception and definition of the ruler, would allow a quasi-religious fervour to permeate all the ranks of the service. Hence Anglicanism and Lutheranism, though otherwise parallel, did not have the same influence on officialdom. The deep admiration of the philosopher Hegel for the *Beamte* of his adopted homeland of Prussia, whom he saw in a supernal light,[1] is nowhere to be encountered on English soil. Ideas on this subject could not be similar, because reality was not similar either.

In the end, however, even the English civil service was made over and – though liberal influences, stemming in the final analysis from the country's Calvinist past and Calvinist descended strata, saw to it that the bureaucracy remained small and poor in power – conditions more comparable to those in other caesaropapist systems arose. It is a fair guess – though, in the absence of hard and fast proof, we would not dare to go further – that the new civil servants, those, for instance, of Queen Victoria, would be proud of their connection with a throne which was not only powerful and prestigious, but also surrounded by a semi-religious aura, and that their loyalty and their performance would increase along with this sentiment so as to become second to none.

After this short sideglance at England, we can again take up the thread of our analysis from the point where we left it on page 322.

One area within which the contrast between the Lutheran and Calvinist cultures and their diverse effects on the economy lies open for all to see, is the area of colonization. Only those could colonize who were strong, independent and aggressive personalities capable of standing alone, if need be even for long stretches of time. Calvinism bred such men; Lutheranism did not. The Lutheran was essentially the state's or the king's subject, always relying on guidance from above, always anxious not to be alone; he was ill fitted for pioneering in a far-off land. He wanted to be at home; he wanted to stay at home; and stay at home he did. 'This lack of initiative in the broad masses of the population,' writes Müller-Armack,[2] 'set obvious limits to the outward expansion of the State. The failure of the colonial policy of Brandenburg makes it clear that a centrally directed political society could achieve little in the field of colonial expansion. All newer colonization was effected, not according to a fixed governmental decree, but by forces which asserted themselves spontaneously and which the administration followed only later on . . . The colonizing power of Holland and especially England lay above all in the front of free energies which began the enterprise . . . It was not the will of the administrative centres, but the religious

---

[1] Cf. Pierre Hassner, in *History of Political Philosophy*, edd. Strauss, L., and Cropsey, J., Chicago 1963, pp. 644 and 645.
[2] Müller-Armack, loc. cit., p. 165.

formation that was given to each one of the pioneers in the mother country, which, in Holland and England, retroactively bestowed unity on the effort. All that was missing in Prussia. It was not to be replaced by any initiative on the part of the State. The fact that all forces were tied up in the interior prevented their activity beyond the frontiers of the State's territory.'

Even this quotation, clear and strong as it is, does not, however, tell the whole story. As Müller-Armack enters into the historical detail, he is again and again induced to return to the same point and to reformulate it in new and more concrete terms.[1] We cannot follow him into all the byways and corners which he explores, but one fact which he brings up deserves to be emphasized in a book like the present: even in Prussia, at the time of the most determined effort under the Great Elector, the driving spirits were foreigners, Dutchmen: Gysels van Lier and Benjamin Raule. On the other hand, Prussia's own 'merchants, entrepreneurs, ship-owners and bankers are missing in the enterprise, and so are pure adventurers'.[2] Even they could thrive only in a Calvinistic – i.e. activity-stimulating – setting. There was no Prussian Drake, no Prussian Raleigh. There could not be. The local culture was against it.

The absence of colonial entrepreneurs in the widest sense of the word was, of course, only a reflection of the weakness of entrepreneurship in general. To pick out another revealing point of detail: banking. Both Prussia and England needed banks in order to advance, but the need was supplied differently: in Prussia by governmental, in England by private initiative. The *Königlich Preussische Bank* founded in 1765 shows its origin even in its name; the *Seehandlung* of 1772 does not, but its proper name was really *Preussische Staatsbank*. It was founded by Frederick II and was concerned, not only with the maritime trade, but also with the financial operations, of the government. How great is the contrast to England and Holland! Not only did they have much older banking institutions, but these were products and possessions of a class of city-men who would need little help from father state and brook no interference on his part in their concerns.[3] Speaking not of colonial and banking enterprise, but of the economy as a whole, Müller-Armack sums up the results of his research by saying: 'While in England and Holland the positive tasks of the age were fulfilled in the forms of private endeavour, Germany instinctively turned to State enterprise . . . It was the period when a cameralist judged that undertakings connected with risk were nothing for the merchants and should be founded by officials . . . The same inclination to decided governmental leadership is noticeable also in the Lutheran countries of Scandinavia.' On the other

[1] Cf. ibid., pp. 145, 165, 261, 262, 269, 272, 276, 277, 280, 312, 321, 323–5; cf. also pp. 259, 260, 265.
[2] Ibid., pp. 270 and 262.
[3] Ibid., p. 164. Cf. also p. 168.

hand, 'there was hardly an important industry that arose in Germany which was not characterized by the presence of a major proportion of members of the Reformed churches and sects among its founders. This fact is proved especially for Western Germany by a multitude of entrepreneurial biographies . . . The Calvinists became in Germany, just as in Holland and England, the agents of the first private developments in the economic sphere. Certainly, Lutherans, too, had a share in the founding of new firms which was not negligible. But they are on the whole partisans of Pietism which was in the final analysis an import from the European West, or Diaspora Lutherans who lived in the vicinity of Calvinism. In the Lutheran heart-land, the predominance of State enterprise swallowed up the tendency towards free entrepreneurial activity . . . In contrast, Calvinism, which represented an ascetic attitude and saw the religious centre not in the crown, but in a Church constitution created by the people, was an educator towards personal initiative.'[1] Calvinist Kassel had the first private bank in Germany – an eloquent fact!

But we must move on to a new point. Both variants of classical Protestantism, Lutheranism and Calvinism, contributed, though in a very different manner and measure, to the formation of capitalist society while they were in the ascendant – but what about their decline? At the end of the seventeenth century, the first impetus of these great religious movements had exhausted itself and their grip on life relaxed. They were succeeded by other intellectual fashions, but, characteristically, sharply contrasting ones. Lutheranism spawned, and was succeeded in influence by, men and ideas that were largely alien to ongoing reality: by German idealistic philosophy and by German classical literature, by Goethe and Kant and their likes. There was nothing here that was 'practical': neither Goethe's idealizations nor Kant's speculations could impart direction to the stream of history, of human endeavour. In the West, on the other hand, Calvinism gave way to thoroughly 'practical' attitudes, and these were the fruits of Calvinism itself as well as counterblasts to it. We need only think of one figure in order to recognize how true this is: Joseph Priestley. His Unitarianism was a form of religiosity into which Calvinism (as we have explained on p. 308) all too easily decayed. But he was not only a dissenting minister: he was also a scientific discoverer. What he discovered was above all the element oxygen (for his 'dephlogisticated air' is just that) – no mean contribution to the advance of chemistry. Other cases were not so dramatic, but they followed the same pattern. There was thus brought out, on a fairly broad front, one of the possible implications of the Calvinist creed, a turning of interest from metaphysical and religious to scientific and technological preoccupations. And so the impetus born of the Genevan inspiration towards modern, nineteenth-century capitalism

[1] Ibid., pp. 126 and 156. Cf. also important passages on pp. 122, 124, 127, 128 and 153

was not arrested, as that of Wittenberg was, when faith began to wane and soberness began to wax strong.[1]

If there was any break in the history of Calvinism, any critical transition to a sober, scientific world-view, it occurred already in Calvin's own mind. At first, it is true, and in his more violent moments, Calvin regarded nature with the same dismay as he did man. Both were fallen. 'We know that every creature groaneth and travaileth in pain, even till now' – these words of St. Paul (Romans VIII, 22) were ever before his eyes. Quoting them in his *Institutes*, he adds that Adam 'perverted the whole order of nature in heaven and on earth'.[2] But this is a conviction which links him to the past. The Jews of old had been inclined to think in this way, and such a mode of thinking is thoroughly natural in all societies where integrational thinking prevails. If one is corrupted, all are corrupted; if all are corrupted, everything – including every thing – is corrupted, for one and all, and all and their appurtenances, are but one integrated, co-fated totality. A Calvin who looked, not backward, but ahead, could hardly philosophize in this way. If he was inclined to believe that everybody damned only himself, then he had *a fortiori* to assume that nature could remain unscathed by the sin of man. Man is, after all, a separated substance. The more Calvin and Calvinism weaned themselves from inherited philosophical realism, the more fully they drew the consequences from the modern philosophical nominalism which they had embraced, the more they had to consider that the creature who groaneth and travaileth was *only* man, the one failure in God's fine creation; the more they had to assume that nature was and had remained God's handiwork; and the more attractive had physical reality to appear as a possible field of study. 'They were quite content with their universe, even though it had been the scene of man's fall,' writes Perry Miller of the seventeenth-century Calvinists of America, in whom the tendency of which we are speaking came to full fruition. 'They believed that God had created it by perfect wisdom, and that it was just such a universe as men should live in.'[3] Anybody who could feel like that, would have, to say the least, no disinclination to become a man of science.

But we are understating the case. So loosely does the idea that everything is interconnected with everything else sit on Jehan Calvin that he sometimes holds up nature as a field – perhaps even as *the* field – in which we can find God, as if he did not on other occasions assure us that it, too, was corrupted. 'He . . . revealed Himself and daily discloses Himself in the whole workmanship of the universe,' Calvin writes. 'Indeed, His essence is incomprehensible . . . But upon His individual works He has engraved unmistakable marks of His glory . . . The reason

---

[1] Cf. Müller-Armack, loc. cit., pp. 114–17, for similar considerations.
[2] II, I, 5; op. cit., p. 246.
[3] Miller, loc. cit., p. 366.

why the author of The Letter to the Hebrews elegantly calls the universe the appearance of things invisible is that this skilful ordering of the universe is for us a sort of mirror in which we can contemplate God, who is otherwise invisible.'[1] We can best appreciate what this meant for the livening up of nature studies when we remember Calvin's basic and never abandoned hostility to fallen man. In the depths of fallen man's self nothing of God could ever be discovered, apart from the naked knowledge that He existed, the knowledge which God Himself had left there simply to convict man of sin; nothing could be discovered there than what is opposite to God – darkness and death. But out in the open spaces, under His own sky, in the movement of the stars, in the sprouting of the fields, in the wilderness, there God's imprint, if not indeed God himself, could be discerned, a blessing to the pious soul.

Where Calvin develops these ideas, so important for the direction which his teaching imparted to the attitudes and to the activities of his followers, he is particularly clear. Taking a leaf out of the otherwise despised schoolmen, he begins with a neat distinction: 'There is one kind of understanding of earthly things; another of heavenly. I call "earthly things" those which do not pertain to God or His Kingdom, to true justice or to the blessedness of the future life, but which have their significance and relationship with regard to the present life and are, in a sense, confined within its bounds. I call "heavenly things" the pure knowledge of God, the nature of true righteousness and the mysteries of the Heavenly Kingdom.'[2] The importance of this dichotomy rests on the fact that in the former area man may be, and is, successful; in the latter, he is not and cannot be.[3]

So far as the knowledge of heavenly matters is concerned, 'spiritual insight consists chiefly in three things: 1. knowing God; 2. knowing His fatherly favour in our behalf, in which our salvation consists; 3. knowing how to frame our life according to the rule of His law. In the first two points – and especially in the second – the greatest geniuses are blinder than moles . . . Human reason, therefore, neither approaches, nor strives toward, nor even takes a straight aim at, this truth: to understand who the true God is or what sort of God He wishes to be toward us.'[4] It is only in the area of ethical conduct (of the third point) that we are better off, for we have the Decalogue, YHWH's binding commandments, to keep us straight.

Theological searching is therefore – excepting always the revealed Word – a totally unpromising, nay impossible, enterprise – a sheer waste of time. The power of human understanding is nil with regard to it.

[1] *Institutes*, I, V, 1; ed. cit., pp. 52 and 53. The reference in the Epistle to the Hebrews is xi, 3.

[2] *Institutes*, II, II, 13; ed. cit., p. 272.

[3] Concerning somewhat similar ideas in Luther, cf. Maritain, as quoted, pp. 32–4. and the references given there.

[4] II, II, 18; pp. 277 and 278.

'Yet its efforts do not always become so worthless as to have no effect, especially when it turns its attention to things below.' They include above all the liberal arts and the mechanical skills. Here man scores: 'Human acuteness . . . appears in learning these . . .'. Indeed, 'there are at hand energy and ability, not only to learn, but also to devise something new in each art or to perfect and polish what one has learned from a predecessor'. Calvin has at this point an argument at his disposal which must have carried great weight with his contemporaries, still steeped in the humanistic admiration of antiquity. God gave *all* men the capacity for scientific and technological work, even to those who are not 'within the covenant'. The heathens, for instance the Greeks, knew their way about in these fields: they were first-class mathematicians and medical men. 'Those . . . whom Scripture calls "natural men" were, indeed, sharp and penetrating in their investigation of inferior things. Let us, accordingly, learn by their example, how many gifts the Lord left to human nature after it was [by the fall] despoiled of its true good.'[1]

If Calvin had said no more than this, he would already have done a great deal to direct men into the lines of endeavour which we know as specifically modern. But he did a good deal more. We are not only invited into these pathways of investigation, we are commanded to enter into them. 'If the Lord has willed that we be helped in physics, dialectic, mathematics, and other like disciplines, by the work and ministry of the ungodly, let us use this assistance. For if we neglect God's gift freely offered in these arts, we ought to suffer just punishment for our sloths'[2]. These words are in many ways characteristic of Calvin's mentality. There is the emphasis on penalty rather than encouragement; there is the insistence that what we do must be done in fulfilment of divine behests and not in gratification of human preferences; there is above all the injunction to be up and doing, to be active and effective; and there is finally the counsel that we should choose nature for the employment of our energies. For although he brackets political and household management with the mechanical skills and liberal arts as legitimate areas of exploration and cultivation,[3] the emphasis falls heavily on the latter two. The following words give us, in a nutshell, Calvin's whole message on the matter which we have just considered. 'The most perfect way of seeking God, and the most suitable order, is not for us to attempt with bold curiosity to penetrate to the investigation of His essence which we ought more to adore than meticulously to search out, but for us to contemplate Him in His works whereby He

[1] II, II, 13–15; pp. 271–5. The Scripture passage alluded to is I Corinthians II, 14. The Douai version reads: 'sensual man'.
[2] II, II, 16; p. 275.
[3] II, II, 13; p. 272. On all that has gone before, cf. also the passages quoted in Torrence, T. F., *Calvin's Doctrine of Man*, London 1949, p. 150; further pp. 37, 38, 40, 155, 164, 169, 170, 172.

renders Himself near and familiar to us and in some manner communicates Himself.'[1] If some have summed up the result of Weber's analysis by saying that, as he has shown, the Calvinist tried to serve God in the counting-house, we may now add, with equal assurance, that he also tried to serve God in the laboratory, behind retort and microscope.

We have so far spoken of science and technology together and that was justified because they are like the two arms of one creature, organically connected with each other. But the right arm may be stronger than the left, and Calvinism did strengthen the technological drift even more decidedly than the scientific, a fact not without its influence on the unfolding of the capitalist system which is, after all, in the first place a system of production. Technology – *applied* science in the widest sense of the word – received its impetus from Calvin's doctrine that God had created the universe not only for His own glory, but also for the service of man. 'God has destined all things for our good,' he writes. 'God himself has shown by the order of creation that He created all things for man's sake . . . We ought in the very order of things diligently to contemplate God's fatherly love toward mankind in that He did not create Adam until He had lavished upon the universe all manner of good things. For if He had put him in an earth as yet sterile and empty, if He had given him life before light, He would have seemed to provide insufficiently for his welfare. Now when He disposed the movements of the sun and stars to human uses, filled the earth, waters, and air with living things and brought forth an abundance of fruits to suffice as foods . . . He shows His wonderful goodness toward us . . . From Moses we hear that, through His liberality, all things on earth are subject to us.'[2] In Moses' own day, however, they were subject to us *in posse* rather than *in esse*. God made man the destined rather than the actual controller of lower creation; we are a race called to the high office of explorer and exploiter of the universe and – this is the clear implication – we must accept that call. In this respect, as in all others, we must carry out what God has commanded. And so a man or a nation or a humanity which considers the world as a mechanism to be manipulated and constructs machines to manipulate it is, according to Calvin's convictions, engaged in a godly task. This teaching has legitimated and thereby supported, if it has not indeed evoked, innumerable feats of technology, and even the astronauts' journeyings to the moon still owe something, on the intellectual side, to the Calvinic inspiration.

Thus this 'Protestant ethic' did much for the 'spirit of capitalism',

[1] I, V, 9; p. 62.
[2] I, XIV, 22, and I, XIV, 2; pp. 181, 182, and 163, 164. The Bible reference at the end is to Genesis I, 28, and IX, 2. Cf. also the passages given in Torrence, loc. cit., pp. 23, 24, 48, 147.

not only on its economic, but also on its technical side. It was a spirit afloat which came to Calvin from others and went to others from him. Its disciples were legion. We cannot even hope to enumerate, far less discuss them. Yet there is one man who is so much of a link between the first formulation of the new creed and its after-effects in intellectual and practical life that we must give him a passing glance: Pierre de la Ramée, or, to call him by the name by which he wished to be called, Petrus or Peter Ramus, a leading Huguenot who met his sad end in the Bartholomew massacres. It is curious that Max Weber does not even mention him, for there is no historical figure who better illustrates Weber's contention that there was a correlation and connection between the Reformed Religion on the one side and a reality reforming itself so as to become a capitalist dispensation on the other. Nor was his appearance an isolated phenomenon. His mentality is akin to Jeremy Bentham's Utilitarianism as well as to the Logical Positivism of the twentieth century, and thus forms a link, the first link, in a chain of philosophies or semi-philosophies which have accompanied mankind through the modern age and are expressions of its deeper drifts, or rather of its deeper onesidedness.

The influence of Ramus on the Calvinist, proto-capitalist world was massive. 'One of the persistent puzzles concerning Peter Ramus and his followers is the extraordinary diffusion of their works during the sixteenth and seventeenth centuries,' writes Walter J. Ong, whose elaborate *Ramus and Talon Inventory*[1] has laid solid scholarly foundations for the study of that diffusion. 'These works run to nearly 800 known and identified editions represented by extant copies, or, if one numbers separately works published together, to some 1,100 editions.' If this is astounding, as indeed it is, it is even more astounding to hear that this figure is sure to be an understatement rather than an overestimate. The final tally may come to 230 more, or even go above that count.[2] 'The general pathway of this diffusion ... proceeds chiefly through bourgeois Protestant groups of merchants and artisans more or less tinged with Calvinism. These groups are found not only in Ramus' native France, but especially in Germany, Switzerland, the Low Countries, England, Scotland, Scandinavia and New England.'[3] Perry Miller's *The New England Mind* is almost exclusively a study in Ramism. We see, then, that in Ramus we are confronted with a master of the Calvinist *oikumene*.

What was it that this great teacher of many disciples had to offer? Essentially, we should say, a new model. The ideal of earlier generations had been the Socrates of Plato, a sage who wanted to turn the

---

[1] Cambridge, Mass., 1958. Omer Talon was Ramée's *alter ego*, or rather his second pen, and may be regarded as one hand with him. He predeceased Ramée.
[2] Ong, W. J., 'Ramist Method and the Commercial Mind', *Studies in the Renaissance*, 1961, pp. 155 and 156.
[3] Ibid., p. 155.

mind of man towards divine verities and eternal truths. Ramus endeavoured to put into his place the Socrates of Xenophon, a far more sober philosopher, who condemned all theoretic studies and recommended in their stead the pursuit of concrete, usable knowledge.[1] The Socrates of Ramus was a utilitarian; indeed, one might almost go so far as to say that he was a banausic Socrates. The word is hard, but we are using it advisedly in order to show that in Ramism we are encountering a thoroughly modern mentality.

While Ramus rejected metaphysics, he vigorously developed what he regarded as its counterpart and due replacement, namely logic. He was above all an instructor in method. Men should learn to do things the right way. They should, for instance, learn how to marshal and arrange their ideas so as to be clear, to convince and to compel. The Ramean rhetoric had no aesthetic aim; it was much rather forensic in the wider sense of the word, a weapon in the war of ideas. Harvard graduates, for instance, were drilled with the aid of the Ramean manual. What was suggested to them was a particular, on the whole rather simple technique: to proceed from the more general to the less general, from the general to the specific. The general was presumed to be known and accepted already. By advancing from it, i.e. from its relative certainties, towards the concrete, i.e. the relatively unknown and problematic, it was hoped to carry the interlocutor along, indeed, to force him towards the position which one wanted him to occupy, towards the ideas which one wanted him to embrace.

This recommended mode of argumentation was, as is obvious, essentially deductive. Some students of Ramus have therefore considered him as a pre-, if not, indeed, as an anti-scientific thinker, for the natural sciences, as they were just then taking shape under the influence of Francis Bacon, were predominantly and almost exclusively inductive. From fact to proposition, was their device, from concrete description to abstract generalization. It was especially Charles Waddington, whose book Ramus: sa vie, ses écrits et ses opinions (Paris 1855) was for a long time the most authoritative study of the great Huguenot, who pinned the label 'enemy of the inductive method' to Ramée's lapel.[2] But this is thoroughly misleading. A thinker of Ramée's stature must, surely, be given a little credit for sophistication; he must be expected to have, not one method to be mechanically applied all along the line, but several, each adjusted to a different purpose. And this is what we in fact find. Debate, he knew, was one thing, research quite another. Some two hundred years later, Jeremy Bentham expressed himself on this topic as follows: 'Principles, it is said, ought to precede consequences; and the first being established, the others will follow of course. What are the principles here meant?

[1] Cf. Hooykaas, R., Humanisme, Science et Réforme: Pierre de la Ramée, Leyden 1958, pp. 59 et seq.
[2] Cf. ibid., esp. p. 52.

General propositions, and those of the widest extent. What by consequences? Particular propositions, included under those general ones.
That this order is favourable to demonstration, if by demonstration be
meant personal debate and argumentation, is true enough. Why? Because, if you can get a man to admit the general proposition, he cannot,
without incurring the reproach of inconsistency, reject a particular
proposition that is included in it. But that this order is not the order of
conception, of investigation, of invention, is equally undeniable. In this
order, particular propositions always precede general ones. The assent
to the latter is preceded by and grounded on the assent to the former.
If we prove the consequences from the principle, it is only from the
consequences that we learn the principle.'[1] This was precisely Ramée's
conviction. He could not have expressed it more clearly than his distant comrade-in-arms.

In the end, therefore, Ramus came down, so far as research strategy,
the quest for *new* knowledge, was concerned, on the side of induction,
just like Francis Bacon did in his day. Anticipating, on his first page,
the final conclusions of his study, Hooykaas writes in the book which
we have quoted that 'the natural evolution of the humanist conception
of the essential unity of rhetoric and logic towards the utilitarianism
and empiricism of Ramus ends by leading to the utilitarianism and
empiricism of Bacon which have had so great an influence on science
and its integration into modern culture.' And in another context he
says, more simply and more straightforwardly: 'It is evident that Ramus
shows a clear tendency towards induction and empiricism.'[2] Perhaps we
must not see Ramée and Bacon side by side; comparatively speaking, the
former is merely a distant relation of the latter; but even that is something; even that is much.

If we had the leisure, we could prove the correctness of this interpretation of Peter Ramus by a good deal of detail; we could, for instance,
show how he turns away from Aristotle's bookish physics, as contained
in his *Physicorum Libri Octo*, towards his more descriptive *opuscula*,
those on meteors and natural history which, he knew, would yield
more experiential and experimental knowledge than the major work;[3]
but we have to pass all that by, because we have yet a major point to
make. Ramus was like Bacon in that both were empiricists and utili-
tarians. But there remained a difference between them which Hooykaas has expressed by saying that 'whereas Bacon calls for the inductive study of nature, Ramus does not, in the final analysis, aim at the
discovery of nature, but at the restauration of the arts'.[4] We can formulate the same idea by saying that Bacon was interested in knowledge

---

[1] *Jeremy Bentham's Economic Writings*, ed. Stark, W., vol. I, London 1952, pp. 97 and 98.
[2] Hooykaas, loc. cit., pp. 1 and 53.
[3] Cf. ibid., pp. 33, 34, 41, 54.
[4] Ibid., pp. 100 and 101.

rather than in knowhow, Ramus in knowhow rather than in knowledge. This, however, was not a purely or mainly intellectual difference: it had important sociological implications. Bacon dreamt of living in a *république des professeurs*; Ramée was thinking rather of a society of artisans. His aim was – in spite of the fact that he was a proper academic – above all the enlivening of production. 'There is no mathematician in Paris whose friendship I have not cultivated,' he asserted on one occasion, but significantly added, 'there is no *artisan mécanicien* whose workshop I have not searched out and examined.'[1] Thus he sought contact with the middle classes, and the middle classes repaid his interest in kind: they sought contact with him and even more with his ideas which appear to have suited them very well.

'Ramus' works,' Ong tells us, and the fact is essential in our context, 'enjoyed particular favour not in highly sophisticated intellectual circles but rather in elementary and secondary schools or along the fringe where secondary schooling and university education meet.' Ramism was a rising philosophy plainly destined to meet and to marry a rising societal class, the bourgeoisie: we have before us a case which illustrates Max Weber's conception of an 'elective affinity' between real substructure and intellectual superstructure, men and ideas.[2] 'I should like to suggest,' writes Ong, and his suggestion is certain to be welcomed by sociologists, 'that one of the major features of Ramism is its tendency to reduce knowledge to something congenial to the artists' and burghers' commercial views ... The affinity between Ramist method ... and the practical down-to-earth outlook of burghers and artisans exists not as an explicit, declared relationship but rather in terms of a state of mind. Ramist method presented a view of the intellectual world congenial to the dealer in physical wares. The merchant and artisan were concerned with commodities, with things visible, definite, and things moreover demanding itemization and inventory . . . Ramist method appealed primarily to a desire for order . . . Ramus takes what might be called an itemizing approach . . .'. To the capitalist mind, ever bent on clarity, consistency and systemizing conspectus, this must have meant much; but Ramus' 'enthusiasm for *usus*' meant even more. 'Ramus' commitment to the ideals of the bourgeois world,' says Ong, 'shown for example in his desire to found mathematics on the practice of bankers, merchants, architects, painters and mechanics, is [to be] interpreted ... as favouring a more empirical approach to science on the grounds that these last-named occupational groups were dealing with new problems and techniques which tended to encourage more empirical and experimental approaches to knowledge.'[3] All in all, Ramism was a product and a producer of the modern capitalist world – product of its earliest

---

[1] Ibid., p. 45; cf. also pp. 2, 89, 91, 92, 93, 125.
[2] Cf. Stark, W., *The Sociology of Knowledge*, London 1958, pp. 256 et seq.
[3] Ong, as quoted, pp. 155, 160, 164, 165, 159.

stirrings, producer of its maturer form and fulfilment – and in this respect it is typically part and parcel of the Calvinist outlook as a whole of which it is one of the most characteristic manifestations.

In so far as the bourgeois, too, felt the need of a supporting philosophy, Ramism could be of help to them: the older systems were no longer appealing to them for theirs was a new kind of life experience. 'The world with which they habitually dealt day by day was somewhat less than Neoplatonic,' writes Ong. 'It was concrete, resistant, sensible, and, if one was to make a profit, it had to be kept in a certain physical order. When a man accustomed to such a world turned from it to the unfamiliar and misty realms of learning, Ramist method could be highly reassuring . . . The mysterious realm of knowledge was reduced to something one could manage, almost palpably handle. The arts and sciences could be viewed as a mass of "wares" . . . Ramist method offered the vision of a world of knowledge levelled in much the same businesslike way. A young boy taught the principles of method could feel assured in advance of control of any body of knowledge which might come his way. If he were intelligent, he might set out to organize all human knowledge according to some simple principle of method, confident even before he approached a new field that he would know quite well how to deal with it . . . All these approaches to knowledge are approaches congenial to persons who habitually deal with reality in terms of accounting rather than in terms of meditation or wisdom. "Method" is an early step in the procedures which encode knowledge in a neutral, levelling format, reducing it to bits of information such as those which will eventually make their way into electronic computers.'[1]

So writes Walter Ong. His last jump from the sixteenth to the twentieth century may appear over-bold to some, but there is little or no exaggeration in it. A computer is in principle hardly more complex a piece of mechanism than a pocket- or wrist-watch, and these were the foremost of the great innovations which Ramée's Calvinist co-religionists bestowed upon the world. Among the workshops which Ramée visited, there may well have been some watchmakers' *boutiques* for this industry was to all intents and purposes in the hands of his fellow-Huguenots. Even today the world-capital of chronometry is also the world-capital of Calvinism: the city of Geneva. This is no accident. There was an elective affinity between the Calvinist bourgeoisie and watchmaking as there was an elective affinity between the bourgeoisie *tout court* and Calvinism. The chain of interdependences has many links and stretches far.

Watchmaking is in fact an industry which has great importance in our context, and that not only because it soberly illustrates our thesis of the connection between Calvinism and modern technology, but also because it is symbolical of that relationship which, with the appropriate

[1] Ibid., pp. 164, 169, 170, 171, 172.

explanations, modifications and restrictions, might even be called causal. It is true that the decisive invention was made in a Lutheran, not a Calvinist, city, in Nuremberg: the egg-shaped pocket-watch of Peter Henlein, known as the *Nurembergisch Eierlein*, was first set going there in 1510. But Nuremberg was both economically far advanced and religiously far to the left: so far as to be in both respects comparable to the Swiss cities of Basle, Zürich and Geneva; and, still more importantly, it was the French Huguenots – typical Calvinists – who took the manufacture of the new chronometers most energetically in hand and pushed it in the direction of mass production. When they had to leave their native country, they took the whole industry with them. Charles Weiss, whose *Histoire des Réfugiés Protestants de France depuis la Révocation de l'Edit de Nantes jusqu'à nos Jours* (1853) is still the classical study of the subject, writes this about the detail which interests us at the moment: 'Among the divers mechanics who flocked into Geneva, a considerable number of watchmakers were remarked, above all, whose industry was not slow to prosper in that city and all the country which surrounded it. In 1685 could be counted as yet but a hundred master watchmakers and three hundred journeymen who supplied to commerce five thousand watches yearly. A hundred years afterward, that same branch of industry employed, in the city alone, six thousand workmen, who manufactured each year more than fifty thousand watches, and since that time it has increased still more.'[1] More recent research has amplified, but not controverted this evidence for the Calvinistic character of the whole branch. It has above all shown that the hundred or so master watchmakers who were already established when the influx came after 1685 had themselves originally been Huguenot refugees – or rather their fathers had, which makes little difference. 'There were two important waves of Protestant immigration from France,' we are told.[2] 'The first occurred in the fifty years preceding the Edict of Nantes (1598), and the second came a century later when the edict was revoked. The first wave profoundly affected the political, social and economic life of Geneva and resulted in the establishment of many new trades, such as clockmaking. Those who sought refuge in the city at the end of the seventeenth century . . . apprenticed themselves to watch- and clock-makers [already there] who were on the average far more skilled than they.' No matter: it was in any event Calvinists who started the Genevan preeminence in this industry, and Calvinists who preferred and strengthened it by joining it when they arrived in search of a new hope and a new home. Those of their fellow-sufferers who turned to England rather than to Switzerland when they had to emigrate also included

[1] *History of the French Protestant Refugees from the Revocation of the Edict of Nantes to our own Days*, transl. Herbert, H. W., New York 1854, vol. II, pp. 188 and 189.
[2] Scoville, W. C., *The Persecution of Huguenots and French Economic Development, 1680–1720*, Berkeley and Los Angeles 1960, p. 360.

many goldsmiths and watchmakers, or men who changed over into the related branches when they had to make a fresh start on another shore.[1]

Perhaps it will be said that France cannot have remained without watchmakers when the Huguenot crowd left, and that may indeed be so, but the argument, if it is properly handled, only goes to show that the difference between the directions imparted by Calvinism and Catholicism respectively to artisan activity was even deeper than might be assumed at first sight. Charles Weiss makes an apposite remark which is eye-opening: 'If the Parisian watchmakers preserve their reputation for the excellence of their productions,' he writes, 'the Genevese excel them in cheapness.'[2] Not only two variants of a branch of industry, but even two variants of an inclusive culture come into view here. Watchmaking in a Catholic country is attuned to the needs of an aristocratic public, and its products have as much of an aesthetic as of a utilitarian function; watchmaking in a Calvinist setting, on the other hand, is purely utilitarian; it aims at the provision of everybody with a time-piece, and not only of some, and thereby it becomes a powerful agent for the modernization, the rationalization, of a whole economy, a whole society, a whole world. There are few areas in which we can perceive more clearly that Calvinism was indeed the pioneer of capitalism: without the pocket- and wrist-watch whose mass production it inspired, there would have been no labour-force checking in and checking out at factory gates, no breaking down of the process of manufacture into measurable and measured performances, no postal and railway systems working with maximum precision, and, indeed, no journey to the moon. Capitalism needs the clock, and it received it from Calvinist hands.

True, Catholics also built chronometers, but of what kind were they? First of all, there was a heavy preference for public clocks as against private watches. Cathedral clocks and clocks on town halls delighted the burgher who was still, *au fond*, a medieval child, but he looked askance at the new contraptions which brought a hard discipline and a sickening haste to which he was not accustomed into his life. And even the public clocks were, if we may so express it, pre-Calvinist and pre-capitalist in character. They were play-things rather than serious measuring instruments. They showed, as a rule, not only hours and minutes which alone are important in the conduct of workaday life, but also the rising and setting of sun and moon, the movement of the tides, and all manner of esoteric information the meaning of which is known only to astronomers. They did not say: now it is time to go to work; they said: look, what intricate mechanisms we can manage to contrive! The clock was in intention a 'wonder-work': Meraviglia-clocks is a technical

[1] Ibid., p. 330.
[2] Weiss, loc. cit., p. 189.

expression used for them.[1] For such child's play, for such toys, the man made in the image of Calvinism had no sympathy – 'no time'.

All men must experience the passing of time as a melancholy and menacing process for all men must know that every tick brings them nearer to the grave. There can be no difference in this respect between Catholic and Calvinist: both have to agree that the Scots poet Dunbar struck a universally human note when he wrote of Death;

> He spairis no lord for his piscence,
> Na clerk for his intelligence;
> His awfull strak may no man flé;
> *Timor mortis conturbat me.*[2]

And yet – so great is the influence of religion on culture – starting from this common sentiment, Catholicism and Calvinism shaped even the attitude to time differently. The Catholic concept is close to organicism; it resembles what Bergson described as duration. It is akin to the unsophisticated awareness of sheer existence and has in it something of the pure joy of being alive. Being in time is pleasurable rather than otherwise. The Calvinist idea, on the other hand, is colder: it is closer to the mechanistic definition of time. The passing of the hours is a running out of the sands: it is part and parcel of man's punishment for sin, for it was sin that brought death into the world, and our being in time is a being unto death. When this sombre sentiment began to spread through Europe in the late sixteenth and early seventeenth centuries, the Catholic cultures felt hurt and revolted. A typical Catholic reaction, deep in experience and noble in form, is that of the Spanish poet Luis de Góngora who wrote nine poems on the passage of time,[3] referring in one sorrowfully to

> the hours whose file outwears the golden day;
> the days that gnaw the year till life is slain.[4]

It was a Spanish clock from which Mr. Strether, in *The Ambassadors*, learnt the Latin adage placed as a motto on its face: *Omnes vulnerant, ultima necat* – All hours hurt us, and the last one kills.[5] This hostility, not to time, but to measured time, has remained in Spanish culture. The paintings of Salvador Dali evince it even more than the poems of Luis de Góngora. Some show us watches running over the edges of tables, as if they were over-ripe cheeses: the artist has deprived them (so we

[1] Cf. Hocke, G. R., *Die Welt als Labyrinth*, Hamburg 1957, pp. 81 et seq. and 119 et seq. Cf. further, Vallentin, A., *Leonardo da Vinci*, New York 1952, pp. 137 and 138.

[2] 'Lament for the Makaris' (=poets), *The Poems of William Dunbar*, ed. Small, J., vol. I, Edinburgh and London 1884, p. 49.

[3] Cf. Hocke, op. cit., p. 82, note 1.

[4] Churton, E., *Gongora*, London 1862, vol. II, p. 226.

[5] James, H., *The Ambassadors*, as quoted, p. 64.

may perhaps interpret his meaning) of their stiffness, their strength and their power. Their tyranny, as it were, is denied. One canvas is particularly clear: not only has it the features just mentioned, but it shows a human figure prostrate on the ground, with a watch straddling him as if it were a monster sucking out his life's blood . . .[1]

These are not only metaphysical attitudes: they are that, but they are also thoroughly practical. The Spaniard does not hurry: *mañana* is a word he loves. *Do it now* is the injunction of the Calvinist conscience. *Time is money*, say the Anglo-Saxon cultures; the Irish, on the other hand, assure their guests that 'when God made time, He made enough of it'.[2] Economists would say that to the Anglo-Saxons time is a scarce, to the Irish a free commodity – a very different thing. It is immediately clear that economic action as a whole cannot be quite the same in the one cultural and religious matrix as in the other. We have studied the inner springs of Calvinist conduct: let us now contrast it with Catholic customs.

EXCURSUS: THE CATHOLIC ATTITUDE TO
ECONOMIC LIFE AND TECHNOLOGY

To the points of disagreement which define and delimit the Catholic and the Calvinist culture areas belongs *inter alia* a contrasting attitude to a small fraction of a versicle contained in the sixth chapter of St. Luke's Gospel. Even the correct reading of the text is in dispute. The Vulgate has: *mutuum date, nil inde sperantes*; the Calvinist versions offer: *mutuum date, nil desperantes*. To the human ear, there seems hardly any difference at all. Yet the difference is in fact striking and important. The translations indicate it. The Douai version runs: 'Lend, hoping for nothing thereby.' English Bibles in the Calvinist tradition, on the other hand, give: 'Lend, never despairing.'[3] But even these formulations, unlike each other as they are, do not reveal the full measure of the contrast. The truth is that the Catholic wording forbids and the Calvinist permits the taking of *interest*. And not only one institution is outlawed or legitimized by these four or five words, but a whole economic order, that of capitalism, for without the yielding of interest capital is not what it is supposed to be in a capitalist society.

Calvin knew, of course, that Christ's teaching reported in Luke vi, 35, echoes Old Testament conceptions, and that the Old Testament presents several passages which put a determined ban on interest, for

[1] Cf. Soby, J. Thr., *Paintings, Drawings, Prints: Salvador Dali*, New York 1941, painting 'The Persistence of Memory' in the Museum of Modern Art, New York, plate 9, p. 39.
[2] Heinrich Böll, *Werke*, Stuttgart, Zürich, Salzburg n.d., p. 273 (from *Irisches Tagebuch*). Cf. also Connery, D. S., *The Irish*, New York 1968, p. 93.
[3] Cf. *The Complete Bible: An American Translation*, The New Testament, transl. Goodspeed, E. J., ed. Chicago 1948, p. 60.

instance Leviticus xxv, 36, and Deuteronomy xxiii, 19 and 20, not to speak of Ezechiel xviii, 5 and 8. But he soon got rid of these norms, even though they were contained in Holy Writ. We must distinguish, he argued, between universally binding norms and norms meant only for, and therefore obligating only, the Jewish people. The prohibition of usury, Calvin decreed, belongs to the latter category. The Christian business man may take what the market offers him. A great step towards the legitimation of capitalism was thus put in hand.

Aquinas and the other Catholic teachers of morality got their ideas on this point as much from Aristotle as from the Bible, and Aristotle had declared (to give the terse formula usually quoted) that money cannot breed. In his *Politics*, he indulges, where he discusses the use of money, in a little linguistic criticism and takes up an in his opinion misleading word, the word τόκος. This means 'the young of animals', but it also means 'interest from capital', probably because a calf resembles the cow in much the same way as 5 drachmae resemble 100: both are different in size, but identical in kind with the original. This linguistic usage, Aristotle urges, is stultifying. Money cannot breed; cows can. 'Of all modes of making money,' he concludes, 'this is the most unnatural . . . For money was intended to be used in exchange, but not to increase at interest.' Aquinas agreed. '*Pecunia pecuniam non parit*,' he wrote in his *Summa Theologiae*. Money is, properly speaking, a medium of exchange. In its essence it is not, and it cannot legitimately be used as, capital.[1]

If we look behind and beneath this surface norm, we soon find deeper disagreements. Jeremy Bentham's great little work, *Defence of Usury*, contains an amusing passage which can lead us to one of them. Speaking of Aristotle, 'that celebrated heathen who, in all matters wherein heathenism did not destroy his competence, had established a despotic empire over the Christian world,' Bentham remarks: 'As fate would have it, that great philosopher, with all his industry, and all his penetration, notwithstanding the great number of pieces of money that had passed through his hands, and notwithstanding the uncommon pains he had bestowed on the subject of generation, had never been able to discover, in any one piece of money, any organs for generating any other such piece. Emboldened by so strong a body of negative proof, he ventured at last to usher into the world the result of his observations in the form of an universal proposition that *all money is in its nature barren*.'[2] Facetious as the words are, they can yet open our eyes to an analytically important fact, namely that the thought of Aristotle and Aquinas was attuned to the realm and reality of life, whereas the thought of the defenders of usury, Calvin and Bentham, was attuned to the

[1] *Politics*, I, 10, transl. Jowett, B., ed. Davis, H. W. C., Oxford 1905, p. 46; *Summa Theologiae*, IIa IIae, qu. 78, art. 1. The '*Summa Theologica*', as quoted, vol. X, London 1918, p. 331.
[2] *Jeremy Bentham's Economic Writings*, ed. Stark, W., vol. 1, London 1952, p. 158.

realm and reality of matter, of inanimate creation. For this deep reason alone, interest in and emphasis on mechanical production could never be as intense in the Catholic (or in the Greek) culture area as it was in the Calvinist which came to join it at the beginning of the modern age.

But the sociology of knowledge can lead us even further in our analysis. It invites us to investigate whether behind 'is-sentences', there do not hide 'ought-sentences', in our given case, whether behind the assertion that 'money does not breed' there does not hide the wish that money should not be *allowed* to breed. This suspicion would appear to be entirely justified.[1] Aristotle's ideal was the still largely agricultural society, Aquinas' the pacified, wall-enclosed town; both were aiming at a condition of stability; both desired to reduce the harmony-destroying selfish urges of the individual – Aristotle to secure the golden mean which was the Grecian dream, Aquinas to further the sanctification of souls which is the Christian's prayer. Neither had much sympathy for the business man whose aim is the earning, not of a sufficient, but of a maximal, income, and the accumulation, not of measured, but of unlimited wealth. Man, they felt, was greedy enough as he is; his *concupiscentia* should not be further aggravated; but this was precisely what interest did. They saw the prohibition of usury essentially as an ingredient in the system of social control, like the suppression of gluttony-fostering table manners or of the distribution of sexually stimulating pornographic literature and 'art'.

To the defenders of capitalist society, or indeed of any society with a desire for an ever-increasing supply of material goods without regard to the social costs of such economic advance, the prohibition of interest must necessarily appear as the height of folly. Indeed, many have gone so far as to say – taking a leaf out of Aristotle's book, but turning his main proposition inside out – that the prohibition of usury is 'unnatural', and they have meant thereby that it is unenforceable. They have pointed triumphantly to the virtual acceptance, by the Catholic Church, of the phenomenon of interest which is now a tolerated, if not a welcomed, reality. So far as this acceptance is concerned, its bearing has never been properly spelled out. What determined the change-over from a negative to a more positive point of view was above all the redistribution, brought on by capitalism, of relative power as between creditor and debtor. In pre-capitalist societies, the creditor (the full money-bag) is strong, the debtor (an empty stomach) is weak, and the weaker has to be protected. But in a full-fledged capitalist society the debtor (a bank which works with its customer's deposits, a joint-stock company which sells debentures and shares) is strong, and the creditor (the little depositor, the small man who has a few modest investments) is weak. In such a world, the payment of interest does not betoken, but

[1] Cf. Stark, W., *The Contained Economy: An Interpretation of Medieval Economic Thought*, Aquinas paper no. 26, London 1956, passim.

does in fact prevent, the exploitation of the weaker hand. A productive loan simply is not the same thing as a consumptive loan, a loan to a man whose crops have failed or whose house has burnt to the ground – the cases of which the Bible is thinking. 'If thy brother be impoverished,' says Leviticus xxv, 35 and 36, 'take not usury of him nor more than thou gavest.' Aristotle and Aquinas, and the Gospel according to St. Luke, too, must be seen against the same background. As for the ban on interest as a stimulator to human greed, of an unlimited desire for unlimited enrichment, it must be very doubtful whether that has been lifted, or, more clearly expressed, whether interest has been legitimized in so far as it is an agency which makes for selfishness and works against social peace.

One point, of course, has to be conceded: in a capitalist society which is totally geared to material values, and which is prepared to sacrifice social harmony to these material values, a norm such as the outlawing of interest is well-nigh impossible to enforce. But the question is whether the situation is the same in other societies. The usual argument to the effect that in the Middle Ages many subterfuges were used to avoid the prescriptions of the canon code (*lucrum cessans, damnum emergens, poena conventionalis*, and so on), and that therefore the usury laws were unenforceable even then, is not convincing. Quite apart from the fact that the dodgers' tricks which we have mentioned appeared more massively only towards the end of the medieval dispensation, *no* system of social control is totally watertight. Our modern laws ordain that nobody shall pay the tax authorities less than the finance bills prescribe; but all men attempt to do just that, and many are, to say the least, not unsuccessful. This does not mean that, by and large, taxes are not dutifully surrendered. What we have to see is to what extent the commandment 'thou shalt not be over-greedy in thy economic pursuits' was internalized in times when the Catholic Church was truly powerful, and to what extent it became, *in praxi*, a real determinant of human conduct.

We possess one in-depth study of a leading case, the case of Francesco di Marco Datini, who was born some time around 1335 (the exact date is unknown) and died on 16 August 1410 at Prato in Tuscany. His life is, if not *the* most amazing success story of the *quattrocento*, then at least one of most amazing ones. The Marchesa Iris Origo has retold it in a book which is as beautiful in form as it is rich in content: *The Merchant of Prato*, published at London in 1957.[1]

Datini was the son of a tavern-keeper who had managed to put aside small savings, though he could by no stretch of the imagination be called rich. The Great Plague of 1348 carried him off, together with his wife, Monna Vermiglia, and two of his four children. The survivors, Francesco and Stefano, inherited 'a house, a little land and forty-seven

---

[1] Cf. my review broadcast, 'For God and Gain', reprinted in *The Listener*, 30 May 1957, pp. 879 et seq.

florins' – a poor enough beginning. But Francesco was destined to become affluent. 'Soon after his fifteenth birthday he sold a small piece of land for 150 florins and – probably in the company of some Florentine merchants . . . – set off for Avignon'.[1] That city was at the time the seat of the papacy and thus in some respects the hub and centre of the world. It offered splendid business opportunities for one who knew how to see and grasp them, and this precisely – the eye for the main chance – was young Messer Datini's greatest natural strength.

'How he succeeded in raising a small capital to start with is not known,' writes the biographer. 'Perhaps he worked first as an apprentice with one of the Florentine merchants whose firm was already established; perhaps some "fine cloth" which was sent to him in 1356 by his guardian, by means of a wandering friar, formed the basis of his stock. All that is certain is that he did not send his tutor any requests for money and that by 1358 he was doing sufficiently well for his brother to join him in Avignon.' From then onward, it was smooth sailing. 'The first steps in the foundation of Datini's fortune were probably the hardest, but he was swift to follow them up with further ventures. In 1367 . . . he . . . entered into partnership with another Tuscan, Tuccio Lambertucci, and so greatly did their affairs prosper that, in a letter written some years later, Datini states that 800 florins put up by himself and his partner had brought in, in the course of less than eight years, no less than 10,000 florins.' Anything and everything that was going was grist to this man's money mill: he traded in arms, supplying without hesitation both warring parties; he imported salt, a desperately needed commodity; he hawked spices such as saffron, in those days a most profitable line of business; he opened a wine tavern and a draper's shop; he supplied priests with the precious materials for their vestments and lay-folk with religious pictures which were decidedly less than precious, in fact the same kind of junk which is still to be seen before some church doors even today; in 1376 he set up a money-changer's counter – but why enumerate the ventures which he launched? They had all the same effect: they made the young genius rich. 'By the age of thirty-five, Francesco di Marco was a man of substance.'[2]

Returning to his home town in 1382 or 1383, Datini could have closed his account books and retired into private life. He did not. A cat will not stop catching mice. Soon Prato was too narrow for him, and he set up business in near-by Florence, though he left his family in the smaller city. His closing years were also spent there. They cannot interest us over-much. Suffice it to say that, when he died, his fortune amounted to 70,000 gold florins.[3] At a rough estimate, that was something like 200 times the sum with which he had started out.

[1] Origo, loc. cit., pp. 30 and 31.
[2] Ibid., pp. 35, 37, 36, 38, 41, 42. For the variety of Francesco's speculations and enterprises, cf. also pp. 88 and 89.   [3] Ibid., p. 11.

Looking at this well-nigh incredible story of steep ascent, one might almost be tempted to throw the whole Weberian theory out of the window, and there are writers who have done just that with less dramatic material at their disposal. Here was a Catholic within a Catholic country and within a Catholic period, and yet there seems to have been no inhibition to crude acquisitiveness in his heart. What more could Calvinism do to release the springs of economic action than a Catholic culture had done in this case? What was the difference between Francesco di Marco Datini and, say, John D. Rockefeller, capitalists both? Is the *auri sacra fames*, the frail thirst for gold, not simply a genetically human trait, only more veiled in some societies than in others, but underneath always the same?

Those who would argue in this way, would base themselves only on part of the source material, not on the whole, and would in fact stick to the outer appearances, to the mere surface of things. What makes the Datini case so interesting and revealing is the sheer mass of information at our disposal: 150,000 letters, not to speak of ledgers, deeds, insurance policies and the like. 'The flavour of these letters is completely consistent,' writes Iris Origo. 'In the vision of life they present, only two things have any importance – religion and trade. On the first page of Datini's great ledgers stood the words, "In the name of God and of profit", and these were the only goals to which these merchants aspired: profit in this world or in the next, as if the whole of life were one vast counting-house – and in the end, the final Day of Accounting.'[1] The modern cynical reader will react here by asserting that God was the pretended and profit the real aim of Datini's endeavours – that what mattered to Datini was the balance of gain and loss, not the balance of sanctity and sin. What if there was an overplus of sin, so long as there was also an overplus of gain? Who really cares about the judgment? Francesco di Marco certainly did. His ethos was not as blunt as that of the modern business man, nor was it relieved by the doctrine of predestination according to which a person's fate in eternity depended, not on his action, but on God's decree fixed 'before the foundations of the world were laid'. Datini must have heard Thomas of Celano's *Dies Irae* often, and it let run shivers down his spine.

> Of each deed is record made.
> When the book is open laid,
> No guilt's price remains unpaid.

'His life was not a serene one', reports our searching and deeply understanding historian. 'The canker which ate all joy away, both in youth and old age, and which is revealed by almost every line of this correspondence, was anxiety . . . He was an astute and successful merchant; but he was, above all, an uneasy man.' For long stretches of time he

[1] Ibid., p. 13; cf. p. 11.

worried, of course, about his business. Risk taking was of the essence of it, and risk taking is not conducive to good sleep. But it robs its victim not only of sleep as such, physiological sleep, it also robs him of the sleep of the just, and Datini was not blind to this factor. In any case, 'with old age came the last and worst anxiety: overwhelming fear of what would happen to him in a future life. Pilgrimages and periods of fasting, gifts of pictures to churches and of lands to convents and, finally, the bestowal of all his great fortune to charitable work – none of these sufficed to dispel the haunting sense of guilt that darkened his last years – a gnawing anguish, a perpetual *malinconia*'. Just how deep the *angoisse*, the *Lebensangst* of Francesco di Marco sat can be seen from a dream which he once had and which has come down to us in the sources. He saw a vulture swooping down on him; he offered the bird of vengeance a piece of gold, but the beast scorned it and seized some lumps of flesh instead before beating its wings and flying off.[1] Datini needed neither soothsayer nor psychiatrist to enlighten him on the meaning of his nocturnal experience. All too clearly had it told him that money is not everything, and that it will be no help beyond the grave.

A merchant who, because of the religious ethic which he has internalized, could feel in this way, cannot possibly be compared to those of his confrères whose religion assured them, and that again on the deepest level of the soul, that enrichment was a sign of divine favour and not an occasion of divine wrath. Yet it may be argued, especially by those who are inclined towards behaviourism and think that inner states are irrelevant, if they do not lead to outer actions, that Datini's fears did not prevent him from making his pile, and that therefore the contrast to Calvinist entrepreneurship is greater in the imagination than it was in reality. To such an assertion, two considerations can be opposed, both, it would seem, equally conclusive.

The first is that Datini's environment exerted a strongly restraining influence on him. Even if his greed was great, that of those around him was small, and they did their best to make his smaller. His foster-mother, Monna Piera di Pratese, had a neighbour, Niccolozzo di Ser Naldo, who was a correspondent of Francesco's and a good friend to boot. 'You know God has granted you to acquire great riches in this world, may He be praised,' so one letter to Avignon runs. 'Pray toil not so hard . . . Crave not all: you have already enough to suffice you!' This was a basic theme, for some time later Niccolozzo returns to it: 'Give thanks to God, for you already have enough. Crave not for all, crave not for all!'[2]

Yet Niccolozzo was but an ordinary fellow-citizen and not a closer associate. His admonitions may be written off as the opinion of an

[1] Ibid., pp. 15, 16, 219.
[2] Ibid., pp. 45 and 49.

outsider to the business world, comparable to the vain sermonizing that comes from so many pulpits today. What about, for instance, Datini's lawyers? Did they perhaps hold him back? Strange to say – and this is truly decisive – *they did*. If there is a figure which emerges as fully and lightfully from Iris Origo's pages as Francesco di Marco himself, it is his notary, Ser Lapo Mazzei. Also of humble origin, he too had risen in the world, but it was characteristic of the man that the activity in which he took the greatest pride was his service to the Hospital of Santa Maria Nuova, Florence's finest charitable institution.[1]

Ser Lapo once formulated his basic philosophy in a brief statement, and it is a personal confession of adherence to Catholicism's Aristotelianism and Thomism: 'Measure is God's demand, and no immoderate thing was ever pleasing to that Eternal Equity.' This is what he said; this is what he believed; and this is what he took for his rule of conduct. After Datini had visited Mazzei on his little farm at Grignano, Mazzei wrote to this client: 'I was glad you took pleasure in my little kitchen-garden. I call it so, because so small a thing cannot be called a farm, but to my mind, which desires but little, it is great enough. And this absence of desire seems to me the height of wealth.' 'Believe me, believe me,' he says on another occasion. 'I live in the world, but I am not of it. I dare not say, I serve God . . . but of this I am very sure, to serve the world is an evil thing.' Proudly he warns Datini not to expect of him anything that is less than right: 'Though I am yours . . . as I am, yet I have kept my soul and mind for a greater Lord than you, and I study to keep them for him, as He gave them to me.'[2] 'Blandly, persistently, unceasingly,' the Marchesa Origo tells us, 'during the thirty years of their friendship, he attempted to persuade Francesco to find room, in the midst of business cares, both for human affections and pious thoughts – "To treat God as a master and the world as a servant – that is a thing we can and must do".' Only one of his appeals to the Dives of Prato can be quoted, but it will suffice, because it is truly moving. 'When I think of the cares of the house you are building, of your warehouses in far-off lands, your banquets and your accounts, and of many other matters, they seem to me so far beyond what is needful that I realize it cannot be that you should seize an hour from the world and its snares. Yet God has granted you an abundance of earthly goods, and has given you, too, a thousand warnings to awaken you; and now you are nearly sixty . . . Are you to wait until your death-bed, when the door-latch of death is lifted, to change your heart?' Few letters of this content leave lawyers' offices nowadays, and this must make us feel that cultures are different, even if acquisitiveness is present in them all. It was, in all probability, Mazzei's influence which induced Datini to leave all he had to the poor. The last piece of legal business Ser Lapo ever performed was to draw up a similar

---

[1] Ibid., p. 202.
[2] Ibid., pp. 202, 215, 209. Cf. also pp. 16 and 17.

will – that of Lazzaro Fei of Arezzo, like Datini a rich man who bequeathed his whole property to charity.[1]

The question, of course, remains as to what extent a moralist like Mazzei could influence a money-maker like Datini, and this brings us to our second point. Datini knew a last limit beyond which he was not prepared to go. Ser Lapo, who held very definitely that 'no interest should be taken on a loan of money', warned him against 'dry exchanges', i.e. transactions with deferred payment which were veiled 'usury', and told him to lay off them. Francesco took his advice. He wrote as follows to his associate Simone d'Andrea in Barcelona: 'I have told you ere now that for no man on earth will I agree to the company's exchange dealings . . . If you are not so disposed, you will see how swiftly any agreement between us can be brought to an end.' Six years later, he shows that he has maintained his principles. 'If you feel inclined,' he tells d'Andrea once again, 'to buy or sell money on the exchange . . . find someone else who is of a like mind, for I will not be caught to satisfy your hunger . . .'[2]

But being a fully-fledged capitalist does not only presuppose taking the bridle off certain desires which medieval textbooks of ethics were inclined to qualify as vices; it also means possessing certain positive properties which according to these textbooks – and even more, of course, according to later ones – must count as virtues, and in these, too, Datini was deficient. There is, for instance, the chapter of self-indulgence, more concretely, self-control at the table. Datini had little of it as compared to the Calvinist-bred entrepreneur; he ate more like a medieval *grand seigneur*. Writing home from Avignon, he asks his foster-mother not to feed him on leeks or roots when he returns and lets her know that capons please him better than cockerels. When he had finally settled at Prato, his fellow citizens were amazed at the rare foods that were arriving at his house: 'Cheeses from Pisa, Sardinia and Sicily, barrels of tunny-fish, oranges and dates from Catalonia, besides sugar, pepper and all sorts of spices – cassia, clove, ginger and saffron.' At his wedding, 2 quarters of an ox, 16 quarters of mutton, 37 capons, 11 chickens, 2 boars' heads, 250 eggs and 100 pounds of cheese were eaten, in addition to an unspecified number of pigeons and sea-fowl, all washed down by choice Chianti and Carmignano wine.[3]

Mention of the wedding-breakfast leads us from gluttony to ostentation – to that Veblenian 'conspicuous waste' which is a sign of the decay of classical capitalism and certainly irreconcilable with its pure archetypal form. Datini indulged in it as he did in the pleasures of the palate. 'While his new walls were still rising, he planted before the house, not a

[1] Ibid., pp. 217, 218, 11, 220. Cf. also p. 154 for another strong letter of Ser Lapo to Messer Francesco di Marco.

[2] Ibid., pp. 150, 152, 153.

[3] Ibid., pp. 44, 45, 48, 67; cf. also p. 43.

vegetable-plot or orchard, but a pleasure-garden – 32 *braccia* by 14 – "full of oranges, roses and violets and other lovely flowers". He himself considered later on that this had been "a great piece of folly", for it cost no less than 600 florins.' The neighbours stood amazed. 'Sometimes, too, a crate of exotic creatures for the new garden would be unpacked before their startled eyes – "a monkey, a porcupine in a cage, two pea-cocks (male and female) and a sea-gull".' Entertaining guests was a great pastime. When Louis II of Anjou, the self-styled 'King of Sicily and Jerusalem', came to dinner, 30 florins were spent in a day. But worse followed. The 'king' borrowed 500 florins, never, we can be sure, to be returned. Later 'His Majesty' appeared again with a boon-companion and stayed eighteen days. When he left, he gave Datini the right to add the royal lily of France to his coat of arms, 'gold, on an azure ground'. Francesco, a true child, was thrilled. Not so his friends, especially when they learned that Louis had left with another 'loan' of 1,000 florins in his pocket.[1] Clearly, the Merchant of Prato was not like his Calvinist suc-cessors whose faces were always set against what the Scots call 'bawbees' and who always asked the searching question: what do I get for my money? Is it worth having it?

Vanity is a vice, to be sure, but it is a human one, and Datini was very human. In a sense it was because he was so human that he made less than a complete capitalist. For capitalism properly so called presupposes a certain depersonalization of life. It is *the firm* that looms largest in the typical capitalist's mind, not the owner, and even less, of course, the employees. But Datini's way of conducting business was still intensely personal and therefore entirely pre-capitalist. 'When I formed a company with Toro di Berto in Avignon,' he wrote to Cristofano di Bartolo on 27 February 1402, 'many laughed at me, saying "you were free and have now made yourself a servant; you could rise and go to bed when you pleased, and now you must follow your partner's bidding". I replied I was glad to have a partner for diverse reasons – first, to have a brother, and then, to have someone to keep me from the follies of youth.' To have a brother – what an unbusinesslike view of a commercial partner-ship! 'Many passages of his letters show how deep-rooted the tradition was that the tie between partners should be as close as a family one, a truly fraternal bond,' writes Iris Origo. As the senior shareholder, Francesco considered himself as the *padre* of his associates, and, when they fell ill, he 'watched over his employees with a quasi-paternal solici-tude . . . We find him taking on, as a matter of course, the full obliga-tions of the *capo del parentado* . . . towards the families of his partners, managers and servants. When one of his partners in Avignon, Bonaccorso di Vanni, left at his death four little daughters whom he had had by one of his slaves, Francesco took all four of them into his own house and engaged a woman to look after them'. Such and similar

[1] Ibid., pp. 66, 67, 235; cf. also pp. 226, 16, 98, 145, 236.

actions explain the inscription which his fellow-citizens put over the entrance to his house turned orphanage: 'Mercantante dei Poveri di Christo – "Merchant of Christ's Poor".' They make it much more understandable than it otherwise would be.[1] But above all we must remember at this point that the capital Datini had formed was not kept together in an abiding firm; he had no concept at all of such a firm;[2] it was left for good works and thereby, as capital, deflected, scattered and annihilated; and so his capitalism, if it ever properly existed, was ephemeral, a wonder of nine days.

It was not, however, only the dissolution of the capitals formed (a dissolution, incidentally, of which we have examples from several countries),[3] it was also their mode of employment while they were yet intact which prevented the development of a capitalist economy in the proper sense of the word. Datini was a trader; so were the Fuggers, to cite another well-known instance of medieval enrichment. They knew how to make money in and out of commerce, but they did not venture into production.[4] But modern capitalism is essentially an industrial capitalism; in Marx's classical phrase, it is a 'mode of production'. With such a mode of production Francesco Datini and Jakob Fugger had little to do; and it is perhaps characteristic, or at least symbolical, that Datini never closed his little mercer's shop in the Por S. Maria district of Florence: he thought of himself, even as he was growing rich, as merely a glorified shopkeeper, a glorified grocer.[5]

In this way, even 'the Merchant of Prato', a true prodigy of business acumen, shows up the inherent limitations of capitalist entrepreneurship in a Catholic society. And these limitations are still more obvious in the national economies under the aegis of the Roman faith than they are in the case of one of the faithful. Speaking of Italy, Spain, Portugal, Austria and those parts of Germany which the Reformation did not wean from their pristine allegiance, Müller-Armack writes: 'What they all have in common is the absence of a national ideology and of economic dynamism. They preserve a political and economic structure which is tied to the *ancien* estate *régime*; the power apparatus of a strong absolutist state and the energies of broad liberated bourgeois strata are lacking.'[6] Lacking was also a working class prepared to submit to modern methods of organization and discipline.[7] In one word, the basic preconditions of modern capitalism were not given.

That they were in fact not given can also be seen from the failure of these cultures to develop a mercantilist or even cameralist literature of

---

[1] Ibid., pp. 109, 108, 179, 180, 221. [2] Cf. ibid., p. 110.
[3] Müller-Armack, loc. cit., p. 87. [4] Ibid., p. 210.
[5] Origo, loc. cit., p. 89; Müller-Armack, loc. cit., pp. 94 et seq.
[6] Müller-Armack, p. 145.
[7] Ibid., p. 149. Cf. also p. 311 on the unwillingness or inability of the Catholic states to stamp out begging.

their own. 'Already a first sifting of the biographical material,' writes Müller-Armack, 'forces one statement upon us: the Catholic territories have to be counted out, so far as the learned elaboration of the new economic mentality is concerned. Cameralist and mercantilist literature was written by Protestants.'[1] What is sometimes called Austrian mercantilism refers in reality to a group of immigrants from the Protestant world: J. J. Becher, Hörnigk, Bornitz and von Schröder, all four are Austrians only by adoption. Sonnenfels was a convert from Judaism, hence another kind of naturalized alien. Of the two Spaniards, Uztariz and Ulloa, whose activity, such as it was, falls into the eighteenth century, who therefore were campfollowers rather than pioneers, we shall speak later on.[2] One Catholic country whose case might be thought to be somewhat different is France. But the contrast to, say, Austria or Bavaria is much weaker than would appear at first sight. Quite apart from the fact (which we wish neither to emphasize nor to forget in this discussion) that the official religion of the realm was Gallicanism rather than pure Catholicism, and that therefore at least the state gained something from the currents of the Reformation age, it must be pointed out that two new ideological tendencies broke into the French intellectual tradition and deflected it from its original direction – Calvinism and Enlightenment: 'Huguenots and rationalists dominate here the economic literature. Unbroken Catholicism remains disinterested even in France.'[3]

What is called Cameralism or Mercantilism abroad, is called Colbertism in France, and this shows that a powerful minister of the crown, Jean Baptiste Colbert (1619–83), made the programme of economic and technological modernization his own. In a sense, Colbertism combined the other two, vastly more important variants: it was like cameralism, in so far as the call to modernize came from the administrative centre; it was like mercantilism, in so far as there were strata in the country who took that call up because it corresponded to what they themselves wanted to do and would have done spontaneously anyway. These were the Huguenots. Such economic advancement as France achieved in the seventeenth century would have been impossible without Protestants such as Sully and de Laffemas. It is, of course, beyond our power to estimate with any degree of exactitude how much this limited group in the population contributed to general progress: one thing, however, we can say with some assurance, namely that the contribution was considerable. Our proof must be the manifest blow dealt to the French economy by the revocation of the Edict of Nantes in 1685. Confronted with a choice between a flourishing production and consumption on the one hand and the welding of the population into one unified mass of subjects on the other – more simply expressed: with a choice between

[1] Ibid., pp. 182 and 183.   [2] Cf. below, p. 362.
[3] Müller-Armack, p. 184. Cf. also p. 142.

wealth and power – Louis XIV preferred the latter alternative. He drove
the dissenters out and thereby inhibited capitalism in the full sense of
the word from developing. In 1686, Marshal Vauban, in his *Mémoire
pour le Rappel des Huguenots*, presented the king with the bill, as it were:
see here, he said, what the expulsion of these people costs us. But Louis,
bent on the creation of a manageable *massa subjectionis,* remained deaf.
The result was that the French economy attuned itself to the needs of
the restricted upper strata and became a luxury industry, as we saw
already when we cast a glance at watchmaking. Gobelins, silken goods,
perfumes, knick-knacks and expensive furniture became its chief lines.
Instead of moving forward into full capitalism, it subordinated itself to
decaying feudalism; and so even the French economy was, without the
Calvinist element in its population, unable to achieve all that modernization which the Anglo-Saxon civilizations easily made their own. The
French Canadians show the relative Catholic disinterest in economic
activity and aggressivism to this day.[1]

It is in any case not France, that curious hybrid, which should claim
the main attention in a typological investigation like the present; it is
Spain, the Catholic country *kat exochen*; and how Spain fared in the
period which saw the take-off towards the capitalist dispensation is
sufficiently attested by the general habit, on the part of economic
historians, of speaking of an 'economic decline' in the seventeenth
century. More critically considered, we are confronted with two
phenomena in this context rather than with one: there is the failure of
Spain to keep pace with Calvinist Europe's upward development; and
there is, beyond this failure, a definite sliding back in production and
consumption which some students of the epoch have asserted.[2] The
latter aspect is of less interest to us: accidental causes seem to have
brought it about, above all the two great epidemics of 1599–1600 and
1648–50. The former, however, is crucial to our analysis. Why could
Spain not step out boldly as Holland did and England? The answer can
only be that she did not possess the chief dynamism of the northern
nations, the Protestant ethic.

First, one negative point has to be dealt with. What the expulsion of
the Huguenots in 1685 was to France, that the expulsion of the Jews in
1942 and of the Moriscos in 1609 was to Spain. Unavoidably, voices have
been raised which have considered the later economic woes of the
country as the consequence, if not indeed as the condign punishment,
of these political acts.[3] But the parallel does not in fact hold good. There
was a great difference between the two cases. Many Spanish Jews pre-

[1] Ibid., pp. 143, 144, 145, 212. Cf. also Hughes, E. C., *French Canada in Transition,*
Toronto 1943.
[2] Hamilton, E. J., *American Treasure and the Price Revolution in Spain, 1501–1650,*
Cambridge, Mass., 1934, p. 304.
[3] Cf. Hamilton, E. J., 'American Treasure and the Rise of Capitalism (1500–1700)',
Economica, 1929, p. 356.

ferred conversion to emigration. Indeed, one of our leading specialists has asserted that it was Portuguese rather than Spanish Jews who left the land. Another consideration weighs perhaps still heavier in the scales. A country loses much, so far as the development of industrial capitalism is concerned, if it is abandoned by its artisans; it loses little – it loses at any rate less – if the money-dealers go. But the Spanish Jews were mostly of this latter avocation. So far as the Moriscos are concerned, our expert is equally disinclined to see their disappearance as catastrophic. The settlers from the north-west and from the foothills of the Pyrenees, who were brought to the south to replace them, proved as able as they had been.[1]

The roots of the trouble lie deeper, and we can dig for them with the help of contemporary economic conceptions, which have remained enlightening, even if the science of economics has turned to different ideas since then. If a country is to progress, the mercantilists taught, it must not export its raw materials but, so far as humanly possible, only finished goods, for then it need not remain agricultural but can turn industrial. If – foolishly – it does export its raw materials and imports finished goods, it allows another economy, a neighbouring economy, to modernize its production. From this point of view, Spain was at the end of the Middle Ages in a parlous position. 'What Spain exported was the crude produce of her soil. She provided the north of Europe with wool, iron ore, the skins of sheep and cattle and heavy wines. In mediterranean trade, too, wine and wool played a preponderant part, and beside these the south of Spain delivered oil, fruit and silks . . . Industrial products formed the most important objects of importation. The wool, which left the land in its raw condition, was bought back at high prices as Flanders, French or Florentine cloth. The northern countries sent linens and the Italian towns brocades.'[2] That was bad. But there was, in the narrowest sense of the word, a silver lining, and a broad one at that. For the mercantilists further taught that the transition from medieval to modern conditions depended above all on the possession, or the procurement, of specie. Without the precious metals, the volume of economic transactions could not be increased, and everything depended on this increase, the widening of the market, even technological development. But in this respect Spain was well off, not badly – indeed, she was uniquely favoured. For she could lay hold on the Aztec and Inca gold, and – more importantly still – she could exploit the silver mines of Potasi, Zacatecas and Guanajuato. What if her acres were dry and barren: rain from the New World could easily turn them green and growing!

[1] Cf. van Klaveren, J., *Europäische Wirtschaftsgeschichte Spaniens im 16. und 17. Jahrhundert*, Stuttgart 1960, pp. 32–5, 262, 264.
[2] Häbler, K., *Die wirtschaftliche Blüte Spaniens im 16. Jahrhundert und ihr Verfall*, Berlin 1888, pp. 44 and 45.

The earliest forms of this doctrine were based more on vague intuitions than on clear analyses, and though these intuitions were pragmatically correct, they were theoretically less than satisfactory. But in the end the mercantilistic school won through to deeper insights, especially in the person of David Hume. If specie is imported, if a stream of additional money is poured into the markets, prices will rise. But not all prices will and can rise at the same rate. Some will go up earlier than others, and those who pocket them will reap the benefit. The prices usually called prices, i.e. the prices of finished products, belong to this privileged category. They may be jerked up at a moment's notice. The prices more properly to be called costs, on the other hand, are relatively fixed. They tend to lag behind the increase of the 'final' prices. The rent of land is as a rule settled for several years; so are the wages of labour. In the end, they, too, will be adjusted – but only in the end. In the meantime profits will have accrued to the producers and providers of industrial goods; their equipment will have been built up through the investment of capital; they will be better off all round. If the national product is divided into three shares – rent, wages and profits – an inflation favours the latter one against the former two and that means that it fosters the whole economic system based on profit-making, that it fosters capitalism.[1]

There are economies for which the plain truth of this analysis can be demonstrated. England is a clear case in point. 'In England,' writes Earl J. Hamilton, 'the vast discrepancy between prices and wages, born of the price revolution [of the sixteenth century, the great universal inflation], deprived labourers of a large part of the incomes they had hitherto enjoyed and diverted this wealth to the recipients of other distributive shares . . . Rents, as well as wages, lagged behind prices; so landlords gained nothing from labour's loss . . . The landowning class suffered a diminution of income.'[2] No wonder that the emerging seventeenth century saw the capitalist class moving from strength to strength, and that the next gave birth to the factory system!

Spain might have gone the same way; indeed, she might have done so before England, for the enlivening stream of specie, American in origin, came to her well before other lands received their share. Yet she did not. She was hardly further forward in the year 1700 than she had been in the year 1650 or 1600. Why, is a question which belongs very largely in the sociology of religion. We shall first state the facts, and then endeavour to account for them.

One branch of industry which is very apt to illustrate the condition in all others is shipping and ship-building. It is well known how much England owed to her Navigation Acts, the first of which was due to the

[1] Cf. Stark, W., *The History of Economics*, London 1944, p. 13, and Heimann, E., *History of Economic Doctrines*, London, New York, Toronto, 1945, pp. 44 et seq.
[2] Hamilton in *Economica*, as quoted, pp. 355 and 350.

activity and acumen of the Cromwell administration. In Spain the *Flota*, at any rate, which brought the treasure from overseas, was supposed to contain only Castilian ships, but the regulations had a very big hole. If the *Casa de la Contratación* had no 'suitable' Castilian bottoms at her disposal – locally at her disposal, i.e. at Seville or Cadiz – foreign vessels might be used. We hear that frequently Basque ships offered their services, but the officials, many of them highly corrupt, were quick to declare them 'unsuitable'. The result was that more and more Dutch-owned or at least Dutch-built sails entered the American service, with consequences which may be imagined. The balance of trade, so far as shipping services were concerned, was passive. In the end, even the productive capacity of the Basque dockyards began to go down. 'What is certain is,' says van Klaveren, 'that the shipping and the ship-building of the Basques almost came to a standstill in the seventeenth century.' The situation in the south and east was no better than that in the north and west. As the Castilians lost their trade, so did the Catalonians. The transport of mediterranean products drifted into the hands of the canny Dutch.[1]

A further branch in which the Spaniards did not fare much better, was banking. 'The Sevillian banks were in reality Genovese banks, even if the management consisted of local people. This is, in principle, true of all so-called Spanish bankers of this period. They were go-betweens, impresarios of the Genovese whose interests *vis-à-vis* the authorities they were expected to defend . . . With the help of their moneys . . . the Genovese inserted themselves into all the departments of the Castilian import- and export-economy.' Nor were the merchants of Seville more independent than the bankers. 'With regard to . . . the industrial products of foreign countries, they had, already before 1598, become pure agents . . . The real merchants were foreigners.'[2]

But what about exports to America? That continent was under the Spanish crown and should, in accordance with contemporary convictions, have been made into a preserve of Spanish industry and trade. In point of fact, it was not. 'Castile, and even the whole of Spain, always had a relatively small share in the exports to America . . . Correspondingly small was at that time her share in "private silver",' i.e. the silver paid by Mexican or Peruvian importers for imported wares. One reason was the feudal style of life in the colonies. 'The extraordinarily luxurious standard of living in Mexico and especially in Peru favoured the sale of mirrors, gold and silver textiles and ornamental furniture.' These, however, the Spaniards did not have for sale, and so the payments went elsewhere. When, at the beginning of the seventeenth century, the

---

[1] Van Klaveren, loc. cit., pp. 164, 224, 226, 255; quotation from p. 226.
[2] Ibid., pp. 244, 159, 110. Concerning the curious legal constructions whereby the Seville traders freed themselves of what, properly speaking, constitutes trade, especially capitalist trade, namely risk-taking, cf. ibid., p. 111.

silver mines were more or less worked out, the colonists, used to fine things, were prevented by pride, if not by other incentives, from reducing their purchases of them, and so had to finance their imports by sending circulating silver to their purveyors instead of that new-won metal with which they had paid before. The result was a local deflation which hit the Spanish exporters, such as they were, more than all others. All in all, the miraculous multiplication of productive capacity expected by the mercantilists failed to materialize in Spain. The image of the early modern economy of the Iberian peninsula which the historians have painted for us shows that medieval conditions continued to prevail. The main export article of the country was still wool; and Spanish iron ore was still bought by the French who returned it in the form of hammers and tongues and daggers and knives.[1]

Of course, the mercantilists had not promised that the economic renewal would come of itself. They had expected it from a definite and determined economic policy. Such a one was initiated by Spain as by all other European countries, but the energy put into it was only small. Van Klaveren goes so far as to deny that we can reasonably speak of a Spanish mercantilism in the sixteenth and seventeenth century for such measures as were passed into law remained a dead letter.[2] A memorial submitted to the government in 1606 by one of the more active towns, Medina del Campo, pointed out, with all desirable openness, that the very opposite of the situation envisaged by the mercantilists existed: there was a large consumption of foreign commodities, and it was not domestic articles that were paying for them.[3]

In this discussion, the fact of war must not be forgotten. Spain was determined to uphold the unity of Europe; her rebellious subjects in the Netherlands were as determined to gain their independence. Taxation on a vast scale became an inescapable necessity, if the overall political aim was to be pursued. This alone kept Spain back, if it did not indeed set her back. When Alba tried to introduce a tax in Holland similar to the *alcabalà* in Spain, he achieved nothing, and all the cash needed had to come from Castile. But this was by far not the worst. It is an astounding, but at the same time an incontrovertible, fact that the unhappy mother-country financed her adversaries as well as her own effort. How could it come to that? There seems to be a puzzle before us, but it is easily solved. Philip II allowed the trade of the rebels with Spain and Portugal to go on. He had no choice in the matter for he needed timber, pitch and tar for his ships, butter and cheese for their crews, corn and flour for the civilian population at home. None of these things could be supplied in sufficient quantities from domestic sources. 'The Dutchmen provided the goods and the Spaniards the cash; with-

---

[1] Ibid., pp. 170, 70, 44, 202, 231.
[2] Ibid., p. 53.
[3] Häbler, loc. cit., p. 84.

out the cash the Dutchmen could not continue the war, without the goods the Spaniards could not continue it.' A curious co-operation indeed! Spain was very much the loser in this game.[1] The greater her martial efforts, the greater became the monetary power of the Dutch.

We are now ready to look at the causes of this state of things, but before we do so, one more fact has to be emphasized. Wars are powerful engines of economic progress, and they were so in the earlier modern period as much as before and since. But Spain failed to modernize even her fighting forces. We have adverted to this fact already in volume III.[2] We may add here that, in the estimate of historians, the battle of Rocroi was lost in 1643 because her artillery, and the methods of employing it, were behind the times.[3]

This leads us immediately to the main cause, and it can be summed up in one word – conservatism. Spain failed to achieve the take-off towards modern capitalism which Holland and England so fully performed because she held fast to her traditional culture, the culture of Catholicism – a culture, that is, under which material values are occupying a modest position in the established *ordo amoris*, and consequently in the modes of action in which that *ordo* becomes actualized. We must not, however, oversimplify things. Keynesian economics has helped to explain many facts of economic history not understood before, and we should call it in to help us even here. Experts tell us that the Spanish economy fared so ill because periods of deflation were intermixed with periods of inflation: in the latter periods, industry was stimulated, as expected; in the former, it was diminished and deadened, again as expected. This may be so. The introduction of copper money into circulation seems indeed to have enlivened production, while the attempted return to a currency of precious metals only seems to have dampened it down.[4] These factors have to be given their due weight, and we are not inclined to play them down. Nevertheless, the main reason for Spain's failure to rise to her opportunities was not economic. It was her ethos, the ethos of her population, that prevented her transformation into a capitalist society on the model of the Calvinist countries in the north.

In popular summations of the Keynesian doctrine, it is sometimes said that certain acts of economic policy, like deficit-financing on the part of government, are like the pressing of the starter button of a motor car or any other power-driven machine: they set the wheels turning. This simile logically presupposes that there is an appropriate ready-to-work engine behind the starter-mechanism: otherwise the desired result will fail to materialize. This engine, in our case, is what Weber called 'the spirit of capitalism'. In Spain, it simply did not exist. Let us look at

---

[1] Van Klaveren, loc. cit., pp. 78, 97, 82, 86, 217; quotation from p. 79.
[2] Cf. p. 200.   [3] Van Klaveren, loc. cit., p. 62.
[4] Ibid., p. 191. Cf. also pp. 60, 61, 90, 185, 186.

the different classes of Iberian society one by one: we shall find that none of them was prepared for a push in the direction of modern capitalism.

The aristocracy was nowhere a major agent of economic and technological renewal, but two features distinguish its specifically Spanish form from similar strata in other countries. There is, first of all, a definite contempt for money-making and 'banausic' occupations which contrasts with the simple disinterest elsewhere, notably in England. And there is, secondly, the fact that the Spanish nobility was much more the model, the object of emulation, of the other layers of the population than the nobilities of neighbouring cultures, notably again the English. This latter statement is almost a re-formulation, in different terms, of the Weberian thesis: Calvinism changed the world where, and in so far as, it offered the middle classes, the burghers, an ideal drawn from their own life: the trader was to become the hard-working, honest, successful trader, the artisan the hard-working, honest, successful artisan. Catholicism failed to change the world, so far as economic action was concerned, because it left the medieval ideal, the nobleman, or rather the noble man, unimpaired, undeflated, un-dethroned. Every Spaniard wanted to be an *hidalgo*: but *hidalgos* did not take pride in counting money and making things.

'The laws of the land,' writes Häbler, 'forbade the nobility, not only to carry on a trade, but even to invest its wealth in the enterprises of tradesmen . . . An ancient law counts the following professions among those which lead to loss of aristocratic privileges: tailor, tanner, timberman, stonemason, sword-smith, fuller, barber, druggist, hawker, cobbler, and similar *oficios viles y bajos*' (low and mean occupations).[1] In the mercantilistic age, attempts were made to tone down these traditional attitudes. 'An enactment of the Cortes [of Aragón] declared in 1626, that the nobilitarian privileges should remain unimpaired if a nobleman engaged in trade, provided that he did not himself work by hand or have the shop in his house and did not spend time in the latter.' 'These provisos,' Häbler remarks, and that justly, 'are sufficient proof that the new norms could not expect to be successful'. They were not; nor was a similar law, dated 1682, of Castile which permitted the ownership of factories to members of the premier estate.[2] As for money dealings, they never got rid of the medieval stigma, the ill odour of usuriousness. 'In the nation of the *hidalgos*, commerce was since time immemorial considered as demeaning . . . The trader and the producer were not acknowledged to be of high status and, so far as possible, [even] kept out of urban administration.'[3]

Where such opinions are held by small minorities, however prestigious, they need not inhibit the development of trade and enterprise. The trader and the entrepreneur may shrug their shoulders and go on their way. But it is different where the values of the aristocracy are the values

[1] Häbler, loc. cit., p. 45.   [2] Ibid., pp. 86, 87, 89.   [3] Ibid., pp. 51 and 61.

of the nation, and that was the case in Spain. Elsewhere noblemen and peasants were considered as contrasting classes with the life-style of the one inapplicable to, even ridiculous in, the other. Not so here. Charles V travelled in Spain for the first time in 1517 and 1518 and Laurent Vital has left an account of his journey. In it, we read the following highly revealing remarks about the population of Asturias (*l'Esture*): 'I believe that, if the people here were as diligent at their work as people are elsewhere, and would cultivate the land, they would be beyond comparison better provided with possessions than they are: but they do not choose to labour beyond only what they find convenient to provide for themselves and their households, for they base themselves for the better part on the idea of gentility, even though they are poor; they assert that they are nobles by virtue of certain privileges which they have received from the kings of Castile for the services which their mountain-dwelling forefathers have rendered to the kingdom . . . against the pagans who, without their resistance, would have conquered the whole of the monarchy. In order that their good help should not remain unrewarded, the kings of Castile have regarded them, and still regard them, as free and exempt from all taxes (*tailles*) and imposts, as if they were gentlemen. But, however much they may have become ennobled, they have not become rich; men, women and young girls walk commonly without hose (*chausses*). I do not know whether this is [simply] the popular costume, or whether the cloth is too dear.'[1]

Their sham-nobility did not, of course, make it possible for these 'nobles' to live without labour. It induced them to work less than they would otherwise have worked, but work they did, because they had to. Yet there was another stratum whose members, possessed by the same desire for noble status, often managed to acquire the legal substance of it, and not only a fancy claim – the stratum whose perseverance in their 'calling' would have been a tremendous help in the development of Spain towards the capitalist dispensation: the merchant class. They, too, liked to turn their backs on their economic function. As soon as a merchant had accumulated enough money to buy himself a landed estate, he did so, and he acquired by preference one with the possession of which noble status was connected. Certain crown-lands (at times situated close to towns such as Seville) retained their royal character throughout the period of Arab control and even after the Reconquista, and whoever bought them could easily rise into the *hidalgo* class. Many *nouveaux riches* made use of this convenient ladder. It contributed in fair measure to the thinning out of the commercial community which was never very numerous anyway and carried off precisely those who were (as they had proved by their enrichment) its most valuable elements.[2]

[1] *Collection des Voyages des Souverains des Pays-Bas*, edd. Gachard, L. P., and Piot, Ch., vol. III, Bruxelles 1881, p. 94.
[2] Van Klaveren, loc. cit., pp. 28, 159.

Turning now to the lower classes, our eyes fall first of all on those who were most closely connected with the upper classes: the domestic servants. In a typically capitalist society this contingent can never be more than small and marginal. A capitalist employer will not spend money on services he does not really need: he is not likely to engage numerous footmen. A capitalist worker, on the other hand, will resent personal subjection which domestic service entails and prefer the impersonality of a factory regime, just as the bourgeois state prefers control by the impersonal law to direction by a king's personal will. In a feudal society, the situation is entirely different, and that on both counts. A grandee has the desire to surround himself with a well-sized retinue: the more retainers he has, the better a man he is. Conspicuous waste does not appal him: on the contrary, it is of the essence of his culture. A domestic employee, on his part, will be pleased by his attachment to an aristocratic master rather than otherwise. Where there is a primary élite, there a secondary élite will also tend to appear – an élite whose élitist standing is due precisely to its connection with one who is part of the top echelon by his own right. Spain's abidingly pre-capitalist character is seen in the fact that the class of which we are speaking was exceptionally large.

That this was indeed so, is a point on which the historians agree. Häbler speaks of the 'mischief (*Unwesen*) of an innumerable class of servants', and van Klaveren writes: 'The throngs of domestic attendants were large; their function was in truth only to give emphasis to the distinction of their masters . . . Even in eighteenth-century England, a very great part of the "working class" consisted of domestic servants . . . In Castile, however, the group of domestic personnel had to be very much greater because it had to serve there as a façade' – as conspicuous waste, as Veblen would have said. Van Klaveren speaks of this over-proliferation of a non-productive stratum as 'the result of a social psychosis which considered the *hidalgo* as the ideal type of the Castilian who would have lost his *hidalgunia* if he had done his domestic chores himself'. A law of the year 1623 restricted the permissible number of attendants per grandee to eighteen. Even if it had been implemented, which is doubtful, it would surely not have created Puritan conditions in this respect![1]

Most important, however, and most characteristic of the difficulties which blocked the transition of Spain to a modern industrial economy, was the unwillingness of her masses to accept the harsh realities of a factory regime. Vagrancy was rampant both in the England of the first Elizabeth and in the Iberia of the second Philip, but England knew how to deal with it and Iberia did not. In England we see the coming of the cruel Elizabethan poor law; in Iberia we observe the continuation of medieval charity, the feeding of every beggar at every convent door, a

[1] Häbler, loc. cit., p. 155; van Klaveren, loc. cit., pp. 188 and 189.

feeding which was, no doubt, not very lavish, but sufficient to keep going any *sopista* (literally a 'souper', 'one living on convent soups') who preferred freedom to wages. Anyone who has acquainted himself with the Spanish literature of this period knows that it is distinguished from other European literatures of the same time by the presence of a special *genre*, the picaresque novel (from *picaro*, a rogue, describing the same kind of hobo as the word *sopista*). *Lazarillo de Tormes* (probably by Hurtado de Vendoza) and *Rinconete y Cortadillo* (by Miguel de Cervantes) are good examples of great interest to the social historian. Concerning the question as to what proportion of the population led this footloose existence, 'nearly one third' has been mentioned as a reasonable estimate.[1] This figure is hard to believe, but even if it is exaggerated, it proves that the numbers involved were substantial.

Speaking, in the economist's sober fashion, of the 'causes for the inelasticity of production' in Castile – more simply worded, for the inability of the Spanish economy to respond positively to the classical stimulants – van Klaveren has this to say: 'An explanation can only lie in the fact that . . . a major proportion of the population acted as consumers, but not as producers, the fact that a large number of people were employed in unproductive lines. Differently expressed, the cause must have been a disproportion between the population able to work and the population actually at work. There must have been a great body of men who eked out a livelihood as beggars, vagabonds, superfluous servants and criminals, a phenomenon which, for its part, must be seen as connected with a disinclination to toil: the so-called "disutility of labour" must have been very great in Castile.' Van Klaveren goes on to report that many statements to the effect that 'the Spaniards were lazy' were made at the time, both by Spaniards themselves and by foreigners, but he pleads that such judgments be avoided. The difference between the standard of living achievable by wage-earning and that available by begging was so small that it was not economically irrational to prefer the latter way of life to the former.[2] Thus we see in the end that the *causa causarum* of the failure of the Iberian economy to modernize itself was, in the instance of the lower, as in that of the upper classes, the absence of the 'spirit of capitalism', of the Protestant ethic, of that Puritan attitude which accepted hard effort for low reward or even no reward as inherently meaningful. When an anonymous memorial submitted to Carlos II in 1686 insisted that the acquisition of gold and silver will do nothing for a country – that the metal will, in fact, not remain in the country – unless the inhabitants are prepared to shed their sweat, 'the most indispensable of all "metals",'[3] it summed up in a nutshell why mercantilism was never a success in Spain.

[1] Cf. Marañon, G., *Olivares: Der Niedergang Spaniens als Weltmacht*, transl. Pfandl, L., München 1939, p. 214.
[2] Van Klaveren, pp. 187-9.   [3] Häbler, pp. 19 and 20.

Spain, however, was a non-performer, not only if we measure her with the mercantilistic, but even if we apply to her the milder cameralistic yard-stick. Not only did she not keep pace with the Calvinist countries, but she even failed to follow the Lutheran lands. These latter developed at any rate a modernized bureaucracy; Spain did not. In the year 1606, the town of Medina del Campo petitioned that the control of the export of precious metals be entrusted to the Inquisition: that clerical body alone was expected to do the job properly, the secular officials of the state obviously were not. In fact, the civil servants were often described as venal or corrupt, but, as in the case of labour, so here, a careless moralizing attitude would be unscholarly.[1] What we must remember is that feudal societies make public offices into private prerogatives. When William the Conqueror invested Hugh of Montgomery with wide possessions, he gave him the right rather than the duty to administer 'his' lands, and it was understood that this should be so. It was only the modern age which – not without the help of religious developments – produced the civil servant fully paid by the state and fully placed under its discipline, the Prussian type of official who was a Kantian (i.e. a post-Calvinist and near-Calvinist) in upbringing and attitude as well as in everyday action. That modern age, Spain was not ready to enter for a long time.

It is a final confirmation of our whole analysis that Spanish mercantilism, when it at long last developed in the eighteenth century, urged Spain to cease to be herself and change her whole being so as to conform to the image and to the reality of her erstwhile enemies, England and Holland.[2] Gerónimo de Uztariz bases himself largely on Huet's *Mémoires sur le Commerce des Hollandais*; no fewer than eleven chapters of his *Theoria y Práctica de Comercio y de Marina* (1724 and 1742) are devoted to that admired nation. Bernardo de Ulloa gives it as his opinion that nature has equipped Spain better than the Netherlands: she is richer in material resources. Why then does Spain lose her wealth to the Netherlands? Because, the *Restabilimiento de las Fábricas y Comercio Español* (1740) answers, the foreigners are stronger in industry and industriousness. The enterprise the Northern Calvinists have shown in founding and running their East and West Indian Companies alone explains their flourishing state, sadly contrasting with Iberia's decayed condition.[3]

So much about the economy; now a brief word about science. As all development is one, as it was the same impetus which raised both industrial production and the applied arts, and scientific research and the theoretical sciences to the heights, we must expect that the Catholic

[1] Cf. van Klaveren, pp. 47–9, 54, 55; also pp. 144, 153, 175, 176.
[2] Cf. Wirminghaus, A., *Zwei spanische Merkantilisten (Gerónimo de Uztariz und Bernardo de Ulloa)*, Jena 1886.
[3] Ibid., pp. 7, 10, 52, 61, 63, 75, 85.

cultures were camp-followers rather than pioneers even in this particular field. This was indeed so, and one outstanding observer has given us the chief reason for this lag: 'The purely religious philosophy of an Erigena or an Anselm sees in nature only the symbol and shadow of spiritual reality and consequently leaves no room for a science of things; while the thoroughgoing theologism of Peter Damian . . . rejects even the principles of causality and the uniformity of nature in the interests of the divine omnipotence . . . In the eyes of the theologians, there was no room for an independent science . . . which based itself on human reason and could dispense with the light of revelation. The true wisdom was essentially theocentric. It sought the explanation of all things in God and related every fact of experience, every form of art and science, to its divine source and center. For the universe is nothing but a reflection or image of the glory of God.'[1] Of course, this point must not be exaggerated. Dawson goes on to quote St. Thomas Aquinas whose system leaves wide latitude to scientific research and even calls for it – the reason why the Catholics of the scientific centuries have tended to place the Doctor Angelicus higher than the Seraphicus.

Still, Dawson's assertion stands. The Catholic ages had a totally different approach to nature, even down to the level of awareness, to the very mode of *seeing* the physical environment. Macaulay, in one of his finest critical essays, draws attention to this fact. 'No person can have attended to the Divine Comedy,' he writes, 'without observing how little impression the forms of the external world appear to have made on the mind of Dante. His temper and his situation led him to fix his observation almost exclusively on human nature. The exquisite opening of the eighth[2] canto of the Purgatorio affords a strong instance of this. He leaves to others the earth, the ocean, and the sky. His business is with man. To other writers, evening may be the season of dews and stars and radiant clouds. To Dante it is the hour of fond recollection and passionate devotion – the hour which melts the heart of the mariner and kindles the love of the pilgrim . . . The feeling of the present age has taken a direction diametrically opposite. The magnificence of the physical world, and its influence upon the human mind, have been the favourite themes of our most eminent poets . . . The orthodox poetical creed is

[1] Dawson, Chr., *The Formation of Christendom*, New York 1967, pp. 234, 235, 238.
[2] This passage which describes the first sunset experienced in purgatory, (cf. Temple Classics ed., London 1933, p. 92), may be freely translated as follows:

> The hour it was when in the journeying souls
> Desire is stilled, and when their heart is softened,
> The day they said farewell to friends belov'd;

> The hour the pilgrim newly setting out
> Is pierced by love when from afar
> He hears a bell that mourns the dying day.

more Catholic. The noblest earthly object of the contemplation of man is man himself. The universe, and all its fair and glorious forms, are indeed included in the wide empire of the imagination; but she has placed her home and her sanctuary amidst the inexhaustible varieties and the impenetrable mysteries of the mind.'[1]

Here again, exaggeration must be carefully avoided. As we pointed out not long ago,[2] the attitude of St. Francis to the landscape and all that lives and moves and has its being in it, is proof that the medieval disinterest in the material creation is waning in his day, and that a new interest is waxing strong, an interest which, even if it was at first merely one of childlike wonder and enjoyment, could yet become soberly operational and domination-directed. Still, Macaulay is ultimately as correct as Dawson. In its core of cores, the Catholic culture properly so called is symbolistic, not activistic; and that is the reason why it has always led in the fine arts, above all in painting and in music, while it has lagged in the mechanical and commercial arts, in factory and counting-house.

A culture-lag, however, is not something that lasts for ever. Even he who dawdles will ultimately come to the same point as he who runs; indeed, he may overtake him, if the runner slackens because he has lost his spirit. Today, the distance between England and Italy is but small, and it may even be doubtful who is ahead; tomorrow the relationship between North America and the Hispanic world may well be in the same case. Two influences, one minor and one major, have imparted economic and technological dynamism to the countries under the Roman obedience. The minor influence is the interest in the machine as a work of art. The medieval producer was an artisan and often half an artist; he loved his tools, but he would have looked askance at a contraption tending to make a tool of him; yet that contraption would have fascinated him all the same as a piece of ingenuity, a product of human skill, a proof of man's mind and mastery. When the great automobile firms started to open repair shops in such countries as Mexico, they found that they could attract keen young men, not only because they offered good wages, but also because there were some who found the work enjoyable. To put a motor right that has gone wrong is a challenge which even he may gladly accept who is by his whole culture and upbringing still inclined to old-style craftsmanship. We see here a gate through which capitalism could enter into substantially pre-capitalist, because traditionally Catholic, societies.

But these societies accepted in the end the factory system also, with all its painful impersonality and harsh mechanization of work and life. There were initial difficulties, of course: to mention but one, it was not

[1] Macaulay, T. B., *Critical, Historical and Miscellaneous Essays*, New York 1893, vol. I, pp. 72 and 73.
[2] Cf. above, p. 310.

easy to make the newly acquired workers clock in and clock out exactly on time, because in many of the cultures concerned eight o'clock meant *about* eight o'clock, and not eight o'clock *sharp*. But these bairns' troubles were overcome. How was the feat accomplished? The answer is extremely simple: by the most natural of all means – by the operation of the desire, inborn in men, to enjoy, or, to be more specific, by the removal of the limitations to the desire for enjoyment which earlier systems of social control had imposed on it.

When Calvinism ascribed to economic action a religious meaning, it meant to foster a virtue, not a vice: the virtue of work, of hard, unremitting, methodical devotion to duty. The material reward as such was regarded as unimportant: you toiled, not in order to earn, and even less in order to spend, but in order to be able to feel yourself a child of God, one predestined to eternal blessedness in heaven. As for the money that flowed into one's pockets, it was not to be lightheartedly disbursed; it was a temptation to be resisted, a danger, something of an unvalue rather than a value. It is almost a definition of a Puritan to say that he was one who was in fact rich, yet preferred to live as if he were poor. Such a life-policy is possible in a religious movement's heroic days, but it is impossible in the long run. On the pioneers follow the less pioneering later generations, the sons and grandsons who feel differently from their fathers and grandfathers. In spite of all preachings, the craving for an easier life wins the day and the standard of enjoyment is allowed to rise. The Dutch burghers portrayed by Rembrandt and Hals are ascetics no longer: their portraitists and their portraits tell us in no uncertain manner that they are *gourmands* and *gourmets*. But if the operation of men's natural urge towards a good life could change the stern Calvinists, subjected to a rigorous system of social control, how could it fail to change the much more relaxed Catholics whose Church was, by comparison, the mildest of task-masters? The truth is that, as the modern age progressed, both variants of Christianity lost their grip on the masses of men. So far as the Catholic cultures are concerned, what happened was that a revaluation of values took place: while the *picaro* of the sixteenth or seventeenth century preferred freedom to toil, even if this meant poverty, the proletarian of the nineteenth and twentieth centuries prefers toil without freedom, so long as this secures higher material well-being. And this gave capitalism the chance it needed to transform even those cultures which, to start with, were resistant to it.

In what we have said in the last paragraph we have turned back, from our excursus, to the main theme of the present chapter: the study of Protestantism, more especially Calvinism, and its role in the transition from community to association, from a society devoted to the ideals of sociality to a society given to the pursuit of the overriding aim of world-domination. This aim, as it was at first envisaged, had little in it that was materialistic. It was, in fact, a totally religious aim inspired by the wish to subject nature to the will of man, and man, for his part, to the will of God. Jehan Calvin's disciples, no less than those of Iñigo Loyola, knew only one purpose: to do all they could *ad majorem Dei gloriam*. But in the process, things got changed. The same nations which produced Puritanism, also produced Utilitarianism; the call for the greatest godliness, gave way to the call for the greatest happiness, of the greatest number; the open pursuit of self-interest was proclaimed a right of the liberated individual; and thus a world arose which no Christian, whether of the Roman variety or the Genevan, could recognize as reconcilable with his Master's behests.

THE COMING OF A SECULAR CIVILIZATION

Max Weber's essay on *The Protestant Ethic and the Spirit of Capitalism* contains in addition to the famous theory which we have so fully discussed and, in most things, so loyally supported in these pages, the sketch of a philosophy of much wider, not to say universal, import. It is an interpretation of history which, if it had ever been fully worked out, would have exhibited the same grandeur as that of, say, Comte or Hegel. But there is one essential aspect of it which distinguishes it from these two, and most other, efforts to see and interpret history as a whole: its inherent pessimism. Unlike practically all other children of the nineteenth century, Weber did not equate process with progress; and least of all was he inclined to assume, as the optimists of the eighteenth century had done, that the process was progress because in it evil was transmuted into good. The easy belief of Leibniz and the Leibnizians that a beneficent Providence was combining the selfish deeds of each into social forms advantageous to all, the belief soaked up and poured forth, in a technicized form, by the science of Political Economy,[1] was not for him. Indeed, his conviction was that things worked the other way around. Individuals were often activated by the finest motives: life twisted their ideals out of shape until they were unrecognizable, the very opposite of the original intention. A book on the sociology of religion need not go far afield in order to find evidence of Weber's grim outlook: the doctrine of the 'routinization of charisma' (which we have rejected in our fourth volume) is a prime exemplification of it. The charismatic man breaks into reality like a ray of sunshine into a dusky and depressing day. He gives meaning to many lives; he offers, receives, and spreads love; everything, absolutely everything, seems to be changed in the twinkling of an eye. But, alas, not for long. The leader must die and disappear, and the shadows at once close in. Love degener-

[1] Cf. Stark, W., *The Ideal Foundations of Economic Thought*, London 1943, esp. chapter 1, 'The Philosophical Foundations of Classical Economics'.

ates into law; the direct apprehension of God becomes dry-as-dust theology; the place of true worship is usurped by dead ritual. In the end, the name of the prophet is merely a label which covers – misleadingly – a structure opposed to everything he felt, thought and longed for when he prayed.

Interestingly enough, this doctrine is yet another proof of the tremendous influence of Calvinism on modern life. For what was it that induced Weber to see universal history in so sombre a light? Clearly, it was the conviction that this is a fallen world in which good must for ever be a stranger: it may impinge on it from the outside, it may – like the seed in the Gospel parable (Matthew xiii) – lie on the surface for a while, but it will not have the moisture needed to sprout and to strike root, and so it will wither away and die. Weber, who thought of himself as an irreligious man, and that not without sufficient reason, had – unbeknown to himself – received this subconscious metaphysic from a religious source: his mother, a deeply believing woman who, in turn, had received it from her own mother, Emilia Fallenstein, née Souchay.[1] The Souchays, however, were a typical Calvinist family. Their forebears had left Catholic France in order to be able freely to follow their Huguenot creed, and they had settled in Germany, working as goldsmiths (presumably also as watchmakers, or at least sellers of watches) and amassing a fortune – a prime illustration, surely, of the theory developed by Emilia Fallenstein's sociologist grandson. Arthur Mitzmann calls Emilia Fallenstein-Souchay a 'paragon of sorrowing ethical religiosity', and though every word in this statement deserves emphasis, the word 'sorrowing' needs, in our context, particular stress. There was, however, this difference between Emilia Fallenstein-Souchay and her daughter Helene Weber-Fallenstein, on the one hand, and Helene's son Max on the other, that Max took over the Calvinist outlook without the Calvinist theology. A religious philosophy became in his hands a philosophy without religion. In this way, not only Weber's family, but even Weber himself is an illustration of the 'routinization', and more especially of the rationalization, of religion in our workaday world.

The essay on *The Protestant Ethic and the Spirit of Capitalism* is, as we can see, not merely an investigation of the rise of an economic order, but also an elucidation of the fall of a religious system. Weber's discussion is brief, but clear. 'The full economic effects of those great religious movements, whose significance for economic development lay above all in their ascetic educative influence, generally came only after the peak of the purely religious enthusiasm was past,' he writes. 'Then the intensity of the search for the Kingdom of God commenced gradually to pass over into sober economic virtue; the religious roots died

[1] Cf. Mitzmann, loc. cit., p. 18.

out slowly, giving way to utilitarian worldliness . . . Since asceticism undertook to remodel the world and to work out its ideals in the world, material goods have gained an increasing and finally an inexorable power over the lives of men as at no previous period in history . . . In the field of its highest development, in the United States, the pursuit of wealth, stripped of its religious and ethical meaning, tends to become associated with purely mundane passions . . .'[1] Asceticism has spawned hedonism, religiousness, materialism – a transvaluation of values, perhaps even a devaluation of values, which, to the extent that it is true, may well induce a man to embrace Weber's tragic view of human destiny.

The Weberian theory which we have just outlined belongs to a group of doctrines which Wilhelm Wundt has brought together under the concept of 'the heteronomy of purposes'.[2] In addition to men's individual wills, the thinkers involved have felt, yet another will – a heterogeneous purpose – seems to be working in the world. Adam Smith spoke of an 'invisible hand' and asserted that it turns selfish actions into social results.[3] 'Private vices' become according to Bernard de Mandeville 'public benefits'.[4] The desire for enrichment, for instance, fosters savings, i.e. the formation of capital, which raises the whole economy to a higher level and thereby helps even those who do not and cannot save, the poor. This is the optimistic version of the doctrine. It still has a religious tinge. An 'invisible hand' is and must be something mysterious. The simple truth is that the upholders of the optimistic version of the heterogony of purposes were all still influenced by credal traditions; they were at the very least deists. Max Weber was not; he was at most an agnostic. The only tradition of the religious past which he carried forward was a negative one – the Calvinist conviction that the children of Adam are for ever abandoned by the powers above, and that their efforts for good, because they are so abandoned, must inevitably fail.

If one were to look for a pendant to Adam Smith's 'invisible hand' in Max Weber, one would have to assume that it is the devil's hand, as Smith's is, even if we are not told so, God's. But no such metaphysical personage is needed to make sense of Weber's analysis. It is only too clear why the religious upsurge of the sixteenth century ended in the upsurge of materialism in the nineteenth. Calvinism meant to liberate man's desire to create, not his desire to enjoy. Work for the purpose of working, it preached, not for an ulterior purpose; earn for the purpose of earning, not for the purpose of spending, of 'riotous living'. The

[1] *The Protestant Ethic*, as quoted, pp. 176, 181, 182.
[2] Cf. *System der Philosophie*, ed. Leipzig 1897, p. 328. Cf. also Stark, W., 'Max Weber and the Heterogony of Purposes', *Social Research*, 1967, pp. 249 et seq.
[3] *An Inquiry into the Nature and Causes of the Wealth of Nations*, ed. Eliot, C. W., New York 1909, p. 282.
[4] Subtitle of *The Fable of the Bees*.

term 'human nature' has so often been misused that the social scientist should be reluctant to apply it. Yet here it is, for once, justified. It is *not* human nature to work for the purpose of working; it *is* human nature to work in order to earn, and to earn in order to spend. The Calvinist may have prayed, like any Christian: lead us not into temptation, but there was one temptation into which he led himself, and to which he ultimately succumbed. A world totally devoted to the pursuit of material values, of physical enjoyment even – the world bemoaned by Max Weber – was the result. In the Puritan's view, 'the care for external goods should only lie on the shoulders of the "saint like a light cloak which can be thrown aside at any moment". But fate decreed that the cloak should become an iron cage'.[1]

All in all, then, Weber's final theory is something like *a* doctrine, or *the* doctrine, of the Fall – the fall of the Calvinist culture from grace and godliness into greed; the fall of the West from Calvinism into capitalism. If things are seen from the point of view of asceticism – and Weber tends to see them from this angle – there is indeed descent, a negative heteronomy of purposes. If, on the other hand, they are seen from the point of view of hedonism – and there is no reason why they should not be considered from this side – there is ascent, a positive result. Calvinism may then appear, according to Hegel's and Marx's way of thinking, as a 'ruse of reason' (*List der Vernunft*), initiated by the aim-directed forces of history in order to stimulate the productive capacities of man and ultimately to lead him into a materialistic paradise. No matter: in either case, it is a secular civilization that is the outcome of the religious upheaval, and so far as the end result of the development is concerned, the theory would appear to be entirely correct. Capitalist hedonism has replaced Calvinist asceticism, and nothing can be historically more true than this fact.

One final point needs to be added. By the Industrial Revolution, the one-time uniform bourgeoisie was split into an entrepreneurial and a hand-working class, and it became increasingly impossible that the latter should continue to carry the traditional philosophies of the past. The entrepreneurs could still feel close to Calvinism: they indeed received the wages of work which the Protestant ethic had promised – a feeling of effectiveness, of power, of achievement, of creativeness. It is highly characteristic that Alfred Marshall's classical *Principles of Economics*, first published in 1890 – a late product of the Reformation outlook in so far as the author was in his underlying ethos to some extent influenced by Evangelicalism – considered the privilege of the entrepreneur to lie, not in his higher income, but in the greater meaningfulness, or, to repeat the irreplaceable key-term, in the creativeness,

---

[1] *The Protestant Ethic*, as quoted, p. 181. The quotation within the quotation is from the twelfth chapter of William Baxter's *The Saints' Everlasting Rest* (no page reference given).

of his effort.[1] No such creativity could be experienced by the operative, the proletarian. His whole life came to be dominated by the machine, and there simply was nothing that could give meaning to his drudgery except the wage-packet which he received and the enjoyments which it mediated. Thus a materialistic outlook was very nearly forced on the bulk of the population, and this not only spelled the end of the ascendancy of Calvinism, but threw all religiosity into a deepening crisis.

[1] This creativity of the entrepreneur rested on the fact that it was his function to combine the factors of production, and that he could therefore combine them in ever new ways. Cf. the discussion of Marshall in Parsons, T., *The Structure of Social Action*, New York and London 1937, pp. 129 et seq., esp. 161 et seq.

3 · THE AGE OF ASSOCIATION AND ITS SECULAR CIVILIZATION

The sociology of religion, as it is at present constituted, is characterized by a deep division of labour which, on the whole, must be regarded as helpful and healthy.[1] There are some workers in the field who concentrate on description, and there are others who concern themselves with analysis: in Dilthey's terminology, there are some who want to 'know about' the sector of reality involved, know ever more, know as much as we can know, and there are others who aim at 'understanding', an inner comprehension which, if possible, is to penetrate to ever more basic, ever more hidden, layers. The present work, as every reader of it knows, belongs to the second category. It continues the endeavours of the social theorists such as Durkheim, Tönnies and Weber; it has not made use of the instrumentarium developed by the social statisticians. Where, and in so far as, naked facts are concerned, it must avail itself of the information which fellow-workers across the fence have managed to provide. Their main insight, however, has been that wherever 'modernity' has advanced, religiosity has recoiled. It is no accident that a recent summing-up work speaks, even on its title-page, of an 'eclipse of the sacred in industrial civilization'.[2] We shall not stay to parade the figures which the investigators have amassed. There is no need for it, for what they have to offer is merely a more precise confirmation of the facts which are notorious anyway.

Of course, there is always the question as to what the statistics really mean. Church-going has declined: but does that signify that religiosity, in the proper sense of the word, has lost ground? Not necessarily.[3] The times are not so long past when an American business man had to attend a house of worship on a Sunday morning because this helped him in his affairs, for instance in the procurement of bankers' credit. If bank managers no longer set great store by this outer evidence of respectability or character, and their clients stay in bed instead of hurrying to church or chapel, the loss to faith is really small. For centuries, loyalty to the state was expressed by attending one type of service, while revolutionary sentiments were abreacted by attending another. If these days are over and church-going or chapel-going are today due

[1] Cf. Stark, W., 'Description and Theory: A Plea for Cooperation', *Sociological Analysis*, 1971, pp. 209 et seq.
[2] Cf. Acquaviva, S. S., *L'Eclipse du Sacré dans la Civilisation Industrielle*, Tours 1967.
[3] Cf. the warnings given by that great pioneer of the descriptive sociology of religion, Gabriel Le Bras, in his *Études de Sociologie Religieuse*, vol. II, Paris 1956, p. 561.

more to an inner, truly religious need, then the talk about a shrinkage of religiosity may very well be misleading. Hypocrites need not be counted in God's house.

Of course, our statisticians have not been satisfied with so crude an index as church-going. They have searched for more suitable yardsticks and believe they have found them. It is not for us to evaluate their efforts, nor need we do so, for we are accepting their results. The caution we have given is justified, but scepticism *vis-à-vis* statistical tables can easily be overdone. Outer evidences are but *outer* evidences, but they are at the same time outer *evidences*. It is not to be doubted that religion does not mean in the twentieth century what it meant in the twelfth, or the sixteenth, or even at the beginning of the nineteenth. The fact is there and has to be taken for granted. Above all, it has to be explained. The theoretician's task is to raise the question, *why?*

THE INNER CONDITION OF CHRISTENDOM IN MODERN TIMES

We have in various places, but above all in our fourth volume, given as our conviction that religion is part of life rather than part of thought,[1] and if this is so, then it will only perform its function and therefore remain in undiminished vigour, if it is blended into the totality of culture, truly one with it, as the principle of vitality is part of the body which it animates. There are, even today, still societies, or at least sub-societies, in which this condition conducive to an unproblematical religiosity still persists: the little town in Germany in which the poet Carl Zuckmayer was born is obviously one. 'I was a Catholic,' he writes in his book of recollections, and 'I consider this as one of the fortunate accidents of my youth. Fortunate was above all the matter-of-fact character of this belonging to a religious community whose ritual is rooted in ancient forms, to a church, in which the mystery of incarnation, the miracle of transubstantiation, is again and again taking place in every mass. The child runs into the church as it does into a baker's shop; there is nothing pietistically dignified or solemn about it. Here you smell the warm bread, there the stone-cool incense. The genuflecting, the kneeling down, the folding of the hands, the making of the sign of the cross, the ringing of the altar bell, the raising of the monstrance, the beating of the breast during the deep stillness of the transubstantiation, all this fits into daily life, just like going to bed, getting up, putting on one's clothes, learning and play. It simply is the Sunday which all have in common, and on which the fat black man from the presbytery is transformed into a sacred figure with resplendent vestments . . . My religion offered me, in my childhood, the awakening of an inner life which penetrated flesh and blood; it offered me, for a while, the happiness of an unconditional faith, and later, in my adolescence, all the

[1] Cf. our vol. IV. p. 74.

struggles, doubts and spiritual crises which belong to a productive existence, right to estrangement, but never to indifference; and it offered me in the end, beyond all obstacles, the quiet knowledge that my childhood faith was true. That extraordinary enchantment which dwells in the mystery of the sacraments, from the whisper of the first confession to the swallowing of the host in the first communion, even such rituals which are often smiled at as superstitious, mechanical or magical, like the dipping of the finger tips into blessed water, the rosary, the eternal light above the altar, exert a symbolic power and give to the heart a simple assurance . . . In mysticism and the veneration of the Virgin, too, there is nothing that could be called obscurantist or narcotic. A lived faith does not inhibit, but arouses and stimulates the urge to know and gain insight. This synthesis is as old as the primal questionings of mankind, as philosophy and theism, but it is also as new and inexhaustible as no other experience or doctrine which is being offered to men today.'[1]

Zuckmayer relates on the next page, how he was for a while taken in by the philosophy of Nietzsche, with its cry that 'God is dead', and how this infatuation was countered by the reading of St. Augustine's *Confessions*; how he came to the conclusion that what had attracted him in *Zarathustra*, for instance, was merely a kind of poetry without deeper spiritual implications. But from all that he tells us it is clear that it was not argument that defeated argument in his mind, but rather life – the wave of atheism that washed against him was thrown back by the rock-like foundation of his self, or rather of the culture of which that self was a product and a constitutive element. 'The heart has its reasons which reason does not know,' says Pascal in a passage which cannot be quoted too often.[2] It was the reason of Zuckmayer's heart, his vital or existential reason, so to speak, which defeated Nietzsche's discursive cleverness, and it found the task easy because it knew itself closer to the core and mystery of things.

Zuckmayer happened to be born a Catholic, but other faiths (as he acknowledges) may also achieve that deep identification with a perennial culture of which he is speaking, and which puts religion beyond difficulty and danger. What Catholicism is to Zuckmayer's native Kurhessen, that Calvinism is to Skye off the Caledonian shore and Lutheranism to the Dalarna district of central Sweden. How is it that such faiths, which represent part and parcel of the submerged metaphysics of their societies and are, as an integral aspect of the collective unconscious, beyond attack, become vulnerable and can be defeated? That is the great question with which our investigation, in these closing stages, has still to grapple.

[1] Zuckmayer, C., *Als wärs ein Stück von mir*, Konstanz 1960, pp. 152 and 153. My translation.

[2] *The Thoughts of Blase Pascal*, transl. Kegan Paul, C., London 1905, p. 306.

The answer will have to be given in two stages: both the inner condition of Christendom since the Reformation and the outer conditions of Christianity since the coming of capitalism have contributed to the crisis which grips belief today. The whole phenomenon of religiosity has been shaken from its moorings. What was taken at one time as 'given' and hence as 'matter of fact' like the air we breathe, has become problematic to the bulk of men.

So far as the inner condition of Christendom since the Reformation is concerned, it is clear that the very fact of dividedness had, perforce, to exert a deleterious, destructive influence. Even a man from Kurhessen or Skye or Dalarna will remain settled only so long as creeds not his own are no more than distant phenomena on the horizon, not realities which force their way into the centre of his consciousness. In a religiously mixed society, religion must be problematic: it is as simple as that. It is dragged from its anchor-ground in the depths of life and thrown on to the surface, to be tossed about by the waves of polemics and politics. It is then no longer a matter of certainties and certainty. The *furor theologicus*, displayed by well-meaning protagonists on either side of the arena, has only benefited the laughing thirds: agnosticism and atheism. 'It is natural that schism should lead to incredulity', writes Chateaubriand,[1] and he is right.

A historical analysis of this first cause for the recoil of faith can be fairly precise. Up to the Thirty Years' War, the unity of Europe was not yet irretrievably lost. There was perhaps as yet a possibility of reconciliation: who knows? – especially as a common danger, and a mortal one to boot, was looming ever larger in the east: the Turk. Every time he made one step westward, the tone of religious squabbling lost something of its acidity (though it unhappily regained that acidity as soon as he retreated one step). And there was, of course, still the possibility of defeating the one party or the other. The Habsburgs, busily building a bridge from their Spanish peninsula to their possessions in Italy and Austria, might hope that they might yet achieve universal ascendancy. The Calvinists, possessing themselves of Bohemia, and anticipating Bismarck's opinion that he who controls that heartland of Europe, controls Europe as a whole, might yet entertain the same delusion. It was only the course of the great war itself, revealing as it did the existence of an equilibrium of forces between the warring confessions, which created political, social and intellectual conditions which perpetuated religious division and disunity and thereby shifted religion from the area of agreed truths to that of doubtful opinions.

In a sense, the cause of European unity was lost almost at once. For when Frederick, the Winter-King, as he has been so pathetically dubbed, had to flee from Prague after the Battle of the White Mountain

[1] Chateaubriand, F. R., *Génie du Christianisme*, ed. Paris 1966, vol. I, p. 55. My translation.

(8 November 1620), the power positions on his own side of the fighting line began to change. The Calvinist influence began to wane, that of the Lutheran forces to wax strong, and this shift was confirmed and made final when, in Gustavus Adolfus, a saviour appeared for the hard-pressed Protestant cause. Gustavus Adolfus was a Lutheran; more importantly, he was a caesaropapist; there was nothing in him of that internationalism which was characteristic of the Calvinist outlook and made it, in one important aspect at least, a true pendant to Catholicism. After the summer of 1630, it was understood, in the Protestant camp, that the world consisted of sovereign states, each with its own established religion. Multiplicity had in this way gained the upper hand of unity. But on the Catholic side, similar developments had taken place, or were taking place. Both pope and emperor, of course, stuck to the vision of an *orbis terrarum* safely integrated under the aegis of Rome (though, as to the detail, it must be emphasized, they entertained very different, indeed discordant, opinions); but there was also France, a Gallican country, we must remember, rather than a Catholic one. Under the able leadership of Richelieu and his *Eminence Grise*, François Joseph du Tremblay, she charted a course which was designed to secure the hegemony of France, and not the glory of the House of Habsburg. As Sweden and France became the leading powers, the possibility of a united Europe with a unified and unifying religion died, to continue only as a ghost and a dream.

Significantly, it was a military man who first realized that the cause of European unity was lost: Albrecht von Wallenstein, the imperial commander-in-chief. He became increasingly convinced that – given the hard facts of the situation, the forces available to either side – there could only be one outcome of the struggle, namely compromise. Actuated also by personal ambitions (which do not concern us here), he started to make overtures to his adversaries, with the result that he became guilty of treason, and was removed on 25 February 1634 – murdered, as the Protestants were to say, executed after due process of law, as the Catholics would have it.[1] Later history has not perhaps justified Wallenstein's breach of trust, but it has vindicated his political judgment. What he wanted, namely a return to the conditions of 1618 and their acceptance as permanent, was implemented at the peace treaties concluded in the Westfalian towns after 1648. Countries like Spain or Scotland or Sweden, and territories like Kurhessen, might then continue the medieval condition of one culture, one religion, but Europe was split for good, with the consequences for the life of faith which we have already characterized.

The simple split, however, was only the beginning. It is not unnatural

---

[1] The most prestigious study of this subject is Srbik, H. Ritter von, *Wallensteins Ende.* Cf. ed. Salzburg 1952, esp. pp. 34, 36, 278; cf. also pp. 56 and 98. Cf. furthermore p. 280 *re* Paul Wiegler's *Wallenstein*, Berlin 1920.

for societies, especially new ones, to define themselves, both by working at their self-identification and by trying to set themselves off from others. This is what happened. The contrasts grew. In addition to the polemics on fundamentals which sprang up, there was also a less dramatic, but at the same time more insidious divergence in cultural detail. The Catholics would say hallelúja, as in the olden times; the Protestants halléluja. A petty matter? Certainly. But life is composed of such, and between them they give character to culture and cultures and determine their contrasts. By 1680, it was hardly an exaggeration to speak of Christendoms and Christianities.

But the growing estrangement between Catholicism and Protestantism was not the only – and perhaps was not even the most serious – factor which made theology, and with it religion, problematical. Disagreements had always existed, and some of them had been considerable even in the days when the Universal Church was at its zenith point. The contrast between Franciscanism (a religion of the heart rather than of the head, a movement tending towards more pantheistic conceptions) and Dominicanism (at first a religion of the head rather than of the heart, and a movement tending towards a sharper integration of the individual), springs to mind at once. But so great was the inherent drive for synthesis that, if there were tensions at all, they did not lead to uncertainties or unsettlements – a fact all the more surprising as the two mendicant orders were in many respects competitors, sharing the same field of action, the towns, appealing to the same social strata, the burghers, and so on. Synthesis, as we have seen all along, is simply of the essence of Catholicism. Protestantism, on the other hand, is given to the principles of multiplicity and antithesis. Its very name is expressive of the fact. Hardly had the Reformation started, when it broke in two, a more conservative and a more radical wing facing each other across a sharp divide. But it is somewhat misleading to speak of a 'more conservative' and a 'more radical' wing, as if there had been *one* movement with only differences in shading, a more purple part adjoining another of more pinkish colour. No, there were *two* movements, separated by essentials. Rigorism is the very opposite of antinomianism; Calvin's doctrine of total perversion is *totally* irreconcilable with Fox's conviction that there is an inner light in every man who comes to be born. The overstrict upbringing which went with Puritanism (Robert Burns's 'we piss'd wi' dread . . .')[1] was bound to produce an entirely different type of man from the overpermissive pedagogy which was laid on in Quaker beliefs and has left a very large legacy today. But most important perhaps is the fact that the fissiparous tendency has affected even the palladium of Protestantism – the trust in the Bible, in 'the Word'. This was the rock on which Luther and Calvin based their churches when

---

[1] 'Holy Willie's Prayer', *The Poetical Works of Robert Burns* ed. Robertson J. Logie, ed. London 1936, p. 89.

Peter and the Pope were abandoned. But soon the hoped-for bond of unity was a focus of disunity. Fundamentalism and Higher Criticism are both products of the same Reformation, and it is impossible to imagine more hostile brothers. Fundamentalism, a sticking to the letter, ossifies, but criticism, a search for historical interpretations, dissolves. Naturally, many have tried to steer a middle course – have even known how to steer a middle course. But the positions themselves have remained as wide apart as ever, and they must remain so for logic alone would seem to make a proper fusion impossible. But how can the great masses of men hold fast to religion, how can they use it as a sheet-anchor among the uncertainties of existence, if it is itself nothing but uncertainty?

Wherever the same society was composed of different confessional elements, there was, as soon as the credal positions had hardened, only one solution to the problem of peaceful coexistence, and that was toleration. Toleration is more than a virtue in a religiously complex country: it is a necessity. That precisely was the grand idea which animated Albrecht von Wallenstein, and which has induced many to see him as a hero rather than as a traitor. Live and let live, was his recommendation to both sides. But with the great good which such a policy represents, there is also connected a great evil. Toleration leads to indifference; indeed, it is barely an exaggeration to say that it *is* to some extent indifference. Frederick of Prussia is known to have said: 'In my state, everybody can go to heaven in his own fashion.'[1] But we can almost hear him add: what do I care? Nor would it be unfair to assert that this great champion of tolerance might also have formulated his conviction by saying: in my state everybody may go, in his own fashion, to hell, if he so chooses. The truth of the matter is that toleration is connected, both historically and logically, with individualism, with the idea that the individual is the ultimate arbiter of right and wrong in matters religious. The sociologist will not impugn this position: that is not his office; the good neighbour will not impugn it either: he knows that a fine and – within limits – even a full life in common is possible under an agreement to disagree on the last questions. But everybody will have to acknowledge that, where the principle of toleration reigns supreme, religion can no longer be an integral element in the inclusive culture; it can no longer be a layer in the foundations of the structure, those foundations which are taken for granted and on which absolute unanimity exists so that nobody will even think of challenging them. Religion is bound, under these circumstances, to become something of an 'extra', an accidental rather than an essential concern, in other words, a de-emphasized inheritance from the past. But this alone must spell decay.

In order to combat, and, if this is possible, to compensate for, the weakening which has befallen Christianity as a consequence of schism,

[1] Cf. Büchmann, G., *Geflügelte Worte und Zitatenschatz*, ed. Stuttgart 1953, p. 316.

the ecumenical movement has sprung up in recent times, with the aim of bringing together again what was divided and divorced in the sixteenth century. The question as to what extent it will succeed is still *sub judice*, and will remain so for a long time yet. The contrasts have hardened too much to hope for an easy disappearance of barriers, and processes of unification, if they are to take place on the deeper cultural, and not only on the more superficial organizational, level, are in any case bound to be protracted. The sociologist, who is not a prophet, can therefore voice an opinion only on the present situation, or rather its attendant problems. He will, in the first place, raise the question as to whether ecumenicalism has sprung from a positive or a negative root. Is it due to a revival of fellow-feeling among the Christian denominations, to a sentiment of shame in face of the mutual estrangements, the traditional hates, of those who confess one Lord and Master, or is it merely due to a desire to organize against a common enemy, the laughing third as we have called him a little while ago, to a desire to press back the forces of atheism and agnosticism and the couldn't-care-less-about-religion attitudes which are so widespread in modern urban societies? It is fair to assume that both motives are present, but it is impossible to judge which is the more powerful incentive. Here again, the difference of levels is decisive. What, if anything, is at work in the collective subconscious of the divided Christians? Only if a will to unity is stirring there, will ecumenism be truly successful. Otherwise it will remain a matter of politics.

But the problem of ecumenicalism concerns not only the depths from which the propulsive force, if there is any, takes its origin; it concerns also the direction in which it is thrusting, and this is even more important. Unity may, in principle, be achieved in two ways, one of which we may, for brevity, call synthesis, the other compromise. Synthesis, such as Hegel and Marx have classically analysed it, leads to an end result in which the antithetic position and its opposition, are at the same time reconciled *and* preserved. To use Hegel's expository device, a^2 bears in itself both $+a$ and $-a$. The dialectical evolution is thus essentially a process of summing up, and it travels towards a point of maximum. Not so compromise. It begins by discarding some elements which are objectionable to the intended partner, on condition that he do likewise. Hence contraction is of the essence of it, and the more participants are to be brought in, the more must be sacrificed for such agreement as may be achievable. The overall direction is therefore towards a point of minimum. The matter is more than purely academical. In some countries, there has been experimentation, in religious education, with what is known as an 'agreed syllabus', and what was offered to the oncoming generation was often an indistinct, not to say nebulous, doctrine, as little attractive as mushy features are in a human face when compared to a forceful profile. The more thoughtful protagonists of ecumenism have been well aware of the danger of emaciation lurking here; they have been worried about it. Some have, understandably, even gone so far as to plead that confessional confrontations be not entirely abandoned. 'A new comprehension of the causes of our differences . . . and not a despairing agreement to ignore them, is the only effective first step to their removal,' writes Gregory Dix.[1] He is right, if true synthesis is to be the overall aim. The fate of the ecumenical movement will depend on its ability to take this first step, which is not conceived as compromise but as clarification, and on its subsequent willingness to take further and further steps, in a spirit of construction rather than contraction, towards an ever-fuller Christianity and not towards an ever-emptier deism. But this may be rather difficult, for since about two hundred and fifty years ago forces have been at work in wider society which have made precisely such a faceless deism a highly recommended philosophy of life.

THE OUTER CONDITIONS OF CHRISTIANITY IN MODERN TIMES

Any attempt to understand the modern age, or rather the nineteenth and twentieth centuries which comprise that age, must start from the all-decisive fact that it is the outcome of a series of revolutions which, between them, form in truth but one – a total upheaval of which the French Revolution may serve as the symbol and prototype. A close consideration of its many antecedents would take us far too far afield here; suffice it to say that the core of that historical evolution which ended in political, social, cultural and all-round revolution was the formation of a new class, the bourgeoisie, and its rise to power. Its victory over all adversaries was most spectacularly consummated in 1789.

We have spoken of a total upheaval and all-round revolution, and we have implied therefore that the development also had its religious side. In the Reformation, the bourgeoisie created for itself an outlook which suited it, and its maturest formulation was the great Calvinistic creed, that 'Protestant ethic' which we know to be deeply connected with the 'spirit of capitalism'. But the Reformed Church was not a point of arrival, a building site on which the human race could erect a permanent home; it was much rather a point of departure, a temporary camping ground which enabled the progressive forces to gather more strength, and from which they could go out and conquer and remake the world. The Genevan faith was as yet the faith of a small contained class, the world-view of the bourgeoisie of a *bourg* or city, and however wide it spread, however close it came to being a national religion here or there, as in Scotland or Holland, something of an old-world character continued to cling to it. It was not yet the creed of those whose mentality the Abbé Sieyès summed up when he asked his famous double question: 'What is the third estate? Nothing. What does it aspire to? Everything.'

[1] Loc. cit., p. IX.

As the hour of fulfilment came closer, the usefulness of the Calvinistic philosophy of life became smaller. In the end something like the opposite of Calvinism was needed, and because it was needed, it was provided and produced.

Calvinism, because of the circumstances which presided over its birth, was above all a disciplining force. The burgher had to learn how to be thrifty, how to be hard-working, how to be devoted to the duties of his estate. Without going through this tough school, he would not have been able to achieve what he was to achieve later on. But the social control to which he was subjected was bound in due course to turn from an encouraging into an inhibiting factor. Take away the iron rod, Calvin taught, and you have before you an evil beast. A tamer is needed to keep it in order. Thomas Hobbes was to reformulate these conceptions for the last time in the middle of the seventeenth century, about a century after his master's death. His *Leviathan* characteristically ends in the glorification of the king, 'a mortal god, to which we owe, under the immortal God, our peace and defence'.[1] It is immediately obvious that such an ideology is conservative through and through: the alternative it puts before man lies between obedience and annihilation. A class getting ready for a revolution had to throw it off, or else it would be inhibited from taking even one single step in the direction of its aim, in the direction of its dream. It had to replace the inherited creed with a new ideology which would foster rather than discourage social experimentation, which would spread the conviction that the liberation of man from social controls would be blessing and not curse, and that the risks involved in a destruction of contemporary institutions were practically nil. A hundred years after the *Leviathan*, Jean-Jacques Rousseau gave the word, and he was immediately believed. His deistic creed replaced the theistic creed of his fellow-Genevan of two centuries before; his kindly conception of man the harsh anthropology of the stern preacher of St. Pierre.

The historical and political situation as we have described it would alone suffice to explain the coming and the character of Rousseauan deism. On the eve of every battle, the combatants try, and must try, to raise their spirits and to stir their courage. This is what happened before the storming of the Bastille, and nothing is less surprising. And yet, there is more behind Rousseauism than meets the eye. Subconsciously, the revolutionary forces were not as sure of the future as they pretended to be on the conscious and propagandist level. The fear of freedom is a very real fear, and it is difficult to see how any man can avoid it who knows, simply by knowing himself, what great potentialities for evil are laid on in every human self. That fear had to be overcompensated. Optimism had to receive – if possible – a deep metaphysical foundation. It had to be magnified into a religion of a kind. And thus a competitor to

[1] *Leviathan*, Everyman ed., n.d., p. 89.

Christianity had to appear which was as dangerous to it, if not more so, than the ruler-deification of yore, that pseudo-faith of which Thomas Hobbes was one of the last full representatives. There were only few who would venture openly to deify man; but the deification of man – indeed, even the deification of the common man – was the direction in which much of eighteenth-century speculation was travelling.

Considered purely from the logical point of view, deism and Christianity are irreconcilable. Unless the word is used in a totally indistinct sense, Christianity is a religion centred on Christ, and more particularly on the Cross of Christ, on Christ's redemptive deed on behalf of mankind. The faith called Christianity therefore presupposes the concept of the fall, for it is only because mankind fell, i.e. forfeited the friendship of Almighty God, that there was a need for that vicarious satisfaction which Christ took upon Himself, for that mediation of which He was the author, for that atonement which was bought by His sacrificial death. But all these considerations are alien to deist thinking simply because it rejected the idea, or the fact, of original sin. No original sin, no estrangement from God; no estrangement from God, no need for an incarnation of the Divine Principle of Love; no need for an incarnation of the Divine Principle of Love, no Christianity. The figure of Jesus may indeed formally remain; He may be held up as the Great Teacher of Morality as He is in Jean Jacques' *Confession de Foi d'un Vicaire Savoyard*; but He can no longer be the Saviour, the Son of God—in one word, Christ. The relation between the new deism and traditional Christianity was therefore in principle that of a simple either-or: in principle, but not in practice. What happened was that a desultory attempt was made, in many cultures, to mix the unmixables. Deist interpretations were laid on Christian doctrines, if not openly and professedly, then stealthily and factually, with the result that Christianity lost, in the popular mind, much that is properly its own. If we may for once borrow a metaphor from the world of organicism, we can say that it underwent a softening of the bones.

What is apt to happen in these circumstances can easily be seen from the case of two American presidents, Herbert Hoover and Richard Nixon: both Quakers, but both also Americans in the sense of belonging to the American civic religion (a form of deism), which coexisted and became confused with Quakerism as it did with the more orthodox versions of Christianity. Almost from its inception, the Society of Friends considered the rejection of violence as one of its most sacred principles; so much so that Friends would not even buy toy guns for their children. Yet neither Hoover nor Nixon had any qualms about becoming commanders-in-chief of the world's biggest military machine. On another level, less important politically, but more important intellectually, Quakers have historically declined to take oaths, in obedience to Christ's words recorded in Matthew v, 34: 'Swear not at all.' There was no necessity for either Hoover or Nixon to swear an oath on entering office. The Constitution would have allowed a solemn asseveration not calling God to witness instead. But both Quaker presidents acted like their predecessors: they willingly embraced the common form. The reason? Easy to see. The common form was in line with a common faith; that faith is shared by non-alienated Americans whatever their denomination. Even Catholics, though tending to be somewhat more tradition-bound than their neighbours, are no exception. A flood of evidence could be offered, if it were needed; but it is not. Nor is the phenomenon restricted to the United States, where it is merely most easily observed. The Bishop of Rotterdam, Ad. J. Simonis, a conservative in spite of his young years, said of his country: 'We have lost a great deal of the Christian faith. We face a pure humanism that masks as Christianity but does not even believe in the possibility of sin any more.'[1] In other words, there is pure deism.

At first sight it might appear surprising that the conflict between Christianity and deism was not sharper than we find it to have been, at least in the West. But the puzzle can be solved and due explanations can be given. For one thing, the Christian Churches were too well organized, too firmly established, to be easily shaken. Deism, assuming as it does that man is not in need of redemption or even of social control, assuming in fact that man is born good, representing, moreover, an advanced form of individualism, has no indwelling Church-building power: the very need for a Church is not given. It is surely characteristic that the Quakers, in more senses than one the forerunners of the deists, achieved on their part only a semi-Church for themselves. But where the contest lies between an organized creed on the one hand and an unorganized one, a spirit afloat, on the other, the organized contestant will be too strong to be defeated, even where the unorganized competitor has the spirit of the age on his side. But there is more. Deism had *only* the spirit of the age on its side; it failed in so far as some of the more perennial – and, indeed, some of the more profound – religious needs of mankind are concerned. It has nothing very convincing to say on death. Most of its protagonists, such as Rousseau and Kant, asserted the immortality of the soul, but without any great conviction. Nor did the naked fact of mortality make much sense in their philosophy. If life is a time of testing, if death is a punishment for sin and eternal blessedness a premium for those who have fought a good fight, there is meaning in the pattern. But if there is no original sin to start with, why does Providence, asserted to be beneficent, force us through this vale of tears? Deism was too happy-go-lucky, too superficial a philosophy to still the

[1] *The New York Times*, 15 January 1969 ('Official Prayer Service to open Nixon Inauguration'); 26 January 1969 ('Nixon's Brand of Quakerism De-emphasizes Pacifism'); 7 September 1969 ('Many Problems face Dutch Catholicism despite its Reforms').

searchings of the human heart. In spite of the fact that it had the wind of history in its sails, it was not really the stronger vessel.

Indeed, it soon became the weaker of the two. Leibniz's assertion that this is the best of all possible worlds was absurd from the very start and deserved all the ridicule which Voltaire so mercilessly poured on it in his *Candide*. Locke's and Rousseau's sobered version, according to which this might be a very good world, if only some basic social reforms were carried out, if only liberty and equality were introduced into society, was not absurd from the very start; it was appealing, not to say convincing, so long as it was not put to the test. The French Revolution, however, and its contemporary and co-ordinated upheavals, did put it to the test, and it was found wanting. Liberty and equality did not, between them, engender fraternity as promised; far from it; they seemed, in 1794, five short years after the onset of the new dispensation, to have led to a war of all against all. Leibniz, it was seen, was wrong; so were Locke and Rousseau; Hobbes was right, and so were Calvin and Pascal, and, beyond them, St. Augustine and the Fathers. The lesson of realism which the human race learned as it emerged from the great cataclysm brought on that mighty revival of Christianity which is known as Romanticism. In such figures as John Henry Newman and Sören Kierkegaard it rose triumphant over its fallen foe.

But the renascence of Christian orthodoxy was brief, and deistic secularism was soon on the advance once more. Two reasons seem to explain why the waves of faith which, for a while, had been rolling in, were, by 1840 or so, again receding. Deistic optimism with regard to man was at first mainly a reaction to Calvinistic pessimism, as the Methodist heart religion was a reaction to the head religion of the Presbyterians. No more appeared, to begin with, to be involved than the normal swing of the pendulum. But the pendulum could not freely swing back; it became stuck, so to speak. The explanation for this is almost shamefully simple. Christianity was a stern, even a forbidding religion; it tells us that we are sinners, that we deserve, and that we need, the rod. Deism had sweeter stuff to offer. It asserted that man is kind and had only to be as he was, as he came from the hands of nature, in order to be perfect. Who would not prefer this doctrine to the other? Who would not rather have sugar than vinegar and gall? Who would not prefer the promise of freedom, of do-as-you-please, to the necessity of obedience, of do-as-you-are-told? After deism had spread its message, the dice were permanently loaded against Christianity – real Christianity – real Christianity, that is, not the softened pseudo-Christianity that started to develop in the West, notably the United States of America. Men were offered an escape from the tyranny of Presbyterian control and from the humiliations of the confessional box. No wonder that many slipped through the door that had been opened to them.

Still, the experiences of the human race – both the temporary experience after 1789 and the permanent experience throughout history – showed that the Rousseauan doctrine of man is deeply unrealistic, that man is not angelic and needs control. Deistic secularism would not have recovered as it did, if it had not changed its form, more concretely speaking, if it had not substituted for the disappointed and lost hope – the Christian might write: for the disappointed and lost delusion – a new one, the doctrine of progress. This is not the best of all possible worlds, it was admitted by 1850, not even if liberty and equality in the sense of the French Revolution are included in its cadres; but it may become the best of all possible worlds if development is allowed to proceed, and especially if man consciously helps it on its way. The ideologies of the eighteenth century had been essentially static, Newtonian: bliss was to come from the liberation of the individual which would lead to an equilibrium of individual forces and hence to a natural order which would combine the maximum of personal independence with the maximum of neighbourliness. This dream had been exploded, but it could be replaced by another doctrine essentially dynamical, Lamarckian: bliss would come from the ever-better mutual adjustment of discordant elements so that in the end the utopia of the eighteenth century would after all be realized. Indeed, some of the thinkers of the new pseudo-religion, with a Lamarckian rather than Newtonian, organismic rather than mechanical, background went further than their predecessors: they promised, in lieu of an ever unstable equilibrium of individual forces, the firmer integration of a body social, a body reminiscent, in its assured unity, of the body physical in health and vigour.

Thus a new secular gospel of salvation came into being. Socialism joined liberalism. While the liberals had cried, 'Let us return to nature,' the socialists shouted, 'Let us enter into history and drive it forward to its appointed consummation!' If we compare them with each other, liberalism and socialism, Rousseauism and Marxism, appear as enemies. It is one thing to expect the perfect society from an egalitarian distribution of property into *per capita* shares, from a commonwealth of cottages; it is another thing to expect it from the concentration of property in the hands of the public, from the superstate of communism. But when we compare the two modern pseudo-religions just considered with Christianity, we see that they are but hostile twins. For Christianity has no confidence in any re-arrangement of outer conditions, for instance of property alone. It teaches that there is only one road to perfect society, and that is the conquest of sin – a new inner condition, a purified heart. It was thus not only the assault of the left wing bourgeoisie that tended to push religion into the corner, it was also the assault of the left wing proletariat. Between them, the two promises of salvation through secular means – comparatively speaking, promises of salvation without tears – pressed hard on Christianity and diminished its hold on the human race.

Of course, the hope in communism underwent the same decisive test, the test of practice, and was found to be as delusionary as the older ideology. The Russian Revolution has led to the same sobering experience as the French: ideal life developed as little on the Moskva as it did on the Seine. Christianity was wiser than Marxism in that it operated with a multicausal, and not a monocausal, theory of evil. According to Marx, the ills of humanity are due to the principle of private property; remove private property and they will disappear. According to Christianity, fallen man has a general tendency to selfishness and sin which can work itself out in various ways. In feudal society, it was not the monopolization of the means of production that caused the class struggle; Marx knew very well that land ownership was divided between feu superior and feu inferior and, indeed, created a bond between them; it was the monopolization of the means of warfare. The upper classes were those armed and in armour on horseback, the lower classes those who, defenceless, walked and worked on foot. In post-capitalist society, just as in pre-capitalist, private property does not exist, but there is a new dividing line between upper class and lower: the possession, or otherwise, of administrative power. The commissars, those who sit at the controls, are the lords, the masses are once again the serfs as they have always been. Yet this outcome of the communist experiment has as little returned the apostates to Christianity as the outcome of the liberal experiment, and the reasons are similar. Marx, like Rousseau, promised a life that suits the Old Adam: plenty rather than freedom, it is true, but yet a material value which appeals to materialistic man and attracts him as powerfully as Christianity's demand: confess, repent, be better than yourself, dismays and repels.

Many of the attributes which theology had ascribed to the Deity were transferred by the deists to nature. Nature has a purpose (even though it has none); nature is beneficent (even though she is red in tooth and claw); and so on. The new pseudo-religion substituted history for nature: history is a process of salvation; it will lead mankind to a condition under which the domination of man over man will be replaced by the administration of things. However complex the detail of the Marxian theory, it is clear that it thinks of history in terms of development and even of progress. Intellectually, it is here that its deepest problem lies. We must consider it, not in order to controvert it, but in order to show (which alone is appropriate in a *Sociology of Religion*) why it could drive Christianity back and yet could not totally defeat it.

Alfred Weber, in his profound, if difficult, books, has taught us to distinguish between the cosmos of culture and the cosmos of civilization.[1] Civilization is concerned with man's relation to matter rather than with his relation to man or to God; culture is concerned with man's relation to man and to God, rather than with his relation to matter. Some societies are cultures rather than civilizations; others are civilizations rather than cultures; each one is to some extent mixed. What interests us here is above all the dynamical aspect of things: culture and civilization do not react in the same manner to the flow of time; they are not in the same way involved in it. So far as civilization is concerned, it is progressive; the knowledge which it achieves is addable. Not so in the realm of culture; its achievements are largely relative; its styles are alternatives. Every society is a unity and in one sense all its phenomena are interconnected; but every society is also a complexity and in another sense its phenomena are divided. There is one natural science, and the progress of chemistry is not, and cannot be, out of keeping with that of physics; but still, each has to go its own way. So also here: a highly cultured society will also tend to be a highly civilized one and vice versa; yet it may direct its energies by preference into the one realm rather than the other; and it is because modern society pushed much more energetically along civilizational than along cultural lines that we have given this last chapter the title which we have in fact given it.

Now in the realm of civilization there is undoubtedly upward development, progress; who can doubt it? Riding on horseback is faster than walking on foot; travelling by train or motor car is faster than riding on horseback; flying through the air is faster than travelling by train or motor car, the supersonic aeroplane is faster than its predecessor, the subsonic plane. We have the most incontrovertible evidence that progress is real in this realm: measurement. But no measurement is applicable to, and no progress is provable for, the phenomena of culture. To say that the music of Dmitri Shostakovich is superior to that of Johann Sebastian Bach because two hundred and twenty-one years have elapsed between the birth of the one and the birth of the other is sheer lunacy. Nor is the case much changed if we read 'twentieth-century music' for Shostakovich and 'early eighteenth-century music' for Bach. Styles appear after each other in time, but in quality they are equal because they are equal in possibilities.

Where, in this scheme, does religion stand? It is hardly necessary to say it: it belongs to culture and not to civilization. Its quest is always the same: call it, if you will, with Herbert Spencer, the contemplation of the unknowable. The fact remains that it cannot be helped by the perfection of the techniques of scientific knowledge-gathering, for these are simply inapplicable and obviously so. Modern man is not one whit better off

[1] Cf. Neumann, S., 'Alfred Weber's Conception of Historicocultural Sociology', in *An Introduction to the History of Sociology*, ed. Barnes, H. E., ed. Chicago and London 1965, pp. 353 et seq.

than medieval man, or ancient man for that matter. The only consistent attitude for the scientist to take is that which Spencer in fact did take: to say *ignoramus, ignorabimus*; in other words, to embrace agnosticism. But Spencer equated scientific knowledge with all knowledge; he knew no way to truth except through the physical senses aided by material apparatus, lens for instance, telescope or microscope. To the religious man this must appear as narrowmindedness. He will insist that there are other – proper – avenues of access to mystery. But in taking them he will feel, if he is fair, that he is not one who has left earlier generations behind, but rather one who walks side by side with the searchers of all times.

Spencer, for all his limitations, was a careful man. Others are not so careful. They maintain that material progress makes the abandonment of traditional religion necessary. The main assertion of modern developmental, dynamical secularism is that its philosophy (even concerning metaphysical questions) must be superior to that of age-old Christianity because the twentieth century is superior in technology to the sixteenth or the twelfth or the first. Critically considered, this is simply a *non sequitur*. Yet it is widely believed, and this belief constitutes the strength of the anti-religious forces in the modern world – those forces which have driven Christianity into the crisis from which it is suffering in our day. If we could manage to find out from whence this strength is coming, we should not only possess the clue to the understanding of the world success of the two great competitors of Christianity, the pseudo-religions of liberalism and socialism, but we should also be in a better position to assess Christianity's chances of survival and perhaps of ultimate victory over its opponents.

Equipped as we are with the insights of the sociology of knowledge, our task is a good deal less daunting than might appear at first blush. Wilhelm Dilthey, who knew the history of human philosophizing like no other man, came to the conclusion that there are, in the final analysis, only three types of basic world-view. He calls them naturalism, objective idealism and subjective idealism, but the more widely current terms mechanicism, organicism and culturalism are perhaps more expressive. Each society has a basic intuition in terms of which it tends to interpret all phenomena. In the case of those who have embraced mechanicism, this basic intuition is taken from, and determined by, the observation of matter, lifeless matter to be exact. The laws of physics are supposed to be the key which unlocks all doors. Such societies will, of course, score their greatest successes in the area of mechanics, pure and applied. They will be, in the first place, machine-building and machine-using societies, but in the areas beyond the confines of mechanics, their step will be less assured. There they will face an inescapable alternative: either to abandon their pet principles, or to produce fictitious models assimilated to mechanical patterns and, when the truth is told, no longer representative of the reality which they are supposed to stand for. To take but one step beyond the natural limits, the rational limits, of mechanicism: when basically mechanicist cultures study life, they must either forget their basic philosophy (which is not easy) or assert that living things, for instance the human body, are essentially – substantially – automata (which lands them in absurdity). Lamettrie's *L'Homme Machine*, one of the greatest absurdities ever to be put into print, is a warning example of this latter tendency. Subjective idealism, or culturalism, as we have called it, is apt to commit the corresponding opposite blunder. It takes its cue from the experience of moral conflict. There is the flesh, and there is the spirit. They clash. The spirit is often willing, while the flesh is weak. We have a dualistic philosophy here which, simply because it is dualistic, is somewhat less likely to go astray than mechanicism, i.e. consistent – monistic – materialism. It can allow that there is a physical realm with its own absolute regularities, and a 'higher' realm (the term is accepted, but perhaps not entirely happy) in which volition (human and conceivably superhuman) has its being. But in naïve minds, a simplistic panidealism may develop which is not one whit better than simplistic mechanicism-materialism. The idea may be entertained that it is wills that move the stars or make the corn sprout, and then we get fetishism or other forms of primitive religiosity. As can be seen, the phrase 'to each his own' contains a warning and a prescription to which all those must anxiously keep who desire, not a uniform world-formula, but a system of thought which does equal justice to all aspects of reality.[1]

Of all societies that have ever existed, modern society, capitalist society, is the one most deeply associated with the mechanicist-materialist world-view. It is the machine-building society *kat exochen*. Its claims to glory, like the journey to the moon, lie in this field. True, it has had its successes in the biological sciences also because it has learned that it must make concessions to reality when it undertakes to study the realm of life. But two facts are undeniable: firstly, that the biological sciences have not advanced nearly so far as the physical sciences have; and secondly, that such advances as have been achieved were mainly in the area of control, in the area of the manipulation of vital phenomena for the benefit of man, in other words in the area most closely paralleling the realities and potentialities of inanimate creation. Confronted with religion, the modern mentality is simply baffled. Its phenomena lie outside the cadres of understandability as laid down by its basic 'naturalism'. Agnosticism would appear to be the proper attitude to the 'metaphysical' for any society that has restricted itself to the physical. But for two very understandable reasons, agnosticism is not a general, or even widespread, attitude. For one thing, it is too negative. Spencer spoke of a 'contemplation of the unknowable' which, he recommended, should

[1] On all this, cf. Stark, W., *The Fundamental Forms of Social Thought*, London 1962, pp. 7 et seq. and 257 et seq.

replace religion. But if you contemplate the unknowable, you will wish to know it all the same. Puzzles are challenges, and it is not possible to arrest the human mind in its quest. More important, however, is the other factor. Passive agnosticism will tend to become active and aggressive atheism because the assertions of religion threaten the peace and quiet of the panmechanistic mind. The modern nothing-but-scientist will often be driven to say to the man of faith what Archimedes said to the invading soldier: Do not disturb my circles! Modern man, bent on total control, i.e. purposive manipulation, of the universe, knows full well that he can only succeed in so far as the universe is a comprehensive mechanism. If there are elements in it which defy his wishes, like a superior will, for instance, limits are set to his cherished opportunities, and they will be no more welcome than the plague. But from the proposition 'I hate to see a superior will active in reality' to the proposition 'there is no superior will active in reality', there is only one step. As every student of ideologies knows, ought-sentences are all too easily transmuted into is-sentences if wishful thinking is present, be it on the conscious, be it on the subconscious level. Thus, in a sense, all modern society is directed against the religious mood. Theism, in all its forms, runs counter to the machine-builder's and matter-manipulator's outlook. That Christianity is in crisis should not surprise us, but that it is still alive should do. The desire to expel it operates not only on the surface; it can be seen to be rooted in the very subsoil which determines the patterns of any culture or civilization, mental as well as material: its fundamental, direction-giving order of values. We can see here, incidentally, again, to what extent Calvinism prepared capitalism: though personally quite willing to pay homage to the Mother of God, Calvin excluded her, and all the saints, from the picture of heaven, because he feared that their assumed power of intercession must destroy the fixity of the predestined order of the universe. It did not suit him to have more than one will active in the universe; it does not suit the modal man of capitalism to have any will whatever (except his own) in action there.

The elevation of the desire to dominate the physical universe to the position of supreme value does not, however, do only direct damage to the chances for survival and success of religion in general and Christianity in particular: it does serious indirect damage as well. Not surprisingly, those are respected, those receive (in Max Weber's terminology) a high public estimation of honour, who score in the fields of science and technology or economics; those who are less attuned to these pursuits, even if they are contributing greatly in other areas, are but scantily rewarded and esteemed. Art springs to mind at once as an incontrovertible example;[1] since the Renaissance, the artist is merely a marginal man and treated accordingly; what is most vital in modern art,

[1] Cf. Read, H., *The Philosophy of Modern Art*, New York 1953, pp. 26 et seq. and 58 et seq.

for instance in painting, is therefore revolutionary, and conservative, i.e. friendly to capitalist society and its value system, are only those who allow themselves to be driven or lured in the direction of flat academicism. But the men of religion appear in a yet more unfavourable light than the men of palette and paint. Measured by the yardsticks of capitalist materialism, they are merely supernumeraries in the life process of society, almost drones. Oscar Wilde – the young Wilde yet frivolous, not the older man, tried and chastened and converted – made the point most pungently in Act Three of *The Importance of Being Earnest*:

Jack: Had I been christened already?

Lady Bracknell: Every luxury that money could buy . . . had been lavished on you by your fond and doting parents.[1]

There is no doubt that modern society which always asks: what does this person contribute to production? and: how does he get on in the world?, has a general tendency to think and feel like Lady Bracknell; and so religion is under a cloud.

To some extent, all denominations have experienced demotion since the onset of the Industrial Revolution: before the face of victorious rationalism, which styled itself 'enlightened', they all appeared by comparison 'obscurantist'. But some forms of Christianity have suffered more than others. Calvinism, for the reasons which we have so fully given, managed to produce monster fortunes like those of the Vanderbilt and Rockefeller and Carnegie; it had therefore to be treated with some respect. Catholicism, on the other hand, could not match this achievement; it was, to start with, a religion of the poor; it remained throughout its history a religion of the poor; and it is a religion of the poor even now: of the absolutely poor in such countries as Mexico or Peru where capitalism is of tardy growth; and of the relatively poor even in economies where capitalism has become predominant and raised the standard of living – welfare and wealth – for all and sundry. It is particularly in these latter countries that Catholics have developed something like a psychology of relative deprivation. They compare themselves to their neighbours; they see that they have not done equally well; and they come away with a feeling of inferiority which may deeply affect their religion and its prospects in the world. Either they blame their creed and culture; then the consequences are obvious: apostasy, open or dissimulated, will take place. Or they blame, not their Church, but themselves: in this case they will indeed remain attached, but diffident and defensive, and in this case they may, by a dialectical denouement, turn revolutionary and destructive in the end. In either eventuality the cause of religion, to put it mildly, is not served.

Canada is a good illustration. When the long-smouldering tensions

[1] Oscar Wilde, *Complete Plays*, London, 1954, p. 71.

in the bilingual and biconfessional province of Quebec broke out into open acts of lawlessness in the autumn of 1970, *The New York Times* published a report on the background of the disorders which is highly informative. 'The English,' so we read, a Royal Commission being quoted as the statistical source of the statement, 'earn more than do the French and hold a disproportionately large number of middle and high salaried jobs. The typical English Montreal resident lives in a house or new apartment in the western half of the city. French Canadians . . . live in the faded brick tenements of the east or the newer cramped duplex houses on the north side. The English . . . run all five of Canada's biggest banks, most of the insurance and securities houses and the country's biggest conglomerate, the Canadian Pacific. To be sure, a great number of Montreal's English hold ordinary jobs and live modestly – but proportionately more of the French do. The French also account for nearly all Quebec's chronically high unemployment.' And the reason? Among them, we are told, is this, that 'the Roman Catholic Church discouraged the pursuit of profit, while the Protestant ethic encouraged it among the English'.[1] The picture given owes something, but certainly not much, to local circumstances. Indeed, it is widely typical. Read 'Northern Ireland' for 'the Province of Quebec' and you have substantially the same situation. But most interesting of all is the troubled history of Belgium. Nominally, both nations in the country, Walloons and Flemings, are Catholics, but the Walloons, predominantly town-dwellers, are not untouched by rationalistic currents, while the Flemings have preserved a fuller faith. There has been no decade since 1945 in which the 'language question' has not caused deep disturbances. But the language question, the question as to whether the Flemish tongue shall receive equality of status with the French spoken by the Walloons, was really only a symptom of the deeper disease – the dissatisfactions of the economically less advanced sections of the population.

At this point, we are less interested in the facts themselves or in the political forms in which they work themselves out than in the psychological consequences which they entail. We are confronted here with a very common phenomenon, or rather with a specific variant of it. Wherever an overprivileged and an underprivileged group divide a society, the underprivileged will tend to share the order of values of their 'betters'. Until their hour of rebellion or liberation draws near, they will see themselves to a large extent through the eyes of the top-layer – which means, in practice, that they will see themselves, at least unadmittedly and subconsciously, as inferior types. In an interesting review of women's novels, entitled 'Women beware women, or Cows on a dark hillside', Janice Elliott has drawn our attention to the fact that much of the fiction to come from feminine authors is full of feminine

[1] *The New York Times*, 18 October 1970, Section 4, p. 1.

self-contempt.[1] Theodor Lessing asserted and analysed a parallel tendency for another segment of the population – the Jews. The very title
of his volume is revealing: *Der jüdische Selbsthass*.[2] 'Jewish antisemitism'
may be a curious notion in theory, but there are plenty of examples in
practice (even more than Lessing adduces). Within the cadres of this
book, the salient fact is that the Catholic community, wherever it has
coexisted with a Protestant and especially with a Calvinist majority, has
been afflicted with the same bent towards self-condemnation, with the
result that its attitude to the inherited creed and Church has been sensibly affected. 'I think being a woman is like being Irish,' says a character
in Iris Murdoch's novel, *The Red and the Green*, which Janice Elliott
quotes. 'Everyman says you're important and nice, but you take second
place all the same.' The statement is, of course, convertible. Being Irish
was, for many centuries, like being a woman, a second-rater, in the
judgment of the dominant English and male strata, and the twin result
was a combination of depression and aggression by which, we repeat
it, the cause of the Catholic religion was not served.

The case of Ireland is particularly interesting, partly because of the
deeply Catholic character of the Irish culture, and partly because from
there the self-depreciating mood travelled to one of the world's most
important centres, the United States of America. Only a comprehensive study of Irish literature could provide adequate documentation, and
we simply cannot undertake it in this work. A prominent factor in the
literary tradition of Ireland is its inherent anti-clericalism. Works like
George Moore's *Home Sickness* and Liam O'Flaherty's *Skerrett* are
widely characteristic. Anti-clericalism is not, of course, identical with
disloyalty to the Church, and precisely in Ireland it can be seen that the
former does not necessarily have to engender the latter. But it is a weakening influence, even if we make the best of it. There is, however, in
addition to anti-clericalism, also a more radical current, and its logical
outcome is apostasy. In one author, Ireland's greatest – James Joyce –
it led to this dire result. *Ulysses* is full of blasphemy. It is revealing that
Joyce was distressed when he heard that Oscar Wilde had turned
Catholic, and he expressed the fervent wish that the news of his conversion were not true.[3] Others have not gone to the same length, but it
is to be assumed that the tendencies which come to the surface in one
are subterraneously present in some others also.

Why did Joyce flee in disgust from the realities around him? His
autobiography, *A Portrait of the Artist as a Young Man*, gives us the
unvarnished answer. Stephen Dedalus, that is, Joyce himself, holds up

[1] Cf. *The Sunday Times* (of London), 6 March 1966; cf. also Nora Sayre in *The New
York Times Book Review*, 14 September 1969.
[2] 'Jewish Self-Hatred', Berlin 1930. Cf. esp. p. 31; also pp. 34 and 35. Cf. further
Loewenstein, R. M., *Christians and Jews*, New York 1951, pp. 144 et seq.
[3] O'Connor, Fr., *Short History of Irish Literature*, New York 1967, p. 195.

his father, Simon Dedalus, as typically Irish. And who or what was Simon Dedalus? Here are the exact words: 'A medical student, an oarsman, a tenor, an amateur actor, a shouting politician, a small landlord, a small investor, a drinker, a good fellow, a storyteller, somebody's secretary, something in a distillery, a taxgatherer, a bankrupt and at present a praiser of his own past.'[1] Perhaps the most decisive terms in this whole string of epithets are the first and the last: he was to begin with a medical student who never made the grade, and he was in the end a beggar who had lost all. He was 'feckless'. Compared with this failure, such amiable and positive features as the old man possessed – and they were not wanting[2] – were but dust in the balance. They certainly did not impress the less than admiring and forgiving son. But the father–son relationship counts for little here, for Dedalus senior is the symbol of his kind. This is clearly expressed in an episode in *Ulysses*. Stephen drifts into a cabmen's shelter for rest and refreshment and meets a garrulous sailor there who is evidently acquainted with his father:

– You know Simon Dedalus, he asked at length.

– I've heard of him, Stephen said . . .

– He's Irish, the seaman bold affirmed, staring still in much the same way and nodding. All Irish.

– All too Irish, Stephen rejoined.[3]

The bitterness of the passage proves that Irish self-contempt could certainly reach the intensity of that by females or Jews. But perhaps it could go even further. For belonging to a sex or to a race is an unalterable fact. You may be unhappy about it, but you have nothing with which to reproach yourself. Belonging to a religion is not equally inescapable. And yet a Catholic upbringing has, as a rule, the power of capturing a soul for life. For it appeals to the whole man, and especially to the imaginative, artistic side of man and thereby penetrates deep into the unconscious. Even Joyce was its prisoner, for all his voluntary life-long emigration. It tells us a good deal that his favourite composer was Palestrina and his favourite sculptor Mestrovic, two archetypally Catholic artists. The taunt of his foe-friend Mulligan that he is but a priest *manqué* is certainly not without truth.[4] But this made matters worse. To wish, on the rational level, to be free, and to feel, on the sub-rational level, to be caught, produces a particularly bitter attitude. No horse is so rebellious as the one which bridles at the bit. In his discussion

---

[1] Viking Press ed., New York 1964, p. 241.
[2] Cf. Budgen, Fr., *James Joyce and the Making of Ulysses,* ed. Bloomington 1960, p. 143.
[3] Random House ed. n.d., p. 607.
[4] Budgen, loc. cit., pp. 182, 183, 40, 186, 316, 317.

of *Othello*, Stephen Dedalus = James Joyce refers to 'the hornmad Iago ceaselessly willing that the moor in him shall suffer'.[1] That Iago's *alter ego* was he himself.

Even a Catholic may therefore, under modern conditions, become decidedly anti-Catholic, be it overtly, like James Joyce, be it covertly, like half-known or unknown others. The strong desire of many to reform the Church has had, on occasions at any rate, its roots in this psychology, with the subconscious feeling, totally irrational as it is, that change is bound to be improvement. But the Irish – and to them we must at once add the Poles – have a very powerful countermanding incentive for remaining loyal to Rome, and this explains why the other tendency has done so little damage to the religious tradition among them. Irish and Polish Catholicism are at peace with Irish and Polish nationalism. If you are Irish, you are anti-English and therefore anti-Anglican and anti-Presbyterian; if you are Polish, you are anti-Russian, and therefore anti-Orthodox. But modern life has made the nation the social framework *par excellence*, and therefore the Catholic religion draws strength, in these countries, from its compatibility with patriotism. The case is very different in England and America, the countries to which so many Irishmen have emigrated. In England, a Catholic is looked at askance because he is a man with a 'foreign allegiance', and in America the situation was, for a long time, only little different. Even now, Washington has no full representation at the Vatican, and President Kennedy had to go out of his way, in his election campaign, to swear that he was American first and Catholic second. If hostility to Catholicism has greatly waned in the United States, if it has somewhat abated even in England, the reason is, not that the others have become attuned to internationalism, but, on the contrary, that the Catholics have become attuned to nationalism. A study of the English Catholic poets is very informative. Coventry Patmore and Francis Thompson felt unhappy about the suspicions that lay over their patriotism; they had an inferiority complex in this respect and overcompensated it. They were, in this particular, in line with the bulk of their fellow-believers. Only some stronger personalities, such as Wilfrid Blunt and Alice Meynell, set their face resolutely against nationalism: they accepted the fact of an international Church and all it stood for, and the full obligation that arises from venerating Christ as King.[2] Speaking generally, one English Catholic has expressed the suspicion that English Catholics taken in the lump are 'more eager, perhaps, to show themselves patriots than prove themselves Christians'.[3] The word is hard. But in a world in

---

[1] Ed. cit., p. 210.
[2] De la Gorce, A., *Francis Thompson*, transl. Kynaston-Snell, H. F., London 1933, pp. 160-2, 176 (*re* Thompson), 56, 174, 175 (*re* Blunt), 81 (*re* Meynell); Patmore, D., *The Life and Times of Coventry Patmore*, New York 1949, p. 211.
[3] Cecil, A., *A House in Bryanston Square*, New York, n.d., p. 356.

which nationalism is a basic sentiment – *the* basic sentiment even – it is difficult to be a fully-fledged 'Roman'.

As for the United States, the presence of a strong nationalistic tendency among its Catholics was demonstrated, in no uncertain fashion, by the attitudes, often voiced, of Francis Spellman, Cardinal Archbishop of New York to 1967; but the shepherd only expressed what the flock felt. The width and depth of the attempt to fuse local patriotism with global religiosity, an attempt in which the latter element will often be the weaker partner, has been well documented in Dorothy Dohen's book already quoted.[1] So far as America is concerned, this matter is not without its tragic edge. A continent, a country, that was thrown open to all and that recruited her citizens from all the four corners of the earth, could not but develop the ambition to become representative of humanity in general, to produce a culture that would be a combination of all cultures of the world. To achieve this aim, it would have been necessary to open the door wide to Catholic influences. For the America that emerged in the nineteenth century as a great power still bore the imprint – in our context, we are entitled to say, the onesidedness – of her Puritan beginnings. Her chief interests and achievements are technological; her human relations amorphous and atomistic. Catholic art and Catholic social idealism would have righted the balance. A land rich in wealth would have become a land richer in beauty; a society riddled with competition, with all the human estrangements which it brings, would have become a society more appreciative of co-operation, and hence a human environment more conducive to warmth and contentment. To press Catholic principles on the country was a duty which the country's Catholics owed, not only to Catholicism, but also to Americanism. But the energy behind this drive was small. Not only has Catholicism come to accommodate itself to an uncorrected Americanism, but wider and deeper demands in this direction have increasingly been voiced. A book of Edward Wakin and Joseph Scheuer, with the characteristic title, *The De-Romanisation of the American Catholic Church*,[2] is an example; and if it has gone further than some think prudent, the tendencies at least which it evinces are widespread.

There are plenty of reasons, then, why, in the second half of the twentieth century, Christianity in general and Catholicism in particular should be in retreat, especially in the western world. Traditional religiosity has, however, been able to put up a stiff and not entirely hopeless fight. We shall see in the closing section wherein its perennial, if sometimes ebbing, strength resides. What we have before us in the real world now is a mixture of surviving Christianity and secularist ideologies, and though these two do not, in logic, mix, they mix well enough in life, for life does not shun, but rather seeks, compromises, however foul. It is not

[1] *Nationalism and American Catholicism*, New York 1967. Cf. our vol. III, p. 247.
[2] New York 1966.

for us to investigate in what numerical proportion the ingredients are combined: let the quantifying describer find this out, if he can. Our self-imposed task is typological and has been so throughout the preceding 1,850 pages of this work. The question which we must ask therefore, as we are drawing to a close, is this: is there an imaginable type of religion which would correspond to, and blend with, a generally secularized society? Assuming that the tendencies which we have found at work since a hundred and fifty years ago, or even three hundred and fifty years ago, were to advance even further, as far perhaps as the limitation of all human things allows, what then would be the form of religiosity (if any) that would emerge?

These questions are far less speculative than would appear at first sight. For in the most advanced country of the western world, in the United States of America, a variant of religiosity (to give it the name by which it wishes to be known) has been offered on the market and bought by many, which bids fair to reflect the needs and the strivings of the age. If Norman Vincent Peale's *The Power of Positive Thinking* has sold two million copies, if Ralph Trine's *In Tune with the Infinite* a million and a half, and Catherine Marshall's *A Man called Peter*, Joshua Liebman's *Peace of Mind* and Charles Wagner's *The Simple Life* one million or more, it must be presumed that they are a fair guide to the psychology of the masses in our day, and to the direction in which their search for a religion deemed appropriate is probing. These are not propaganda publications of existing churches; they operate rather on the rim of settled religiosity; their authors feel for the shape of the things to come so far as their lights enable them to do so.

It is fortunate that two outstanding sociologists, Louis Schneider and Sanford M. Dornbusch, have investigated this literature for us.[1] We gladly avail ourselves of their results, emphasizing, as we must, that we are offering them, not as mirrorings of the actually ongoing religious life of an advanced capitalist country, but as indications of what a public largely freed of firm traditions in matters religious may envisage as an acceptable coverage of their religious, or near-religious, wants, in a civilization that is the very archetype of modernity, if not indeed of futurism.

Four features are mentioned by the two authors as jointly characteristic of the spirit of these works.[2] They are activism, optimism, individualism and pragmatism. We need only set them down here in order to show that they are fully in line with the developmental tendencies as identified in the present book. Activism and optimism are inheritances of the past; so is individualism, but we are now encountering it in a still

---

[1] *Popular Religion: Inspirational Books in America*, Chicago 1958. Forty-six best-selling volumes have been meticulously examined. Cf. p. 3 and appendices.
[2] Pp. 18 and 44.

further intensified form; pragmatism, on the other hand, is new, and typologically it is by far the most important element.

Looking at things more in a historical perspective, it is clear that activism is the remaining piece of an otherwise dismantled Puritanism. It was Calvin who, not in so many words, but in fact and in truth, set the busy Martha above the contemplative Mary, and thereby reversed the order of religious values which had held sway from Gospel days to the doom of the Middle Ages. The new 'religion' outlined in the 'inspirational' publications is conceived as a faith for people at work, indeed, for men in business. Optimism, too, is a product of the past, but of a different layer of the past. It reflects the subsequent conquest rather than the abiding power of the Calvinist dispensation. Man who is becoming master of material creation does not have to think meanly of himself. Much rather may he conceive of himself as one of creation's lords. About these two aspects, we need say no more. They are understandable from the analyses which have gone before.

Individualism and pragmatism may be handled together, for they are really only the two sides of the same coin; and so far as they are concerned, our two authors offer us a splendid summation of the whole drift of the literature when they speak of an 'instrumentalization of religion'.[1] 'The findings allow us to continue to remark,' they write, that there is 'a very significant strain toward instrumentalization of God and religion.' It involves 'the adaptation of the one, the other, or both to the uses of man that he may live a better life on this earth'.[2] Being somewhat less careful and a lot cruder than Schneider and Dornbusch, we can present the plea of the Peales and Trines and Marshalls and their fellows in a short formula: Buy religion, folks, for it is good for you! 'A man who practices the laws of prayer correctly,' writes Glenn Clark in *The Soul's Sincere Desire*, 'should be able to play golf better, do business better, work better, love better, serve better.'[3] That these things, and especially the first two or three, are the soul's or souls' sincere desire, is hardly to be denied; but it is to be doubted that such a soul or souls are specifically religious in the sense in which the term has been understood by all Christian denominations up and down the centuries.

The whole outlook of this type of 'religiosity' is determined by the basic desire to 'instrumentalize'. Under the heading 'constant elements', Schneider and Dornbusch set down the following seven items as the leading ones. '1. The writers of the literature hold to the view that religion gives life meaning by providing a feeling of individual worth or significance. 2. Religious faith is said to ease the making of decisions: one needs only to surrender to God and the right decision will be forthcoming. 3. The writers insist that religion gives power to live by. 4. Religion promotes success, successful living, life-mastery. 5. It is true both that religious faith is asserted to bring happiness and satisfaction

[1] Loc. cit., pp. 32 and 34.   [2] Ibid.   [3] Cit. ibid., p. 6.

in this world and that man is said to be able to expect happiness in this world. It is further claimed that religion brings emotional security. 6. Religious faith is viewed as likely to bring either wealth or emotional or physical health. 7. The individual can make changes beneficial to himself by religious means.'[1]

If these are indeed the tenets of 'popular religion', or at least of the popular 'inspirational books', in America, then it is surely justifiable to call the whole outlook egocentric; and if it is egocentric, it is the very opposite of theocentric. St. Augustine, in *De Civitate Dei*,[2] contrasts those who love self to the contempt of God, and those who love God to the contempt of self; the latter belong to the heavenly city, the former to the world; they are therefore irreligious. Perhaps it would be unduly harsh to men like Peale to say that they support a philosophy which condones the love of self to the contempt of God; contempt is too strong a word to use. And yet, two points stand well out in the literature: man is not depicted, as he is in traditional Christianity, and most of all in Calvinism, as a sinner; the whole concept of original sin is alien to these writers. Hence there is no contempt of self in their 'religion', not even that contempt which is the result of searching self-examination and the basis of a healthy humility. And, secondly, God is not depicted, as He is in traditional Christianity, and, again, most of all in Calvinism, as Judge; judgment – the day of reckoning – is once again a concept alien to these writers. But to deny to God, be it only by implication, the most awesome of all His attributes is surely to deny Him that veneration which is due to Him, and so you get close to contempt after all. He is, in fact, spoken of by one of the writers (Marshall) as 'the chief' and by another (Russell) even as a 'livin' doll'.[3]

No doubt, the whole literature, well-meaning as it is, must seem shocking to Christians of the traditional cast, and even Schneider and Dornbusch, whose attitude is throughout that of objective describers and, indeed, scientists, betray at times a certain muted sense of outrage. But if the writers of today's inspirational books shock old-style Christians, old-style Christians for their part must shock these writers. For these writers aim at happiness; happiness is their supreme value; Christianity properly so called is, however, a religion which insists, not only on the reality of suffering, but also on the value of it. It is through suffering that man atones for his sins; it is through suffering that he associates himself with the Bleeding Victim on the Cross; it is through suffering that salvation was and is achieved. Those who set their hearts on making man happy in this life, have often hated Christianity and Christ with a surprisingly intense hatred. An impressive example of this is Algernon Swinburne's poem 'Before a Crucifix'.

[1] Ibid., pp. 38 and 39.
[2] XIV, 28. Cf. *The City of God*, transl. Dods, M., New York 1950, vol. I, p. 477.
[3] Schneider and Dornbusch, p. 109.

> The nineteenth wave of the ages rolls
> Now deathward since thy death and birth.
> Hast thou fed full men's starved-out souls?
> Hast thou brought freedom upon earth? . . .
> This dead God here against my face
> Hath help for no man; who hath seen
> The good works of it, or such grace
> As thy grace in it Nazarene . . .
> Thou bad'st let children come to thee;
> What children now but curses come?
> What manhood in that God can be
> Who sees their worship, and is dumb?
> No soul that lived, loved, wrought, and died,
> Is this their carrion crucified.[1]

Rainer Maria Rilke, too, entertained similar sentiments. His *Marienleben* carries in it the reproach to Jesus of having inflicted on His mother too much pain. The men of the pulpit whose products Schneider and Dornbusch are studying, simply leave this stern and stark aspect of religious tradition out of the picture as one, in company, avoids mentioning an unpleasant fact. There is no intention of making an issue of it, as Swinburne and Rilke do. But we must not forget the claims of logic. To the extent that you transform religion into an agency of this-worldly contentment, you rob it of its function of chastisement, purification and preparation for the life to come. To the extent that you make God your coadjutor and your pal, you rob Him of His majesty, His power and His glory. It is not easy to bring this supposed 'religion of the future' on to a common denominator with the religion of the past. If materialistic secularism wishes to expel Christianity from the cadres of life, this remnant-religion which sees itself surviving in it in order to take care of the 'ineliminable minimum of anxiety',[2] tends to expel, for its part, at the very least, the scourging and crowning with thorns, the carrying of the cross and the threefold fall under its weight, the ascent to Calvary and the Crucifixion – in one word, the Suffering Christ. Thus, however it is presented, it is, at the core, no longer Christianity.

We have neither time nor space to discuss the vast literature which has been put out by those who, unlike the writers just surveyed, wish to preserve *traditional* Christianity – preserve it by 'reforming' it and so making it more 'relevant' to contemporary life. We would make only one point in fulfilling the role which we have taken upon our shoulders,

---

[1] *The Complete Works of Algernon Charles Swinburne*, edd. Gosse, Sir E., and Wise, Th.J., *Poetical Works*, vol. II, London and New York 1925, pp. 147, 151, 152.
[2] Ibid., p. 32.

that of the typologist. There are logically two directions in which a would-be reformer can go, back or forward. The great prophets of the past chose the first alternative when they called: *Jerusalem, Jerusalem revertere ad Dominum Deum Tuum* – turn again, return again, to the Lord, the Lord thy God. Those who operate on the moving frontiers of contemporary society, on the other hand, show a tendency to go forward, to push into the future. But where shall they ultimately arrive? At some accommodation, no doubt, with one or other of the characteristics which, as Schneider and Dornbusch have shown, are inherent in, and central to, the thinking of modern secularized culture: activism, optimism, individualism and pragmatism. It is difficult to see what else 'modernization' can mean. If John A. T. Robinson, in *Honest to God*, calls for a theology which would assert that God lives in man, and *only* in man, he makes a vast concession to individualism.[1] If Harvey Cox, in *The Secular City*, pleads that the religious-minded should make it their first concern to 'heal urban fractures', he makes an equally vast concession to pragmatism.[2] Surveying American Protestantism as a whole, and more particularly its advanced sections, Will Oursler has reported that even now the traditional concerns of *homines religiosi*, such as prayer, do not receive the highest priority. As the *de facto* leading preoccupations he lists 'racism, hunger, drugs, pollution, war, wage scales, peace marches, riots, ghettos, protests and nudity'.[3]

Catholicism has as yet been less affected by activism and pragmatism. But individualism and optimism have penetrated it deeply. Even the ritual already reflects these specifically American and hardly Catholic features. If Catholics in America have changed to white vestments for Requiem masses, because it is a joy to see another soul go to God, they tend to forget that it is not only appointed for us to die, but – more seriously – that there is after that the judgment. Who knows that he *will* go to God? Who can presume even to expect it? The greatest saints assuredly did not. They died in the fear of God which the Bible calls the beginning of wisdom. They remembered Christ's words: 'Narrow is the gate ... that leadeth to life: and few there are that find it!' (Matthew VII, 14). And if, in addition to this, the great sequence of the *Dies irae* is omitted from the service, the tremendous hymn which reminds us, in accents almost too powerful to bear, of sin and its consequence, the judgment, the possibility of damnation, what else is this but a step in the direction of Peale and Trine?

We are back, then, with Peale and Trine and their whole school, and

---

[1] Philadelphia 1963. Cf. esp. p. 62: 'God is the "depth" of common non-religious experience'; p. 76: 'God, the ultimate "depth" of our being'. Cf. also pp. 48, 49, 52, 53, 60, 62, 76, 115, 129.

[2] New York 1966. Cf. esp. p. 115. Cf. also pp. 198, 199, 207, 231, 232.

[3] Cf. *Protestant Power and the Coming Revolution*, New York 1971. We have quoted from a preview published in *The New York Times* on 11 January 1971 under the title 'Oursler says God is put aside by many Modern Protestants'.

well we might be, for their attitude is the modern attitude *kat exochen*. In a book on the sociology of religion, this can best be shown by a comparison between religious and sociological thought. The great break in social thinking came, when philosophers ceased to regard society as the wider life into which the individual has to fit himself and which he has to serve, and began to consider it in sharp contrast as a public utility, a tool even, which men fashion for themselves because it is of use to them in the pursuit of their personal purposes. John Locke, to name but one, took precisely this line. According to his theories, not only the state, but even the nation, indeed, the whole social bond, was created by people in order to be, each of them taken singly, better off, more secure, more affluent, more happy. The 'popular religion' depicted by Schneider and Dornbusch does exactly the same with religion, and we must emphasize, in this statement, the term *exactly*. A wider life dominating men is reduced to a narrow instrument subservient to them. Locke and Rousseau brought the instrumentalization of government and society; these their disciples – and they are their disciples, for they take their cue, *via* the French and American Revolutions, from a current born of their ideas – add the 'instrumentalization of religion', the 'instrumentalization of God'. They only complete what the fathers of modern civilization have begun. The historian of ideas will describe these developments with unconcern; the sociologist of knowledge will find them interesting and use them in his analyses; but the man of faith will feel and fear that there broods over them the curse of human *hybris*.

There is, however, only one way of judging a doctrine fairly, and that is judging it on its own terms. Does the 'spiritual technology' offered by the 'popular religion in America' provide that freedom from pain and acquisition of bliss which it promises, and can it do so? – these are the questions which should be raised and which are, in the last resort, decisive. Schneider and Dornbusch answer them in the negative, and we are entirely on their side. A theologian and a psychologist whom they quote give the reason why. 'The instrumental value of faith,' writes Richard H. Niebuhr, 'is dependent on faith's conviction that it has more than instrumental value. Faith could not defend men if it believed that defence was its meaning. The godliness which is profitable to all things becomes unprofitable when profit rather than God comes to be its interest.'[1] And J. B. Pratt: 'If the subjective value of prayer be all the value it has, we wise psychologists of religion had best keep the fact to ourselves; otherwise the game will soon be up ... and we shall have killed the goose that laid our golden egg.'[2] More tersely worded: the instrument ceases to be a usable instrument if it is only an

---

[1] Cit. ibid., p. 65. Cf. Niebuhr, R. H., *The Kingdom of God in America*, Chicago and New York 1937, p. 12.

[2] Cit. ibid. Cf. Pratt, J. B., *The Religious Consciousness*, New York 1920, p. 336.

instrument. Schneider and Dornbusch call this 'the paradox of instrumentalization' and write: 'The inspirational . . . literature puts into
jeopardy the very instrumental value it seeks . . . The deliberate and concentrated effort to make [religion] "useful" carries with it the distinct
possibility of being self-defeating.'[1]

'Possibility' is too weak a word to apply here. Of course, in life old-
style genuine faith and new-style utilitarian technique may mingle and
combine, but typologically they remain irreconcilables. There is obviously a clear either/or. Either there is, as the Creed has it, an Omnipo-
tent Father, Maker of Heaven and Earth, and of all things seen and
unseen; then He is Majesty Itself and cannot be treated as a mere con-
venience. Then whatever He sends, be it blessing and bliss, or be it
punishment and pain, will have to be accepted without demur. Or there
is no such divinity; then a reference to it can be of no avail. You cannot
use an instrument that does not exist. The so-called inspirational
writers have tried to steer unscathed through Scylla and Charybdis, but
this is impossible. Religion can have its effect only if it is unconditionally
accepted; more religiously expressed, if there is total surrender to God.
It does not belong to the sphere of utility, but to the realm of being.
Through it, the mysterious inside us takes cognizance of, and estab-
lishes harmony with, the mysterious outside us. A world-view like that
of materialism which sees nothing but what the animal senses have to
offer, can never hope to understand it, let alone bend it to its purposes
and force it to do its will.

THE PERENNIAL NEED FOR RELIGION

Those who are totally enclosed in the materialistic world-view and who
equate the physical universe with the totality of being cannot admit so
much as the possibility of a religious need on the part of man. Religion
can be only one thing for them, namely erroneous science. Hence with
every step that science properly so called takes forward, religion must
take one step back. When the progress of science will have reached its
predestined end, religion will have to vanish, or will have vanished,
altogether. Even now its hold on the human race, or at least on the more
highly developed portions of it, is very weak. Speaking of the 'technopolitan man' of today and tomorrow, Harvey Cox has this to say:
'Life for him is a set of problems, not an unfathomable mystery. He
brackets off the things that cannot be dealt with and deals with those
that can. He wastes little time thinking about "ultimate" questions . . .
He sees the world not so much as an awesome enigma evoking a sense
of hushed reverence, but as a series of complex and interrelated projects
requiring the application of competence. He rarely ponders what we
usually call religious questions because he feels he can handle this world
[1] Schneider and Dornbusch, as quoted, pp. 60, 72, 69.

adequately without them.' On another page, this argument is repeated with a slightly different twist: 'The gods and their pale children, the ciphers and symbols of metaphysics, are disappearing. The world is becoming more and more "mere world". It is being divested of its sacral and religious character. Man is becoming more and more "man" and losing the mythical meanings and cultic afterglows that marked him during the "religious" stage of history, a stage now coming to its end.'[1]

The assumed and asserted passage of mankind from an 'ontological' to a 'functional' period – Comte, whose distant disciple Cox is, would have said: from a metaphysical to a positive stage – does not fill this observer with misgivings, even though he presents himself to us as a religiously committed person. 'The fact that urban-secular man is incurably and irreversibly pragmatic,' he writes, 'is in no sense a disaster. It means [merely] that he is shedding the lifeless cuticles of the mythical and ontological periods . . .'.[2] The loss of what up till now was considered religion appears in this statement almost as gain. You march much better if you do not carry a lot of deadweight in your knapsack.

It is interesting to compare the assertion of the professing Christian Harvey Cox that the religious dispensation is about to phase out, with the considered opinion of a professed Anti-Christian, Georg Lukàcs. 'I have a radical atheistic viewpoint and am convinced that history will justify me,' Lukàcs wrote recently. But, he went on to say, 'we cannot conceal the fact that religious ideology [still] exercises a great influence [even] on some Marxists . . . The withering away of the state lies in the most distant future. The same applies to religion. Today hundreds of millions still believe, and Marxists must take this into account.'[3] The passage is revealing, and it concedes even more than it appears to do. For if religion is to disappear when the State does, it will never disappear. The state will exist so long as men are given to self-preference and therefore may, on occasions, clash with others and commit crimes. Barring a miracle, they will always be like that, and there is no future of society we can foresee in which policemen, judges and jailers will not be needed. A Christian might formulate this by saying that men will always be in the grip of original sin. But then they will continue to need, not only law-enforcement agencies to protect them, but also religious institutions to educate them and to bring them to the knowledge that they can rise above themselves, that they can be redeemed.

Taking the part and the position he does, Cox must necessarily drift into collision with his fellow-theologians, and his conflict with one of them, Paul Tillich, soon comes into the open. Tillich believed – and this was the very foundation of his system – that man *must* ask the ultimate questions to which science has no answer and on which only religion

[1] Cox, loc. cit., pp. 55 and 190.
[2] Ibid., p. 60.
[3] *The New York Times*, 26 November 1970, p. 31.

can speak with an assured voice; he *must* ask them because they are inherent in the whole structure of human existence. Not every age will necessarily be preoccupied with the same aspect of mystery, but each will confront – each will have to confront – mystery in *some* form and deal with it as best it can. Though the concrete formulations may change, the ultimate concern remains. Cox will have none of this. Religious questions, he writes, 'are obviously *not* questions which occur to everyone, or indeed to the vast majority of people'. In particular, 'they do not trouble the newly emergent urban-secular man very frequently'. In Europe, it is true, existentialism has in recent decades given new urgency to the old searchings; but then Europe is not yet really emancipated from its obscurantist past and still has a lot to learn. 'In pragmatic America,' on the other hand, the most advanced of all civilizations, 'the existentialist anxiety never really took root.'[1]

Cox is in all probability right when he suggests, or if he suggests, that religious questions do not trouble the newly emergent urban-secular man very frequently *on the conscious level*. He has no time and, what is more important, he has no guts to confront them. Whenever they arise – and arise they must, for who has not encountered the fact of death? – he thrusts them away, he 'suppresses' them, to use the technical term current among psychologists. But what is suppressed, is not annihilated. The besetting problems are merely shifted from the conscious to the subconscious self, but there they lurk and trouble the newly emergent urban-secular man very frequently indeed. The incredible error which Cox commits consists in considering conscious man as identical with the whole man, in disregarding the unconscious in man which is yet, as twentieth-century psychology has so conclusively, so incontrovertibly, shown, the better part of him. In other words, Cox falls a victim to the *pars-pro-toto* fallacy. It is true that existentialism has failed to spread to America, but why? Because there is no anxiety? Surely not. The reason is simply that Calvinism has convinced the American people that philosophizing is a waste of time, that man is incapable of achieving reliable insights in this field, that the solution to men's problems does not lie in that direction. If he is up against a difficulty, the American, descendant of the Puritans, will try to help himself by material, not by intellectual, means. He will try to make, to manufacture, something that will be of use to him. In this case, it is the chemical industry on which he has decided to rely. There is anxiety and plenty of it, but the tranquillizer pill is supposed to take care of it, along with other drugs, be they of the alcoholic, be they of an otherwise narcotic kind. Technopolitan civilization, to retain Cox's term, is shot through by a plaguing restlessness which is due above all to its failure to achieve embeddedness in a wider, stability-providing, peace-bestowing order.

Let us see, by considering a leading case, what is apt to happen to

[1] Ibid., pp. 69 and 221. Author's emphasis.

man and his mind when he radically breaks with faith. James Joyce's masterly autobiography, *A Portrait of the Artist as a Young Man*, supplemented by the autobiographical elements in *Ulysses*, gives us a deep insight into the psyche of one archetypally modern person. Born into a strongly Catholic environment and brought up by Jesuits, he is at first a child of faith. When, at the age of sixteen, he commits his first truly serious sin, he feels himself cast off by Almighty God, but clings in desperation to Mary, the Comforter of the Afflicted. He goes and confesses to a Capuchin priest and experiences all the happiness which comes with one's re-instatement in grace. The account of this phase is written years later by a man who no longer believes, but – so great is Joyce's artistry, and, above all, so vivid are his memories – the story he tells of innocence lost and restored can hardly be read without emotion. Yet, as adolescence proceeds, there is more and more estrangement from the Church and all she stands for. We can appreciate the great change which came over Joyce if we contrast two passages in the book. This is how he speaks of his visit to the Capuchin friary in order to do penance. 'He approached timidly and knelt at the last bench in the body, thankful for the peace and silence and fragrant shadow of the church. The board on which he knelt was narrow and worn and those who knelt near him were humble followers of Jesus. Jesus too had been born in poverty and had worked in the shop of a carpenter, cutting boards and planing them, and had first spoken of the kingdom of God to poor fishermen, teaching all men to be meek and humble of heart. He bowed his head upon his hands, bidding his heart be meek and humble that he might be like those who knelt beside him and his prayer as acceptable as theirs. He prayed beside them but it was hard. His soul was foul with sin and he dared not ask forgiveness with the simple trust of those whom Jesus, in the mysterious ways of God, had called first to His side, the carpenters, the fishermen, poor and simple people following a lowly trade, handling and shaping the wood of trees, mending their nets with patience.'[1]

It is nothing less than a shock to turn from these words and the mood they embody to another passage which reveals the scorner and scoffer of later years. 'On Sunday mornings as he passed the churchdoor he glanced coldly at the worshippers who stood bareheaded, four deep, outside the church, morally present at the mass which they could neither see nor hear. Their dull piety and the sickly smell of a cheap hairoil with which they had anointed their heads repelled him from the altar they prayed at.'[2] What had happened to this soul? The answer is, surely, clear: humility had given way to arrogance. There was stirring in him the same sentiment which, the theologians of the ages of faith tell us, induced Satan to rise up in rebellion and to fall in defeat, the sentiment

[1] *A Portrait*, as quoted, pp. 141 and 142.
[2] Ibid., p. 104.

they call *superbia*. Throughout his work, Joyce uses the concrete and singular in order to describe and discuss the universal. We may take a leaf out of his own book here and handle him in the same way. The Stephen Dedalus of the novel is not only one person, James Joyce, he is all those who will not bend their heads like the humble fishermen and carpenters of Galilee.

But Stephen Dedalus is specifically the model of modern man, of that technopolitan man, of whom Harvey Cox has spoken to us. The very choice of the cover-name Dedalus is revealing. For the Daidalos of ancient Greece was the mythical representative of the formgiving arts, the artificer *kat exochen*, the inventor, the contriver, the builder of clever machines. His greatest achievement was to swing himself up to the sun. Joyce himself calls him 'a symbol of the artist forging anew in his work-shop out of the sluggish matter of the earth a new soaring impalpable imperishable being'.[1] He may stand therefore also as the ideal represent-ative of a civilization which has made the taming of the elements and the transformation of raw materials into enjoyable objects its overriding aim. Joyce wanted to fit into this civilization. He wanted to shape lang-uage as the metallurgist does gold or silver or vanadium or cobalt. Daidalos was the inspirer of both of them. 'This was the call of life to his soul . . . not the inhuman voice that had called him to the pale service of the altar . . . His soul had arisen from the grave of boyhood, spurning her graveclothes. Yes! Yes! Yes! He would create proudly, out of the freedom and power of his soul, as the great artificer whose name he bore, a living thing, new and soaring and beautiful, impalpable, imperishable.'[2]

The aspiration, the *élan* is strong, nay, overwhelmingly so. And yet – Dedalus-Joyce is full of apprehensions even while he is spreading his wings, even as he is taking off on his flight.[3] 'A sense of fear of the unknown moved in the heart of his weariness,' he confesses, 'a fear of symbols and portents, of the hawklike man whose name he bore soaring out of his captivity on osierwoven wings . . . Was it for this folly that he was about to leave for ever the house of prayer and prudence into which he had been born and the order of life out of which he had come?'[4] The question is merely rhetorical. James Joyce *did* leave the tents as well as the altars of his fathers and never returned to them. His conscious will told him he had to take the step, but his subconscious sentiment warned him that he was unwise in taking it. Here, then, we see, in sharp profile, the image of modern man, internally divided as he is: above the limit of awareness, enterprising, bold and aggressive; below it, in the dark and

[1] Ibid., p. 169.
[2] Ibid., pp. 169 and 170.
[3] For the curiously parallel case of Beethoven, cf. Stark, W., *The Sociology of Know-ledge*, as quoted, p. 6.
[4] *A Portrait*, as quoted, p. 225.

yet so dominant layers of the soul, hesitant, unsure and apprehensive. Folly is a strong word, and yet Stephen Dedalus uses it advisedly to stigmatize the adventure on which his rebelliousness invites him to embark. 'Old father, old artificer,' he cries, and with this invocation of Daidalos closes *A Portrait of the Artist as a Young Man*, 'stand me now and ever in good stead!'

In *Ulysses*, Joyce sneers about his own childlike attachment to the Queen of Heaven, Refuge of Sinners: 'Cousin Stephen,' he writes, 'you will never be a saint . . . You were awfully holy, weren't you. You prayed to the Blessed Virgin that you might not have a red nose.'[1] But he pours no less scorn on his Daidalian hopes, and this is where his tragedy and the tragedy of his kind lies: 'Your name is strange enough,' he says in one of his soliloquies. 'Fabulous artificer, the hawklike man. You flew. Whereto?' To heavenly spheres? Far from it! 'You flew. Whereto? Newhaven-Dieppe, steerage passenger. Paris and back . . . Seabedabbled, fallen, weltering . . .'.[2] A bitter admission, this: there is no salvation for man, so we must understand the great writer, in imitating Daidalos. He perhaps flew; but all Stephen Dedalus could do was to flee, and this is not quite the same thing.

Joyce's changed mood, the sobering realization that the man freed from the shackles of religion is not necessarily a man liberated, by his creativeness, from the besetting pains of human existence, is visible not only in the one stray passage of his great work which we have quoted, but manifestly informs the whole of it. The title itself reflects it. Daidalos is the hero who raises himself, on wings he himself has fashioned, to the skies. But Ulysses is the hapless wanderer on the face of the sea, driven hither and thither by the capricious will of powers greater than himself, not a master of the air, but a prisoner of the waves. There is a kind of link – tenuous, it is true, but not uncommon in Joyce's thought – between the two eponyms. Daidalos was, according to the legend, the builder of the great Labyrinth of Crete, the apparently issue-less maze in which King Minos sought to incarcerate him. But the Ocean was to Ulysses also a kind of labyrinth, a trap in which he was caught, and sailing it a frustrating search for an exit which for years appeared to be ever far, to be simply unattainable. Both central figures in *Ulysses*, Stephen Dedalus and Leopold Bloom, are modern replicas of the actors in the Greek saga, searchers who cannot find. And so are all men – all wanderers on the face of the deep.[3]

The labyrinth, with all its negative implications, emerges in this fashion as the prime symbol of the human condition in the artistic work of the mature Joyce. And this links him with a broad tradition which started in the age of the Renaissance, in the age, that is, which first

---

[1] *Ulysses*, as quoted, p. 41.
[2] Ibid., p. 208.
[3] Cf. Daiches, D., *The Novel and the Modern World*, Chicago 1939, pp. 135 and 136.

experienced a sensible loss of faith. A decorative ceiling in the ducal palace at Mantua is one of its first, as it is surely one of its most impressive, plastic representations. It carries, ever repeated, the legend: *Forse si, forse no* - perhaps, perhaps not. Perhaps there is a meaning in my life, but perhaps there is not (K's query in Kafka's *Das Schloss*); perhaps I shall survive in a changed form after death, but perhaps I shall not; and so on. Many questions of the deepest significance may be poured into, and expressed in, this matrix; questions which men cannot simply switch off, as it were, whatever anyone may say, questions which will stay with us even if we tell them to go away. Between them, they build up to a sentiment of insecurity which spells unsettlement, unrest, unhappiness. 'God is engaged in a war with the Devil and God may lose,' writes Norman Mailer in *An American Dream*,[1] and this reveals all the anxiety inherent in American reality. How different is Christianity! 'The prince of this world is already judged,' Jesus said to His disciples at the Last Supper, on the very eve of His catastrophe. 'Have confidence, I have overcome the world' (John xvi, 11 and 33). Scepticism will, of course, urge here that such assurances are unavailing, that there is no guarantee that they will prove reliable, and that therefore in the end the *forse si, forse no* remains. But if the assurances are lodged in the unconscious, then scepticism (whether generated within or suggested from without) will not be able to touch and trouble them; then they will be, as Lévy-Bruhl used to say of a society's submerged metaphysics, *imperméable à l'expérience*, and in certain societies – societies embedded in the matrix of a truly religious culture, such as the one we have heard Carl Zuckmayer describing – they are so lodged, rooted so firmly in the subsoil of life that even the strongest winds cannot dislodge them.

In an unusually interesting book, *Die Welt als Labyrinth*,[2] Gustav René Hocke has shown how frequently the plaguing, peace-destroying image of the labyrinth has risen from the depths of modern man's tortured soul. Since his work has been published, more has been added to his already long list – to mention but one example: Michael Tippett's opera, *The Knot Garden*, where the characters are shown incomprehendingly confronting each other in a maze. Men see themselves as captives, as animals trapped. Calvin, with his remarkable insight, predicted that this would happen: abandon faith, he preaches in his *Institutes*,[3] and reality will be no more to you than 'an inexplicable labyrinth', a prison-

[1] Paperback ed., reprint of 1969, p. 221.
[2] Already quoted (cf. p. 144). Concerning James Joyce, cf. pp. 230 and 231; also 204 et seq. On Dublin as a symbol of the outer labyrinth, cf. Budgen, Fr., *James Joyce and the Making of Ulysses*, ed. Bloomington 1960, p. 123; on the maternity hospital as a symbol of 'the spaceless labyrinth of the human conscience', cf. ibid., p. 216.
[3] Ed. cit., vol. I, p. 73 (I, IV, 3). Cf. also pp. 64 and 65 and especially footnote 36 where many passages are enumerated in which Calvin makes use of the labyrinth metaphor.

house without escape, a nightmare, an evil dream. The Positivists from Comte to Cox have tried to counter this prophecy by asserting that work *alone* is a *sufficient* content for men's lives. They have advocated a Protestant ethic *minus* Protestantism, so to speak,, but this nostrum is in the last resort unavailing. Certainly, work offers satisfactions which it is difficult to overestimate. But it has to be meaningful from every point of view and futile from none, and it can be so only if it is enclosed in a totally – and that means also metaphysically – meaningful existence. Even those few privileged persons who had a chance of being truly creative – captains in industry and similar leaders – whose duties were enjoyable in themselves, have often betrayed, by the very feverishness of their efforts, that the stabilizing factor of religiosity was missing from their lives and that, in the midst of their successes, they were less than happy.

We are saying all this, not in order to denigrate unbelief and to exalt belief – more coarsely expressed, not in order to sell something which many nowadays are unwilling to buy – but in order to show, as factually as we can, that the metaphysical need, too, has to be met, if man and society are to function in the best possible manner. To say that there is a physical hunger which must be stilled, if man is to be physically healthy, is a scientific statement of the purest water. The parallel assertion that there is a psychic hunger which must be stilled if man is to be psychically healthy is no less so, even if many do not see it. True, the psychic hunger does not become conscious as the physical hunger does, but that does not mean that it is less real.

We owe the understanding of these momentous matters to the genius of Carl Gustav Jung. In one of his minor, yet rather significant writings, *Flying Saucers*,[1] he has raised the question as to why so many people should be asserting that they had seen disc-like objects floating through the air, if there are in reality, scientifically speaking, no such things, and he explains the phenomenon as an effect of the 'psychic dissociation' or 'split-mindedness' of our age.[2] Our age does not satisfy the conscious and the unconscious parts of our selves in the same measure and manner: it gives consciousness, and the rationality that is characteristic of it, free rein, but it does little or nothing to still the cravings of our unconscious and of the emotionality which it harbours. 'In the midst of our civilized, conscious existence,' the great psychiatrist and psychologist writes, 'we have lost wholeness ... All feeling for value is repressed in the interests of a narrow intellect and biased reason ... Belief in this world and in the power of man has, despite assurances to the contrary, become a practical and, for the time being, irrefragable truth. This attitude on the part of the overwhelming majority provides the most favourable basis for a

---

[1] First published under the title *Ein moderner Mythus von Dingen, die am Himmel gesehen werden*, Zürich 1958.
[2] Engl. transl. by R. F. C. Hull, New York 1959, pp. 9 and 21.

projection, that is, for a manifestation of the unconscious background. Undeterred by rationalistic criticism, it thrusts itself to the forefront in the form of a symbolic rumour, accompanied and reinforced by the appropriate visions . . . In the individual, too, such phenomena as abnormal convictions, visions, illusions etc., only occur when he is suffering from a psychic dissociation, that is, when there is a split between the conscious attitude and the unconscious contents opposed to it. Precisely because the conscious mind does not know about them and is therefore confronted with a situation from which there seems to be no way out, these strange contents cannot be integrated directly but seek to express themselves indirectly, thus giving rise to unexpected and apparently inexplicable opinions, beliefs, illusions, visions, and so forth . . . The "unidentified flying object" [thus] comes from the unconscious background which has always expressed itself in numinous ideas and images.' It is 'a gesture on the part of the unconscious' which spontaneously appears 'when feelings of . . . the senselessness of a merely functional existence threaten to stifle the personality'. It is, properly understood, a not unhealthy reaction to an unhealthy situation. Though there is physical delusion, there is no mental pathology. The eyes may be wrong, but the psyche is right. 'This case,' Jung adds, 'may serve as a paradigm for the widespread anxiety and insecurity of . . . people today, while at the same time revealing the compensating power of the unconscious.'[1]

The unidentified flying objects are, briefly expressed, 'subliminal contents that have become visible'; they are 'in a word, archetypal figures'.[2] We must look closely at the archetype that is being activated and shown forth in these visions; it will teach us a good deal about modern man. The alleged 'saucers' are always depicted as round or spherical or cylindrical, and these are the forms which have 'always expressed order, deliverance, salvation and wholeness'. This, then, is what modern 'fragmented' man is longing for. He is longing for, in the first place, integration of his self. 'Psychologically,' Jung writes, 'the *rotundum* . . . is a symbol of the self. The self is the archetype of order *par excellence*'. But the self is not to be confused with the ego. The ego, i.e. conscious man, is never identical with the true self, the whole man. Modern associational, mechanistic, atheistic society is composed of egos, who are not at peace with themselves because they wish, in the depths of their being, to become selves, to be 'made whole', as the Gospels so often express it. This desire for wholeness is a desire for salvation whether it may be admitted or not. 'A political, social, philosophical and religious conflict of unprecedented proportions has split the consciousness of our age,' Jung writes. 'When such tremendous opposites split asunder, we may expect with certainty that the need for

[1] Ibid., pp. 100, 37, 22, 8, 9, 40, 56.
[2] Cf. above, p. 114.

a saviour will make itself felt. Experience has amply confirmed that, in the psyche as in nature, a tension of opposites creates a potential which may express itself at any time in a manifestation of energy. Between above and below flows the waterfall, and between hot and cold there is a turbulent exchange of molecules. Similarly, between the psychic opposites there is generated a "uniting symbol", at first unconscious. This process is running its course in the unconscious of modern man. Between the opposites there arises spontaneously a symbol of unity and wholeness, no matter whether it reaches consciousness or not.'[1]

The circle or ball 'seen' in the sky is in this manner not only a symbol of the self: it is also a visible sign of the self's search for salvation. He who would be whole looks for one who can make him whole, and this, in our tradition, is Jesus Christ. Christ, then, is the archetype made manifest, as well as, and as much as, the self. He is the perfection of the personality towards which every person strives, or rather towards which the unconscious of every person strives, for the conscious may be unaware of the longing and striving, and indeed repudiate it. 'Christ . . . was long ago characterized by totality symbols, because He was understood to be all-embracing and to unite all opposites . . . It is this fact which also makes it possible to say that whoever believes in Christ is not only contained in Him, but that Christ then dwells in the believer as the perfect man formed in the image of God, the second Adam . . . It is the ascendancy of the "complete" or total human being, consisting of the totality of the psyche, of conscious and unconscious, over the ego, which represents only consciousness and its contents and knows nothing of the unconscious, although in many respects it is dependent on the unconscious and is often decisively influenced by it. This relationship of the self to the ego is reflected in the relationship of Christ to man.'[2] Thus far the great psychologist. The sociologist will only wish to insert a third term between the soul and its saviour (understood in the Jungian sense) and that is, of course, society. Unity of the self and unitedness of the community and union of them both with the centre of being is the threefold condition which must be fulfilled if all men's longings are to be stilled.

All men as we know them, i.e. all men endowed with intelligence, bear within them the split between the conscious and the unconscious of which Jung is speaking. All therefore also long for wholeness. It is modern man's special problem and predicament that he longs with much greater intensity than his predecessors (even if he experiences his longing merely as a dark wish for he-knows-not-what); and, more importantly still, that he is inclined to push from him the remedies of his malady

[1] Ibid., pp. 119, 22, 23, 152, 163, 148. Cf. also pp. 142, 143, 162.
[2] Jung, C. G., *Answer to Job*, transl. Hull, R. F. C., New York 1960, pp. 134, 152, 153. Cf. also note 47 on p. 210.

which his own deeper self spontaneously offers – the ideas, or the realities, by which his longing might be laid to rest.

The relation between the conscious and the unconscious, as Jung has analysed it, is one of mutual compensation. 'As a totality, the self is by definition always a *complexio oppositorum*, and the more consciousness insists on its own luminous nature and lays claim to moral authority, the more the self will appear as something dark and menacing.'[1] Perhaps it is at this point that we can best see the realism of Jung's depth-psychology, for we all have observed in recent history, and are still observing, how the advances of rationality are bringing with them, like a shadow that cannot be discarded, equipollent advances of irrationality. The demoniac hatred, on the part of a great cultural nation, of a small minority group within its midst which led to the horror of the gas chambers, and the no less demoniac headlong rush of many into drug addiction, the voluntary self-destruction of young lives for the sake of hallucinatory experiences, are only too convincing proofs of the fact that you cannot have intensifying rationalization without intensifying irrationality. The theory of ever-advancing reasonableness, be it in its optimistic shape, as we find it in such writers as William Godwin, be it in its pessimistic shape, as we find it in such writers as Max Weber, is wrong. There are two sides to the coin and they cannot be separated from each other.

The call of the unconscious, however, presents in and for itself no insoluble problem, for it can be answered. In primitive or 'heathen' times, there was, for instance, the symbolic figure of the sacred king who reconciles man with his fellow men and with the powers above and thus gives integration – roundedness – to the self, or, more simply expressed, inner peace. We started our first volume with a reference to that far-flung phenomenon, the ultimate root of monarchical religious-ness.[2] In Christian times, or rather during the transition to Christianity, the sacred king becomes the Christomimetes, one who shows forth Christ, a sub-symbol as it were under the uprising master-symbol of Christ. In the fullness of time, Christ then enters into His central position. He becomes the Symbol of Unity *kat exochen*.

But – and this is where the problematic of modern religion, which is also the problematic of modern man, arises – in the rationalistic and technocratic environment which the twentieth century has developed, one half of the personality denies to the other half what it needs. The *ratio* would be all, forgetting the ever-true words of one of the greatest of all rationalists, Blaise Pascal, which, as we said before, cannot be quoted too often, namely that 'the heart has its reasons which reason does not know'. The *ratio* sets itself up as a censor which condemns everything that is not rational, and has the power to make its judgment

[1] Ibid., p. 155.
[2] Cf. loc. cit., p. 8.

prevail. The 'flying saucers' are a convincing proof even of this censorship. 'It is characteristic of our time,' Jung writes, 'that, in contrast to its previous expressions, the archetype should now take the form of an object, a technological construction, in order to avoid the odiousness of a mythological personification.'[1] But that 'mythological personification' who, to the believer, is a real person, was men's redeemer through the ages, and would be so now, if only their hearts would lay hold on Him.

There is, says Jung, and we agree with him, a 'crass undervaluation of the psyche', i.e. the inner world, 'in our predominantly materialistic and statistical age' which, as we would like to add, in order to be balanced and fair, is essentially the seamy side of the great successes which we have achieved in our dealings with the outer world. 'People imagine that only the things they are conscious of affect them . . . But in that way we succumb to the greatest psychic danger that now threatens us – rootless intellectualisms which one and all reckon without their host, i.e without real man.' For the modern mentality only that is real which is tangible, real in the physical sense. It therefore refuses to deal with, and scorns, the realities which can be apprehended only through the intermediacy of symbols. The realities of religion are of this kind. They get short shrift. 'The most important of the fundamental instincts,' Jung explains, 'the religious instinct for wholeness, plays the least conspicuous part in contemporary consciousness.' Drives like those for sex satisfaction and personal power dominate the scene. 'These can constantly appeal to common, everyday facts known to everyone, but the religious instinct requires for its evidence a more highly differentiated consciousness, thoughtfulness, reflection, responsibility, and sundry other virtues. Therefore it does not commend itself to . . . man [if he is] driven by his natural impulses, because, imprisoned in his familiar world, he clings to the commonplace, the obvious, the probable . . . It is an enormous relief to him when something that looks complicated, unusual, puzzling and problematical can be reduced to something ordinary and banal . . . The most convenient explanations are invariably sex and the power instinct, and reduction to these two dominants gives rationalists and materialists an ill-concealed satisfaction: they have neatly disposed of an intellectually and morally uncomfortable difficulty, and on top of that can enjoy the feeling of having accomplished a useful work of enlightenment which will free the individual from unnecessary moral and social burdens . . . This is the exact opposite of what the striving for wholeness wants, namely to free the individual from the compulsion of the other two instincts. The task before him comes back with all its energies unused, and reinforces, to an almost pathological degree, the very instincts that have always stood in the way of man's higher development. At all events, it has a neuroticizing

[1] *Flying Saucers*, as quoted, p. 23.

effect characteristic of our time and must bear most of the blame for the splitting of the individual and of the world in general.'[1]

In view of all that has gone before, it is almost unnecessary to say that the conscious mind cannot provide what the unconscious self needs: the two are simply not attuned to each other. The primordial images, Jung maintains, which constitute the religion of Christianity 'cannot simply be replaced by a new rational configuration, for this would be moulded too much by the outer situation and not enough by man's biological needs . . . Today, our basic convictions have become increasingly rationalistic. Our philosophy is no longer a way of life, as it was in antiquity: it has turned into an exclusively intellectual and academic affair. Our denominational religions with their archaic rites and conceptions – justified enough in themselves – express a view of the world which caused no great difficulties in the Middle Ages but has become strange and unintelligible to the man of today. Despite this conflict with the modern scientific outlook, a deep instinct bids him hang on to ideas which, if taken literally, leave out of account all the mental developments of the last five hundred years. The obvious purpose of this is to prevent him from falling into the abyss of nihilistic despair. But even when, as rationalists, we feel impelled to criticize contemporary religion as . . . obsolescent, we should never forget that the creeds proclaim a doctrine whose symbols, although their interpretation may be disputed, nevertheless possess a life of their own on account of their archetypal character'.[2]

A life of their own, Jung says in this passage. In others he goes further and gives as his opinion that the credal symbols possess a truth of their own: 'The unconscious mind of man sees correctly even when conscious reason is blind and impotent . . . The statements of the conscious mind may easily be snares and delusions, lies or arbitrary opinions, but this is certainly not true of the statements of the soul: to begin with, they always go over our heads because they point to realities that transcend consciousness. These *entia* are the archetypes of the collective unconscious, and they precipitate complexes of ideas in the form of mythological motifs. Ideas of this kind are never invented, but enter the field of perception as finished products . . .'.[3] They are, therefore, in a sense, facts. We may well wish, in religion, for the same sort of literal truth which we get in science; but our wish cannot be fulfilled. 'The reality [of the unconscious] we can experience only in parables.'[4] But it is a reality all the same.

One point at which we can see that 'obscurantist religion' brings us

---

[1] Ibid., pp. 48, 86, 85, 46, 47. Cf. also 39 and 40. Cf. further *The Undiscovered Self*, transl. Hull, R. F. C., ed. New York n.d., pp. 77 and 86.
[2] *The Undiscovered Self*, as quoted. pp. 84 and 85.
[3] *Answer to Job*, as quoted, pp. 55 and 18.
[4] *Flying Saucers*, as quoted, pp. 118 and 119.

much closer to truth than 'enlightened reason' is self-knowledge, an area of unsurpassable importance from every point of view. When it became known that six million men, women and children had been burnt to death in gas chambers, the secularists of the Rousseauan tradition stood aghast: how *could* this have happened? Christians of the Augustinian tradition were equally appalled, but they were less surprised. They knew better what beast is slumbering in the depths of man. 'The evil that comes to light in man and that undoubtedly dwells within him is of gigantic proportions, so that for the Church to talk of original sin and to trace it back to Adam's relatively innocent slip-up with Eve is almost a euphemism . . . Since it is universally believed that man *is* merely what his consciousness knows of itself, he regards himself as harmless and so adds stupidity to iniquity.' Here reason obfuscates: it certainly does not enlighten. 'The evil, the guilt, the profound unease of conscience, the obscure misgiving are there before our eyes, if only we would see.' Religious man does see: rational man does not. 'He does not deny that terrible things have happened and still go on happening, but it is always "the others" who do them . . . We prefer to localize the evil with individual criminals or groups of criminals, while washing our hands in innocence and ignoring the general proclivity to evil.' As against this Rousseauan I-am-born-good philosophy, Jung reasserts the insights of the Fiftieth Psalm: 'I know my iniquity, and my sin is always before me': 'Man has done these things; I am a man, who has his share of human nature; therefore I am guilty with the rest and bear unaltered and indelibly within me the capacity and the inclination to do them again at any time . . . None of us stands outside humanity's black collective shadow.'[1]

Religion, then, does give us truth, just as reason does. It is not in this that the difference between the two prongs of exploration rests. Their dissimilarity stems rather from the fact that reason deals with that which is within our grip – which is, so to speak, smaller than us, and religion with that which is beyond our grip – which is, as is but all too certain, bigger than us. 'Whenever we speak of religious contents, we move in a world of images that point to something ineffable. We do not know how clear or unclear these images, metaphors, and concepts are in respect of their transcendental object . . . There is no doubt [however] that there is something behind these images that . . . operates in such a way that the statements [we may make about it] do not vary limitlessly and chaotically, but clearly all relate to a few basic principles or archetypes . . . We are dealing with psychic facts which logic can overlook but not eliminate.'[2] For an *imago mundi* which aims at wholeness, and even more for a life which does so, religion is therefore as necessary as science.

[1] *The Undiscovered Self*, pp. 107–10.
[2] *Answer to Job*, pp. 15–17.

In sum: what this great healer of minds recommends to modern man, unhappy in the midst of all his achievements, is a certain re-mythologization which stands in the sharpest possible contrast to that de-mythologization for which a strong call has recently gone forth.[1] We usually connect it with the name of Rudolf Bultmann, but it is characteristic of contemporary rationalism as a whole. Commenting on the state of the confessions in the second half of the twentieth century, Norman Bellah has recently written: 'Much of the excitement of the present moment is the willingness . . . to think things through again from the foundations.' To *think* things through again! If the problems of religion could be *thought* through, i.e. solved by rational means, there would be no need for religion; science would do it all. But this is impossible. What we have before us in the case of this and all similar-minded men is, to vary Bellah's own words, a 'failure of critical intelligence' when applied to intelligence itself.[2] For intelligence is never more intelligent than when it discovers its own inherent limitations.

The simplest thing the *ratio* can do when it is faced with the religious needs of the human self is to deny their existence. It only reveals its own impotence when it undertakes to deal with them, as has often been proved by experience. It is, for instance, an ever-repeated fact that symbols which are artificially manufactured, so to speak, and offered out, fail to develop that numinous quality which surrounds the grown *symbolum*, i.e. the *symbolum* which, like folk-poetry, has risen from the collective unconscious. But perhaps the most massive and impressive failure of the intellect in this field which is simply closed to it, is the fate of Auguste Comte's Religion of Humanity. This grand attempt to reconcile the head and the heart had everything in its favour. A religion which is at the same time also science – what more can be wanted, so it was argued. Moreover, the propagator of the idea was a charismatic person – a *saint manqué*, as his countrymen might call him; and the *manqué* is not even quite fair for there are features of genuine saintliness about this man. It is impossible to read the hymns which were proposed for the new cult without emotion. But, to use a phrase formulated by Carl Gustav Jung and quoted above, he had not reckoned with the host of the intended unmystical mysticism, the real man, or rather the real man's real unconscious which reason does not know. And so the so-called Religion of Humanity which its clever father and founder had confidently expected would sweep the world and be the Catholicism of the future never gathered as much as a thousand adherents.

If the intellect thus does not have the word that is needed, what has? We have given the answer already: it is life. More concretely: it is those institutions which agree to allow the life of the unconscious free play, even if its results shock the conscious ego. Jung is very explicit on this

[1] Cf. ibid., p. 95.
[2] Cf. *Sociological Analysis*, 1968, pp. 161 and 160.

point also. 'The religious need longs for wholeness,' he writes, 'and therefore lays hold of the images of wholeness offered by the unconscious which, independently of the conscious mind, rise up from the depths of our psychic nature . . . Whatever man's wholeness, or the self, may mean *per se*, empirically it is an image of the goal of life spontaneously produced by the unconscious . . . The symbols that rise up out of the unconscious . . . show it . . . as a confrontation of opposites, and the images of the goal represent their successful reconciliation. Something empirically demonstrable comes to our aid from the depths of our unconscious nature.'[1] To turn away from that 'something' means losing the chance of developing a viable religion, as the psychologist must say, whether he happens to be a believer or not. The man of faith can go further and assert that it means losing the chance of salvation for that 'something' is the Ultimate showing itself to us, the ground of being.

Born and bred a Protestant, Jung drew, in the course of time, closer to Catholicism because he felt that Rome was less rationalistic than Geneva and therefore a more reliable source of a religiosity which would really satisfy the unconscious self. 'The Catholic outlook,' he confesses, 'gives the archetypal symbolisms the necessary freedom and space in which to develop over the centuries while at the same time insisting on their original form, unperturbed by intellectual difficulties and the objections of rationalists. In this way the Catholic Church demonstrates her maternal character, because she allows the tree growing out of her matrix to develop according to its own laws.'[2] Jung even goes so far as to comment favourably on the promulgation of the Dogma of the Assumption in 1950, although this greatly shocked the rationalists both outside and inside the Catholic Church herself. He shows by a depth-psychological analysis that this act, too, met one of the psychological needs of the present time.[3]

In the passage from Jung which we have just quoted there is contained a piece of analysis which we might easily lose and should try to retain. Jung commends Rome for allowing the basic religious intuitions freely to develop 'while at the same time insisting on their original form'. Many are the writers, close either to evolutionism or to historicism, who have asserted that the religion of yesterday was right for yesteryear, but that something else is needed now because we have 'advanced'. Jung does not deny the need for adjustment to changing situations, but he is even firmer (as he must be) in his insistence that there have to be adjustments only, no new creations. What came to the surface in the man-killing orgies of the thirties and forties, and what comes to the surface in any and every war, is a primitive trait of the human psyche, an ever-present element of it and in it. This is characteristic of the unconscious as a whole. Its contents are, as Jung proves in

---

[1] *Answer to Job*, pp. 200, 183, 184; cf. also p. 198.
[2] Ibid., p. 194. [3] Ibid., pp. 197 et seq. and 210 et seq.

many discussions which we cannot detail here, archaic. We live with them; we must live with them. The answers to the perennial questions which it asks have to be perennial also although their formulation may require timely revisions. How could there be anything radically new about them? There is nothing new in the fact that we are born and that we have to die – nothing new in the facts with which religious life is centrally concerned. Christianity has not, therefore, been superseded. 'The Christian symbol is a living thing that carries in itself the seeds of further development. It can go on developing; it depends only on us whether we can make up our minds to meditate again, and more thoroughly, on the Christian promises.'[1]

In taking up this twosided and yet unitary position, Jung comes close to a great Christian thinker whom, in all probability, he never encountered – John Henry Newman, whose *Essay on the Development of Christian Doctrine* moves, in its basic analyses, along exactly the same lines. While yet an Anglican, and hence closer to Protestantism, Newman thought deeply about the 'additions' to the original revelation laid down in the Gospels which were charged against Rome, and he came to the conclusion that these 'additions' (which in fact existed) were no falsifications but unfoldings of the depositum of faith and hence acceptable to the religious consciousness. The dogmatic structure of the nineteenth century was different from that of the first, and yet the same – as the grown tree is different from, and yet identical with, the seedling of the first days.[2]

In trying to justify his new-won conviction (which was the cause of his conversion to Catholicism), the future Cardinal did not rely on inductive demonstration, on point for point explications, such as showing that all the later Mariological dogmas are contained, in outline, in the unique honour shown by primitive Christians to the Mother of Jesus, and indeed in her whole function in the economy of salvation. He added to descriptive material an analytical argument, and that brings him even nearer to Carl Gustav Jung. The original intuitions, he points out, *and* the later developments come from the same source – from what Newman, in a phrase to which the modern sociologist is likely to take exception, described as the mind of the Church. Protestants, of course, cannot and will not concede this. The original depositum, they will say, is a revelation from God, the later accretions creations of men. They are in line with their basic conviction if they argue in this way; they cannot

[1] *The Undiscovered Self*, as quoted, pp. 74 and 75. In taking leave of Jung (there will only be one more – critical – reference to him later on), we would repeat what we said before (cf. p. 122), that we do not find all his theories acceptable. Our allegiance is given to the scientific core of his work, not to its more imaginative fringes. Especially in *Answer to Job* there is much that gives one pause.

[2] I have spoken in detail about Newman in my book *Social Theory and Christian Thought* (London 1959, pp. 106 et seq.), and so will say no more here. The reader is referred to my original essay.

see matters differently from their point of view. But Newman's point of view was otherwise. The Church was to him the Body of Christ; its thought, its voice, its developments were therefore from Christ. *Mutatis mutandis*, Jung felt similarly, and so we cannot really be surprised to find that he ended a philo-Catholic. The very logic of his science drove him in that direction, as the logic of Newman's theology did a century before.

We can, as sociologists, sum up both Jung and Newman by saying that a religion, properly so called, is the product of the vital and not of the calculating will, of Tönnies' *Wesenwille* or existential striving, not of his *Kürwille* or purposive choosing. Christianity in general, and Catholicism in particular, is the mental pendant, the 'superstructure' of community in real, 'substructural' life. This truth has to be strongly underlined; even Jung tends to forget it, for all too often he talks as if the conscious ego and the unconscious self were attributes exclusively of the individual person. It is true that he knows full well that this is not so, and that the analysis must not be narrowed down to a consideration of isolated man. He writes for instance: 'As experience shows, the archetypes possess the quality of "transgressiveness"; they can sometimes manifest themselves in such a way that they seem to belong as much to society as to the individual; they are therefore numinous and contagious in their effects.'[1] This is correct, but the formulation is far too weak. We must remember that Jung's basic explorations operated with the concept of a *collective* unconscious, and on this concept the sociologist has to insist. In saying this, we do not wish to resuscitate the unsound and exploded notion of a collective mind. A society has neither a collective sensorium, as Schaeffle thought, nor yet a communal soul or entelechy as, for instance, Alfred Weber was inclined to believe. Such metaphysical assumptions do not belong in a factual science such as sociology. But if an extreme philosophical realism is forbidden us, if we must be aware of the fact that philosophical nominalism also holds part of the truth, then we are all the more justified in thinking of religion in terms of *intersubjectivity*. Sumner was far from being a collectivist; indeed, this is a strong understatement. Folkways are to be observed only in individual conduct; but they link individuals together and create out of them a society. They are a social 'cement'. Thus they are also societal. They inhere in the society's culture; they *are* society's culture, and in that sense real. The young confront them as facts and internalize them as data. So also with religious notions. They belong, in settled social systems, no less than norms of action do, to the folkway complex.

This insistence on the collective character of the unconscious, and especially on the all-important fact that the symbols which it produces, and with the help of which it stills men's existential fears and strivings,

[1] *Flying Saucers*, p. 54.

are the results of a collective-unconscious process, shows us a second reason why religion is certain to remain a feature, however reduced, of the sociocultural scene. Not only is there a mysterious self in us which will ever tend to meet with the Mysterious Self outside us which we call God, but there is also an irreducible minimum of community in every society, however individualistic and associational it otherwise might be, and, through the existential will or *Wesenwille*, it, too, ties us to mystery, to the double mystery of which we have just spoken. Tönnies emphasized all along that community and association are contrasts only in theory, as 'normal concepts' or ideal types; in practice, they are intermixed, though in very varying proportions. As there is no community, however closely knit, in which there is not a modicum of individualism and utilitarianism, so there is no association, however little emphasis it may put on collective values, which does not harbour a trace of collectivism and emotional fusion. A social life totally severed from its communal roots is unimaginable. Tönnies is right in this respect, and so is Durkheim. And therefore it is not only the unconscious, *tout court*, which will always be with us, but even the collective unconscious – that source of all living religion, of Christianity in general and more particularly Catholicism, the variant of Christianity which is willing to follow wherever the mysterious forces of reality are tending to lead.

The strong emphasis which we are placing – even, in part, against our own mentor – on the collectivity of the unconscious which is finding its complement in religion is necessary to reinforce a point which, as we have seen, is made by Jung himself, but which can hardly be rendered secure enough. Jung asserts that there is definite truth about the symbols of faith, though it is not truth as defined in the physical sciences. There is a truth of their own about them in so far as they correspond to the archetypes, the basic realities of our souls. The sociologist will call in here a helpful concept provided by Alfred Weber, the concept of *Ausdruckswahrheit*,[1] or expressive truth, as distinguished from scientific truth, i.e. truth based on systematic observation of the outer world (impression-truth, if we may so call it, knowledge in the sense of truths impressed upon us). This expressive truth, if it is to be effectively expressed, must be expressed by the collectivity itself. It will, of course, always be individuals who first suggest modes of expression which seem to them subjectively appropriate, but this will merely be the beginning of a collective development in which statements will be worked out which are also objectively, in the sense of collectivity, appropriate – a language which corresponds, not to the individual, but to the collective unconscious. It is in this process of trial and testing that the symbols of religion find, not only their form, but also their strength. Men will not easily throw them off, for men have so tailored them that they fit them. This basically was Newman's argument though he worded

[1] Cf. Stark, W., *The Sociology of Knowledge*, as quoted, p. 179.

it differently; it was also the argument of Edmund Burke who formulated it in an unforgettable phrase. 'We are afraid to put men to live and trade each on his own private stock of reason; because we suspect that the stock in each man is small, and that the individuals would do better to avail themselves of the general bank and capital of nations and of ages.' Burke speaks of politics, but what he says applies to religion as well – both concerns of the common life. 'Political arrangement, as it is a work for social ends, is to be only wrought by social means. There mind must conspire with mind. Time is required to produce that union of minds which alone can produce all the good we aim at.'[1] A Church, so we may utilize another passage, like a nation, 'is not an idea only of local extent and individual momentary aggregation, but it is an idea of continuity which extends in time as well as in numbers and in space'. It must select its governing principles, just as a nation must, and it will only find what it really needs, if it allows them to emerge, after a long period of gestation, out of a collective effort, if it does not manufacture them, but allows them to grow. If it permits its symbols (both in the sense of emblems and in the sense of creeds) to be fashioned in this way, it exercises its right to choose, but 'this is a choice not of one day, or one set of people, not a tumultuary and giddy choice; it is a deliberate election of ages and of generations . . . made by what is ten thousand times better than choice, it is made by the peculiar circumstances, occasions, tempers, dispositions, and moral, civil and social habitudes of the people' – in our case, the *plebs Christi* organized in His *corpus mysticum* – 'which disclose themselves only in a long space of time . . . The individual is foolish . . . but the species is wise, and when time is given to it, as a species, it almost always acts right'.[2] The classical variants of Christianity, and more particularly Catholicism, have always lived by this maxim, and this is why they are still with us. Nor will they disappear tomorrow – unless, wantonly, they cut the roots which connect them with the subsoil of life. They are too deeply anchored in the collective unconscious to wither away spontaneously.

There may be some, and perhaps even many, who are prepared to accept the arguments which we have put forward and yet reject the assessment of religion's, or Christianity's, or Catholicism's chances of survival at which we have arrived. They will say that rationality is our fate for better or worse. Granting that in an associational-individualistic-rationalistic civilization something is missing which the human self cannot really do without, we have to reconcile ourselves to the loss of it, for it is irretrievable. In an extreme form, this opinion was voiced by Theodor Lessing when he spoke of the 'destruction of the world by the

---

[1] *Reflections on the Revolution in France, The Works of the Right Honourable Edmund Burke*, London 1826, vol. V, pp. 168 and 305.
[2] *On the Reform of the Representation in the House of Commons, Works*, as quoted, vol. X, p. 97.

intellect',[1] a formulation which has gained more poignancy by the invention, since his day, of the atomic bomb. Max Weber would never have gone so far. The possible 'death of a society' would have appeared to him as an objectionable metaphysical notion. Yet he talked, in sorrow, of a 'disenchantment of the world'. Neither the hero, nor the entrepreneur, nor yet the proletarian, but the bureaucrat is on the march. We may, we shall, achieve a scientific administration; but its hand will be icy cold. Weber felt a little like Burke, who wrote with a tragic pen: 'The age of chivalry is gone. That of sophisters, economists and calculators has succeeded; and the glory of Europe is extinguished for ever.'[2]

Such cultural pessimism is not, strictly speaking, necessary. We are aware, in saying this, that we are stepping out of the area of objective fact and into the area of subjective opinion; that we are entering, as we expressed it in a parallel place before,[3] into a 'concluding unscientific postscript'. But there can be no reasonable objection to the expression of opinions, provided they are not given for more than they are, impressions which a man has received in pursuing his life's work, or convictions which have formed in his mind in the course of time.

Lessing and Weber – and Weber even more than Lessing – were close to believing that there is an iron law of rationalization of which bureaucratization is merely an outer evidence and application. There is, however, no such iron law. Rationalization, with the deadening consequences which Weber feared, will – quite apart from the violent reactions to it, like the present drugging epidemic – draw ahead only if men lazily give in to the tendencies which arise from the economic and technological sectors of modern society, but there is no reason why they should do so. There is no reason, in other words, why they should not indulge in a little auto-criticism and decide that rationalization has its legitimate place within the rationalizable departments of life (within the field described by Alfred Weber as civilization), but that it should not be extended to the concerns which, by their very nature, are incapable of it (to the concerns which Alfred Weber specifically called culture). Such a decision would not presuppose a tremendous intellectual effort; it would demand only a little common sense. Nobody would go to a physicist, if he needed a medical man to heal his body. The habit of looking to the physical sciences when confronted with metaphysical problems is not one whit more reasonable than looking to mechanics for help with chemical conundrums or to students of the bone structure for help with malfunctions of an inner organ. *Suum cuique.* Today, no educated person would consult the Bible when exploring geology. Why then should geology, or any other natural science, be consulted when exploring, not tangible facts, but intangible mysteries?

[1] Subtitle of his book, *Europa und Asien*, fifth edition, Leipzig 1930.
[2] *Reflections on the Revolution in France*, as quoted, p. 149.
[3] Vol. III, p. 438.

But, it may be said, we need a closed and unified world-vie
cannot have one approach during the week and another on S
There is truth in this assertion, but the question is, how far will it
A purely formally integrated world-view, a unity mechanically
by spreading the concepts and the propositions appropriate to (
of reality to all others, whether or not they fit, would be totally
Everybody wishes to apply what is (incorrectly, as it happens) k
Ockham's razor: *entia non sunt multiplicanda*. But a razor is not a (
It is supposed to remove the superfluous hair, but not to slice (
organ like the nose. A philosophy, to be viable, must allow the
within reality to be real and do justice, on its own terms,
department of it. It must offer a biology which allows that
reducible to matter; it must offer a sociology which allows th
is not fully reducible to its constituent individuals; and it
contain an attitude to mystery which concedes that the m(
cannot be conjured away by dissolving it into physical elem

When we move downward from that highest level of
where the physical and the metaphysical – the seen and the
such – meet, and where there is a danger that the one will (
blot out the other, when we come to the lower levels of the
crete, we find that even highly scientific thinking does n
monist solutions. Staying, for one more minute, within phi
Kantian system is a case in point. We are calling it a system,
everybody else, for it is systemic, that is, integrated and i
ordinated. And yet it is dualistic. It teaches that there are t\
man irreducible to each other. There is man as a natural be\
enal man, subject to the laws of determinacy, and there
moral being, noumenal man, endowed with a will of his (
ject to outer laws, but internally free. It simply makes n
that 'spirit' can control bodily developments, or, vice \
body controls the motions of the will. A philosophical
that is to convince must be complex. Of course, the co
the two realities which have to enter into it raises difficul\
excruciating ones, but these have to be faced, and only
fool will shirk them.

If it be said that philosophy is not science, and that
rate – according to modern man, the superior pursuit –
all of one piece, it has to be emphasized that even scienc
dualism where the facts demand it. There are, at the p
two theories of light which hold sway side by side: the
the corpuscular theory. Physicists are not overly concer
go out of their way to force them into one framewor\
that, by submitting to the demands of formal logic
material damage to their work. There are areas of e\
which we get further, if we start with the wave theor\

such areas within which the corpuscular theory serves us better. Again, there is the coexistence of relativity theory and quantum mechanics. It cannot be asserted that they have ever been properly reconciled – which has not prevented physics from becoming the most successful of all the sciences. Physicists simply get on with their business as best they can. But men in general also have business with which they have to get on, the business of living, and it is amply evident that they would get on with it better than they do if only they realized that our outer needs, the needs arising from our desire to understand and to control nature, demand a different approach from our inner needs, the longing to find an ultimate meaning in existence and to come to terms with its mysterious beginning and end.

We cannot, of course, underline the diversity of experience without at the same time throwing the problem of its unity into sharp relief. Is it possible to solve it? On the pragmatic level certainly, as we have just indicated; on the philosophical level probably not: one of man's inherent and inescapable limitations seems to lie here. The sociologist, in so far as he has to face it at all, will be inclined to point to the greatest of all social institutions, namely language, and say that it clearly is a vital system, a unity of life, without at the same time being systemic and integrated in the logical sense of the word. Life has ever rejected logically constructed idioms, idioms which would force us to say 'teach' and 'teached', because we are saying 'preach' and 'preached'. Those who demand that the modern world-view should become monistic, and that religion be expelled from it in order to achieve that monism, would, to be consistent, also have to abandon the language which they are speaking, a step which even the Logical Positivists, for all their linguistic criticism, have been loath to take. Reason itself puts a negative on any imperialistic desires on the part of monism, for it is not reasonable to sacrifice the living variety of existence to the dead unity of a formal principle.

A society is very largely what its system of values makes it. But a system of values is not imposed on men, it is chosen by them, and when a condition is reached under which material ends have outstripped and undercut all others, a change is entirely possible. The reason why we are fully justified in rejecting the pessimism and fatalism of men like Lessing and Weber is that nobody is a slave to his own doings. It is another question as to how *likely* the human race is to reconsider and to redirect its willing, and pessimism may be based, not on something like a law of spiritual entropy, which does not exist, but on something like a law of axiological inertia, on the improbability – often observed – that men will in fact restructure their order of preferences. Yet even in this respect, the prospect is not entirely bleak. Capitalism has, it is true, in the current colloquialism, which is totally appropriate in this context, 'delivered the goods', i.e. the material goods which people want, but it

has failed to provide other kinds of good, especially in the social field. Its triumphs were largely due to the principle of competition which it has ruthlessly applied: from its first moment of existence, it has pitted man against man in order to coax the last ounce of energy out of him. Of that principle, the world has tired. There is an elementary desire for more co-operation, more integration, more peace. Socialism is the *alter ego* of capitalism, and capitalism has never been able to cast it off. Indeed, it looks already as if the future belongs to a less competitive, i.e. a less individualistic dispensation, as if community values were already in the ascendant. But the more community values are in the ascendant, in other words, the more a society feels itself a unity rather than a multiplicity, the greater is and must be the likelihood that the doctrines of Christianity will appeal to it. In a world in which everyone thinks of himself first and foremost, if not indeed exclusively, as a closed self, the assertion that the whole race fell in Adam and rose in Christ, simply makes no sense. Or rather, it makes no sense to modal man; it will have its attraction only for those who know how to free themselves from prevailing ideologies. But where the word 'we' receives a fuller and fairer meaning, where it comes to be regarded less as a fiction, an empty sound, and more as a reality, there the 'intellectual superstructure' resting on the basic network of human relationships will also receive re-direction. The noon of capitalism is over; its dusk has arrived; more collectivistic conditions are in the offing. This may well give the Christian new hope. Communism, it is true, has not helped, but then communism is merely the hostile twin of capitalism. It, too, allots to material values pride of place; it, too, sacrifices the satisfactions of sociality to the cruder enjoyments of the economic sphere. The future that will overcome materialistic capitalism, will overcome materialistic communism also. Both East and West may yet find their way to a more human and humane order of things. And then the call of Christianity may once again find more receptive ears.

The argument which we have just placed before the reader is lucidly developed in Thomas Mann's great philosophical novel, *The Magic Mountain*, or rather *Der Zauberberg*.[1] It is one enthralling personality, Father Naphta, who puts it forward there, against his liberal antagonist, Professor Settembrini. Not by accident, Settembrini is shown in a defensive posture, as one who fights a rearguard action. The future is sure to belong to science; it is not likely to belong to capitalism. But the men who will make human purposes more predominant in practical life, will also make them more dominant in culture. Science, too, will have to find a new place in the great scheme of things. It will still be one of men's most treasured possessions, but it will no longer be able to

---

[1] Cf. esp. the climactic section of chapter VI, entitled 'Of the City of God, and Deliverance by Evil', transl. Lowe-Porter, H. T., ed. New York 1960, pp. 386 et seq.

blot out all other pursuits, such as the searching for metaphysical and religious truths.

In the natural sciences, man has proved himself master; in the orbit of religion, he must ever see himself as servant. The change-over to a greater emphasis on the latter will assuredly not be easy, but it should not be too difficult for those who wish to be realistic and who know our human weaknesses as well as our strengths. What is needed, in the face of the ultimate questions, is what Chateaubriand once called *une seconde innocence*, 'less assured, but more sublime' than the first.[1] If, in the areas in which we exercise control, we may take pride in the understanding which we have achieved, if we may even be allowed to be, so far as they are concerned, a little *blasé*, we must, as we cross the borderline into another land, where we cannot exercise control, where we cannot hope for understanding, learn once more to feel humility, wonderment and awe. This is one of the preconditions of our liberation – liberation from the shadows which must inescapably lie over those who have not successfully dealt with all the problems posed by their existence, metaphysical as well as physical. We recognize here the meaning of the Gospel words, of the Gospel warning: 'Unless you be converted and become as little children, you shall not enter into the kingdom of heaven' (Matthew XVIII, 3). No 'sacrifice of our intellect' (to use an old phrase) is demanded: all we need do is to acknowledge that there is a frontier beyond which all our scientific sophistication is of no avail. Great scientists have always known this. 'Let us hope we can overcome the myth of omnipotence,' Barry Commoner has pleaded, 'and learn that the proper use of science is not to conquer the world, but to live in it.'[2] And Albert Einstein: 'The fairest thing we can experience is the mysterious . . . He who knows it not, can no longer wonder, no longer feel amazement, is as good as dead, a snuffed-out candle.'[3]

These last words of Albert Einstein may appear as a vast exaggeration to the common run of modern man. As good as dead! Why, we are living better than ever before! Why should we bother about the mysterious? We can very easily do without it. People who argue in this vein, who blithely assume that material satisfactions are all that our race requires in order to be happy, forget how unhappy modern man is in the midst of his wealth. 'Alas for the nineteenth century,' wrote Francis Thompson in *Maestitiae Encomium*, 'with so much pleasure, and so little joy; so much learning, and so little wisdom; so much effort, and so little fruition; so many philosophers, and such little philosophy; so many seers, and such little foresight; so many teachers, and such an infinite wild vortex of doubt! The one divine thing left to us is sadness.'[4]

[1] *Génie du Christianisme*, as quoted, vol. I, p. 405.
[2] Cf. *The New York Times*, 5 January 1969, p. 13E.
[3] *The World as I see it*, New York 1934, p. 242.
[4] *The Works of Francis Thompson*, New York 1913, vol. III, p. 111.

More recently, Gregory Dix has expressed himself in the same vein: 'It is a historical mistake to idealize and romanticize the middle ages. The ordinary mediaeval man lived in a world which was horribly uncomfortable and dangerous, very poor in material resources, and also very sinful. And he knew all that quite well. But his literature, from the popular literature of the ballads up to the great works of genius, reveals a world that was hopeful nevertheless, and had a great zest for living. Our own world . . . is much better equipped with material resources, . . . but it is hardly what one would call hopeful, and it has a fear of living. This is because our world has forgotten or has ceased to believe that it has been redeemed. It is probable that the conventional religion of most men in the "Ages of Faith" went not much deeper really than the conventional irreligion of most men to-day. Yet religion did penetrate all human life then with a hopefulness and a purpose beyond its human littleness which it is very hard to imagine in our secularized society.'[1]

A zest for living! A far-reaching loss of it is indeed part of the heavy price which modern man has been paying for the triumphs he has achieved in his pet pursuits. Should anyone doubt that there has been such loss, let him compare the prevailing mood expressed in contemporary music with that which dominated the classics, almost all of them products of a profoundly Catholic culture. Where is the sun-filled and fun-filled feeling which speaks to us in Vivaldi's *The Seasons*, in Haydn's *Toy* and *Hen* Symphonies, in all of Mozart's early work, in Beethoven's Fourth and Eighth Symphonies, in Schubert's Fifth and in so many of his songs, in Bizet's Symphony in C, in the overtures to Rossini's *The Barber of Seville* and to Smetana's *The Bartered Bride*, in Dvořák's *Slavonic Dance Number 1* – to mention only a few of the inspired works whose list might be vastly enlarged? Of course, we must not exaggerate. There is also Schubert's poignant Ninth; there is Mozart's sombre *Requiem*; there are Beethoven's tragic Third and Fifth. And the optimism is, in some of the composers we have adduced, also due to a touch of the Leibnizian belief in a *harmonia prestabilità* which stemmed from rationalism and not from Christianity. But in Haydn that touch is only slight; in Beethoven, indeed, it is strong, but then it also accounts for his despairing and defiant attitude which came with his disappointments after the French Revolution, the Napoleonic Wars and the first economic crisis of the eighteen-twenties. As for Schubert and Mozart, their unhappiness was due, partly to cruel disease, partly to economic trouble, the inability to make ends meet or to find a job. It was the personal foreground that cast a shadow over them, not the cultural and religious background which remained attuned to a smiling sense of life. Perhaps we can make our point best if we concentrate for a moment on Haydn, Dvořák and Smetana. All three were children of peasant societies permeated by Catholicism as a healthy body is by vitality in all

[1] *The Shape of the Liturgy*, as quoted, p. 604.

427

its fibres. Their music was essentially an externalization of an inherent mood which took many shocks but never went into a decline. What we are speaking about now is, of course, common knowledge. It is agreed on all hands that Vienna and Paris are the gayest cities in the world, and they are so because they are but overgrown villages of the kind which gave birth to Haydn, to Dvořák, to Smetana, and to their music also.

When the science of sociology was founded, its first protagonist, Auguste Comte, pointed out that the needs of man point in two directions: they are partly material, partly spiritual. The former are well taken care of in modern society, the latter are not. Yet they, too, are real. As Gabriel Marcel has expressed it, in a distinction which we can adapt to our purposes, there is not only *homo spectans*, man as he looks out on the physical environment and deals with it, but also *homo particeps*, man who would be embedded in an encompassing system, in a matrix of life.[1] Three harmonies, Comte taught, are required to still the longings of *homo particeps*: harmony with himself, harmony with his neighbours, and harmony with the wider frame of existence at the edges of which mystery becomes visible. The first, or inner, harmony will ever be a reflection of the other two, social and religious integration. What can provide them? Only a living faith which is as religious as it is social, and as social as it is religious. It alone can heal the sickness of modern man which is due to his human and cosmic loneliness; it alone can offer to him the gift which the Gospel carries in its hands: that feeling of total belonging, of contentment and of peace, which came over the Beloved Disciple when, on the night of the Last Supper, he leaned his head against the Master's breast and heard the beating of His most loving heart.

[1] *The Mystery of Being*, vol. I, transl. Fraser, G. S., London 1950, p. 122.

APPENDIX I · THE CULTURE OF THE SECT

This volume has been concerned with inclusive cultures, and little has therefore been said about religious establishments (as defined in our volume I) and religious sects (as defined in our volume II). A state church is, in law and in fact, part and parcel of the state whose church it is. The same culture permeates them both. Its study is not, therefore, a specific task of the sociology of religion – which does not mean, of course, that the culture concerned is political, i.e. secular, rather than religious. It may, indeed, be highly and deeply religious. The facts alone can decide whether it is or not. All we are saying is that he who would know the culture of the Church of England must study England, not forgetting the Christian heritage, in so far as it has entered English reality.

The case of the sect is somewhat different. True, it, too, is included in a society rather than inclusive of it, but as it tends to contract out, it has, to some extent, a culture of its own – a contraculture, as it must be called, if it is considered from the point of view of the establishment.[1] This raises the question as to whether, and in what sense, the categories of Tönnies can be applied to it. Is the typical sect an association, or is it a community? And, if associational and communal features are intermixed, what is their relation to each other?

The answer to these queries cannot be simple, but it can be clear. Basically, a sect is an association rather than a community. According to Ernst Troeltsch's classical definition, the sect is a 'voluntary' society whose members join it 'of their own free will'.[2] The part is therefore prior to the whole, the individual more 'real' than the group, and this is the decisive hallmark of an association as contrasted with a community, where the whole is prior to the part and the community more 'real' than the individual person.

This does not, however, exclude the possibility that the sect may have character traits reminiscent of community. A description of associations as weakly coherent societies, and of communities as strongly coherent societies, would be somewhat vague, but it would have an element of truth in it, and according to it, the sect would be communal rather than associational in nature. A sect is not like a business partnership (Tönnies' chief example of an association); it is much rather like a family

---

[1] Cf. our vol. II, pp. 128 et seq.
[2] *The Social Teaching of the Christian Churches*, transl. Wyon, O., ed. New York and Evanston 1960, p. 339.

(Tönnies' chief example of a community); its near-communal facets must be duly taken into account.

To accommodate them, and so be fair to the realities of sect life, one of Tönnies' critics, Hermann Schmalenbach, has suggested that we need a third category which he calls *der Bund*.[1] The term is not easy to translate. The sound pattern suggests the English expression *the band*, and Schmalenbach's main illustration is in fact the war-band of young men such as we find it from the Blackfoot and Navaho to the Normans and Franks. But the word hardly has the right overtones and undertones, if it is to be applied to a form of religious association. Perhaps *friendship league* would do; it would be closer to the German meaning than the etymologically-phonetically more similar pendant. The *Bund* or friendship league is not – like a business firm – association, for there is emotional fusion among those who join it; it is not community for – unlike a primitive clan – it has not grown from the anonymous forces of life; it is therefore a *tertium quid*.

The point is well taken and may be conceded. No objection can reasonably be raised if a trichotomy is proposed instead of Tönnies' classical dichotomy. Others among us may wish to stick to the latter and understand the sect, and also the primitive war-band, as a variant of association because it is called into being by its members rather than the other way round. In any event, no violent discussions are needed around such formal points.

So far as the more material aspects of the sect phenomenon are concerned, Schmalenbach asserts that the dissenting group cannot be bracketed with the typical association because the latter is entered by dint of a sober, purely rational contract, the former with the aid of a soul-shaking, deeply emotional ceremony – the oath of fealty sworn by the young warrior, the rite of immersion undergone by the religious neophyte. He expresses the contrast also by saying that joining an association involves only the conscious self whereas entry into the sect touches the unconscious also. All this is true. But Schmalenbach himself has to add that the psychological act of conversion, so far as it concerns sociality, only 'inflames' the unconscious and does not become 'rooted' in it. 'The experiences which create the *Bund*,' he writes, 'are happenings to the individual.'[2] The Jew of patriarchal times was for ever a *we*, the sectarian as we know him remains an *I*. A consequence of this persistence of full ego-integration is the short life-expectation of the community sentiment. 'For the *Bund*, instability is inherently symptomatic. So long as it lasts, it does not, by any means, consist merely of and in separate, discrete acts . . . . But the waves of sentiment which carry it and in which it exists, always more or less a kind of intoxication,

---

[1] Cf. 'Die soziologische Kategorie des Bundes', in the yearbook *Die Dioskuren*, München 1922, pp. 35 et seq.
[2] Loc. cit., pp. 67 and 72. My translation.

are in their whole nature transitory. They may indeed deeply stir our souls; they may be strong enough utterly to destroy a man, to drive him into madness or death. But they are not permanent. The drunkenness wears off.'[1] The sect becomes a denomination, and the community-like character disappears.

We see, then, that, on Schmalenbach's own showing, the sect is associational when it is formed (because it is founded by the assertion of individual willing, by the action of individual selves), and associational also when it has decayed (because then the emotional fusion of the members has faded and the fibres of the body social have relaxed). This leaves us with the question of whether friendship leagues are not at least temporarily communities, communities in their halcyon days. In answering, we shall be well advised to make a distinction which Schmalenbach fails to draw: a distinction between *Bünde* which, like the primitive war-bands, arise within the matrix of a community-type society, and others which, like the modern Protestant sects, take shape within the cadres of an associational life. The primitive war-band was in its heyday more communal than associational because it was an organization of a grown age group or age class, as Varagnac has so impressively shown.[2] Nature is behind it, as well as the human will. But the modern Protestant sect is, even in its early years, more associational than communal because it is the meeting of persons who are in no way organically connected. It does not have nature behind it, only the human will. This does not mean that deep attachments do not occur within it. Assuredly they do. The 'fraternal' element should not be discounted or played down; indeed, it should be insisted on, and it even deserves admiration. But, in Martin Buber's language, there is and remains only an 'I and you', a 'society of friends', as the Quakers so well express it. Modern religious non-conformity, simply because it is modern, is shot through with individualism. Does it not energetically, indeed with passion, insist on the 'supremacy of private judgment'? And is there a principle more clearly characteristic and constitutive of Protestantism in all its forms than this?

Roger Mehl, in his *Traité de Sociologie du Protestantisme*[3] does not deny it. And yet he asserts that not only sects, but even all Protestant Churches are communities. This opinion seems so diametrically opposed to the convictions put forward in the present book that we must have a brief glance at it.

It may be said at once that the differences are far smaller than they appear to be. Mehl does not use the term 'community' in the specific, technical sense given to it by Ferdinand Tönnies (whom he nowhere mentions), but in the much vaguer, much more colloquial sense in

---

[1] Ibid., pp. 73 and 74.
[2] *Civilisation Traditionelle et Genres de Vie*, as quoted, esp. pp. 138 et seq.
[3] Neuchâtel 1965.

which we sometimes speak of 'the Negro community' or 'the Jewish community' as if they were more than multiplicities of men in similar life conditions – with parallel 'chances in life', as Max Weber would have expressed it. Mehl's attitude is largely determined, not by scientific nomenclature, but by the accidental environment in which he finds himself. A Protestant in France is the member of a small minority; a Protestant in the Alsace is still the member of a minority, though of a more substantial one. Minorities, however, stick together, as everyone knows. This is due to their being a minority rather than to their being denominational (or racial or what not). It is not likely that the Catholics of, say, Sweden, are less inclined to cluster around their priests than the Protestants of France around their pastors.

The main and perhaps the only reason which Mehl gives for using the term 'community' as he does, i.e. as an epithet applicable to all variants of Protestantism, is the assertion that the local grouping is characteristic of these Churches and the decisive, truly operative unit. 'The internal organization of Protestantism rests on the building up of parishes,' he says. There is an inherent tendency towards congregationalism in the tradition which took its rise in the Reformation.[1] But, once again, all depends on the given circumstances. The principle 'to assemble Christians according to laws of human proximity'[2] is common to all Christians, and for a Tyrolean peasant his parish and his parish church are as much the decisive, truly operative centre of religious life as they are for an Alsatian wine-grower around Strasbourg.

Later on in the book, when the eye is raised from the local circumstances and allowed to roam over the wider expanse of Protestantism, the equation between Protestantism and at least *de facto* congregationalism is dropped. It is admitted that there are 'two ecclesiastical structures' which can be distinguished, namely 'episcopalianism and the presbyterian synodal system on the one hand, and congregationalism on the other'. Episcopalianism and Presbyterianism, however, are not so strongly or exclusively parish-centred as Mehl's original statements on Protestantism in general would lead one to believe, and for the latter, the Calvinist Churches, he expressly concedes that authority does not belong to the individual pastor, but to 'consistories, synods, synodal councils'.[3] Sweden and Scotland simply are not the Alsace. We must not take *pars pro toto*.

Yet later the suggested principle according to which the Protestant Churches are essentially associations of parishes is further reduced. Halfway through the book it is admitted that it does not apply over the greater part of the Protestant area; in the end it is conceded, at least by

[1] Engl. transl., *The Sociology of Protestantism*, transl. Farley, J. H., Philadelphia 1970, p. 45; cf. also pp. 42, 119, 120, 146.
[2] Ibid., p. 42.
[3] Ibid., pp. 158 and 157.

implication, that it is not essential to Protestantism in any form or shape. 'Congregationalism is losing pace in Protestantism,' we read. 'The centralization of the government of the Church is being accomplished . . .'.[1] Here the author, in order to be consistent, would have to complain that Protestantism is losing something of its pristine self and soul. But he does not. Far from considering the change as loss, he depicts it as gain: 'The Reformation doctrine of the equality of all ministers is turning out to be incompatible with an effective government.'[2]

If we wish to see the real self and soul of Protestantism, we must not look to little Alsace, nor even to Sweden and Scotland, but to the Anglo-Saxon cultures which border the Atlantic on either side, for it was there that Calvinism, its climactic form, could most freely unfold. What we find there in the fullness of time is a breaking asunder into two forms, Presbyterianism properly so called, in design an integrated Church, and Congregationalism properly so called, a collection of independent localized formations. But Congregationalism was sectarian. And this fact leads us back from Mehl to Schmalenbach. In its heroic period, a congregation of the Congregationalist type was a *Bund* and thus had its quasi-communal aspects. When it declined into a denomination, these were more or less lost – the common fate. But *both* Congregationalist sect and Presbyterian Church were essentially, archetypally *covenantal*, a fact which Mehl, almost incredibly, does not mention, even though it filled all vital utterances of the Calvinist groupings, especially in America, and that is what really matters; and because they were so, they were associations in the sense which Tönnies has given to the term.

[1] Ibid., p. 217.
[2] Ibid.

433

APPENDIX II. ESSAYS ON MAX WEBER

Throughout our investigation, the name of Max Weber has cropped up again and again, and this is not surprising, for his thought has more deeply influenced the sociology of religion in this century than any other. Our attitude to him has been partly positive, partly negative. We have rejected his concept of the 'routinization of charisma', but we have accepted his thesis that the Calvinist ethic sped the formation of capitalist society. So far as the latter aspect is concerned, we have indeed pushed beyond Weber's famous book, but we have advanced in the direction which he indicated.

Needless to say, there are more facets to Weber's position than two, and a discussion of all of them would have been desirable. We could not possibly undertake it, but we have selected the most significant of them and commented on them in occasional writings (originally mostly lectures). In the subjoined list, the first seven are critical, the remaining three constructive. Numbers 2, 4, 8 and 9 overlap with passages contained in our five volumes; the rest do not.

1. Max Weber's Sociology of Religious Belief, *Sociological Analysis*, Spring 1964, pp. 41–9.
2. The Routinization of Charisma: A Consideration of Catholicism, *Sociological Analysis*, Winter 1965, pp. 203–11.
3. Max Weber and the Heteronomy of Purposes, *Social Research*, Summer 1967, pp. 249–64; also in *Humanitas*, Winter 1968, pp. 307–20.
4. Die Sektenethiken und der Geist des Kapitalismus, *Revista Internacional de Sociologia*, Julio-Diciembre 1967, pp. 5–15.
5. The Agony of Righteousness: Max Weber's Moral Philosophy, *Thought*, Autumn 1968, pp. 380–92.
6. The Place of Catholicism in Max Weber's Sociology of Religion, *Sociological Analysis*, Winter 1968, pp. 202–10.
7. The Rational and Social Foundations of Religious Dogma, in *Festschrift für Wilhelm Mühlmann*, J. C. B. Mohr (Paul Siebeck), Tübingen 1969, pp. 303–14.
8. Capitalism, Calvinism and the Rise of Modern Science, *The Sociological Review*, vol. XLIII, 5, 1951, pp. 95–104; also in *Readings in Philosophy of Science*, ed. P. P. Wiener, New York, N.Y.: Charles

Scribner's Sons, 1953, pp. 340–8; Spanish translation (abbreviated) in *Ciencias Sociales*, Agosto y Octubre 1952, pp. 76–8.

9. The Socio-religious Origins of Modern Science, *Revista Internacional de Sociologia*, Julio-Septiembre 1962, pp. 322–31.

10. The Protestant Ethic and the Spirit of Sociology, *Social Compass*, vol. XIII, 5–6, 1966, pp. 373–7.

Index

Caravaggio, M. de, 153, 154, 155, 198, 201, 203
Carlyle, Thomas, 119
Carracci, A., 153, 154, 155
Cassirer, E., 24, 25, 26, 120, 121
Cathedrals, *see* Architecture *and under individual cathedrals*
Catholic Church, The, 3, 65, 67, 69, 73, 79, 97, 98, 171, 180, 185, 198n., 275, 285, 342, 343, 390, 391, 392, 394, 405, 417, *see also* Church, the
Puritanism in, 155, 157-9
Catholicism, 1, 3, 4, 5, 8, 37, 65, 67-71, 75, 83, 84, 85, 87-92, 94, 98-100, 102, 105, 109, 110, 121, 122, 123, 124, 128, 134, 139, 143, 146, 149, 152, 153, 159, 160, 161, 164-7, 173-6, 178, 179, 180, 189, 190, 193, 195, 196, 198, 202-4, 206, 207, 210-12, 220-3, 229, 230, 234, 240, 247, 248, 249, 257, 259, 261, 262, 265, 266, 272, 274, 276, 279, 280, 281, 282, 338, 339, 341, 342, 345, 347, 350, 351, 352, 358, 363, 364, 365, 372, 373, 375, 376, 390, 391, 392, 393, 394, 395, 405, 416, 417, 418, 419, 420, 421, 432, *see also* Self-depreciation, Catholic
American, 382, 390, 392, 394, 395, 400
and Calvinism contrasted, 140, 141, 264, 267, 298, 340
Culture of, 91, 108, 110, 121, 140, 150, 155, 158, 159, 180, 182, 184, 185, 212, 213, 276, 357, 362, 363, 364, 385, 427
English, 394
Irish, 394
Polish, 394
Sociology of, 75
Censers, Symbolism of, 132, 133, *see also* Symbolism
Charisma, Routinization of, 366, 367, 434
Charlemagne, 22, 108
Chartres cathedral, 132, 166, 167, 178, 179, 286, *see also* Adams H.; Architecture
Chateaubriand, F. R. de, 221, 374, 426
Christ, 37, 63, 64, 65, 68, 69, 77, 106, 126, 129, 155, 190, 191, 205, 220, 229, 231, 232, 253, 254, 265, 273,

280, 281, 286, 300, 312, 381, 399, 400, 411, 412
Divinity of, *see* Christology
Humanity of, *see* Christology
Representation of, in visual art, 138, 151, 152, 153, 154, 155, 213, 214
Christianity, 1, 2, 4, 6, 8, 17, 23, 25, 26, 29, 30, 33, 34, 35, 45, 50, 52, 54, 55, 57, 63, 69, 71, 77, 78, 79, 82, 85, 86, 87, 88, 99, 102, 104, 105, 106, 109, 118, 120, 121, 122, 123, 124, 128, 137, 139, 141, 145, 152, 153, 191, 192, 193, 195, 196, 210, 211, 213, 215, 219, 221, 223, 228, 229, 231, 232, 234, 237, 240, 247, 248, 252, 253, 254, 257, 259, 261, 264, 273, 274, 279, 281, 282, 284, 296, 302, 309, 312, 365, 366, 374, 376, 377, 378, 379, 381, 382, 383, 384, 385, 387, 389, 390, 395, 397, 398, 399, 403, 408, 412, 414, 415, 418, 419, 420, 421, 425, 427, 432
Primitive, *see* Church, Early
Christology, 81-9, 94, 128-33, *see also* Church, Early, Theology of
Christomimetes, 412
Church, The, 21, 63, 66, 67, 68, 69, 70, 71, 72, 73, 74, 78, 79, 80, 84, 88, 93, 94, 97, 99, 106, 123, 124, 127, 130, 131, 159, 210, 216, 218, 226, 229, 248, 253, 254, 267, 274, 275, 277, 278, 281, 291, 376, 382, 415, 418, 421
as an institution, 75
Calvin's view of, 256, 257
the mystical body of Christ, 66-75, 110, 247, 253, 282, 287, 288, 290, 299, 419
Church as a building, *see* Architecture; Symbolism
Church, Early, 98, 99, 106, 107, 108, 109, 111, 120, 128, 129, 130, 156, 215, 383
Liturgy of, 146
Theology of, 78-91
Church covenant, *see* Covenant
Church-going, 371, 372
Church music, *see* Liturgy; Mass, The; Music, Liturgical; Palestrina; Worship
Civil service, *see* Bureaucracy
Civilization, 369, 401
as defined by Alfred Weber, 386, 389, 422
Clan and clans, *see* Family